SO-AZT-033

THE GULAG ARCHIPELAGO

Also by Aleksandr I. Solzhenitsyn

The Nobel Lecture on Literature
August 1914
A Lenten Letter to Pimen, Patriarch of All Russia
Stories and Prose Poems
The Love Girl and the Innocent
The Cancer Ward
The First Circle
For the Good of the Cause
We Never Make Mistakes
One Day in the Life of Ivan Denisovich

Aleksandr I. Solzhenitsyn

THE GULAG ARCHIPELAGO

1918 – 1956

An Experiment in Literary Investigation

I - II

Translated from the Russian by **Thomas P. Whitney**

WestviewPress
A Division of HarperCollins*Publishers*

Portions of this work previously appeared in the *New York Times*.

A hardcover edition of this book was published in 1973 by Harper & Row, Publishers.

THE GULAG ARCHIPELAGO 1918–1956: AN EXPERIMENT IN LITERARY INVESTIGATION. Copyright
© 1973 by Aleksandr I. Solzhenitsyn. English language translation copyright © 1973, 1974 by
Harper & Row, Publishers, Inc. All rights reserved. Printed in the United States of America. No
part of this book may be used or reproduced in any manner whatsoever without written
permission except in the case of brief quotations embodied in critical articles and reviews. For
information address HarperCollins Publishers, 10 East 53rd Street, New York, NY 10022.

First HarperPerennial edition published 1991.

Designed by Sidney Feinberg

Library of Congress Cataloging-in-Publication Data

Solzhenitsyn, Aleksandr Isayevich, 1918–
    The Gulag archipelago, 1918–1956.
    Translated from the Russian.
    1. Political prisoners—Russia. I. Title.
HV9713.S6413   365'.45'0947   73–22756
ISBN 0-8133-3289-3

98 99 RRD   10 9 8 7 6 5 4

I dedicate this
to all those who did not live
to tell it.
And may they please forgive me
for not having seen it all
nor remembered it all,
for not having divined all of it.

Author's Note

For years I have with reluctant heart withheld from publication this already completed book: my obligation to those still living outweighed my obligation to the dead. But now that State Security has seized the book anyway, I have no alternative but to publish it immediately.

In this book there are no fictitious persons, nor fictitious events. People and places are named with their own names. If they are identified by initials instead of names, it is for personal considerations. If they are not named at all, it is only because human memory has failed to preserve their names. But it all took place just as it is here described.

Contents

ILLUSTRATIONS

page 2   Aleksandr Isayevich Solzhenitsyn
                  In the army
                  In detention
                  After his release from camp

page 488   Viktor Petrovich Pokrovsky
              Aleksandr Shtrobinder
              Vasily Ivanovich Anichkov
              Aleksandr Andreyevich Svechin
              Mikhail Aleksandrovich Reformatsky
              Yelizaveta Yevgenyevna Anichkova

Preface

In 1949 some friends and I came upon a noteworthy news item in *Nature*, a magazine of the Academy of Sciences. It reported in tiny type that in the course of excavations on the Kolyma River a subterranean ice lens had been discovered which was actually a frozen stream—and in it were found frozen specimens of prehistoric fauna some tens of thousands of years old. Whether fish or salamander, these were preserved in so fresh a state, the scientific correspondent reported, that those present immediately broke open the ice encasing the specimens and devoured them *with relish* on the spot.

The magazine no doubt astonished its small audience with the news of how successfully the flesh of fish could be kept fresh in a frozen state. But few, indeed, among its readers were able to decipher the genuine and heroic meaning of this incautious report.

As for us, however—we understood instantly. We could picture the entire scene right down to the smallest details: how those present broke up the ice in frenzied haste; how, flouting the higher claims of ichthyology and elbowing each other to be first, they tore off chunks of the prehistoric flesh and hauled them over to the bonfire to thaw them out and bolt them down.

We understood because we ourselves were the same kind of people as *those present* at that event. We, too, were from that powerful tribe of *zeks*, unique on the face of the earth, the only people who could devour prehistoric salamander *with relish*.

And the Kolyma was the greatest and most famous island, the

pole of ferocity of that amazing country of *Gulag* which, though scattered in an Archipelago geographically, was, in the psychological sense, fused into a continent—an almost invisible, almost imperceptible country inhabited by the zek people.

And this Archipelago crisscrossed and patterned that other country within which it was located, like a gigantic patchwork, cutting into its cities, hovering over its streets. Yet there were many who did not even guess at its presence and many, many others who had heard something vague. And only those who had been there knew the whole truth.

But, as though stricken dumb on the islands of the Archipelago, they kept their silence.

By an unexpected turn of our history, a bit of the truth, an insignificant part of the whole, was allowed out in the open. But those same hands which once screwed tight our handcuffs now hold out their palms in reconciliation: "No, don't! Don't dig up the past! Dwell on the past and you'll lose an eye."

But the proverb goes on to say: "Forget the past and you'll lose both eyes."

Decades go by, and the scars and sores of the past are healing over for good. In the course of this period some of the islands of the Archipelago have shuddered and dissolved and the polar sea of oblivion rolls over them. And someday in the future, this Archipelago, its air, and the bones of its inhabitants, frozen in a lens of ice, will be discovered by our descendants like some improbable salamander.

I would not be so bold as to try to write the history of the Archipelago. I have never had the chance to read the documents. And, in fact, will anyone ever have the chance to read them? Those who do not wish to *recall* have already had enough time— and will have more—to destroy all the documents, down to the very last one.

I have absorbed into myself my own eleven years there not as something shameful nor as a nightmare to be cursed: I have come almost to love that monstrous world, and now, by a happy turn of events, I have also been entrusted with many recent reports and letters. So perhaps I shall be able to give some account of the bones and flesh of that salamander—which, incidentally, is still alive.

This book could never have been created by one person alone. In addition to what I myself was able to take away from the Archipelago—on the skin of my back, and with my eyes and ears —material for this book was given me in reports, memoirs, and letters by 227 witnesses, whose names were to have been listed here.

What I here express to them is not personal gratitude, because this is our common, collective monument to all those who were tortured and murdered.

From among them I would like to single out in particular those who worked hard to help me obtain supporting bibliographical material from books to be found in contemporary libraries or from books long since removed from libraries and destroyed; great persistence was often required to find even one copy which had been preserved. Even more would I like to pay tribute to those who helped me keep this manuscript concealed in difficult periods and then to have it copied.

But the time has not yet come when I dare name them.

The old Solovetsky Islands prisoner Dmitri Petrovich Vitkovsky was to have been editor of this book. But his half a lifetime spent *there*—indeed, his own camp memoirs are entitled "Half a Lifetime"—resulted in untimely paralysis, and it was not until after he had already been deprived of the gift of speech that he was able to read several completed chapters only and see for himself that everything *will be told*.

And if freedom still does not dawn on my country for a long time to come, then the very reading and handing on of this book will be very dangerous, so that I am bound to salute future readers as well—on behalf of *those* who have perished.

When I began to write this book in 1958, I knew of no memoirs nor works of literature dealing with the camps. During my years of work before 1967 I gradually became acquainted with the *Kolyma Stories* of Varlam Shalamov and the memoirs of Dmitri Vitkovsky, Y. Ginzburg, and O. Adamova-Sliozberg, to which I refer in the course of my narrative as literary facts known to all (as indeed they someday shall be).

Despite their intent and against their will, certain persons provided invaluable material for this book and helped preserve many important facts and statistics as well as the very air they breathed: M. I. Sudrabs-Latsis, N. V. Krylenko, the Chief State Prosecutor for many years, his heir A. Y. Vyshinsky, and those jurists who were his accomplices, among whom one must single out in particular I. L. Averbakh.

Material for this book was also provided by *thirty-six* Soviet writers, headed by *Maxim Gorky*, authors of the disgraceful book on the White Sea Canal, which was the first in Russian literature to glorify slave labor.

PART I

The Prison Industry

■

"In the period of dictatorship, surrounded on all sides by enemies, we sometimes manifested unnecessary leniency and unnecessary softheartedness."

KRYLENKO,
speech at the Promparty trial

Aleksandr Isayevich Solzhenitsyn—in the army

... in detention

... after his release from camp

Chapter 1

■

Arrest

How do people get to this clandestine Archipelago? Hour by hour planes fly there, ships steer their course there, and trains thunder off to it—but all with nary a mark on them to tell of their destination. And at ticket windows or at travel bureaus for Soviet or foreign tourists the employees would be astounded if you were to ask for a ticket to go there. They know nothing and they've never heard of the Archipelago as a whole or of any one of its innumerable islands.

Those who go to the Archipelago to administer it get there via the training schools of the Ministry of Internal Affairs.

Those who go there to be guards are conscripted via the military conscription centers.

And those who, like you and me, dear reader, go there to die, must get there solely and compulsorily via arrest.

Arrest! Need it be said that it is a breaking point in your life, a bolt of lightning which has scored a direct hit on you? That it is an unassimilable spiritual earthquake not every person can cope with, as a result of which people often slip into insanity?

The Universe has as many different centers as there are living beings in it. Each of us is a center of the Universe, and that Universe is shattered when they hiss at you: *"You are under arrest."*

If *you* are arrested, can anything else remain unshattered by this cataclysm?

But the darkened mind is incapable of embracing these dis-placements in our universe, and both the most sophisticated and

3

the veriest simpleton among us, drawing on all life's experience, can gasp out only: "Me? What for?"

And this is a question which, though repeated millions and millions of times before, has yet to receive an answer.

Arrest is an instantaneous, shattering thrust, expulsion, somersault from one state into another.

We have been happily borne—or perhaps have unhappily dragged our weary way—down the long and crooked streets of our lives, past all kinds of walls and fences made of rotting wood, rammed earth, brick, concrete, iron railings. We have never given a thought to what lies behind them. We have never tried to penetrate them with our vision or our understanding. But there is where the *Gulag* country begins, right next to us, two yards away from us. In addition, we have failed to notice an enormous number of closely fitted, well-disguised doors and gates in these fences. All those gates were prepared for us, every last one! And all of a sudden the fateful gate swings quickly open, and four white male hands, unaccustomed to physical labor but nonetheless strong and tenacious, grab us by the leg, arm, collar, cap, ear, and drag us in like a sack, and the gate behind us, the gate to our past life, is slammed shut once and for all.

That's all there is to it! You are arrested!

And you'll find nothing better to respond with than a lamblike bleat: "Me? What for?"

That's what arrest is: it's a blinding flash and a blow which shifts the present instantly into the past and the impossible into omnipotent actuality.

That's all. And neither for the first hour nor for the first day will you be able to grasp anything else.

Except that in your desperation the fake circus moon will blink at you: "It's a mistake! They'll set things right!"

And everything which is by now comprised in the traditional, even literary, image of an arrest will pile up and take shape, not in your own disordered memory, but in what your family and your neighbors in your apartment remember: The sharp nighttime ring or the rude knock at the door. The insolent entrance of the unwiped jackboots of the unsleeping State Security operatives. The frightened and cowed civilian witness at their backs. (And what function does this civilian witness serve? The victim doesn't even dare think about it and the operatives don't remember, but that's what the regulations call for, and so he has to sit there all night long and sign in the morning.[1] For the witness, jerked from his bed, it is torture too—to go out night after night to help arrest his own neighbors and acquaintances.)

The traditional image of arrest is also trembling hands packing for the victim—a change of underwear, a piece of soap, something to eat; and no one knows what is needed, what is permitted, what clothes are best to wear; and the Security agents keep interrupting and hurrying you:

"You don't need anything. They'll feed you there. It's warm there." (It's all lies. They keep hurrying you to frighten you.)

The traditional image of arrest is also what happens afterward, when the poor victim has been taken away. It is an alien, brutal, and crushing force totally dominating the apartment for hours on end, a breaking, ripping open, pulling from the walls, emptying things from wardrobes and desks onto the floor, shaking, dumping out, and ripping apart—piling up mountains of litter on the floor —and the crunch of things being trampled beneath jackboots. And nothing is sacred in a search! During the arrest of the locomotive engineer Inoshin, a tiny coffin stood in his room containing the body of his newly dead child. The *"jurists"* dumped the child's body out of the coffin and searched it. They shake sick people out of their sickbeds, and they unwind bandages to search beneath them.[2]

Nothing is so stupid as to be inadmissible during a search! For example, they seized from the antiquarian Chetverukhin "a certain number of pages of Tsarist decrees"—to wit, the decree on ending the war with Napoleon, on the formation of the Holy Alliance, and a proclamation of public prayers against cholera during the epidemic of 1830. From our greatest expert on Tibet, Vostrikov, they confiscated ancient Tibetan manuscripts of great value; and it took the pupils of the deceased scholar thirty years to wrest them from the KGB! When the Orientalist Nevsky was

---

1. The regulation, purposeless in itself, derives, N.M. recalls, from that strange time when the citizenry not only was supposed to but actually dared to verify the actions of the police.
2. When in 1937 they wiped out Dr. Kazakov's institute, the "commission" broke up the jars containing the *lysates* developed by him, even though patients who had been cured and others still being treated rushed around them, begging them to preserve the miraculous medicines. (According to the official version, the lysates were supposed to be poisons; in that case, why should they not have been kept as material evidence?)

arrested, they grabbed Tangut manuscripts—and twenty-five years later the deceased victim was posthumously awarded a Lenin Prize for deciphering them. From Karger they took his archive of the Yenisei Ostyaks and vetoed the alphabet and vocabulary he had developed for this people—and a small nationality was thereby left without any written language. It would take a long time to describe all this in educated speech, but there's a folk saying about the search which covers the subject: *They are looking for something which was never put there.* They carry off whatever they have seized, but sometimes they compel the arrested individual to carry it. Thus Nina Aleksandrovna Palchinskaya hauled over her shoulder a bag filled with the papers and letters of her eternally busy and active husband, the late great Russian engineer, carrying it into *their* maw—once and for all, forever.

For those left behind after the arrest there is the long tail end of a wrecked and devastated life. And the attempts to go and deliver food parcels. But from all the windows the answer comes in barking voices: "Nobody here by that name!" "Never heard of him!" Yes, and in the worst days in Leningrad it took five days of standing in crowded lines just to get to that window. And it may be only after half a year or a year that the arrested person responds at all. Or else the answer is tossed out: "Deprived of the right to correspond." And that means once and for all. "No right to correspondence"—and that almost for certain means: "Has been shot."[3]

That's how we picture arrest to ourselves.

The kind of night arrest described is, in fact, a favorite, because it has important advantages. Everyone living in the apartment is thrown into a state of terror by the first knock at the door. The arrested person is torn from the warmth of his bed. He is in a daze, half-asleep, helpless, and his judgment is befogged. In a night arrest the State Security men have a superiority in numbers; there are many of them, armed, against one person who hasn't

3. In other words, "We live in the cursed conditions in which a human being can disappear into the void and even his closest relatives, his mother and his wife . . . do not know for years what has become of him." Is that right or not? That is what Lenin wrote in 1910 in his obituary of Babushkin. But let's speak frankly: Babushkin was transporting arms for an uprising, and was caught with them when he was shot. He knew what he was doing. You couldn't say that about helpless rabbits like us.

even finished buttoning his trousers. During the arrest and search it is highly improbable that a crowd of potential supporters will gather at the entrance. The unhurried, step-by-step visits, first to one apartment, then to another, tomorrow to a third and a fourth, provide an opportunity for the Security operations personnel to be deployed with the maximum efficiency and to imprison many more citizens of a given town than the police force itself numbers.

In addition, there's an advantage to night arrests in that neither the people in neighboring apartment houses nor those on the city streets can see how many have been taken away. Arrests which frighten the closest neighbors are no event at all to those farther away. It's as if they had not taken place. Along that same asphalt ribbon on which the Black Marias scurry at night, a tribe of youngsters strides by day with banners, flowers, and gay, untroubled songs.

But those who *take*, whose work consists solely of arrests, for whom the horror is boringly repetitive, have a much broader understanding of how arrests operate. They operate according to a large body of theory, and innocence must not lead one to ignore this. The science of arrest is an important segment of the course on general penology and has been propped up with a substantial body of social theory. Arrests are classified according to various criteria: nighttime and daytime; at home, at work, during a journey; first-time arrests and repeats; individual and group arrests. Arrests are distinguished by the degree of surprise required, the amount of resistance expected (even though in tens of millions of cases no resistance was expected and in fact there was none). Arrests are also differentiated by the thoroughness of the required search;[4] by instructions either to make out or not to

4. And there is a separate Science of Searches too. I have had the chance to read a pamphlet on this subject for correspondence-school law students in Alma-Ata. Its author praises highly those police officials who in the course of their searches went so far as to turn over two tons of manure, eight cubic yards of firewood, or two loads of hay; cleaned the snow from an entire collective-farm vegetable plot, dismantled brick ovens, dug up cesspools, checked out toilet bowls, looked into doghouses, chicken coops, birdhouses, tore apart mattresses, ripped adhesive tape off people's bodies and even tore out metal teeth in the search for microfilm. Students were advised to begin and to end with a body search (during the course of the search the arrested person might have grabbed up something that had already been examined). They were also advised to return to the site of a search at a different time of day and carry out the search all over again.

make out an inventory of confiscated property or seal a room or apartment; to arrest the wife after the husband and send the children to an orphanage, or to send the rest of the family into exile, or to send the old folks to a labor camp too.

No, no: arrests vary widely in form. In 1926 Irma Mendel, a Hungarian, obtained through the Comintern two front-row tickets to the Bolshoi Theatre. Interrogator Klegel was courting her at the time and she invited him to go with her. They sat through the show very affectionately, and when it was over he took her—straight to the Lubyanka. And if on a flowering June day in 1927 on Kuznetsky Most, the plump-cheeked, redheaded beauty Anna Skripnikova, who had just bought some navy-blue material for a dress, climbed into a hansom cab with a young man-about-town, you can be sure it wasn't a lovers' tryst at all, as the cabman understood very well and showed by his frown (he knew the *Organs* don't pay). It was an arrest. In just a moment they would turn on the Lubyanka and enter the black maw of the gates. And if, some twenty-two springs later, Navy Captain Second Rank Boris Burkovsky, wearing a white tunic and a trace of expensive eau de cologne, was buying a cake for a young lady, do not take an oath that the cake would ever reach the young lady and not be sliced up instead by the knives of the men searching the captain and then delivered to him in his first cell. No, one certainly cannot say that daylight arrest, arrest during a journey, or arrest in the middle of a crowd has ever been neglected in our country. However, it has always been clean-cut—and, most surprising of all, the victims, in cooperation with the Security men, have conducted themselves in the noblest conceivable manner, so as to spare the living from witnessing the death of the condemned.

Not everyone can be arrested at home, with a preliminary knock at the door (and if there is a knock, then it has to be the house manager or else the postman). And not everyone can be arrested at work either. If the person to be arrested is vicious, then it's better to seize him *outside* his ordinary milieu—away from his family and colleagues, from those who share his views, from any hiding places. It is essential that he have no chance to destroy, hide, or pass on anything to anyone. VIP's in the military or the Party were sometimes first given new assignments, ensconced in a private railway car, and then arrested en route. Some obscure, ordinary mortal, scared to death by epidemic arrests all around him and already depressed for a week by sinister glances from his chief, is suddenly summoned to the local Party committee, where he is beamingly presented with a vacation ticket to a Sochi sanatorium. The rabbit is overwhelmed and immediately concludes that his fears were groundless. After expressing his gratitude, he hurries home, triumphant, to pack his suitcase. It is only two hours till train time, and he scolds his wife for being too slow. He arrives at the station with time to spare. And there in the waiting room or at the bar he is hailed by an extraordinarily pleasant young man: "Don't you remember me, Pyotr Ivanich?" Pyotr Ivanich has difficulty remembering: "Well, not exactly, you see, although . . ." The young man, however, is overflowing with friendly concern: "Come now, how can that be? I'll have to remind you. . . ." And he bows respectfully to Pyotr Ivanich's wife: "You must forgive us. I'll keep him only *one minute*." The wife accedes, and trustingly the husband lets himself be led away by the arm—forever or for ten years!

The station is thronged—and no one notices anything. . . . Oh, you citizens who love to travel! Do not forget that in every station there are a GPU Branch and several prison cells.

This importunity of alleged acquaintances is so abrupt that only a person who has not had the wolfish preparation of camp life is likely to pull back from it. Do not suppose, for example, that if you are an employee of the American Embassy by the name of Alexander D. you cannot be arrested in broad daylight on Gorky Street, right by the Central Telegraph Office. Your unfamiliar friend dashes through the press of the crowd, and opens his plundering arms to embrace you: "Saaasha!" He simply shouts at you, with no effort to be inconspicuous. "Hey, pal! Long time no see! Come on over, let's get out of the way." At that moment a Pobeda sedan draws up to the curb. . . . And several days later TASS will issue an angry statement to all the papers alleging that informed circles of the Soviet government have no information on the disappearance of Alexander D. But what's so unusual about that? Our boys have carried out such arrests in Brussels—which was where Zhora Blednov was seized—not just in Moscow.

One has to give the *Organs* their due: in an age when public speeches, the plays in our theaters, and women's fashions all seem to have come off assembly lines, arrests can be of the most varied kind. They take you aside in a factory corridor after you have had your pass checked—and you're arrested. They take you from a military hospital with a temperature of 102, as they did with Ans Bernshtein, and the doctor will not raise a peep about your arrest—just let him try! They'll take you right off the operating table—as they took N. M. Vorobyev, a school inspector, in 1936, in the middle of an operation for stomach ulcer—and drag you off to a cell, as they did him, half-alive and all bloody (as Karpunich recollects). Or, like Nadya Levitskaya, you try to get information about your mother's sentence, and they give it to you, but it turns out to be a confrontation—and your own arrest! In the Gastronome—the fancy food store—you are invited to the special-order department and arrested there. You are arrested by a religious pilgrim whom you have put up for the night "for the sake of Christ." You are arrested by a meterman who has come to read your electric meter. You are arrested by a bicyclist who has run into you on the street, by a railway conductor, a taxi driver, a savings bank teller, the manager of a movie theater. Any one of them can arrest you, and you notice the concealed maroon-colored identification card only when it is too late.

Sometimes arrests even seem to be a game—there is so much superfluous imagination, so much well-fed energy, invested in them. After all, the victim would not resist anyway. Is it that the Security agents want to justify their employment and their numbers? After all, it would seem enough to send notices to all the rabbits marked for arrest, and they would show up obediently at the designated hour and minute at the iron gates of State Security with a bundle in their hands—ready to occupy a piece of floor in the cell for which they were intended. And, in fact, that's the way collective farmers are arrested. Who wants to go all the way to a hut at night, with no roads to travel on? They are summoned to the village soviet—and arrested there. Manual workers are called into the office.

Of course, every machine has a point at which it is overloaded, beyond which it cannot function. In the strained and overloaded years of 1945 and 1946, when trainload after trainload poured in from Europe, to be swallowed up immediately and sent off to

Gulag, all that excessive theatricality went out the window, and the whole theory suffered greatly. All the fuss and feathers of ritual went flying in every direction, and the arrest of tens of thousands took on the appearance of a squalid roll call: they stood there with lists, read off the names of those on one train, loaded them onto another, and that was the whole arrest.

For several decades political arrests were distinguished in our country precisely by the fact that people were arrested who were guilty of nothing and were therefore unprepared to put up any resistance whatsoever. There was a general feeling of being destined for destruction, a sense of having nowhere to escape from the GPU-NKVD (which, incidentally, given our internal passport system, was quite accurate). And even in the fever of epidemic arrests, when people leaving for work said farewell to their families every day, because they could not be certain they would return at night, even then almost no one tried to run away and only in rare cases did people commit suicide. And that was exactly what was required. A submissive sheep is a find for a wolf.

This submissiveness was also due to ignorance of the mechanics of epidemic arrests. By and large, the *Organs* had no profound reasons for their choice of whom to arrest and whom not to arrest. They merely had over-all assignments, quotas for a specific number of arrests. These quotas might be filled on an orderly basis or wholly arbitrarily. In 1937 a woman came to the reception room of the Novocherkassk NKVD to ask what she should do about the unfed unweaned infant of a neighbor who had been arrested. They said: "Sit down, we'll find out." She sat there for two hours—whereupon they took her and tossed her into a cell. They had a total plan which had to be fulfilled in a hurry, and there was no one available to send out into the city —and here was this woman already in their hands!

On the other hand, the NKVD did come to get the Latvian Andrei Pavel near Orsha. But he didn't open the door; he jumped out the window, escaped, and shot straight to Siberia. And even though he lived under his own name, and it was clear from his documents that he had come from Orsha, he was *never* arrested, nor summoned to the Organs, nor subjected to any suspicion whatsoever. After all, search for wanted persons falls into three categories: All-Union, republican, and provincial. And the pursuit of nearly half of those arrested in those epidemics would have been confined to the provinces. A person marked for arrest by virtue of chance circumstances, such as a neighbor's denunciation, could be easily replaced by another neighbor. Others, like Andrei Pavel, who found themselves in a trap or an ambushed apartment by accident, and who were bold enough to escape immediately, before they could be questioned, were never caught and never charged; while those who stayed behind to await justice got a term in prison. And the overwhelming majority—almost all—behaved just like that: without any spirit, helplessly, with a sense of doom.

It is true, of course, that the NKVD, in the absence of the person it wanted, would make his relatives guarantee not to leave the area. And, of course, it was easy enough *to cook up* a case against those who stayed behind to replace the one who had fled.

Universal innocence also gave rise to the universal failure to act. Maybe they *won't take* you? Maybe it will all blow over? A. I. Ladyzhensky was the chief teacher in a school in remote Kologriv. In 1937 a peasant approached him in an open market and passed him a message from a third person: "Aleksandr Ivanich, get out of town, *you are on the list!*" But he stayed: After all, the whole school rests on my shoulders, and *their own* children are pupils here. How can they arrest me? (Several days later he was arrested.) Not everyone was so fortunate as to understand at the age of fourteen, as did Vanya Levitsky: "Every honest man is sure to go to prison. Right now my papa is serving time, and when I grow up they'll put me in too." (They put him in when he was twenty-three years old.) The majority sit quietly and dare to hope. Since you aren't guilty, then how can they arrest you? *It's a mistake!* They are already dragging you along by the collar, and you still keep on exclaiming to yourself: "It's a mistake! *They'll set things straight and let me out!*" Others are being arrested en masse, and that's a bothersome fact, but in those other cases there is always some dark area: "Maybe *he* was guilty . . . ?" But as for you, you are obviously innocent! You still believe that the *Organs* are humanly logical institutions: they will set things straight and let you out.

Why, then, should you run away? And how can you resist right then? After all, you'll only make your situation worse; you'll make it more difficult for them to sort out the mistake. And it isn't just that you don't put up any resistance; you even walk down the stairs on tiptoe, as you are ordered to do, so your neighbors won't hear.[5]

At what exact point, then, should one resist? When one's belt is taken away? When one is ordered to face into a corner? When one crosses the threshold of one's home? An arrest consists of a series of incidental irrelevancies, of a multitude of things that do not matter, and there seems no point in arguing about any one of them individually—especially at a time when the thoughts of the person arrested are wrapped tightly about the big question: "What for?"—and yet all these incidental irrelevancies taken together implacably constitute the arrest.

Almost anything can occupy the thoughts of a person who has just been arrested! This alone would fill volumes. There can be feelings which we never suspected. When nineteen-year-old

5. And how we burned in the camps later, thinking: What would things have been like if every Security operative, when he went out at night to make an arrest, had been uncertain whether he would return alive and had to say good-bye to his family? Or if, during periods of mass arrests, as for example in Leningrad, when they arrested a quarter of the entire city, people had not simply sat there in their lairs, paling with terror at every bang of the downstairs door and at every step on the staircase, but had understood they had nothing left to lose and had boldly set up in the downstairs hall an ambush of half a dozen people with axes, hammers, pokers, or whatever else was at hand? After all, you knew ahead of time that those bluecaps were out at night for no good purpose. And you could be sure ahead of time that you'd be cracking the skull of a cutthroat. Or what about the Black Maria sitting out there on the street with one lonely chauffeur—what if it had been driven off or its tires spiked? The Organs would very quickly have suffered a shortage of officers and transport and, notwithstanding all of Stalin's thirst, the cursed machine would have ground to a halt!

If . . . if . . . We didn't love freedom enough. And even more—we had no awareness of the real situation. We spent ourselves in one unrestrained outburst in 1917, and then we *hurried* to submit. We submitted *with pleasure!* (Arthur Ransome describes a workers' meeting in Yaroslavl in 1921. Delegates were sent to the workers from the Central Committee in Moscow to confer on the substance of the argument about trade unions. The representative of the opposition, Y. Larin, explained to the workers that their trade union must be their defense against the administration, that they possessed rights which they had won and upon which no one else had any right to infringe. The workers, however, were completely indifferent, simply *not comprehending* whom they still needed to be defended against and why they still needed any rights. When the spokesman for the Party line rebuked them for their laziness and for getting out of hand, and demanded sacrifices from them—overtime work without pay, reductions in food, military discipline in the factory administration—this aroused great elation and applause.) We purely and simply *deserved* everything that happened afterward.

Yevgeniya Doyarenko was arrested in 1921 and three young Chekists were poking about her bed and through the underwear in her chest of drawers, she was not disturbed. There was nothing there, and they would find nothing. But all of a sudden they touched her personal diary, which she would not have shown even to her own mother. And these hostile young strangers reading the words she had written was more devastating to her than the whole Lubyanka with its bars and its cellars. It is true of many that the outrage inflicted by arrest on their personal feelings and attachments can be far, far stronger than their political beliefs or their fear of prison. A person who is not inwardly prepared for the use of violence against him is always weaker than the person committing the violence.

There are a few bright and daring individuals who understand instantly. Grigoryev, the Director of the Geological Institute of the Academy of Sciences, barricaded himself inside and spent two hours burning up his papers when they came to arrest him in 1948.

Sometimes the principal emotion of the person arrested is relief and even *happiness!* This is another aspect of human nature. It happened before the Revolution too: the Yekaterinodar schoolteacher Serdyukova, involved in the case of Aleksandr Ulyanov, felt only relief when she was arrested. But this feeling was a thousand times stronger during epidemics of arrests when all around you they were hauling in people like yourself and still had not come for you; for some reason they were taking their time. After all, that kind of exhaustion, that kind of suffering, is worse than any kind of arrest, and not only for a person of limited courage. Vasily Vlasov, a fearless Communist, whom we shall recall more than once later on, renounced the idea of escape proposed by his non-Party assistants, and pined away because the entire leadership of the Kady District was arrested in 1937, and they kept delaying and delaying his own arrest. He could only endure the blow head on. He did endure it, and then he relaxed, and during the first days after his arrest he felt marvelous. In 1934 the priest Father Irakly went to Alma-Ata to visit some believers in exile there. During his absence they came three times to his Moscow apartment to arrest him. When he returned, members of his flock met him at the station and refused to let him go home, and for eight years hid him in one apartment after another. The priest suffered so painfully from this harried life that when he was finally arrested in 1942 he sang hymns of praise to God.

In this chapter we are speaking only of the masses, the helpless rabbits arrested for no one knows what reason. But in this book we will also have to touch on those who in postrevolutionary times remained genuinely *political*. Vera Rybakova, a Social Democratic student, *dreamed* when she was in freedom of being in the detention center in Suzdal. Only there did she hope to encounter her old comrades—for there were none of them left in freedom. And only there could she work out her world outlook. The Socialist Revolutionary—the SR—Yekaterina Olitskaya didn't consider herself *worthy* of being imprisoned in 1924. After all, Russia's best people had served time and she was still young and had not yet done anything for Russia. But *freedom* itself was expelling her. And so both of them went to prison—with pride and happiness.

"Resistance! Why didn't you resist?" Today those who have continued to live on in comfort scold those who suffered.

Yes, resistance should have begun right there, at the moment of the arrest itself.

But it did not begin.

And so they are *leading* you. During a daylight arrest there is always that brief and unique moment when they are *leading* you, either inconspicuously, on the basis of a cowardly deal you have made, or else quite openly, their pistols unholstered, through a crowd of hundreds of just such doomed innocents as yourself. You aren't gagged. You really can and you really ought to *cry out*—to *cry out* that you are being arrested! That villains in disguise are trapping people! That arrests are being made on the strength of false denunciations! That millions are being subjected to silent reprisals! If many such outcries had been heard all over the city in the course of a day, would not our fellow citizens perhaps have begun to bristle? And would arrests perhaps no longer have been so easy?

In 1927, when submissiveness had not yet softened our brains to such a degree, two Chekists tried to arrest a woman on Serpukhov Square during the day. She grabbed hold of the stanchion of

a streetlamp and began to scream, refusing to submit. A crowd
gathered. (There had to have been that kind of woman; there had
to have been that kind of crowd too! Passers-by didn't all just
close their eyes and hurry by!) The quick young men immediately
became flustered. They can't *work* in the public eye. They got
into their car and fled. (Right then and there she should have
gone to a railroad station and left! But she went home to spend
the night. And during the night they took her off to the Lubyanka.)

Instead, not one sound comes from *your* parched lips, and
that passing crowd naïvely believes that you and your executioners are friends out for a stroll.

I myself often had the chance to *cry out.*

On the eleventh day after my arrest, three SMERSH bums,
more burdened by four suitcases full of war booty than by me
(they had come to rely on me in the course of the long trip),
brought me to the Byelorussian Station in Moscow. They were
called a *Special Convoy*—in other words, a special escort guard
—but in actual fact their automatic pistols only interfered with
their dragging along the four terribly heavy bags of loot they
and their chiefs in SMERSH counterintelligence on the Second
Byelorussian Front had plundered in Germany and were now
bringing to their families in the Fatherland under the pretext of
convoying me. I myself lugged a fifth suitcase with no great joy
since it contained my diaries and literary works, which were
being used as evidence against me.

Not one of the three knew the city, and it was up to me to pick
the shortest route to the prison. I had personally to conduct them
to the Lubyanka, where they had never been before (and which,
in fact, I confused with the Ministry of Foreign Affairs).

I had spent one day in the counterintelligence prison at army
headquarters and three days in the counterintelligence prison at
the headquarters of the front, where my cellmates had educated
me in the deceptions practiced by the interrogators, their threats
and beatings; in the fact that once a person was arrested he was
never released; and in the inevitability of a *tenner,* a ten-year
sentence; and then by a miracle I had suddenly burst out of there
and for four days had traveled like a *free* person among *free*
people, even though my flanks had already lain on rotten straw

beside the latrine bucket, my eyes had already beheld beaten-up and sleepless men, my ears had heard the truth, and my mouth had tasted prison gruel. So why did I keep silent? Why, in my last minute out in the open, did I not attempt to enlighten the hoodwinked crowd?

I kept silent, too, in the Polish city of Brodnica—but maybe they didn't understand Russian there. I didn't call out one word on the streets of Bialystok—but maybe it wasn't a matter that concerned the Poles. I didn't utter a sound at the Volkovysk Station—but there were very few people there. I walked along the Minsk Station platform beside those same bandits as if nothing at all were amiss—but the station was still a ruin. And now I was leading the SMERSH men through the circular upper concourse of the Byelorussian-Radial subway station on the Moscow circle line, with its white-ceilinged dome and brilliant electric lights, and opposite us two parallel escalators, thickly packed with Muscovites, rising from below. It seemed as though they were all looking at me! They kept coming in an endless ribbon from down there, from the depths of ignorance—on and on beneath the gleaming dome, reaching toward me for at least one word of truth—so why did I keep silent?

Every man always has handy a dozen glib little reasons why he is right not to sacrifice himself.

Some still have hopes of a favorable outcome to their case and are afraid to ruin their chances by an outcry. (For, after all, we get no news from that other world, and we do not realize that from the very moment of arrest our fate has almost certainly been decided in the worst possible sense and that we cannot make it any worse.) Others have not yet attained the mature concepts on which a shout of protest to the crowd must be based. Indeed, only a revolutionary has slogans on his lips that are crying to be uttered aloud; and where would the uninvolved, peaceable average man come by such slogans? He simply *does not know what* to shout. And then, last of all, there is the person whose heart is too full of emotion, whose eyes have seen too much, for that whole ocean to pour forth in a few disconnected cries.

As for me, I kept silent for one further reason: because those Muscovites thronging the steps of the escalators were too few for me, *too few!* Here my cry would be heard by 200 or twice 200, but what about the 200 million? Vaguely, unclearly, I had a vision that someday I would cry out to the 200 million.

But for the time being I did not open my mouth, and the escalator dragged me implacably down into the nether world.

And when I got to Okhotny Ryad, I continued to keep silent.

Nor did I utter a cry at the Metropole Hotel.

Nor wave my arms on the Golgotha of Lubyanka Square.

■

Mine was, probably, the easiest imaginable kind of arrest. It did not tear me from the embrace of kith and kin, nor wrench me from a deeply cherished home life. One pallid European February it took me from our narrow salient on the Baltic Sea, where, depending on one's point of view, either we had surrounded the Germans or they had surrounded us, and it deprived me only of my familiar artillery battery and the scenes of the last three months of the war.

The brigade commander called me to his headquarters and asked me for my pistol; I turned it over without suspecting any evil intent, when suddenly, from a tense, immobile suite of staff officers in the corner, two counterintelligence officers stepped forward hurriedly, crossed the room in a few quick bounds, their four hands grabbed simultaneously at the star on my cap, my shoulder boards, my officer's belt, my map case, and they shouted theatrically:

"You are under arrest!"

Burning and prickling from head to toe, all I could exclaim was:

"Me? What for?"

And even though there is usually no answer to this question, surprisingly I received one! This is worth recalling, because it is so contrary to our usual custom. Hardly had the SMERSH men finished "plucking" me and taken my notes on political subjects, along with my map case, and begun to push me as quickly as possible toward the exit, urged on by the German shellfire rattling the windowpanes, than I heard myself firmly addressed—yes! Across the sheer gap separating me from those left behind, the gap created by the heavy-falling word "arrest," across that quarantine line not even a sound dared penetrate, came the unthinkable, magic words of the brigade commander:

"Solzhenitsyn. Come back here."

With a sharp turn I broke away from the hands of the SMERSH men and stepped back to the brigade commander. I had never known him very well. He had never condescended to run-of-the-mill conversations with me. To me his face had always conveyed an order, a command, wrath. But right now it was illuminated in a thoughtful way. Was it from shame for his own involuntary part in this dirty business? Was it from an impulse to rise above the pitiful subordination of a whole lifetime? Ten days before, I had led my own reconnaissance battery almost intact out of the *fire pocket* in which the twelve heavy guns of his artillery battalion had been left, and now he had to renounce me because of a piece of paper with a seal on it?

"You have . . ." he asked weightily, "a friend on the First Ukrainian Front?"

"It's forbidden! You have no right!" the captain and the major of counterintelligence shouted at the colonel. In the corner, the suite of staff officers crowded closer to each other in fright, as if they feared to share the brigade commander's unbelievable rashness (the political officers among them already preparing to present *materials* against him). But I had already understood: I knew instantly I had been arrested because of my correspondence with a school friend, and understood from what direction to expect danger.

Zakhar Georgiyevich Travkin could have stopped right there! But no! Continuing his attempt to expunge his part in this and to stand erect before his own conscience, he rose from behind his desk—he had never stood up in my presence in my former life—and reached across the quarantine line that separated us and gave me his hand, although he would never have reached out his hand to me had I remained a free man. And pressing my hand, while his whole suite stood there in mute horror, showing that warmth that may appear in an habitually severe face, he said fearlessly and precisely:

"I wish you happiness, Captain!"

Not only was I no longer a captain, but I had been exposed

as an enemy of the people (for among us every person is totally exposed from the moment of arrest). And he had wished happiness—to an enemy?[6]

The panes rattled. The German shells tore up the earth two hundred yards away, reminding one that *this* could not have happened back in the rear, under the ordinary circumstances of established existence, but only out here, under the breath of death, which was not only close by but in the face of which all were equal.

This is not going to be a volume of memoirs about my own life. Therefore I am not going to recount the truly amusing details of my arrest, which was like no other. That night the SMERSH officers gave up their last hope of being able to make out where we were on the map—they never had been able to read maps anyway. So they politely handed the map to me and asked me to tell the driver how to proceed to counterintelligence at army headquarters. I, therefore, led them and myself to that prison, and in gratitude they immediately put me not in an ordinary cell but in a punishment cell. And I really must describe that closet in a German peasant house which served as a temporary punishment cell.

It was the length of one human body and wide enough for three to lie packed tightly, four at a pinch. As it happened, I was the fourth, shoved in after midnight. The three lying there blinked sleepily at me in the light of the smoky kerosene lantern and moved over, giving me enough space to lie on my side, half between them, half on top of them, until gradually, by sheer weight, I could wedge my way in. And so four overcoats lay on the crushed-straw-covered floor, with eight boots pointing at the door. They slept and I burned. The more self-assured I had been as a captain half a day before, the more painful it was to crowd onto the floor of that closet. Once or twice the other fellows woke up numb on one side, and we all turned over at the same time.

6. Here is what is most surprising of all: one *can* be a human being despite everything! Nothing happened to Travkin. Not long ago, we met again cordially, and I really got to know him for the first time. He is a retired general and an inspector of the Hunters' Alliance.

Toward morning they awoke, yawned, grunted, pulled up their legs, moved into various corners, and our acquaintance began.

"What are you in for?"

But a troubled little breeze of caution had already breathed on me beneath the poisoned roof of SMERSH and I pretended to be surprised:

"No idea. Do the bastards tell you?"

However, my cellmates—tankmen in soft black helmets—hid nothing. They were three honest, openhearted soldiers—people of a kind I had become attached to during the war years because I myself was more complex and worse. All three had been officers. Their shoulder boards also had been viciously torn off, and in some places the cotton batting stuck out. On their stained field shirts light patches indicated where decorations had been removed, and there were dark and red scars on their faces and arms, the results of wounds and burns. Their tank unit had, unfortunately, arrived for repairs in the village where the SMERSH counterintelligence headquarters of the Forty-eighth Army was located. Still damp from the battle of the day before, yesterday they had gotten drunk, and on the outskirts of the village broke into a bath where they had noticed two raunchy broads going to bathe. The girls, half-dressed, managed to get away all right from the soldiers' staggering, drunken legs. But one of them, it turned out, was the property of the army Chief of Counterintelligence, no less.

Yes! For three weeks the war had been going on inside Germany, and all of us knew very well that if the girls were German they could be raped and then shot. This was almost a combat distinction. Had they been Polish girls or our own displaced Russian girls, they could have been chased naked around the garden and slapped on the behind—an amusement, no more. But just because this one was the "campaign wife" of the Chief of Counterintelligence, right off some deep-in-the-rear sergeant had viciously torn from three front-line officers the shoulder boards awarded them by the front headquarters and had taken off the decorations conferred upon them by the Presidium of the Supreme Soviet. And now these warriors, who had gone through the whole war and who had no doubt crushed more than one line of enemy trenches, were waiting for a court-martial, whose members, had it not been for their tank, could have come no-where near the village.

We put out the kerosene lamp, which had already used up all the air there was to breathe. A *Judas hole* the size of a postage stamp had been cut in the door and through it came indirect light from the corridor. Then, as if afraid that with the coming of daylight we would have too much room in the punishment cell, they *tossed in* a fifth person. He stepped in wearing a newish Red Army tunic and a cap that was also new, and when he stopped opposite the peephole we could see a fresh face with a turned-up nose and red cheeks.

"Where are you from, brother? Who are you?"

"From the *other* side," he answered briskly. "A shhpy."

"You're kidding!" We were astounded. (To be a spy and to admit it—Sheinin and the brothers Tur had never written that kind of spy story!)

"What is there to kid about in wartime?" the young fellow sighed reasonably. "And just how else can you get back home from being a POW? Well, you tell me!"

He had barely begun to tell us how, some days back, the Germans had led him through the front lines so that he could play the spy and blow up bridges, whereupon he had gone im-mediately to the nearest battalion headquarters to turn himself in; but the weary, sleep-starved battalion commander hadn't believed his story about being a spy and had sent him off to the nurse to get a pill. And at that moment new impressions burst upon us:

"Out for toilet call! Hands behind your backs!" hollered a master sergeant *hardhead* as the door sprang open; he was just built for swinging the tail of a 122-millimeter cannon.

A circle of machine gunners had been strung around the peasant courtyard, guarding the path which was pointed out to us and which went behind the barn. I was bursting with indigna-tion that some ignoramus of a master sergeant dared to give orders to us officers: "Hands behind your backs!" But the tank officers put their hands behind them and I followed suit.

Back of the barn was a small square area in which the snow had been all trampled down but had not yet melted. It was soiled all over with human feces, so densely scattered over the whole square that it was difficult to find a spot to place one's two feet and squat. However, we spread ourselves about and the five of us did squat down. Two machine gunners grimly pointed their machine pistols at us as we squatted, and before a minute had passed the master sergeant brusquely urged us on:

"Come on, hurry it up! With us they do it quickly!"

Not far from me squatted one of the tankmen, a native of Rostov, a tall, melancholy senior lieutenant. His face was blackened by a thin film of metallic dust or smoke, but the big red scar stretching across his cheek stood out nonetheless.

"What do you mean, *with us?*" he asked quietly, indicating no intention of hurrying back to the punishment cell that still stank of kerosene.

"In SMERSH counterintelligence!" the master sergeant shot back proudly and more resonantly than was called for. (The counterintelligence men used to love that tastelessly concocted word "SMERSH," manufactured from the initial syllables of the words for "death to spies." They felt it intimidated people.)

"And *with us* we do it slowly," replied the senior lieutenant thoughtfully. His helmet was pulled back, uncovering his still untrimmed hair. His oaken, battle-hardened rear end was lifted toward the pleasant coolish breeze.

"Where do you mean, *with us?*" the master sergeant barked at him more loudly than he needed to.

"In the Red Army," the senior lieutenant replied very quietly from his heels, measuring with his look the cannon-tailer that never was.

Such were my first gulps of prison air.

Chapter 2

■

The History of Our Sewage Disposal System

When people today decry *the abuses of the cult*, they keep getting hung up on those years which are stuck in our throats, '37 and '38. And memory begins to make it seem as though arrests were never made *before* or *after*, but only in those two years.

Although I have no statistics at hand, I am not afraid of erring when I say that the *wave* of 1937 and 1938 was neither the only one nor even the main one, but only one, perhaps, of the three biggest waves which strained the murky, stinking pipes of our prison sewers to bursting.

Before it came the wave of 1929 and 1930, the size of a good River Ob, which drove a mere fifteen million peasants, maybe even more, out into the taiga and the tundra. But peasants are a silent people, without a literary voice, nor do they write complaints or memoirs. No interrogators sweated out the night with them, nor did they bother to draw up formal indictments—it was enough to have a decree from the village soviet. This wave poured forth, sank down into the permafrost, and even our most active minds recall hardly a thing about it. It is as if it had not even scarred the Russian conscience. And yet Stalin (and you and I as well) committed no crime more heinous than this.

And *after* it there was the wave of 1944 to 1946, the size of a good Yenisei, when they dumped whole *nations* down the sewer pipes, not to mention millions and millions of others who (because of us!) had been prisoners of war, or carried off to Germany and subsequently repatriated. (This was Stalin's method of cauterizing the wounds so that scar tissue would form more quickly, and thus the body politic as a whole would not have to rest up, catch its breath, regain its strength.) But in this wave, too, the people were of the simpler kind, and they wrote no memoirs.

But the wave of 1937 swept up and carried off to the Archipelago people of position, people with a Party past, yes, educated people, around whom were many who had been wounded and remained in the cities . . . and what a lot of them had pen in hand! And today they are all writing, speaking, remembering: "Nineteen thirty-seven!" A whole Volga of the people's grief!

But just say "Nineteen thirty-seven" to a Crimean Tatar, a Kalmyk, a Chechen, and he'll shrug his shoulders. And what's 1937 to Leningrad when 1935 had come before it? And for the *second-termers* (i.e., *repeaters*), or people from the Baltic countries—weren't 1948 and 1949 harder on them? And if sticklers for style and geography should accuse me of having omitted some Russian rivers, and of not yet having named some of the waves, then just give me enough paper! There were enough waves to use up the names of all the rivers of Russia!

It is well known that any *organ* withers away if it is not used. Therefore, if we know that the Soviet Security organs, or *Organs* (and they christened themselves with this vile word), praised and exalted above all living things, have not died off even to the extent of one single tentacle, but, instead, have grown new ones and strengthened their muscles—it is easy to deduce that they have had *constant* exercise.

Through the sewer pipes the flow pulsed. Sometimes the pressure was higher than had been projected, sometimes lower. But the prison sewers were never empty. The blood, the sweat, and the urine into which we were pulped pulsed through them continuously. The history of this sewage system is the history of an endless swallow and flow; flood alternating with ebb and ebb again with flood; waves pouring in, some big, some small; brooks and rivulets flowing in from all sides; trickles oozing in through gutters; and then just plain individually scooped-up droplets.

The chronological list which follows, in which waves made up of millions of arrested persons are given equal attention with ordinary streamlets of unremarkable handfuls, is quite incomplete, meager, miserly, and limited by my own capacity to penetrate the past. What is really needed is a great deal of additional work by survivors familiar with the material.

■

In compiling this list the most difficult thing is to *begin,* partly because the further back into the decades one goes, the fewer the eyewitnesses who are left, and therefore the light of common knowledge has gone out and darkness has set in, and the written chronicles either do not exist or are kept under lock and key. Also, it is not entirely fair to consider in a single category the especially brutal years of the Civil War and the first years of peacetime, when mercy might have been expected.

But even before there was any Civil War, it could be seen that Russia, due to the makeup of its population, was obviously not suited for any sort of socialism whatsoever. It was totally polluted. One of the first blows of the dictatorship was directed against the Cadets—the members of the *Constitutional Democratic Party.* (Under the Tsar they had constituted the most dangerous ranks of revolution, and under the government of the proletariat they represented the most dangerous ranks of reaction.) At the end of November, 1917, on the occasion of the first scheduled convening of the Constituent Assembly, which did not take place, the Cadet Party was outlawed and arrests of its members began. At about the same time, people associated with the "Alliance for the Constituent Assembly" and the students enrolled in the "soldiers' universities" were being *thrown in the jug.*

Knowing the sense and spirit of the Revolution, it is easy to guess that during these months such central prisons as Kresty in Petrograd and the Butyrki in Moscow, and many provincial prisons like them, were filled with wealthy men, prominent public figures, generals and officers, as well as officials of ministries and of the state apparatus who refused to carry out the orders of the new authority. One of the first operations of the Cheka was to arrest the entire committee of the All-Russian Union of Employees.

One of the first circulars of the NKVD, in December, 1917, stated: "In view of sabotage by officials . . . use maximum initiative in localities, *not excluding* confiscations, compulsion, and arrests."[1]

And even though V. I. Lenin, at the end of 1917, in order to establish "strictly revolutionary order," demanded "merciless suppression of attempts at anarchy on the part of drunkards, hooligans, counterrevolutionaries, and other persons"[2]—in other words, foresaw that drunkards and hooligans represented the principal danger to the October Revolution, with counterrevolutionaries somewhere back in third place—he nonetheless put the problem more broadly. In his essay "How to Organize the Competition" (January 7 and 10, 1918), V. I. Lenin proclaimed the common, united purpose of "purging the Russian land of all kinds of harmful insects."[3] And under the term *insects* he included not only all class enemies but also "workers malingering at their work"—for example, the typesetters of the Petrograd Party printing shops. (That is what time does. It is difficult for us nowadays to understand how workers who had just become *dictators* were immediately inclined to malinger at work they were doing for themselves.) And then again: "In what block of a big city, in what factory, in what village . . . are there not . . . saboteurs who call themselves intellectuals?"[4] True, the forms of insect-purging which Lenin conceived of in this essay were most varied: in some places they would be placed under arrest, in other places set to cleaning latrines; in some, "after having served their time in punishment cells, they would be handed yellow tickets"; in others, *parasites would be shot*; elsewhere you could take your pick of imprisonment "or punishment at forced labor of the hardest kind."[5] Even though he perceived and suggested the basic directions punishment should take, Vladimir Ilyich proposed that "communes and communities" should compete to find the best methods of purging.

It is not possible for us at this time fully to investigate exactly

1. *Vestnik NKVD* (*NKVD Herald*), 1917, No. 1, p. 4.
2. Lenin, *Sobrannye Sochineniya* (*Collected Works*), fifth edition, Vol. 35, p. 68.
3. *Ibid.*, p. 204.
4. *Ibid.*
5. *Ibid.*, p. 203.

who fell within the broad definition of *insects*; the population of Russia was too heterogeneous and encompassed small, special groups, entirely superfluous and, today, forgotten. The people in the local zemstvo self-governing bodies in the provinces were, of course, insects. People in the cooperative movement were also insects, as were all owners of their own homes. There were not a few insects among the teachers in the gymnasiums. The church parish councils were made up almost exclusively of insects, and it was insects, of course, who sang in church choirs. All priests were insects—and monks and nuns even more so. And all those Tolstoyans who, when they undertook to serve the Soviet government on, for example, the railroads, refused to sign the required oath to defend the Soviet government with *gun* in hand thereby showed themselves to be insects too. (We will later see some of them on trial.) The railroads were particularly important, for there were indeed many insects hidden beneath railroad uniforms, and they had to be *rooted out* and some of them *slapped down*. And telegraphers, for some reason, were, for the most part, inveterate insects who had no sympathy for the Soviets. Nor could you say a good word about *Vikzhel,* the All-Russian Executive Committee of the Union of Railroad Workers, nor about the other trade unions, which were often filled with insects hostile to the working class.

Just those groups we have so far enumerated represent an enormous number of people—several years' worth of purge activity.

In addition, how many kinds of cursed intellectuals there were —restless students and a variety of eccentrics, truth-seekers, and holy fools, of whom even Peter the Great had tried in vain to purge Russia and who are always a hindrance to a well-ordered, strict regime.

It would have been impossible to carry out this hygienic purging, especially under wartime conditions, if they had had to follow outdated legal processes and normal judicial procedures. And so an entirely new form was adopted: *extrajudicial reprisal,* and this thankless job was self-sacrificingly assumed by the Cheka, the Sentinel of the Revolution, which was the only punitive organ in human history that combined in one set of hands investigation, arrest, interrogation, prosecution, trial, and execution of the *verdict.*

In 1918, in order to speed up the cultural victory of the Revolution as well, they began to ransack the churches and throw out the relics of saints, and to carry off church plate. Popular disorders broke out in defense of the plundered churches and monasteries. Here and there the alarm bells rang out, and the true Orthodox believers rushed forth, some of them with clubs. Naturally, some had to be *expended* right on the spot and others arrested.

In considering now the period from 1918 to 1920, we are in difficulties: Should we classify among the prison waves all those who were done in before they even got to prison cells? And in what classification should we put those whom the Committees of the Poor took behind the wing of the village soviet or to the rear of the courtyard, and *finished off* right there? Did the participants in the clusters of plots uncovered in every province (two in Ryazan; one in Kostroma, Vyshni Volochek, and Velizh; several in Kiev; several in Moscow; one in Saratov, Chernigov, Astrakhan, Seliger, Smolensk, Bobruisk, the Tambov Cavalry, Chembar, Velikiye Luki, Mstislavl, etc.) at least succeed in setting foot on the land of the Archipelago, or did they not— and are they therefore not related to the subject of our investigations? Bypassing the repression of the now famous rebellions (Yaroslavl, Murom, Rybinsk, Arzamas), we know of certain events only by their names—for instance, the Kolpino executions of June, 1918. What were they? Who were they? And where should they be classified?

There is also no little difficulty in deciding whether we should classify among the prison waves or on the balance sheets of the Civil War those tens of thousands of *hostages*, i.e., people not personally accused of anything, those peaceful citizens not even listed by name, who were taken off and destroyed simply to terrorize or wreak vengeance on a military enemy or a rebellious population. After August 30, 1918, the NKVD ordered the localities "to arrest immediately *all* Right Socialist Revolutionaries and to take *a significant number of hostages* from the bourgeoisie and military officers."[6] (This was just as if, for example, after the attempt of Aleksandr Ulyanov's group to assassinate the Tsar, not only its members but *all* the students in Russia and a *significant number of zemstvo officials* had been arrested.) By

6. *Vestnik NKVD*, 1918, No. 21–22, p. 1.

a decree of the Defense Council of February 15, 1919—apparently with Lenin in the chair—the Cheka and the NKVD were ordered to take hostage *peasants* from those localities where the removal of snow from railroad tracks "was not proceeding satisfactorily," and "if the snow removal did not take place they were to be shot."[7] (At the end of 1920, by decree of the Council of People's Commissars, permission was given to take Social Democrats as hostages too.)

But even restricting ourselves to ordinary arrests, we can note that by the spring of 1918 a torrent of socialist traitors had already begun that was to continue without slackening for many years. All these parties—the SR's, the Mensheviks, the Anarchists, the Popular Socialists—had for decades only pretended to be revolutionaries; they had worn socialism only as a mask, and for that they went to hard labor, still pretending. Only during the violent course of the Revolution was the bourgeois essence of these socialist traitors discovered. What could be more natural than to begin arresting them! Soon after the outlawing of the Cadets, the dispersal of the Constituent Assembly, the disarming of the Preobrazhensky and other regiments, they began in a small way to arrest, quietly at first, both SR's and Mensheviks. After June 14, 1918, the day members of these parties were excluded from all the soviets, the arrests proceeded in a more intensive and more coordinated fashion. From July 6 on, they began to deal with the Left SR's in the same way, though the Left SR's had been cleverer and had gone on pretending longer that they were allies of the one and only consistent party of the proletariat. From then on, it was enough for a workers' protest, a disturbance, a strike, to occur at any factory or in any little town (and there were many of them in the summer of 1918; and in March, 1921, they shook Petrograd, Moscow, and then Kronstadt and forced the inauguration of the NEP), and— coinciding with concessions, assurances, and the satisfaction for the just demands of the workers—the Cheka began silently to pick up Mensheviks and SR's at night as being the people truly to blame for these disorders. In the summer of 1918 and in April and October of 1919, they jailed Anarchists right and

7. *Dekrety Sovetskoi Vlasti* (*Decrees of the Soviet Regime*), Vol. 4, Moscow, 1968, p. 627.

left. In 1919 they arrested all the members of the SR Central Committee they could catch—and kept them imprisoned in the Butyrki up to the time of their trial in 1922. In that same year, Latsis, a leading Chekist, wrote of the Mensheviks: "People of this sort are more than a mere hindrance to us. That is why we remove them from our path, so they won't get under our feet. . . . We put them away in a secluded, cozy place, in the Butyrki, and we are going to keep them there until the struggle between capital and labor comes to an end."[8] In 1919, also, the delegates to the Non-Party Workers Congress were arrested; as a result, the Congress never took place.[9]

In 1919, suspicion of our Russians returning from abroad was already having its effect (Why? What was their alleged assignment?)—thus the officers of the Russian expeditionary force in France were imprisoned on their homecoming.

In 1919, too, what with the big hauls in connection with such actual and pseudo plots as the "National Center" and the "Military Plot," executions were carried out in Moscow, Petrograd, and other cities *on the basis of lists*—in other words, free people were simply arrested and executed immediately, and right and left those elements of the intelligentsia considered *close to the Cadets* were raked into prison. (What does the term "close to the Cadets" mean? *Not* monarchist and *not* socialist: in other words, all scientific circles, all university circles, all artistic, literary, yes, and, of course, all engineering circles. Except for the extremist writers, except for the theologians and theoreticians of socialism, all the rest of the intelligentsia, 80 percent of it, was "close to the Cadets.") In that category, for example, Lenin placed the writer Korolenko—"a pitiful petty bourgeois, imprisoned in bourgeois prejudices."[10] He considered it was "not amiss" for such "talents" to spend a few weeks in prison.[11] From Gorky's protests we learn of individual groups that were arrested. On September 15, 1919, Lenin replied to him: "It is clear to us that there were some mistakes." But: "What a

8. M. I. Latsis, *Dva Goda Borby na Vnutrennom Fronte; Populyarni Obzor Deyatelnosti ChK (Two Years of Struggle on the Home Front; Popular Review of the Activity of the Cheka)*, Moscow, GIZ, 1920, p. 61.

9. *Ibid.*, p. 60.

10. Lenin, fifth edition, Vol. 51, pp. 47, 48.

11. *Ibid.*, p. 48.

misfortune, just think about it! What injustice!"[12] And he advised Gorky "not to waste [his] energy whimpering over rotten intellectuals."[13]

From January, 1919, on, food requisitioning was organized and food-collecting detachments were set up. They encountered resistance everywhere in the rural areas, sometimes stubborn and passive, sometimes violent. The suppression of this opposition gave rise to an abundant flood of arrests during the course of the next two years, not counting those who were shot on the spot.

I am deliberately bypassing here the major part of the grinding done by the Cheka, the Special Branches, and the Revolutionary Tribunals as the front line advanced and cities and provinces were occupied. And that same NKVD directive of August 30, 1918, ordered that efforts be made to ensure "the unconditional execution of all who had been involved in White Guard work." But sometimes it is not clear where to draw the line. By the summer of 1920, for example, the Civil War had not entirely ended everywhere. But it was over on the Don; nonetheless officers were sent from there en masse—from Rostov, and from Novocherkassk—to Archangel, whence they were transported to the Solovetsky Islands, and, it is said, several of the barges were sunk in the White Sea and in the Caspian Sea. Now should this be billed to the Civil War or to the beginning of peacetime reconstruction? In Novocherkassk, in the same year, they shot the pregnant wife of an officer because she had hidden her husband. In what classification should she be put?

In May, 1920, came the well-known decree of the Central Committee "on Subversive Activity in the Rear." We know from experience that every such decree is a call for a new wave of widespread arrests; it is the outward sign of such a wave.

A particular difficulty—and also a particular advantage—in the organization of all these waves was the absence of a criminal code or any system of criminal law whatsoever before 1922. Only a revolutionary sense of justice (always infallible) guided those doing the purging and managing the sewage system when they were deciding whom to *take* and what to do with them.

In this survey we are not going to investigate the successive

12. *Ibid.*, p. 47.
13. *Ibid.*, p. 49.

waves of habitual criminals (ugolovniki) and nonpolitical offenders (bytoviki). Therefore we will merely recall that the country-wide poverty and shortages during the period when the government, all institutions, and the laws themselves were being reorganized could serve only to increase greatly the number of thefts, robberies, assaults, bribes, and the resale of merchandise for excessive profit (speculation). Even though these crimes presented less danger to the existence of the Republic, they, too, had to be repressed, and their own waves of prisoners served to swell the waves of counterrevolutionaries. And there was *speculation*, too, of a purely political character, as was pointed out in the decree of the Council of People's Commissars signed by Lenin on July 22, 1918: "Those guilty of selling, or buying up, or keeping for sale in the way of business food products which have been placed under the monopoly of the Republic [A peasant keeps grains for sale in the way of business. What else is his business anyway?] . . . imprisonment for a term of *not less* than ten years, combined with the *most severe* forced labor and confiscation of *all* their property."

From that summer on, the countryside, which had already been strained to the utmost limits, gave up its harvest year after year without compensation. This led to peasant revolts and, in the upshot, suppression of the revolts and new arrests.[14] It was in 1920 that we knew (or failed to know) of the trial of the "Siberian Peasants' Union." And at the end of 1920 the repression of the Tambov peasants' rebellion began. There was no trial for them.

But the main drive to uproot people from the Tambov villages took place mostly in June, 1921. Throughout the province concentration camps were set up for the families of peasants who had taken part in the revolts. Tracts of open field were enclosed with barbed wire strung on posts, and for three weeks every family of a suspected rebel was confined there. If within that time the man of the family did not turn up to buy his family's way out with his own head, they sent the family into exile.[15]

Even earlier, in March, 1921, the rebellious Kronstadt sailors,

14. "The hardest-working sector of the nation was positively uprooted." Korolenko, letter to Gorky, August 10, 1921.
15. Tukhachevsky, "Borba s Kontrrevolyutsionnymi Vostaniyami" ("The Struggle Against Counterrevolutionary Revolts"), in *Voina i Revolyutsiya* (*War and Revolution*), 1926, No. 7/8.

minus those who had been shot, were sent to the islands of the Archipelago via the Trubetskoi bastion of the Peter and Paul Fortress.

That same year, 1921, began with Cheka Order No. 10, dated January 8: "To *intensify* the repression of the bourgeoisie." Now, when the Civil War had ended, repression was not to be reduced but *intensified!* Voloshin has pictured for us in several of his poems how this worked out in the Crimea.

In the summer of 1921, the State Commission for Famine Relief, including Kuskova, Prokopovich, Kishkin, and others, was arrested. They had tried to combat the unprecedented famine in Russia. The heart of the matter, however, was that theirs were the *wrong hands* to be offering food and could not be allowed to feed the starving. The chairman of this commission, the dying Korolenko, who was pardoned, called the destruction of the commission "the worst of dirty political tricks, a dirty political trick by the government."[16]

In that same year the practice of arresting *students* began (for example, the group of Yevgeniya Doyarenko in the Timiryazev Academy) for "criticism of the system" (not in public, merely in conversation among themselves). Such cases, however, were evidently few, because the group in question was interrogated by Menzhinsky and Yagoda personally.

Also in 1921 the arrests of members of all non-Bolshevik parties were expanded and systematized. In fact, all Russia's political parties had been buried, except the victorious one. (Oh, do not dig a grave for someone else!) And so that the dissolution of these parties would be irreversible, it was necessary that their members should disintegrate and their physical bodies too.

Not one citizen of the former Russian state who had ever joined a party other than the Bolshevik Party could avoid his fate. He was condemned unless, like Maisky or Vyshinsky, he succeeded in making his way across the planks of the wreck to the Bolsheviks. He might not be arrested in the first group. He might live on, depending on how dangerous he was believed to be, until 1922, 1932, or even 1937, but the lists were kept; his

16. Korolenko's letter to Gorky, September 14, 1921. Korolenko also reminds us of a particularly important situation in the prisons of 1921: "Everywhere they are saturated with typhus." This has been confirmed by Skripnikova and others imprisoned at the time.

turn would and did come; he was arrested or else politely invited to an interrogation, where he was asked just one question: Had he been a member of such and such, from then till then? (There were also questions about hostile activity, but the first question decided everything, as is clear to us now, decades later.) From there on his fate might vary. Some were put immediately in one of the famous Tsarist central prisons—fortunately, all the Tsarist central prisons had been well preserved—and some socialists even ended up in the very same cells and with the very same jailers they had had before. Others were offered the opportunity of going into exile—oh, not for long, just for two or three years. And some had it even easier: they were merely given a *minus* (a certain number of cities were forbidden) and told to pick out a new place of residence *themselves,* and for the future would they please be so kind as to stay fixed in that one place and await the pleasure of the GPU.

This whole operation was stretched out over many years because it was of primary importance that it be stealthy and unnoticed. It was essential to clean out, conscientiously, socialists of every other stripe from Moscow, Petrograd, the ports, the industrial centers, and, later on, the outlying provinces as well. This was a grandiose silent game of solitaire, whose rules were totally incomprehensible to its contemporaries, and whose outlines we can appreciate only now. Someone's far-seeing mind, someone's neat hands, planned it all, without letting one wasted minute go by. They picked up a card which had spent three years in one pile and softly placed it on another pile. And the person who had been imprisoned in a central prison was thereby shifted into exile—and a good way off. Someone who had served out a "minus" sentence was sent into exile, too, but out of sight of the rest of the "minus" category, or else from exile to exile, and then back again into the central prison—but this time a different one. Patience, overwhelming patience, was the trait of the person playing out the solitaire. And without any noise, without any outcry, the members of all the other parties slipped gradually out of sight, lost all connection with the places and people where they and their revolutionary activities were known, and thus—imperceptibly and mercilessly—was prepared the annihilation of those who had once raged against tyranny at student meetings and had clanked their Tsarist shackles in pride.[17]

In this game of the Big Solitaire, the majority of the old political prisoners, survivors of hard labor, were destroyed, for it was primarily the SR's and the Anarchists—not the Social Democrats—who had received the harshest sentences from the Tsarist courts. They in particular had made up the population of the Tsarist hard-labor political prisons.

There was justice in the priorities of destruction, however; in 1920 they were all offered the chance to renounce in writing their parties and party ideologies. Some declined—and they, naturally, came up first for annihilation. Others signed such renunciations, and thereby added a few years to their lifetimes. But their turn, too, came implacably, and their heads rolled implacably from their shoulders.[18]

In the spring of 1922 the Extraordinary Commission for Struggle Against Counterrevolution, Sabotage, and Speculation, the Cheka, recently renamed the GPU, decided to intervene in church affairs. It was called on to carry out a "church revolution"—to remove the existing leadership and replace it with one which would have only one ear turned to heaven and the other to the Lubyanka. The so-called "Living Church" people seemed to go along with this plan, but without outside help they could not gain control of the church apparatus. For this reason, the Patriarch Tikhon was arrested and two resounding trials were held, followed by the execution in Moscow of those who had publicized the Patriarch's appeal and, in Petrograd, of the Metropolitan Veniamin, who had attempted to hinder the transfer of ecclesiastical power to the "Living Church" group. Here and there in the provincial centers and even further down in the

17. V. G. Korolenko wrote to Gorky, June 29, 1921: "History will someday note that the Bolshevik Revolution used the same means to deal with true revolutionaries and socalists as did the Tsarist regime, in other words, purely police measures."

18. Sometimes, reading a newspaper article, one is astonished to the point of disbelief. In *Izvestiya* of May 24, 1959, one could read that a year after Hitler came to power Maximilian Hauke was arrested for belonging to none other than the Communist Party. Was he destroyed? No, they sentenced him to *two* years. After this was he, naturally, sentenced to a second term? No, he was released. You can interpret that as you please! He proceeded to live quietly and build an underground organization, in connection with which the *Izvestiya* article on his courage appeared.

administrative districts, metropolitans and bishops were arrested, and, as always, in the wake of the big fish, followed shoals of smaller fry: archpriests, monks, and deacons. These arrests were not even reported in the press. They also arrested those who refused to swear to support the "Living Church" "renewal" movement.

Men of religion were an inevitable part of every annual "catch," and their silver locks gleamed in every cell and in every prisoner transport en route to the Solovetsky Islands.

From the early twenties on, arrests were also made among groups of theosophists, mystics, spiritualists. (Count Palen's group used to keep official transcripts of its communications with the spirit world.) Also, religious societies and philosophers of the Berdyayev circle. The so-called "Eastern Catholics"—followers of Vladimir Solovyev—were arrested and destroyed in passing, as was the group of A. I. Abrikosova. And, of course, ordinary Roman Catholics—Polish Catholic priests, etc.—were arrested, too, as part of the normal course of events.

However, the root destruction of religion in the country, which throughout the twenties and thirties was one of the most important goals of the GPU-NKVD, could be realized only by mass arrests of Orthodox believers. Monks and nuns, whose black habits had been a distinctive feature of Old Russian life, were intensively rounded up on every hand, placed under arrest, and sent into exile. They arrested and sentenced active laymen. The circles kept getting bigger, as they raked in ordinary believers as well, old people, and particularly women, who were the most stubborn believers of all and who, for many long years to come, would be called "nuns" in transit prisons and in camps.

True, they were supposedly being arrested and tried not for their actual faith but for openly declaring their convictions and for bringing up their children in the same spirit. As Tanya Khodkevich wrote:

> You can pray *freely*
> But just so God alone can hear.

(She received a ten-year sentence for these verses.) A person convinced that he possessed spiritual truth was required to conceal it from his own children! In the twenties the religious education of children was classified as a political crime under Article 58-10 of the Code—in other words, counterrevolutionary propaganda! True, one was still permitted to renounce one's religion at one's trial: it didn't often happen but it nonetheless did happen that the father would renounce his religion and remain at home to raise the children while the mother went to the Solovetsky Islands. (Throughout all those years women manifested great firmness in their faith.) All persons convicted of religious activity received *tenners*, the longest term then given.

(In those years, particularly in 1927, in purging the big cities for the pure society that was coming into being, they sent prostitutes to the Solovetsky Islands along with the "nuns." Those lovers of a sinful earthly life were given *three*-year sentences under a more lenient article of the Code. The conditions in prisoner transports, in transit prisons, and on the Solovetsky Islands were not of a sort to hinder them from plying their merry trade among the administrators and the convoy guards. And three years later they would return with laden suitcases to the places they had come from. Religious prisoners, however, were prohibited from ever returning to their children and their home areas.)

As early as the early twenties, waves appeared that were purely national in character—at first not very large in proportion to the populations of their homelands, especially by Russian yardsticks: Mussavatists from Azerbaijan; Dashnaks from Armenia; Georgian Mensheviks; and Turkmenian Basmachi, who were resisting the establishment of Soviet power in Central Asia. (The first Central Asian soviets were Russian in makeup by an overwhelming majority, and were therefore seen as outposts of Russian power.) In 1926 the Zionist society of "Hehalutz" was exiled in toto—since it had failed to respond to the all-powerful upsurge of internationalism.

Among subsequent generations, a picture has evolved of the twenties as some kind of holiday of totally unlimited freedom. In this book we shall encounter people who viewed the twenties quite differently. The non-Party students at this time sought "autonomy for higher educational institutions," the right of assembly, and the removal from the curriculum of excessive political indoctrination. Arrests were the answer. These were intensified during holidays— for example, on May 1, 1924. In 1925, about one hundred Leningrad students were sentenced to three years in political detention for reading the *Sotsialistichesky Vestnik*—the organ of the Mensheviks abroad—and for studying Plekhanov. (In his youth Plekhanov himself had gotten off far more lightly for speaking out against the government in front of Kazan Cathedral.) In 1925 they had already begun to arrest the first (young) Trotskyites. (Two naïve Red Army men, remembering the Russian tradition, began to collect funds for the arrested Trotskyites—and they, too, were put in political detention.)

And, of course, it is obvious that the exploiting classes were not spared. Throughout the twenties the hunt continued for former officers who had managed to survive: "Whites" (those who had not already earned execution during the Civil War); "White-Reds," who had fought on both sides; and "Tsarist Reds," Tsarist officers who had gone over to the Red Army but had not served in it for the whole period or who had gaps in their army service records and no documents to account for them. They were truly put through the mill because instead of being sentenced immediately they, too, were put through the solitaire game: endless verifications, limitations on the kind of work they could do and on where they could live; they were taken into custody, released, taken into custody again. And only gradually did they proceed to the camps, from which they did not return.

However, sending these officers to the Archipelago did not end the problem but only set it in motion. After all, their mothers, wives, and children were still at liberty. With the help of unerring social analysis it was easy to see what kind of mood they were in after the heads of their households had been arrested. And thus they simply compelled their own arrest too! And one more wave was set rolling.

In the twenties there was an amnesty for Cossacks who had taken part in the Civil War. Many of them returned from the island of Lemnos to the Kuban, where they were given land. All of them were subsequently arrested.

And, of course, all former state officials had gone into hiding and were likewise liable to be hunted down. They had hidden well and disguised themselves cleverly, making use of the fact that there was as yet no internal passport system nor any unified system of work-books in the Republic—and they managed to creep into

Soviet institutions. In such cases, slips of the tongue, chance recognitions, and the denunciations of neighbors helped battle-intelligence—so to speak. (Sometimes sheer accident took a hand. Solely out of a love of order, a certain Mova kept at home a list of all former employees of the provincial judiciary. This was discovered by accident in 1925, and they were all arrested and shot.)

And so the waves rolled on—for "concealment of social origin" and for "former social origin." This received the widest interpretation. They arrested members of the nobility for their social origin. They arrested members of their families. Finally, unable to draw even simple distinctions, they arrested members of the *"individual nobility"*—i.e., anybody who had simply graduated from a university. And once they had been arrested, there was no way back. You can't undo what has been done! The Sentinel of the Revolution never makes a mistake!

(No. There were a few ways back! The *counterwaves* were thin, sparse, but they did sometimes break through. The first is worthy of mention right here. Among the wives and daughters of the nobility and the officers there were quite often women of outstanding personal qualities and attractive appearance. Some succeeded in breaking through in a small *reverse* wave! They were the ones who remembered that life is given to us only once and that nothing is more precious to us than *our own life*. They offered their services to the Cheka-GPU as informers, as colleagues, in any capacity whatsoever—and those who were liked were accepted. These were the most fertile of all informers! They helped the GPU a great deal, because "former" people trusted them. Here one can name the last Princess Vyazemskaya, a most prominent postrevolutionary informer [as was her son on the Solovetsky Islands]. And Konkordiya Nikolayevna Iosse was evidently a woman of brilliant qualities: her husband was an officer who had been shot in her presence, and she herself was exiled to the Solovetsky Islands. But she managed to beg her way out and to set up a salon near the Big Lubyanka which the important figures of that establishment loved to frequent. She was not arrested again until 1937, along with her Yagoda customers.)

It is strange to recount, but as a result of an absurd tradition the Political Red Cross had been preserved from Old Russia.

There were three branches: the Moscow branch (Y. Peshkova-Vinaver); the Kharkov (Sandormirskaya); and the Petrograd. The one in Moscow behaved itself and was not dissolved until 1937. The one in Petrograd (the old Narodnik Shevtsov, the cripple Gartman, and Kocherovsky) adopted an intolerably impudent stance, mixed into political cases, tried to get support from such former inmates of the Schlüsselburg Prison as Novorussky, who had been convicted in the same case as Lenin's brother, Aleksandr Ulyanov, and helped not only socialists but also KR's —Counter-Revolutionaries. In 1926 it was shut down and its leaders were sent into exile.

The years go by, and everything that has not been freshly recalled to us is wiped from our memory. In the dim distance, we see the year 1927 as a careless, well-fed year of the still untruncated NEP. But in fact it was tense; it shuddered as newspaper headlines exploded; and it was considered at the time, and portrayed to us then, as the threshold of a war for world revolution. The assassination of the Soviet ambassador in Warsaw, which filled whole columns of the papers that June, aroused Mayakovsky to dedicate four thunderous verses to the subject.

But here's bad luck for you: Poland offered an apology; Voikov's lone assassin was arrested there—and so how and against whom was the poet's appeal to be directed?[19]

> With cohesion,
>> construction,
>>> grit,
>>>> and *repression*
>
> Wring the neck
>> of this gang run riot!

Who was to be repressed? Whose neck should be wrung? It was then that the so-called *Voikov draft* began. As always happened when there were incidents of disturbance or tension, they arrested *former* people: Anarchists, SR's, Mensheviks, and also *the intel-*

19. Evidently, the monarchist in question assassinated Voikov as an act of private vengeance: it is said that as Urals Provincial Commissar of Foodstuffs, in July, 1918, P. L. Voikov had directed the destruction of all traces of the shooting of the Tsar's family (the dissection and dismemberment of the corpses, the cremation of the remains, and the dispersal of the ashes).

ligentsia as such. Indeed, who else was there to arrest in the cities? Not the working class!

But the old "close-to-the-Cadets" intelligentsia had already been thoroughly shaken up, starting in 1919. Had the time not come to shake up that part of the intelligentsia which imagined itself to be progressive? To give the students a once-over? Once again Mayakovsky came to the rescue:

> Think
> > about the Komsomol
> > > for days and for weeks!
>
> Look over
> > your ranks,
> > > watch them with care.
>
> Are all of them
> > really
> > > Komsomols?
>
> Or are they
> > only
> > > pretending to be?

A convenient world outlook gives rise to a convenient juridical term: *social prophylaxis*. It was introduced and accepted, and it was immediately understood by all. (Lazar Kogan, one of the bosses of the White Sea Canal construction, would, in fact, soon say: "I believe that you personally were not guilty of anything. But, as an educated person, you have to understand that social prophylaxis was being widely applied!") And when else, in fact, should unreliable fellow travelers, all that shaky intellectual rot, be arrested, if not on the eve of the war for world revolution? When the big war actually began, it would be too late.

And so in Moscow they began a systematic search, block by block. Someone had to be arrested everywhere. The slogan was: "We are going to bang our fist on the table so hard that the world will shake with terror!" It was to the Lubyanka, to the Butyrki, that the Black Marias, the passenger cars, the enclosed trucks, the open hansom cabs kept moving, even by day. There was a jam at the gates, a jam in the courtyard. They didn't have time to unload and register those they'd arrested. (And the same situation existed in other cities. In Rostov-on-the-Don during those days the floor was so crowded in the cellar of House 33 that the newly arrived Boiko could hardly find a place to sit down.)

A typical example from this wave: Several dozen young people got together for some kind of musical evening which had not been authorized ahead of time by the GPU. They listened to music and then drank tea. They got the money for the tea by voluntarily contributing their own kopecks. It was quite clear, of course, that this music was a cover for counterrevolutionary sentiments, and that the money was being collected not for tea but to assist the dying world bourgeoisie. And they were *all* arrested and given from three to ten years—Anna Skripnikova getting five, while Ivan Nikolayevich Varentsov and the other organizers of the affair who refused to confess were *shot!*

And in that same year, somewhere in Paris, a group of Russian émigré Lycée graduates gathered to celebrate the traditional Pushkin holiday. A report of this was published in the papers. It was clearly an intrigue on the part of mortally wounded imperialism, and as a result *all* Lycée graduates still left in the U.S.S.R. were arrested, as were the so-called "law students" (graduates of another such privileged special school of prerevolutionary Russia).

Only the size of SLON—the Solovetsky Special Purpose Camp—limited for the time being the scale of the Voikov draft. But the Gulag Archipelago had already begun its malignant life and would shortly metastasize throughout the whole body of the nation.

A new taste had been acquired and a new appetite began to grow. The time had long since arrived to crush the technical intelligentsia, which had come to regard itself as too irreplaceable and had not gotten used to catching instructions on the wing.

In other words, we never did trust the engineers—and from the very first years of the Revolution we saw to it that those lackeys and servants of former capitalist bosses were kept in line by healthy suspicion and surveillance by the workers. However, during the reconstruction period, we did permit them to work in our industries, while the whole force of the class assault was directed against the rest of the intelligentsia. But the more our own economic leadership matured—in VSNKh (the Supreme Council of the Economy) and Gosplan (the State Planning Commission) —the more the number of plans increased, and the more those plans overlapped and conflicted with one another, the clearer became the old engineers' basic commitment to wrecking, their insincerity, slyness, venality. The Sentinel of the Revolution narrowed its eyes with even greater vigilance—and wherever it directed its narrowed gaze it immediately discovered a nest of wreckers.

This therapy continued full speed from 1927 on, and immediately exposed to the proletariat all the causes of our economic failures and shortages. There was wrecking in the People's Commissariat of Railroads—that was why it was hard to get aboard a train, why there were interruptions in supplies. There was wrecking in the Moscow Electric Power System—and interruptions in power. There was wrecking in the oil industry—hence the shortage of kerosene. There was wrecking in textiles—hence nothing for a workingman to wear. In the coal industry there was colossal wrecking—hence no heat! In the metallurgy, defense, machinery, shipbuilding, chemical, mining, gold and platinum industries, in irrigation, everywhere there were these pus-filled boils of wrecking! Enemies with slide rules were on all sides. The GPU puffed and panted in its efforts to grab off and drag off the "wreckers." In the capitals and in the provinces, GPU collegiums and proletarian courts kept hard at work, sifting through this viscous sewage, and every day the workers gasped to learn (and sometimes they didn't learn) from the papers of new vile deeds. They learned about Palchinsky, von Meck, and Velichko,[20] and how many others who were nameless. Every industry, every factory, and every handicraft artel had to find wreckers in its ranks, and no sooner had they begun to look than they found them (with the help of the GPU). If any prerevolutionary engineer was not yet exposed as a traitor, then he could certainly be suspected of being one.

And what accomplished villains these old engineers were! What diabolical ways to sabotage they found! Nikolai Karlovich von Meck, of the People's Commissariat of Railroads, pretended to

20. A. F. Velichko, a military engineer, former professor of the Military Academy of the General Staff, and a lieutenant general, had been in charge of the Administration for Military Transport in the Tsarist War Ministry. He was shot. Oh, how useful he would have been in 1941!

be terribly devoted to the development of the new economy, and would hold forth for hours on end about the economic problems involved in the construction of socialism, and he loved to give advice. One such pernicious piece of advice was to increase the size of freight trains and not worry about heavier than average loads. The GPU exposed von Meck, and he was shot: his objective had been to wear out rails and roadbeds, freight cars and locomotives, so as to leave the Republic without railroads in case of foreign military intervention! When, not long afterward, the new People's Commissar of Railroads, Comrade Kaganovich, ordered that average loads should be increased, and even doubled and tripled them (and for this discovery received the Order of Lenin along with others of our leaders)—the malicious engineers who protested became known as *limiters*. They raised the outcry that this was too much, and would result in the breakdown of the rolling stock, and they were rightly shot for their lack of faith in the possibilities of socialist transport.

These *limiters* were pursued for several years. In all branches of the economy they brandished their formulas and calculations and refused to understand that bridges and lathes could respond to the enthusiasm of the personnel. (These were the years when all the norms of folk psychology were turned inside out: the circumspect folk wisdom expressed in such a proverb as "Haste makes waste" was ridiculed, and the ancient saying that "The slower you go, the farther you'll get" was turned inside out.) The only thing which at times delayed the arrest of the old engineers was the absence of a new batch to take their place. Nikolai Ivanovich Ladyzhensky, chief engineer of defense plants in Izhevsk, was first arrested for "limitation theories" and "blind faith in safety factors" (which explained why he considered inadequate the funds allocated by Ordzhonikidze for factory expansion).[21] Then they put him under house arrest and ordered him back to work in his old job. Without him the work was collapsing. He put it back in shape. But the funds allocated were just as inadequate as they had been earlier, and so once again he was thrown in prison, this time for "incorrect use of funds": the funds were insufficient, they

21. They say that when Ordzhonikidze used to talk with the old engineers, he would put one pistol on his desk beside his right hand and another beside his left.

charged, because the chief engineer had used them inefficiently! Ladyzhensky died in camp after a year of timbering.

Thus in the course of a few years they broke the back of the Old Russian engineers who had constituted the glory of the country, who were the beloved heroes of such writers as Garin-Mikhailovsky, Chekhov, and Zamyatin.

It is to be understood, of course, that in this wave, as in all of them, other people were taken too: for example, those who had been near and dear to and connected with those doomed. I hesitate to sully the shining bronze countenance of the Sentinel of the Revolution, yet I must: they also arrested persons who refused to become informers. We would ask the reader to keep in mind at all times, but especially in connection with the first postrevolutionary decade, this entirely secret wave, which never surfaced in public: at that time people still had their pride, and many of them quite failed to comprehend that morality is a relative thing, having only a narrow class meaning, and they dared to reject the employment offered them, and they were all punished without mercy. In fact, at this time young Magdalena Edzhubova was supposed to act as an informer on a group of engineers, and she not only dared to refuse but also told her guardian (it was against him she was supposed to inform). However, he was arrested soon anyway, and in the course of the investigation he confessed everything. Edzhubova, who was pregnant, was arrested for "revealing an operational secret" and was sentenced to be shot—but subsequently managed to get off with a twenty-five-year string of sentences. In that same year, 1927, though in a completely different milieu, among the leading Kharkov Communists, Nadezhda Vitalyevna Surovets refused to become an informer and spy on members of the Ukrainian government. For this she was arrested by the GPU, and not until a quarter of a century later did she manage to emerge, barely alive, in the Kolyma. As for those who didn't survive—of them we know nothing.

(In the thirties this wave of the disobedient fell off to zero: if they asked you to, then it meant you had to inform—where would you hide? "The weakest go to the wall." "If I don't, someone else will." "Better me than someone bad." Meanwhile there were plenty of volunteers; you couldn't get away from them: it was both profitable and praiseworthy.)

In 1928 in Moscow the big Shakhty case came to trial—big in terms of the publicity it was given, in the startling confessions and self-flagellation of the defendants (though not yet all of them). Two years later, in September, 1930, the *famine organizers* were tried with a great hue and cry. (They were the ones! There they are!) There were forty-eight wreckers in the food industry. At the end of 1930, the trial of the Promparty was put on with even greater fanfare. It had been faultlessly rehearsed. In this case every single defendant took upon himself the blame for every kind of filthy rubbish—and then, like a monument unveiled, there arose before the eyes of the workers the grandiose, cunningly contrived skein in which all the separate wrecking cases previously exposed were tied into one diabolical knot along with Milyukov, Ryabushinsky, Deterding, and Poincaré.

As we begin to understand our judicial practices, we realize now that the public trials were only the surface indications of the mole's tunnel, and that all the main digging lay beneath the surface. At these trials only a small number of those arrested were produced in court—only those who agreed to the unnatural practice of accusing themselves and others in the hope of getting off more easily. The majority of the engineers, who had the courage and intelligence to reject and refute the interrogators' stupidities, were tried out of earshot. But even though they did not confess, they got the same *tenners* from the Collegium of the GPU.

The waves flowed underground through the pipes; they provided sewage disposal for the life flowering on the surface.

It was precisely at this moment that an important step was taken toward universal participation in sewage disposal, universal distribution of responsibility for it. Those who had not yet been swept bodily down the sewer hatches, who had not yet been carried through the pipes to the Archipelago, had to march up above, carrying banners praising the trials, and rejoicing at the judicial reprisals. (And this was very farsighted! Decades would pass, and history would have its eyes opened, but the interrogators, judges, and prosecutors would turn out to be no more guilty than you and I, fellow citizens! The reason we possess our worthy gray heads is that in our time we worthily voted *"for."*)

Stalin carried out the first such effort in connection with the trial of the *famine organizers*—and how could it not succeed when everyone was starving in bounteous Russia, and everyone was always looking about and asking: "Where did all our dear bread get to?" Therefore, before the court verdict, the workers and employees wrathfully voted for the death penalty for the scoundrels on trial. And by the time of the Promparty trial, there were universal meetings and demonstrations (including even schoolchildren). It was the newspaper march of millions, and the roar rose outside the windows of the courtroom: "Death! Death! Death!"

At this turning point in our history, there were some lonely voices of protest or abstention—and very, very great bravery was required to say "No!" in the midst of that roaring chorus of approval. It is incomparably easier today! (Yet even today people don't very often vote "*against*.") To the extent that we know about them, it was those same spineless, slushy intellectuals. At the meeting of the Leningrad Polytechnic Institute, Professor Dmitri Apollinaryevich Rozhansky *abstained* (he was an enemy of capital punishment *in general*, you see; in the language of science, you see, this was an *irreversible* process), and he was arrested then and there! The student Dima Olitsky abstained and was arrested then and there! Thus all these protests were silenced at the very source.

So far as we know, the gray-mustached working class approved these executions. So far as we know, from the blazing Komsomols right up to the Party leaders and the legendary army commanders, the entire vanguard waxed unanimous in approving these executions. Famous revolutionaries, theoreticians, and prophets, seven years before their own inglorious destruction, welcomed the roar of the crowd, not guessing then that their own time stood on the threshold, that soon their own names would be dragged down in that roar of *"Scum!" "Filth!"*

In fact, for the engineers the rout soon came to an end. At the beginning of 1931 Iosif Vissarionovich spake his "Six Conditions" for construction. And His Autocracy vouchsafed as the fifth condition: We must move from a policy of destruction of the old technical intelligentsia to a policy of concern for it, of making use of it.

Concern for it! What had happened in the meantime to our just wrath? Where had all our terrible accusations gone to? At this very moment, as it happened, a trial of "wreckers" in the porcelain industry was under way (they had been playing their filthy tricks even there!). All the defendants had damned each other in unison and confessed to everything—and suddenly they cried out in unison again: "We are innocent!" And they were freed!

(There was even a small reverse wave to be remarked in this particular year: some engineers who had already been sentenced or put under interrogation were released. Thus D. A. Rozhansky came back. Should we not say he had won his duel with Stalin? And that if people had been heroic in exercising their civil responsibilities, there would never have been any reason to write either this chapter or this whole book?)

That same year Stalin was still engaged in grinding beneath his hoof the long-since prostrate Mensheviks. (There was a public trial in March, 1931, of the "All-Union Bureau of Mensheviks," Groman, Sukhanov,[22] and Yakubovich, and a certain number of small, scattered, unannounced arrests took place in addition.)

And suddenly Stalin "reconsidered."

The White Sea folk say of the tide, the water *reconsiders,* meaning the moment just before it begins to fall. Well, of course, it is inappropriate to compare the murky soul of Stalin with the water of the White Sea. And perhaps he didn't reconsider anything whatever. Nor was there any ebb tide. But one more miracle happened that year. In 1931, following the trial of the Promparty, a grandiose trial of the Working Peasants Party was being prepared—on the grounds that they existed (never, in actual fact!) as an enormous organized underground force among the rural intelligentsia, including leaders of consumer and agricultural cooperatives and the more advanced upper layer of the peasantry, and supposedly were preparing to overthrow the dictatorship of the proletariat. At the trial of the Promparty this Working Peasants Party—the TKP—was referred to as if it were already well known and under detention. The interrogation apparatus of

22. The Sukhanov referred to here was the same Sukhanov in whose apartment, on the Karpovka, in Petrograd, and with whose knowledge (and the guides there nowadays are lying when they say it was *without* his knowledge), the Bolshevik Central Committee met on October 10, 1917, and adopted its decision to launch an armed uprising.

the GPU was working flawlessly: *thousands* of defendants had already fully *confessed* their adherence to the TKP and participation in its criminal plans. And no less than *two hundred thousand* "members" altogether were promised by the GPU. Mentioned as "heading" the party were the agricultural economist Aleksandr Vasilyevich Chayanov; the future "Prime Minister" N. D. Kondratyev; L. N. Yurovsky; Makarov; and Aleksei Doyarenko, a professor from the Timiryazev Academy (future Minister of Agriculture).[23]

Then all of a sudden, one lovely night, Stalin *reconsidered*. Why? Maybe we will never know. Did he perhaps wish to save his soul? Too soon for that, it would seem. Did his sense of humor come to the fore—was it all so deadly, monotonous, so bitter-tasting? But no one would ever dare accuse Stalin of having a sense of humor! Likeliest of all, Stalin simply figured out that the whole countryside, not just 200,000 people, would soon die of famine anyway, so why go to the trouble? And instantly the whole TKP trial was called off. All those who had "confessed" were told they could *repudiate* their confessions (one can picture their happiness!). And instead of the whole big catch, only the small group of Kondratyev and Chayanov was hauled in and tried.[24] (In 1941, the charge against the tortured Vavilov was that the TKP had existed and he had been its head.)

Paragraph piles on paragraph, year on year—and yet there is no way we can describe in sequence everything that took place (but the GPU did its job effectively! The GPU never let anything get by!). But we must always remember that:

• Religious believers, of course, were being arrested uninterruptedly. (There were, nonetheless, certain special dates and peak periods. There was a "night of struggle against religion" in Leningrad on Christmas Eve, 1929, when they arrested a large part of the religious intelligentsia and held them—not just until morning either. And that was certainly no "Christmas tale."

23. He might well have been a better one than those who held the job for the next forty years! But how strange is human fate! As a matter of principle, Doyarenko was always nonpolitical! When his daughter used to bring home fellow students who expressed opinions savoring of Socialist Revolutionary views, he made them leave!

24. Kondratyev, sentenced to solitary confinement, became mentally ill there and died. Yurovsky also died. Chayanov was exiled to Alma-Ata after five years in solitary and was arrested again there in 1948.

Then in February, 1932, again in Leningrad, many churches were closed simultaneously, while, at the same time, large-scale arrests were made among the clergy. And there are still more dates and places, but they haven't been reported to us by anyone.)

• Non-Orthodox *sects* were also under constant attack, even those sympathetic to Communism. (Thus, in 1929, they arrested every last member of the *communes* between Sochi and Khosta. These communes ran everything—both production and distribution—on a Communist basis, and it was all done fairly and honestly, in a way the rest of the country won't achieve in a hundred years. But, alas, they were too literate; they were well read in religious literature; and atheism was not their philosophy, which combined Baptist and Tolstoyan beliefs with those of Yoga. It appeared that such a *commune* was criminal and that it could not bring people happiness.)

In the twenties, a large group of Tolstoyans was exiled to the foothills of the Altai and there they established communal settlements jointly with the Baptists. When the construction of the Kuznetsk industrial complex began, they supplied it with food products. Then arrests began—first the teachers (they were not teaching in accordance with the government programs), and the children ran after the cars, shouting. And after that the commune leaders were taken.

• The Big Solitaire game played with the socialists went on and on uninterruptedly—of course.

• In 1929, also, those historians who had not been sent abroad in time were arrested: Platonov, Tarle, Lyubavsky, Gotye, Likhachev, Izmailov, and the outstanding literary scholar M. M. Bakhtin.

• From one end of the country to the other, nationalities kept pouring in. The Yakuts were imprisoned after the revolt of 1928. The Buryat-Mongols were imprisoned after the uprising of 1929 —and they say about 35,000 were shot, a figure it has been impossible to verify. The Kazakhs were imprisoned after Budenny's cavalry heroically crushed their revolt in 1930 and 1931. The Union for Liberation of the Ukraine was put on trial at the beginning of 1930 (Professor Yefremov, Chekhovsky, Nikovsky, etc.), and, knowing the ratio in our country of what is public to what is secret, how many others followed in their footsteps? How many were secretly arrested?

Then came the time—slowly, it is true, but surely—when it was the turn of the members of the ruling Party to do time in prison! At first—from 1927 to 1929—it was a question of the "workers' opposition," in other words, the Trotskyites, who had chosen themselves such an unsuccessful leader. They numbered, hundreds at the start; soon there would be thousands. But it's the first step that's the hardest! Just as these Trotskyites had observed with approval the arrest of members of other parties, so the rest of the Party now watched approvingly as the Trotskyites were arrested. But everyone would have his turn. The nonexistent "rightist opposition" would come later, and, limb by limb, beginning with its own tail, the ravenous maw would devour itself . . . right up to its head.

From 1928 on, it was time to call to a reckoning those late stragglers after the bourgeoisie—the NEPmen. The usual practice was to impose on them ever-increasing and finally totally intolerable taxes. At a certain point they could no longer pay; they were immediately arrested for bankruptcy, and their property was confiscated. (Small tradesmen such as barbers, tailors, even those who repaired primus stoves, were only deprived of their licenses to ply their trade.)

There was an economic purpose to the development of the NEPmen wave. The state needed property and gold, and there was as yet no Kolyma. The famous *gold fever* began at the end of 1929, only the fever gripped not those looking for gold but those from whom it was being shaken loose. The particular feature of this new, "gold" wave was that the GPU was not actually accusing these rabbits of anything, and was perfectly willing not to send them off to Gulag country, but wished only to take away their gold by main force. So the prisons were packed, the interrogators were worn to a frazzle, but the transit prisons, prisoner transports, and camps received only relatively minor reinforcements.

Who was arrested in the "gold" wave? All those who, at one time or another, fifteen years before, had had a private "business," had been involved in retail trade, had earned wages at a craft, and *could have,* according to the GPU's deductions, hoarded gold.

But it so happened that they often had no gold. They had put their money into real estate or securities, which had melted away or been taken away in the Revolution, and nothing remained. They had high hopes, of course, in arresting dental technicians, jewelers, and watch repairmen. Through denunciations, one could learn about gold in the most unexpected places: a veteran lathe worker had somewhere gotten hold of, and held on to, sixty gold five-ruble pieces from Tsarist times. The famous Siberian partisan Muravyev had come to Odessa, bringing with him a small bag full of gold. The Petersburg Tatar draymen all had gold hidden away. Whether or not these things were so could be discovered only inside prison walls. Nothing—neither proletarian origin nor revolutionary services—served as a defense against a gold denunciation. All were arrested, all were crammed into GPU cells in numbers no one had considered possible up to then—but that was all to the good: they would *cough it up* all the sooner! It even reached a point of such confusion that men and women were imprisoned in the same cells and used the latrine bucket in each other's presence—who cared about those niceties? Give up your gold, vipers! The interrogators did not write up charge sheets because no one needed their papers. And whether or not a sentence would be pasted on was of very little interest. Only one thing was important: Give up your gold, viper! The state needs gold and you don't. The interrogators had neither voice nor strength left to threaten and torture; they had one universal method: feed the prisoners nothing but salty food and give them no water. Whoever coughed up gold got water! One gold piece for a cup of fresh water!

People perish for cold metal.

This wave was distinguished from those that preceded and followed it because, even though fewer than half its victims held their fate in their own hands, some did. If you in fact had no gold, then your situation was hopeless. You would be beaten, burned, tortured, and steamed to the point of death or until they finally came to believe you. But if you had gold, you could determine the extent of your torture, the limits of your endurance, and your own fate. Psychologically, this situation was, incidentally, not easier but more difficult, because if you made an error you would always be ridden by a guilty conscience. Of course, anyone who had already mastered the rules of the institution would yield and give up his gold—that was easier. But it was a mistake to give it up too readily. They would refuse to believe you had coughed it all up, and they would continue to hold you. But you'd be wrong, too, to wait too long before yielding: you'd end up kicking the bucket or they'd paste *a term* on you out of meanness. One of the Tatar draymen endured all the tortures: he had no gold! They imprisoned his wife, too, and tortured her, but the Tatar stuck to his story: no gold! Then they arrested his daughter: the Tatar couldn't take it any more. He coughed up 100,000 rubles. At this point they let his family go, but slapped a prison term on him. The crudest detective stories and operas about brigands were played out in real life on a vast national scale.

The introduction of the passport system on the threshold of the thirties also provided the camps with a good-sized draft of reinforcements. Just as Peter I simplified the social structure, sweeping clean all the nooks and crannies of the old Russian class system, so our socialist passport system swept out, in particular, the betwixt-and-between insects. It hit at the clever, homeless portion of the population which wasn't tied down to anything. In the early stages, people made many mistakes with those passports—and those not registered at their places of residence, and those not registered as having left their former places of residence, were raked into the Archipelago, if only for a single year.

And so the waves foamed and rolled. But over them all, in 1929–1930, billowed and gushed the multimillion wave of *dispossessed kulaks*. It was immeasurably large and it could certainly not have been housed in even the highly developed network of Soviet interrogation prisons (which in any case were packed full by the "gold" wave). Instead, it bypassed the prisons, going directly to the transit prisons and camps, onto prisoner transports, into the Gulag country. In sheer size this nonrecurring tidal wave (it was an ocean) swelled beyond the bounds of anything the penal system of even an immense state can permit itself. There was nothing to be compared with it in all Russian history. It was the forced resettlement of a whole people, an ethnic catastrophe. But yet so cleverly were the channels of the GPU-

Gulag organized that the cities would have noticed nothing had they not been stricken by a strange three-year famine—a famine that came about without drought and without war.

This wave was also distinct from all those which preceded it because no one fussed about with taking the head of the family first and then working out what to do with the rest of the family. On the contrary, in this wave they burned out whole nests, whole families, from the start; and they watched jealously to be sure that none of the children—fourteen, ten, even six years old—got away: to the last scrapings, all had to go down the same road, to the same common destruction. (This was the *first* such experiment—at least in modern history. It was subsequently repeated by Hitler with the Jews, and again by Stalin with nationalities which were disloyal to him or suspected by him.)

This wave included only pathetically few of those *kulaks* for whom it was named, in order to draw the wool over people's eyes. In Russian a *kulak* is a miserly, dishonest rural trader who grows rich not by his own labor but through someone else's, through usury and operating as a middleman. In every locality even before the Revolution such kulaks could be numbered on one's fingers. And the Revolution totally destroyed their basis of activity. Subsequently, after 1917, by a transfer of meaning, the name *kulak* began to be applied (in official and propaganda literature, whence it moved into general usage) to all those who in any way hired workers, even if it was only when they were temporarily short of working hands in their own families. But we must keep in mind that after the Revolution it was impossible to pay less than a fair wage for all such labor—the Committees of the Poor and the village soviets looked after the interests of landless laborers. Just let somebody try to swindle a landless laborer! To this very day, in fact, the hiring of labor at a fair wage is permitted in the Soviet Union.

But the inflation of this scathing term *kulak* proceeded relentlessly, and by 1930 *all strong peasants in general* were being so called—all peasants strong in management, strong in work, or even strong merely in convictions. The term *kulak* was used to smash the *strength* of the peasantry. Let us remember, let us open our eyes: only a dozen years had passed since the great Decree on the Land—that very decree without which the peasants would have refused to follow the Bolsheviks and without which the October Revolution would have failed. The land was allocated in accordance with the number of "mouths" per family, equally. It had been only nine years since the men of the peasantry had returned from the Red Army and rushed onto the land they had wrested for themselves. Then suddenly there were kulaks and there were poor peasants. How could that be? Sometimes it was the result of differences in initial stock and equipment; sometimes it may have resulted from luck in the mixture of the family. But wasn't it most often a matter of hard work and persistence? And now these peasants, whose breadgrain had fed Russia in 1928, were hastily uprooted by local good-for-nothings and city people sent in from outside. Like raging beasts, abandoning every concept of "humanity," abandoning all humane principles which had evolved through the millennia, they began to round up the very best farmers and their families, and to drive them, stripped of their possessions, naked, into the northern wastes, into the tundra and the taiga.

Such a mass movement could not help but develop subsequent ramifications. It became necessary to rid the villages also of those peasants who had merely manifested an aversion to joining the collective farms, or an absence of inclination for the collective life, which they had never seen with their own eyes, about which they knew nothing, and which they suspected (we now know how well founded their suspicions were) would mean a life of forced labor and famine under the leadership of loafers. Then it was also necessary to get rid of those peasants, some of them not at all prosperous, who, because of their daring, their physical strength, their determination, their outspokenness at meetings, and their love of justice, were favorites with their fellow villagers and by virtue of their independence were therefore dangerous to the leadership of the collective farm.[25] Beyond this, in every village there were people who in one way or another had *personally* gotten in the way of the local *activists*. This was the perfect time to settle accounts with them of jealousy, envy, insult. A new word was needed for all these new victims as a class—and it was born. By this time it had no "social" or "economic" content whatsoever, but it had a marvelous sound: *podkulachnik—"a person aiding*

25. This kind of peasant and his fate were portrayed immortally in the character of Stepan Chausov in S. Zalygin's novel.

the kulaks." In other words, I consider you an accomplice of the enemy. And that finishes you! The most tattered landless laborer in the countryside could quite easily be labeled a *podkulachnik.*[26]

And so it was that these two terms embraced everything that constituted the essence of the village, its energy, its keenness of wit, its love of hard work, its resistance, and its conscience. They were torn up by the roots—and collectivization was accomplished.

But new waves rolled from the collectivized villages: one of them was a wave of agricultural *wreckers.* Everywhere they began to discover *wrecker* agronomists who up until that year had worked honestly all their lives but who now purposely sowed weeds in Russian fields (on the instructions, of course, of the Moscow institute, which had now been totally exposed; indeed, there were those same 200,000 unarrested members of the Working Peasants Party, the TKP!). Certain agronomists failed to put into effect the profound instructions of Lysenko—and in one such wave, in 1931, Lorkh, the so-called "king" of the potato, was sent to Kazakhstan. Others carried out the Lysenko directives too precisely and thus exposed their absurdity. (In 1934 Pskov agronomists sowed flax on the snow—exactly as Lysenko had ordered. The seeds swelled up, grew moldy, and died. The big fields lay empty for a year. Lysenko could not say that the snow was a kulak or that he himself was an ass. He accused the agronomists of being kulaks and of distorting his technology. And the agronomists went off to Siberia.) Beyond all this, in almost every Machine and Tractor Station wrecking in the repairing of tractors was discovered—and that is how the failures of the first collective farm years were explained!

There was a wave "for harvest losses" (losses in comparison with the arbitrary harvest figures announced the preceding spring by the "Commission for Determination of the Harvest").

There was a wave "for failure to fulfill obligations undertaken for delivery to the state of breadgrains"—the District Party Committee had undertaken the obligation, and the collective farm had not fulfilled it: go to prison!

There was a wave for *snipping ears,* the nighttime snipping of individual ears of grain in the field—a totally new type of

26. I remember very well that in our youth this term seemed quite logical; there was nothing in the least unclear about it.

agricultural activity, a new type of harvesting! The wave of those caught doing this was not small—it included many tens of thousands of peasants, many of them not even adults but boys, girls, and small children whose elders had sent them out at night to *snip*, because they had no hope of receiving anything from the collective farm for their daytime labor. For this bitter and not very productive occupation (an extreme of poverty to which the peasants had not been driven even in serfdom) the courts handed out a full measure: *ten* years for what ranked as an especially dangerous theft of socialist property under the notorious law of August 7, 1932—which in prisoners' lingo was known simply as *the law of Seven-eighths*.

This law of "Seven-eighths" produced another big, separate wave from the construction projects of the First and Second Five-Year Plans, from transport, trade, and industry. Big thefts were turned over to the NKVD. This wave must further be kept in mind as one that kept on flowing steadily for the next fifteen years, until 1947, especially during the war years. (Then in 1947 the original law was expanded and made more harsh.)

Now at last we can catch our breath! Now at last all the mass waves are coming to an end! Comrade Molotov said on May 17, 1933: "We do not see our task as being mass repressions." Whew! At last! Begone, nighttime fears! But what's that dog howling out there? Go get 'em. Go get 'em.

And here we are! The *Kirov* wave from Leningrad has begun. While it lasted the tension was acknowledged to be so great that special staffs of the NKVD were set up in each and every District Executive Committee of the city and an "accelerated" judicial procedure was introduced. (Even earlier, it had not been famous for being slow.) And there was no right of appeal. (There had been no appeal earlier.) It is also believed that one-quarter of Leningrad was purged—*cleaned out*—in 1934–1935. Let this estimate be disproved by those who have the exact statistics and are willing to publish them. (To be sure, this wave took in much more than Leningrad alone. It had a substantial impact on the rest of the country in a form that was consistent though chaotic: the firing from the civil service of all those still left there whose fathers had been priests, all former noble-women, and all persons having relatives abroad.)

Among such lashing waves as this, certain modest, changeless wavelets always got lost; they were little heard of, but they, too, kept flowing on and on:

- There were Schutzbündlers who had lost the class battles in Vienna and had come to the Fatherland of the world proletariat for refuge.
- There were Esperantists—a harmful group which Stalin undertook to smoke out during the years when Hitler was doing the same thing.
- There were the unliquidated remnants of the Free Philosophic Society—illegal philosophical circles.
- There were teachers who disagreed with the advanced laboratory-team system of instruction. (In 1933, for instance, Natalya Ivanovna Bugayenko was arrested by the Rostov GPU —but in the third month of her interrogation, a government decree suddenly announced that the system was a faulty one. And she was let go.)
- There were employees of the Political Red Cross, which, through the efforts of Yekaterina Peshkova, was still defending its existence.
- There were mountain tribes of the North Caucasus who were arrested for their 1935 revolt. And non-Russian nationalities kept rolling in from one area, then another. (On the Volga Canal construction site newspapers were published in four national languages: Tatar, Turkish, Uzbek, and Kazakh. And, of course, there were readers to read them!)
- There were once again believers, who this time were unwilling to work on Sundays. (They had introduced the five- and the six-day week.) And there were collective farmers sent up for sabotage because they refused to work on religious feast days, as had been their custom in the era of individual farms.
- And, always, there were those who refused to become NKVD informers. (Among them were priests who refused to violate the secrecy of the confessional, for the *Organs* had very quickly discovered how useful it was to learn the content of confessions—the only use they found for religion.)
- And members of non-Orthodox sects were arrested on an ever-wider scale.
- And the Big Solitaire game with the socialists went on and on.

And last of all there was a category I have not yet named, a wave that was continually flowing: *Section 10*, also known as KRA (Counter-Revolutionary Agitation) and also known as ASA (Anti-Soviet Agitation). The wave of Section 10 was perhaps the most constant of all. It never stopped, and whenever there was another big wave, as, for instance, in 1937, 1945, and 1949, its waters became particularly swollen.[27]

Paradoxically enough, every act of the all-penetrating, eternally wakeful *Organs,* over a span of many years, was based solely on *one* article of the 140 articles of the nongeneral division of the Criminal Code of 1926. One can find more epithets in praise of this article than Turgenev once assembled to praise the Russian language, or Nekrasov to praise Mother Russia: great, powerful, abundant, highly ramified, multiform, wide-sweeping 58, which summed up the world not so much through the exact terms of its sections as in their extended dialectical interpretation.

Who among us has not experienced its all-encompassing embrace? In all truth, there is no step, thought, action, or lack of action under the heavens which could not be punished by the heavy hand of Article 58.

The article itself could not be worded in such broad terms, but it proved possible to interpret it this broadly.

Article 58 was not in that division of the Code dealing with political crimes; and nowhere was it categorized as "political." No. It was included, with crimes against public order and organized gangsterism, in a division of "crimes against the state." Thus the Criminal Code starts off by refusing to recognize anyone under its jurisdiction as a political offender. All are simply criminals.

Article 58 consisted of fourteen sections.

In Section 1 we learn that any action (and, according to

27. This particular unremitting wave grabbed up anyone at all at any moment. But when it came to outstanding intellectuals in the thirties, they sometimes considered it cleverer to fabricate a case based on some conspicuously shameful violation (like pederasty; or, in the case of Professor Pletnev, the allegation that, left alone with a woman patient, he bit her breast. A national newspaper reports such an incident—and just try to deny it!).

Article 6 of the Criminal Code, any absence of action) directed toward the weakening of state power was considered to be counterrevolutionary.

Broadly interpreted, this turned out to include the refusal of a prisoner in camp to work when in a state of starvation and exhaustion. This was a weakening of state power. And it was punished by execution. (The execution of *malingerers* during the war.)

From 1934 on, when we were given back the term *Motherland*, subsections were inserted on *treason to the Motherland*— 1a, 1b, 1c, 1d. According to these subsections, all actions directed against the military might of the U.S.S.R. were punishable by execution (1b), or by ten years' imprisonment (1a), but the lighter penalty was imposed only when mitigating circumstances were present and upon civilians only.

Broadly interpreted: when our soldiers were sentenced to only ten years for allowing themselves to be taken prisoner (action injurious to Soviet military might), this was humanitarian to the point of being illegal. According to the Stalinist code, they should all have been shot on their return home.

(Here is another example of broad interpretation. I remember well an encounter in the Butyrki in the summer of 1946. A certain Pole had been born in Lemberg when that city was part of the Austro-Hungarian Empire. Until World War II he lived in his native city, by then located in Poland; then he went to Austria, where he entered the service, and in 1945 he was arrested there by the Russians. Since by this time Austrian Lemberg had become Ukrainian Lvov, he received a *tenner* under Article 54-1a of the Ukrainian Criminal Code: i.e., for treason to his motherland, *the Ukraine!* And at his interrogation the poor fellow couldn't prove that treason to the Ukraine had not been his purpose when he went to Vienna! And that's how he conned his way into becoming a traitor.)

One important additional broadening of the section on treason was its application "via Article 19 of the Criminal Code"—"via intent." In other words, no treason had taken place; but the interrogator envisioned an *intention* to betray— and that was enough to justify a full term, the same as for actual treason. True, Article 19 proposes that there be no penalty for intent, but only for *preparation*, but given a dialectical reading one can understand intention as preparation. And "preparation is punished in the same way [i.e., with the same penalty] as the crime itself" (Criminal Code). In general, "we draw no distinction between *intention* and the *crime* itself, and this is an instance of the *superiority* of Soviet legislation to bourgeois legislation."[28]

Section 2 listed armed rebellion, seizure of power in the capital or in the provinces, especially for the purpose of severing any part of the U.S.S.R. through the use of force. For this the penalties ranged up to and included execution (as in *every* succeeding section).

This was expanded to mean something which could not be explicitly stated in the article itself but which revolutionary sense of justice could be counted on to suggest: it applied to every attempt of any national republic to act upon its right to leave the U.S.S.R. After all, the word "force" is not defined in terms of *whom* it applies to. Even when the entire population of a republic wants to secede, if Moscow is opposed, the attempted secession will be *forcible*. Thus, all Estonian, Latvian, Lithuanian, Ukrainian, and Turkestan nationalists very easily received their *tens* and their *twenty-fives* under this section.

Section 3 was "assisting in any way or by any means a foreign state at war with the U.S.S.R."

This section made it possible to condemn *any* citizen who had been in occupied territory—whether he had nailed on the heel of a German soldier's shoe or sold him a bunch of radishes. And it could be applied to any citizeness who had helped lift the fighting spirit of an enemy soldier by dancing and spending the night with him. Not everyone *was* actually sentenced under this section—because of the huge numbers who had been in occupied territory. But everyone who had been in occupied territory *could* have been sentenced under it.

Section 4 spoke about (fantastic!) aid to the international bourgeoisie.

28. A. Y. Vyshinsky (editor), *Ot Tyurem k Vospitatelnym Uchrezhdeniyam* (*From Prisons to Rehabilitative Institutions*), a collection of articles published by the Criminal Policy Institute, Moscow, Sovetskoye Zakonodatelstvo Publishing House, 1934.

To whom, one wonders, could this possibly refer? And yet, broadly interpreted, and with the help of a revolutionary conscience, it was easy to find categories: All émigrés who had left the country before 1920, i.e., several years before the Code was even written, and whom our armies came upon in Europe a quarter-century later—in 1944 and 1945—received 58-4: ten years or execution. What could they have been doing abroad other than aiding the international bourgeoisie? (In the example of the young people's musical society already cited, we have seen that the international bourgeoisie could also be aided from inside the U.S.S.R.) They were, in addition, aided by all SR's, all Mensheviks (the section was drafted with them in mind), and, subsequently, by the engineers of the State Planning Commission and the Supreme Council of the Economy.

Section 5 was inciting a foreign state to declare war against the U.S.S.R.

A chance was missed to apply this section against Stalin and his diplomatic and military circle in 1940–1941. Their blindness and insanity led to just that. Who if not they drove Russia into shameful, unheard-of defeats, incomparably worse than the defeats of Tsarist Russia in 1904 or 1915? Defeats such as Russia had never known since the thirteenth century.

Section 6 was espionage.

This section was interpreted so broadly that if one were to count up all those sentenced under it one might conclude that during Stalin's time our people supported life not by agriculture or industry, but only by espionage on behalf of foreigners, and by living on subsidies from foreign intelligence services. Espionage was very convenient in its simplicity, comprehensible both to an undeveloped criminal and to a learned jurist, to a journalist and to public opinion.[29]

The breadth of interpretation of Section 6 lay further in

29. And very likely spy mania was not merely the narrow-minded predilection of Stalin alone. It was very useful for everyone who possessed any privileges. It became the natural justification for increasingly widespread secrecy, the withholding of information, closed doors and security passes, fenced-off dachas and secret, restricted special shops. People had no way of penetrating the armor plate of spy mania and learning how the bureaucracy made its cozy arrangements, loafed, blundered, ate, and took its amusements.

the fact that people were sentenced not only for actual espionage but also for:

PSh—Suspicion of Espionage—or NSh—Unproven Espionage —for which they gave the whole works.

And even SVPSh—Contacts Leading to (!) Suspicion of Espionage.

In other words, let us say that an acquaintance of an ac-quaintance of your wife had a dress made by the same seam-stress (who was, of course, an NKVD agent) used by the wife of a foreign diplomat.

These 58-6 PSh's and SVPSh's were sticky sections. They re-quired the strict confinement and incessant supervision of those convicted (for, after all, an intelligence service might reach out its tentacles to its protégé even in a camp); also, such prisoners could be moved only under convoy—armed escort. In general, all the *lettered articles*—which were, in fact, not articles of the Code at all but frightening combinations of capital letters (and we shall encounter more of them in this chapter)—always contained a touch of the enigmatic, always remained incompre-hensible, and it wasn't at all clear whether they were offshoots of Article 58 or independent and extremely dangerous. In many camps prisoners convicted under the provisions of these lettered articles were subjected to restrictions even more stringent than those of the ordinary 58's.

Section 7 applied to subversion of industry, transport, trade, and the circulation of money.

In the thirties, extensive use was made of this section to catch masses of people—under the simplified and widely under-stood catchword *wrecking*. In reality, everything enumerated under Section 7 was very obviously and plainly being sub-verted daily. So didn't someone have to be guilty of it all? For centuries the people had built and created, always honor-ably, always honestly, even for serf-owners and nobles. Yet no one, from the days of Ryurik on, had ever heard of *wreck-ing*. But now, when for the first time all the wealth had come to belong to the people, hundreds of thousands of the best sons of the people inexplicably rushed off to *wreck*. (Section 7 did not provide for wrecking in *agriculture*, but since it was impossible otherwise to explain rationally how and why the fields were choked with weeds, why harvests were falling off, why machines were breaking down, then dialectic sensitivity brought agriculture, too, under its sway.)

Section 8 covered terror (not that terror from above for which the Soviet Criminal Code was supposed to "provide a foundation and basis in legality,"[30] but terrorism from below).

Terror was construed in a very broad sense, not simply a matter of putting bombs under governors' carriages, but, for example, smashing in the face of a personal enemy if he was an activist in the Party, the Komsomol, or the *police!*—that was already terror. The *murder* of an activist, especially, was always treated more seriously than the murder of an ordinary person (as in the Code of Hammurabi in the eighteenth century B.C.). If a husband killed his wife's lover, it was very fortunate for him if the victim turned out not to be a Party member; he would be sentenced under Article 136 as a common criminal, who was a "social ally" and didn't require an armed escort. But if the lover turned out to have been a Party member, the husband became an enemy of the people, with a 58-8 sentence.

An even more important extension of the concept was attained by interpreting Section 8 in terms of that same Article 19, i.e., intent in the sense of *preparation*, to include not only a direct threat against an activist uttered near a beer hall ("Just you wait!") but also the quick-tempered retort of a peasant woman at the market ("Oh, drop dead!"). Both qualified as TN—Terrorist Intent—and provided a basis for applying the article in all its severity.[31]

Section 9 concerned destruction or damage by explosion or arson (always with a counterrevolutionary purpose), for which the abbreviated term was "diversion"—in other words, sabotage.

The expansion of this section was based on the fact that the counterrevolutionary purpose could be discerned by the interrogator, who knew best what was going on in the criminal's mind. And every human error, failure, mistake at work or in the production process, remained unforgiven, and was therefore considered to be a case of "diversion."

But there was no section in Article 58 which was interpreted as broadly and with so ardent a revolutionary conscience as

---

30. *Lenin*, fifth edition, Vol. 45, p. 190.
31. This sounds like an exaggeration, a farce, but it was not I who invented that farce. I was in prison with these individuals.

Section 10. Its definition was: "Propaganda or agitation, containing an appeal for the overthrow, subverting, or weakening of the Soviet power . . . and, equally, the dissemination or preparation or possession of literary materials of similar content." For this section in *peacetime* a minimum penalty only was set (not any less! not too light!); *no upper limit* was set for the maximum penalty.

Such was the fearlessness of the great Power when confronted by the *word* of a subject.

The famous extensions of this famous section were as follows: The scope of "agitation containing an appeal" was enlarged to include a face-to-face conversation between friends or even between husband and wife, or a private letter. The word "appeal" could mean personal advice. And we say "could mean" because, in fact, *it did.*

"Subverting and weakening" the government could include any idea which did not coincide with or rise to the level of intensity of the ideas expressed in the newspaper on any particular day. After all, anything which *does not strengthen* must *weaken*: Indeed, anything which does not completely fit in, coincide, *subverts!*

> And he who sings not with us today
>   is against
>   us!
>   —MAYAKOVSKY

The term "preparation of literary materials" covered every letter, note, or private diary, even when only the original document existed.

Thus happily expanded, what *thought* was there, whether merely in the mind, spoken aloud, or jotted down, which was not covered by Section 10?

Section 11 was a special one; it had no independent content of its own, but provided for an aggravating factor in any of the preceding ones: if the action was undertaken by an organization or if the criminal joined an organization.

In actual practice, the section was so broadened that no organization whatever was required. I myself experienced the subtle application of this section. *Two* of us had secretly exchanged thoughts—*in other words* we were the beginnings of an organization, *in other words* an organization!

Section 12 concerned itself closely with the conscience of our citizens: it dealt with the *failure to make a denunciation* of any action of the types listed. And the penalty for the mortal sin of failure to make a denunciation *carried no maximum limit!*

This section was in itself such a fantastic extension of everything else that no further extension was needed. *He knew and he did not tell* became the equivalent of "He did it himself"!

Section 13, presumably long since out of date, had to do with service in the Tsarist secret police—the Okhrana.[32] (A subsequent form of analogous service was, on the contrary, considered patriotic.)

Section 14 stipulated the penalties for "conscious failure to carry out defined duties or intentionally careless execution of same." In brief this was called "sabotage" or "economic counter-revolution"—and the penalties, of course, included execution.

It was only the interrogator who, after consulting his revolutionary sense of justice, could separate what was intentional from what was unintentional. This section was applied to peasants who failed to come across with food deliveries. It was also applied to collective farmers who failed to work the required minimum number of "labor days"; to camp prisoners who failed to complete their work norms; and, in a peculiar ricochet, after the war it came to be applied to members of Russia's organized underworld of thieves, the blatnye or blatari, for escaping from camp. In other words, by an extension, a thief's flight from camp was interpreted as subversion of the camp system rather than as a dash to freedom.

Such was the last rib of the fan of Article 58—a fan whose spread encompassed all human existence.

Now that we have completed our review of this great Article of the Criminal Code, we are less likely to be astounded further on. Wherever the law is, crime can be found.

32. There are psychological bases for suspecting I. Stalin of having been liable under this section of Article 58 also. By no means all the documents relating to this type of service survived February, 1917, to become matters of public knowledge. V. F. Dzhunkovsky a former Tsarist police director, who died in the Kolyma, declared that the hasty burning of police archives in the first days of the February Revolution was a joint effort on the part of certain self-interested revolutionaries.

■

The damascene steel of Article 58, first tried out in 1927, right after it was forged, was wetted by all the waves of the following decade, and with whistle and slash was used to the full to deal telling blows in the law's attack upon the people in 1937–1938.

Here one has to make the point that the 1937 operation was not arbitrary or accidental, but well planned well ahead of time, and that in the first half of that year many Soviet prisons were re-equipped. Cots were taken out of the cells and continuous one- or two-storied board benches or bunks were built.[33] Old prisoners claim to remember that the first blow allegedly took the form of mass arrests, striking virtually throughout the whole country on one single August night. (But, knowing our clumsiness, I don't really believe this.) In that autumn, when people were trustingly expecting a big, nationwide amnesty on the twentieth anniversary of the October Revolution, Stalin, the prankster, added unheard-of fifteen- and twenty-year prison terms to the Criminal Code.[34]

There is hardly any need to repeat here what has already been widely written, and will be written many times more, about 1937: that a crushing blow was dealt the upper ranks of the Party, the government, the military command, and the GPU-NKVD itself.[35] There was hardly one province of the Soviet Union in which the first secretary of the Party Committee or the Chairman of the Provincial Executive Committee survived. Stalin picked more suitable people for his purposes.

Olga Chavchavadze tells how it was in Tbilisi. In 1938 the Chairman of the City Executive Committee, his first deputy, department chiefs, their assistants, all the chief accountants, all the chief economists were arrested. New ones were appointed in their places. Two months passed, and the arrests began again: the

33. It was similarly not by chance that the "Big House" in Leningrad was finished in 1934, just in time for Kirov's asassination.
34. The twenty-five-year term was added for the thirtieth anniversary of the Revolution in 1947.
35. These days, as we observe the Chinese Cultural Revolution at the same stage—in the seventeenth year after its final victory—we can begin to consider it very likely that there exists a fundamental law of historical development. And even Stalin himself begins to seem only a blind and perfunctory executive agent.

chairman, the deputy, all eleven department chiefs, all the chief accountants, all the chief economists. The only people left at liberty were ordinary accountants, stenographers, charwomen, and messengers. . . .

In the arrest of rank-and-file members of the Party there was evidently a hidden theme not directly stated anywhere in the indictments and verdicts: that arrests should be carried out predominantly among Party members who had joined *before* 1924. This was pursued with particular rigor in Leningrad, because all of them there had signed the "platform" of the New Opposition. (And how could they have refused to sign? How could they have refused to "trust" their Leningrad Provincial Party Committee?)

Here is one vignette from those years as it actually occurred. A district Party conference was under way in Moscow Province. It was presided over by a new secretary of the District Party Committee, replacing one recently *arrested*. At the conclusion of the conference, a tribute to Comrade Stalin was called for. Of course, everyone stood up (just as everyone had leaped to his feet during the conference at every mention of his name). The small hall echoed with "stormy applause, rising to an ovation." For three minutes, four minutes, five minutes, the "stormy applause, rising to an ovation," continued. But palms were getting sore and raised arms were already aching. And the older people were panting from exhaustion. It was becoming insufferably silly even to those who really adored Stalin. However, who would dare be the *first* to stop? The secretary of the District Party Committee could have done it. He was standing on the platform, and it was he who had just called for the ovation. But he was a newcomer. He had taken the place of a man who'd been arrested. He was afraid! After all, NKVD men were standing in the hall applauding and watching to see *who* quit first! And in that obscure, small hall, unknown to the Leader, the applause went on —six, seven, eight minutes! They were done for! Their goose was cooked! They couldn't stop now till they collapsed with heart attacks! At the rear of the hall, which was crowded, they could of course cheat a bit, clap less frequently, less vigorously, not so eagerly—but up there with the presidium where everyone could see them? The director of the local paper factory, an independent and strong-minded man, stood with the presidium. Aware of all the falsity and all the impossibility of the situation, he still kept on applauding! Nine minutes! Ten! In anguish he watched the secretary of the District Party Committee, but the latter dared not stop. Insanity! To the last man! With make-believe enthusiasm on their faces, looking at each other with faint hope, the district leaders were just going to go on and on applauding till they fell where they stood, till they were carried out of the hall on stretchers! And even then those who were left would not falter. . . . Then, after eleven minutes, the director of the paper factory assumed a businesslike expression and sat down in his seat. And, oh, a miracle took place! Where had the universal, uninhibited, indescribable enthusiasm gone? To a man, everyone else stopped dead and sat down. They had been saved! The squirrel had been smart enough to jump off his revolving wheel.

That, however, was how they discovered who the independent people were. And that was how they went about eliminating them. That same night the factory director was arrested. They easily pasted ten years on him on the pretext of something quite different. But after he had signed Form 206, the final document of the interrogation, his interrogator reminded him:

"Don't ever be the first to stop applauding!"[36]

(And just what are we supposed to do? How are we supposed to stop?)

Now that's what Darwin's natural selection is. And that's also how to grind people down with stupidity.

But today a new myth is being created. Every story of 1937 that is printed, every reminiscence that is published, relates without exception the tragedy of the Communist leaders. They have kept on assuring us, and we have unwittingly fallen for it, that the history of 1937 and 1938 consisted chiefly of the arrests of the big Communists—and virtually no one else. But out of the *millions* arrested at that time, important Party and state officials could not possibly have represented more than 10 percent. Most of the relatives standing in line with food parcels outside the Leningrad prisons were lower-class women, the sort who sold milk.

36. Told me by N. G——ko.

The composition of the hordes who were arrested in that powerful wave and lugged off, half-dead, to the Archipelago was of such fantastic diversity that anyone who wants to deduce the rationale for it scientifically will rack his brain a long time for the answer. (To the contemporaries of the purge it was still more incomprehensible.)

The real law underlying the arrests of those years was *the assignment of quotas,* the norms set, the planned allocations. Every city, every district, every military unit was assigned a specific quota of arrests to be carried out by a stipulated time. From then on everything else depended on the ingenuity of the Security operations personnel.

The former Chekist Aleksandr Kalganov recalls that a telegram arrived in Tashkent: "Send 200!" They had just finished one clean-out, and it seemed as if there was "no one else" to take. Well, true, they had just brought in about fifty more from the districts. And then they had an idea! They would reclassify as 58's all the nonpolitical offenders being held by the police. No sooner said than done. But despite that, they had still not filled the quota. At that precise moment the police reported that a gypsy band had impudently encamped on one of the city squares and asked what to do with them. Someone had another bright idea! They surrounded the encampment and raked in all the gypsy men from seventeen to sixty as 58's! They had fulfilled the plan!

This could happen another way as well: according to Chief of Police Zabolovsky, the Chekists of Ossetia were given a quota of five hundred to be shot in the Republic. They asked to have it increased, and they were permitted another 250.

Telegrams transmitting instructions of this kind were sent via ordinary channels in a very rudimentary code. In Temryuk the woman telegrapher, in holy innocence, transmitted to the NKVD switchboard the message that 240 boxes of soap were to be shipped to Krasnodar the following day. In the morning she learned about a big wave of arrests and guessed the meaning of the message! She told her girl friend what kind of telegram it was—and was promptly arrested herself.

(Was it indeed totally by chance that the code words for human beings were *a box of soap?* Or were they familiar with soap-making?)

Of course, certain patterns could be discerned.

Among those arrested were:

Our own real spies abroad. (These were often the most dedicated Comintern workers and Chekists, and among them were many attractive women. They were called back to the Motherland and arrested at the border. They were then confronted with their former Comintern chief, for example, Mirov-Korona, who confirmed that he himself had been working for one of the foreign intelligence services—which meant that his subordinates were automatically guilty too. And the more dedicated they were, the worse it was for them.)

Soviet employees of the Chinese Eastern Railroad, the KVZhD, were one and all arrested as Japanese spies, including their wives, children, and grandmothers. But we have to admit these arrests had already begun several years earlier.

Koreans from the Far East were sent into exile in Kazakhstan —the first experiment in mass arrests *on the basis of race.*

Leningrad Estonians were all arrested on the strength of having Estonian family names and charged with being anti-Communist Estonian spies.

All Latvian Riflemen and all Latvian Chekists were arrested. Yes, indeed, those very Latvians who had been the midwives of the Revolution, who just a short while before had constituted the nucleus and the pride of the Cheka! And with them were taken even those Communists of bourgeois Latvia who had been exchanged in 1921—and been freed thereby from their dreadful Latvian prison terms of two and three years. (In Leningrad, the Latvian Department of the Herzen Institute, the House of Latvian Culture, the Estonian Club, the Latvian Technicum, and the Latvian and Estonian newspapers were all closed down.)

In the midst of the general to-do, the Big Solitaire game was finally wound up. All those not yet taken were raked in. There was no longer any reason to keep it secret. The time had come to write "finis" to the whole game. So now the socialists were taken off to prison in whole "exiles" (for example, the Ufa "exile" and the Saratov "exile"), and they were all sentenced together and driven off in herds to the slaughterhouses of the Archipelago.

Nowhere was it specifically prescribed that more members of the intelligentsia should be arrested than of other groups. But just as the intelligentsia had never been overlooked in previous waves, it was not neglected in this one. A student's denunciation (and this combination of words, "student" and "denunciation," had ceased to sound outlandish) that a certain lecturer in a higher educational institution kept citing Lenin and Marx frequently but Stalin not at all was all that was needed for the lecturer not to show up for lectures any more. And what if he *cited no one?* All Leningrad Orientalists of the middle and younger generation were *arrested.* The entire staff of the Institute of the North, except for its NKVD informers, was *arrested.* They even went after schoolteachers. In Sverdlovsk one *case* involved thirty secondary schoolteachers and the head of the Provincial Education Department, Perel.[37] One of the terrible accusations against them was that they had made arrangements to have a New Year's tree *in order to burn down the school.* And the club fell with the regularity of a pendulum on the heads of the engineers—who by this time were no longer "bourgeois" but a whole Soviet generation of engineers.

Because of an irregularity in the geological strata two mine tunnels which mine surveyor Nikolai Merkuryevich Mikov had calculated would meet failed to do so. He got Article 58-7—twenty years.

Six geologists (the Kotovich group) were sentenced to ten years under 58-7 "for intentionally concealing reserves of tin ore in underground sites in anticipation of the arrival of the Germans." (In other words, they had failed to find the deposits.)

On the heels of the main waves followed an additional, *special* wave—of *wives* and the so-called "ChS" (Members of Families). Among them were the wives of important Party leaders and also, in certain places, Leningrad, for example, the wives of all those who had been sentenced to "ten years without the right to correspond"—in other words, those who were no longer among the living. The "ChS," as a rule, all got *eights*—eight years. (Well,

---

37. Five of them died before trial from tortures suffered during interrogation. Twenty-four died in camps. The thirtieth, Ivan Aristaulovich Punich, returned after his release and rehabilitation. (Had he died, we would have known nothing about the thirty, just as we know nothing about millions of others.) And the many "witnesses" who testified against them are still there in Sverdlovsk today—prospering, occupying responsible positions, or living on as special pensioners. Darwinian selection!

that was still less than the dispossessed kulaks got and their children did not go to the Archipelago.)

Piles of victims! Hills of victims! A frontal assault of the NKVD on the city: In one wave, for example, G. P. Matveyeva saw not only her husband but all three of her brothers arrested, and all in *different* cases. (Of the four, three never returned.)

An electrician had a high-tension line break in his sector: 58-7—twenty years.

A Perm worker, Novikov, was accused of planning to blow up a Kama River Bridge.

In that same city of Perm, Yuzhakov was arrested during the day, and at night they came for his wife. They presented her with a list of names and demanded that she sign a confession that they had all met in her house at a Menshevik-SR meeting (of course, they had not). They promised in return to let her out to be with her three children. She signed, destroying all those listed, and, of course, she herself remained in prison.

Nadezhda Yudenich was arrested because of her family name. True, they established, after nine months, that she was not related to the White general, and they let her out (a mere trifle: during that time her mother had died of worry).

The film *Lenin in October* was shown in Staraya Russa. Someone present noticed the phrase in the film, "Palchinsky must know!" Palchinsky was defending the Winter Palace. But we have a nurse working here named Palchinskaya! Arrest her! They did arrest her. And it turned out that she actually was his wife— who had hidden in the provinces following his execution.

In 1930, as *small boys,* the three brothers Pavel, Ivan, and Stepan Borushko came to the Soviet Union from Poland to live with their parents. Now as young men they were arrested for PSh—Suspicion of Espionage—and got ten years.

A streetcar motorwoman of Krasnodar was returning on foot late at night from the car depot; on the outskirts of the city, to her misfortune, she passed some people working to free a truck that had gotten stuck. It turned out to be full of corpses—hands and legs stuck out from beneath the canvas. They wrote down her name and the next day she was arrested. The interrogator asked her what she had seen. She told him truthfully. (Darwinian selection!) Anti-Soviet Agitation—ten years.

A plumber turned off the loudspeaker in his room every time

the endless letters to Stalin were being read.[38] His next-door neighbor denounced him. (Where, oh where, is that neighbor today?) He got SOE—"Socially Dangerous Element"—eight years.

A half-literate stovemaker used to enjoy writing his name in his free time. This raised his self-esteem. There was no blank paper around, so he wrote on newspapers. His neighbors found his newspaper in the sack in the communal toilet, with pen-and-ink flourishes across the countenance of the Father and Teacher. Anti-Soviet Agitation—ten years.

Stalin and those close to him loved their portraits and splashed them all over the newspapers and issued them in millions of copies. The flies paid little heed to their sanctity, and it was a pity not to make use of the paper—and how many unfortunates got a term for that!

Arrests rolled through the streets and apartment houses like an epidemic. Just as people transmit an epidemic infection from one to another without knowing it, by such innocent means as a handshake, a breath, handing someone something, so, too, they passed on the infection of inevitable arrest by a handshake, by a breath, by a chance meeting on the street. For if you are destined to confess tomorrow that you organized an underground group to poison the city's water supply, and if today I shake hands with you on the street, that means I, too, am doomed.

Seven years earlier the city had watched while they massacred the countryside and considered it only natural. Now the country-side might have watched them massacre the city, but the country-side itself was too dark for that, and was still undergoing the finishing touches of its own slaughter.

The surveyor (!) Saunin got fifteen years for . . . cattle plague (!) in the district and for bad harvests (!) (and the entire leader-ship of the district was shot for the same reason).

The secretary of a District Party Committee went into the fields to speed up the plowing, and an old peasant asked him whether he *knew* that for *seven years* the collective farmers had received not one single ounce of grain in return for their "labor days"—only *straw* and very little of that. For his question the peasant got ASA—Anti-Soviet Agitation—ten years.

38. Who remembers them? They went on and on every day for hours! Stupefyingly identical! Levitan, the announcer, probably remembers them well: he used to read them in rolling tones, with great expression!

Another peasant, with six children, met a different fate. Because he had six mouths to feed he devoted himself wholeheartedly to collective farm work, and kept hoping he would get some return for his labor. And he did—they awarded him a decoration. They awarded it at a special assembly, made speeches. In his reply, the peasant got carried away. He said, "Now if I could just have a sack of flour instead of this decoration! Couldn't I somehow?" A wolflike laugh rocketed through the hall, and the newly decorated hero went off to exile, together with all six of those dependent mouths.

Should we wrap it all up and simply say that they arrested the *innocent?* But we omitted saying that the very concept of *guilt* had been repealed by the proletarian revolution and, at the beginning of the thirties, was defined as *rightist opportunism!*[39] So we can't even discuss these out-of-date concepts, guilt and innocence.

■

The *reverse wave* of 1939 was an unheard-of incident in the history of the *Organs,* a blot on their record! But, in fact, this reverse wave was not large; it included about 1 to 2 percent of those who had been arrested but not yet convicted, who had not yet been sent away to far-off places and had not yet perished. It was not large, but it was put to effective use. It was like giving back one kopeck change from a ruble, but it was necessary in order to heap all the blame on that dirty Yezhov, to strengthen the newcomer, Beria, and to cause the Leader himself to shine more brightly. With this kopeck they skillfully drove the ruble right into the ground. After all, if "they had sorted things out and freed some people" (and even the newspapers wrote intrepidly about *individual* cases of persons who had been slandered), it meant that the rest of those arrested were indeed scoundrels! And those who returned kept silent. They had signed pledges not to speak out. They were mute with terror. And there were very few who knew even a little about the secrets of the Archipelago. The distinction was as before: Black Marias at night and demonstrations by day.

But for that matter they soon took that kopeck back—during

39. Vyshinsky, *op. cit.*

those same years and via those same sections of the boundless Article 58. Well, who in 1940 noticed the wave of wives arrested for *failure to renounce* their husbands? And who in Tambov remembers that during that year of peace they arrested an entire jazz orchestra playing at the "Modern" Cinema Theatre because they all turned out to be enemies of the people? And who noticed the thirty thousand Czechs who in 1939 fled from occupied Czechoslovakia to their Slavic kinfolk in the U.S.S.R.? It was impossible to guarantee that a single one of them was not a spy. They sent them all off to northern camps. (And it was out of those camps that the "Czechoslovak Corps" materialized during the war.) And was it not, indeed, in 1939 that we reached out our helping hands to the West Ukrainians and the West Byelorussians, and, in 1940, to the Baltic states and to the Moldavians? It turned out that our brothers badly needed to be purged, and from them, too, flowed waves of *social prophylaxis*. They took those who were too independent, too influential, along with those who were too well-to-do, too intelligent, too noteworthy; they took, particularly, many Poles from former Polish provinces. (It was then that ill-fated Katyn was filled up; and then, too, that in the northern camps they stockpiled fodder for the future army of Sikorski and Anders.) They arrested officers everywhere. Thus the population was shaken up, forced into silence, and left without any possible leaders of resistance. Thus it was that wisdom was instilled, that former ties and former friendships were cut off.

Finland ceded its isthmus to us with zero population. Nevertheless, the removal and resettlement of all persons with Finnish blood took place throughout Soviet Karelia and in Leningrad in 1940. We didn't notice that wavelet: we have no Finnish blood.

In the Finnish War we undertook our first experiment in convicting our war prisoners as traitors to the Motherland. The first such experiment in human history; and would you believe it?—we didn't notice!

That was the rehearsal—just at that moment the war burst upon us. And with it a massive retreat. It was essential to evacuate swiftly everyone who could be got out of the western republics that were being abandoned to the enemy. In the rush, entire military units—regiments, antiaircraft and artillery batteries—were left behind intact in Lithuania. But they still managed to get out several thousand families of unreliable Lithuanians. (Four thousand of them were subsequently turned over to be plundered by thieves in camp at Krasnoyarsk.) From June 23 on, in Latvia and Estonia, they speeded up the arrests. But the ground was burning under them, and they were forced to leave even faster. They forgot to take whole fortresses with them, like the one at Brest, but they did not forget to shoot down political prisoners in the cells and courtyards of Lvov, Rovno, Tallinn, and many other Western prisons. In the Tartu Prison they shot 192 prisoners and threw their corpses down a well.

How can one visualize it? You know nothing. The door of your cell opens, and they shoot you. You cry out in your death agony, and there is no one to hear your cries or tell of them except the prison stones. They say, however, that there were some who weren't successfully finished off, and we may someday read a book about that too.

In the rear, the first wartime wave was for *those spreading rumors and panic*. That was the language of a special decree, outside the Code, issued in the first days of the war.[40] This was just a trial bloodletting in order to maintain a general state of tension. They gave everyone ten years for it, but it was not considered part of Article 58, and therefore those few who survived the wartime camps were amnestied in 1945.

Then there was a wave of those who *failed to turn in radio receivers* or radio parts. For one radio tube found (as a result of denunciation) they gave ten years.

Then there was the wave of *Germans*—Germans living on the Volga, colonists in the Ukraine and the North Caucasus, and all Germans in general who lived anywhere in the Soviet Union. The determining factor here was *blood*, and even heroes of the Civil War and old members of the Party who were German were sent off into exile.[41]

40. I myself almost felt the impact of that decree. I was standing in line at the bread store, when a policeman called me out and took me off for the sake of his score. If it had not been for a fortunate intervention, I might have started out in Gulag right away instead of going off to war.
41. They judged blood by family name. The design engineer Vasily Okorokov had found it inconvenient to sign his drawings with his real name. Consequently, in the thirties, when it was still legally possible, he had changed his name to Robert Shtekker. It was elegant, and he was able to work up a good-looking professional signature with it. Now he was arrested as a German—and given

In essence, the exile of the Germans was similar to the dispossession of the kulaks. But it was less harsh, since the Germans were allowed to take more of their possessions with them and were not sent off to such fatal, deadly areas. As had been the case with the kulaks, the German exile had no juridical basis. The Criminal Code in itself was one thing, and the exile of hundreds of thousands of people was something else entirely. It was the personal edict of a monarch. In addition, this was his first experiment of the sort with an entire nationality, and he found it extremely interesting from a theoretical point of view.

By the end of the summer of 1941, becoming bigger in the autumn, the wave of *the encircled* was surging in. These were the defenders of their native land, the very same warriors whom the cities had seen off to the front with bouquets and bands a few months before, who had then sustained the heaviest tank assaults of the Germans, and in the general chaos, and through no fault of their own, had spent a certain time as isolated units not in enemy imprisonment, not at all, but in temporary encirclement, and later had broken out. And instead of being given a brotherly embrace on their return, such as every other army in the world would have given them, instead of being given a chance to rest up, to visit their families, and then return to their units—they were held on suspicion, disarmed, deprived of all rights, and taken away in groups to identification points and screening centers where officers of the Special Branches started interrogating them, distrusting not only their every word but their very identity. Identification consisted of cross-questioning, confrontations, pitting the evidence of one against another. Afterward, some of those who had been encircled were restored to their former names, ranks, and responsibilities and went off to military units. Others, fewer in number at the start, constituted the first wave of *traitors of the Motherland* under 58-1b. But at first, until the standard penalty was finally determined, they got less than ten years.

That was how the active army was kept purged. But there was also an enormous inactive army in the Far East and in Mongolia,

---

no chance to prove he was not. So he was exiled. "Is this your real name? What assignments were you given by the Fascist intelligence service?" Then there was that native of Tambov whose real name was Kaverznev, and who changed it to Kolbe in 1918. At what point did he share Okorokov's fate?

and it was the noble task of the Special Branches to keep that army from growing rusty. And for lack of anything to do, the heroes of Khalkhin-Gol and Khasan began to let their tongues wag, especially after they were permitted to examine the Degtyarev automatic pistols and the regimental mortars, which until then had been kept secret even from Soviet soldiers. With such weapons in their hands, it was hard for them to understand why we were retreating in the west. With all Siberia and the Urals between them and European Russia, it was not easy for them to grasp that in retreating seventy miles a day we were simply repeating the Kutuzov entrapment maneuver. Their comprehension could be helped along only by means of a *wave* from the Eastern Army. And at that point lips tightened and faith became steely.

It was obvious that a wave had also to roll in high places—of those to blame for the retreat. (After all, it was not the Great Strategist who was at fault!) It was a small wave, just half a hundred men, a *generals'* wave. They were in Moscow prisons by the summer of 1941, and in October, 1941, they were sent off on a prisoner transport. Most of the generals were from the air force; among them were Air Force Commander Smushkevich and General Ptukhin, who was known to have said: "If I had known, I would have first bombed our Dear Father, and then gone off to prison!" And there were others.

The victory outside Moscow gave rise to a new wave: guilty Muscovites. Looking at things after the event, it turned out that those Muscovites who had not run away and who had not been evacuated but had fearlessly remained in the threatened capital, which had been abandoned by the authorities, were by that very token under suspicion either of subverting governmental authority (58-10); or of staying on to await the Germans (58-1a, via 19, a wave which kept on providing fodder for the interrogators of Moscow and Leningrad right up to 1945).

It need hardly be said that 58-10, ASA—Anti-Soviet Agitation—never let up but hovered over the front and in the rear throughout the war. Sentences under 58-10 were handed out to evacuees who talked about the horrors of the retreat (it was clear from the newspapers that the retreat was proceeding according to plan); to those in the rear who were guilty of the slanderous rumor that rations were meager; to those at the front who were guilty of the slanderous rumor that the Germans had excellent equipment; and to those everywhere who, in 1942, were guilty of the slanderous rumor that people were dying of starvation in blockaded Leningrad.

During that same year, after the disasters at Kerch (120,000 prisoners), at Kharkov (even more), and in the course of the big southern retreat to the Caucasus and the Volga, another very important wave of officers and soldiers was pumped through—those who refused to stand to the death and who retreated without permission, the men whom, in the words of Stalin's immortal Order No. 227, the Motherland could not forgive for the shame they had caused her. This wave, however, never reached Gulag: after accelerated processing by divisional tribunals, it was, to a man, herded into punishment battalions, and was soaked up in the red sand of advanced positions, leaving not a trace. Thus was cemented the foundation of the Stalingrad victory, but it has found no place in the usual Russian history and exists only in the private history of the sewage system.

(Incidentally, we are here trying to identify only those waves which came into Gulag from outside. There was, after all, an incessant internal recirculation from reservoir to reservoir, through the system of so-called *sentencing in camp*, which was particularly rampant during the war years. But we are not considering those in this chapter.)

Conscientiousness requires that we recall also the reverse waves of wartime: the previously mentioned Czechs and Poles who were released; as well as criminals released for service at the front.

From 1943 on, when the war turned in our favor, there began the multimillion wave from the occupied territories and from Europe, which got larger every year up to 1946. Its two main divisions were:

• Civilians who had lived under the Germans or among Germans—hung with a *tenner* under the letter "a": 58-1a.
• Military personnel who had been POW's—who were nailed with a *tenner* under the letter "b": 58-1b.

Everyone living under the occupation wanted, of course, to survive, and therefore could not remain with *hands folded*, and thereby theoretically earned, along with his daily bread, a future sentence—if not for treason to the Motherland, then at least for aiding and abetting the enemy. However, in actual practice, it was enough to note in the passport serial number that a person had been in occupied territory. To arrest all such persons would have been, from the economic point of view, irrational, because it would have depopulated such enormous areas. All that was required in order to heighten the general consciousness was to arrest a certain percentage—of those guilty, those half-guilty, those quarter-guilty, and those who had hung out their footcloths to dry on the same branch as the Germans.

After all, even one percent of just one million fills up a dozen full-blooded camps.

And dismiss the thought that honorable participation in an underground anti-German organization would surely protect one from being arrested in this wave. More than one case proved this. For instance, there was the Kiev Komsomol member whom the underground organization sent to serve in the Kiev police during the German occupation in order to obtain inside information. The boy kept the Komsomol honestly informed about everything, but when our forces arrived on the scene, he got his *tenner* because he couldn't, while serving in the police, fail to acquire some of the enemy's spirit or to carry out some enemy orders.

Those who were in Europe got the stiffest punishments of all, even though they went there as conscripted German slaves. That was because they had seen something of European life and could talk about it. And their stories, which made unpleasant listening for us (except, of course, for the travel notes of sensible writers), were especially unpleasant during the postwar years of ruin and disorganization; not everyone, after all, was able to report that things in Europe were hopelessly bad and that it was absolutely impossible to live there.

That also was the reason why they sentenced the majority of *war prisoners* (it was not simply because they had allowed themselves to be captured), particularly those POW's who had seen a little more of the West than a German death camp.[42] This was

42. That was not such a clear-cut decision at the start. Even in 1943 there were certain separate waves which were like no others—like the so-called "Africans," who bore this nickname for a long time at the Vorkuta construction projects. These were Russian war prisoners of the Germans, who had been taken prisoner a second time when the Americans captured them from Rommel's army in Africa (the "Hiwi"). In 1943 they were sent in Studebakers, through Egypt, Iraq, and Iran, to their Motherland. And on a desert gulf of the

obvious from the fact that *interned persons* were sentenced as severely as POW's. For example, during the first days of the war one of our destroyers went aground on Swedish territory. Its crew proceeded to live freely in Sweden during all the rest of the war, and in such comfort and plenty as they had never experienced before and would never experience again. The U.S.S.R. retreated, attacked, starved and died, while those scoundrels stuffed their *neutral* mugs. After the war Sweden returned them to us along with the destroyer. Their treason to the Motherland was indubitable—but somehow the case didn't get off the ground. They let them go their different ways and then pasted them with Anti-Soviet Agitation for their lovely stories in praise of freedom and good eating in capitalist Sweden. (This was the Kadenko group.)[43]

Caspian, they were immediately put behind barbed wire. The police who received them ripped off their military insignia and liberated them of all things the Americans had given them (keeping them for themselves, of course, not turning them over to the state); then they sent them off to Vorkuta to await special orders, without (due to inexperience) sentencing them to a specific term under any article of the Code. These "Africans" lived in Vorkuta in a betwixt-and-between condition. They were not under guard, but they were given no passes, and without passes they could not take so much as one step in Vorkuta. They were paid wages at the same rate as free workers, but they were treated like prisoners. And the special orders never did come. They were forgotten men.

43. What happened to this group later makes an anecdote. In camp they kept their mouths shut about Sweden, fearing they'd get a second term. But people in Sweden somehow found out about their fate and published slanderous reports in the press. By that time the boys were scattered far and near among various camps. Suddenly, on the strength of special orders, they were all yanked out and taken to the Kresty Prison in Leningrad. There they were fed for two months as though for slaughter and allowed to let their hair grow. Then they were dressed with modest elegance, rehearsed on what to say and to whom, and warned that any bastard who dared to squeak out of turn would get a bullet in his skull—and they were led off to a press conference for selected foreign journalists and some others who had known the entire crew in Sweden. The former internees bore themselves cheerfully described where they were living, studying, and working, and expressed their indignation at the bourgeois slander they had *read* about not long before in the Western press (after all, Western papers are sold in the Soviet Union at every corner newsstand!). And so they had written to one another and decided to gather in Leningrad. (Their travel expenses didn't bother them in the least.) Their fresh, shiny appearance completely gave the lie to the newspaper canard. The discredited journalists went off to write their apologies. It was wholly inconceivable to the Western imagination that there could be any other explanation. And the men who had been the subjects of the interview were taken off to a bath, had their hair cut off again, were dressed in their former rags, and sent back to the same camps. But because they had conducted themselves properly, none of them was given a second term.

Within the over-all wave of those from formerly occupied areas, there followed, one after another, the quick and compact waves of the nationalities which had transgressed:

- In 1943, the Kalmyks, Chechens, Ingush, and Balkars.
- In 1944, the Crimean Tatars.

They would not have been pushed out into eternal exile so energetically and swiftly had it not been that regular army units and military trucks were assigned to help the *Organs*. The military units gallantly surrounded the auls, or settlements, and, within twenty-four hours, with the speed of a parachute attack, those who had nested there for centuries past found themselves removed to railroad stations, loaded by the trainload, and rushed off to Siberia, Kazakhstan, Central Asia, and the Russian North. Within one day their land and their property had been turned over to their "heirs."

What had happened to the Germans at the beginning of the war now happened to these nationalities: they were exiled solely on the basis of *blood*. There was no filling out of questionnaires; Party members, Heroes of Labor, and heroes of the still-unfinished war were all sent along with the rest.

During the last years of the war, of course, there was a wave of German *war criminals* who were selected from the POW camps and transferred by court verdict to the jurisdiction of Gulag.

In 1945, even though the war with Japan didn't last three weeks, great numbers of Japanese war prisoners were raked in for urgent construction projects in Siberia and Central Asia, and the same process of selecting *war criminals* for Gulag was carried out among them.[44]

At the end of 1944, when our army entered the Balkans, and especially in 1945, when it reached into Central Europe, a wave of Russian *émigrés* flowed through the channels of Gulag. Most were old men, who had left at the time of the Revolution, but there were also young people, who had grown up outside Russia. They usually dragged off the menfolk and left the women and

44. Without knowing the details, I am nevertheless convinced that a great many of these Japanese could not have been sentenced legitimately. It was an act of revenge, as well as a means of holding onto manpower for as long a period as possible.

children where they were. It is true that they did not take every-one, but they took all those who, in the course of twenty-five years, had expressed even the mildest political views, or who had expressed them earlier, during the Revolution. They did not touch those who had lived a purely vegetable existence. The main waves came from Bulgaria, Yugoslavia, and Czechoslovakia; there were fewer from Austria and Germany. In the other countries of Eastern Europe, there were hardly any Russians.

As if in response to 1945, a wave of émigrés poured from Manchuria too. (Some of them were not arrested immediately. Entire families were encouraged to return to the homeland as free persons, but once back in Russia they were separated and sent into exile or taken to prison.)

All during 1945 and 1946 a big wave of genuine, at-long-last, enemies of the Soviet government flowed into the Archipelago. (These were the Vlasov men, the Krasnov Cossacks, and Moslems from the national units created under Hitler.) Some of them had acted out of conviction; others had been merely involuntary participants.

Along with them were seized *not less than one million fugitives from the Soviet government*—civilians of all ages and of both sexes who had been fortunate enough to find shelter on Allied territory, but who in 1946–1947 were perfidiously returned by Allied authorities into Soviet hands.[45]

45. It is surprising that in the West, where political secrets cannot be kept long, since they inevitably come out in print or are disclosed, the secret of *this* particular act of betrayal has been very well and carefully kept by the British and American governments. This is truly the last secret, or one of the last, of the Second World War. Having often encountered these people in camps, I was unable to believe for a whole quarter-century that the public in the West knew *nothing* of this action of the Western governments, this massive handing over of ordinary Russian people to retribution and death. Not until 1973—in the *Sunday Oklahoman* of January 21—was an article by Julius Epstein published. And I am here going to be so bold as to express gratitude on behalf of the mass of those who perished and those few left alive. One random little document was published from the many volumes of the hitherto concealed case history of forced repatriation to the Soviet Union. "After having remained unmolested in British hands for two years, they had allowed themselves to be lulled into a false sense of security and they were therefore taken completely by surprise. . . . They did not realize they were being re-patriated. . . . They were mainly simple peasants with bitter personal grievances against the Bolsheviks." The English authorities gave them the treatment "reserved in the case of every other nation for war criminals alone: that of being handed over against their will to captors who, incidentally, were not expected to give them a fair trial." They were all sent to destruction on the Archipelago. (Author's note, dated 1973.)

A certain number of *Poles*, members of the Home Army, followers of Mikolajczyk, arrived in Gulag in 1945 via our prisons.

There were a certain number of *Rumanians* and *Hungarians*.

At war's end and for many years after, there flowed uninterruptedly an abundant wave of Ukrainian nationalists (the "Banderovtsy").

Against the background of this enormous postwar displacement of millions, few paid much attention to such small waves as:

- *Foreigners' girl friends* (in 1946–1947)—in other words,
Soviet girls who went out with foreigners. They sentenced these
girls under Article 7-35—SOE—Socially Dangerous Element.
- *Spanish children*—the same children who had been taken
from their homeland during the Spanish Civil War, but who
were adults by the end of World War II. Raised in our boarding schools, they nonetheless fitted very poorly into our life.
Many longed to go "home." They, too, were given 7-35—SOE
—Socially Dangerous Element. And those who were particularly stubborn got 58-6—espionage on behalf of America.

(In fairness we must not forget the brief reverse wave of priests
in 1947. Yes, a miracle! For the first time in thirty years they
freed priests! They didn't actually go about seeking them out in
camps, but whenever a priest was known to people in freedom,
and whenever a name and exact location could be provided, the
individual priests in question were sent out to freedom in order to
strengthen the church, which at that time was being revived.)

■

We have to remind our readers once again that this chapter
does not attempt by any means to list *all* the waves which fertilized
Gulag—but only those which had a political coloration. And
just as, in a course in physiology, after a detailed description of
the circulation of the blood, one can begin over again and describe in detail the lymphatic system, one could begin again and
describe the waves of *nonpolitical offenders* and *habitual criminals*
from 1918 to 1953. And this description, too, would run long.
It would bring to light many famous decrees, now in part for-

gotten (even though they have never been repealed), which supplied abundant human material for the insatiable Archipelago. One was the Decree on Absenteeism. One was the Decree on Production of Bad Quality Goods. Another was on samogon [moonshine] distilling. Its peak period was 1922—but arrests for this were constant throughout the twenties. And the Decree on the Punishment of Collective Farmers for Failure to Fulfill the Obligatory Norm of Labor Days. And the Decree on the Introduction of Military Discipline on Railroads, issued in April, 1943 —not at the beginning of the war, but when it had already taken a turn for the better.

In accordance with the ancient Petrine tradition, these decrees always put in an appearance as the most important element in all our legislation, but without any comprehension of or reference to the whole of our previous legislation. Learned jurists were supposed to coordinate the branches of the law, but they were not particularly energetic at it, nor particularly successful either.

This steady pulse of decrees led to a curious national pattern of violations and crimes. One could easily recognize that neither burglary, nor murder, nor samogon distilling, nor rape ever seemed to occur at random intervals or in random places throughout the country as a result of human weakness, lust, or failure to control one's passions. By no means! One detected, instead, a surprising unanimity and monotony in the crimes committed. The entire Soviet Union would be in a turmoil of rape alone, or murder alone, or samogon distilling alone, each in its turn—in sensitive reaction to the latest government decree. Each particular crime or violation seemed somehow to be playing into the hands of the latest decree so that it would disappear from the scene that much faster! At that precise moment, the particular crime which had just been foreseen, and for which wise new legislation had just provided stricter punishment, would explode simultaneously everywhere.

The Decree on the militarization of railroads crowded the military tribunals with the women and adolescents who did most of the work on the railroads during the war years and who, having received no barracks training beforehand, were those mostly involved in delays and violations. The Decree on Failure to Fulfill the Obligatory Norm of Labor Days greatly simplified the procedure for removing from the scene those collective farmers who were dissatisfied with receiving for their labor mere "labor day" *points* in the farm account books and wanted produce instead. Whereas previously their cases had required a trial, based on the article of the Code relating to "economic counterrevolution," now it was enough to produce a collective farm decree confirmed by the District Executive Committee. And even then these collective farmers, although they were sent into exile, must have been relieved to know that they were not listed as enemies of the people. The obligatory norm of "labor days" was different in different areas, the easiest of all being among the peoples of the Caucasus—seventy-five "labor days" a year; but despite that, many of them were also sent off to Krasnoyarsk Province for eight years.

As we have said, we are not going to go into a lengthy and lavish examination of the waves of nonpolitical offenders and common criminals. But, having reached 1947, we cannot remain silent about one of the most grandiose of Stalin's decrees. We have already mentioned the famous law of "Seven-Eight" or "Seven-eighths," on the basis of which they arrested people right and left—for taking a stalk of grain, a cucumber, two small potatoes, a chip of wood, a spool of thread—all of whom got ten years.[46]

But the requirements of the times, as Stalin understood them, had changed, and the *tenner*, which had seemed adequate on the eve of a terrible war, seemed now, in the wake of a world-wide historical victory, inadequate. And so again, in complete disregard of the Code, and totally overlooking the fact that many different articles and decrees on the subject of thefts and robberies already existed, on June 4, 1947, a decree was issued which outdid them all. It was instantly christened "Four-sixths" by the undismayed prisoners.

The advantages of the new decree lay first of all in its newness. From the very moment it appeared, a torrent of the crimes it specified would be bound to burst forth, thereby providing an abundant wave of newly sentenced prisoners. But it offered an

---

46. In the actual documents of the "spool of thread" case, they wrote down "200 meters of sewing material." The fact remains that they were ashamed to write "a spool of thread."

even greater advantage in prison terms. If a young girl sent into the fields to get a few ears of grain took along two friends for company ("an organized gang") or some twelve-year-old youngsters went after cucumbers or apples, they were liable to get *twenty* years in camp. In factories, the maximum sentence was raised to *twenty-five years.* (This sentence, called the *quarter,* had been introduced a few days earlier to replace the death penalty, which had been abolished as a humane act.)[47]

And then, at long last, an ancient shortcoming of the law was corrected. Previously the only failure to make a denunciation which qualified as a crime against the state had been in connection with political offenses. But now simple failure to report the theft of state or collective farm property earned three years of camp or seven years of exile.

In the years immediately following this decree, whole "divisions" from the countryside and the cities were sent off to cultivate the islands of Gulag in place of the natives who had died off there. True, these waves were processed through the police and the ordinary courts, and did not clog the channels of State Security, which, even without them, were overstrained in the postwar years.

Stalin's new line, suggesting that it was necessary, in the wake of the victory over fascism, *to jail* more people more energetically and for longer terms than ever before, had immediate repercussions, of course, on political prisoners.

The year 1948–1949, notable throughout Soviet public life for intensified persecution and vigilance, was marked by one tragicomedy hitherto unheard of even in Stalinist antijustice—that of the *repeaters.*

That is what, in the language of Gulag, they called those still undestroyed unfortunates of 1937 vintage, who had succeeded in surviving ten impossible, unendurable years, and who in 1947–1948, had timidly stepped forth onto the land of *freedom* . . . worn out, broken in health, but hoping to live out in peace what little of their lives remained. But some sort of savage fantasy (or stubborn malice, or unsated vengeance) pushed the Victorious

47. And the death penalty itself was kept veiled for a brief period only; the veil was removed, amid a show of bared fangs, two and a half years later —in January, 1950.

Generalissimo into issuing the order to arrest all those cripples over again, without any new charges! It was even disadvantageous, both economically and politically, to clog the meat grinder with its own refuse. But Stalin issued the order anyway. Here was a case in which a historical personality simply behaved capriciously toward historical necessity.

And so it was necessary to *take* all of them though they had hardly had a chance to attach themselves to new places or new families. They were rounded up with much the same weary indolence they themselves now returned with. They knew beforehand the whole way of the cross ahead. They did not ask "What for?" And they did not say to their families: "I'll be back." They put on their shabbiest rags, poured some makhorka into their camp tobacco pouches, and went off to sign the deposition. (Only one question: "Are you the one who was in prison?" "Yes." "Take *ten* more.")

At this point the Autocrat decided it wasn't enough to arrest just those who had survived since 1937! What about the *children* of his sworn enemies? They, too, must be imprisoned! They were growing up, and they might have notions of vengeance. (He may have had a heavy dinner and had a nightmare about those children.) They went through the lists, looked around, and arrested children—but not very many. They arrested the children of the purged army commanders, but not all the children of Trotskyites. And so the wave of the *vengeful children* came into being. (Among such children were seventeen-year-old Lena Kosaryeva and thirty-five-year-old Yelena Rakovskaya.)

By 1948, after the great European displacement, Stalin had succeeded once again in tightly barricading himself in and pulling the ceiling down closer to him: in this reduced space he had recreated the tension of 1937.

And so in 1948, 1949, and 1950 there flowed past:

- Alleged spies (ten years earlier they had been German and Japanese, now they were Anglo-American).
- Believers (this wave non-Orthodox for the most part).
- Those geneticists and plant breeders, disciples of the late Vavilov and of Mendel, who had not previously been arrested.
- Just plain ordinary thinking people (and students, with particular severity) who had not been sufficiently scared away

from the West. It was fashionable to charge them with:

- VAT—Praise of American Technology;
- VAD—Praise of American Democracy; and
- PZ—Toadyism Toward the West.

These waves were not unlike those of 1937, but the *sentences* were different. The standard sentence was no longer the patriarchal *ten-ruble bill*, but the new Stalinist *twenty-five*. By now the *tenner* was for *juveniles*.

There was a good-sized wave from the new Decree on Revealing State Secrets. (State secrets included such things as: the district harvest; any figure on epidemics; the type of goods produced by any workshop or mini-factory; mention of a civil airport, municipal transport routes, or the family name of any prisoner imprisoned in any camp.) For violations of this decree they gave fifteen years.

The waves of nationalities were not forgotten either. The Ukrainian nationalists, the "Banderovtsy," taken in the heat of struggle from the forests where they fought, kept flowing all this time. Simultaneously, all West Ukrainian country people received *tenners* and *fivers* in camps and exile—presumably for having had connections with the partisans: someone had let them spend the night; someone had once fed them; someone had not reported them. For about a year, starting in 1950, a wave of *wives* of Banderovtsy was under way. They gave them each ten years for failure to make a denunciation—so as to finish off their husbands faster.

By this time resistance in Lithuania and Estonia had already come to an end. But in 1949 new waves of new "social prophylaxis" to assure collectivization kept coming. They took whole trainloads of city dwellers and peasants from the three Baltic republics into Siberian exile. (The historical rhythm was disrupted in these republics: they were forced to recapitulate in brief, limited periods the more extended experience of the rest of the country.)

In 1948 one more nationalist wave went into exile—that of the *Greeks* who inhabited the areas around the Sea of Azov, the Kuban, and Sukhumi. They had done nothing to offend the Father during the war, but now he avenged himself on them for his failure in Greece, or so it seemed. This wave, too, was evidently the fruit of his personal insanity. The majority of the Greeks ended up in Central Asian exile; those who voiced their discontent were thrown into political prisons.

Around 1950, to avenge the same lost war, or perhaps just to balance those already in exile, the Greek rebels from Markos' army, who had been turned over to us by Bulgaria, were themselves shipped off to the Archipelago.

During the last years of Stalin's life, a wave of *Jews* became noticeable. (From 1950 on they were hauled in little by little as *cosmopolites*. And that was why the *doctors'* case was cooked up. It would appear that Stalin intended to arrange a great massacre of the Jews.)[48]

But this became the first plan of his life to fail. God told him —apparently with the help of human hands—to depart from his rib cage.

The preceding exposition should have made it clear, one would think, that in the removal of millions and in the populating of Gulag, consistent, cold-blooded planning and never-weakening persistence were at work.

That we never did have any *empty* prisons, merely prisons which were full or prisons which were very, very overcrowded.

And that while you occupied yourself to your heart's content studying the safe secrets of the atomic nucleus, researching the influence of Heidegger on Sartre, or collecting Picasso reproductions; while you rode off in your railroad sleeping compartment to vacation resorts, or finished building your country house near Moscow—the Black Marias rolled incessantly through the streets and the gaybisty—the State Security men—knocked at doors and rang doorbells.

And I think this exposition proves that the *Organs* always earned their pay.

---

48. It has always been impossible to learn the truth about anything in our country—now, and always, and from the beginning. But, according to Moscow rumors, Stalin's plan was this: At the beginning of March the "doctor-murderers" were to be hanged on Red Square. The aroused patriots, spurred on, naturally, by instructors, were to rush into an anti-Jewish pogrom. At this point the government—and here Stalin's character can be divined, can it not? —would intervene generously to save the Jews from the wrath of the people, and that same night would remove them from Moscow to the Far East and Siberia—where barracks had already been prepared for them.

Chapter 3

■

The Interrogation

If the intellectuals in the plays of Chekhov who spent all their time guessing what would happen in twenty, thirty, or forty years had been told that in forty years interrogation by torture would be practiced in Russia; that prisoners would have their skulls squeezed within iron rings;[1] that a human being would be lowered into an acid bath;[2] that they would be trussed up naked to be bitten by ants and bedbugs; that a ramrod heated over a primus stove would be thrust up their anal canal (the "secret brand"); that a man's genitals would be slowly crushed beneath the toe of a jackboot; and that, in the luckiest possible circumstances, prisoners would be tortured by being kept from sleeping for a week, by thirst, and by being beaten to a bloody pulp, not one of Chekhov's plays would have gotten to its end because all the heroes would have gone off to insane asylums.

Yes, not only Chekhov's heroes, but what normal Russian at the beginning of the century, including any member of the Russian Social Democratic Workers' Party, could have believed, would have tolerated, such a slander against the bright future? What had been acceptable under Tsar Aleksei Mikhailovich in the seventeenth century, what had already been regarded as barbarism under Peter the Great, what might have been used against ten or twenty people in all during the time of Biron in the

---

1. Dr. S., according to the testimony of A.P.K——va.
2. K. S. T——e.

mid-eighteenth century, what had already become totally impossible under Catherine the Great, was all being practiced during the flowering of the glorious twentieth century—in a society based on socialist principles, and at a time when airplanes were flying and the radio and talking films had already appeared—not by one scoundrel alone in one secret place only, but by tens of thousands of specially trained human beasts standing over millions of defenseless victims.

Was it only that explosion of atavism which is now evasively called "the cult of personality" that was so horrible? Or was it even more horrible that during those same years, in 1937 itself, we celebrated Pushkin's centennial? And that we shamelessly continued to stage those self-same Chekhov plays, even though the answers to them had already come in? Is it not still more dreadful that we are now being told, thirty years later, "Don't talk about it!"? If we start to recall the sufferings of millions, we are told it will distort the historical perspective! If we doggedly seek out the essence of our morality, we are told it will darken our material progress! Let's think rather about the blast furnaces, the rolling mills that were built, the canals that were dug . . . no, better not talk about the canals. . . . Then maybe about the gold of the Kolyma? No, maybe we ought not to talk about that either. . . . Well, we can talk about anything, so long as we do it adroitly, so long as we glorify it. . . .

It is really hard to see why we condemn the Inquisition. Wasn't it true that beside the autos-da-fé, magnificent services were offered the Almighty? It is hard to see why we are so down on serfdom. After all, no one forbade the peasants to work every day. And they could sing carols at Christmas too. And for Trinity Day the girls wove wreaths. . . .

■

The exceptional character which written and oral legend nowadays assigns to the year 1937 is seen in the creation of fabricated charges and tortures. But this is untrue, wrong. Throughout the years and decades, interrogations under Article 58 were *almost never* undertaken to elicit the truth, but were simply an exercise in an inevitably filthy procedure: someone who had been free only a little while before, who was sometimes proud and always unprepared, was to be bent and pushed through a narrow pipe where his sides would be torn by iron hooks and where he could not breathe, so that he would finally pray to get to the other end. And at the other end, he would be shoved out, an already processed native of the Archipelago, already in the promised land. (The fool would keep on resisting! He even thought there was a way back out of the pipe.)

The more time that passes without anything being written about all this, the harder it becomes to assemble the scattered testimony of the survivors. But they tell us that the creation of *fabricated* cases began back in the early years of the *Organs* so their constant salutary activity might be perceived as essential. Otherwise, what with a decline in the number of enemies, the *Organs* might, in a bad hour, have been forced to *wither away*. As the case of Kosyrev makes clear,[3] the situation of the Cheka was shaky even at the beginning of 1919. Reading the newspapers of 1918, I ran into the official report of a terrible plot that had just been discovered: A group of ten people wanted to (it seems they only *wanted to!*) drag *cannon* onto the roof of an orphanage (let's see—how high was it?) and shell the Kremlin. There were *ten* of them (including, perhaps, women and youngsters), and it was not reported how many cannon there were to be—nor where the cannon were to come from. Nor what caliber they were. Nor how they were to be carried up the stairs to the attic. Nor how they were to be set up, on the steeply sloping roof, and so they wouldn't recoil when fired! How was it that the Petersburg police, when they were fighting to put down the February Revolution, took nothing heavier than a machine gun up to the roofs? Yet this fantasy, exceeding even the fabrications of 1937, was read and believed! Apparently, it will be proved to us in time that the Gumilyev case of 1921 was also fabricated.[4]

In that same year, 1921, the Ryazan Cheka fabricated a false case of a "plot" on the part of the local intelligentsia. But the protests of courageous people could still reach Moscow, and they dropped the case. That year, too, the whole Sapropelite Com-

---

3. Cf. Part I, Chapter 8, below.
4. A. A. Akhmatova told me she was convinced that this was so. She even gave me the name of the Chekist who cooked up the *case*—Y. Agranov, it seems.

mittee, part of the Commission on the Use of Natural Forces, was shot. Familiar enough with the attitude and the mood of Russian scientists at that time, and not being shut off from those years by a smoke screen of fanaticism, we can, indeed, figure out, even without archaeological excavations, the precise validity of that case.

Here is what Y. Doyarenko remembers about 1921: the Lubyanka reception cell for those newly arrested, with forty to fifty trestle beds, and women being brought in one after another all night long. None of them knew what she was supposed to be guilty of, and there was a feeling among them that people were being arrested for no reason at all. Only one woman in the whole cell knew why she was there—she was an SR. The first question asked by Yagoda: "Well, *what* are you here for?" In other words, you tell me, and help me cook up the case! And they say *absolutely the same thing* about the Ryazan GPU in 1930! People all felt they were being imprisoned for no reason. There was so little on which to base a charge that they accused I. D. T——v of using a false name. (And even though his name was perfectly real, they handed him three years via a Special Board—OSO—under 58-10.) Not knowing what to pick on, the interrogator asked: "What was your job?" Answer: "A planner." The interrogater: "Write me a statement that explains 'planning at the factory and how it is carried out.' After that I will let you know why you've been arrested." (He expected the explanation to provide the hook on which to hang a charge.)

Here is the way it went in the case of the Kovno Fortress in 1912: Since the fortress served no useful military purpose, it was decided to eliminate it. At that point the fortress command, thoroughly alarmed, arranged a "night attack" simply to prove its usefulness and in order to stay where they were!

The theoretical view of the suspect's *guilt* was, incidentally, quite elastic from the very beginning. In his instructions on the use of Red Terror, the Chekist M. I. Latsis wrote: "In the interrogation do not seek evidence and proof that the person accused acted in word or deed against Soviet power. The first questions should be: What is his class, what is his origin, what is his education and upbringing? [There is your Sapropelite Committee for you!] These are the questions which must determine the fate of the accused." On November 13, 1920, Dzerzhinsky reported in a letter to the Cheka that "slanderous declarations are often given the green light" in the Cheka.

After so many decades have they not taught us that people do not return *from there?* Except for the small, brief, intentional reverse wave of 1939, one hears only the rarest, isolated stories of someone being turned loose as the result of an interrogation. And in such cases, the person was either imprisoned soon again or else he was let out so he could be kept under surveillance. That is how the tradition arose that *the Organs do not make mistakes.* Then what about those who were innocent?

In his *Dictionary of Definitions* Dal makes the following distinction: "An *inquiry* is distinguished from an *investigation* by the fact that it is carried out to determine whether there is a basis for proceeding to an *investigation.*"

On, sacred simplicity! The *Organs* have never heard of such a thing as an *inquiry!* Lists of names prepared up above, or an initial suspicion, or a denunciation by an informer, or any anonymous denunciation,[5] were all that was needed to bring about the arrest of the suspect, followed by the inevitable formal charge. The time allotted for investigation was not used to unravel the crime but, in ninety-five cases out of a hundred, to exhaust, wear down, weaken, and render helpless the defendant, so that he would want it to end at any cost.

As long ago as 1919 the chief method used by the interrogator was *a revolver on the desk.* That was how they investigated not only political but also ordinary misdemeanors and violations. At the trial of the Main Fuels Committee (1921), the accused Makhrovskaya complained that at her interrogation she had been drugged with cocaine. The prosecutor replied: "If she had declared that she had been treated rudely, that they had *threatened to shoot her, this might be just barely believable.*"[6] The frightening revolver lies there and sometimes it is aimed at you, and the interrogator doesn't tire himself out thinking up what you are

---

5. Article 93 of the Code of Criminal Procedure has this to say: "An anonymous declaration *can* serve as reason for beginning a criminal case"! (And there is no need to be surprised at the word "criminal" here, since all "politicals" were considered criminals, too, under the Code.)

6. N. V. Krylenko, *Za Pyat Let (1918–1922)* (*The Last Five Years [1918–1922]*), Moscow-Petrograd, GIZ, 1923, p. 401.

guilty of, but shouts: "Come on, talk! You know what about!" That was what the interrogator Khaikin demanded of Skripnikova in 1927. That was what they demanded of Vitkovsky in 1929. And twenty-five years later nothing had changed. In 1952 Anna Skripnikova was undergoing her *fifth* imprisonment, and Sivakov, Chief of the Investigative Department of the Ordzhonikidze State Security Administration, said to her: "The prison doctor reports you have a blood pressure of 240/120. That's too low, you bitch! We're going to drive it up to 340 so you'll kick the bucket, you viper, and with no black and blue marks; no beatings; no broken bones. We'll just not let you sleep." She was in her fifties at the time. And if, back in her cell, after a night spent in interrogation, she closed her eyes during the day, the jailer broke in and shouted: "Open your eyes or I'll haul you off that cot by the legs and tie you to the wall standing up."

As early as 1921 interrogations usually took place at night. At that time, too, they shone automobile lights in the prisoner's face (the Ryazan Cheka—Stelmakh). And at the Lubyanka in 1926 (according to the testimony of Berta Gandal) they made use of the hot-air heating system to fill the cell first with icy-cold and then with stinking hot air. And there was an airtight cork-lined cell in which there was no ventilation and they cooked the prisoners. The poet Klyuyev was apparently confined in such a cell and Berta Gandal also. A participant in the Yaroslavl uprising of 1918, Vasily Aleksandrovich Kasyanov, described how the heat in such a cell was turned up until your blood began to ooze through your pores. When they saw this happening through the peephole, they would put the prisoner on a stretcher and take him off to sign his confession. The "hot" and "salty" methods of the "gold" period are well known. And in Georgia in 1926 they used lighted cigarettes to burn the hands of prisoners under interrogation. In Metekhi Prison they pushed prisoners into a cesspool in the dark.

There is a very simple connection here. Once it was established that charges had to be brought at any cost and despite everything, threats, violence, tortures became inevitable. And the more fantastic the charges were, the more ferocious the interrogation had to be in order to force the required confession. Given the fact that the cases were always fabricated, violence and torture had to accompany them. This was not peculiar to 1937 alone. It was a chronic, general practice. And that is why it seems strange today to read in the recollections of former zeks that "torture was permitted from the spring of 1938 on."[7] There were never any spiritual or moral barriers which could have held the Organs back from torture. In the early postwar years, in the *Cheka Weekly, The Red Sword,* and *Red Terror,* the admissibility of torture from a Marxist point of view was openly debated. Judging by the subsequent course of events, the answer deduced was positive, though not universally so.

It is more accurate to say that if before 1938 some kind of formal documentation was required as a preliminary to torture, as well as specific permission for each case under investigation (even though such permission was easy to obtain), then in the years 1937–1938, in view of the extraordinary situation prevailing (the specified millions of admissions to the Archipelago had to be ground through the apparatus of individual interrogation in specified, limited periods, something which had simply not happened in the mass waves of kulaks and nationalities), interrogators were allowed to use violence and torture on an unlimited basis, at their own discretion, and in accordance with the demands of their work quotas and the amount of time they were given. The types of torture used were not regulated and every kind of ingenuity was permitted, no matter what.

In 1939 such indiscriminate authorization was withdrawn, and once again written permission was required for torture, and perhaps it may not have been so easily granted. (Of course, simple threats, blackmail, deception, exhaustion through enforced sleeplessness, and punishment cells were never prohibited.) Then, from the end of the war and throughout the postwar years, certain *categories* of prisoners were established by decree for whom a broad range of torture was automatically permitted. Among these were nationalists, particularly the Ukrainians and the Lithuanians, especially in those cases where an underground organization

7. Y. Ginzburg writes that permission for "physical measures of persuasion" was given in April, 1938. V. Shalamov believes that tortures were permitted from the middle of 1938 on. The old prisoner M——ch is convinced that there was an "order to simplify the questioning and to change from psychological methods to physical methods." Ivanov-Razumnik singles out the middle of 1938 as the "period of the most cruel interrogations."

existed (or was suspected) that had to be completely uncovered, which meant obtaining the names of everyone involved from those already arrested. For example, there were about fifty Lithuanians in the group of Romualdas Skyrius, the son of Pranus. In 1945 they were charged with posting anti-Soviet leaflets. Because there weren't enough prisons in Lithuania at the time, they sent them to a camp near Velsk in Archangel Province. There some were tortured and others simply couldn't endure the double regime of work plus interrogation, with the result that all fifty, to the very last one, *confessed.* After a short time news came from Lithuania that the real culprits responsible for the leaflets had been discovered, *and none of the first group had been involved at all!* In 1950, at the Kuibyshev Transit Prison, I encountered a Ukrainian from Dnepropetrovsk who had been tortured many different ways in an effort to squeeze "contacts" and names out of him. Among the tortures to which he had been subjected was a punishment cell in which there was room only to stand. They shoved a pole inside for him to hold on to so that he could sleep —for four hours a day. After the war, they tortured Corresponding Member of the Academy of Sciences Levina because she and the Alliluyevs had acquaintances in common.

It would also be incorrect to ascribe to 1937 the "discovery" that the personal confession of an accused person was more important than any other kind of proof or facts. This concept had already been formulated in the twenties. And 1937 was just the year when the brilliant teaching of Vyshinsky came into its own. Incidentally, even at that time, his teaching was transmitted only to interrogators and prosecutors—for the sake of their morale and steadfastness. The rest of us only learned about it twenty years later—when it had already come into disfavor— through subordinate clauses and minor paragraphs of newspaper articles, which treated the subject as if it had long been widely known to all.

It turns out that in that terrible year Andrei Yanuaryevich (one longs to blurt out, "Jaguaryevich") Vyshinsky, availing himself of the most flexible dialectics (of a sort nowadays not permitted either Soviet citizens or electronic calculators, since to them *yes* is *yes* and *no* is *no*), pointed out in a report which became famous in certain circles that it is never possible for mortal men to establish absolute truth, but relative truth only. He then proceeded to a further step, which jurists of the last two thousand years had not been willing to take: that the truth established by interrogation and trial could not be absolute, but only, so to speak, relative. Therefore, when we sign a sentence ordering someone to be shot we can never be *absolutely* certain, but only approximately, in view of certain hypotheses, and in a certain sense, that we are punishing a *guilty person*.[8] Thence arose the most practical conclusion: that it was useless to seek absolute evidence—for evidence is always relative—or unchallengeable witnesses—for they can say different things at different times. The proofs of guilt were *relative,* approximate, and the interrogator could find them, even when there was no evidence and no witness, without leaving his office, "basing his conclusions not only on his own intellect but also on his Party sensitivity, his *moral forces*" (in other words, the superiority of someone who has slept well, has been well fed, and has not been beaten up) "and on his *character*" (i.e., his willingness to apply cruelty!).

Of course, this formulation was much more elegant than Latsis' instructions. But the essence of both was the same.

In only one respect did Vyshinsky fail to be consistent and retreat from dialectical logic: for some reason, the executioner's *bullet* which he allowed was not relative but *absolute*. . . .

Thus it was that the conclusions of advanced Soviet jurisprudence, proceeding in a spiral, returned to barbaric or medieval standards. Like medieval torturers, our interrogators, prosecutors, and judges agreed to accept the confession of the accused as the chief proof of guilt.[9]

However, the simple-minded Middle Ages used dramatic and

8. Perhaps Vyshinsky, no less than his listeners, needed this ideological comfort at this time. When he cried out from the prosecutor's platform: "Shoot them all like mad dogs!" he, at least, who was both evil and quick of mind, understood that the accused were innocent. And in all probability he and that whale of Marxist dialectics, the defendant Bukharin, devoted themselves with all the greater passion to the dialectical elaboration of the judicial lie: for Bukharin it was too stupid and futile to die if he was altogether innocent (thus he *needed* to find his own guilt!); and for Vyshinsky it was more agreeable to see himself as a logician than as a plain downright scoundrel.

9. Compare the Fifth Amendment to the Constitution of the United States: "Nor shall [any person] be compelled in any criminal case to be a witness against himself." *Not be compelled!* (The same thing appears in the seventeenth-century Bill of Rights.)

picturesque methods to squeeze out the desired confessions: the rack, the wheel, the bed of nails, impalement, hot coals, etc. In the twentieth century, taking advantage of our more highly developed medical knowledge and extensive prison experience (and someone seriously defended a doctoral dissertation on this theme), people came to realize that the accumulation of such impressive apparatus was superfluous and that, on a mass scale, it was also cumbersome. And in addition . . .

In addition, there was evidently one other circumstance. As always, Stalin did not pronounce that final word, and his subordinates had to guess what he wanted. Thus, like a jackal, he left himself an escape hole, so that he could, if he wanted, beat a retreat and write about "dizziness from success." After all, for the first time in human history the calculated torture of millions was being undertaken, and, even with all his strength and power, Stalin could not be absolutely sure of success. In dealing with such an enormous mass of material, the effects of the experiment might differ from those obtained from a smaller sample. An unforeseen explosion might take place, a slippage in a geological fault, or even world-wide disclosure. In any case, Stalin had to remain innocent, his sacred vestments angelically pure.

We are therefore forced to conclude that no list of tortures and torments existed in printed form for the guidance of interrogators! Instead, all that was required was for every Interrogation Department to supply the tribunal within a specified period with a stipulated number of rabbits who had confessed everything. *And it was simply stated,* orally but often, that any measures and means employed were good, since they were being used for a lofty purpose; that no interrogator would be made to answer for the death of an accused; and that the prison doctor should interfere as little as possible with the course of the investigation. In all probability, they exchanged experiences in comradely fashion; "they learned from the most successful workers." Then, too, "material rewards" were offered—higher pay for night work, bonus pay for fast work—and there were also definite warnings that interrogators who could not cope with their tasks . . . Even the chief of some provincial NKVD administration, if some sort of mess developed, could show Stalin his hands were clean: he had issued no direct instructions to use torture! But at the same time he had ensured that torture would be used!

Understanding that their superiors were taking precautions for self-protection, some of the rank-and-file interrogators—not, however, those who drank like maniacs—tried to start off with milder methods, and even when they intensified them, they tried to avoid those that left obvious marks: an eye gouged out, an ear torn off, a backbone broken, even bruises all over the body.

That is why in 1937 we observe no general consistency of methods—except for enforced sleeplessness—in the administrations of the various provinces, or for that matter among the different interrogators of a single administration.[10]

What they did have in common, however, was that they gave precedence to the so-called *light* methods (we will see what they were immediately). This way was sure. Indeed, the actual boundaries of human equilibrium are very narrow, and it is not really necessary to use a rack or hot coals to drive the average human being out of his mind.

Let us try to list some of the simplest methods which break the will and the character of the prisoner without leaving marks on his body.

Let us begin with *psychological* methods. These methods have enormous and even annihilating impact on rabbits who have never been prepared for prison suffering. And it isn't easy even for a person who holds strong convictions.

1. First of all: *night*. Why is it that all the main work of breaking down human souls went on at *night*? Why, from their very earliest years, did the *Organs* select the *night*? Because at night, the prisoner torn from sleep, even though he has not yet been tortured by sleeplessness, lacks his normal daytime equanimity and common sense. He is more vulnerable.

2. *Persuasion* in a sincere tone is the very simplest method. Why play at cat and mouse, so to speak? After all, having spent some time among others undergoing interrogation, the prisoner has come to see what the situation is. And so the interrogator says to him in a lazily friendly way: "Look, you're going to get a prison term whatever happens. But if you resist, *you'll croak* right here in prison, you'll lose your health. But if you go to camp, you'll have fresh air and sunlight. . . . So why not sign right now?" Very logical. And those who agree and sign are

10. It is common talk that Rostov-on-the-Don and Krasnodar were particularly distinguished for the cruelty of their tortures, but this has not been proved.

smart, if . . . if the matter concerns only themselves! But that's rarely so. A struggle is inevitable.

Another variant of persuasion is particularly appropriate to the Party member. "If there are shortages and even famine in the country, then you as a Bolshevik have to make up your mind: can you admit that the whole Party is to blame? Or the whole Soviet government?" "No, of course not!" the director of the flax depot hastened to reply. "Then be brave, and shoulder the blame yourself!" And he did!

3. *Foul language* is not a clever method, but it can have a powerful impact on people who are well brought up, refined, delicate. I know of two cases involving priests, who capitulated to foul language alone. One of them, in the Butyrki in 1944, was being interrogated by a woman. At first when he'd come back to our cell he couldn't say often enough how polite she was. But once he came back very despondent, and for a long time he refused to tell us how, with her legs crossed high, she had begun to *curse*. (I regret that I cannot cite one of her little phrases here.)

4. *Psychological contrast* was sometimes effective: sudden reversals of tone, for example. For a whole or part of the interrogation period, the interrogator would be extremely friendly, addressing the prisoner formally by first name and patronymic, and promising everything. Suddenly he would brandish a paperweight and shout: "Foo, you rat! I'll put nine grams of lead in your skull!" And he would advance on the accused, clutching hands outstretched as if to grab him by the hair, fingernails like needles. (This worked very, very well with women prisoners.)

Or as a variation on this: two interrogators would take turns. One would shout and bully. The other would be friendly, almost gentle. Each time the accused entered the office he would tremble —which would it be? He wanted to do everything to please the gentle one because of his different manner, even to the point of signing and confessing to things that had never happened.

5. Preliminary *humiliation* was another approach. In the famous cellars of the Rostov-on-the-Don GPU (House 33), which were lit by lenslike insets of thick glass in the sidewalk above the former storage basement, prisoners awaiting interrogation were made to lie face down for several hours in the main corridor and forbidden to raise their heads or make a

sound. They lay this way, like Moslems at prayer, until the guard touched a shoulder and took them off to interrogation. Another case: At the Lubyanka, Aleksandra O——va refused to give the testimony demanded of her. She was transferred to Lefortovo. In the admitting office, a woman jailer ordered her to undress, allegedly for a medical examination, took away her clothes, and locked her in a "box" naked. At that point the men jailers began to peer through the peephole and to appraise her female attributes with loud laughs. If one were systematically to question former prisoners, many more such examples would certainly emerge. They all had but a single purpose: to dishearten and humiliate.

6. Any method of inducing extreme *confusion* in the accused might be employed. Here is how F.I.V. from Krasnogorsk, Moscow Province, was interrogated. (This was reported by I. A. P——ev.) During the interrogation, the interrogator, a woman, undressed in front of him by stages (a striptease!), all the time continuing the interrogation as if nothing were going on. She walked about the room and came close to him and tried to get him to give in. Perhaps this satisfied some personal quirk in her, but it may also have been cold-blooded calculation, an attempt to get the accused so muddled that he would sign. And she was in no danger. She had her pistol, and she had her alarm bell.

7. *Intimidation* was very widely used and very varied. It was often accompanied by *enticement* and by *promises* which were, of course, false. In 1924: "If you don't confess, you'll go to the Solovetsky Islands. Anybody who confesses is turned loose." In 1944: "Which camp you'll be sent to depends on us. Camps are different. We've got hard-labor camps now. If you confess, you'll go to an easy camp. If you're stubborn, you'll get twenty-five years in handcuffs in the mines!" Another form of intimidation was threatening a prisoner with a prison worse than the one he was in. "If you keep on being stubborn, we'll send you to Lefortovo" (if you are in the Lubyanka), "to Sukhanovka" (if you are at Lefortovo). "They'll find another way to talk to you there." You have already gotten used to things where you are; the regimen seems to be *not so bad;* and what kind of torments await you *elsewhere?* Yes, and you also have to be transported there. . . . Should you give in?

Intimidation worked beautifully on those who had not yet

been arrested but had simply received an official summons to the Bolshoi Dom—the Big House. He (or she) still had a lot to lose. He (or she) was frightened of everything—that they wouldn't let him (or her) out today, that they would confiscate his (or her) belongings or apartment. He would be ready to give all kinds of testimony and make all kinds of concessions in order to avoid these dangers. She, of course, would be ignorant of the Criminal Code, and, at the very least, at the start of the questioning they would push a sheet of paper in front of her with a fake citation from the Code: "I have been warned that for giving false testimony . . . five years of imprisonment." (In actual fact, under Article 95, it is two years.) "For refusal to give testimony—five years . . ." (In actual fact, under Article 92, it is up to three months.) Here, then, one more of the interrogator's basic methods has entered the picture and will continue to re-enter it.

8. The *lie*. We lambs were forbidden to lie, but the interrogator could tell all the lies he felt like. Those articles of the law did not apply to him. We had even lost the yardstick with which to gauge: what does he get for lying? He could confront us with as many documents as he chose, bearing the forged signatures of our kinfolk and friends—and it would be just a skillful interrogation technique.

Intimidation through enticement and lies was the fundamental method for bringing pressure on the *relatives* of the arrested person when they were called in to give testimony. "If you don't tell us such and such" (whatever was being asked), "it's going to be the worse for *him*. . . . You'll be destroying him completely." (How hard for a mother to hear that!) [11] "Signing this paper" (pushed in front of the relatives) "is the only way you can save him" (destroy him).

9. *Playing on one's affection* for those one loved was a game that worked beautifully on the accused as well. It was the most effective of all methods of intimidation. One could break even a totally fearless person through his concern for those he loved. (Oh, how foresighted was the saying: "A man's family are his

11. Under the harsh laws of the Tsarist Empire, close relatives could refuse to testify. And even if they gave testimony at a preliminary investigation, they could choose to repudiate it and refuse to permit it to be used in court. And, curiously enough, kinship or acquaintance with a criminal was never in itself considered evidence.

enemies.") Remember the Tatar who bore his sufferings—his own and those of his wife—but could not endure his daughter's! In 1930, Rimalis, a woman interrogator, used to threaten: "We'll arrest your daughter and lock her in a cell with syphilitics!" And that was a woman!

They would threaten to arrest everyone you loved. Sometimes this would be done with sound effects: Your wife has already been arrested, but her further fate depends on you. They are questioning her in the next room—just listen! And through the wall you can actually hear a woman weeping and screaming. (After all, they all sound alike; you're hearing it through a wall; and you're under terrific strain and not in a state to play the expert on voice identification. Sometimes they simply play a recording of the voice of a "typical wife"—soprano or contralto —a labor-saving device suggested by some inventive genius.) And then, without fakery, they actually show her to you through a glass door, as she walks along in silence, her head bent in grief. Yes! Your own wife in the corridors of State Security! You have destroyed her by your stubbornness! She has already been arrested! (In actual fact, she has simply been summoned in connection with some insignificant procedural question and sent into the corridor at just the right moment, after being told: "Don't raise your head, or you'll be kept here!") Or they give you a letter to read, and the handwriting is exactly like hers: "I renounce you! After the filth they have told me about you, I don't need you any more!" (And since such wives do exist in our country, and such letters as well, you are left to ponder in your heart: Is that the kind of wife she really is?)

The interrogator Goldman (in 1944) was trying to extort testimony against other people from V. A. Korneyeva with the threat: "We'll confiscate your house and toss your old women into the street." A woman of deep convictions, and firm in her faith, Korneyeva had no fear whatever for herself. She was prepared to suffer. But, given our laws, Goldman's threats were all too real, and she was in torment over the fate of her loved ones. When, by morning, after a night of tearing up rejected depositions, Goldman began to write a fourth version accusing Korneyeva alone, she signed it happily and with a feeling of spiritual victory. We fail to hang on to the basic human instinct to prove our innocence when falsely accused. How can we there? We were even glad when we succeeded in taking all the guilt on our own shoulders.[12]

Just as there is no classification in nature with rigid boundaries, it is impossible rigidly to separate psychological methods from *physical* ones. Where, for example, should we classify the following amusement?

10. *Sound effects*: The accused is made to stand twenty to twenty-five feet away and is then forced to speak more and more loudly and to repeat everything. This is not easy for someone already weakened to the point of exhaustion. Or two megaphones are constructed of rolled-up cardboard, and two interrogators, coming close to the prisoner, bellow in both ears: "Confess, you rat!" The prisoner is deafened; sometimes he actually loses his sense of hearing. But this method is uneconomical. The fact is that the interrogators like some diversion in their monotonous work, and so they vie in thinking up new ideas.

11. *Tickling*: This is also a diversion. The prisoner's arms and legs are bound or held down, and then the inside of his nose is tickled with a feather. The prisoner writhes; it feels as though someone were drilling into his brain.

12. *A cigarette is put out* on the accused's skin (already mentioned above).

13. *Light effects* involve the use of an extremely bright electric light in the small, white-walled cell or "box" in which the accused is being held—a light which is never extinguished. (The electricity saved by the economies of schoolchildren and housewives!) Your eyelids become inflamed, which is very painful. And then in the interrogation room searchlights are again directed into your eyes.

14. Here is another imaginative trick: On the eve of May 1, 1933, in the Khabarovsk GPU, for *twelve* hours—all night—Chebotaryev was not interrogated, no, but was simply kept in a continual state of being *led to* interrogation. "Hey, you—hands

12. Today she says: "After eleven years, during rehabilitation proceedings they let me reread those 'depositions,' and I was gripped by a feeling of spiritual nausea. What was there to be proud of?" I myself, during the rehabilitation period, felt the very same way on hearing excerpts from my earlier depositions. As the saying goes: They bent me into a bow, and I became someone else. I did not recognize myself—how could I have signed them and still think I had not gotten off too badly?

behind your back!" They led him out of the cell, up the stairs quickly, into the interrogator's office. The guard left. But the interrogator, without asking one single question, and sometimes without even allowing Chebotaryev to sit down, would pick up the telephone: "Take away the prisoner from 107!" And so they came to get him and took him back to his cell. No sooner had he lain down on his board bunk than the lock rattled: "Chebotaryev! To interrogation. Hands behind your back!" And when he got there: "Take away the prisoner from 107!"

For that matter, the methods of bringing pressure to bear can begin a long time before the interrogator's office.

15. Prison begins with the *box*, in other words, what amounts to a closet or packing case. The human being who has just been taken from freedom, still in a state of inner turmoil, ready to explain, to argue, to struggle, is, when he first sets foot in prison, clapped into a "box," which sometimes has a lamp and a place where he can sit down, but which sometimes is dark and constructed in such a way that he can only stand up and even then is squeezed against the door. And he is held there for several hours, or for half a day, or a day. During those hours he knows absolutely nothing! Will he perhaps be confined there all his life? He has never in his life encountered anything like this, and he cannot guess at the outcome. Those first hours are passing when everything inside him is still ablaze from the unstilled storm in his heart. Some become despondent—and that's the time to subject them to their first interrogation. Others become angry—and that, too, is all to the good, for they may insult the interrogator right at the start or make a slip, and it will be all the easier to cook up their case.

16. When boxes were in short supply, they used to have another method. In the Novocherkassk NKVD, Yelena Strutinskaya was forced to remain seated on a stool in the corridor for six days in such a way that she did not lean against anything, did not sleep, did not fall off, and did not get up from it. Six days! Just try to sit that way for six hours!

Then again, as a variation, the prisoner can be forced to sit on a tall chair, of the kind used in laboratories, so that his feet do not reach the floor. They become very numb in this position. He is left sitting that way from eight to ten hours.

Or else, during the interrogation itself, when the prisoner is out in plain view, he can be forced to sit in this way: as far forward as possible on the front edge ("Move further forward! Further still!") of the chair so that he is under painful pressure during the entire interrogation. He is not allowed to stir for several hours. Is that all? Yes, that's all. Just try it yourself!

17. Depending on local conditions, a *divisional pit* can be substituted for the box, as was done in the Gorokhovets army camps during World War II. The prisoner was pushed into such a pit, ten feet in depth, six and a half feet in diameter; and beneath the open sky, rain or shine, this pit was for several days both his cell and his latrine. And ten and a half ounces of bread, and water, were lowered to him on a cord. Imagine yourself in this situation just after you've been arrested, when you're all in a boil.

Either identical orders to all Special Branches of the Red Army or else the similarities of their situations in the field led to broad use of this method. Thus, in the 36th Motorized Infantry Division, a unit which took part in the battle of Khalkhin-Gol, and which was encamped in the Mongolian desert in 1941, a newly arrested prisoner was, without explanation, given a spade by Chief of the Special Branch Samulyev and ordered to dig a pit the exact dimensions of a *grave*. (Here is a hybridization of physical and psychological methods.) When the prisoner had dug deeper than his own waist, they ordered him to stop and sit down on the bottom: his head was no longer visible. One guard kept watch over several such pits and it was as though he were surrounded by empty space.[13] They kept the accused in this desert with no protection from the Mongolian sun and with no warm clothing against the cold of the night, but no tortures—why waste effort on tortures? The ration they gave was *three and a half ounces of bread* per day and *one glass of water*. Lieutenant Chulpenyev, a giant, a boxer, twenty-one years old, spent *a month* imprisoned this way. Within ten days he was swarming with lice. After fifteen days he was summoned to interrogation for the first time.

---

13. This, evidently, is a Mongolian theme. In the magazine *Niva* (March 15, 1914, p. 218) there is a drawing of a Mongolian prison: each prisoner is shut in a separate trunk with a small opening for his head or for food. A jailer patrols between the trunks.

18. The accused could be compelled *to stand on his knees*—not in some figurative sense, but literally: on his knees, without sitting back on his heels, and with his back upright. People could be compelled to kneel in the interrogator's office or the corridor for twelve, or even twenty-four or forty-eight hours. (The interrogator himself could go home, sleep, amuse himself in one way or another—this was an organized system; watch was kept over the kneeling prisoner, and the guards worked in shifts.)[14] What kind of prisoner was most vulnerable to such treatment? One already broken, already inclined to surrender. It was also a good method to use with women. Ivanov-Razumnik reports a variation of it: Having set young Lordkipanidze on his knees, the interrogator urinated in his face! And what happened? Unbroken by anything else, Lordkipanidze was broken by this. Which shows that the method also worked well on proud people. . . .

19. Then there is the method of simply compelling a prisoner to *stand there*. This can be arranged so that the accused stands only while being interrogated—because that, too, exhausts and breaks a person down. It can be set up in another way—so that the prisoner sits down during interrogation but is forced to stand up between interrogations. (A watch is set over him, and the guards see to it that he doesn't lean against the wall, and if he goes to sleep and falls over he is given a kick and straightened up.) Sometimes even one day of standing is enough to deprive a person of all his strength and to force him to *testify* to *anything at all*.

20. During all these tortures which involved standing for three, four, and five days, they ordinarily *deprived a person of water*.

The most natural thing of all is to *combine* the psychological and physical methods. It is also natural to combine all the preceding methods with:

21. *Sleeplessness*, which they quite failed to appreciate in medieval times. They did not understand how narrow are the limits within which a human being can preserve his personality

---

14. That, after all, is how somebody's career was launched—standing guard over a prisoner on his knees. And now, in all probability, that somebody has attained high rank and his children are already grown up.

intact. Sleeplessness (yes, combined with standing, thirst, bright light, terror, and the unknown—what other tortures are needed!?) befogs the reason, undermines the will, and the human being ceases to be himself, to be his own "I." (As in Chekhov's "I Want to Sleep," but there it was much easier, for there the girl could lie down and slip into lapses of consciousness, which even in just a minute would revive and refresh the brain.) A person deprived of sleep acts half-unconsciously or altogether unconsciously, so that his testimony cannot be held against him.[15]

They used to say: "You are *not truthful* in your testimony, and *therefore* you will not be allowed to sleep!" Sometimes, as a refinement, instead of making the prisoner stand up, they made him *sit down* on a *soft* sofa, which made him want to sleep all the more. (The jailer on duty sat next to him on the same sofa and kicked him every time his eyes began to shut.) Here is how one victim—who had just sat out days in a box infested with bedbugs—describes his feelings after this torture: "Chill from great loss of blood. Irises of the eyes dried out as if someone were holding a red-hot iron in front of them. Tongue swollen from thirst and prickling as from a hedgehog at the slightest movement. Throat racked by spasms of swallowing."[16]

Sleeplessness was a great form of torture: it left no visible marks and could not provide grounds for complaint even if an inspection—something unheard of anyway—were to strike on the morrow.[17]

"They didn't let you sleep? Well, after all, this is not supposed to be a *vacation resort*. The Security officials were awake too!" (They would catch up on their sleep during the day.) One can say that sleeplessness became the universal method in the *Organs*. From being one among many tortures, it became *an integral part of the system* of State Security; it was the cheapest possible

15. Just picture a foreigner, who knows no Russian, in this muddled state, being given something to sign. Under these conditions the Bavarian Jupp Aschenbrenner signed a document admitting that he had worked on wartime gas vans. It was not until 1954, in camp, that he was finally able to prove that at the time he had been in Munich, studying to become an electric welder.

16. G. M——ch.

17. Inspection, by the way, was so totally impossible and had so emphatically *never* taken place that in 1953, when real inspectors entered the cell of former Minister of State Security Abakumov, himself a prisoner by that time, he roared with laughter, thinking their appearance was a trick intended to confuse him.

method and did not require the posting of sentries. In all the interrogation prisons the prisoners were forbidden to sleep even one minute from reveille till taps. (In Sukhanovka and several other prisons used specifically for interrogation, the cot was folded into the wall during the day; in others, the prisoners were simply forbidden to lie down, and even to close their eyes while seated.) Since the major interrogations were all conducted at night, it was automatic: whoever was undergoing interrogation got no sleep for at least five days and nights. (Saturday and Sunday nights, the interrogators themselves tried to get some rest.)

22. The above method was further implemented by *an assembly line of interrogators*. Not only were you not allowed to sleep, but for three or four days *shifts of interrogators kept up a continuous interrogation*.

23. *The bedbug-infested box* has already been mentioned. In the dark closet made of wooden planks, there were hundreds, maybe even thousands, of bedbugs, which had been allowed to multiply. The guards removed the prisoner's jacket or field shirt, and immediately the hungry bedbugs assaulted him, crawling onto him from the walls or falling off the ceiling. At first he waged war with them strenuously, crushing them on his body and on the walls, suffocated by their stink. But after several hours he weakened and let them drink his blood without a murmur.

24. *Punishment cells.* No matter how hard it was in the ordinary cell, the punishment cells were always worse. And on return from there the ordinary cell always seemed like paradise. In the punishment cell a human being was systematically worn down by starvation and also, usually, by *cold*. (In Sukhanovka Prison there were also *hot* punishment cells.) For example, the Lefortovo punishment cells were entirely unheated. There were radiators in the corridor only, and in this "heated" corridor the guards on duty *walked* in felt boots and padded jackets. The prisoner was forced to undress down to his underwear, and sometimes to his undershorts, and he was forced to spend from three to five days in the punishment cell without moving (since it was so confining). He received hot gruel on the third day only. For the first few minutes you were convinced you'd not be able to last an hour. But, by some miracle, a human being would in-

deed sit out his five days, perhaps acquiring in the course of it an illness that would last him the rest of his life.

There were various aspects to punishment cells—as, for instance, dampness and water. In the Chernovtsy Prison after the war, Masha G. was kept barefooted for two hours *and up to her ankles* in icy water—confess! (She was eighteen years old, and how she feared for her feet! She was going to have to live with them a long time.)

25. Should one consider it a variation of the punishment cell when a prisoner was *locked in an alcove?* As long ago as 1933 this was one of the ways they tortured S. A. Chebotaryev in the Khabarovsk GPU. They locked him naked in a concrete alcove in such a way that he could neither bend his knees, nor straighten up and change the position of his arms, nor turn his head. And that was not all! They began to drip cold water onto his scalp— a classic torture—which then ran down his body in rivulets. They did not inform him, of course, that this would go on for only twenty-four hours. It was awful enough at any rate for him to lose consciousness, and he was discovered the next day apparently dead. He came to on a hospital cot. They had brought him out of his faint with spirits of ammonia, caffeine, and body massage. At first he had no recollection of where he had been, or what had happened. For a whole month he was useless even for interrogation. (We may be so bold as to assume that this alcove and dripping device had not been devised for Chebotaryev alone. In 1949 my Dnepropetrovsk acquaintance had been similarly confined, without the dripping attachment, however. On a line joining Khabarovsk and Dnepropetrovsk, and over a period of sixteen years, were there not other such points as well?)

26. *Starvation* has already been mentioned in combination with other methods. Nor was it an unusual method: to starve the prisoner into confession. Actually, the starvation technique, like interrogation at night, was an integral element in the entire system of coercion. The miserly prison bread ration, amounting to ten and a half ounces in the peacetime year of 1933, and to one pound in 1945 in the Lubyanka, and permitting or prohibiting food parcels from one's family and access to the commissary, were universally applied to everyone. But there was also

the technique of intensified hunger: for example, Chulpenyev was kept for a month on three and a half ounces of bread, after which—when he had just been brought in from the pit—the interrogator Sokol placed in front of him a pot of thick borscht, and half a loaf of white bread sliced diagonally. (What does it matter, one might ask, how it was sliced? But Chulpenyev even today will insist that it was really sliced very attractively.) However, he was not given a thing to eat. How ancient it all is, how medieval, how primitive! The only thing new about it was that it was applied in a socialist society! Others, too, tell about such tricks. They were often tried. But we are going to cite another case involving Chebotaryev because it combined so many methods. They put him in the interrogator's office for seventy-two hours, and the only thing he was allowed was to be taken to the toilet. For the rest, they allowed him neither food nor drink —even though there was water in a carafe right next to him. Nor was he permitted to sleep. Throughout there were three interrogators in the office, working in shifts. One kept writing something—silently, without disturbing the prisoner. The second slept on the sofa, and the third walked around the room, and as soon as Chebotaryev fell asleep, beat him instantly. Then they switched roles. (Maybe they themselves were being punished for failure to deliver.) And then, all of a sudden, they brought Chebotaryev a meal: fat Ukrainian borscht, a chop, fried potatoes, and red wine in a crystal carafe. But because Chebotaryev had had an aversion to alcohol all his life, he refused to drink the wine, and the interrogator couldn't go too far in forcing him to, because that would have spoiled the whole game. After he had eaten, they said to him: "Now here's what you have *testified to in the presence of two witnesses*. Sign here." In other words, he was to sign what had been silently composed by one interrogator in the presence of another, who had been asleep, and a third, who had been actively working. On the very first page Chebotaryev learned he had been on intimate terms with all the leading Japanese generals and that he had received espionage assignments from all of them. He began to cross out whole pages. They beat him up and threw him out. Blaginin, another Chinese Eastern Railroad man, arrested with him, was put through the same thing; but he drank the wine and, in a state of pleasant intoxication, signed the confession—and was shot. (Even one tiny glass can have an enormous effect on a famished man—and that was a whole carafe.)

27. *Beatings*—of a kind that leave no marks. They use rubber truncheons, and they use wooden mallets and small sandbags. It is very, very painful when they hit a bone—for example, an interrogator's jackboot on the shin, where the bone lies just beneath the skin. They beat Brigade Commander Karpunich-Braven for twenty-one days in a row. And today he says: "Even after thirty years all my bones ache—and my head too." In recollecting his own experience and the stories of others, he counts up to fifty-two methods of torture. Here is one: They grip the hand in a special vise so that the prisoner's palm lies flat on the desk—and then they hit the joints with the thin edge of a ruler. And one screams! Should we single out particularly the technique by which teeth are knocked out? They knocked out eight of Karpunich's.[18]

As everyone knows, a blow of the fist in the solar plexus, catching the victim in the middle of a breath, leaves no mark whatever. The Lefortovo Colonel Sidorov, in the postwar period, used to take a "penalty kick" with his overshoes at the dangling genitals of male prisoners. Soccer players who at one time or another have been hit in the groin by a ball know what that kind of blow is like. There is no pain comparable to it, and ordinarily the recipient loses consciousness.[19]

28. In the Novorossisk NKVD they invented a machine for squeezing fingernails. As a result it could be observed later at transit prisons that many of those from Novorossisk had lost their fingernails.

29. And what about the *strait jacket?*

30. And *breaking the prisoner's back?* (As in that same Khabarovsk GPU in 1933.)

18. In the case of the Secretary of the Karelian Provincial Party Committee, G. Kupriyanov, arrested in 1949, some of the teeth they knocked out were just ordinary ones, of no particular account, but others were gold. At first they gave him a receipt that said his gold teeth were being kept for him. And then they caught themselves just in time and took away his receipt.

19. In 1918 the Moscow Revolutionary Tribunal convicted the former Tsarist jailer Bondar. The *most extreme* measure of his cruelty that was cited was the accusation that "in *one* case he had struck a political prisoner with such force that his eardrum had burst." (Krylenko, *op. cit.*, p. 16.)

31. Or *bridling* (also known as "the swan dive")? This was a Sukhanovka method—also used in Archangel, where the interrogator Ivkov applied it in 1940. A long piece of rough toweling was inserted between the prisoner's jaws like a bridle; the ends were then pulled back over his shoulders and tied to his heels. Just try lying on your stomach like a wheel, with your spine breaking—and without water and food for two days![20]

Is it necessary to go on with the list? Is there much left to enumerate? What won't idle, well-fed, unfeeling people invent?

Brother mine! Do not condemn those who, finding themselves in such a situation, turned out to be weak and confessed to more than they should have. . . . Do not be the first to cast a stone at them.

■

But here's the point! Neither these methods nor even the "lightest" methods of all are needed to wring testimony from the majority . . . for iron jaws to grip lambs who are unprepared and longing to return to their warm hearths. The relationship of forces to situations is too unequal.

Oh, in how new a light does our past life appear when re-examined in the interrogator's office: abounding in dangers, like an African jungle. And we had considered it so simple!

You, A, and your friend, B, have known each other for years and have complete faith in one another. When you met, you spoke out boldly about political matters large and small. No one else was present. There was no one who could have overheard you. And you have not denounced each other—not at all.

But at this point, for some reason, you, A, have been marked, hauled out of the herd by the ears, and arrested. And for some reason—well, maybe not without a denunciation on somebody's part, and not without your apprehensions as to the fate of your loved ones, and not without a certain lack of sleep, and not without a bit of punishment cell—you have decided to write yourself off but at the same time not to betray anyone else at any price.

You have therefore confessed in four depositions, and signed them—declaring yourself to be a sworn enemy of Soviet power

20. N.K.G.

—because you used to tell jokes about the Leader, because you thought there should be a choice of candidates at elections, because you went into the voting booth only in order to cross out the name of the only candidate and would have done so except there was no ink in the inkwell, and because there was a 16-meter band on your radio on which you tried to catch parts of Western broadcasts through the jamming. Your own *tenner* has been assured, yet your ribs have remained whole, and so far you have not caught pneumonia. You have not sold anyone out; and it seems to you that you have worked things out sensibly. You have already informed your cellmates that in your opinion your interrogation is probably coming to an end.

But lo and behold! Admiring his own handwriting, and with deliberation, the interrogator begins to fill out deposition No. 5. Question: Were you friendly with B? Answer: Yes. Question: Were you frank with him about politics? Answer: No, no, I did not trust him. Question: But you met often? Answer: Not very. Question: What does that mean, not very? According to testimony from your neighbors, he was at your house on such and such a day, and on such and such, and on such and such just in the past month. Was he? Answer: Maybe. Question: And it was observed that on these occasions, as always, you did not drink, you did not make any noise, you spoke very quietly, and you couldn't be overheard even in the corridor? (Well, friends, drink up! Break bottles! Curse at the top of your lungs! On that basis you will be considered reliable.) Answer: Well, what of it? Question: And you used to visit him too. And you said to him on the phone, for example: "We spent such an interesting evening." Then they saw you on the street at an intersection. You were standing there together in the cold for half an hour, and you both had gloomy faces and dissatisfied expressions; in fact, they even took photographs of you during that meeting. (The technological resources of agents, my friends, the technology of agents!) So *what did you talk about* during these meetings?

What about? That's a leading question! Your first idea is to say that you've forgotten what you talked about. Are you really obliged to remember? So! You've forgotten your first conversation. And the second one too? And the third? And even your interesting evening? And that time at the intersection? And your conversations with C? And your conversations with D? No, you think: "I forgot" is not the way out; you will be unable to maintain that position. And your mind, still shocked by your arrest, in the grip of fear, muddled by sleeplessness and hunger, seeks a way out: how to play it shrewdly in a manner that will have some verisimilitude and outsmart the interrogator.

What about? It is fine if you talked about hockey—that, friends, is in all cases the least troublesome! Or about women, or even about science. Then you can repeat what was said. (Science is not too far removed from hockey, but in our time everything to do with science is classified information and they may get you for a violation of the Decree on Revealing State Secrets.) But what if you did in actual fact talk about the latest arrests in the city? Or about the collective farms? (Of course, critically—for who has anything good to say about them?) Or about reducing the rate of pay for piecework? The fact remains that you frowned for half an hour at the intersection—what were you talking about there?

Maybe B has already been arrested. The interrogator assures you that he has been, and that he has already given evidence against you, and that they are about to bring him in for a confrontation with you. Maybe he is sitting home very calmly and quietly, but they might very well bring him in for questioning and then they will find out from him what you were frowning about for half an hour at that intersection.

At this point, too late, you have come to understand that, because of the way life is, you and he ought to have reached an agreement every time you parted and remembered clearly *what you were going to say if you were asked what you had talked about that day.* Then, regardless of interrogations, your testimony and his would agree. But you had not made any such agreement. You had unfortunately not understood what kind of a jungle you lived in.

Should you say that you were talking about going on a fishing trip? But then B might say that there was never any discussion of fishing, that you talked about correspondence-school courses. In that case, instead of causing the investigation to ease up a bit, you would only tie the noose tighter: what about, what about, what about?

And the idea flashes through your mind—is it a brilliant or a fatal one?—that you ought to come as close as you can to the truth of what was actually said—of course rounding off the sharp edges and skipping the dangerous parts. After all, people say that when you lie you should always stay as close to the truth as possible. And maybe B will guess what's up and say approximately the same thing and then your testimony will coincide in some respects and they will leave you in peace.

Many years later you will come to understand that this was not really a wise idea, and that it is much smarter to play the role of someone so improbably imbecile that he can't remember one single day of his life even at the risk of being beaten. But you have been kept awake for three days. You have hardly strength enough to follow the course of your own thoughts and to maintain an imperturbable expression. And you don't have even a minute to think things over. Suddenly two interrogators—for they enjoy visiting one another—are at you: What were you talking about? What about? What about?

And you testify: We were talking about collective farms—to the effect that not everything had as yet been set to rights on them but it soon would be. We talked about the lowering of piece rates. . . . And what in particular did you say about them? That you were delighted they had been reduced? But that wasn't the way people normally talked—it was too implausible. And so as to make it seem an altogether believable conversation, you concede that you complained just a little that they were putting on the squeeze a bit with piece rates.

The interrogator writes down the deposition himself, translating it into *his own* language: At this meeting we slandered Party and government policy in the field of wages.

And someday B is going to accuse you: "Oh, you blabbermouth, and I said we were making plans to go fishing."

But you tried to outsmart your interrogator! You have a quick, abstruse mind. You are an intellectual! And you outsmarted yourself. . . .

In *Crime and Punishment,* Porfiri Petrovich makes a surprisingly astute remark to Raskolnikov, to the effect that he could have been found out only by someone who had himself gone through that same cat-and-mouse game—implying, so to speak: "I don't even have to construct my own version with you intellectuals. You will put it together yourselves and bring it to me all wrapped up." Yes, that's so! An intellectual cannot reply with the delightful incoherence of Chekhov's "Malefactor." He is bound to try to build up in logical form the whole story he is being accused of, no matter how much falsehood it contains.

But the interrogator-butcher isn't interested in logic; he just wants to catch two or three phrases. He knows what he wants. And as for us—we are totally unprepared for anything.

From childhood on we are educated and trained—for our own profession; for our civil duties; for military service; to take care of our bodily needs; to behave well; even to appreciate beauty (well, this last not really all that much!). But neither our education, nor our upbringing, nor our experience prepares us in the slightest for the greatest trial of our lives: being arrested for nothing and interrogated about nothing. Novels, plays, films (their authors should themselves be forced to drink the cup of Gulag to the bottom!) depict the types one meets in the offices of interrogators as chivalrous guardians of truth and humanitarianism, as our loving fathers. We are exposed to lectures on everything under the sun—and are even herded in to listen to them. But no one is going to lecture to us about the true and extended significance of the Criminal Code; and the codes themselves are not on open shelves in our libraries, nor sold at newsstands; nor do they fall into the hands of the heedless young.

It seems a virtual fairy tale that somewhere, at the ends of the earth, an accused person can avail himself of a lawyer's help. This means having beside you in the most difficult moment of your life a clear-minded ally who knows the law.

The principle of our interrogation consists further in depriving the accused of even a knowledge of the law.

An indictment is presented. And here, incidentally, is how it's presented: "Sign it." "It's not true." "Sign." "But I'm not guilty of anything!" It turns out that you are being indicted under the provisions of Articles 58-10, Part 2, and 58-11 of the Criminal Code of the Russian Republic. "Sign!" "But what do these sections say? Let me read the Code!" "I don't have it." "Well, get it from your department head!" "He doesn't have it either. Sign!" "But I want to see it." "You are not supposed to see it. It isn't written for you but for us. You don't need it. I'll tell you what it says: these sections spell out exactly what you are guilty of. And anyway, at this point your signature doesn't mean that you agree with the indictment but that you've read it, that it's been presented to you."

All of a sudden, a new combination of letters, UPK, flashes by on one of the pieces of paper. Your sense of caution is aroused. What's the difference between the UPK and the UK— the Criminal Code? If you've been lucky enough to catch the interrogator when he is in a good mood, he will explain it to you: the UPK is the Code of Criminal Procedure. What? This means that there are two distinct codes, not just one, of whose contents you are completely ignorant even as you are being trampled under their provisions.

Since that time ten years have passed; then fifteen. The grass has grown thick over the grave of my youth. I served out my term and even "eternal exile" as well. And nowhere—neither in the "cultural education" sections of the camps, nor in district libraries, nor even in medium-sized cities, have I seen with my own eyes, held in my own hands, been able to buy, obtain, or even *ask for* the Code of Soviet law![21]

And of the hundreds of prisoners I knew who had gone through interrogation and trial, and more than once too, who had served sentences in camp and in exile, none had ever seen the Code or held it in his hand!

It was only when both codes were thirty-five years old and on the point of being replaced by new ones that I saw them, two little paperback brothers, the UK or Criminal Code, and the UPK or Code of Criminal Procedure, on a newsstand in the Moscow subway (because they were outdated, it had been decided to release them for general circulation).

I read them today touched with emotion. For example, the UPK—the Code of Criminal Procedure:

"Article 136: The interrogator does not have the right to extract testimony or a confession from an accused by means of compulsion and threats." (It was as though they had foreseen it!)

---

21. Those familiar with our atmosphere of suspicion will understand why it was impossible to ask for the Code in a people's court or in the District Executive Committee. Your interest in the Code would be an extraordinary phenomenon: you must either be preparing to commit a crime or be trying to cover your tracks.

"Article 111: The interrogator is obliged to establish clearly all the relevant facts, both those tending toward acquittal and any which might lessen the accused's measure of guilt."

But it was I who helped establish Soviet power in October! It was I who shot Kolchak! I took part in the dispossession of the kulaks! I saved the state ten million rubles in lowered production costs! I was wounded twice in the war! I have three orders and decorations.

"You're not being tried for that!" History . . . the bared teeth of the interrogator: "Whatever good you may have done has nothing to do with the case."

"Article 139: The accused has the right to set forth his testimony in his own hand, and to demand the right to make corrections in the deposition written by the interrogator."

Oh, if we had only known that in time! But what I should say is: If that were only the way it really was! We were always vainly imploring the interrogator not to write "my repulsive, slanderous fabrications" instead of "my mistaken statements," or not to write "our underground weapons arsenal" instead of "my rusty Finnish knife."

If only the defendants had first been taught some prison science! If only interrogation had been run through first in rehearsal, and only afterward for real. . . . They didn't, after all, play that interrogation game with the *second-termers* of 1948: it would have gotten them nowhere. But *newcomers* had no experience, no knowledge! And there was no one from whom to seek advice.

The loneliness of the accused! That was one more factor in the success of unjust interrogation! The entire apparatus threw its full weight on one lonely and inhibited will. From the moment of his arrest and throughout the entire *shock* period of the interrogation the prisoner was, ideally, to be kept entirely alone. In his cell, in the corridor, on the stairs, in the offices, he was not supposed to encounter others like himself, in order to avoid the risk of his gleaning a bit of sympathy, advice, support from someone's smile or glance. The *Organs* did everything to blot out for him his future and distort his present: to lead him to believe that his friends and family had all been arrested and that material proof of his guilt had been found. It was their habit to exaggerate their power to destroy him and those he loved as well as their authority to pardon (which the *Organs* didn't even have). They pretended that there was some connection between the sincerity of a prisoner's "repentance" and a reduction in his sentence or an easing of the camp regimen. (No such connection ever existed.) While the prisoner was still in a state of shock and torment and totally beside himself, they tried to get from him very quickly as many irreparably damaging items of evidence as possible and to implicate with him as many totally innocent persons as possible. Some defendants became so depressed in these circumstances that they even asked not to have the depositions read to them. They could not stand hearing them. They asked merely to be allowed to sign them, just to sign and get it over with. Only after all this was over would the prisoner be released from solitary into a large cell, where, in belated desperation, he would discover and count over his mistakes one by one.

How was it possible not to make mistakes in such a duel? Who could have failed to make a mistake?

We said that "ideally he was to be kept alone." However, in the overcrowded prisons of 1937, and, for that matter, of 1945 as well, this ideal of solitary confinement for a newly arrested defendant could not be attained. Almost from his first hours, the prisoner was in fact in a terribly overcrowded common cell.

But there were virtues to this arrangement, too, which more than made up for its flaws. The overcrowding of the cells not only took the place of the tightly confined solitary "box" but also assumed the character of a first-class *torture* in itself . . . one that was particularly useful because it continued for whole days and weeks—with no effort on the part of the interrogators. The prisoners tortured the prisoners! The jailers pushed so many prisoners into the cell that not every one had even a piece of floor; some were sitting on others' feet, and people walked on people and couldn't even move about at all. Thus, in the Kishinev KPZ's —Cells for Preliminary Detention—in 1945, they pushed *eighteen* prisoners into a cell designed for the solitary confinement of one person; in Lugansk in 1937 it was *fifteen*.[22] And in 1938

22. And the interrogation there lasted eight to ten months at a time. "Maybe Klim [Voroshilov] had one of these to himself," said the fellows there. (Was he, in fact, ever imprisoned?)

Ivanov-Razumnik found *one hundred forty* prisoners in a standard Butyrki cell intended for twenty-five—with toilets so overburdened that prisoners were taken to the toilet only once a day, sometimes at night; and the same thing was true of their outdoor walk as well.[23] It was Ivanov-Razumnik who in the Lubyanka reception "kennel" calculated that for weeks at a time there were *three* persons for each square yard of floor space (just as an experiment, try to fit three people into that space!).[24] In this "kennel" there was neither ventilation nor a window, and the prisoners' body heat and breathing raised the temperature to 40 or 45 degrees Centigrade—104 to 113 degrees Fahrenheit—and everyone sat there in undershorts with their winter clothing piled beneath them. Their naked bodies were pressed against one another, and they got eczema from one another's sweat. They sat like that for *weeks at a time,* and were given neither fresh air nor water—except for gruel and tea in the morning.[25]

And if at the same time the latrine bucket replaced all other types of toilet (or if, on the other hand, there was no latrine bucket for use between trips to an outside toilet, as was the case in several Siberian prisons); and if four people ate from one bowl, sitting on each other's knees; and if someone was hauled out for interrogation, and then someone else was pushed in beaten up, sleepless, and broken; and if the appearance of such broken men was more persuasive than any threats on the part of the interrogators; and if, by then, death and any camp whatever seemed easier to a prisoner who had been left unsummoned for months than his tormented current situation—perhaps this really

23. That same year in the Butyrki, those newly arrested, who had already been processed through the bath and the boxes, sat on the stairs for several days at a stretch, waiting for departing prisoner transports to leave and release space in the cells. T——v had been imprisoned in the Butyrki seven years earlier, in 1931, and says that it was overcrowded under the bunks and that prisoners lay on the asphalt floor. I myself was imprisoned seven years later, in 1945, and it was just the same. But recently I received from M. K. B——ch valuable personal testimony about overcrowding in the Butyrki in *1918.* In October of that year—during the second month of the Red Terror—it was so full that they even set up a cell for seventy women in the laundry. When, then, was the Butyrki not crowded?

24. But this, too, is no miracle: in the Vladimir *Internal Prison* in 1948, thirty people had to stand in a cell ten feet by ten feet in size! (S. Potapov.)

25. By and large there is a good deal in Ivanov-Razumnik's book that is superficial and personal, and there are many exhaustingly monotonous jokes. But the real life of the cells in the 1937–1938 period is very well described there.

did replace the theoretically ideal isolation in solitary. And you could not always decide in such a porridge of people with whom to be forthright; and you could not always find someone from whom to seek advice. And you would believe in the tortures and beatings not when the interrogator threatened you with them but when you saw their results on other prisoners.

You could learn from those who had suffered that they could give you a salt-water douche in the throat and then leave you in a box for a day tormented by thirst (Karpunich). Or that they might scrape the skin off a man's back with a grater till it bled and then oil it with turpentine. (Brigade Commander Rudolf Pintsov underwent both treatments. In addition, they pushed needles under his nails, and poured water into him to the bursting point—demanding that he confess to having *wanted* to turn his brigade of tanks against the government during the November parade.)[26] And from Aleksandrov, the former head of the Arts Section of the All-Union Society for Cultural Relations with Foreign Countries, who has a broken spinal column which tilts to one side, and who cannot control his tear ducts and thus cannot stop crying, one can learn how *Abakumov* himself could beat—in 1948.

Yes, yes, Minister of State Security Abakumov himself did not by any means spurn such menial labor. (A Suvorov at the head of his troops!) He was not averse to taking a rubber truncheon in his hands every once in a while. And his deputy Ryumin was even more willing. He did this at Sukhanovka in the "Generals'" interrogation office. The office had imitation-walnut paneling on the walls, silk portieres at the windows and doors, and a great Persian carpet on the floor. In order not to spoil all this beauty, a dirty runner bespattered with blood was rolled out on top of the carpet when a prisoner was being beaten. When Ryumin was doing the beating, he was assisted not by some ordinary guard but by a colonel. "And so," said Ryumin politely, stroking his rubber truncheon, which was four centimeters—an inch and a half—thick, "you have survived trial by sleeplessness with honor." (Alexander D.

---

26. In actual fact, he did *lead* his brigade at the parade, but for some reason he did *not* turn it against the government. But this was not taken into account. However, after these most varied tortures, he was sentenced to ten years by the OSO. To that degree, the gendarmes themselves had no faith in their achievements.

had cleverly managed to last a month "without sleep" by sleeping while he was standing up.) "So now we will try the club. Prisoners can't take more than two or three sessions of this. Let down your trousers and lie down on the runner." The colonel sat down on the prisoner's back. A.D. was going to *count* the blows. He didn't yet know about a blow from a rubber truncheon on the sciatic nerve when the buttocks have disappeared as a consequence of prolonged starvation. The effect is not felt in the place where the blow is delivered—it explodes inside the head. After the first blow the victim was mad with pain and broke his nails on the carpet. Ryumin beat away, trying to hit accurately. The colonel pressed down on A.D.'s torso—this was just the right sort of work for three big shoulder-board stars, assisting the all-powerful Ryumin! (After the beating the prisoner could not walk and, of course, was not carried. They just dragged him along the floor. What was left of his buttocks was soon so swollen that he could not button his trousers, and yet there were practically no scars. He was hit by a violent case of diarrhea, and, sitting there on the latrine bucket in solitary, A.D. guffawed. He went through a second and a third session, and his skin cracked, and Ryumin went wild, and started to beat him on the stomach, breaking through the intestinal wall and creating an enormous hernia through which A.D.'s intestines protruded. The prisoner was taken off to the Butyrki hospital with a case of peritonitis, and for the time being their attempts to compel him to commit a foul deed were suspended.)

That is how they can torture you too! After that it could seem a simple fatherly caress when the Kishinev interrogator Danilov beat Father Viktor Shipovalnikov across the back of the head with a poker and pulled him by his long hair. (It is very convenient to drag a priest around in that fashion; ordinary laymen can be dragged by the beard from one corner of the office to the other. And Richard Ohola—a Finnish Red Guard, and a participant in the capture of British agent Sidney Reilly, and commander of a company during the suppression of the Kronstadt revolt—was lifted up with pliers first by one end of his great mustaches and then by the other, and held for ten minutes with his feet off the floor.)

But the most awful thing they can do with you is this: undress you from the waist down, place you on your back on the floor, pull your legs apart, seat assistants on them (from the glorious corps of sergeants!) who also hold down your arms; and then the interrogator (and women interrogators have not shrunk from this) stands between your legs and with the toe of his boot (or of her shoe) gradually, steadily, and with ever greater pressure crushes against the floor those organs which once made you a man. He looks into your eyes and repeats and repeats his questions or the betrayal he is urging on you. If he does not press down too quickly or just a shade too powerfully, you still have fifteen seconds left in which to scream that you will confess to everything, that you are ready to see arrested all twenty of those people he's been demanding of you, or that you will slander in the newspapers everything you hold holy. . . .

And may you be judged by God, but not by people. . . .

"There is no way out! You have to confess to everything!" whisper the stoolies who have been planted in the cell.

"It's a simple question: hang onto your health!" say people with common sense.

"You can't get new teeth," those who have already lost them nod at you.

"They are going to convict you in any case, whether you confess or whether you don't," conclude those who have got to the bottom of things.

"Those who don't sign get shot!" prophesies someone else in the corner. "Out of vengeance! So as not to risk any leaks about how they conduct interrogations."

"And if you die in the interrogator's office, they'll tell your relatives you've been sentenced to camp without the right of correspondence. And then just let them look for you."

If you are an orthodox Communist, then another orthodox Communist will sidle up to you, peering about with hostile suspicion, and he'll begin to whisper in your ear so that the uninitiated cannot overhear:

"It's our duty to support Soviet interrogation. It's a combat situation. We ourselves are to blame. We were too softhearted; and now look at all the rot that has multiplied in the country. There is a vicious secret war going on. Even here we are surrounded by enemies. Just listen to what they are saying! The

Party is not obliged to account for what it does to every single one of us—to explain the whys and wherefores. If they ask us to, that means we should sign."

And another orthodox Communist sidles up:

"I signed denunciations against thirty-five people, against all my acquaintances. And I advise you too: Drag along as many names as you can in your wake, as many as you can. That way it will become obvious that the whole thing is an absurdity and they'll let everyone out!"

But that is precisely what the *Organs* need. The conscientiousness of the orthodox Communist and the purpose of the NKVD naturally coincide. Indeed, the NKVD needs just that arched fan of names, that fat multiplication of them. That is the mark of quality of their work, and these are also new patches of woods in which to set out snares. "Your accomplices, accomplices! Others who share your views!" That is what they keep pressing to shake out of everyone. They say that R. Ralov named Cardinal Richelieu as one of his accomplices and that the Cardinal was in fact so listed in his depositions—and no one was astonished by this until Ralov was questioned about it at his rehabilitation proceedings in 1956.

Apropos of the orthodox Communists, Stalin was necessary, for such a *purge* as that, yes, but a Party like that was necessary too: the majority of those in power, up to the very moment of their own arrest, were pitiless in arresting others, obediently destroyed their peers in accordance with those same instructions and handed over to retribution any friend or comrade-in-arms of yesterday. And all the big Bolsheviks, who now wear martyrs' halos, managed to be the executioners of other Bolsheviks (not even taking into account how *all of them* in the first place had been the executioners of non-Communists). Perhaps 1937 was *needed* in order to show how little their whole ideology was worth —that *ideology* of which they boasted so enthusiastically, turning Russia upside down, destroying its foundations, trampling everything it held sacred underfoot, that Russia where *they themselves* had never been threatened by *such* retribution. The victims of the Bolsheviks from 1918 to 1946 never conducted themselves so despicably as the leading Bolsheviks when the lightning struck them. If you study in detail the whole history of the arrests and trials of 1936 to 1938, the principal revulsion you feel is not against Stalin and his accomplices, but against the humiliatingly repulsive defendants—nausea at their spiritual baseness after their former pride and implacability.

So what is the answer? How can you stand your ground when you are weak and sensitive to pain, when people you love are still alive, when you are unprepared?

What do you need to make you stronger than the interrogator and the whole trap?

From the moment you go to prison you must put your cozy past firmly behind you. At the very threshold, you must say to yourself: "My life is over, a little early to be sure, but there's nothing to be done about it. I shall never return to freedom. I am condemned to die—now or a little later. But later on, in truth, it will be even harder, and so the sooner the better. I no longer have any property whatsoever. For me those I love have died, and for them I have died. From today on, my body is useless and alien to me. Only my spirit and my conscience remain precious and important to me."

Confronted by such a prisoner, the interrogation will tremble.

Only the man who has renounced everything can win that victory.

But how can one turn one's body to stone?

Well, they managed to turn some individuals from the Berdyayev circle into puppets for a trial, but they didn't succeed with Berdyayev. They wanted to drag him into an open trial; they arrested him twice; and (in 1922) he was subjected to a night interrogation by Dzerzhinsky himself. Kamenev was there too (which means that he, too, was not averse to using the Cheka in an ideological conflict). But Berdyayev did not humiliate himself. He did not beg or plead. He set forth firmly those religious and moral principles which had led him to refuse to accept the political authority established in Russia. And not only did they come to the conclusion that he would be useless for a trial, but they liberated him.

A human being has *a point of view!*

N. Stolyarova recalls an old woman who was her neighbor on the Butyrki bunks in 1937. They kept on interrogating her every night. Two years earlier, a former Metropolitan of the Orthodox Church, who had escaped from exile, had spent a night at her home on his way through Moscow. "But he wasn't the former Metropolitan, he was the Metropolitan! Truly, I was worthy of receiving him." "All right then. To whom did he go when he left Moscow?" "I know, but I won't tell you!" (The Metropolitan had escaped to Finland via an underground railroad of believers.) At first the interrogators took turns, and then they went after her in groups. They shook their fists in the little old woman's face, and she replied: "There is nothing you can do with me even if you cut me into pieces. After all, you are afraid of your bosses, and you are afraid of each other, and you are even afraid of killing me." (They would lose contact with the underground railroad.) "But I am not afraid of anything. I would be glad to be judged by God right this minute."

There were such people in 1937 too, people who did not return to their cell for their bundles of belongings, who chose death, who *signed* nothing denouncing anyone.

One can't say that the history of the Russian revolutionaries has given us any better examples of steadfastness. But there is no comparison anyway, because none of our revolutionaries ever knew what a really *good* interrogation could be, with fifty-two different methods to choose from.

Sheshkovsky did not subject Radishchev to torture. And because of contemporary custom, Radishchev knew perfectly well that his sons would serve as officers in the imperial guard no matter what happened to him, and that their lives wouldn't be cut short. Nor would anyone confiscate Radishchev's family estate. Nonetheless, in the course of his brief two-week interrogation, this outstanding man renounced his beliefs and his book and begged for mercy.

Nicholas I didn't have enough imagination to arrest the wives of the Decembrists and compel them to scream in the interrogation room next door, or even to torture the Decembrists themselves. But in any case he didn't need to. Even Ryleyev "answered fully, frankly, and hid nothing." Even Pestel *broke down* and named comrades (who were still free) assigned to bury *Russkaya Pravda* and the very place where it had been buried.[27] There were very few who, like Lunin, expressed disdain and contempt for the investigating commission. The majority behaved badly and got one another more deeply involved. Many of them begged abjectly to be pardoned! Zavalishin put all the blame on Ryleyev. Y. P. Obolensky and S. P. Trubetskoi couldn't wait to slander Griboyedov—which even Nicholas I didn't believe.

Bakunin in his *Confessions* abjectly groveled before Nicholas I—thereby avoiding execution. Was this wretchedness of soul? Or revolutionary cunning?

One would think that those who decided to assassinate Alexander II must have been people of the highest selflessness and dedication. After all, they knew what the stakes were! Grinyevitsky shared the fate of the Tsar, but Rysakov remained alive and was held for interrogation. And *that very day* he *blabbed* on the participants in the plot and identified their secret meeting places. Out of fear for his young life he rushed to give the government more information than he could ever have been suspected of having. He nearly choked with repentance; he proposed to "expose all the secrets of the Anarchists."

At the end of the last century and the beginning of this one, the Tsarist interrogator immediately *withdrew* his question if the prisoner found it inappropriate or too intimate. But in Kresty Prison in 1938, when the old political hard-labor prisoner Zelensky was whipped with ramrods with his pants pulled down like a small boy, he wept in his cell: "My Tsarist interrogator didn't even dare address me rudely."

Or, for example, we learn from recently published research[28] that the Tsarist gendarmes seized the manuscript of Lenin's essay "What Are Our Ministers Thinking Of?" but were *unable* to get at its author:

"At the interrogation the gendarmes, *just as one might have expected,* learned very little from the student Vaneyev. [The

27. In part, the reason for this was the same as in the case of Bukharin many years later. They were, after all, being interrogated by their social equals, their class brothers, and so their desire to *explain* everything was only natural.
28. R. Peresvetov, *Novy Mir*, No. 4, 1962.

italics here and throughout this quotation are my own.] He informed them *only* that the manuscripts found at his place had
been brought to him in one package for safekeeping several days
before the search by a certain person *whom he did not wish to
name*. Therefore the interrogator's *sole alternative* was to turn
the manuscripts over for expert analysis." The experts learned
nothing. (What did he mean—his "sole alternative"? What about
icy water up to the ankles? Or a salt-water douche? Or Ryumin's
truncheon?) It would seem that the author of this article, R.
Peresvetov, himself *served time* for several years and might easily
have enumerated what "alternatives" the interrogator actually
had when confronting the guardian of Lenin's "What Are Our
Ministers Thinking Of?"

As S. P. Melgunov recollects: "That was a Tsarist prison, a
prison of blessed memory, which political prisoners nowadays
can only recall with a feeling almost of gladness."[29]

But that is a case of displaced concepts. The yardstick is totally
different. Just as oxcart drivers of Gogol's time could not have
imagined the speed of a jet plane, those who have never gone
through the receiving-line meat grinder of Gulag cannot grasp
the true possibilities of interrogation.

We read in *Izvestiya* for May 24, 1959, that Yulipa Rumyan-
tseva was confined in the internal prison of a Nazi camp while
they tried to find out from her the whereabouts of her husband,
who had escaped from that same camp. She knew, but she refused
to tell! For a reader who is not in the know this is a model of
heroism. For a reader with a bitter Gulag past it's a model of in-
efficient interrogation: Yuliya did not die under torture, and she
was not driven insane. A month later she was simply released—
still very much alive and kicking.

All these thoughts about standing firm as a rock were quite
unknown to me in February, 1945. Not only was I not in the
least prepared to cut my cozy ties with earth, I was even quite

29. S. P. Melgunov, *Vospominaniya i Dnevniki*, (*Memoirs and Diaries*),
Vol. 1, Paris, 1964, p. 139.

angry for a long time because a hundred or so Faber pencils had been taken away from me when I was arrested. Looking back on my interrogation from my long subsequent imprisonment, I had no reason to be proud of it. I might have borne myself more firmly; and in all probability I could have maneuvered more skillfully. But my first weeks were characterized by a mental blackout and a slump into depression. The only reason these recollections do not torment me with remorse is that, thanks be to God, I avoided getting anyone else arrested. But I came close to it.

Although we were front-line officers, Nikolai V. and I, who were involved in the same case, got ourselves into prison through a piece of childish stupidity. He and I corresponded during the war, between two sectors of the front; and though we knew perfectly well that wartime censorship of correspondence was in effect, we indulged in fairly outspoken expressions of our political outrage and in derogatory comments about the Wisest of the Wise, whom we labeled with the transparently obvious nickname of Pakhan or *Ringleader of the Thieves*. (When, later on, I reported our *case* in various prisons, our naïveté aroused only laughter and astonishment. Other prisoners told me that two more such stupid jackasses couldn't exist. And I became convinced of it myself. Then suddenly, one day, reading some documents on the case of Aleksandr Ulyanov, Lenin's elder brother, I learned that he and his confederates got caught in exactly the same way—a careless exchange of letters. And that was the only reason Alexander III didn't die on March 1, 1887.)[30]

The office of my interrogator, I. I. Yezepov, was high-ceilinged, spacious and bright, with an enormous window. (The Rossiya Insurance Company had not been built with torture in mind.) And, putting to use its seventeen feet of height, a full-length, vertical, thirteen-foot portrait of that powerful Sovereign hung

30. A member of the group, Andreyushkin sent a frank letter to his friend in Kharkov: "I am firmly convinced that we are going to have the most merciless terror—and in the fairly near future too. . . . Red Terror is my hobby. . . . I am worried about my addressee. . . . If he gets *it*, then I may get *it* too, and that will be unfortunate because I will drag in a lot of very effective people." It was not the first such letter he had written! And the unhurried search this letter initiated continued for five weeks, via Kharkov, in order to discover who in St. Petersburg had written it. Andreyushkin's identity was not established until February 28. On March 1, the bomb throwers, bombs in hand, were arrested on Nevsky Prospekt just before the attempted assassination.

there, toward whom I, grain of sand that I was, had expressed my hatred. Sometimes the interrogator stood in front of the portrait and declaimed dramatically: "We are ready to lay down our lives for him! We are ready to lie down in the path of oncoming tanks for his sake!" Face to face with the altarlike grandeur of that portrait, my mumbling about some kind of purified Leninism seemed pitiful, and I myself seemed a blasphemous slanderer deserving only death.

The contents of our letters provided more than enough, in keeping with the standards of those times, to sentence us both. Therefore my interrogator did not have to invent anything. He merely tried to cast his noose around everyone I had ever written to or received a letter from. I had expressed myself vehemently in letters to friends my own age and had been almost reckless in spelling out seditious ideas, but my friends for some reason had continued to correspond with me! And some suspicious phrases could be found in their replies to my letters.[31] And then Yezepov, like Porfiri Petrovich, demanded that I explain it all in a coherent way: if we had expressed ourselves in such a fashion in letters that we knew were subject to censorship, what could we have said to each other face to face? I could not convince him that all my fire-eating talk was confined to my letters. And at that point, with muddled mind, I had to undertake to weave something credible about my meetings with my friends—meetings referred to in my letters. What I said had to jibe with the letters, in such a way as to be on the very edge of political matters and yet not fall under that Criminal Code. Moreover, these explanations had to pour forth quickly, all in one breath, so as to convince this veteran interrogator of my naïveté, my humility, my total honesty. The main thing was not to provoke my lazy interrogator to any interest in looking through that accursed load of stuff I had

31. One of our school friends was nearly arrested because of me at this time. It was an enormous relief to me to learn later that he was still free! But then, twenty-two years later, he wrote to me: "On the basis of your published works I conclude that you take a one-sided view of life. . . . Objectively speaking, you have become the standard-bearer of Fascist reactionaries in the West, in West Germany and the United States, for example. . . . Lenin, whom, I'm convinced, you love and honor just as much as you used to, yes, and old Marx and Engels, too, would have condemned you in the severest fashion. Think about that!" Indeed, I do think about that: How sorry I am that you didn't get arrested then! How much you lost!

brought in my accursed suitcase—including many notebooks of my "War Diary," written in hard, light pencil in a needle-thin handwriting, with some of the notes already partially washed out. These diaries constituted my claim to becoming a writer. I had not believed in the capacities of our amazing memory, and throughout the war years I had tried to write down everything I saw. That would have been only half a catastrophe: I also wrote down everything I *heard* from other people. But opinions and stories which were so natural in front-line areas seemed to be treasonable here in the rear and reeked of raw imprisonment for my front-line comrades. So to prevent that interrogator from going to work on my "War Diary" and mining from it a whole case against a free front-line tribe, I repented just as much as I had to and pretended to see the light and reject my political mistakes. I became utterly exhausted from this balancing on a razor's edge, until I recognized that no one was being hauled in for a confrontation with me and distinguished the clear signs that the interrogation was drawing to an end . . . until, in the fourth month, all the notebooks of my "War Diary" were cast into the hellish maw of the Lubyanka furnace, where they burst into flame—the red pyre of one more novel which had perished in Russia—and flew out of the highest chimney in black butterflies of soot.

We used to walk in the shadow of that chimney, our exercise yard a boxlike concrete enclosure on the roof of the Big Lubyanka, six floors up. The walls rose around us to approximately three times a man's height. With our own ears we could hear Moscow—automobile horns honking back and forth. But all we could see was that chimney, the guard posted in a seventh-floor tower, and that segment of God's heaven whose unhappy fate it was to float over the Lubyanka.

Oh, that soot! It kept falling on and on in that first postwar May. So much of it fell during each of our walks that we decided the Lubyanka must be burning countless years of files. My doomed diary was only one momentary plume of that soot. I recalled a frosty sunny morning in March when I was sitting in the interrogator's office. He was asking his customary crude questions and writing down my answers, distorting my words as he did so. The sun played in the melting latticework of the frost on the wide window, through which at times I felt very much like jumping, so as to flash through Moscow at least in death and smash onto the sidewalk five floors below, just as, in my childhood, my unknown predecessor had jumped from House 33 in Rostov-on-the-Don. In the gaps where the frost had melted, the rooftops of Moscow could be seen, rooftop after rooftop, and above them merry little puffs of smoke. But I was staring not in that direction but at a mound of piled-up manuscripts—someone else's—covering the entire center of the floor in this half-empty room, thirty-six square yards in area, manuscripts which had been dumped there a little while before and had not yet been examined. In notebooks, in file folders, in homemade binders, in tied and untied bundles, and simply in loose pages. The manuscripts lay there like the burial mound of some interred human spirit, its conical top rearing higher than the interrogator's desk, almost blocking me from his view. And brotherly pity ached in me for the labor of that unknown person who had been arrested the previous night, these spoils from the search of his premises having been dumped that very morning on the parquet floor of the torture chamber, at the feet of that thirteen-foot Stalin. I sat there and I wondered: Whose extraordinary life had they brought in for torment, for dismemberment, and then for burning?

Oh, how many ideas and works had perished in that building —a whole lost culture? Oh, soot, soot, from the Lubyanka chimneys! And the most hurtful thing of all was that our descendants would consider our generation more stupid, less gifted, less vocal than in actual fact it was.

■

One needs to have only two points in order to draw a straight line between them.

In 1920, as Ehrenburg recalls, the Cheka addressed him as follows:

"*You* prove to us that you are *not* Wrangel's agent."

And in 1950, one of the leading colonels of the MGB, Foma Fomich Zheleznov, said to his prisoners: "We are not going to sweat to prove the prisoner's guilt to him. Let *him* prove to *us* that he did *not* have hostile intent."

And along this cannibalistically artless straight line lie the recollections of countless millions.

What a speed-up and simplification of criminal investigation previously unknown to mankind! The *Organs* altogether freed themselves of the burden of obtaining proof! Trembling and pale, the rabbit who had been caught, deprived of the right to write anyone, phone anyone, bring anything with him from freedom, deprived too of sleep, food, paper, pencils, and even buttons, seated on a bare stool in the corner of an office, had to try to find out for *himself* and display to that loafer of an interrogator *proof* that he did *not* have hostile *intentions*. If he could not discover such proof (and where would he find it?), by that very failure he provided the interrogation with *approximate* proof of his guilt!

I knew of a case in which a certain old man who had been a prisoner in Germany managed nonetheless, sitting there on his bare stool and gesturing with his cold fingers, to prove to his monster of an interrogator that he did *not* betray his Motherland and even that he did *not* have any such intention! It was a scandal! And what happened? Did they free him? Of course not —after all, he told me about this in Butyrki and not on Tverskoi Boulevard in the middle of Moscow. At that point a second interrogator joined the first and they spent a quiet evening reminiscing with the old man. Then the two interrogators signed witnesses' affidavits stating that in the course of the evening the hungry, sleepy old man had engaged in anti-Soviet propaganda! Things were said innocently—but they weren't listened to innocently. The old man was then turned over to a third interrogator, who quashed the treason indictment and neatly nailed him with that very same *tenner* for Anti-Soviet Agitation during his interrogation.

Given that interrogations had ceased to be an attempt to get at the truth, for the interrogators in difficult cases they became a mere exercise of their duties as executioners and in easy cases simply a pastime and a basis for receiving a salary.

And easy cases always existed, even in the notorious year 1937. For example, Borodko was accused of having visited his parents in Poland sixteen years before without having a passport for foreign travel. (His papa and mama lived all of ten versts—six miles—away, but the diplomats had signed away that part of Byelorussia to Poland, and in 1921 people had not yet gotten used to that fact and went back and forth as they pleased.) The interrogation took just half an hour. Question: Did you go there?

Answer: I did. Question: How? Answer: Horseback, of course. Conclusion: Take ten years for KRD.[32]

But that sort of pace smells of the Stakhanovite movement, a movement which found no disciples among the bluecaps. According to the Code of Criminal Procedure every interrogation was supposed to take two months. And if it presented difficulties, one was allowed to ask the prosecutor for several continuations of a month apiece (which, of course, the prosecutors never refused). Thus it would have been stupid to risk one's health, not to take advantage of these postponements, and, speaking in factory terms, to raise one's work norms. Having worked with voice and fist in the initial assault week of every interrogation, and thereby expended one's will and *character* (as per Vyshinsky), the interrogators had a vital interest in dragging out the remainder of every case as long as possible. That way more old, subdued cases were on hand and fewer new ones. It was considered just indecent to complete a political interrogation in two months.

The state system itself suffered from its own lack of trust and from its rigidity. These interrogators were selected personnel, but they weren't trusted either. In all probability they, too, were required to check in on arriving and check out on leaving, and the prisoners were, of course, checked in and out when called for questioning. What else could the interrogators do to keep the bookkeepers' accounts straight? They would summon one of their defendants, sit him down in a corner, ask him some terrifying question—and then forget about him while they themselves sat for a long time reading the paper, writing an outline for a political indoctrination course or personal letters, or went off to visit one another, leaving guards to act as watchdogs in their place. Peacefully batting the breeze on the sofa with a colleague who had just dropped in, the interrogator would come to himself once in a while, look threateningly at the accused, and say:

"Now there's a rat! There's a real rat for you! Well, that's all right, we'll not be stingy about his *nine grams!*"

My interrogator also made frequent use of the telephone. For example, he used to phone home and tell his wife—with his sparkling eyes directed at me—that he was going to be working all night long so she mustn't expect him before morning. (My

32. KRD = Counter-Revolutionary Activity.

heart, of course, fell. That meant he would be working *me* over all night long!) But then he would immediately dial the phone number of his mistress and, in purring tones, make a date with her for the night. (So: I would be able to get some sleep! I felt relieved.)

Thus it was that the faultless system was moderated only by the shortcomings of those who carried it out.

Certain of the more curious interrogators used to enjoy using "empty" interrogations to broaden their knowledge of life. They might ask the accused prisoner about the front (about those very German tanks beneath which they never quite managed to find the time to throw themselves). Or perhaps about the customs of European countries and lands across the sea which the prisoner had visited: about the stores and the merchandise sold in them, and particularly about procedures in foreign whorehouses and about all kinds of adventures with women.

The Code of Criminal Procedure provided that the prosecutor was to review continuously the course of every interrogation to ensure its being conducted correctly. But no one in our time ever saw him face to face until the so-called "questioning by the prosecutor," which meant the interrogation was nearing its end. I, too, was taken to such a "questioning." Lieutenant Colonel Kotov, a calm, well-nourished, impersonal blond man, who was neither nasty nor nice but essentially a cipher, sat behind his desk and, yawning, examined for the first time the file on my case. He spent fifteen minutes acquainting himself with it while I watched. (Since this "questioning" was quite unavoidable and since it was also recorded, there would have been no sense at all in his studying the file at some earlier, unrecorded time and then having had to remember details of the case for a certain number of hours.) Finally, he raised his indifferent eyes to stare at the wall and asked lazily what I wanted to add to my testimony.

He was required by law to ask what complaints I had about the conduct of the interrogation and whether coercion had been used or any violations of my legal rights had occurred. But it had been a long time since prosecutors asked such questions. And what if they had? After all, the existence of that entire Ministry building with its thousands of rooms, and of all five thousand of the Ministry's other interrogation buildings, railroad cars, caves, and dugouts scattered throughout the Soviet Union, was based on violations of legal rights. And it certainly wasn't up to Lieutenant Colonel Kotov and me to reverse that whole process.

Anyway, all the prosecutors of any rank at all held their positions with the approval of that very same State Security which . . . they were supposed to check up on.

His own wilted state, his lack of combativeness, and his fatigue from all those endless stupid cases were somehow transmitted to me. So I didn't raise questions of truth with him. I requested only that one too obvious stupidity be corrected: two of us had been indicted in the same case, but our interrogations were conducted in different places—mine in Moscow and my friend's at the front. Therefore I was processed *singly,* yet charged under Section 11— in other words, as a *group,* an *organization.* As persuasively as possible, I requested him to cancel this additional charge under Section 11.

He leafed through the case for another five minutes, sighed, spread out his hands, and said:

"What's there to say? One person is a person and two persons are . . . people."

But one person and a half—is that an organization?

And he pushed the button for them to come and take me away.

Soon after that, late one evening in late May, in that same office with a sculptured bronze clock on the marble mantel, my interrogator summoned me for a "206" procedure. This was, in accordance with the provisions of the Code of Criminal Procedure, the defendant's review of the case before his final signature. Not doubting for one moment that I would sign, the interrogator was already seated, writing the conclusion of the indictment.

I opened the cover of the thick file, and there, on the inside of the cover in printed text, I read an astonishing statement. It turned out that during the interrogation I had had the right to make written complaints against anything improper in its conduct, and that the interrogator was obliged to staple these complaints into my record! During the interrogation! Not at its end.

Alas, not one of the thousands with whom I was later imprisoned had been aware of this right.

I turned more pages. I saw photocopies of my own letters and a totally distorted interpretation of their meaning by unknown commentators (like Captain Libin). I saw the hyperbolized lie in which Captain Yezepov had wrapped up my careful testimony. And, last but not least, I saw the idiocy whereby I, one individual, was accused as a "group"!

"I won't sign," I said, without much firmness. "You conducted the interrogation improperly."

"All right then, let's begin it all over again!" Maliciously he compressed his lips. "We'll send you off to the place where we keep the Polizei."

He even stretched out his hand as though to take the file away from me. (At that point I held onto it.)

Somewhere outside the fifth-floor windows of the Lubyanka, the golden sunset sun glowed. Somewhere it was May. The office windows, like all the windows facing outward, were tightly closed and had not yet been unsealed after the winter—so that fresh air and the fragrance of things in bloom should not creep into those hidden rooms. The bronze clock on the mantel, from which the last rays of the sun had disappeared, quietly chimed.

Begin all over again? It seemed to me it would be easier to die than to begin all over again. Ahead of me loomed at least some kind of life. (If I had only known what kind!) And then what about that place where they kept the Polizei? And, in general, it was a bad idea to make him angry. It would influence the tone in which he phrased the conclusion of the indictment.

And so I signed. I signed it complete with Section 11, the significance of which I did not then know. They told me only that it would not add to my prison term. But because of that Section 11 I was later put into a hard-labor camp. Because of that Section 11 I was sent, even after "liberation," and without any additional sentence, into eternal exile.

Maybe it was all for the best. Without both those experiences, I would not have written this book.

My interrogator had used no methods on me other than sleeplessness, lies, and threats—all completely legal. Therefore, in the course of the "206" procedure, he didn't have to shove at me —as did interrogators who had made a mess of things and wanted to play safe—a document on nondisclosure for me to sign: that I, the undersigned, under pain of criminal penalty, swore never to tell anyone about the methods used in conducting my interrogation. (No one knows, incidentally, what article of the Code this comes under.)

In several of the provincial administrations of the NKVD this measure was carried out in sequence: the typed statement on nondisclosure was shoved at a prisoner along with the verdict of the OSO. And later a similar document was shoved at prisoners being released from camp, whereby they guaranteed never to disclose to anyone the state of affairs in camp.

And so? Our habit of obedience, our bent (or broken) backbone, did not suffer us either to reject this gangster method of burying loose ends or even to be enraged by it.

We have lost *the measure of freedom.* We have no means of determining where it begins and where it ends. We are an Asiatic people. On and on and on they go, taking from us those endless pledges of nondisclosure—everyone not too lazy to ask for them.

By now we are even unsure whether we have the right to talk about the events of our own lives.

Chapter 4

■

The Bluecaps

Throughout the grinding of our souls in the gears of the great Nighttime Institution, when our souls are pulverized and our flesh hangs down in tatters like a beggar's rags, we suffer too much and are too immersed in our own pain to rivet with penetrating and far-seeing gaze those pale night executioners who torture us. A surfeit of inner grief floods our eyes. Otherwise what historians of our torturers we would be! For it is certain they will never describe themselves as they actually are. But alas! Every former prisoner remembers his own interrogation in detail, how they squeezed him, and what foulness they squeezed out of him —but often he does not even remember their names, let alone think about them as human beings. So it is with me. I can recall much more—and much more that's interesting—about any one of my cellmates than I can about Captain of State Security Yezepov, with whom I spent no little time face to face, the two of us alone in his office.

There is one thing, however, which remains with us all as an accurate, generalized recollection: foul rot—a space totally infected with putrefaction. And even when, decades later, we are long past fits of anger or outrage, in our own quieted hearts we retain this firm impression of low, malicious, impious, and, possibly, muddled people.

There is an interesting story about Alexander II, the Tsar surrounded by revolutionaries, who were to make seven attempts on his life. He once visited the House of Preliminary Detention on Shpalernaya—the uncle of the Big House—where he ordered them to lock him up in solitary-confinement cell No. 227. He stayed in it for more than an hour, attempting thereby to sense the state of mind of those he had imprisoned there.

One cannot but admit that for a monarch this was evidence of moral aspiration, to feel the need and make the effort to take a spiritual view of the matter.

But it is impossible to picture any of our interrogators, right up to Abakumov and Beria, wanting to slip into a prisoner's skin even for one hour, or feeling compelled to sit and meditate in solitary confinement.

Their branch of service does not require them to be educated people of broad culture and broad views—and they are not. Their branch of service does not require them to think logically—and they do not. Their branch of service requires only that they carry out orders exactly and be impervious to suffering—and that is what they do and what they are. We who have passed through their hands feel suffocated when we think of that legion, which is stripped bare of universal human ideals.

Although others might not be aware of it, it was clear to the interrogators at least that the *cases* were fabricated. Except at staff conferences, they could not seriously say to one another or to themselves that they were exposing criminals. Nonetheless they kept right on producing depositions page after page to make sure that we rotted. So the essence of it all turns out to be the credo of the blatnye—the underworld of Russian thieves: "You today; me tomorrow."

They understood that the cases were fabricated, yet they kept on working year after year. How could they? Either they forced themselves *not to think* (and this in itself means the ruin of a human being), and simply accepted that this was the way it had to be and that the person who gave them their orders was always right . . .

But didn't the Nazis, too, it comes to mind, argue that same way?[1]

1. There is no way of sidestepping this comparison: both the years and the methods coincide too closely. And the comparison occurred even more naturally to those who had passed through the hands of both the Gestapo and the MGB. One of these was Yevgeny Ivanovich Divnich, an émigré and preacher of Orthodox Christianity. The Gestapo accused him of Communist activities among Russian workers in Germany, and the MGB charged him with having ties to the international bourgeoisie. Divnich's verdict was unfavorable to the MGB. He was tortured by both, but the Gestapo was nonetheless trying to get at the truth, and when the accusation did not hold up, Divnich was released. The MGB wasn't interested in the truth and had no intention of letting anyone out of its grip once he was arrested.

Or else it was a matter of the Progressive Doctrine, the granite ideology. An interrogator in awful Orotukan—sent there to the Kolyma in 1938 as a penalty assignment—was so touched when M. Lurye, former director of the Krivoi Rog Industrial Complex, readily agreed to sign an indictment which meant a second camp term that he used the time they had thus saved to say: "You think we get any satisfaction from using *persuasion?*[2] We have to do what the Party demands of us. You are an old Party member. Tell me what would you do in my place?" Apparently Lurye nearly agreed with him, and it may have been the fact that he had already been thinking in some such terms that led him to sign so readily. It is after all a convincing argument.

But most often it was merely a matter of cynicism. The blue-caps understood the workings of the meat grinder and loved it. In the Dzhida camps in 1944, interrogator Mironenko said to the condemned Babich with pride in his faultless logic: "Interrogation and trial are merely judicial corroboration. They cannot alter your fate, which was *previously* decided. If it is necessary to shoot you, then you will be shot even if you are altogether innocent. If it is necessary to acquit you,[3] then no matter how guilty you are you will be cleared and acquitted." Kushnaryev, Chief of the First Investigation Department of the West Kazakhstan Provincial State Security Administration, laid it on the line in just that way to Adolf Tsivilko. "After all, we're not going to let you out if you're a Leningrader!" (In other words, a Communist Party member with seniority.)

"Just give us a person—and we'll create the *case!*" That was what many of them said jokingly, and it was their slogan. What we think of as torture they think of as good work. The wife of the interrogator Nikolai Grabishchenko (the Volga Canal Project) said touchingly to her neighbors: "Kolya is a very good worker. One of them didn't confess for a long time—and they gave him to Kolya. Kolya talked with him for one night and he confessed."

What prompted them all to slip into harness and pursue so zealously not truth but *totals* of the processed and condemned? Because it was *most comfortable* for them not to be different from the others. And because these totals meant an easy life, supple-

2. An affectionate term for *torture*.
3. This evidently refers to *their own people*.

mentary pay, awards and decorations, promotions in rank, and the expansion and prosperity of the *Organs* themselves. If they ran up high totals, they could loaf when they felt like it, or do poor work or go out and enjoy themselves at night. And that is just what they did. Low totals led to their being kicked out, to the loss of their feedbag. For Stalin could never be convinced that in any district, or city, or military unit, he might suddenly cease to have enemies.

That was why they felt no mercy, but, instead, an explosion of resentment and rage toward those maliciously stubborn prisoners who opposed being fitted into the totals, who would not capitulate to sleeplessness or the punishment cell or hunger. By refusing to confess they menaced the interrogator's personal standing. It was as though they wanted to bring *him* down. In such circumstances all measures were justified! If it's to be war, then war it will be! We'll ram the tube down your throat—swallow that salt water!

Excluded by the nature of their work and by deliberate choice from the *higher* sphere of human existence, the servitors of the Blue Institution lived in their lower sphere with all the greater intensity and avidity. And there they were possessed and directed by the two strongest instincts of the lower sphere, other than hunger and sex: greed for *power* and greed for *gain*. (Particularly for power. In recent decades it has turned out to be more important than money.)

Power is a poison well known for thousands of years. If only no one were ever to acquire material power over others! But to the human being who has faith in some force that holds dominion over all of us, and who is therefore conscious of his own limitations, power is not necessarily fatal. For those, however, who are unaware of any higher sphere, it is a deadly poison. For them there is no antidote.

Remember what Tolstoi said about power? Ivan Ilyich had accepted an official position which gave him authority to *destroy any person he wanted to! All* without exception *were in his hands, and anyone, even the most important, could be brought before him as an accused*. (And that is just where our blueboys are! There is nothing to add to the description.) The consciousness of this power (and "the possibilities of using it mercifully"—so Tolstoi qualifies the situation, but this does not in any way apply to our boys) constituted for Ivan Ilyich *the chief interest and attraction of the service.*

But attraction is not the right word—it is *intoxication!* After all, it *is* intoxicating. You are still young—still, shall we say parenthetically, a sniveling youth. Only a little while ago your parents were deeply concerned about you and didn't know where to turn to launch you in life. You were such a fool you didn't even want to study, but you got through three years of *that* school—and then how you took off and flew! How your situation changed! How your gestures changed, your glance, the turn of your head! The learned council of the scientific institute is in session. You enter and everyone notices you and trembles. You don't take the chairman's chair. Those headaches are for the rector to take on. You sit off to one side, but everyone understands that you are head man there. You are the Special Department. And you can sit there for just five minutes and then leave. You have that advantage over the professors. You can be called away by more important business—but later on, when you're considering their decision, you will raise your eyebrows or, better still, purse your lips and say to the rector: "You can't do that. There are *special considerations* involved." That's all! And it won't be done. Or else you are an osobist—a State Security representative in the army—a SMERSH man, and a mere lieutenant; but the portly old colonel, the commander of the unit, stands up when you enter the room and tries to flatter you, to play up to you. He doesn't even have a drink with his chief of staff without inviting you to join them. The fact that you have only two tiny stars on your shoulder boards doesn't mean a thing; it is even amusing. After all, your stars have a very different weight and are measured on a totally different scale from those of ordinary officers. (On special assignments you are sometimes even authorized to wear major's insignia, for example, which is a sort of incognito, a convention.) You have a power over all the people in that military unit, or factory, or district, incomparably greater than that of the military commander, or factory director, or secretary of the district Communist Party. These men control people's military or official duties, wages, reputations, but you control people's freedom. And no one dares speak about you at meetings, and no one will ever dare write about you in the newspaper—not only something bad but anything *good!* They don't dare. Your name, like that of a jealously guarded deity, cannot even be mentioned. You are there; everyone feels your presence; but it's as though you didn't exist. From the moment you don that heavenly blue service cap, you stand higher than the publicly acknowledged power. No one dares check up on what *you* do. But no one is exempt from your checking up on him. And therefore, in dealing with ordinary so-called citizens, who for you are mere blocks of wood, it is altogether appropriate for you to wear an ambiguous and deeply thoughtful expression. For, of course, you are the one—and no one else—who knows about the *special considerations*. And therefore you are always right.

There is just one thing you must never forget. You, too, would have been just such a poor block of wood if you had not had the luck to become one of the little links in the *Organs*—that flexible, unitary organism inhabiting a nation as a tapeworm inhabits a human body. Everything is yours now! Everything is for you! Just be true to the *Organs!* They will always stand up for you! They will help you swallow up anyone who bothers you! They will help move every obstacle from your path! But—be true to the *Organs!* Do everything they order you to! They will do the thinking for you in respect to your functions too: today you serve in a special unit; tomorrow you will sit in an interrogator's armchair; and then perhaps you will travel to Lake Seliger as a folklorist,[4] partly, it may be, to get your nerves straightened out. And next you may be sent from a city where you are too well known to the opposite end of the country as a Plenipotentiary in Charge of Church Affairs.[5] Or perhaps you will become Executive Secretary of the Union of Soviet Writers.[6] Be surprised at nothing. People's true appointments and true ranks are known only to the *Organs*. The rest is merely play-acting. Some Honored Artist or other, or Hero of Socialist Agriculture, is here today, and tomorrow, puff! he's gone.[7]

The duties of an interrogator require work, of course: you have

4. Ilin in 1931.

5. The violent Yaroslavl interrogator Volkopyalov, appointed Plenipotentiary in Charge of Church Affairs in Moldavia.

6. Another Ilin—this one Viktor Nikolayevich, a former lieutenant general of State Security.

7. "Who are you?" asked General Serov in Berlin of the world-renowned biologist Timofeyev-Ressovsky, offensively using the familiar form of address. And the scientist, who was undismayed and who possessed a Cossack's hereditary daring, replied, using the same familiar form: "And who are you?" Serov corrected himself and, this time using the formal and correct form, asked: "Are you a scientist?"

to come in during the day, at night, sit for hours and hours—but not split your skull over "proof." (Let the prisoner's head ache over that.) And you don't have to worry whether the prisoner is guilty or not but simply do what the *Organs* require. And everything will be all right. It will be up to you to make the interrogation periods pass as pleasurably as possible and not to get overly fatigued. And it would be nice to get some good out of it—at least to amuse yourself. You have been sitting a long time, and all of a sudden a new method of *persuasion* occurs to you! Eureka! So you call up your friends on the phone, and you go around to other offices and tell them about it—what a laugh! Who shall we try it on, boys? It's really pretty monotonous to keep doing the same thing all the time. Those trembling hands, those imploring eyes, that cowardly submissiveness—they are really a bore. If you could just get one of them to resist! "I love strong opponents! *It's such fun to break their backs!*" said the Leningrad interrogator Shitov to G. G——v.

And if your opponent is so strong that he refuses to give in, all your methods have failed, and you are in a rage? Then don't control your fury! It's tremendously satisfying, that outburst! Let your anger have its way; don't set any bounds to it! Don't hold yourself back! That's when interrogators spit in the open mouth of the accused! And shove his face into a full cuspidor![8] That's the state of mind in which they drag priests around by their long hair! Or urinate in a kneeling prisoner's face! After such a storm of fury you feel yourself a real honest-to-God man!

Or else you are interrogating a "foreigner's girl friend."[9] So you curse her out and then you say: "Come on now, does an American have a special kind of ——? Is that it? Weren't there enough Russian ones for you?" And all of a sudden you get an idea: maybe she learned something from those foreigners. Here's a chance not to be missed, like an assignment abroad! And so you begin to interrogate her energetically: *How?* What positions? More! In detail! Every scrap of information! (You can use the information yourself, and you can tell the other boys too!) The girl is blushing all over and in tears. "It doesn't have anything to do with the case," she protests. "Yes, it does, speak up!" That's

8. As happened with Vasilyev, according to Ivanov-Razumnik.
9. Esfir R., 1947.

power for you! She gives you the full details. If you want, she'll draw a picture for you. If you want, she'll demonstrate with her body. She has no way out. In your hands you hold the punishment cell and her *prison term*.

And if you have asked for a stenographer[10] to take down the questions and answers, and they send in a pretty one, you can shove your paw down into her bosom right in front of the boy being interrogated.[11] He's not a human being after all, and there is no reason to feel shy in his presence.

In fact, there's no reason for you to feel shy with anyone. And if you like the broads—and who doesn't?—you'd be a fool not to make use of your position. Some will be drawn to you because of your power, and others will give in out of fear. So you've met a girl somewhere and she's caught your eye? She'll belong to you, never fear; she can't get away! Someone else's wife has caught your eye? She'll be yours too! Because, after all, there's no problem about removing the husband.[12] No, indeed! To know what it meant to be a bluecap one had to experience it! Anything you saw was yours! Any apartment you looked at was yours! Any woman was yours! Any enemy was struck from your path! The

10. Interrogator Pokhilko, Kemerovo State Security Administration.
11. The schoolboy Misha B.
12. For a long time I've been hanging on to a theme for a story to be called "The Spoiled Wife." But it looks as though I will never get the chance to write it, so here it is. In a certain Far Eastern aviation unit before the Korean War, a certain lieutenant colonel returned from an assignment to find his wife in a hospital. The doctors did not hide the truth from him: her sexual organs had been injured by perverted sexual practices. The lieutenant colonel got in to see his wife and wrung from her the admission that the man responsible was the osobist in their unit, a senior lieutenant. (It would seem, by the way, that this incident had not occurred without some cooperation on her part.) In a rage the lieutenant colonel ran to the osobist's office, took out his pistol, and threatened to kill him. But the senior lieutenant very quickly forced him to back down and leave the office defeated and pitiful. He threatened to send the lieutenant colonel to rot in the most horrible of camps, where he'd pray to be released from life without further torment, and he *ordered* him to take his wife back just as he found her—with an injury that was to some extent incurable—and to live with her, not to dare get a divorce, and not to dare complain. And all this was the price for not being arrested! The lieutenant colonel did just as he was ordered. (I was told the story by the osobist's chauffeur.)
There must have been many such cases, because the abuse of power was particularly attractive in this area. In 1944, another gaybist—State Security officer—forced the daughter of an army general to marry him by threatening to arrest her father. The girl had a fiancé, but to save her father she married the gaybist. She kept a diary during her brief marriage, gave it to her true love, and then committed suicide.

earth beneath your feet was yours! The heaven above you was yours—it was, after all, like your cap, sky blue!

The passion for gain was their universal passion. After all, in the absence of any checking up, such power was inevitably used for personal enrichment. One would have had to be *holy* to refrain!

If we were able to discover the hidden motivation behind individual arrests, we would be astounded to find that, granted the rules governing *arrests* in general, 75 percent of the time the particular choice of *whom* to arrest, the personal cast of the die, was determined by human greed and vengefulness; and of that 75 percent, half were the result of material self-interest on the part of the local NKVD (and, of course, the prosecutor too, for on this point I do not distinguish between them).

How, for example, did V. G. Vlasov's nineteen-year-long journey through the Archipelago begin? As head of the District Consumer Cooperatives he arranged a sale of textiles for the activists of the local Party organization. (These materials were of a sort and quality which no one nowadays would even touch.) No one was bothered, of course, by the fact that this sale was not open to the general public. But the prosecutor's wife was unable to buy any: She wasn't there at the time; Prosecutor Rusov himself had been shy about approaching the counter; and Vlasov hadn't thought to say: "I'll set some aside for you." (In fact, given his character, he would never have said this anyway.) Furthermore, Prosecutor Rusov had invited a friend to dine in the restricted Party dining room—such restricted dining rooms used to exist in the thirties. This friend of his was not high enough in rank to be admitted there, and the dining room manager refused to serve him. The prosecutor demanded that Vlasov punish the manager, and Vlasov refused. Vlasov also managed to insult the district NKVD, and just as painfully. And he was therefore added to the rightist opposition.

The motivations and actions of the bluecaps are sometimes so petty that one can only be astounded. Security officer Senchenko took a map case and dispatch case from an officer he'd arrested and started to use them right in his presence, and, by manipulating the documentation, he took a pair of foreign gloves from another prisoner. (When the armies were advancing, the bluecaps were especially irritated because they got only second pick of the booty.) The counterintelligence officer of the Forty-ninth Army who arrested me had a yen for my cigarette case—and it wasn't even a cigarette case but a small German Army box, of a tempting scarlet, however. And because of that piece of shit he carried out a whole maneuver: As his first step, he omitted it from the list of belongings that were confiscated from me. ("You can keep it.") He thereupon ordered me to be searched again, knowing all the time that it was all I had in my pockets. "Aha! what's that? Take it away!" And to prevent my protests: "Put him in the punishment cell!" (What Tsarist gendarme would have dared behave that way toward a defender of the Fatherland?)

Every interrogator was given an allowance of a certain number of cigarettes to encourage those willing to confess and to reward stool pigeons. Some of them kept all the cigarettes for themselves.

Even in accounting for hours spent in interrogating, they used to cheat. They got higher pay for night work. And we used to note the way they wrote down more hours on the night interrogations than they really spent.

Interrogator Fyodorov (Reshety Station, P. O. Box No. 235) stole a wristwatch while searching the apartment of the free person Korzukhin. During the Leningrad blockade Interrogator Nikolai Fyodorovich Kruzhkov told Yelizaveta Viktorovna Strakhovich, wife of the prisoner he was interrogating, K. I. Strakhovich: "I want a quilt. Bring it to me!" When she replied: "All our warm things are in the room they've sealed," he went to her apartment and, without breaking the State Security seal on the lock, unscrewed the entire doorknob. "That's how the MGB works," he explained gaily. And he went in and began to collect the warm things, shoving some crystal in his pocket at the same time. She herself tried to get whatever she could out of the room, but he stopped her.[13] "That's enough for you!"—and he kept on raking in the booty.

13. In 1954, although her husband, who had forgiven them everything, including a death sentence that had been commuted, kept trying to persuade her not to pursue the matter, this energetic and implacable woman testified against Kruzhkov at a trial. Because this was not Kruzhkov's first offense, and because the interests of the *Organs* had been violated, he was given a twenty-five-year sentence. Has he really been in the jug that long?

There's no end to such cases. One could issue a thousand "White Papers" (and beginning in 1918 too). One would need only to question systematically former prisoners and their wives. Maybe there are and were bluecaps who never stole anything or appropriated anything for themselves—but I find it impossible to imagine one. I simply do not understand: given the bluecaps' philosophy of life, what was there to restrain them if they liked some particular thing? Way back at the beginning of the thirties, when all of us were marching around in the German uniforms of the Red Youth Front and were building the First Five-Year Plan, they were spending their evenings in salons like the one in the apartment of Konkordiya Iosse, behaving like members of the nobility or Westerners, and their lady friends were showing off their foreign clothes. Where were they getting those clothes?

Here are their family names—and one might almost think they were hired because of those names. For example, in the Kemerovo Provincial State Security Administration, there were: a prosecutor named *Trutnev*, "drone"; a chief of the interrogation section Major *Shkurkin*, "self-server"; his deputy, Lieutenant Colonel *Balandin*, "soupy"; and an interrogator *Skorokhvatov*, "quick-grabber." When all is said and done, one could not invent names more appropriate. And they were all right there together! (I need hardly bother to mention again Volkopyalov—"wolf-skin-stretcher"—or Grabishchenko—"plunderer.") Are we to assume that nothing at all is expressed in people's family names and such a concentration of them?

Again the prisoner's faulty memory. I. Korneyev has forgotten the name of the colonel of State Security who was also Konkordiya Iosse's friend (they both knew her, it turned out), who was in the Vladimir Detention Prison at the same time as Korneyev. This colonel was a living embodiment of the instincts for power and personal gain. At the beginning of 1945, during the height of the "war booty" period, he got himself assigned to that section of the *Organs,* headed by Abakumov himself, which was supposed to keep watch over the plundering—in other words, they tried to grab off as much as possible for themselves, not for the state. (And succeeded brilliantly.) Our hero pulled in whole freight car loads and built several dachas, one of them in Klin. After the war he operated on such a scale that when he arrived at the Novosibirsk Station he ordered all the customers chased out of the station restaurant and had girls and women rounded up and forced to dance naked on the tables to entertain him and his drinking companions. He would have gotten away with this too, but he violated another important rule. Like Kruzhkov, he went against *his own kind*. Kruzhkov deceived the *Organs*. And this colonel did perhaps even worse. He laid bets on which wives he could seduce, and not just ordinary wives, but the wives of his colleagues in the Security police. And he was not forgiven! He was sentenced to a political prison under Article 58, and was serving out his time fuming at their having *dared* to arrest him. He had no doubt they would change their minds. (And perhaps they did.)

That dread fate—*to be thrown into prison* themselves—was not such a rarity for the bluecaps. There was no genuine insurance against it. But somehow these men were slow to sense the lessons of the past. Once again this was probably due to their having no higher powers of reason; their low-grade intellect would tell them: It happens only rarely; very few get caught; it may pass me by; my friends won't let me down.

Friends, as a matter of fact, did try not to leave their friends in a bad spot. They had their own unspoken understanding: at least to arrange favorable conditions for *friends*. (This was the case, for example, with Colonel I. Y. Vorobyev in the Marfino Special Prison, and with the same V. N. Ilin who was in the Lubyanka for more than eight years.) Thanks to this caste spirit, those arrested singly, as a result of only personal shortcomings, usually did not do too badly. And that was how they were able to justify their sense of immunity from punishment in their day-to-day work in the service. But there were several known cases when camp Security officers were tossed into ordinary camps to serve out their sentences. There were even instances when as prisoners they ran into zeks who had once been under their thumb and came off badly in the encounter. For example, Security officer Munshin, who cherished a particularly violent hatred toward the 58's in camp and had relied heavily on the support of the blatnye, the habitual thieves, was driven right under the board bunks by those very same thieves. However, we have no way to learn more details about these cases in order to be able to explain them.

But those gaybisty—the State Security officers—who got

caught in a *wave* were in very serious danger. (They had their own *waves!*) A wave is a natural catastrophe and is even more powerful than the *Organs* themselves. In this situation, no one was going to help anyone else lest he be drawn into the same abyss himself.

The possibility did exist, however, if you were well informed and had a sharp Chekist sensitivity, of getting yourself out from under the avalanche, even at the last minute, by proving that you had no connection with it. Thus it was that Captain Sayenko (not the Kharkov Chekist carpenter of 1918–1919, who was famous for executing prisoners with his pistol, punching holes in bodies with his saber, breaking shinbones in two, flattening heads with weights, and branding people with hot irons,[14] but, perhaps, a relative) was weak enough to marry for love an ex-employee of the Chinese Eastern Railroad named Kokhanskaya. And suddenly he found out, right at the beginning of the wave, that all the Chinese Eastern Railroad people were going to be arrested. At this time he was head of the Security Operations Department of the Archangel GPU. He acted without losing a moment. How? He *arrested his own beloved wife!* And not on the basis of her being one of the Chinese Eastern Railroad people—but on the basis of a case he himself cooked up. Not only did he save himself, but he moved up and became the Chief of the Tomsk Province NKVD.[15]

The *waves* were generated by the *Organs'* hidden law of *self-renewal*—a small periodic ritual sacrifice so that the rest could take on the appearance of being purified. The *Organs* had to change personnel faster than the normal rate of human growth and aging would ensure. Driven by that same implacable urgency that forces the sturgeon to swim upriver and perish in the shallows, to be replaced by schools of small fry, a certain number of "schools" of gaybisty had to sacrifice themselves. This law was easily apparent to a higher intelligence, but the bluecaps themselves did not want to accept the fact of its existence and make provision for it. Yet, at the hour appointed in their stars, the kings of the *Organs,* the aces of the *Organs,* and even the ministers themselves laid their heads down beneath their own guillotine.

14. Roman Gul, *Dzerzhinsky. Menzhinsky—Peters—Latsis—Yagoda*, Paris, 1936.

15. This, too, is a theme for a story—and how many more there are in this field! Maybe someone will make use of them someday.

Yagoda took one such school of fish along with him. No doubt many of those whose glorious names we shall come to admire when we come to the White Sea Canal were taken in this school and their names thenceforward expunged from the poetic eulogies.

Very shortly, a second school accompanied the short-lived Yezhov. Some of the finest cavaliers of 1937 vanished in this one. (Yet one ought not to exaggerate their number. It did not by any means include all the best.) Yezhov himself was beaten during his interrogation. He was pitiful. And Gulag was orphaned during this wave of arrests. For example, arrested with Yezhov were the Chief of the Financial Administration of Gulag, the Chief of the Medical Administration of Gulag, the Chief of the Guard Service of Gulag (VOKhR),[16] and even the Chief of the Security Operations Department of Gulag, who oversaw the work of the camp "godfathers."

And later there was the school of Beria.

The corpulent, conceited Abakumov had fallen earlier, separately.

Someday—if the archives are not destroyed—the historians of the *Organs* will recount all this step by step, with all the figures and all the glittering names.

Therefore, I am going to write only briefly about Ryumin and Abakumov, a story I learned only by chance. I will not repeat what I have already written about them in *The First Circle*.

Ryumin had been raised to the heights by Abakumov and was very close to him. At the end of 1952, he came to Abakumov with the sensational report that Professor Etinger, a physician, had confessed to intentional malpractice when treating Zhdanov and Shcherbakov, with the purpose of killing them. Abakumov refused to believe him. He knew the whole cookery and decided Ryumin was getting too big for his britches. (But Ryumin had a better idea of what Stalin wanted!) To verify the story, they arranged to cross-question Etinger that very evening. But each of them drew different conclusions from his testimony. Abakumov concluded that there was no such thing as a "doctors' case." And Ryumin concluded that there was. A second attempt at verification was to take place the following morning, but, thanks to the miraculous attributes of the Nighttime Institution, *Etinger died*

16. VOKhR: Militarized Guard Service, formerly the Internal Guard Service of the Republic.

that very night! In the morning, Ryumin, bypassing Abakumov and without his knowledge, telephoned the Central Committee and asked for an appointment with Stalin! (My own opinion, however, is that this was not his most decisive step. Ryumin's decisive action, following which his life hung in the balance, was in not going along with Abakumov earlier. And perhaps in having Etinger killed that same night. Who knows the secrets of those *courtyards!* Had Ryumin's contact with Stalin begun earlier perhaps?) Stalin received Ryumin, set in motion the "doctors' case" and *arrested Abakumov.* From that point on it would seem that Ryumin conducted the "doctors' case" independently of and even despite Beria! There were signs before Stalin's death that Beria was in danger—and perhaps it was he who arranged to have Stalin done away with. One of the first acts of the new government was to dismiss the "doctors' case." At that time *Ryumin was arrested* (while Beria was still in power), but *Abakumov was not released!* At the Lubyanka a new order of things was introduced. And for the first time in its entire existence a prosecutor crossed its threshold—D. Terekhov. Imprisoned, Ryumin was fidgety and subservient: "I am not guilty. I am here for no reason." He asked to be interrogated. As was his custom, he was sucking a hard candy at the time, and when Terekhov rebuked him for it, he spat it out on the palm of his hand. "Pardon me." As we have already reported, Abakumov roared with laughter: "Hocus-pocus!" Terekhov showed him the document authorizing him to inspect the Internal Prison of the Ministry of State Security. Abakumov brushed it away: "You can forge five hundred of those!" As an organizational "patriot," he was principally offended not by being in prison but by this encroachment on the power of the *Organs,* which could not be subordinate to anything in the world! In July, 1953, Ryumin was tried in Moscow and shot. And Abakumov remained in prison! During one interrogation he said to Terekhov: "Your eyes are too beautiful. *I am going to be sorry to have to shoot you!*[17] Leave my case alone. Leave it while you still have time." On another occasion Terekhov

17. This is true. On the whole, D. Terekhov is a man of uncommon strength of will and courage (which were what was required in bringing the big Stalinists to justice in an uneasy situation). And he evidently has a lively mind as well. If Khrushchev's reforms had been more thoroughgoing and consistent, Terekhov might have excelled in carrying them out. That is how historic leaders fail to materialize in our country.

called him in and handed him the newspaper which carried the announcement of Beria's exposure. At the time this was virtually a cosmic upheaval. Abakumov read it and, with not so much as the twitch of an eyebrow, he turned the page and started to read the sports news! On another occasion, during an interrogation in the presence of a high-ranking gaybist who had, in the recent past, been his subordinate, Abakumov asked him: "How could you have permitted the investigation of the Beria case to be conducted by the prosecutor's office instead of by the MGB?" (Everything in his own domain kept nagging him.) He went on: "Do you really believe they are going to put me, the Minister of State Security, on trial?" The answer was "Yes." And he replied: "Then put on your *top hat!* The *Organs* are finished!" (He was, of course, too pessimistic, uneducated courier that he was.) But when he was in the Lubyanka, Abakumov was not afraid of being tried; he was afraid of being poisoned. (This, too, showed what a worthy son of the *Organs* he was!) He started to reject the prison food altogether and would eat only eggs that he bought from the prison store. (In this case, he simply lacked technical imagination. He thought one couldn't poison eggs.) The only books he borrowed from the well-stocked Lubyanka library were the works of, believe it or not, Stalin! (Who had imprisoned him.) But in all likelihood this was for show rather than the result of any calculation that Stalin's adherents would gain power. He spent two years in prison. Why didn't they release him? The question is not a naïve one. In terms of his crimes against humanity, he was over his head in blood. But he was not the only one! And all the others came out of it safe and sound. There is some hidden secret here too: there is a vague rumor that in his time he had personally beaten Khrushchev's daughter-in-law Lyuba Sedykh, the wife of Khrushchev's older son, who had been condemned to a punishment battalion in Stalin's time and who died as a result. And, so goes the rumor, this was why, having been imprisoned by Stalin, he was tried—in Leningrad—under Khrushchev and shot on December 18, 1954.[18] But Abakumov had no real reason to be depressed: the *Organs* still didn't perish because of that.

18. Here is one more of his eccentricities as a VIP: he used to change into civilian clothes and walk around Moscow with Kuznetsov, the head of his bodyguard, and whenever he felt like it, he would hand out money from the Cheka operations funds. Does not this smell of Old Russia—charity for the sake of one's soul?

■

As the folk saying goes: *If you speak for the wolf, speak against him as well.*

Where did this wolf-tribe appear from among our people? Does it really stem from our own roots? Our own blood?

It is our own.

And just so we don't go around flaunting too proudly the white mantle of the just, let everyone ask himself: "If my life had turned out differently, might I myself not have become just such an executioner?"

It is a dreadful question if one really answers it honestly.

I remember my third year at the university, in the fall of 1938. We young men of the Komsomol were summoned before the District Komsomol Committee not once but twice. Scarcely bothering to ask our consent, they shoved an application form at us: You've had enough physics, mathematics, and chemistry; it's more important to your country for you to enter the NKVD school. (That's the way it always is. It isn't just some person who needs you; it is always your Motherland. And it is always some official or other who speaks on behalf of your Motherland and who knows what she needs.)

One year before, the District Committee had conducted a drive among us to recruit candidates for the air force schools. We avoided getting involved that time too, because we didn't want to leave the university—but we didn't sidestep recruitment then as stubbornly as we did this time.

Twenty-five years later we could think: Well, yes, we understood the sort of arrests that were being made at the time, and the fact that they were torturing people in prisons, and the slime they were trying to drag us into. But it isn't true! After all, the Black Marias were going through the streets at night, and we were the same young people who were parading with banners during the day. How could we know anything about those arrests and why should we think about them? All the provincial leaders had been removed, but as far as we were concerned it didn't matter. Two or three professors had been arrested, but after all they hadn't been our dancing partners, and it might even be easier to pass our exams as a result. Twenty-year-olds, we marched in the ranks of those born the year the Revolution took place, and because we were the same age as the Revolution, the brightest of futures lay ahead.

It would be hard to identify the exact source of that inner intuition, not founded on rational argument, which prompted our refusal to enter the NKVD schools. It certainly didn't derive from the lectures on historical materialism we listened to: it was clear from them that the struggle against the internal enemy was a crucial battlefront, and to share in it was an honorable task. Our decision even ran counter to our material interests: at that time the provincial university we attended could not promise us anything more than the chance to teach in a rural school in a remote area for miserly wages. The NKVD school dangled before us special rations and double or triple pay. Our feelings could not be put into words—and even if we had found the words, fear would have prevented our speaking them aloud to one another. It was not our minds that resisted but something inside our breasts. People can shout at you from all sides: "You must!" And your own head can be saying also: "You must!" But inside your breast there is a sense of revulsion, repudiation. I don't want to. *It makes me feel sick.* Do what you want without me; I want no part of it.

This came from very far back, quite likely as far back as Lermontov, from those decades of Russian life when frankly and openly there was no worse and no more vile branch of the service for a decent person than that of the gendarmerie. No, it went back even further. Without even knowing it ourselves, we were ransomed by the small change in copper that was left from the golden coins our great-grandfathers had expended, at a time when morality was not considered relative and when the distinction between good and evil was very simply perceived by the heart.

Still, some of us were recruited at that time, and I think that if they had really put the pressure on, they could have broken everybody's resistance. So I would like to imagine: if, by the time war broke out, I had already been wearing an NKVD officer's insignia on my blue tabs, what would I have become? Nowadays, of course, I can console myself by saying that my heart wouldn't have stood it, that I would have objected and at some point slammed the door. But later, lying on a prison bunk, I began to

162162162

1 | THE GULAG ARCHIPELAGO
162 | THE GULAG ARCHIPELAGO

look back over my actual career as an officer and I was horrified.

I did not move in one stride from being a student worn out by mathematics to officer's rank. Before becoming an officer I spent a half-year as a downtrodden soldier. And one might think I would have gotten through my thick skull what it was like always to obey people who were perhaps not worthy of your obedience and to do it on a hungry stomach to boot. Then for another half-year they tore me to pieces in officer candidate school. So I ought to have grasped, once and for all, the bitterness of service as a rank-and-file soldier and remembered how my hide froze and how it was flayed from my body. But did I? Not at all. For consolation, they pinned two little stars on my shoulder boards, and then a third, and then a fourth. And I forgot every bit of what it had been like!

Had I at least kept my student's love of freedom? But, you see, we had never had any such thing. Instead, we loved forming up, we loved marches.

I remember very well that right after officer candidate school I experienced the *happiness of simplification,* of being a military man and *not having to think things through; the happiness of being immersed* in the life *everyone else lived,* that was *accepted* in our military milieu; the happiness of forgetting some of the spiritual subtleties inculcated since childhood.

We were constantly hungry in that school and kept looking around to see where we could grab an extra bite, and we watched one another enviously to see who was the cleverest. But most of all we were afraid we wouldn't manage to stay in until the time came to graduate and receive our officer's insignia. (They sent those who failed to the battle for Stalingrad.) And they trained us like young beasts, so as to infuriate us to the point where we would later want to take it out on someone else. We never got enough sleep because after taps, as punishment, we might be forced to go through the drill alone under the eyes of a sergeant. Or the entire squad might be routed out at night and made to form up because of one uncleaned boot: there he is, the bastard, and he'll keep on cleaning it, and until he gets a shine on it you're all going to stay standing there.

In passionate anticipation of those insignia, we developed a tigerlike stride and a metallic voice of command.

Then the officer's stars were fastened on our tabs. And only one month later, forming up my battery in the rear, I ordered a careless soldier named Berbenyev to march up and down after taps under the eyes of my insubordinate Sergeant Metlin. (And do you know, I had *forgotten* all about it until now. I honestly forgot about it for years! Only now, seated in front of this sheet of paper, have I remembered.) Some elderly colonel, who was an inspector, happened to be there, and he called me in and put me to shame. And I (and this after I'd left the university!) tried to justify my action on the grounds that it was what we had been taught in school. In other words, I meant: What humane views can there be, given the fact that we are in the army?

(And the more so in the *Organs.*)

Pride grows in the human heart like lard on a pig.

I tossed out orders to my subordinates that I would not allow them to question, convinced that no orders could be wiser. Even at the front, where, one might have thought, death made equals of us all, my power soon convinced me that I was a superior human being. Seated there, I heard them out as they stood at attention. I interrupted them. I issued commands. I addressed fathers and grandfathers with the familiar, downgrading form of address—while they, of course, addressed me formally. I sent them out to repair wires under shellfire so that my superiors should not reproach me. (Andreyashin died that way.) I ate my officer's ration of butter with rolls, without giving a thought as to why I had a right to it, and why the rank-and-file soldiers did not. I, of course, had a personal servant assigned to me—in polite terms, an "orderly"—whom I badgered one way or another and ordered to look after my person and prepare my meals separately from the soldiers'. (After all, the Lubyanka interrogators don't have orderlies—that's one thing you can't say about them.) I forced my soldiers to put their backs into it and dig me a special dugout at every new bivouac and to haul the heaviest beams to support it so that I should be as comfortable and safe as possible. And wait a minute, yes, my battery always had a guardhouse too. What kind of guardhouse could there be in the woods? It was a pit, of course, although a better one than those at the Gorokhovets division camps which I have described, because it had a roof and the man confined got a soldier's ration. Vyushkov was imprisoned there for losing his horse and Popkov for maltreating his carbine. Yes, just a moment, I can remember more. They sewed me a map case out of German hide—not human, but from a car seat. But I didn't have a strap for it, and I was unhappy about that. Then all of a sudden they saw some partisan commissar, from the local District Party Committee, wearing just the right kind of strap—and they took it away from him: we are the army; we have seniority! (Remember Senchenko, the Security officer, who stole a map case and a dispatch case?) Finally, I coveted that scarlet box, and I remember how they took it away and got it for me.

That's what shoulder boards do to a human being. And where have all the exhortations of grandmother, standing before an ikon, gone! And where the young Pioneer's daydreams of future sacred Equality!

And at the moment when my life was turned upside down and the SMERSH officers at the brigade command point tore off those cursed shoulder boards, and took my belt away and shoved me along to their automobile, I was pierced to the quick by worrying how, in my stripped and sorry state, I was going to make my way through the telephone operator's room. The rank and file must not see me in that condition!

The day after my arrest my march of penance began: the most recent "catch" was always sent from the army counterintelligence center to the counterintelligence headquarters of the front. They herded us on foot from Osterode to Brodnica.

When they led me out of the punishment cell, there were already seven prisoners there in three and a half pairs standing with their backs to me. Six of them had on well-worn Russian Army overcoats which had been around for a long time, and on their backs had been painted, in indelible white paint, "SU," meaning "Soviet Union." I already knew that mark, having seen it more than once on the backs of our Russian POW's as they wandered sadly and guiltily toward the army that was approaching to *free* them. They had been freed, but there was no shared happiness in that liberation. Their compatriots glowered at them even more grimly than at the Germans. And as soon as they crossed the front lines, they were arrested and imprisoned.

The seventh prisoner was a German civilian in a black three-piece suit, a black overcoat, and black hat. He was over fifty, tall, well groomed, and his white face had been nurtured on gentleman's food.

I completed the fourth pair, and the Tatar sergeant, chief of the convoy, gestured to me to pick up my sealed suitcase, which stood off to one side. It contained my officer's equipment as well as all the papers which had been seized as evidence when I was arrested.

What did he mean, carry my suitcase? He, a sergeant, wanted me, an officer, to pick up my suitcase and carry it? A large, heavy object? Despite the new regulations? While beside me six men *from the ranks* would be marching empty-handed? And one representative of a conquered nation?

I did not express this whole complex set of ideas to the sergeant. I merely said: "I am an officer. Let the German carry it."

None of the prisoners turned around at my words: turning around was forbidden. Only my mate in the fourth pair, also an "SU," looked at me in astonishment. (When he had been captured, our army wasn't yet like that.)

But the sergeant from counterintelligence was not surprised. Even though I was not, of course, an officer in his eyes, still his indoctrination and mine coincided. He summoned the innocent German and ordered him to carry the suitcase. It was just as well the latter had not understood our conversation.

The rest of us put our hands behind our backs. The former POW's did not have even one bag among them. They had left the Motherland with empty hands and that is exactly how they returned to her. So our column marched off, four pairs in file. We did not converse with our convoy. And it was absolutely forbidden to talk among ourselves whether on the march, during a halt, or at overnight stops. As accused prisoners we were required to move as though separated by invisible partitions, as though suffocated, each in his own solitary-confinement cell.

The early spring weather was changeable. At times a thin mist hung in the air, and even on the firm highway the liquid mud squelched dismally beneath our boots. At times the heavens cleared and the soft yellow sun, still uncertain of its talent, warmed the already thawing hillocks and showed us with perfect clarity the world we were about to leave. At times a hostile squall flew to the attack and tore from the black clouds a snow that was not really even white, which beat icily on faces and backs and feet, soaking through our overcoats and our footcloths.

Six backs ahead of me, six constant backs. There was more than enough time to examine and re-examine the crooked, hideous brands "SU" and the shiny black cloth on the German's back. There was more than enough time to reconsider my former life and to comprehend my present one. But I couldn't. I had been smashed on the head with an oak club—but I still didn't comprehend.

Six backs! There was neither approval nor condemnation in their swing.

The German soon tired. He shifted the suitcase from hand to hand, grabbed at his heart, made signs to the convoy that he couldn't carry it any further. At that point his neighbor in the pair, a POW who only a little while before had experienced God knows what in German captivity (but, perhaps, mercy too), took the suitcase of his own free will and carried it.

After that the other POW's carried it in turn, also without being ordered to; and then the German again.

All but me.

And no one said a word to me.

At one point we met a long string of empty carts. The drivers studied us with interest, and some of them jumped up to full height on top of the carts and stared. I understood very quickly that their stares and their malice were directed toward me. I was very sharply set off from the others: my coat was new, long, and cut to fit my figure snugly. My tabs had not yet been torn off, and in the filtered sunlight my buttons, also not cut off, burned with the glitter of cheap gold. It was easy to see I was an officer, with a look of newness, too, and newly taken into custody. Perhaps this very fall from the heights stimulated them and gave them pleasure, suggesting some gleam of justice, but more likely they could not get it into their heads, stuffed with political indoctrination, that one of their own company commanders could be arrested in this way, and they all decided unanimously I had come from the *other* side.

"Aha, the Vlasov bastard got caught, did he! Shoot the rat!"

They were vehement in their rear-line wrath (the most intense patriotism always flourishes in the rear), and they added a good deal more in mother oaths.

They regarded me as some kind of international operator who had, nonetheless, been caught—and as a result the advance at the front would move along faster and the war would come to an end sooner.

How was I to answer them? I was forbidden to utter a single word, and I would have had to explain my entire life to each and every one of them. What could I do to make them understand that I was not a spy, a saboteur? That I was their friend? That it was because of them that I was here? I smiled. Looking up at them, I smiled at them from a column of prisoners under escort! But my bared teeth seemed to them the worst kind of mockery, and they shook their fists and bellowed insults at me even more violently than before.

I smiled in pride that I had been arrested not for stealing, nor treason, nor desertion, but because I had discovered through my power of reasoning the evil secrets of Stalin. I smiled at the thought that I wanted, and might still be able, to effect some small remedies and changes in our Russian way of life.

But all that time my suitcase was being carried by others.

And I didn't even feel remorseful about it! And if my neighbor, whose sunken cheeks were already covered with a soft two-week growth of beard and whose eyes were filled to overflowing with suffering and knowledge, had then and there reproached me in the clearest of clear Russian words for having disgraced the honor of a prisoner by appealing to the convoy for help and had accused me of haughtiness, of setting myself above the rest of them, I would *not have understood* him! I simply would not have understood *what he was talking about*. I was an officer!

And if seven of us had to die on the way, and the eighth could have been saved by the convoy, what was to keep me from crying out: "Sergeant! Save *me*. I am an officer!"

And that's what an officer is even when his shoulder boards aren't blue!

And if they are blue? If he has been indoctrinated to believe that even among other officers he is the salt of the earth? And that he knows more than others and is entrusted with more responsibility than others and that, consequently, it is his duty to force a prisoner's head between his legs, and then to shove him like that into a pipe . . .

Why shouldn't he?

I credited myself with unselfish dedication. But meanwhile I had been thoroughly prepared to be an executioner. And if I had gotten into an NKVD school under Yezhov, maybe I would have matured just in time for Beria.

So let the reader who expects this book to be a political exposé slam its covers shut right now.

If only it were all so simple! If only there were evil people somewhere insidiously committing evil deeds, and it were necessary only to separate them from the rest of us and destroy them. But the line dividing good and evil cuts through the heart of every human being. And who is willing to destroy a piece of his own heart?

During the life of any heart this line keeps changing place; sometimes it is squeezed one way by exuberant evil and sometimes it shifts to allow enough space for good to flourish. One and the same human being is, at various ages, under various circumstances, a totally different human being. At times he is close to being a devil, at times to sainthood. But his name doesn't change, and to that name we ascribe the whole lot, good and evil.

Socrates taught us: *Know thyself!*

Confronted by the pit into which we are about to toss those who have done us harm, we halt, stricken dumb: it is after all only because of the way things worked out that they were the executioners and we weren't.

If Malyuta Skuratov had summoned *us*, we, too, probably would have done our work well!

From good to evil is one quaver, says the proverb.

And correspondingly, from evil to good.

From the moment when our society was convulsed by the reminder of those illegalities and tortures, they began on all sides to explain, to write, to protest: *Good people* were *there* too —meaning in the NKVD-MGB!

We know which "good" people they are talking about: they were the ones who whispered to the old Bolsheviks: "Don't weaken," or even sneaked a sandwich in to them, and who kicked all the rest around wherever they found them. But weren't there also some who rose above the Party—who were good in a general, human sense?

Broadly speaking, they should not have been *there*. The Organs avoided employing such people, eliminating them at the recruitment stage. And such people played their hand shrewdly so as to get out of it.[19] Whoever got in by mistake either adjusted to the milieu or else was thrown out, or eased out, or even fell across the rails himself. Still . . . were there no good people left there?

In Kishinev, a young lieutenant gaybist went to Father Viktor Shipovalnikov a full month before he was arrested: "Get away from here, go away, they plan to arrest you!" (Did he do this on his own, or did his mother send him to warn the priest?) After the arrest, this young man was assigned to Father Viktor as an escort guard. And he grieved for him: "Why didn't you go away?"

Or here's another. I had a platoon commander named Lieutenant Ovsyannikov. At the front no one was closer to me than he was. During half the war we ate from the same pot; even under enemy shellfire we would gulp down our food between explosions, so the stew wouldn't get cold. He was a peasant lad with a clean soul and a view of life so undistorted that neither officer candidate school nor being an officer had spoiled him in any degree. He even did what he could to soften my hard edges in many ways. Throughout his service as an officer he concentrated on one thing only: preserving the lives and strength of his soldiers, many of whom were no longer young. He was the first to tell me what the Russian villages were like then and what the collective farms were like. He talked about all this without resentment, without protest, very simply and straightforwardly—just as a forest pool reflects the image of a tree and all its branches, even the smallest. He was deeply shocked by my arrest. He wrote me a combat reference containing the highest praise and got the divisional commander to sign it. After he was demobilized he continued to try to help me, through my relatives. And this, mind you, was in 1947, which was not very different from 1937. At my interrogation I had many reasons to be afraid on his account, especially lest they

19. During the war, a certain Leningrad aviator, after being discharged from the hospital in Ryazan, went to a TB clinic and begged: "Please find something wrong with me! I'm under orders to go into the *Organs!*" The radiologists dreamed up a touch of TB for him—and the *Organs* dropped him posthaste.

read my "War Diary," which contained the stories he'd told me. When I was rehabilitated in 1957, I very much wanted to find him. I remembered his village address and wrote once, and then again, but there was no reply. I discovered one thread I could follow— that he had graduated from the Yaroslavl Pedagogical Institute. When I inquired there, they replied: "He was sent to work in the Organs of State Security." Fine! All the more interesting! I wrote to him at his city address, but there was no reply. Several years passed and *Ivan Denisovich* was published. Well, I thought, now he'll turn up. No! Three years later I asked one of my Yaroslavl correspondents to go to him and personally hand him a letter. My correspondent did as I asked and wrote me: "Evidently he has never read *Ivan Denisovich*." And truly, why should they know how things go with prisoners after they've been sentenced? This time Ovsyannikov couldn't keep silent any longer. He wrote: "After the Institute they offered me work in the *Organs,* and it seemed to me I would be just as successful there." (What did he mean, *successful?*) "I cannot say that I have prospered remarkably in my new walk of life. There are some things I did not like, but I work hard, and, if I am not mistaken, I shall not let my comrades down." (And that's the justification—comradeship!) He ended: "I no longer think about the future."

And that is all. Allegedly, he had not received my previous letters. Evidently, he doesn't want to see me. (But if we had met, I think this would have been a better chapter.) In Stalin's last years he had already become an interrogator—during those very years when they handed out a *twenty-five-year sentence* to everyone who came along. How did everything in his consciousness recircuit itself? How did everything black out? But remembering the once selfless, dedicated boy, as fresh as spring water, can I possibly believe that everything in him changed beyond recall, that there are no living tendrils left?

When the interrogator Goldman gave Vera Korneyeva the "206" form on nondisclosure to sign, she began to catch on to her rights, and then she began to go into the *case* in detail, involving as it did all seventeen members of their "religious group." Goldman raged, but he had to let her study the file. In order not to be bored waiting for her, he led her to a large office, where half a dozen employees were sitting, and left her there. At first she read quietly, but then a conversation began—perhaps because the others were bored—and Vera launched aloud into a real religious sermon. (One would have had to know her to appreciate this to the full. She was a luminous person, with a lively mind and a gift of eloquence, even though in freedom she had been no more than a lathe operator, a stable girl, and a housewife.) They listened to her impressively, now and then asking questions in order to clarify something or other. It was catching them from an unexpected side of things. People came in from other offices, and the room filled up. Even though they were only typists, stenographers, file clerks, and not interrogators, in 1946 this was still their milieu, the *Organs*. It is impossible to reconstruct her monologue. She managed to work in all sorts of things, including the question of "traitors of the Motherland." Why were there no traitors in the 1812 War of the Fatherland, when there was still serfdom? It would have been natural to have traitors then! But mostly she spoke about religious faith and religious believers. *Formerly*, she declared, unbridled passions were the basis for everything—"Steal the stolen goods"—and, in that state of affairs, religious believers were naturally a hindrance to you. But now, when you want to *build* and prosper in this world, why do you persecute your best citizens? They represent your most precious material: after all, believers don't need to be watched, they do not steal, and they do not shirk. Do you think you can build a just society on a foundation of self-serving and envious people? Everything in the country is falling apart. Why do you spit in the hearts of your best people? Separate church and state properly and do not touch the church; you will not lose a thing thereby. Are you materialists? In that case, put your faith in education—in the possibility that it will, as they say, disperse religious faith. But why arrest people? At this point Goldman came in and started to interrupt rudely. But everyone shouted at him: "Oh, shut up! Keep quiet! Go ahead, woman, talk." (And how should they have addressed her? Citizeness? Comrade? Those forms of address were forbidden, and these people were bound by the conventions of Soviet life. But "woman"—that was how Christ had spoken, and you couldn't go wrong there.) And Vera continued in the presence of her interrogator.

So there in the MGB office those people listened to Korneyeva

—and why did the words of an insignificant prisoner touch them so near the quick?

That same D. Terekhov I mentioned earlier remembers to this day the first prisoner he sentenced to death. "I was sorry for him." His memory obviously clings to something that came from his heart. (But after that first one, he forgot many and no longer kept count any more.)[20]

No matter how icy the jailers in the Big House in Leningrad, the innermost nucleus of the nucleus of the heart—for a nucleus has its own nucleus—had to continue to exist, did it not? N. P———va recalls the time when she was being taken to interrogation by an impassive, silent woman guard with unseeing eyes —when suddenly the bombs began to explode right next to the Big House and it sounded as if at the next moment they would fall directly on them. The terrified guard threw her arms around her prisoner and embraced her, desperate for human companionship and sympathy. Then the bombing stopped. And her eyes became unseeing again. "Hands behind your back! Move along."

Well, of course, there was no great merit in that—to become a human being at the moment of death. Similarly, loving one's own children is no proof of virtue. (People often try to excuse scoundrels by saying: "He's a good family man!") The Chairman of the Supreme Court, I. T. Golyakov, is praised: he enjoyed digging in his garden, he loved books, he used to browse around used- and rare-book stores, he knew the work of Tolstoi, Korolenko, and Chekhov. Well, what did he learn from them? How many thousands did he destroy? Or, for example, that colonel, Konkordiya Iosse's friend, who had roared with laughter in the Vladimir Detention Prison at the memory of locking up a group of old Jews in an ice-filled root cellar, had been afraid of one thing only during all his debaucheries: that his wife might find out about them. She believed in him, regarded him as noble, and this faith of hers was precious to him. But do we dare accept that feeling as a bridgehead to virtue in his heart?

20. An episode with Terekhov: Attempting to prove to me the fairness of the judicial system under Khrushchev, he energetically struck the plate-glass desk top with his hand and cut his wrist on the edge. He rang for help. His subordinates were at the ready. The senior officer on duty brought him iodine and hydrogen peroxide. Continuing the conversation, he helplessly held dampened cotton to the wound: it appears that his blood coagulates poorly. And thus God showed him clearly the limitations of the human being! And he had delivered verdicts, imposed death sentences on others.

And why is it that for nearly two hundred years the Security forces have hung onto the color of the heavens? That was what they wore in Lermontov's lifetime—"and you, blue uniforms!" Then came blue service caps, blue shoulder boards, blue tabs, and then they were ordered to make themselves less conspicuous, and the blue brims were hidden from the gratitude of the people and everything blue on heads and shoulders was made narrower —until what was left was piping, narrow rims . . . but still blue.

Is this only a masquerade?

Or is it that even blackness must, every so often, however rarely, partake of the heavens?

It would be beautiful to think so. But when one learns, for example, the nature of Yagoda's striving toward the sacred . . . An eyewitness from the group around Gorky, who was close to Yagoda at the time, reports that in the vestibule of the bathhouse on Yagoda's estate near Moscow, ikons were placed so that Yagoda and his comrades, after undressing, could use them as targets for revolver practice before going in to take their baths.

Just how are we to understand that? As the act of an *evildoer?* What sort of behavior is it? Do such people really exist?

We would prefer to say that such people cannot exist, that there aren't any. It is permissible to portray evildoers in a story for children, so as to keep the picture simple. But when the great world literature of the past—Shakespeare, Schiller, Dickens—inflates and inflates images of evildoers of the blackest shades, it seems somewhat farcical and clumsy to our contemporary perception. The trouble lies in the way these classic evildoers are pictured. They recognize themselves as evildoers, and they know their souls are black. And they reason: "I cannot live unless I do evil. So I'll set my father against my brother! I'll drink the victim's sufferings until I'm drunk with them!" Iago very precisely identifies his purposes and his motives as being black and born of hate.

But no; that's not the way it is! To do evil a human being must first of all believe that what he's doing is good, or else that it's a well-considered act in conformity with natural law. Fortunately, it is in the nature of the human being to seek a *justification* for his actions.

Macbeth's self-justifications were feeble—and his conscience devoured him. Yes, even Iago was a little lamb too. The imagination and the spiritual strength of Shakespeare's evildoers stopped short at a dozen corpses. Because they had no *ideology*.

Ideology—that is what gives evildoing its long-sought justification and gives the evildoer the necessary steadfastness and determination. That is the social theory which helps to make his acts seem good instead of bad in his own and others' eyes, so that he won't hear reproaches and curses but will receive praise and honors. That was how the agents of the Inquisition fortified their wills: by invoking Christianity; the conquerors of foreign lands, by extolling the grandeur of their Motherland; the colonizers, by civilization; the Nazis, by race; and the Jacobins (early and late), by equality, brotherhood, and the happiness of future generations.

Thanks to *ideology,* the twentieth century was fated to experience evildoing on a scale calculated in the millions. This cannot be denied, nor passed over, nor suppressed. How, then, do we dare insist that evildoers do not exist? And who was it that destroyed these millions? Without evildoers there would have been no Archipelago.

There was a rumor going the rounds between 1918 and 1920 that the Petrograd Cheka, headed by Uritsky, and the Odessa Cheka, headed by Deich, did not shoot all those condemned to death but fed some of them alive to the animals in the city zoos. I do not know whether this is truth or calumny, or, if there were any such cases, how many there were. But I wouldn't set out to look for proof, either. Following the practice of the bluecaps, I would propose that they prove to us that this was impossible. How else could they get food for the zoos in those famine years? Take it away from the working class? Those enemies were going to die anyway, so why couldn't their deaths support the zoo economy of the Republic and thereby assist our march into the future? Wasn't it *expedient*?

That is the precise line the Shakespearean evildoer could not cross. But the evildoer with ideology does cross it, and his eyes remain dry and clear.

Physics is aware of phenomena which occur only at *threshold* magnitudes, which do not exist at all until a certain *threshold* encoded by and known to nature has been crossed. No matter how intense a yellow light you shine on a lithium sample, it will not emit electrons. But as soon as a weak bluish light begins to glow, it does emit them. (The threshold of the photoelectric effect has been crossed.) You can cool oxygen to 100 degrees below zero Centigrade and exert as much pressure as you want; it does not yield, but remains a gas. But as soon as minus 183 degrees is reached, it liquefies and begins to flow.

Evidently evildoing also has a threshold magnitude. Yes, a human being hesitates and bobs back and forth between good and evil all his life. He slips, falls back, clambers up, repents, things begin to darken again. But just so long as the threshold of evildoing is not crossed, the possibility of returning remains, and he himself is still within reach of our hope. But when, through the density of evil actions, the result either of their own extreme degree or of the absoluteness of his power, he suddenly crosses that threshold, he has left humanity behind, and without, perhaps, the possibility of return.

■

From the most ancient times justice has been a two-part concept: virtue triumphs, and vice is punished.

We have been fortunate enough to live to a time when virtue, though it does not triumph, is nonetheless not always tormented by attack dogs. Beaten down, sickly, virtue has now been allowed to enter in all its tatters and sit in the corner, as long as it doesn't raise its voice.

However, no one dares say a word about vice. Yes, they did mock virtue, but there was no vice in that. Yes, so-and-so many millions did get mowed down—but no one was to blame for it. And if someone pipes up: "What about *those who* . . ." the answer comes from all sides, reproachfully and amicably at first: "What are you talking about, comrade! Why *open* old *wounds*?"[21] Then they go after you with an oaken club: "Shut up! Haven't you had enough yet? You think you've been rehabilitated!"

In that same period, by 1966, *eighty-six thousand* Nazi criminals had been convicted in West Germany.[22] And still we choke

21. Even in connection with *One Day in the Life of Ivan Denisovich*, the retired bluecaps living on pensions objected because the book might reopen the wounds of *those who had been imprisoned in camp*. Allegedly, they were the ones to be protected.

22. Meanwhile, in East Germany, nothing of the sort is to be heard. Which means that there they have been *shod with new shoes*; they are valued in the service of the state.

with anger here. We do not hesitate to devote to the subject page after newspaper page and hour after hour of radio time. We even stay after work to attend protest meetings and vote: *"Too few! Eighty-six thousand are too few. And twenty years is too little! It must go on and on."*

And during the same period, in our own country (according to the reports of the Military Collegium of the Supreme Court) about *ten men* have been convicted.

What takes place beyond the Oder and the Rhine gets us all worked up. What goes on in the environs of Moscow and behind the green fences near Sochi, or the fact that the murderers of our husbands and fathers ride through our streets and we make way for them as they pass, doesn't get us worked up at all, doesn't touch us. That would be "digging up the past."

Meanwhile, if we translate 86,000 West Germans into our own terms, on the basis of comparative population figures, it would become *one-quarter of a million.*

But in a quarter-century we have not tracked down anyone. We have not brought anyone to trial. It is their wounds we are afraid to reopen. And as a symbol of them all, the smug and stupid Molotov lives on at Granovsky No. 3, a man who has learned nothing at all, even now, though he is saturated with our blood and nobly crosses the sidewalk to seat himself in his long, wide automobile.

Here is a riddle not for us contemporaries to figure out: *Why* is Germany allowed to punish its evildoers and Russia is not? What kind of disastrous path lies ahead of us if we do not have the chance to purge ourselves of that putrefaction rotting inside our body? What, then, can Russia teach the world?

In the German trials an astonishing phenomenon takes place from time to time. The defendant clasps his head in his hands, refuses to make any defense, and from then on asks no concessions from the court. He says that the presentation of his crimes, revived and once again confronting him, has filled him with revulsion and he no longer wants to live.

That is the ultimate height a trial can attain: when evil is so utterly condemned that even the criminal is revolted by it.

A country which has condemned evil 86,000 times from the rostrum of a court and irrevocably condemned it in literature and among its young people, year by year, step by step, is purged of it.

What are we to do? Someday our descendants will describe our several generations as generations of driveling do-nothings. First we submissively allowed them to massacre us by the millions, and then with devoted concern we tended the murderers in their prosperous old age.

What are we to do if the great Russian tradition of penitence is incomprehensible and absurd to them? What are we to do if the animal terror of hearing even one-hundredth part of all they subjected others to outweighs in their hearts any inclination to justice? If they cling greedily to the harvest of benefits they have watered with the blood of those who perished?

It is clear enough that those men who turned the handle of the meat grinder even as late as 1937 are no longer young. They are fifty to eighty years old. They have lived the best years of their lives prosperously, well nourished and comfortable, so that it is too late for any kind of *equal* retribution as far as they are concerned.

But let us be generous. We will not shoot them. We will not pour salt water into them, nor bury them in bedbugs, nor bridle them into a "swan dive," nor keep them on sleepless "stand-up" for a week, nor kick them with jackboots, nor beat them with rubber truncheons, nor squeeze their skulls in iron rings, nor push them into a cell so that they lie atop one another like pieces of baggage—we will not do any of the things they did! But for the sake of our country and our children we have the duty to *seek them all out and bring them all to trial!* Not to put them on trial so much as their crimes. And to compel each one of them to announce loudly:

"Yes, I was an executioner and a murderer."

And if these words were spoken in our country *only* one-quarter of a million times (a just proportion, if we are not to fall behind West Germany), would it, perhaps, be enough?

It is unthinkable in the twentieth century to fail to distinguish between what constitutes an abominable atrocity that must be prosecuted and what constitutes that "past" which "ought not to be stirred up."

We have to condemn publicly the very *idea* that some people have the right to repress others. In keeping silent about evil, in burying it so deep within us that no sign of it appears on the surface, we are *implanting* it, and it will rise up a thousandfold in the future. When we neither punish nor reproach evildoers, we are not simply protecting their trivial old age, we are thereby ripping the foundations of justice from beneath new generations. It is for this reason, and not because of the "weakness of indoctrinational work," that they are growing up "indifferent." Young people are acquiring the conviction that foul deeds are never punished on earth, that they always bring prosperity.

It is going to be uncomfortable, horrible, to live in such a country!

Chapter 5

■

First Cell, First Love

How is one to take the title of this chapter? A cell and love in the same breath? Ah, well, probably it has to do with Leningrad during the blockade—and you were imprisoned in the Big House. In that case it would be very understandable. That's why you are still alive—because they shoved you in there. It was the best place in Leningrad—not only for the interrogators, who even lived there and had offices in the cellars in case of shelling. Joking aside, in Leningrad in those days no one washed and everyone's face was covered with a black crust, but in the Big House prisoners were given a hot shower every tenth day. Well, it's true that only the corridors were heated—for the jailers. The cells were left unheated, but after all, there were water pipes in the cells that worked and a toilet, and where else in Leningrad could you find that? And the bread ration was just like the ration outside—barely four and a half ounces. In addition, there was broth made from slaughtered horses once a day! And thin gruel once a day as well!

It was a case of the cat's being envious of the dog's life! But what about punishment cells? And what about the *"supreme measure"*—execution? No, that isn't what the chapter title is about.

Not at all.

You sit down and half-close your eyes and try to remember them all. How many different cells you were imprisoned in during your term! It is difficult even to count them. And in each one there were people, people. There might be two people in one, 150 in another. You were imprisoned for five minutes in one and all summer long in another.

But in every case, out of all the cells you've been in, your first cell is a very special one, the place where you first encountered others like yourself, doomed to the same fate. All your life you will remember it with an emotion that you otherwise experience only in remembering your first love. And those people, who shared with you the floor and air of that stone cubicle during those days when you rethought your entire life, will from time to time be recollected by you as members of your own family.

Yes, in those days they were your only family.

What you experience in your first interrogation cell parallels nothing in your entire *previous* life or your whole *subsequent* life. No doubt prisons have stood for thousands of years before you came along, and may continue to stand after you too— longer than one would like to think—but that first interrogation cell is unique and inimitable.

Maybe it was a terrible place for a human being. A lice-laden, bedbug-infested lock-up, without windows, without ventilation, without bunks, and with a dirty floor, a box called a KPZ[1] in the village soviet, at the police station, in the railroad station, or in some port. (The KPZ's and the DPZ's are scattered across the face of our land in the greatest abundance. There are masses of prisoners in them.) Or maybe it was "solitary" in the Archangel prison, where the glass had been smeared over with red lead so that the only rays of God's maimed light which crept in to you were crimson, and where a 15-watt bulb burned constantly in the ceiling, day and night. Or "solitary" in the city of Choibalsan, where, for six months at a time, fourteen of you were crowded onto seven square yards of floor space in such a way that you could only shift your bent legs in unison. Or it was one of the Lefortovo "psychological" cells, like No. 111, which was painted black and also had a day-and-night 25-watt bulb, but was in all other respects like every other Lefortovo cell: asphalt floor; the heating valve out in the corridor where only the guards had access

---

1. KPZ = Cell for Preliminary Detention. DPZ = House of Preliminary Detention. In other words, where interrogations are conducted, not where sentences are served.

to it; and, above all, that interminable irritating roar from the wind tunnel of the neighboring Central Aero- and Hydrodynamics Institute—a roar one could not believe was unintentional, a roar which would make a bowl or cup vibrate so violently that it would slip off the edge of the table, a roar which made it useless to converse and during which one could sing at the top of one's lungs and the jailer wouldn't even hear. And then when the roar stopped, there would ensue a sense of relief and felicity superior to freedom itself.

But it was not the dirty floor, nor the murky walls, nor the odor of the latrine bucket that you loved—but those fellow prisoners with whom you about-faced at command, and that something which beat between your heart and theirs, and their sometimes astonishing words, and then, too, the birth within you, on that very spot, of free-floating thoughts you had so recently been unable to leap up or rise to.

And how much it had cost you to last out until that first cell! You had been kept in a pit, or in a box, or in a cellar. No one had addressed a human word to you. No one had looked at you with a human gaze. All they did was to peck at your brain and heart with iron beaks, and when you cried out or groaned, they laughed.

For a week or a month you had been an abandoned waif, alone among enemies, and you had already said good-bye to reason and to life; and you had already tried to kill yourself by "falling" from the radiator in such a way as to smash your brains against the iron cone of the valve.[2] Then all of a sudden you were alive again, and were brought in to your friends. And reason returned to you.

That's what your first cell is!

You waited for that cell. You dreamed of it almost as eagerly as of freedom. Meanwhile, they kept shoving you around between cracks in the wall and holes in the ground, from Lefortovo into some legendary, diabolical Sukhanovka.

Sukhanovka was the most terrible prison the MGB had. Its very name was used to intimidate prisoners; interrogators would hiss it threateningly. And you'd not be able to question those who had been there: either they were insane and talking only disconnected nonsense, or they were dead.

2. Alexander D.

Sukhanovka was a former monastery, dating back to Catherine the Great. It consisted of two buildings—one in which prisoners served out their terms, and the other a structure that contained sixty-eight monks' cells and was used for interrogations. The journey there in a Black Maria took two hours, and only a handful of people knew that the prison was really just a few miles from Lenin's Gorki estate and near the former estate of Zinaida Volkonskaya. The countryside surrounding it was beautiful.

There they stunned the newly arrived prisoner with a stand-up punishment cell again so narrow that when he was no longer able to stand he had to sag, supported by his bent knees propped against the wall. There was no alternative. They kept prisoners thus for more than a day to break their resistance. But they ate tender, tasty food at Sukhanovka, which was like nothing else in the MGB—because it was brought in from the Architects' Rest Home. They didn't maintain a separate kitchen to prepare hogwash. However, the amount one architect would eat—including fried potatoes and meatballs—was divided among twelve prisoners. As a result the prisoners were not only always hungry but also exceedingly irritable.

The cells were all built for two, but prisoners under interrogation were usually kept in them singly. The dimensions were five by six and a half feet.[3] Two little round stools were welded to the stone floor, like stumps, and at night, if the guard unlocked

3. To be absolutely precise, they were 156 centimeters by 209 centimeters. How do we know? Through a triumph of engineering calculation and a strong heart that even Sukhanovka could not break. The measurements were the work of Alexander D., who would not allow them to drive him to madness or despair. He resisted by striving to use his mind to calculate distances. In Lefortovo he counted steps, converted them into kilometers, remembered from a map how many kilometers it was from Moscow to the border, and then how many across all Europe, and how many across the Atlantic Ocean. He was sustained in this by the hope of returning to America. And in one year in Lefortovo solitary he got, so to speak, halfway across the Atlantic. Thereupon they took him to Sukhanovka. Here, realizing how few would survive to tell of it—and all our information about it comes from him—he invented a method of measuring the cell. The numbers 10/22 were stamped on the bottom of his prison bowl, and he guessed that "10" was the diameter of the bottom and "22" the diameter of the outside edge. Then he pulled a thread from a towel, made himself a tape measure, and measured everything with it. Then he began to invent a way of sleeping *standing up*, propping his knees against the small chair, and of deceiving the guard into thinking his eyes were open. He succeeded in this deception, and that was how he managed not to go insane when Ryumin kept him sleepless for a month.

a cylinder lock, a shelf dropped from the wall onto each stump and remained there for seven hours (in other words, during the hours of interrogation, since there was no daytime interrogation at Sukhanovka at all), and a little straw mattress large enough for a child also dropped down. During the day, the stool was exposed and free, but one was forbidden to sit on it. In addition, a table lay, like an ironing board, on four upright pipes. The "fortochka" in the window—the small hinged pane for ventilation —was always closed except for ten minutes in the morning when the guard cranked it open. The glass in the little window was reinforced. There were never any exercise periods out of doors. Prisoners were taken to the toilet at 6 A.M. only—i.e., when no one's stomach needed it. There was no toilet period in the evening. There were two guards for each block of seven cells, so that was why the prisoners could be under almost constant inspection through the peephole, the only interruption being the time it took the guard to step past two doors to a third. And that was the purpose of silent Sukhanovka: to leave the prisoner not a single moment for sleep, not a single stolen moment for privacy. You were always being watched and always in their power.

But if you endured the whole duel with insanity and all the trials of loneliness, and had stood firm, you deserved your first cell! And now when you got into it, your soul would heal.

If you had surrendered, if you had given in and betrayed everyone, you were also ready for your first cell. But it would have been better for you not to have lived until that happy moment and to have died a victor in the cellar, without having signed a single sheet of paper.

Now for the first time you were about to see people who were not your enemies. Now for the first time you were about to see others who were alive,[4] who were traveling your road, and whom you could join to yourself with the joyous word "we."

Yes, that word which you may have despised out in freedom, when they used it as a substitute for your own individuality ("All of us, like one man!" Or: "We are deeply angered!" Or:

---

4. And if this was in the Big House in Leningrad during the siege, you may also have seen cannibals. Those who had eaten human flesh, those who had traded in human livers from dissecting rooms, were for some reason kept by the MGB with the political prisoners.

"We demand!" Or: "We swear!"), is now revealed to you as
something sweet: you are not alone in the world! Wise, spiritual
beings—*human beings*—still exist.

■

I had been dueling for four days with the interrogator, when the
jailer, having waited until I lay down to sleep in my blindingly
lit box, began to unlock my door. I heard him all right, but
before he could say: "Get up! Interrogation!" I wanted to lie for
another three-hundredths of a second with my head on the pillow
and pretend I was sleeping. But, instead of the familiar command,
the guard ordered: "Get up! Pick up your bedding!"

Uncomprehending, and unhappy because this was my most
precious time, I wound on my footcloths, put on my boots, my
overcoat, my winter cap, and clasped the government-issue mattress in my arms. The guard was walking on tiptoe and kept
signaling me not to make any noise as he led me down a corridor
silent as the grave, through the fourth floor of the Lubyanka, past
the desk of the section supervisor, past the shiny numbers on the
cells and the olive-colored covers of the peepholes, and unlocked
Cell 67. I entered and he locked it behind me immediately.

Even though only a quarter of an hour or so had passed since
the signal to go to sleep had been given, the period allotted the
prisoners for sleeping was so fragile, and undependable, and brief
that, by the time I arrived, the inhabitants of Cell 67 were already
asleep on their metal cots with their hands on top of the blankets.[5]

At the sound of the door opening, all three started and raised
their heads for an instant. They, too, were waiting to learn which
of them might be taken to interrogation.

And those three lifted heads, those three unshaven, crumpled

5. New measures of oppression, additions to the traditional prison regulations, were invented only gradually in the internal prisons of the GPU-NKVD-
MGB. At the beginning of the twenties, prisoners were not subjected to this
particular measure, and lights were turned off at night as in the ordinary world.
But they began to keep the lights on, on the logical grounds that they needed
to keep the prisoners in view at all times. (When they used to turn the lights
on for inspection, it had been even worse.) Arms had to be kept outside the
blanket, allegedly to prevent the prisoner from strangling himself beneath the
blanket and thus escaping his just interrogation. It was demonstrated experi-
mentally that in the winter a human being always wants to keep his arms under
the bedclothes for warmth; consequently the measure was made permanent.

pale faces, seemed to me so human, so dear, that I stood there, hugging my mattress, and smiled with happiness. And they smiled. And what a forgotten look that was—after only one week!

"Are you from freedom?" they asked me. (That was the question customarily put to a newcomer.)

"Nooo," I replied. And that was a newcomer's usual first reply.

They had in mind that I had probably been arrested recently, which meant that I came *from freedom.* And I, after ninety-six hours of interrogation, hardly considered that I was from "freedom." Was I not already a veteran prisoner? Nonetheless I was *from freedom.* The beardless old man with the black and very lively eyebrows was already asking me for military and political news. Astonishing! Even though it was late February, they knew nothing about the Yalta Conference, nor the encirclement of East Prussia, nor anything at all about our own attack below Warsaw in mid-January, nor even about the woeful December retreat of the Allies. According to regulations, those under interrogation were not supposed to know anything about the outside world. And here indeed they didn't!

I was prepared to spend half the night telling them all about it—with pride, as though all the victories and advances were the work of my own hands. But at this point the duty jailer brought in my cot, and I had to set it up without making any noise. I was helped by a young fellow my own age, also a military man. His tunic and aviator's cap hung on his cot. He had asked me, even before the old man spoke, not for news of the war but for tobacco. But although I felt openhearted toward my new friends, and although not many words had been exchanged in the few minutes since I joined them, I sensed something alien in this front-line soldier who was my contemporary, and, as far as he was concerned, I clammed up immediately and forever.

(I had not yet even heard the word "nasedka"—"stool pigeon" —nor learned that there had to be one such "stool pigeon" in each cell. And I had not yet had time to think things over and conclude that I did not like this fellow, Georgi Kramarenko. But a spiritual relay, a sensor relay, had clicked inside me, and it had closed him off from me for good and all. I would not bother to recall this event if it had been the only one of its kind. But soon, with astonishment, and alarm, I became aware of the work of this internal sensor relay as a constant, inborn trait. The years passed and I lay on the same bunks, marched in the same formations, and worked in the same work brigades with hundreds of others. And always that secret sensor relay, for whose creation I deserved not the least bit of credit, worked even before I remembered it was there, worked at the first sight of a human face and eyes, at the first sound of a voice—so that I opened my heart to that person either fully or just the width of a crack, or else shut myself off from him completely. This was so consistently unfailing that all the efforts of the State Security officers to employ stool pigeons began to seem to me as insignificant as being pestered by gnats: after all, a person who has undertaken to be a traitor always betrays the fact in his face and in his voice, and even though some were more skilled in pretense, there was always something fishy about them. On the other hand, the sensor relay helped me distinguish those to whom I could from the very beginning of our acquaintance completely disclose my most precious depths and secrets—secrets for which heads roll. Thus it was that I got through eight years of imprisonment, three years of exile, and another six years of underground authorship, which were in no wise less dangerous. During all those seventeen years I recklessly revealed myself to dozens of people—and didn't make a misstep even once. (I have never read about this trait anywhere, and I mention it here for those interested in psychology. It seems to me that such spiritual sensors exist in many of us, but because we live in too technological and rational an age, we neglect this miracle and don't allow it to develop.)

We set up the cot, and I was then ready to talk—in a whisper, of course, and lying down, so as not to be sent from this cozy nest into a punishment cell. But our third cellmate, a middle-aged man whose cropped head already showed the white bristles of imminent grayness, peered at me discontentedly and said with characteristic northern severity: "Tomorrow! Night is for sleeping."

That was the most intelligent thing to do. At any minute, one of us could have been pulled out for interrogation and held until 6 A.M., when the interrogator would go home to sleep but we were forbidden to.

One night of undisturbed sleep was more important than all the fates on earth!

One more thing held me back, which I didn't quite catch right away but had felt nonetheless from the first words of my story, although I could not at this early date find a name for it: As each of us had been arrested, everything in our world had switched places, a 180-degree shift in all our concepts had occurred, and the good news I had begun to recount with such enthusiasm might not be good news for *us* at all.

My cellmates turned on their sides, covered their eyes with their handkerchiefs to keep out the light from the 200-watt bulb, wound towels around their upper arms, which were chilled from lying on top of the blankets, hid their lower arms furtively beneath them, and went to sleep.

And I lay there, filled to the brim with the joy of being among them. One hour ago I could not have counted on being with anyone. I could have come to my end with a bullet in the back of my head—which was what the interrogator kept promising me—without having seen anyone at all. Interrogation still hung over me, but how far it had retreated! Tomorrow I would be telling them my story (though not talking about my *case,* of course) and they would be telling me their stories too. How interesting tomorrow would be, one of the best days of my life! (Thus, very early and very clearly, I had this consciousness that prison was not an abyss for me, but the most important turning point in my life.)

Every detail of the cell interested me. Sleep fled, and when the peephole was not in use I studied it all furtively. Up there at the top of one wall was a small indentation the length of three bricks, covered by a dark-blue paper blind. They had already told me it was a window. Yes, there was a window in the cell. And the blind served as an air-raid blackout. Tomorrow there would be weak daylight, and in the middle of the day they would turn off the glaring light bulb. How much that meant—to have daylight in daytime!

There was also a table in the cell. On it, in the most conspicuous spot, were a teapot, a chess set, and a small pile of books. (I was not yet aware why they were so conspicuously positioned. It turned out to be another example of the Lubyanka system at work. During his once-a-minute peephole inspection, the jailer was supposed to make sure that the gifts of the prison administration were not being misused: that the teapot was not being used to break down the wall; that no one was swallowing the chessmen and thereby possibly cashing in his chips and ceasing to be a citizen of the U.S.S.R.; and that no one was starting a fire with the books in the hope of burning down the whole prison. And a prisoner's eyeglasses were considered so potentially dangerous that they were not allowed to remain on the table during the night; the prison administration took them away until morning.)

What a cozy life! Chess, books, cots with springs, decent mattresses, clean linen. I could not remember having slept like this during the whole war. There was a worn parquet floor. One could take nearly four strides from window to door in the aisle between the cots. No, indeed! This central political prison was a real resort.

And no shells were falling. I remembered their sounds: the high-pitched sobbing way up overhead, then the rising whistle, and the crash as they burst. And how tenderly the mortar shells whistled. And how everything trembled from the four blasts of what we called "Dr. Goebbels' mortar-rockets." And I remembered the wet snow and mud near Wormditt, where I had been arrested, which our men were still wading through to keep the Germans from breaking out of our encirclement.

All right then, the hell with you; if you don't want me to fight, I won't.

Among our many lost values there is one more: the high worth of those people who spoke and wrote Russian before us. It is odd that they are almost undescribed in our prerevolutionary literature. Only very rarely do we feel their breath—from Marina Tsvetayeva, or from "Mother Mariya" (in her *Recollections of Blok*). They saw too much to settle on any one thing. They reached toward the sublime too fervently to stand firmly on the earth. Before societies fall, just such a stratum of wise, thinking people emerges, people who are that and nothing more. And how they were laughed at! How they were mocked! As though they stuck in the craw of people whose deeds and actions were single-minded and narrow-minded. And the only nickname they were christened with was "rot." Because these people were a flower that bloomed too soon and breathed too delicate a fragrance. And so they were mowed down.

These people were particularly helpless in their personal lives: they could neither bend with the wind, nor pretend, nor get by; every word declared an opinion, a passion, a protest. And it was just such people the mowing machine cut down, just such people the chaff-cutter shredded.[6]

They had passed through these very same cells. But the cell walls—for the wallpaper had long since been stripped off, and they had been plastered, whitewashed, and painted more than once—gave off nothing of the past. (On the contrary, the walls now tried to listen to us with hidden microphones.) Nowhere is anything written down or reported of the former inhabitants of these cells, of the conversations held in them, of the thoughts with which earlier inmates went forth to be shot or to imprisonment on the Solovetsky Islands. And now such a volume, which would be worth forty freight car loads of our literature, will in all probability never be written.

Those still alive recount to us all sorts of trivial details: that there used to be wooden trestle beds here and that the mattresses were stuffed with straw. That, way back in 1920, before they put *muzzles* over the windows, the panes were whitewashed up to the top. By 1923 "muzzles" had been installed (although we unanimously ascribed them to Beria). They said that back in the twenties, prison authorities had been very lenient toward prisoners communicating with each other by "knocking" on the walls: this was a carry-over from the stupid tradition in the Tsarist prisons that if the prisoners were deprived of knocking, they would have no way to occupy their time. And another thing: back in the twenties all the jailers were Latvians, from the Latvian Red Army units and others, and the food was all handed out by strapping Latvian women.

All this was trivial detail, but it was certainly food for thought. I myself had needed very badly to get into this main Soviet

---

6. I am almost fearful of saying it, but it seems as though on the eve of the 1970's these people are emerging once again. That is surprising. It was almost too much to hope for.

political prison, and I was grateful that I had been sent here: I thought about Bukharin a great deal and I wanted to picture the whole thing as it had actually been. However, I had the impression that we were by now merely the remnants, and that in this respect we might just as well have been in any provincial "internal" prison.[7] Still, there was a good deal of status in being here.

And there was no reason to be bored with my companions in my new cell. They were people to listen to and people with whom to compare notes.

The old fellow with the lively eyebrows—and at sixty-three he in no way bore himself like an old man—was Anatoly Ilyich Fastenko. He was a big asset to our Lubyanka cell—both as a keeper of the old Russian prison traditions and as a living history of Russian revolutions. Thanks to all that he remembered, he somehow managed to put in perspective everything that had taken place in the past and everything that was taking place in the present. Such people are valuable not only in a cell. We badly need them in our society as a whole.

Right there in our cell we read Fastenko's name in a book about the 1905 Revolution. He had been a Social Democrat for such a long, long time that in the end, it seemed, he had ceased to be one.

He had been sentenced to his first prison term in 1904 while still a young man, but he had been freed outright under the "manifesto" proclaimed on October 17, 1905.[8]

His story about that amnesty was interesting. In those years,

---

7. One attached to a State Security headquarters.

8. Who among us has not learned by heart from our school history courses, as well as from the *Short Course* in the history of the Soviet Communist Party, that this "provocative and foul manifesto" was a mockery of freedom, that the Tsar had proclaimed: "Freedom for the dead, and prison for the living"? But the epigram was bogus. The manifesto declared that *all* political parties were to be tolerated and that a State Duma was to be convened, and it provided for an amnesty which was honest and extremely extensive. (The fact that it had been issued under duress was something else again.) Indeed, under its terms none other than *all* political prisoners without exception were to be released without reference to the term and type of punishment they had been sentenced to. Only criminals remained imprisoned. The Stalin amnesty of July 7, 1945— true, it was not issued under duress—was exactly the opposite. All the political prisoners remained *imprisoned*.

of course, there were no muzzles on the prison windows, and from the cells of the Belaya Tserkov Prison in which Fastenko was being held the prisoners could easily observe the prison courtyard and the street, and all arrivals and departures, and they could shout back and forth as they pleased to ordinary citizens outside. During the day of October 17, these outsiders, having learned of the amnesty by telegraph, announced the news to the prisoners. In their happiness the political prisoners went wild with joy. They smashed windowpanes, broke down doors, and demanded that the prison warden release them immediately. And were any of them kicked right in the snout with jackboots? Or put in punishment cells? Or was anyone deprived of library and commissary privileges? Of course not! In his distress, the warden ran from cell to cell and implored them: "Gentlemen! I beg of you, please be reasonable! I don't have the authority to release you on the basis of a telegraphed report. I must have direct orders from my superiors in Kiev. Please, I beg of you. You will have to spend the night here." And in actual fact they were most barbarously kept there for one more day.[9]

On getting back their freedom, Fastenko and his comrades immediately rushed to join the revolution. In 1906 he was sentenced to eight years at hard labor, which meant four years in irons and four in exile. He served the first four years in the Sevastopol Central Prison, where, incidentally, during his stay, a mass escape was organized from outside by a coalition of revolutionary parties: the SR's, the Anarchists, and the Social Democrats. A bomb blew a hole in the prison wall big enough for a horse and rider to go through, and two dozen prisoners— not everyone who wanted to escape, but those who had been chosen ahead of time by their parties and, right inside the prison, had been equipped with pistols by the jailers—fled through the hole and escaped. All but one: Anatoly Fastenko was selected by the Russian Social Democratic Party not to escape but to cause a disturbance in order to distract the attention of the guards.

On the other hand, when he reached exile in the Yenisei area,

---

9. After Stalin's amnesty, as I will recount later, those amnestied were held in prison for another two or three months and were forced to *slog away* just as before. And no one considered this illegal.

he did not stay there long. Comparing his stories (and later those of others who had survived) with the well-known fact that under the Tsar our revolutionaries escaped from exile by the hundreds and hundreds, and more and more of them went abroad, one comes to the conclusion that the only prisoners who did not escape from Tsarist exile were the lazy ones—because it was so easy. Fastenko "escaped," which is to say, he simply left his place of exile without a passport. He went to Vladivostok, expecting to get aboard a steamer through an acquaintance there. Somehow it did not work out. So then, still without a passport, he calmly crossed the whole of Mother Russia on a train and went to the Ukraine, where he had been a member of the Bolshevik underground and where he had first been arrested. There he was given a false passport, and he left to cross the Austrian border. That particular step was so routine, and Fastenko felt himself so safe from pursuit, that he was guilty of an astonishing piece of carelessness. Having arrived at the border, and having turned in his passport to the official there, he suddenly discovered he *could not remember* his new name. What was he to do? There were forty passengers altogether and the official had already begun to call off their names. Fastenko thought up a solution. He pretended to be asleep. He listened as the passports were handed back to their owners, and he noted that the name Makarov was called several times without anyone responding. But even at this point he was not absolutely certain it was his name. Finally, the dragon of the imperial regime bent down to the underground revolutionary and politely tapped him on the shoulder: "Mr. Makarov! Mr. Makarov! Please, here is your passport!"

Fastenko headed for Paris. There he got to know Lenin and Lunacharsky and carried out some administrative duties at the Party school at Longjumeau. At the same time he studied French, looked around him, and decided that he wanted to travel farther and see the world. Before the war he went to Canada, where he worked for a while, and he spent some time in the United States as well. He was astonished by the free and easy, yet solidly established life in these countries, and he concluded that they would never have a proletarian revolution and even that they hardly needed one.

Then, in Russia, the long-awaited revolution came, sooner

than expected, and everyone went back to Russia, and then there was one more Revolution. Fastenko no longer felt his former passion for these revolutions. But he returned, compelled by the same need that urges birds to their annual migrations.[10]

There was much about Fastenko I could not yet understand. In my eyes, perhaps the main thing about him, and the most surprising, was that he had known Lenin personally. Yet he was quite cool in recalling this. (Such was my attitude at the time that when someone in the cell called Fastenko by his patronymic alone, without using his given name—in other words simply "Ilyich," asking: "Ilyich, is it your turn to take out the latrine bucket?"—I was utterly outraged and offended because it seemed sacrilege to me not only to use Lenin's patronymic in the same sentence as "latrine bucket," but even to call anyone on earth "Ilyich" except that one man, Lenin.) For this reason, no doubt, there was much that Fastenko would have liked to explain to me that he still could not bring himself to.

Nonetheless, he did say to me, in the clearest Russian: "Thou shalt not make unto thee any graven image!" But I failed to understand him!

Observing my enthusiasm, he more than once said to me insistently: "You're a mathematician; it's a mistake for you to forget that maxim of Descartes: 'Question everything!' Question *everything!*" What did this mean—"everything"? Certainly not *everything!* It seemed to me that I had questioned enough things as it was, and that was enough of that!

Or he said: "Hardly any of the old hard-labor political pris-

10. Soon after Fastenko returned to the Motherland, he was followed by a Canadian acquaintance, a former sailor on the battleship *Potemkin*, one of the mutineers, in fact, who had escaped to Canada and become a well-to-do farmer there. This former *Potemkin* sailor sold everything he owned, his farm and cattle, and returned to his native region with his money and his new tractor to help build sacred socialism. He enlisted in one of the first agricultural communes and donated his tractor to it. The tractor was driven any which way by whoever happened along and was quickly ruined. And the former *Potemkin* sailor saw things turning out very differently from the way he had pictured them for twenty years. Those in charge were incompetents, issuing orders that any sensible farmer could see were wild nonsense. In addition, he became skinnier and skinnier, and his clothes wore out, and nothing was left of the Canadian dollars he had exchanged for paper rubles. He begged to be allowed to leave with his family, and he crossed the border as poor as when he fled from the *Potemkin*. He crossed the ocean, just as he had done then, working his way as a sailor, because he had no money for passages, and back in Canada he began life all over again as a hired hand on a farm.

oners of Tsarist times are left. I am one of the last. All the hard-labor politicals have been destroyed, and they even dissolved our society in the thirties." "Why?" I asked. "So we would not get together and discuss things." And although these simple words, spoken in a calm tone, should have been shouted to the heavens, should have shattered windowpanes, I understood them only as indicating one more of Stalin's evil deeds. It was a trouble-some fact, but without roots.

One thing is absolutely definite: not everything that enters our ears penetrates our consciousness. Anything too far out of tune with our attitude is lost, either in the ears themselves or somewhere beyond, but it is lost. And even though I clearly re-member Fastenko's many stories, I recall his opinions but vaguely. He gave me the names of various books which he strongly advised me to read whenever I got back to freedom. In view of his age and his health, he evidently did not count on getting out of prison alive, and he got some satisfaction from hoping that I would someday understand his ideas. I couldn't write down the list of books he suggested, and even as it was there was a great deal of prison life for me to remember, but I at least remembered those titles which were closest to my taste then: *Untimely Thoughts* by Gorky (whom I regarded very highly at that time, since he had, after all, outdone all the other classical Russian writers in being proletarian) and Plekhanov's *A Year in the Motherland*.

Today, when I read what Plekhanov wrote on October 28, 1917, I can clearly reconstruct what Fastenko himself thought:

. . . I am disappointed by the events of the last days not because I do not desire the triumph of the working class in Russia but precisely because I pray for it with all the strength of my soul. . . . [We must] remember Engels' remark that there could be no greater historical tragedy for the working class than to seize political power when it is not ready for it. [Such a seizure of power] would compel it to retreat far back from the positions which were won in February and March of the present year. [11]

When Fastenko returned to Russia, pressure was put on him, out of respect for his old underground exploits, to accept an

11. G. V. Plekhanov, "An Open Letter to the Workers of Petrograd," in the newspaper *Yedinstvo*, October 28, 1917.

important position. But he did not want to; instead, he accepted a modest post on the newspaper *Pravda* and then a still more modest one, and eventually he moved over to the Moscow City Planning office, where he worked in an inconspicuous job.

I was surprised. Why had he chosen such a cul-de-sac? He explained in terms I found incomprehensible. "You can't teach an old dog to live on a chain."

Realizing that there was nothing he could accomplish, Fastenko quite simply wanted, in a very human way, to stay alive. He had already gotten used to living on a very small pension—not one of the "personal" pensions especially assigned by the government, because to have accepted that sort of thing would have called attention to his close ties to many who had been shot. And he might have managed to survive in this way until 1953. But, to his misfortune, they arrested another tenant in his apartment, a debauched, perpetually drunken writer, L. S——v, who had bragged somewhere while he was drunk about owning a pistol. Owning a pistol meant an obligatory conviction for terrorism, and Fastenko, with his ancient Social Democratic past, was naturally the very picture of a terrorist. Therefore, the interrogator immediately proceeded to *nail* him for terrorism and, simultaneously, of course, for service in the French and Canadian intelligence services and thus for service in the Tsarist *Okhrana* as well.[12] And in 1945, to earn his fat pay, the fat interrogator was quite seriously leafing through the archives of the Tsarist provincial gendarmerie administrations, and composing entirely serious interrogation depositions about conspiratorial nicknames, passwords, and secret rendezvous and meetings in 1903.

On the tenth day, which was as soon as was permitted, his old wife (they had no children) delivered to Anatoly Ilyich such parcels as she could manage to put together: a piece of black bread weighing about ten and a half ounces (after all, it had been bought in the open market, where bread cost 50 rubles a pound), and a dozen peeled boiled potatoes which had been pierced by an awl when the parcel was being inspected. And the

12. This was one of Stalin's pet themes—to ascribe to every arrested Bolshevik, and in general to every arrested revolutionary, service in the Tsarist *Okhrana*. Was this merely his intolerant suspiciousness? Or was it intuition? Or, perhaps, analogy? . . .

sight of those wretched—and truly sacred—parcels tore at one's heartstrings.

That was what this human being had earned for sixty-three years of honesty and doubts.

■

The four cots in our cell left an aisle in the middle, where the table stood. But several days after my arrival, they put a fifth person in with us and inserted a cot crosswise.

They brought in the newcomer an hour before rising time—that brief, sweetly cerebral last hour, and three of us did not lift our heads. Only Kramarenko jumped up, to sponge some tobacco, and maybe, with it, some material for the interrogator. They began to converse in a whisper, and we tried not to listen. But it was quite impossible not to overhear the newcomer's whisper. It was so loud, so disquieting, so tense, and so close to a sob, that we realized it was no ordinary grief that had entered our cell. The newcomer was asking whether many were shot. Nonetheless, without turning my head, I *called them down*, asking them to talk more quietly.

When, on the signal to rise, we all instantly jumped up (lying abed earned you the punishment cell), we saw a general, no less! True, he wasn't wearing any insignia of rank, not even tabs—nor could one see where his insignia had been torn off or unscrewed, but his expensive tunic, his soft overcoat, indeed his entire figure and face, told us that he was unquestionably a general, in fact a typical general, and most certainly a full general, and not one of your run-of-the-mill major generals. He was short, stocky, very broad of shoulder and body, and notably fat in the face, but this fat, which had been acquired by eating well, endowed him, not with an appearance of good-natured accessibility, but with an air of weighty importance, of affiliation with the highest ranks. The crowning part of his face was, to be sure, not the upper portion, but the lower, which resembled a bulldog's jaw. It was there that his energy was concentrated, along with his will and authoritativeness, which were what had enabled him to attain such rank by early middle age.

We introduced ourselves, and it turned out that L. V. Z———v

was even younger than he appeared. He would be thirty-six that year—"If they don't shoot me." Even more surprisingly, it developed that he was not a general at all, not even a colonel, and not even a military man—but an *engineer!*

An engineer? I had grown up among engineers, and I could remember the engineers of the twenties very well indeed: their open, shining intellects, their free and gentle humor, their agility and breadth of thought, the ease with which they shifted from one engineering field to another, and, for that matter, from technology to social concerns and art. Then, too, they personified good manners and delicacy of taste; well-bred speech that flowed evenly and was free of uncultured words; one of them might play a musical instrument, another dabble in painting; and their faces always bore a spiritual imprint.

From the beginning of the thirties I had lost contact with that milieu. Then came the war. And here before me stood—an *engineer*, one of those who had replaced *those* destroyed.

No one could deny him one point of superiority. He was much stronger, more visceral, than *those others* had been. His shoulders and hands retained their strength even though they had not needed it for a long time. Freed from the restraints of courtesy, he stared sternly and spoke impersonally, as if he didn't even consider the possibility of a dissenting view. He had grown up differently from *those others* too, and he worked differently.

His father had plowed the earth in the most literal sense. Lenya Z——v had been one of those disheveled, unenlightened peasant boys whose wasted talents so distressed Belinsky and Tolstoi. He was certainly no Lomonosov, and he could never have gotten to the Academy on his own, but he was talented. If there had been no revolution, he would have plowed the land, and he would have become well-to-do because he was energetic and active, and he might have raised himself into the merchant class.

It being the Soviet period, however, he entered the Komsomol, and his work in the Komsomol, overshadowing his other talents, lifted him out of anonymity, out of his lowly state, out of the countryside, and shot him like a rocket through the Workers' School right into the Industrial Academy. He arrived there in 1929—at the very moment when *those other* engineers were being driven in whole herds into Gulag. It was urgently necessary for those in power to produce their own engineers—politically-conscious, loyal, one-hundred percenters, who were to become bigwigs of production, Soviet businessmen, in fact, rather than people who did things themselves. That was the moment when the famous *commanding heights* overlooking the as-yet-uncreated industries were empty. And it was the fate of Z——v's class in the Industrial Academy to occupy them.

Z——v's life became a chain of triumphs, a garland winding right up to the peak. Those were the exhausting years, from 1929 to 1933, when the civil war was being waged, not as in 1918 to 1920 with tachankas—machine guns mounted on horse-drawn carts—but with police dogs, when the long lines of those dying of famine trudged toward the railroad stations in the hope of getting to the cities, which was where the breadgrains were evidently ripening, but were refused tickets and were unable to leave—and lay dying beneath the station fences in a submissive human heap of homespun coats and bark shoes. In those same years Z——v not only did not know that bread was rationed to city dwellers but, at a time when a manual laborer was receiving 60 rubles a month in wages, he enjoyed a *student's* scholarship of 900 rubles a month. Z——v's heart did not ache for the countryside whose dust he had shaken from his feet. His new life was already soaring elsewhere among the victors and the leaders.

He never had time to be an ordinary, run-of-the-mill foreman. He was immediately assigned to a position in which he had dozens of engineers and thousands of workers under him. He was the chief engineer of the big construction projects outside Moscow. From the very beginning of the war he, of course, had an exemption from military service. He was evacuated to Alma-Ata, together with the department he worked for, and in this area he bossed even bigger construction projects on the Ili River. But in this case his workers were prisoners. The sight of those little gray people bothered him very little at the time, nor did it inspire him to any reappraisals nor compel him to take a closer look. In that gleaming orbit in which he circled, the only important thing was to achieve the projected totals, fulfillment of the plan. And it was quite enough for Z——v merely to punish a particular construction unit, a particular camp, and a particular work superintendent—after that, it was up to them to manage to fulfill their norm with their own resources. How many hours they had to work to do it or what ration they had to get along on were details that didn't concern him.

The war years deep in the rear were the best years in Z——v's life. Such is the eternal and universal aspect of war: the more grief it accumulates at one of its poles, the more joy it generates at the other. Z——v had not only a bulldog's jaw but also a swift, enterprising, businesslike grasp. With the greatest skill he immediately switched to the economy's new wartime rhythm. Everything for victory. Give and take, and the war will write it all off. He made just one small concession to the war. He got along without suits and neckties, and, camouflaging himself in khaki color, had chrome-leather boots made to order and donned a general's tunic—the very one in which he appeared before us. That was fashionable and not uncommon at the time. It provoked neither anger in the war-wounded nor reproachful glances from women.

Women usually looked at him with another sort of glance. They came to him to get well fed, to get warmed up, to have some fun. He had wild money passing through his hands. His billfold bulged like a little barrel with expense money, and to him ten-ruble notes were like kopecks, and thousands like single rubles. Z——v didn't hoard them, regret spending them, or keep count of them. He counted only the women who passed through his hands, and particularly those he had "uncorked." This count was his sport. In the cell he assured us that his arrest had broken off the count at 290 plus, and he regretted that he had not reached 300. Since it was wartime and the women were alone and lonely. And since, in addition to his power and money, he had the virility of a Rasputin, one can probably believe him. And he was quite prepared to describe one episode after another. It was just that our ears were not prepared to listen to him. Even though no danger threatened him during those last years, he had frantically grabbed these women, messed them up, and then thrown them away, like a greedy diner eating boiled crayfish— grabbing one, devouring it, sucking it, then grabbing the next.

He was so accustomed to the malleability of material, to his own vigorous boarlike drive across the land! (Whenever he was especially agitated, he would dash about the cell like a powerful boar who might just knock down an oak tree in his path.) He was so accustomed to an environment in which all the leaders were his own kind of people, in which one could always make a deal, work things out, cover them up! He forgot that the more success one gains, the more envy one arouses. As he found out during his interrogation, a dossier had been accumulating against him since way back in 1936, on the basis of an anecdote he had carelessly told at a drunken party. More denunciations had followed, and more testimony from agents (after all, one has to take women to restaurants, where all types of people see you!). Another report pointed out that he had been in no hurry to leave Moscow in 1941, that he had been waiting for the Germans. He had in actual fact stayed on longer than he should have, apparently because of some woman. Z——v took great care to keep his business deals clean. But he quite forgot the existence of Article 58. Nonetheless, the avalanche might not have overwhelmed him had he not grown overconfident and refused to supply building materials for a certain prosecutor's dacha. That was what caused his dormant case to awaken and tremble and start rolling. (And this was one more instance of the fact that cases begin with the material self-interest of the blueboys.)

The scope of Z——v's concepts of the world can be judged by the fact that he believed there was a *Canadian* language. During the course of two months in the cell, he did not read a single book, not even a whole page, and if he did read a paragraph, it was only to be distracted from his gloomy thoughts about his interrogation. It was clear from his conversation that he had read even less in freedom. He knew of Pushkin—as the hero of bawdy stories. And of Tolstoi he knew only, in all probability, that he was—a Deputy of the Supreme Soviet!

On the other hand, was he a one hundred percent loyal Communist? Was he that same socially-conscious proletarian who had been brought up to replace Palchinsky and von Meck and their ilk? This was what was really surprising—he was most certainly not! We once discussed the whole course of the war with him, and I said that from the very first moment I had never had any doubts about our victory over the Germans. He looked at me sharply; he did not believe me. "Come on, what are you saying?" And then he took his head in his hands. "Oh, Sasha,

Sasha, and I was convinced the Germans would win! That's what
did me in!" There you are! He was one of the "organizers of
victory," but each day he believed in the Germans' success and
awaited their inevitable arrival. Not because he loved them, but
simply because he had so sober an insight into our economy
(which I, of course, knew nothing about and therefore believed
in).

All of us in the cell were deeply depressed, but none of us
was so crushed as Z——v, none took his arrest as so profound
a tragedy. He learned from us that he would get no more than a
tenner, that during his years in camp he would, of course, be a
work superintendent, and that he would not have to experience
real suffering, as indeed he never did. But this did not comfort
him in the least. He was too stricken by the collapse of such a
glorious life. After all, it was his one and only life on earth, and
no one else's, which had interested him all his thirty-six years.
And more than once, sitting on his cot in front of the table,
propping his pudgy head on his short, pudgy arm, he would start
to sing quietly, in a singsong voice and with lost, befogged eyes:

> Forgotten and abandoned
> Since my young, early years,
> I was left a tiny orphan. . . .

He could never get any further than that. At that point, he would
break into explosive sobs. All that bursting strength which could
not break through the walls that enclosed him he turned inward,
toward self-pity.

And toward pity for his wife. Every tenth day (since oftener
was not allowed) his wife, long since unloved, brought him rich
and bountiful food parcels—the whitest of white bread, butter,
red caviar, veal, sturgeon. He would give each of us a sandwich
and a twist of tobacco and then bend down to the provisions he
had set before himself, delighting in odors and colors that con-
trasted vividly with the bluish potatoes of the old underground
revolutionary Fastenko. Then his tears would start to pour again,
redoubled. He recalled out loud his wife's tears, whole years of
tears: some due to love notes she had found in his trousers, some
to some woman's underpants in his overcoat pocket, stuffed
there hurriedly in his automobile and forgotten. And when he
was thus torn by burning self-pity, his armor of evil energy fell

away, and before us was a ruined and clearly a good person.
I was astonished that he could sob so. The Estonian Arnold
Susi, our cellmate with the gray bristles in his hair, explained it
to me: "Cruelty is invariably accompanied by sentimentality.
It is the law of complementaries. For example, in the case of the
Germans, the combination is a national trait."

Fastenko, on the other hand, was the most cheerful person
in the cell, even though, in view of his age, he was the only one
who could not count on surviving and returning to freedom.
Flinging an arm around my shoulders, he would say:

> To *stand up* for the truth is nothing!
> For truth you have to *sit* in jail!

Or else he taught me to sing this song from Tsarist hard-labor
days:

> And if we have to perish
> In mines and prisons wet,
> Our cause will ever find renown
> In future generations yet.

And I believe this! May these pages help his faith come true!

∎

The sixteen-hour days in our cell were short on outward events,
but they were so interesting that I, for example, now find a mere
sixteen minutes' wait for a trolley bus much more boring. There
were no events worthy of attention, and yet by evening I would
sigh because once more there had not been enough time, once
more the day had flown. The events were trivial, but for the first
time in my life I learned to look at them through a magnifying
glass.

The most difficult hours in the day were the first two. At the
rattle of the key in the lock (for at the Lubyanka there were no
"swill troughs,"[13] and it was necessary to unlock the door even

13. Special large openings in the cell doors of many Russian prisons [known
to the prisoners as "kormushki," meaning "swill troughs" or "fodder bins"].
Their lids dropped down to make tiny tables. Conversations with the jailers were
carried on through these openings, food was handed through, and prison papers
were shoved through for the prisoners to sign.

to shout: "Time to get up!"), we jumped up without lingering, made our beds, and sat down on them feeling empty and helpless, with the electric light still burning. This enforced wakefulness from 6 A.M. on—at a time when the brain was still lazy from sleep, the whole world seemed repulsive and all of life wrecked, and there was not a gulp of air in the cell—was particularly ludicrous for those who had been under interrogation all night and had only just been able to get to sleep. But don't try to steal extra sleep! If you should try to doze off, leaning slightly against the wall, or propped over the table as if studying the chessboard, or relaxing over a book lying conspicuously open on your knees, the key would sound a warning knock on the door, or, worse yet, the door with that rattling lock would suddenly open silently, since the Lubyanka jailers were specially trained to do just that, and like a spirit passing through a wall, the swift and silent shadow of the junior sergeant would take three steps into the cell, hook onto you as you slept, and maybe take you off to the punishment cell; or maybe they would take book privileges away from the whole cell or deprive everyone of their daily walk —a cruel, unjust punishment for all, and there were other punishments, too, in the black lines of the prison regulations. Read them! They hang in every cell. If, incidentally, you needed glasses to read, then you wouldn't be reading books or the sacred regulations either during those two starving hours. Eyeglasses were taken away every night, and it was evidently still "dangerous" for you to have them during those two hours when no one brought anything to the cell, and no one came to it. No one asked about anything, and no one was summoned—the interrogators were still sleeping sweetly. And the prison administration was just opening its eyes, coming to. Only the vertukhai, the turnkeys, were active and energetic, opening the peephole cover once a minute for inspection.[14]

But one procedure was carried out during those two hours: the morning trip to the toilet. When the guard roused us, he made an important announcement. He designated the person from our

14. During my time this word "vertukhai" had already come into wide currency for the jailers. It was said to have originated with Ukrainian guards who were always ordering: "Stoi, ta ne vertukhais!" And yet it is also worth recalling the English word for jailer, "turnkey," is "verti klyuch" in Russian. Perhaps a "vertukhai" here in Russia is also "one who turns the key."

cell who was to be entrusted with the responsibility of carrying out the latrine bucket. (In more isolated, ordinary prisons the prisoners had enough freedom of speech and self-government to decide this question themselves. But in the Chief Political Prison such an important event could not be left to chance.) So then you formed up in single file, hands behind your backs, and, at the head of the line, the responsible latrine-bucket-bearer carried chest high the two-gallon tin pail with a lid on it. When you reached your goal, you were locked in again, each having first been handed a small piece of paper, the size of two railway tickets. (At the Lubyanka this was not particularly interesting. The paper was blank and white. But there were enticing prisons where they gave you pages of books—and what reading that was! You could try to guess *whence* it came, read it over on both sides, digest the contents, evaluate the style—and when words had been cut in half that was particularly essential! You could trade with your comrades. In some places they handed out pages from the once progressive *Granat Encyclopedia*, and sometimes, it's awful to say it, from the *classics*, and I don't mean belles-lettres either. Visits to the toilet thus became a means of acquiring knowledge.)

But there's not that much to laugh at. We are dealing with that crude necessity which it is considered unsuitable to refer to in literature (although there, too, it has been said, with immortal adroitness: "Blessed is he who early in the morning . . ."). This allegedly natural start of the prison day set a trap for the prisoner that would grip him all day, a trap for his spirit—which was what hurt. Given the lack of physical activity in prison, and the meager food, and the muscular relaxation of sleep, a person was just not able to square accounts with nature immediately after rising. Then they quickly returned you to the cell and locked you up—until 6 P.M., or, in some prisons, until morning. At that point, you would start to get worried and worked up by the approach of the daytime interrogation period and the events of the day itself, and you would be loading yourself up with your bread ration and water and gruel, but no one was going to let you visit that glorious accommodation again, easy access to which *free people* are incapable of appreciating. This debilitating, banal need could make itself felt day after day shortly after the morning toilet trip and would then torment you the whole day long, oppress you, rob you of the inclination to talk, read, think, and even of any desire to eat the meager food.

People in the cells sometimes discussed how the Lubyanka system and schedule, and those in other prisons as well, had come into being, whether through calculated brutality or as a matter of chance. My opinion is that both factors are involved. The rising time is, obviously, a matter of malicious intent, but much of the rest evolved automatically at first (which is true of many of the brutalities of life generally) and was then discovered by the powers that be to be useful and was therefore made permanent. The shifts change at 8 A.M. and 8 P.M., and it was more convenient for everyone to take the prisoners to the toilet at the end of a shift. (Letting them out singly in the middle of the day was extra trouble and meant extra precautions, and no one got paid for that.) The same was true of the business with eyeglasses: Why should one worry about that at 6 A.M.? They could be returned to the owners just before the end of the shift instead.

So now we heard them being brought around—doors were being opened. We could guess whether someone wore them in the cell next door. (And didn't your codefendant wear spectacles? But we didn't feel up to knocking out a message on the wall. This was punished very severely.) A moment later they would bring the eyeglasses to our cell. Fastenko used them only for reading. But Susi needed them all the time. He could stop squinting once he'd put them on. Thanks to his horn-rimmed glasses and straight lines above the eyes, his face became severe, perspicacious, exactly the face of an educated man of our century as we might picture it to ourselves. Back before the Revolution he had studied at the Faculty of History and Philology of the University of Petrograd, and throughout his twenty years in independent Estonia he had preserved intact the purest Russian speech, which he spoke like a native. Later, in Tartu, he had studied law. In addition to Estonian, he spoke English and German, and through all these years he continued to read the London *Economist* and the German scientific "Berichte" summaries. He had studied the constitutions and the codes of law of various countries—and in our cell he represented Europe worthily and with restraint. He had been a leading lawyer in Estonia and been known as "kuldsuu"—meaning "golden-tongued."

There was new activity in the corridor. A free-loader in a gray smock—a husky young fellow who had certainly not been at the front—brought a tray with our five bread rations and ten lumps of sugar. Our cell stoolie hovered over them, even though we would inevitably cast lots for them—which we did because every least detail of this was important: the heel of the loaf, for instance, and the number of smaller pieces needed to make the total weight come out right, and how the crust adheres, or doesn't, to the inside of the bread—and it was better that fate should decide.[15] But the stoolie felt he just had to hold everything in his hands for at least a second so that some bread and sugar molecules would cling to his palms.

That pound of unrisen wet bread, with its swamplike sogginess of texture, made half with potato flour, was our *crutch* and the main event of the day. Life had begun! The day had begun—this was when it began! And everyone had countless problems. Had he allocated his bread ration wisely the day before? Should he cut it with a thread? Or break it up greedily? Or slowly, quietly nip off pieces one by one? Should he wait for tea or pile into it right now? Should he leave some for dinner or finish it off at lunch? And how much?

In addition to these wretched dilemmas, what wide-ranging discussions and arguments went on (for our tongues had been liberated and with bread we were once more men) provoked by this one-pound chunk in our hand, consisting more of water than of grain. (Incidentally, Fastenko explained that the workers of Moscow were eating the very same bread at that time.) And, generally speaking, was there any real breadgrain in this bread at all? And what additives were in it? (There was at least one person in every cell who knew all about additives, for, after all, who hadn't eaten them during these past decades?) Discussions and reminiscences began. About the white bread they had baked back in the twenties—springy round loaves, like sponge cake inside, with a buttery reddish-brown top crust and a bottom crust that still had a trace of ash from the coals of the hearth—that bread had

15. Where indeed in our country did this casting of lots not happen? It was the result of our universal and endless hunger. In the army, all rations were divided up the same way. And the Germans, who could hear what was going on from their trenches, teased us about it: "Who gets it? The political commissar!"

vanished for good! Those born in 1930 would never know what *bread* is. Friends, this is a forbidden subject! We agreed not to say one word about *food*.

Once again there was movement in the corridor—tea was being brought around. A new young tough in a gray smock carrying pails. We put our teapot out in the corridor and he poured straight into it from a pail without a spout—into the teapot and onto the runner and the floor beneath it. And the whole corridor was polished like that of a first-class hotel.[16]

And that was all they gave us. Whatever cooked food we got would be served at 1 P.M. and at 4 P.M., one meal almost on the heels of the other. You could then spend the next twenty-one hours remembering it. (And that wasn't prison brutality either: it was simply a matter of the kitchen staff having to do its work as quickly as possible and leave.)

At nine o'clock the morning check-up took place. For a long while beforehand, we could hear especially loud turns of the key and particularly sharp knocks on the doors. Then one of the duty lieutenants for the whole floor would march forward and enter, almost as erect as if he were standing at attention. He would take two steps forward and look sternly at us. We would be on our feet. (We didn't even dare remember that political prisoners were once not required to rise.) It was no work at all to count us— he could do it in a glance—but this was a moment for testing our rights. For we did have some rights, after all, although we did not really know them, and it was his job to hide them from us. The whole strength of the Lubyanka training showed itself in a totally machinelike manner: no expression on the face, no inflection, not a superfluous word.

And which of our rights did we know about? A request to have our shoes repaired. An appointment with the doctor. Although if they actually took you to the doctor, you would not be happy

16. Soon the biologist Timofeyev-Ressovsky, whom I have already mentioned, would be brought here from Berlin. There was nothing at the Lubyanka, it appeared, which so offended him as this spilling on the floor. He considered it striking evidence of the lack of professional pride on the part of the jailers, and of all of us in our chosen work. He multiplied the 27 years of Lubyanka's existence as a prison by 730 times (twice for each day of the year), and then by 111 cells—and he would seethe for a long time because it was easier to spill boiling water on the floor 2,188,000 times and then come and wipe it up with a rag the same number of times than to make pails with spouts.

about the consequences. There the machinelike Lubyanka manner would be particularly striking. He didn't ask: "What's your trouble?" That would take too many words, and one couldn't pronounce the phrase without any inflection. He would ask curtly: "Troubles?" And if you began to talk at too great length about your ailment, he would cut you off. It was clear anyway. A toothache? Extract it. You could have arsenic. A filling? We don't fill teeth here. (That would have required additional appointments and created a somewhat humane atmosphere.)

The prison doctor was the interrogator's and executioner's right-hand man. The beaten prisoner would come to on the floor only to hear the doctor's voice: "You can continue, the pulse is normal." After a prisoner's five days and nights in a punishment cell the doctor inspects the frozen, naked body and says: "You can continue." If a prisoner is beaten to death, he signs the death certificate: "Cirrhosis of the liver" or "Coronary occlusion." He gets an urgent call to a dying prisoner in a cell and he takes his time. And whoever behaves differently is not kept on in the prison.[17]

But our *stoolie* was better informed about his rights. (According to him he had already been under interrogation eleven months. And he was taken to interrogation only during the day.) He spoke up and asked for an appointment with the prison chief. What, the chief of the whole Lubyanka? Yes. His name was taken down. (And in the evening, after taps, when the interrogators were already in their offices, he was summoned. And he returned with some makhorka.) This was very crude, of course, but so far they had not been able to think up anything better. It would have been a big expense to convert entirely to microphones in the walls and impossible to listen in on all 111 cells for whole days at a time. Who would do it? Stool pigeons were cheaper and would continue to be used for a long time to come. But Kramarenko had a hard time with us. Sometimes he eavesdropped so hard that the sweat poured from him, and we could see from his face that he didn't understand what we were saying.

There was one additional right—the privilege of writing applications and petitions (which replaced freedom of the press, of assembly, and of the ballot, all of which we had lost when we

17. Dr. F. P. Gaaz would have earned nothing extra in our country.

left freedom). Twice a month the morning duty officer asked: "Who wants to write a petition?" And they listed everyone who wanted to. In the middle of the day they would lead you to an individual box and lock you up in it. In there, you could write whomever you pleased: the Father of the Peoples, the Central Committee of the Party, the Supreme Soviet, Minister Beria, Minister Abakumov, the General Prosecutor, the Chief Military Prosecutor, the Prison Administration, the Investigation Department. You could complain about your arrest, your interrogator, even the chief of the prison! In each and every case your petition would have no effect whatever. It would not be stapled into any file, and the most senior official to read it would be your own interrogator. However, you were in no position to prove this. In fact, it was rather more likely that he would *not read it,* because no one would be able to read it. On a piece of paper measuring seven by ten centimeters—in other words, three by four inches— a little larger than the paper given you each morning at the toilet, with a pen broken in the middle or bent into a hook, and an inkwell with pieces of rag in it and ink diluted with water, you would just be able to scratch out "Petit . . ." Then the letters would all run together on the cheap paper, "ion" couldn't be worked into the line, and everything would come through on the other side of the sheet.

You might have still other rights, but the duty officer would keep quiet about them. And you wouldn't be losing much, truth to tell, even if you didn't find out about them.

The check-up came and went. And the day began. The interrogators were already arriving there somewhere. The turnkey would summon one of us with a great air of secrecy; he called out the first letter of the name only. Like this: "Whose name begins with 'S'?" and: "Whose name begins with 'F'?" Or perhaps: "Whose begins with 'M'?—with 'Am'?" And you yourself had to be quick-witted enough to recognize that it was you he wanted and offer yourself as a victim. This system was introduced to prevent mistakes on the jailer's part. He might have called out a name in the wrong cell, and that way we might have found out who else was in prison. And yet, though cut off from the entire prison, we were not deprived of news from other cells. Because they tried to crowd in as many prisoners as possible, they shuffled them about from cell to cell, and every newcomer brought all his accumulated experience to his new cell. Thus it was that we, imprisoned on the fourth floor, knew all about the cellar cells, about the boxes on the first floor, about the darkness on the second floor, where the women were all kept, about the split-level arrangement of the fifth, and about the biggest cell of all on the fifth floor—No. 111. Before my time, the children's writer Bondarin had been a prisoner in our cell, and before that he had been on the women's floor with some Polish correspondent or other, who had previously been a cellmate of Field Marshal von Paulus—and that was how we learned all the details about von Paulus.

The period for being summoned to interrogation passed. And for those left in the cell a long, pleasant day stretched ahead, lightened by opportunities and not overly darkened by duties. Duties could include sterilizing the cots with a blow torch twice a month. (At the Lubyanka, matches were categorically forbidden to prisoners; to get a light for a cigarette we had to signal patiently with a finger when the peephole was opened, thus asking the jailer for a light. But blow torches were entrusted to us without hesitation.) And once a week we might be called into the corridor to have our faces clipped with a dull clipper—allegedly a right but strongly resembling a duty. And one might be assigned the duty of cleaning the parquet floor in the cell. (Z——v always avoided this work because it was beneath his dignity, like any other work, in fact.) We got out of breath quickly because we were underfed; otherwise we would have considered this duty a privilege. It was such gay, lively work—pushing the brush forward with one's bare foot, torso pulled back, and then turn about; forward-back, forward-back, and forget all your grief! Shiny as a mirror! A Potemkin prison!

Besides, we didn't have to go on being overcrowded in our old Cell 67 any longer. In the middle of March they added a sixth prisoner to our number, and since here in the Lubyanka they did not fill all the cells with board bunks, nor make you sleep on the floor, they transferred all of us into a beauty of a cell—No. 53. (I would advise anyone who has not yet been in it to pay it a visit.) This was not a cell. It was a palace chamber set aside as a sleeping apartment for distinguished travelers! The Rossiya Insurance Company, without a thought for economy, had raised the height of the ceiling in this wing to sixteen and a half feet.[18] (Oh, what four-story bunks the chief of counterintelligence at the front would have slapped in here. And he could have gotten one hundred people in, results guaranteed.) And the window! It was such an enormous window that standing on its sill the jailer could hardly reach the "fortochka," that hinged ventilation pane. One section of this window alone would have made a fine whole window in an ordinary house. Only the riveted steel sheets of the *muzzle* closing off four-fifths of it reminded us that we were not in a palace after all.

Nonetheless, on clear days, above this muzzle, from the wall of the Lubyanka courtyard, from some windowpane or other on the sixth or seventh floor, we now and then got a pale reflection of a ray of sunlight. To us it was a real ray of sunlight—a living, dear being! We followed with affection its climb up the wall. And every step it made was filled with meaning, presaging the time of our daily outing in the fresh air, counting off several half-hours before lunch. Then, just before lunch, it disappeared.

And our rights included being let out for a walk, reading books, telling one another about the past, listening and learning, arguing and being educated! And we would be rewarded by a lunch that included two courses! Too good to be true!

The walk was bad on the first three floors of the Lubyanka. The prisoners were let out into a damp, low-lying little courtyard —the bottom of a narrow well between the prison buildings. But the prisoners on the fourth and fifth floors, on the other hand, were taken to an eagle's perch—on the roof of the fifth floor. It had a concrete floor; there were concrete walls three times the height of a man; we were accompanied by an unarmed jailer; on the watch tower was a sentinel with an automatic weapon. But the air was real and the sky was real! "Hands behind your back! Line up in pairs! No talking! No stopping!" Such were the commands, but they forgot to forbid us to throw back our heads. And, of course, we did just that. Here one could see not a re-

18. This company acquired a piece of Moscow earth that was well acquainted with blood. The innocent Vereshchagin was torn to pieces in 1812 on Furkasovsky, near the Rostopchin house. And the murderess and serf-owner Saltychikha lived—and killed serfs—on the other side of the Bolshaya Lubyanka. (*Po Moskve* [*In Moscow*], edited by N. A. Geinike and others, Moscow, Sabashnikov Publishers, 1917, p. 231.)

flected, not a secondhand Sun, but the real one! The real, eternally living Sun itself! Or its golden diffusion through the spring clouds.

Spring promises everyone happiness—and tenfold to the prisoner. Oh, April sky! It didn't matter that I was in prison. Evidently, they were not going to shoot me. And in the end I would become wiser here. I would come to understand many things here, Heaven! I would correct my mistakes yet, O Heaven, not for *them* but for you, Heaven! I had come to understand those mistakes here, and I would correct them!

As if from a pit, from the far-off lower reaches, from Dzerzhinsky Square, the hoarse earthly singing of the automobile horns rose to us in a constant refrain. To those who were dashing along to the tune of those honkings, they seemed the trumpets of creation, but from here their insignificance was very clear.

The walk in the fresh air lasted only twenty minutes, but how much there was about it to concern oneself with; how much one had to accomplish while it lasted.

In the first place, it was very interesting to try to figure out the layout of the entire prison while they were taking you there and back, and to calculate where those tiny hanging courtyards were, so that at some later date, out in freedom, one could walk along the square and spot their location. We made many turns on the way there, and I invented the following system: Starting from the cell itself, I would count every turn to the right as plus one, and every turn to the left as minus one. And, no matter how quickly they made us turn, the idea was not to try to *picture* it hastily to oneself, but to count up the total. If, in addition, through some staircase window, you could catch a glimpse of the backs of the Lubyanka water nymphs, half-reclining against the pillared turret which hovered over the square itself, and you could remember the exact point in your count when this happened, then back in the cell you could orient yourself and figure out what your own window looked out on.

And during that outdoor walk you concentrated on breathing as much fresh air as possible.

There, too, alone beneath that bright heaven, you had to imagine your bright future life, sinless and without error.

There, too, was the best place of all to talk about the most dangerous subjects. It didn't matter that conversation during the walk was forbidden. One simply had to know how to manage it. The compensation was that in all likelihood you could not be overheard either by a stoolie or by a microphone.

During these walks I tried to get into a pair with Susi. We talked together in the cell, but we liked to try talking about the main things here. We hadn't come together quickly. It took some time. But he had already managed to tell me a great deal. I acquired a new capability from him: to accept patiently and purposefully things that had never had any place in my own plans and had, it seemed, no connection at all with the clearly outlined direction of my life. From childhood on, I had somehow known that my objective was the history of the Russian Revolution and that nothing else concerned me. To understand the Revolution I had long since required nothing beyond Marxism. I cut myself off from everything else that came up and turned my back on it. And now fate brought me together with Susi. He breathed a completely different sort of air. And he would tell me passionately about his own interests, and these were Estonia and democracy. And although I had never expected to become interested in Estonia, much less bourgeois democracy, I nevertheless kept listening and listening to his loving stories of twenty free years in that modest, work-loving, small nation of big men whose ways were slow and set. I listened to the principles of the Estonian constitution, which had been borrowed from the best of European experience, and to how their hundred-member, one-house parliament had worked. And, though the *why* of it wasn't clear, I began to like it all and store it all away in my experience.[19] I listened willingly to their fatal history: the tiny Estonian anvil had, from way, way back, been caught between two hammers, the Teutons and the Slavs. Blows showered on it from East and West in turn; there was no end to it, and there still isn't. And there was the well-known (totally unknown) story of how we Russians wanted to take them over in one fell swoop in 1918, but they refused to yield. And how, later on, Yudenich spoke contemptuously of their Finnish heritage, and we ourselves christened them "White Guard Bandits." Then the Estonian gymnasium students enrolled as volunteers. We struck at Estonia again in 1940, and again in

19. Susi remembered me later as a strange mixture of Marxist and democrat. Yes, things were wildly mixed up inside me at that time.

1941, and again in 1944. Some of their sons were conscripted by the Russian Army, and others by the German Army, and still others ran off into the woods. The elderly Tallinn intellectuals discussed how they might break out of that iron ring, break away somehow, and live for themselves and by themselves. Their Premier might, possibly, have been Tief, and their Minister of Education, say, Susi. But neither Churchill nor Roosevelt cared about them in the least; but "Uncle Joe" did. And during the very first nights after the Soviet armies entered Tallinn, all these dreamers were seized in their Tallinn apartments. Fifteen of them were imprisoned in various cells of the Moscow Lubyanka, one in each, and were charged under Article 58-2 with the criminal desire for national self-determination.

Each time we returned to the cell from our walk was like being arrested again. Even in our very special cell the air seemed stifling after the outdoors. And it would have been good to have a snack afterward too. But it was best not to think about it—not at all. It was bad if one of the prisoners who received food parcels tactlessly spread out his treasures at the wrong time and began to eat. All right, we'll develop self-control! It was bad, too, to be betrayed by the author of the book you were reading—if he began to drool over food in the greatest detail. Get away from me, Gogol! Get away from me, Chekhov, too! They both had too much food in their books. "He didn't really feel like eating, but nevertheless he ate a helping of veal and drank some beer." The son-of-a-bitch! It was better to read spiritual things! Dostoyevsky was the right kind of author for prisoners to read! Yet even in Dostoyevsky you could find that passage "The children went hungry. For several days they had seen nothing but bread and *sausage*."

The Lubyanka library was the prison's principal ornament. True, the librarian was repulsive—a blond spinster with a horsy build, who did everything possible to make herself ugly. Her face was so whitened that it looked like a doll's immobile mask; her lips were purple; and her plucked eyebrows were black. (You might say that was her own business, but we would have enjoyed it more if she had been a charmer. However, perhaps the chief of the Lubyanka had already taken that into consideration?) But here was a wonder: once every ten days, when she came to take away our books, she listened to our requests for new ones! She heard us out in that same machinelike, inhuman Lubyanka manner, and it was impossible to judge whether she had heard the authors' names or the titles, whether, indeed, she had heard our words at all. She would leave, and we would experience several hours of nervous but happy expectation. During those hours all the books we had returned were leafed through and checked. They were examined in case we had left pinpricks or dots underneath certain letters—for there was such a method of clandestine intramural communication—or we had underlined passages we liked with a fingernail. We were worried even though we were totally innocent. They might come to us and say that they had discovered pinpricks. They were always right, of course; and, as always, no proof was required. And on that basis we could be deprived of books for three months—if, indeed, they didn't put the whole cell on a punishment-cell regime. It would be very sad to have to do without books during the best and brightest of our prison months, before we were tossed into the pit of camp. Indeed, we were not only afraid; we actually trembled, just as we had in youth after sending a love letter, while we waited for an answer. Will it come or not? And what will it say?

Then at last the books arrived and determined the pattern of the next ten days. They would decide whether we would chiefly concentrate on reading or, if they had brought us trash, be spending more time in conversation. They brought exactly as many books as there were people in the cell, this being the sort of calculation appropriate to a bread cutter and not a librarian: one book for one person, six books for six persons. The cells with the largest number of prisoners were the best off.

Sometimes the spinster would fill our orders miraculously. But even when she was careless about them, things could turn out interestingly. Because the library of the Big Lubyanka was unique. In all probability it had been assembled out of confiscated private libraries. The bibliophiles who had collected those books had already rendered up their souls to God. But the main thing was that while State Security had been busy censoring and emasculating all the libraries of the nation for decades, it forgot to dig in its own bosom. Here, in its very den, one could read Zamyatin, Pilnyak, Panteleimon Romanov, and any volume at all of the complete works of Merezhkovsky. (Some people wisecracked that they allowed us to read forbidden books because they already regarded us as dead. But I myself think that the Lubyanka librarians hadn't the faintest concept of what they were giving us—they were simply lazy and ignorant.)

We used to read intensively during the hours before lunch. But it sometimes happened that a single phrase would get you going and drive you to pace from window to door, from door to window. And you would want to show somebody what you had read and explain what it implied, and then an argument would get started. It was a time for sharp arguments, as well!

I often argued with Yuri Y.

■

On that March morning when they led the five of us into palatial Cell 53, they had just added a sixth prisoner to our group.

He entered, it seemed, like a spirit, and his shoes made no noise against the floor. He entered and, not sure that he could stay on his feet, leaned against the door frame. The bulb had been turned off in the cell and the morning light was dim. However, the newcomer did not have his eyes wide open. He squinted, and he kept silent.

The cloth of his military field jacket and trousers did not identify him as coming from the Soviet, or the German, or the Polish, or the English Army. The structure of his face was elongated. There was very little Russian in it. And he was painfully thin. And not only very thin but very tall.

We spoke to him in Russian—and he kept silent. Susi addressed him in German—he still kept silent. Fastenko tried French and English—with the same result. Only gradually did a smile appear on his emaciated, yellow, half-dead face—the only such smile I had ever seen in my life.

"Pee–eeple," he uttered weakly, as if he were coming out of a faint, or as if he had been waiting all night long to be executed. And he reached out his weak, emaciated hand. It held a small bundle tied up in a rag. Our stoolie understood instantly what was in it, threw himself on it, grabbed it, and opened it up on the table. There was half a pound of light tobacco. He had instantly managed to roll himself a cigarette four times the size of an ordinary one.

Thus, after three weeks' confinement in a cellar box, Yuri Nikolayevich Y. made his appearance in our cell.

From the time of the 1929 incidents on the Chinese Eastern Railroad, the song had been sung throughout the land:

> Its steel breast brushing aside our enemies,
> The *27th* stands on guard!

The chief of artillery of this 27th Infantry Division, formed back in the Civil War, was the Tsarist officer Nikolai Y. (I remembered the name because it was the name of one of the authors of our artillery textbook.) In a heated freight car that had been converted into living quarters, and always accompanied by his wife, this artillery officer had crossed and recrossed the Volga and the Urals, sometimes moving east and sometimes west. It was in this heated freight car that his son, Yuri, born in 1917, and twin brother, therefore, of the Revolution itself, spent his first years.

That was a long time ago. Since then his father had settled in Leningrad, in the Academy, and lived well and frequented high circles, and the son graduated from the officer candidate school. During the Finnish War, Yuri wanted desperately to fight for the Motherland, and friends of his father got him an appointment as an aide on an army staff. Yuri did not have to crawl on his stomach to destroy the Finns' concrete artillery emplacements, nor get trapped and encircled on a scouting mission, nor freeze in the snow under sniper bullets—but his service was nevertheless rewarded, not with some ordinary decoration, but with the Order of the Red Banner, which fitted neatly on his field shirt. Thus he completed the Finnish War in full consciousness of its justice and his own part in it.

But he didn't have things so easy in the next war. The battery he commanded was surrounded near Luga. They scattered and were caught and driven off into prisoner-of-war camps. Yuri found himself in a concentration camp for officers near Vilnius.

In every life there is one particular event that is decisive for the entire person—for his fate, his convictions, his passions. Two years in that camp shook Yuri up once and for all. It is impossible to catch with words or to circumvent with syllogisms what that camp was. That was a camp to die in—and whoever did not die was compelled to reach certain conclusions.

Among those who could survive were the Ordners—the internal camp police or Polizei—chosen from among the prisoners. Of course, Yuri did not become an Ordner. The cooks managed to survive too. The translators could survive also—they needed them. But though Yuri had a superb command of conversational German, he concealed this fact. He realized that a translator would have to betray his fellow prisoners. One could also postpone dying by digging graves, but others stronger and more dexterous got those jobs. Yuri announced that he was an artist. And, actually, as part of his varied education at home, he had been given lessons in painting. Yuri didn't paint badly in oils, and only his desire to follow in his father's footsteps—for he had been proud of his father—had kept him from entering art school.

Together with an elderly artist (I regret that I don't remember his name) he occupied a separate room in the barracks. And there Yuri painted for nothing schmaltzy pictures such as *Nero's Feast* and the *Chorus of Elves* and the like for the German officers on the commandant's staff. In return, he was given food. The slops for which the POW officers stood in line with their mess tins from 6 A.M. on, while the Ordners beat them with sticks and the cooks with ladles, were not enough to sustain life. At evening, Yuri could see from the windows of their room the one and only picture for which his artistic talent had been given him: the evening mist hovering above a swampy meadow encircled by barbed wire; a multitude of bonfires; and, around the bonfires, beings who had once been Russian officers but had now become beastlike creatures who gnawed the bones of dead horses, who baked patties from potato rinds, who smoked manure and were all swarming with lice. Not all those two-legged creatures had died as yet. Not all of them had yet lost the capacity for intelligible speech, and one could see in the crimson reflections of the bonfires how a belated understanding was dawning on those faces which were descending to the Neanderthal.

Wormwood on the tongue! That life which Yuri had preserved was no longer precious to him for its own sake. He was not one of those who easily agree to forget. No, if he was going to survive, he was obliged to draw certain conclusions.

It was already clear to them that the Germans were not the heart of the matter, or at least not the Germans alone; that among the POW's of many nationalities only the Soviets lived like this and died like this. None were worse off than the Soviets. Even the Poles, even the Yugoslavs, existed in far more tolerable conditions; and as for the English and the Norwegians, they were inundated by the International Red Cross with parcels from home. They didn't even bother to line up for the German rations. Wherever there were Allied POW camps next door, their prisoners, out of kindness, threw our men handouts over the fence, and our prisoners jumped on these gifts like a pack of dogs on a bone.

The Russians were carrying the whole war on their shoulders —and this was the Russian lot. Why?

Gradually, explanations came in from here and there: it turned out that the U.S.S.R. did not recognize as binding Russia's signature to the Hague Convention on war prisoners. That meant that the U.S.S.R. accepted no obligations at all in the treatment of war prisoners and took no steps for the protection of its own soldiers who had been captured.[20] The U.S.S.R. did not recognize the International Red Cross. The U.S.S.R. did not recognize its own soldiers of the day before: it did not intend to give them any help as POW's.

And the heart of Yuri, enthusiastic twin of the October Revolution, grew cold. In their barracks room, he and the elderly artist clashed and argued. It was difficult for Yuri to accept. Yuri resisted. But the old man kept peeling off layer after layer. What was it all about? Stalin? But wasn't it too much to ascribe everything to Stalin, to those stubby hands? He who draws a conclusion only halfway fails to draw it at all. What about the rest of them? The ones right next to Stalin and below him, and everywhere around the country—all those whom the Motherland had authorized to speak for it?

What is the right course of action if our mother has sold us to

20. We did not recognize that 1907 Convention until 1955. Incidentally, in his diary for 1915, Melgunov reports *rumors* that Russia would not let aid go through for its prisoners in Germany and that their living conditions were worse than those of all other Allied prisoners—simply in order to prevent *rumors* about the good life of war prisoners inducing our soldiers to surrender willingly. There was some sort of continuity of ideas here. (Melgunov, *Vospominaniya i Dnevniki*, Vol. I, pp. 199 and 203.)

the gypsies? No, even worse, thrown us to the dogs? Does she really remain our mother? If a wife has become a whore, are we really still bound to her in fidelity? A Motherland that betrays its soldiers—is that really a Motherland?

And everything turned topsy-turvy for Yuri! He used to take pride in his father—now he cursed him! For the first time he began to consider that his father had, in essence, betrayed his oath to that army in which he had been brought up—had betrayed it in order to help establish this system which now betrayed its own soldiers. Why, then, was Yuri bound by his own oath to that traitorous system?

When, in the spring of 1943, recruiters from the first Byelorussian "legions" put in an appearance, some POW's signed up with them to escape starvation. Yuri went with them out of conviction, with a clear mind. But he didn't stay in the legion for long. As the saying goes: "Once they've skinned you, there's no point in grieving over the wool." By this time Yuri had given up hiding his excellent knowledge of German, and soon a certain Chief, a German from near Kassel, who had been assigned to create an espionage school with an accelerated wartime output, took Yuri as his right-hand man. And that was how Yuri began the downward slide he had not foreseen. That was how things got turned around. Yuri passionately desired to free his Motherland, and what did they do but shove him into training spies? The Germans had their own plans. Just where could one draw the line? Which step was the fatal one? Yuri became a lieutenant in the German Army. He traveled through Germany, in German uniform, spent some time in Berlin, visited Russian émigrés, and read authors like Bunin, Nabokov, Aldanov, Amfiteatrov, whose works were forbidden at home. Yuri had anticipated that in all their writing, in Bunin's, for example, the blood flowing from Russia's living wounds would pour from every page. What was wrong with them? To what did they devote their unutterably precious freedom? To the female body, to ecstasy, sunsets, the beauty of noble brows, to anecdotes going back to dusty years. They wrote as if there had been no revolution in Russia, or as if it were too complex for them to explain. They left it to young Russian people to find for themselves what was highest in life. And Yuri dashed back and forth, in a hurry to see, in a hurry to know, and meanwhile, in accordance with ancient Russian tradition, he kept drowning his confusion more and more often and more and more deeply in vodka.

What was their spy school really? It was, of course, not a real one. All they could be taught in six months was to master the parachute, the use of explosives, and the use of portable radios. The Germans put no special trust in them. In sending them across the lines they were simply whistling in the dark. And for those dying, hopelessly abandoned Russian POW's, those schools, in Yuri's opinion, were a good way out. The men ate their fill, got new warm clothing, and, in addition, had their pockets stuffed with Soviet money. The students (and their teachers) acted as if all this nonsense were genuine—as if they would actually carry out spying missions in the Soviet rear, blow up the designated objectives, get back in touch with the Germans via radio, and return to the German lines. But in reality in their eyes this school was simply a means of sidestepping death and captivity. They wanted to live, but not at the price of shooting their own compatriots at the front.[21] The Germans sent them across the front lines, and from then on their free choice depended on their own morality and conscience. They all threw away their TNT and radio apparatus immediately. The only point on which they differed was whether to surrender to the authorities immediately, like the snub-nosed "shhpy" I had encountered at army counterintelligence headquarters, or whether to get drunk first and have some fun squandering all that free money. None of them ever recrossed the front lines to the Germans.

Suddenly, as the new year of 1945 approached, one smart fellow did return and reported he had carried out his assignment. (Just go and check on it!) He created a sensation. The Chief hadn't the slightest doubt that SMERSH had sent him back and decided to shoot him. (The fate of a conscientious spy!) But Yuri insisted that he be given a decoration instead and held up as an

---

21. Of course, our Soviet interrogators did not accept this line of reasoning. What right did *they* have to want to live—at a time when privileged families in the Soviet rear lived well without collaborating? No one ever thought of considering that these boys had refused to take up German arms against their own people. For playing spies, they were nailed with the very worst and most serious charges of all—Article 58-6, plus sabotage with intent. This meant: to be held until dead.

example to the others taking the course. The returned "spy" invited Yuri to drink a quart of vodka with him and, crimson from drink, leaned across the table and disclosed: "Yuri Nikolayevich! The Soviet Command promises you forgiveness if you will come over to us immediately."

Yuri trembled. And that heart which had already grown hard, which had renounced everything, was flooded with warmth. The Motherland? Accursed, unjust, but nonetheless still precious! Forgiveness? And he could go back to his own family? And walk along Kamennoostrovsky in Leningrad? All right, so what? We are Russian! If you will forgive us, we will return, and we will behave ourselves, oh, how well! That year and a half since he had left the POW camp had not brought Yuri happiness. He did not repent, but he could see no future either. And when, while drinking, he encountered other such unrepentant Russians, he learned that they realized clearly that they had nothing to stand on. It wasn't real life. The Germans were twisting them to suit themselves. But now, when the Germans were obviously losing the war, Yuri had been offered an out. His Chief, who liked him, confided that he had a second estate in Spain which they could head for together if the German Reich went up in smoke. But there across the table sat his drunken compatriot, coaxing him at the risk of his own life: "Yuri Nikolayevich! The Soviet Command values your experience and knowledge. They want you to tell them about the organization of the German intelligence service."

For two weeks Yuri was torn by hesitation. But during the Soviet offensive beyond the Vistula, after he had led his school well out of the way, he ordered them to turn in to a quiet Polish farm, lined them all up, and declared: "I am going over to the Soviet side! There is a free choice for everyone!" And these sad-sack spies, with the milk hardly dry on their lips, who just one hour before had pretended loyalty to the German Reich, now cried out with enthusiasm: "Hurrah! Us too!" (They were shouting "hurrah" for their future lives at hard labor.)

Then the entire spy school hid until the arrival of the Soviet tanks; and then came SMERSH. Yuri saw his boys no more. They took him off by himself and gave him ten days to describe the whole history of the school, the programs, the sabotage assignments. He really thought that they valued his "experience and knowledge." They were already talking about his going home to his family.

Only when he arrived at the Lubyanka did he realize that even in Salamanca he would have been closer to his native Neva. He could now await being shot, or, in any case, a sentence of certainly not less than twenty years.

So immutably does a human being surrender to the mist of the Motherland! Just as a tooth will not stop aching until the nerve is killed, so is it with us; we shall probably not stop responding to the call of the Motherland until we swallow arsenic. The lotus-eaters in the *Odyssey* knew of a certain lotus for that purpose. . . .

In all, Yuri spent three weeks in our cell. I argued with him during all those weeks. I said that our Revolution was magnificent and just; that only its 1929 distortion was terrible. He looked at me regretfully, compressing his nervous lips: before trying our hands at revolution, we should have exterminated the bedbugs in this country! (Sometimes, oddly, he and Fastenko arrived at the same conclusions, approaching them from such different beginnings.) I said there had been a long period in which the people in charge of everything important in our country had been people of unimpeachably lofty intentions, and totally dedicated. He said that from the very beginning they were all cut from the same cloth as Stalin. (We agreed that Stalin was a gangster.) I praised Gorky to the skies. What a smart man he had been! How correct his point of view! What a great artist he was! And Yuri parried. He was an insignificant, terribly boring personality! He invented himself; he invented his heroes; and his books were fabrications from beginning to end. Lev Tolstoi—he was the king of our literature.

As a result of these daily arguments, vehement because of our youth, he and I were never able to become really close or to discern and accept in each other more than we rejected.

They took him out of our cell; and since then, no matter how often I have inquired, I have found no one who was imprisoned with him in the Butyrki, and no one who encountered him in a transit prison. Even the rank-and-file Vlasov men have all disappeared without a trace, under the earth, most likely, and even now some of them do not have the documents they need in order to leave the northern wastes. But even among them, the fate of Yuri Y. was not a rank-and-file fate.

■

At long last our Lubyanka lunch arrived. Long before it got
to us we could hear the cheery clatter in the corridor, and then,
as in a restaurant, they brought in a tray with two aluminum
plates—not bowls—for each prisoner. One plate held a ladleful
of soup and the other a ladleful of the thinnest kind of thin gruel,
with no fat in it.

In his first excitement, a prisoner couldn't get anything down
his throat. There were those who didn't touch their bread for
several days, who didn't know where to put it. But gradually
one's appetite returned; and then a chronically famished state
ensued that became almost uncontrollable. Then, if one managed
to get it under control, one's stomach shrank and adapted itself
to inadequate food, at which point the meager Lubyanka fare
became just right. One needed to have self-control to achieve
this, and also needed to stop looking around to see who might
be eating something extra. All those extremely dangerous prison
conversations about food had to be outlawed, and one had to
try to lift oneself, as far as possible, into higher spheres. At the
Lubyanka this was made easier by our being permitted two hours
of rest after lunch—something else that was astonishingly resort-
like. We lay down, our backs to the peephole, set up open books
for appearance' sake, and dozed off. Sleep was forbidden, strictly
speaking, and the guards could see that the pages of the books
hadn't been turned for a long time. But ordinarily they did not
knock during this period. (The explanation for this humanitarianism was that whoever wasn't resting during these hours was undergoing interrogation. Thus, for those who were stubborn, who
had not signed the depositions, the contrast was unmistakable:
they returned to the cell at the very end of the rest period.)

And sleep was the very best thing for hunger and anguish.
One's organism cooled off, and the brain stopped recapitulating
one's mistakes over and over again.

Then they brought in dinner—another ladle of gruel. Life was
setting all its gifts before you. After that, you were not going to
get anything to eat in the five or six hours before bedtime, but
that was not so terrible; it was easy to get used to not eating in

the evenings. That has long been known in military medicine. And in reserve regiments they don't have anything to eat in the evening.

Then came the time for the evening visit to the toilet, for which, in all likelihood, you had waited, all atremble, all day. How relieved, how eased, the whole world suddenly became! How the great questions all simplified themselves at the same instant—did you feel it?

Oh, the weightless Lubyanka evenings! (Only weightless, incidentally, if you were not awaiting a night interrogation.) A weightless body, just sufficiently satisfied by soup so that the soul did not feel oppressed by it. What light, free thoughts! It was as if we had been lifted up to the heights of Sinai, and there the truth manifested itself to us from out the fire. Was it not of this that Pushkin dreamed:

> I want to live to think and suffer!

And there we suffered, and we thought, and there was nothing else in our lives. How easy it turned out to be to attain that ideal.

Some evenings I would get involved in arguments, withdrawing from a chess game with Susi or from a book. Again I would have the sharpest quarrels with Yuri, because the questions were all explosive ones—for example, the question of the outcome of the war. The jailer, without any word or change of expression, would come in and pull down the dark-blue blackout blind on the window. And then, out there on the other side of the blind, evening Moscow would begin to send up salutes. And just as we could not see the salutes lighting up the heavens, we were unable to see the map of Europe. Yet we tried to picture it in all its details and to guess which cities had been taken. Yuri was especially tormented by those salutes. Appealing to fate to correct his own mistakes, he assured us that the war was by no means finished and that the Red Army and the Anglo-American forces would now go for each other's throats: that the real war would really begin now. The others in the cell took a greedy interest in this prediction. How would such a conflict end? Yuri claimed it would end with the easy destruction of the Red Army. (Would this result in our liberation or our execution?) I objected to this, and we got into heated arguments. It was his contention that our army was worn down, bled white, poorly supplied, and, most importantly, that it would not fight with its usual determination against the Allies. I, however, insisted, on the basis of the units I had been familiar with, that the army was not so much worn down as experienced, that it had now become both strong and mean, and that in such an event it would crush the Allies even more thoroughly than it had the Germans. "Never," cried Yuri in a half-whisper. "And what about the Ardennes?" I answered in a half-whisper. Fastenko interrupted us, ridiculing us both, informing us that we did not understand the West and that no one, now or ever, could compel the Allied armies to fight against us.

However, in the evening we didn't want to argue so much as to hear something interesting that might bring us closer together, and to talk in a spirit of fellowship.

One favorite subject of conversation was prison traditions, *how it used to be in prison*. We had Fastenko and were therefore able to hear these stories at first hand. What dismayed us most of all was to learn that it had previously been an honor to be a political prisoner, and that it was not only their relatives who stuck by them and refused to renounce them, but that girls who had never even met them came to visit them, pretending for that purpose to be their fiancées. And what about the once universal tradition of gifts for the prisoners on holidays? No one in Russia ever broke the Lenten fast without first taking gifts for unknown prisoners to the common prison kitchen. They brought in Christmas hams, tarts, and kulichi—the special Russian Easter cakes. One poor old lady even used to bring a dozen colored Easter eggs; it made her feel better. And where had all that Russian generosity gone? It had been replaced by *political consciousness*. That was how cruelly and implacably they had terrified our people and cured them of taking thought for and caring for those who were suffering. Today it would seem silly to do such a thing. If it was proposed today that some institution organize a preholiday collection of gifts for prisoners in the local prison, it would be virtually considered an anti-Soviet revolt! That's how far we have gone along the road to being brutalized!

And what about those holiday gifts? Were they only a matter of tasty food? More importantly, those gifts gave the prisoners the warm feeling that people in freedom were thinking about them and were concerned for them.

Fastenko told us that even in the Soviet period a Political Red Cross had existed. We found this difficult to imagine. It wasn't that we thought he was telling us an untruth. Somehow we just couldn't picture such a thing. He told us that Y. P. Peshkova, taking advantage of her personal immunity, had traveled abroad, collected money there (you'd not collect much here), and then seen to it that foodstuffs were bought in Russia for political prisoners who had no relatives. For all political prisoners? And he explained at this point that the KR's—the so-called "Counter-Revolutionaries"—engineers and priests, for example, weren't included, but only members of former political parties. Well, why didn't you say so right away? Yes, and then for the most part the Political Red Cross, except Peshkova, was itself liquidated and its staff imprisoned.

It was also very pleasant, on those evenings when one wasn't expecting interrogation, to talk about getting out of prison. Yes, they said there had been astonishing instances when they did release someone. One day they took Z——v from our cell, "with his things"—perhaps to free him? But his interrogation could not have been completed so swiftly. Ten days later he returned. They had dragged him off to Lefortovo. When he got there, he had evidently begun *to sign things* very quickly. So they brought him back to us. "Now if they *should* just release you," we would say to a fellow prisoner, "since your case, after all, isn't very serious, as you yourself say, then you must promise to go see my wife and, to show you've done it, tell her, let's say, to put two apples in my next parcel. . . . But there aren't any apples anywhere right now, so tell her to put in three bagels. But then there mightn't be any bagels in Moscow either. So all right, it will just have to be four potatoes!" (That's how the discussion went, and then they actually did take N. off, "with his things," and M. got four potatoes in his next parcel. Truly astonishing! It was more than a coincidence! So they had really let him go! And his case was much more serious than mine. So maybe soon . . . However, what really happened was that M.'s wife brought five potatoes, but one of them got crushed in her bag, and N. was in the hold of a ship en route to the Kolyma.)

And so it went. We talked about all kinds of things and recalled something amusing, and it was all very jolly and delightful to be among interesting people who were so different from those you used to spend your life with, and who came from outside your own circle of experience. Meanwhile the silent evening check-up had come and gone, and they had taken eyeglasses away and the light bulb had blinked three times. That meant that bedtime would be in five minutes.

Quick! Quick! Grab a blanket! Just as you never knew at the front when a hail of shells would begin to fall all around you, here you didn't know which would be your fateful interrogation night. And we would lie down with one arm on top of the blanket and try to expel the whirlwind of thought from our heads. Go to sleep!

And at a certain moment on an April evening, soon after we had seen Yuri off, the lock rattled. Hearts tightened. For whom had they come? Now the jailer would whisper: "Name with 'S'? Name with 'Z'?" But the guard did not whisper anything. The door closed. We raised our heads. There was a newcomer at the door: on the thin side, young, in a cheap blue suit and a dark-blue cap. He had nothing with him. He looked around in a state of confusion.

"What's the cell number?" he asked in alarm.

"Fifty-three."

He shuddered a bit.

"Are you from freedom?" we asked.

"No!" He shook his head in a painful sort of way.

"When were you arrested?"

"Yesterday morning."

We roared. He had a very gentle, innocent sort of face, and his eyebrows were nearly white.

"What for?"

(It was an unfair question. One could not really expect an answer.)

"Oh, I don't know. . . . Nothing much."

That was how they all replied. Everyone here was imprisoned because of nothing much. And to the newly arrested prisoner his own case always seemed especially nothing much.

"But anyway, what was it?"

"Well, you see, I wrote a proclamation. To the Russian people."

"Whaaat?"

(None of us had ever run into that sort of "nothing much.")

"Are they going to shoot me?" His face grew longer. He kept pulling at the visor of the cap he had still not taken off.

"Well, no, probably not," we reassured him. "They don't shoot anyone nowadays. They give out *tenners*—every time the clock strikes."

"Are you a worker? Or a white-collar employee?" asked the Social Democrat, true to his class principles.

"A worker."

Fastenko reached out a hand to him and triumphantly proclaimed to me: "You see, Aleksandr Isayevich, that's the mood of the working class!"

He turned away to go to sleep, assuming that there was nowhere else to go from there and nothing else to listen to.

But he was wrong.

"What do you mean, a proclamation? Just like that? Without any reason? In whose name was it issued?"

"In my own."

"And who are you?"

The newcomer smiled with embarrassment: "The Emperor, Mikhail."

An electric shock ran through us all. Once again we raised ourselves on our cots and looked at him. No, his shy, thin face was not in the least like the face of Mikhail Romanov. And then his age too . . .

"Tomorrow, tomorrow. Time to sleep now," said Susi sternly.

We went to sleep, confident that the two hours before the morning bread ration were not going to be boring.

They brought in a cot and bedding for the Emperor, and he lay down quietly next to the latrine bucket.

■

In 1916 a portly stranger, an elderly man with a light-brown beard, entered the home of the Moscow locomotive engineer Belov and said to the engineer's pious wife: "Pelageya! You have a year-old son. Take good care of him for the Lord. The hour will come—and I will come to you again." Then he left.

Pelageya did not have the faintest idea who this man was. But he had spoken so clearly and authoritatively that her mother's heart accepted his word as law. And she cared for her child like the apple of her eye. Viktor grew up to be quiet, obedient, and pious; and he often saw visions of the angels and the Holy Virgin. But, as he grew up, these visions became less frequent. The elderly man did not come again. Viktor learned to be a chauffeur, and in 1936 he was taken into the army and sent off to Birobidzhan, where he was stationed in an auto transport company. He was not at all overly familiar or cheeky, and perhaps it was his quiet demeanor and modesty, so untypical of a chauffeur, which attracted a civilian girl employee. But the commander of his platoon was after the same girl and found himself out in the cold because of Viktor. At this time, Marshal Blücher came to their area for maneuvers and his personal chauffeur fell seriously ill. Blücher ordered the commander of the motor company to send him the best driver in the company; the company commander summoned the platoon commander, who immediately latched onto the idea of dumping his rival, Belov. (That's the way it often is in the army. The person who deserves promotion doesn't get it, and the person they want to get rid of does.) In addition, Belov was sober, a hard worker, and reliable—he wouldn't let them down.

Blücher liked Belov. So Belov stayed with him. Soon Blücher was summoned to Moscow on a plausible pretext. This was how they separated the marshal from his power base in the Far East before arresting him. He had brought his own chauffeur, Belov, to Moscow with him. Having lost his boss, Belov then landed in the Kremlin garage and began chauffeuring, sometimes for Mikhailov (of the Komsomol), sometimes for Lozovsky or somebody else in the leadership, and, finally, for Khrushchev. He had a close view of things—and he told us a lot, too, about the feasts, the morals, the security precautions. As a representative of the rank-and-file Moscow proletariat, he was also present at the trial of Bukharin in the House of the Unions. Of all those for whom he worked, he spoke well only of Khrushchev. Only in Khrushchev's home was the chauffeur seated at the family table instead of being put in the kitchen. Only there, in those years, did he find the simplicity of the workingman's life preserved. Khrushchev, who enjoyed life hugely, also became attached to Viktor Alekseyevich, and in 1938, when he left for the Ukraine, he tried to get him to go along. "I would have stayed with Khrushchev forever," said Viktor Alekseyevich. But for some reason he felt he should remain in Moscow.

For a while in 1941, before the beginning of the war, he was not employed in the government garage and, having no one to protect him, he was taken into military service. But because his health was poor, he was not sent to the front but to a labor battalion. First they went on foot to Inza, to dig trenches and build roads there. After his secure and prosperous life of the previous few years he found it painful to have his nose shoved in the dirt. He drank a full draft of grief and poverty there, and on every side he saw not only that people had not begun to live better before the war, but that they were deeply impoverished. Just barely surviving himself, and released from the service because of illness, he returned to Moscow and again managed to get himself a job as chauffeur for Shcherbakov,[22] and after that for Sedin, People's Commissar of Petroleum. But Sedin embezzled funds to the tune of 35 million and was quietly removed. And Belov was once again out of a job driving for the leaders. He became a chauffeur at an automobile depot, and in his spare time he used to moonlight with his car on the road to Krasnaya Pakhra.

But his thoughts were already centered elsewhere. In 1943 he had been visiting his mother. She was doing the laundry and had gone out to the hydrant with her pails. The door opened and a portly stranger, an old man with a white beard, entered the house. He crossed himself at the ikon there, looked sternly at Belov, and said to him: "Hail, Mikhail. God gives you his blessing!" Belov replied: "My name is Viktor." "But," the old man continued, "you are destined to become Mikhail, the Emperor of Holy Russia!" Just then Viktor's mother returned and half-collapsed in fright, spilling her pails. It was the very same old man who had come to her twenty-seven years before. He had turned white in the meantime, but it was he. "God bless you,

22. He used to describe how the obese Shcherbakov hated to see people around when he arrived at his Informburo, so they temporarily removed all those who were working in the offices he had to walk through. Grunting because of his fat, he would lean down and pull back a corner of the carpet. And the whole Informburo caught it if he found any dust there.

Pelageya, you have preserved your son," said the old man. And he took the future Emperor aside, like a patriarch preparing to enthrone him, and announced to the astonished young man that in 1953 there would be a change in rule and that he would become Emperor of All Russia.[23] (That is why the number of our cell, 53, shocked him so.) To this end, the old man told him, he was to begin to gather his forces in 1948. The old man didn't instruct him as to how to gather his forces. He departed, and Viktor Alekseyevich didn't get around to asking.

All the peace and simplicity of his life were lost to him now. Perhaps some other individual would have recoiled from the ambitious program, but Viktor, as it happened, had rubbed shoulders with the highest of the high. He had seen all those Mikhailovs, Shcherbakovs, Sedins, and he had heard a lot from other chauffeurs, too, and he had gotten it clear in his own mind that nothing in the least unusual was required—in fact, just the reverse.

The newly anointed Tsar, quiet, conscientious, sensitive, like Fyodor Ivanovich, the last of the line of Ryurik, felt on his brow the heavy pressure of the crown of Monomakh. All around him were the people's poverty and grief, for which he had not until now borne any responsibility. Now all this lay upon his shoulders, and he was to blame for the fact that this misery still existed. It seemed strange to him to wait until 1948, and, therefore, in that very autumn of 1943, he wrote his first proclamation to the Russian people and read it to four of his fellow workers in the garage of the People's Commissariat of Petroleum.

We had surrounded Viktor Alekseyevich from early morning, and he had meekly told us all this. We had still not fathomed his childish trustfulness—we were absorbed in his unusual story and —it was our fault—we forgot to warn him about the stoolie. In fact, we never even thought for one minute that there was anything in the naïve and simple story he had told us that the interrogator didn't already know.

The instant the story ended, Kramarenko began demanding to be taken either to the "chief of the prison for tobacco" or else to the doctor. At any rate, they summoned him quickly. And as soon as he got there he *put the finger on* those four workers in

---

23. The prophetic old man made only one mistake. He confused the chauffeur with his former employer.

the garage of the People's Commissariat of Petroleum—whose existence no one would ever have suspected. (The next day, returning from his interrogation, Belov was astonished that the interrogator knew about them. And that's when it hit us.) Those workers had heard the proclamation and approved it all, and *no one had turned in* the Emperor! But he himself felt that it was too early, and he burned it.

A year passed. Viktor Alekseyevich was working as a mechanic in the garage of an automobile depot. In the fall of 1944, he again wrote a proclamation and gave it to ten people to read—chauffeurs and lathe operators. All of them approved it. *And no one turned him in.* (It was a surprising thing, indeed, that not one person in that group of ten had turned him in, in that period of ubiquitous stool pigeons! Fastenko had not been mistaken in his deductions about the "mood of the working class.") True, in this case the Emperor had used some innocent tricks. He had thrown out hints that a strong arm inside the government was on his side. And he had promised his supporters travel assignments to rally monarchic sentiment at the grass roots.

Months went by. The Emperor entrusted his secret to two girls at the garage. But this time there was no misfire. These girls turned out to be ideologically sound! And Viktor Alekseyevich's heart sank: he had a premonition of disaster. On the Sunday after the Annunciation he went to the market, carrying the proclamation with him. One of his sympathizers among the old workers saw him there and said: "Viktor, you ought to burn that piece of paper for the time being; how about it?" And Viktor felt clearly that he had written it too soon, and that he should burn it. "I'll burn it right now! You're right." And he started home to burn it. But right there in the market two pleasant young men called out to him: "Viktor Alekseyevich! Come along with us!" And they took him to the Lubyanka in a private car. When they got him there, they had been in such a hurry and were so excited that they didn't search him in the usual way, and there was a moment when the Emperor almost destroyed his proclamation in the toilet. But he decided that it would be the worse for him, that they would keep after him anyway to find out where it was. And they straightaway took him in an elevator up to a general and a colonel, and the general with his own hands grabbed the proclamation from Viktor's pocket.

However, it took only one interrogation for the Big Lubyanka to quiet down again. It turned out to be not so dangerous. Ten arrests in the garage of the auto depot and four in the garage of the People's Commissariat of Petroleum. The interrogation was turned over to a lieutenant colonel, who had a good laugh as he went through the proclamation:

"You write here, Your Majesty: 'In the first spring I will instruct my Minister of Agriculture to dissolve the collective farms.' But how are you going to divide up the tools and live-stock? You haven't got it worked out yet. And then you also write: 'I am going to increase housing construction and house each person next to the place he works, and I am going to raise all the workers' wages.' And where are you going to find the money, Your Majesty? Are you going to have to run the money off on printing presses? You are going to abolish the *state loans*. And then, too: 'I am going to wipe the Kremlin from the face of the earth.' But where are you going to put your own govern-ment? What about the building of the Big Lubyanka? Would you like to take a tour of inspection and look it over?"

Many of the younger interrogators also stopped by to make fun of the Emperor of All Russia. They saw nothing except comedy in all this.

And it was not always easy for us in the cell to keep a straight face. "We hope you aren't going to forget us here in Cell No. 53," said Z——v, winking at the rest of us.

Everyone laughed at him.

Viktor Alekseyevich, with his white eyebrows and innocent simplicity and his callused hands, would treat us when he received boiled potatoes from his unfortunate mother, Pelageya, without ever dividing them into "yours" and mine": "Come on, com-rades, eat up, eat up!"

He used to smile shyly. He understood perfectly well how uncontemporary and funny all this was—to be the Emperor of All Russia. But what could he do if God's choice had fallen on him?

They soon removed him from our cell.[24]

---

24. When they introduced me to Khrushchev in 1962, I wanted to say to him: "Nikita Sergeyevich! You and I have an acquaintance in common." But I told him something else, more urgent, on behalf of former prisoners.

■

Just before May 1 they took down the blackout shade on the window. The war was perceptibly coming to an end.

That evening it was quieter than ever before in the Lubyanka. It was, I remember, almost like the second day of Easter, since May Day and Easter came one after the other that year. All the interrogators were out in Moscow celebrating. No one was taken to interrogation. In the silence we could hear someone across the corridor protesting. They took him from the cell and into a box. By listening, we could detect the location of all the doors. They left the door of the box open, and they kept beating him a long time. In the suspended silence every blow on his soft and choking mouth could be heard clearly.

On May 2 a thirty-gun salute roared out. That meant a European capital. Only two had not yet been captured—Prague and Berlin. We tried to guess which it was.

On the ninth of May they brought us our dinner at the same time as our lunch—which was done at the Lubyanka only on May 1 and November 7.

And that is how we guessed that the war had ended.

That evening they shot off another thirty-gun salute. We then knew that there were no more capitals to be captured. And later that same evening one more salute roared out—forty guns, I seem to remember. And that was the end of all the ends.

Above the muzzle of our window, and from all the other cells of the Lubyanka, and from all the windows of all the Moscow prisons, we, too, former prisoners of war and former front-line soldiers, watched the Moscow heavens, patterned with fireworks and crisscrossed by the beams of searchlights.

Boris Gammerov, a young antitank man, already demobilized because of wounds, with an incurable wound in his lung, having been arrested with a group of students, was in prison that evening in an overcrowded Butyrki cell, where half the inmates were former POW's and front-line soldiers. He described this last salute of the war in a terse eight-stanza poem, in the most ordinary language: how they were already lying down on their board bunks, covered with their overcoats; how they were awakened by the

noise; how they raised their heads; squinted up at the muzzle—
"Oh, it's just a salute"—and then lay down again:

And once again covered themselves with their coats.

With those same overcoats which had been in the clay of the
trenches, and the ashes of bonfires, and been torn to tatters by
German shell fragments.

That victory was not for us. And that spring was not for us
either.

Chapter 6

■

That Spring

Through the windows of the Butyrki Prison every morning and evening in June, 1945, we could hear the brassy notes of bands not far away—coming from either Lesnaya Street or Novoslobodskaya. They kept playing marches over and over.

Behind the murky green "muzzles" of reinforced glass, we stood at the wide-open but impenetrable prison windows and listened. Were they military units that were marching? Or were they workers cheerfully devoting their free time to marching practice? We didn't know, but the rumor had already gotten through to us that preparations were under way for a big Victory Parade on Red Square on June 22—the fourth anniversary of the beginning of the war.

The foundation stones of a great building are destined to groan and be pressed upon; it is not for them to crown the edifice. But even the honor of being part of the foundation was denied those whose doomed heads and ribs had borne the first blows of this war and thwarted the foreigners' victory, and who were now abandoned for no good reason.

"Joyful sounds mean nought to the traitor."

That spring of 1945 was, in our prisons, predominantly the spring of the Russian *prisoners of war*. They passed through the prisons of the Soviet Union in vast dense gray shoals like ocean herring. The first trace of those schools I glimpsed was Yuri Y. But I was soon entirely surrounded by their purposeful motion, which seemed to know its own fated design.

Not only war prisoners passed through those cells. A wave of those who had spent any time in Europe was rolling too: émigrés from the Civil War; the "ostovtsy"—workers recruited as laborers by the Germans during World War II; Red Army officers who had been too astute and farsighted in their conclusions, so that Stalin feared they might bring European freedom back from their European crusade, like the Decembrists 120 years before. And yet it was the war prisoners who constituted the bulk of the wave. And among the war prisoners of various ages, most were of my own age—not precisely my age, but *the twins of October*, those born along with the Revolution, who in 1937 had poured forth undismayed to celebrate the twentieth anniversary of the Revolution, and whose age group, at the beginning of the war, made up the standing army—which had been scattered in a matter of weeks.

That tedious prison spring had, to the tune of the victory marches, become the spring of reckoning for my whole generation.

Over our cradles the rallying cry had resounded: "All power to the Soviets!" It was we who had reached out our suntanned childish hands to clutch the Pioneers' bugle, and who in response to the Pioneer challenge, "Be prepared," had saluted and answered: "We are always prepared!" It was we who had smuggled weapons into Buchenwald and joined the Communist Party there. And it was we who were now in disgrace, only because we had survived.[1]

Back when the Red Army had cut through East Prussia, I had seen downcast columns of returning war prisoners—the only people around who were grieving instead of celebrating. Even then their gloom had shocked me, though I didn't yet grasp the reason for it. I jumped down and went over to those voluntarily formed-up columns. (Why were they marching in columns? Why had they lined themselves up in ranks? After all, no one had compelled them to, and the war prisoners of all other nations went home as scattered individuals. But ours wanted to return as submissively as possible.) I was wearing a captain's shoulder

1. Those prisoners who had been in Buchenwald and survived were, in fact, imprisoned for that very reason in our own camps: How could you have survived an annihilation camp? Something doesn't smell right!

boards, and they, plus the fact that I was moving forward, helped prevent my finding out why our POW's were so sad. But then fate turned me around and sent me in the wake of those prisoners along the same path they had taken. I had already marched with them from army counterintelligence headquarters to the head-quarters at the front, and when we got there I had heard their first stories, which I didn't yet understand; and then Yuri Y. told me the whole thing. And here beneath the domes of the brick-red Butyrki castle, I felt that the story of these several mil-lion Russian prisoners had got me in its grip once and for all, like a pin through a specimen beetle. My own story of landing in prison seemed insignificant. I stopped regretting my torn-off shoulder boards. It was mere chance that had kept me from end-ing up exactly where these contemporaries of mine had ended. I came to understand that it was my duty to take upon my shoulders a share of their common burden—and to bear it to the last man, until it crushed us. I now felt as if I, too, had fallen prisoner at the Solovyev crossing, in the Kharkov encirclement, in the quarries of Kerch, and, hands behind my back, had carried my Soviet pride behind the barbed wire of the concentration camps; that I, too, had stood for hours in the freezing cold for a ladle of cold Kawa (an ersatz coffee) and had been left on the ground for dead, without even reaching the kettle; that in Oflag 68 (Suwalki) I had used my hands and the lid of a mess tin to dig a bell-shaped (upturned, that is) foxhole, so as not to have to spend the winter on the open field; and that a maddened prisoner had crawled up to me as I lay dying to gnaw on the still warm flesh beneath my arm; and with every new day of exacerbated, famished consciousness, lying in a barracks riddled with typhus, or at the barbed wire of the neighboring camp for English POW's, the clear thought had penetrated my dying brain: Soviet Russia has renounced her dying children. She had needed them, "proud sons of Russia," as long as they let the tanks roll over them and it was still possible to rouse them to attack. But to feed them once they were war prisoners? Extra mouths. And extra witnesses to humiliating defeats.

Sometimes we try to lie but our tongue will not allow us to. These people were labeled traitors, but a remarkable slip of the tongue occurred—on the part of the judges, prosecutors, and interrogators. And the convicted prisoners, the entire nation, and the newspapers repeated and reinforced this mistake, involuntarily letting the truth out of the bag. They intended to declare them "traitors *to* the Motherland." But they were universally referred to, in speech and in writing, even in the court documents, as "traitors *of* the Motherland."

You said it! They were not traitors *to her*. They were *her* traitors. It was not they, the unfortunates, who had betrayed the Motherland, but their calculating Motherland who had betrayed them, and not just once but *thrice*.

The first time she betrayed them was on the battlefield, through ineptitude—when the government, so beloved by the Motherland, did everything it could to lose the war: destroyed the lines of fortifications; set up the whole air force for annihilation; dismantled the tanks and artillery; removed the effective generals; and forbade the armies to resist.[2] And the war prisoners were the men whose bodies took the blow and stopped the Wehrmacht.

The second time they were heartlessly betrayed by the Motherland was when she abandoned them to die in captivity.

And the third time they were unscrupulously betrayed was when, with motherly love, she coaxed them to return home, with such phrases as "The Motherland has forgiven you! The Motherland calls you!" and snared them the moment they reached the frontiers.[3]

It would appear that during the one thousand one hundred years of Russia's existence as a state there have been, ah, how many foul and terrible deeds! But among them was there ever so multimillioned foul a deed as this: to betray one's own soldiers and proclaim them traitors?

How easily we left them out of our own accounting! He was a traitor? For shame! Write him off! And our Father *wrote them off*, even before we did: he threw the flower of Moscow's intelligentsia into the Vyazma meat grinder with Berdan single-

2. Now, after twenty-seven years, the first honest work on this subject has appeared—P. G. Grigorenko, "A Letter to the Magazine *Problems of the History of the Communist Party of the Soviet Union*," samizdat, 1968—and such works are going to multiply from here on out. Not all the witnesses died. And soon no one will call Stalin's government anything but a government of insanity and treason.

3. One of the biggest war criminals, Colonel General Golikov, former chief of the Red Army's intelligence administration, was put in charge of coaxing the repatriates home and swallowing them up.

loading rifles, vintage 1866, and only one for every five men at that. What Lev Tolstoi is going to describe *that* Borodino for us? And with one stupid slither of his greasy, stubby finger, the Great Strategist sent *120,000* of our young men, almost as many as all the Russian forces at Borodino, across the Strait of Kerch in December, 1941—senselessly, and exclusively for the sake of a sensational New Year's communiqué—and he turned them all over to the Germans without a fight.

And yet, for some reason, it was not he who was the traitor, but they.

(How easily we let ourselves be taken in by partisan labels; how easily we agreed to regard these devoted men as—traitors! In one of the Butyrki cells that spring, there was an old man, Lebedev, a metallurgist, a professor in rank, and in appearance a stalwart artisan of the last century or maybe even the century before, from, say, the famous Demidov iron foundries. He was broad of shoulder, broad of head, wore a Pugachev-like beard, and the wide span of his hand could lift a 150-pound bucket. In the cell he wore a faded gray laborer's smock over his underwear; he was slovenly and might have been an auxiliary prison worker—until he sat down to read, and then his habitual powerful intelligence lit up his face. The men often gathered around him. He discussed metallurgy very little, but explained to us in his kettledrum bass voice that Stalin was exactly the same kind of dog as Ivan the Terrible: "Shoot!" "Strangle!" "Don't hesitate!" He explained to us also that Maxim Gorky had been a slobbering prattler, an apologist for executioners. I was very much taken with this Lebedev. It was as though the whole Russian people were embodied, there before my eyes, in that one thick-set torso with that intelligent head and the arms and legs of a plowman. He had already thought through so much! I learned from him to understand the world! And suddenly, with a chopping gesture of his huge hand, he thundered out that those charged under Article 58-1b were traitors of the Motherland and must not be forgiven. And those very same *1b's* were piled up on the board bunks all around. And how hurtful to them this was! The old man was pontificating with such conviction in the name of Russia's peasantry and labor that they were abashed and found it hard to defend themselves against the attack from this new direction. I was the one to whom it fell, along with two boys charged under

58-10, to defend them and to argue with the old man. But what depths of enforced ignorance were achieved by the monstrous lies of the state. Even the most broad-minded of us can embrace only that part of the truth into which our own snout has blundered.)[4]

How many wars Russia has been involved in! (It would have been better if there had been fewer.) And were there many traitors in all those wars? Had anyone observed that treason had become deeply rooted in the hearts of Russian soldiers? Then, under the most just social system in the world, came the most just war of all—and out of nowhere millions of traitors appeared, from among the simplest, lowliest elements of the population. How is this to be understood and explained?

Capitalist England fought at our side against Hitler; Marx had eloquently described the poverty and suffering of the working class in that same England. Why was it that in this war only one traitor could be found among *them*, the businessman "Lord Haw Haw"—but in our country millions?

It is frightening to open one's trap about this, but might the heart of the matter not be in the political system?

One of our most ancient proverbs justifies the war prisoner: "The captive will cry out, but the dead man never." During the reign of Tsar Aleksei Mikhailovich, *nobility* was granted for *durance in captivity!* And in *all* subsequent wars it was considered society's duty to exchange prisoners, to comfort one's own and to give them sustenance and aid. Every escape from captivity was glorified as the height of heroism. Throughout World War I, money was collected in Russia to aid our prisoners of war, and our nurses were permitted to go to Germany to help our prisoners, and our newspapers reminded their readers daily that our prisoners of war, our compatriots, were languishing in evil captivity.

---

4. Vitkovsky writes about this, on the basis of the thirties, in more general terms. It was astonishing that the pseudo wreckers, who knew perfectly well that they weren't wreckers, believed that military men and priests were being *shaken up* justifiably. The military men, who knew they hadn't worked for foreign intelligence services and had not sabotaged the Red Army, believed readily enough that the engineers were wreckers and that the priests deserved to be destroyed. Imprisoned, the Soviet person reasoned in the following way: I personally am innocent, but any methods are justified in dealing with those others, the enemies. The lessons of interrogation and the cell failed to enlighten such people. Even after they themselves had been convicted, they retained the blind beliefs of their days in *freedom*: belief in universal conspiracies, poisonings, wrecking, espionage.

All the Western peoples behaved the same in our war: parcels, letters, all kinds of assistance flowed freely through the neutral countries. The Western POW's did not have to lower themselves to accept ladlefuls from German soup kettles. They talked back to the German guards. Western governments gave their captured soldiers their seniority rights, their regular promotions, even their pay.

The only soldier in the world *who cannot surrender* is the soldier of the world's one and only Red Army. That's what it says in our military statutes. (The Germans would shout at us from their trenches: "Ivan plen nicht!"—"Ivan no prisoner!") Who can picture all that means? There is war; there is death—but there is no surrender! What a discovery! What it means is: Go and die; we will go on living. And if you lose your legs, yet manage to return from captivity on crutches, we will convict you. (The Leningrader Ivanov, commander of a machine-gun platoon in the Finnish War, was subsequently thus imprisoned in Ustvymlag, for example.)

Our soldiers alone, renounced by their Motherland and degraded to nothing in the eyes of enemies and allies, had to push their way to the swine swill being doled out in the backyards of the Third Reich. Our soldiers alone had the doors shut tight to keep them from returning to their homes, although their young souls tried hard not to believe this. There was something called Article 58-1b—and, in wartime, it provided only for execution by shooting! For not wanting to die from a German bullet, the prisoner had to die from a Soviet bullet for having been a prisoner of war! Some get theirs from the enemy; we get it from our own!

Incidentally, it is very naïve to say *What for?* At no time have governments been moralists. They never imprisoned people and executed them *for* having done something. They imprisoned and executed them *to keep them from* doing something. They imprisoned all those POW's, of course, not *for* treason to the Motherland, because it was absolutely clear even to a fool that only the Vlasov men could be accused of treason. They imprisoned all of them *to keep them from* telling their fellow villagers about Europe. What the eye doesn't see, the heart doesn't grieve for.

What, then, were the courses of action open to Russian war prisoners? There was only one *legally acceptable* course: to lie

244 THE GULAG ARCHIPELAGO

down and let oneself be trampled to death. Every blade of grass pushes its fragile length upward in order to live. As for you—lie down and be trampled on. Even though you've been slow about it, even though you couldn't do it on the battlefield, at least die now; then you will not be prosecuted.

> The soldiers sleep. They spoke their word
> And they are right for eternity.

And every other path which, in desperation, your mind may invent is going to lead you into conflict with the Law.

Escape and return to the Motherland—past the guards ringing the camp, across half Germany, then through Poland or the Balkans—led straight to SMERSH and prison. They were asked: How did you manage to escape when others couldn't? This stinks! Come on, you rat, what *assignment* did they give you? (Mikhail Burnatsev, Pavel Bondarenko, and many, many others.)[5]

Escaping to the Western partisans, to the Resistance forces,

---

5. It has become the accepted thing for our literary critics to say that Sholokhov, in his immortal story *"Sudba Cheloveka"*—"The Fate of a Man"—spoke the "bitter truth" about "this side of our life" and that he "revealed" the problem. But we must retort that in this story, which is in general very inferior, and in which the passages about the war are pale and unconvincing—since the author evidently knew nothing about the last war—and the descriptions of Germans are unconvincing cartoon clichés (only the hero's wife is successfully portrayed—because she is a pure Christian straight out of Dostoyevsky), in this story about a war prisoner, *the real problem of the war prisoners was hidden or distorted:*

(1) The author picked the least incriminating form of being taken prisoner conceivable—the soldier was captured while unconscious, so as to make him noncontroversial and to bypass the whole poignancy of the problem. (What if he had been conscious when he was taken prisoner, as was most often the case? What would have happened to him then?)

(2) The fact that the Motherland had deserted us, had renounced us, had cursed us, was not presented as the war prisoner's chief problem. Sholokhov says not a word about it. But it was because of *that particular factor* that there was no way out. On the contrary, he identifies the presence of traitors among us as constituting the problem. (But if this really was the main thing, one might then expect him to have investigated further and explained where they came from a full quarter-century after a Revolution that was supported by the entire people!)

(3) Sholokhov dreamed up a fantastic, spy-story escape from captivity, stretching innumerable points to avoid the obligatory, inevitable procedural step of the returned war prisoner's reception in SMERSH—the Identification and Screening Camp. Not only was Sokolov, the hero, not put behind barbed wire, as provided in the regulations, but—and this is a real joke—he was given a month's holiday by his colonel! (In other words: the freedom to carry out the *assignment* given him by the Fascist intelligence service. So his colonel would end up *in the same place* as he!)

only postponed your full reckoning with the military tribunal; also, it made you still more dangerous. You could have acquired a very harmful spirit through living freely among Europeans. And if you had not been afraid to escape and continue to fight, it meant you were a determined person and thus doubly dangerous in the Motherland.

Did you survive POW camp at the expense of your compatriots and comrades? Did you become a member of the camp Polizei, or a commandant, a helper of the Germans and of death? Stalinist law did not punish you any more severely than if you had operated with the Resistance forces. It was the same article of the Code and the same term—and one could guess why too. *Such* a person was less dangerous. But the inert law that is inexplicably implanted in us forbade this path to all except the dregs.

In addition to those four possibilities—either impossible or unacceptable—there was a fifth: to wait for German recruiters, to see what they would summon you to.

Sometimes, fortunately, representatives came from German rural districts to select hired men for their farmers. Sometimes they came from corporations and picked out engineers and mechanics. According to the supreme Stalinist imperative you should have rejected that too. You should have concealed the fact that you were an engineer. You should have concealed the fact that you were a skilled worker. As an industrial designer or electrician, you could have preserved your patriotic purity only if you had stayed in the POW camp to dig in the earth, to rot, to pick through the garbage heap. In that case, for *pure* treason to the Motherland, you could count on getting, your head raised high in pride, ten years in prison and five more "muzzled." Whereas for treason to the Motherland aggravated by working for the enemy, especially in one's own profession, you got, with bowed head, the same ten years in prison and five more muzzled.

And that was the jeweler's precision of a behemoth—Stalin's trademark.

Now and then recruiters turned up who were of quite a different stripe—Russians, usually recent Communist political commissars. White Guards didn't accept that type of employment. These recruiters scheduled a meeting in the camp, condemned the

Soviet regime, and appealed to prisoners to enlist in spy schools
or in Vlasov units.

People who have never starved as our war prisoners did, who
have never gnawed on bats that happened to fly into the barracks,
who have never had to boil the soles of old shoes, will never
understand the irresistible material force exerted by any kind
of appeal, any kind of argument whatever, if behind it, on the
other side of the camp gates, smoke rises from a field kitchen, and
if everyone who signs up is fed a bellyful of kasha right then and
there—if only once! Just once more before I die!

And hovering over the steaming kasha and the inducements of
the recruiter was the apparition of freedom and a real life—
wherever it might call! To the Vlasov battalions. To the Cossack
regiments of Krasnov. To the labor battalions—pouring cement
in the future Atlantic Wall. To the fjords of Norway. To the
sands of Libya. To the "Hiwi" units ("Hilfswillige"—volunteers
in the German Wehrmacht—there being twelve "Hiwi" men in
each German company). And then, finally, to the village Polizei,
who pursued and caught partisans—many of whom the Motherland would also renounce. Wherever it might call, any place at
all, at least anything so as not to stay there and die like abandoned
cattle.

We *ourselves* released from every obligation, not merely to his
Motherland but to all humanity, the human being whom we
drove to gnawing on bats.

And those of our boys who agreed to become half-baked spies
still had not drawn any drastic conclusions from their abandoned
state; they were still, in fact, acting very patriotically. They saw
this course as the least difficult means of getting out of POW
camp. Almost to a man, they decided that as soon as the Germans
sent them across to the Soviet side, they would turn themselves
in to the authorities, turn in their equipment and instructions,
and join their own benign command in laughing at the stupid
Germans. They would then put on their Red Army uniforms and
return to fight bravely in their units. And tell me, *who, speaking
in human terms, could have expected anything else? How could it
have been any other way?* These were straightforward, sincere
men. I saw many of them. They had honest round faces and spoke
with an attractive Vyatka or Vladimir accent. They boldly joined

up as spies, even though they'd had only four or five grades of rural school and were not even competent to cope with map and compass.

It appears that they picked the only way out they could. And one would suppose that the whole thing was an expensive and stupid game on the part of the German Command. But no! Hitler played in rhythm and in tune with his brother dictator! Spy mania was one of the fundamental aspects of Stalin's insanity. It seemed to Stalin that the country was swarming with spies. All the Chinese who lived in the Soviet Far East were convicted as spies—Article 58-6—and were taken to the northern camps, where they perished. The same fate had awaited Chinese participants in the Soviet civil war—if they hadn't cleared out in time. Several hundred thousand Koreans were exiled to Kazakhstan, all similarly accused of spying. All Soviet citizens who at one time or another had lived abroad, who at one time or another had hung around Intourist hotels, who at one time or another happened to be photographed next to a foreigner, or who had themselves photographed a city building (the Golden Gate in Vladimir) were accused of the same crime. Those who stared too long at railroad tracks, at a highway bridge, at a factory chimney were similarly charged. All the numerous foreign Communists stranded in the Soviet Union, all the big and little Comintern officials and employees, one after another, without any individual distinctions, were charged first of all with espionage.[6] And the Latvian Riflemen—whose bayonets were the most reliable in the first years of the Revolution—were also accused of espionage when they were arrested to a man in 1937. Stalin seems somehow to have twisted around and maximized the famous declaration of that coquette Catherine the Great: he would rather that 999 innocent men should rot than miss one genuine spy. Given all this, how could one believe and trust Russian soldiers who had really been in the hands of the German intelligence service? And how it eased the burden for the MGB executioners when thousands of soldiers pouring in from Europe did not even try to conceal that they had voluntarily enlisted as spies. What an astonishing con-

6. Iosip Tito just barely escaped this fate. And Popov and Tanev, fellow defendants of Dimitrov in the Leipzig trial, both got prison terms. (For Dimitrov himself Stalin prepared another fate.)

firmation of the predictions of the Wisest of the Wise! Come on, keep coming, you silly fools! The article and the retribution have long since been waiting for you!

But it is appropriate to ask one thing more. There still were prisoners of war who did not accept recruiting offers, who never worked for the Germans at their profession or trade, and who were not camp police, *who spent the whole war in POW camps, without sticking their noses outside,* and who, in spite of everything, did not die, however unlikely this was. For example, they made cigarette lighters out of scrap metal, like the electrical engineers Nikolai Andreyevich Semyonov and Fyodor Fyodorovich Karpov, and in that way managed to get enough to eat. And did the Motherland forgive them for surrendering?

No, it did not forgive them! I met both Semyonov and Karpov in the Butyrki after they had already received their lawful sentence. And what was it? The alert reader already knows: *ten years of imprisonment and five muzzled.* As brilliant engineers, they had *rejected* German offers to work at their profession. In 1941 Junior Lieutenant Semyonov had gone to the front as a *volunteer.* In 1942 he still didn't have a revolver; instead, he had *an empty holster*—and the interrogator could not understand why he hadn't shot himself with his holster! He had escaped from captivity *three times.* And in 1945, after he had been liberated from a concentration camp, seated atop a tank as a member of a penalty unit of tank-borne infantry, *he took part in the capture of Berlin* and received the Order of the *Red Star.* Yet, after all that, he was finally imprisoned and *sentenced.* All of this mirrored our Nemesis.

Very few of the war prisoners returned across the Soviet border as free men, and if one happened to get through by accident because of the prevailing chaos, he was seized later on, even as late as 1946 or 1947. Some were arrested at assembly points in Germany. Others weren't arrested openly right away but were transported from the border in freight cars, under convoy, to one of the numerous Identification and Screening Camps (PFL's) scattered throughout the country. These camps differed in no way from the common run of Corrective Labor Camps (ITL's) except that their prisoners had not yet been sentenced but would be sentenced there. All these PFL's were also attached to some kind of factory, or mine, or construction project, and the former POW's, looking out on the Motherland newly restored to them through the same barbed wire through which they had seen Germany, could begin work from their first day on a ten-hour work day. Those under suspicion were questioned during their rest periods, in the evenings, and at night, and there were large numbers of Security officers and interrogators in the PFL's for this purpose. As always, the interrogation began with the hypothesis that you were obviously guilty. And you, without going outside the barbed wire, had to prove that you were *not* guilty. Your only available means to this end was to rely on witnesses who were exactly the same kind of POW's as you. Obviously they might not have turned up in your own PFL; they might, in fact, be at the other end of the country; in that case, the Security officers of, say, Kemerovo would send off inquiries to the Security officers of Solikamsk, who would question the witnesses and send back their answers along with new inquiries, and you yourself would be questioned as a witness in some other case. True, it might take a year or two before your fate was resolved, but after all, the Motherland was losing nothing in the process. You were out mining coal every day. And if one of your witnesses gave the wrong sort of testimony about you, or if none of your witnesses was alive, you had only yourself to blame, and you were sure to be entered in the documents as a traitor *of* the Motherland. And the visiting military court would rubber-stamp your *tenner*. And if, despite all their twisting things about, it appeared that you really hadn't worked for the Germans, and if—and this was the main point—you had not had the chance to see the Americans and English with your own eyes (to have been liberated from captivity by *them* instead of by us was a gravely aggravating circumstance), then the Security officers would decide the degree of isolation in which you were to be held. Certain people were ordered to change their place of resi-dence—which always breaks a person's ties with his environment and makes him more vulnerable. Others were valiantly offered the chance to go to work in the VOKhR, the Militarized Guard Service. In that situation, while nominally remaining free, a man lost all his personal freedom and was sent off to some isolated area. There was a third category: after a handshake, some were humanely permitted to return home, although, even without aggravating circumstances, they deserved to be shot for having surrendered. But people in this category celebrated prematurely! Even before the former prisoner arrived home, his *case* had reached his home district through the secret channels of State Security. These people remained eternally *outsiders*. And with the first mass arrests, like those of 1948–1949, they were immediately arrested for hostile propaganda or some other reason. I was imprisoned with people in that category too.

"Oh, if I had only known!" That was the refrain in the prison cells that spring. If I had only known that this was how I would be greeted! That they would deceive me so! That this would be my fate! Would I have really returned to my Motherland? Not for anything! I would have made my way to Switzerland, to France! I would have gone across the sea, across the ocean! Across three oceans![7]

But the more thoughtful prisoners corrected them. They had made their mistake earlier! They were stupid to have dashed off to the front lines in 1941. It takes a fool to rush off to war! Right from the start, they should have gotten themselves set up in the rear. Somewhere quiet. Those who did are heroes now. And it would have been an even surer thing just to desert. Almost certainly, one's skin would be whole. They didn't get ten years either—but eight, or seven. And they weren't excluded from any of the cushy jobs in camp. After all, a deserter was not regarded as an enemy or a traitor or a political prisoner. He was considered not a hostile factor but a friendly one, *a nonpolitical offender,* so to speak. That point of view aroused passionate

7. In actual fact, even when POW's actually *knew* what would happen to them, they behaved in exactly the same way. Vasily Aleksandrov was taken prisoner in Finland. He was sought out there by some elderly Petersburg merchant who asked him his name and patronymic and then said: "In 1917 I owed your grandfather a large debt, and I didn't have the chance to pay it. Here you are—take it!" An old debt is a windfall! After the war Aleksandrov was accepted by the circle of Russian émigrés, and he got engaged to a girl there whom he came to love—and not just casually. To educate him, his future father-in-law gave him a bound set of *Pravda*—just as it was issued from 1918 to 1941, without any deletions or corrections. At the same time, he recounted to him more or less completely the history of the *waves* of arrests, as we have set it forth in Chapter 2, above. And nevertheless . . . Aleksandrov abandoned his fiancée, and his wealth, and returned to the U.S.S.R., where he was given, as one can easily guess, *ten years and disenfranchisement for five more*. In 1953 he was happy to have managed to snag himself a job as foreman in a Special Camp.

argument and objections. The deserters had to spend all those years rotting in prison, and they would not be forgiven. But there would soon be an amnesty for everyone else; they would all be released. (At that time the principal advantage of being a deserter was still unknown.)

Those who had gotten in via 58-10, snatched from their apartments or from the Red Army, often envied the rest. What the hell! For *the very same money,* in other words for the same ten-year sentence, they could have seen so many interesting things, like those other fellows, who had been just about everywhere! And here we are, about to croak in camp, without ever having seen anything beyond our own stinking stairs. Incidentally, those who were in on Article 58-10 could hardly conceal their triumphant presentiment that they would be the first to be amnestied.

The only ones who did not sigh: "Oh, if I had only known"— because they knew very well what they were doing—and the only ones who did not expect any mercy and did not expect an amnesty—were the Vlasov men.

■

I had known about them and been perplexed about them long before our unexpected meeting on the board bunks of prison.

First there had been the leaflets, repeatedly soaked through, dried out, and lost in the high grass—uncut for the third year— of the front-line strip near Orel. In December, 1942, they had announced the creation in Smolensk of a "Russian Committee" —which apparently claimed to be some sort of Russian government and yet at the same time seemed not to be one. Evidently the Germans themselves had not yet made up their minds. For that reason, the communiqué seemed to be a hoax. There was a photograph of General Vlasov in the leaflets, and his biography was outlined. In the fuzzy photograph, his face looked well fed and successful, like all our generals of the new stripe. They told me later that this wasn't so, that Vlasov's face was more like that of a Western general—high, thin, with horn-rimmed glasses. His biography testified to a penchant for success. He had begun in a peasant family, and 1937 had not broken his skyrocketing career; nor was it ruined by his service as a military adviser to

Chiang Kai-shek. The first and only disaster of his earlier life
had occurred when his Second Shock Army, after being encircled, was ineptly abandoned to die of starvation. But how
much of that whole biography could be believed?[8]

8. As far as one can establish at this late date, Andrei Andreyevich Vlasov,
prevented by the Revolution from completing his studies at the Nizhni Novgorod Orthodox Seminary, was drafted into the Red Army in 1919 and fought
as an enlisted man. On the southern front, against Denikin and Wrangel, he
rose to be commander of a platoon, then of a company. In the twenties he
completed the Vystrel courses. He became a member of the Communist Party
in 1930. In 1936, having attained the rank of regimental commander, he was
sent to China as a military adviser. Evidently he had no ties to the top military
and Party circles, and he therefore turned up naturally in that Stalinist "second
echelon" of officers promoted to replace the purged commanders of armies,
divisions, and brigades. From 1938 on he commanded a division. And in
1940, when "new" (in other words, old) officer ranks were created, he became
a major general. From additional information one can conclude that in that
corps of newly made generals, many of whom were totally stupid and inexperienced, Vlasov was one of the most talented. His 99th Infantry Division, which
he had instructed and trained from the summer of 1940 on, was not caught
off balance by the German attack. On the contrary, while the rest of the army
reeled backward, his division advanced, retook Przemysl, and held it for six
days. Quickly skipping the rank of corps commander, in 1941 Lieutenant General Vlasov was in command of the Thirty-seventh Army near Kiev. He made
his way out of the enormous Kiev encirclement and in December, 1941, near
Moscow he commanded the Twentieth Army, whose successful Soviet counter-
offensive for defense of the capital (the taking of Solnechnogorsk) was noted
in the Sovinformburo communiqué for December 12. And the list of generals
mentioned there was as follows: Zhukov, Lelyushenko, Kuznetsov, Vlasov,
Rokossovsky, Govorov. Thanks to the speed with which officers were promoted
in those months, he became Deputy Commander of the Volkhov Front (under
Meretskov), and took over command of the Second Shock Army. On January
7, 1942, at the head of that army, he began a drive to break the Leningrad
blockade—an attack across the Volkhov River to the northwest. This had
been planned as a combined operation, a concerted push from several directions and from Leningrad itself. At scheduled intervals the Fifty-fourth, the
Fourth, and the Fifty-second armies were to take part in it also. But those
three armies either did not advance because they were unready or else came
to a quick halt. At that time we still didn't have the capacity to plan such
complex combined operations, and, more importantly, provide supplies for
them. Vlasov's Second Shock Army, however, was successful in its assault, and
by February, 1942, it was 46 miles deep inside the German lines! And from
then on, the reckless Stalinist Supreme Command could find neither men nor
ammunition to reinforce even those troops. (That's the kind of reserves they
had begun the offensive with!) Leningrad, too, was left to die behind the
blockade, having received no specific information from Novgorod. During
March the winter roads still held up. From April on, however, the entire
swampy area through which the Second Army had advanced melted into mud,
and there were no supply roads, and there was no help from the air. The army
was *without food* and, at the same time, Vlasov *was refused permission to retreat*. For two months they endured starvation and extermination. In the
Butyrki, soldiers from that army told me how they had cut off the hoofs of
dead and rotting horses and boiled the scrapings and eaten them. Then, on
May 14, a German attack was launched from all sides against the encircled

From his photograph, it was impossible to believe that he was an outstanding man or that for long years he had suffered profoundly for Russia. As for the leaflets reporting the creation of the ROA, the "Russian Liberation Army," not only were they written in bad Russian, but they were imbued with an alien spirit that was clearly German and, moreover, seemed little concerned with their presumed subject; besides, and on the other hand, they contained crude boasting about the plentiful chow available and the cheery mood of the soldiers. Somehow one couldn't believe in that army, and, if it really did exist, what kind of cheery mood could it be in? Only a German could lie like that.[9]

---

army. The only planes in the air, of course, were German. And only then, in mockery, were they given permission to pull back behind the Volkhov. They made several hopeless attempts to break through—until the beginning of July.

And so it was that Vlasov's Second Shock Army perished, literally recapitulating the fate of Samsonov's Russian Second Army in World War I, having been just as insanely thrown into encirclement.

Now this, of course, was treason to the Motherland! This, of course, was vicious, self-obsessed betrayal! But it was Stalin's. Treason does not necessarily involve selling out for money. It can include ignorance and carelessness in the preparations for war, confusion and cowardice at its very start, the meaningless sacrifice of armies and corps solely for the sake of saving one's own marshal's uniform. Indeed, what more bitter treason is there on the part of a Supreme Commander in Chief?

Unlike Samsonov, Vlasov did not commit suicide. After his army had been wiped out, he wandered among the woods and swamps and, on July 6, personally surrendered in the area of Siverskaya. He was taken to the German headquarters near Lötzen in East Prussia, where they were holding several captured generals and a brigade political commissar, G. N. Zhilenkov, formerly a successful Party official and secretary of one of the Moscow District Party Committees. These captives had already confessed their disagreement with the policy of the Stalin government. But they had no real leader. Vlasov became it.

9. In reality there was no Russian Liberation Army until almost the very end of the war. Both the name and the insignia devised for it were invented by a German of Russian origin, Captain Strik-Strikfeldt, in the Ost-Propaganda-Abteilung. Although he held only a minor position, he had influence, and he tried to convince the Hitlerite leadership that a German-Russian alliance was essential and that the Russians should be encouraged to collaborate with Germany. A vain undertaking for both sides! Each side wanted only to use and deceive the other. But, in the given situation, the Germans had power—they were on top of the setup. And the Vlasov officers had only their fantasy—at the bottom of the abyss. There was no such army, but anti-Soviet formations made up of Soviet citizens were organized from the very start of the war. The first to support the Germans were the Lithuanians. In the one year we had been there we had aroused their deep, angry hostility! And then the SS-Galicia Division was created from Ukrainian volunteers. And Estonian units afterward. In the fall of 1941, guard companies appeared in Byelorussia. And a Tatar battalion in the Crimea. We ourselves had sowed the seeds of all this! Take,

We soon discovered that there really were Russians fighting against us and that they fought harder than any SS men. In July, 1943, for example, near Orel, a platoon of Russians in German uniform defended Sobakinskiye Vyselki. They fought with the desperation that might have been expected if they had built the place themselves. One of them was driven into a root cellar. They threw hand grenades in after him and he fell silent. But they had no more than stuck their heads in than he let them have another volley from his automatic pistol. Only when they lobbed in an antitank grenade did they find out that, within the root cellar, he had another foxhole in which he had taken shelter from the infantry grenades. Just try to imagine the degree of shock, deafness, and hopelessness in which he had kept on fighting.

They defended, for example, the unshakable Dnieper bridgehead south of Tursk. For two weeks we continued to fight there for a mere few hundred yards. The battles were fierce in December, 1943, and so was the cold. Through many long days both we and they went through the extreme trials of winter, fighting

for example, our stupid twenty-year policy of closing and destroying the Moslem mosques in the Crimea. And compare that with the policy of the farsighted conqueror Catherine the Great, who contributed state funds for building and expanding the Crimean mosques. And the Hitlerites, when they arrived, were smart enough to present themselves as their defenders. Later, Caucasian detachments and Cossack armies—more than a cavalry corps—put in an appearance on the German side. In the first winter of the war, platoons and companies of Russian volunteers began to be formed. But the German Command was very distrustful of these Russian units, and their master sergeants and lieutenants were Germans. Only their noncoms below master sergeant were Russian. They also used such German commands as "Achtung!," "Halt!" etc. More significant and entirely Russian were the following units: a brigade in Lokot, in Bryansk Province, from November, 1941, when a local teacher of engineering, K. P. Voskoboinikov, proclaimed the "National Labor Party of Russia" and issued a manifesto to the citizens of the nation, hoisting the flag of St. George; a unit in the Osintorf settlement near Orsha, formed at the beginning of 1942 under the leadership of Russian émigrés (it must be said that only a small group of Russian émigrés joined this movement, and even they did not conceal their anti-German feelings and allowed many crossovers [including a whole battalion] to the Soviet side . . . after which they were dropped by the Germans); and a unit formed by Gil, in the summer of 1942, near Lublin. (V. V. Gil, a Communist Party member and even, it seems, a Jew, not only survived as a POW but, with the help of other POW's, became the head of a camp near Suwalki and offered to create a "fighting alliance of Russian nationalists" for the Germans.) However, there was as yet no Russian Liberation Army in all of this and no Vlasov. The companies under German command were put on the Russian front, as an experiment, and the Russian units were sent against the Bryansk, Orsha, and Polish partisans.

in winter camouflage cloaks that covered our overcoats and caps. Near Malye Kozlovichi, I was told, an interesting encounter took place. As the soldiers dashed back and forth among the pines, things got confused, and two soldiers lay down next to one another. No longer very accurately oriented, they kept shooting at someone, somewhere over there. Both had Soviet automatic pistols. They shared their cartridges, praised one another, and together swore at the grease freezing on their automatic pistols. Finally, their pistols stopped firing altogether, and they decided to take a break and light up. They pulled back their white hoods —and at the same instant each saw the other's cap . . . the eagle and the star. They jumped up! Their automatic pistols still refused to fire! Grabbing them by the barrel and swinging them like clubs, they began to go at each other. This, if you will, was not politics and not the Motherland, but just sheer caveman distrust: If I take pity on him, he is going to kill me.

In East Prussia, a trio of captured Vlasov men was being marched along the roadside a few steps away from me. At that moment a T-34 tank thundered down the highway. Suddenly one of the captives twisted around and dived underneath the tank. The tank veered, but the edge of its track crushed him nevertheless. The broken man lay writhing, bloody foam coming from his mouth. And one could certainly understand him! He preferred a soldier's death to being hanged in a dungeon.

They had no choice. There was no other way for them to fight. They had no chance to find a way out, to safeguard their lives, by some more cautious mode of fighting. If "pure" surrender was considered unforgivable treason to the Motherland, then what about those who had taken up enemy arms? Our propaganda, in all its crudity, explained their conduct as: (1) treason (was it biologically based? carried in the bloodstream?); or (2) cowardice—which it certainly was not! A coward tries to find a spot where things are easy, soft, safe. And men could be induced to enter the Wehrmacht's Vlasov detachments only in the last extremity, only at the limit of desperation, only out of inexhaustible hatred of the Soviet regime, only with total contempt for their own safety. For they knew they would never have the faintest glimpse of mercy! When we captured them, we shot them as soon as the first intelligible Russian word came from their mouths. In

Russian captivity, as in German captivity, the worst lot of all was reserved for the Russians.

In general, this war revealed to us that the worst thing in the world was to be a Russian.

I recall with shame an incident I observed during the liquidation—in other words, the plundering—of the Bobruisk encirclement, when I was walking along the highway among wrecked and overturned German automobiles, and a wealth of booty lay scattered everywhere. German cart horses wandered aimlessly in and out of a shallow depression where wagons and automobiles that had gotten stuck were buried in the mud, and bonfires of booty were smoking away. Then I heard a cry for help: "Mr. Captain! Mr. Captain!" A prisoner on foot in German britches was crying out to me in pure Russian. He was naked from the waist up, and his face, chest, shoulders, and back were all bloody, while a sergeant osobist, a Security man, seated on a horse, drove him forward with a whip, pushing him with his horse. He kept lashing that naked back up and down with the whip, without letting him turn around, without letting him ask for help. He drove him along, beating and beating him, raising new crimson welts on his skin.

And this was not one of the Punic Wars, nor a war between the Greeks and the Persians! Any officer, possessing any authority, in any army on earth ought to have stopped that senseless torture. In any army on earth, yes, but in ours? Given our fierce and uncompromising method of dividing mankind? (If you are *not with us,* if you are *not our own, etc.,* then you deserve nothing but contempt and annihilation.) So I *was afraid* to defend the Vlasov man against the osobist. *I said nothing and I did nothing. I passed him by as if I could not hear him . . .* so that I myself would not be infected by that universally recognized plague. (What if the Vlasov man was indeed some kind of supervillain? Or maybe the osobist would think something was wrong with me? And then?) Or, putting it more simply for anyone who knows anything about the situation in the Soviet Army at that time: would that osobist have paid any attention to an army captain?

So the osobist continued to lash the defenseless man brutally and drive him along like a beast.

This picture will remain etched in my mind forever. This, after all, is almost a symbol of the Archipelago. It ought to be on the jacket of this book.

The Vlasov men had a presentiment of all this; they knew it ahead of time; nevertheless, on the left sleeve of their German uniforms they sewed the shield with the white-blue-red edging, the field of St. Andrew, and the letters "ROA."[10] The inhabitants

10. These letters became even better known, although, as before, there was still no real Russian Liberation Army. The units were all scattered and kept subordinate to German orders, and the Vlasov generals had nothing to do but play cards in Dahlemdorf, near Berlin. By the middle of 1942, Voskoboinikov's brigade, which, after his death, was commanded by Kaminsky, numbered five infantry regiments of 2,500 to 3,000 men each, with attached artillery crews, a tank battalion consisting of two dozen Soviet tanks, and an artillery battalion with three dozen guns. The commanding officers were POW officers, and the rank and file was made up, in considerable part, of local Bryansk volunteers. This brigade was under orders to guard the area against partisans. In the summer of 1942, the brigade of Gil-Blazhevich was transferred for the same purpose from Poland, where it had been notable for its cruelty toward Poles and Jews, to the area near Mogilev. At the beginning of 1943, its command refused to acknowledge Vlasov's authority, demanding that he explain why, in his stated program, there was no reference to the "struggle against world Jewry and Jew-loving commissars." These were the very men—called the Rodionovites, because Gil had changed his name to Rodionov—who in August, 1943, when Hitler's approaching defeat became apparent, changed their black flag with a silver skull to a red flag, and proclaimed Soviet authority and a large "partisan region" in the northeast corner of Byelorussia.

At that time, Soviet newspapers began to write about the "partisan region," but without explaining its origins. Later on, all surviving Rodionovites were imprisoned. And whom did the Germans immediately throw in against the Rodionovites? The Kaminsky brigade! That was in May, 1944, and they also threw in thirteen of their own divisions in an effort to liquidate the "partisan region." That was the extent to which Germans understood all those tricolor cockades, St. George, and the field of St. Andrew. The Russian and German languages were mutually untranslatable, inexpressible, uncorrelatable. Still worse: in October, 1944, the Germans threw in Kaminsky's brigade—with its Moslem units—to suppress the Warsaw uprising. While one group of Russians sat traitorously dozing beyond the Vistula, watching the death of Warsaw through their binoculars, other Russians crushed the uprising! Hadn't the Poles had enough Russian villainy to bear in the nineteenth century without having to endure more of it in the twentieth? For that matter, was that the last of it? Perhaps more is still to come. The career of the Osintorf Battalion was apparently more straightforward. This consisted of about six hundred soldiers and two hundred officers, with an émigré command, I. K. Sakharov and Lamsdorf, Russian uniforms, and a white-blue-red flag; it was thrown in near Pskov. Then, reinforced to regimental strength, it was readied for a parachute drop on the line of Vologda-Archangel, the idea being to make use of the nest of concentration camps in that area. Throughout 1943, Igor Sakharov managed to prevent his unit from being sent against the partisans. But then he was replaced and the battalion was first disarmed and imprisoned in a camp and then sent off to the Western Front. Then, in the fall of 1943, the Germans decided to send the Russian cannon fodder to the Atlantic Wall, and against the French and Italian Resistance, having lost, forgotten, and not even tried to recall its original purpose. Those among the Vlasov men who had managed to retain some kind of political rationality or hope thereupon lost both.

of the occupied areas held them in contempt as German hire-lings. So did the Germans, because of their Russian blood. Their pitiful little newspapers were worked over with a German cen-sor's broadsword: Greater Germany and the Führer. And the Vlasov men had one way out of all that—to fight to the death, and, when they were not fighting, to down vodka and more vodka. *Foredoomed*—that was their existence during all their years of war and alien lands, and there was no salvation for them from any direction.

Hitler and those around him, even when they were retreating on every front and were staring their own destruction in the face, could still not overcome their intense distrust of wholly separate Russian units; they could not bring themselves to organize divi-sions that were entirely Russian, to allow even the shadow of a Russia that was not totally subject to them. Only in the crack of the final debacle, in November, 1944, was a belated theatrical production at last permitted in Prague: the creation of a "Com-mittee for the Liberation of the Peoples of Russia," combining all the different national groups, and a manifesto, which, like everything that had preceded it, was neither fish nor fowl, since the concept of a Russia independent of Germany and Nazism was still not tolerated. Vlasov became chairman of the commit-tee. And only in the fall of 1944 did they begin to form Vlasov divisions that were exclusively Russian.[11] Probably the wise Ger-man political leaders had concluded that at this point the Russian workers in Germany (the "ostovtsy") would rush to take up arms. But the Red Army was already on the Vistula and the Danube. And ironically, as though to confirm the farsightedness of the very nearsighted Germans, those Vlasov divisions, in their first and last independent action, dealt a blow—to the Germans themselves. In the general disaster, Vlasov gathered up his two and a half divisions near Prague at the end of April, without coordinating his action with the German Supreme Command. It became known at this point that SS General Steiner was pre-paring to destroy the Czech capital rather than surrender it in-tact. And Vlasov ordered his divisions to the aid of the Czech

11. They were: the 1st, based on "the Kaminsky brigade," under S. K. Bunyachenko; the 2nd, under Zverev (former military commandant of Khar-kov); half the 3rd; segments of the 4th; and Maltsev's air force detachment. Only four divisions were authorized.

rebels. And at that point, all the hurt, bitterness, and anger against the Germans that had accumulated during three cruel and futile years in the breasts of the enslaved Russians was vented in the attack on the Germans. They were shoved out of Prague from an unexpected direction. Did all Czechs realize later *which* Russians had saved their city? Our own history is similarly distorted; we claim that Prague was saved by Soviet armies, although they couldn't have gotten there in time.

Then the Vlasov army began to retreat toward Bavaria and the Americans. They were pinning all their hopes on the possibility of being useful to the Allies; in this way their years of dangling in the German noose would finally become meaningful. But the Americans greeted them with a wall of armor and forced them to surrender to Soviet hands, as stipulated by the Yalta Conference. In Austria that May, Churchill perpetrated the same sort of "act of a loyal ally," but, out of our accustomed modesty, we did not publicize it. He turned over to the Soviet command the Cossack corps of 90,000 men.[12] Along with them, he also

12. This surrender was an act of double-dealing consistent with the spirit of traditional English diplomacy. The heart of the matter was that the Cossacks were determined to fight to the death, or to cross the ocean, all the way to Paraguay or Indochina if they had to . . . anything rather than surrender alive. Therefore, the English proposed, first, that the Cossacks give up their arms on the pretext of replacing them with standardized weapons. Then the officers —without the enlisted men—were summoned to a supposed conference on the future of the army in the city of Judenburg in the English occupation zone. But the English had secretly turned the city over to the Soviet armies the night before. Forty busloads of officers, all the way from commanders of companies on up to General Krasnov himself, crossed a high viaduct and drove straight down into a semicircle of *Black Marias*, next to which stood convoy guards with lists in their hands. The road back was blocked by Soviet tanks. The officers didn't even have anything with which to shoot themselves or to stab themselves to death, since their weapons had been taken away. They jumped from the viaduct onto the paving stones below. Immediately afterward, and just as treacherously, the English turned over the rank-and-file soldiers by the train-load—pretending that they were on their way to receive new weapons from their commanders.

In their own countries Roosevelt and Churchill are honored as embodiments of statesmanlike wisdom. To us, in our Russian prison conversations, their consistent shortsightedness and stupidity stood out as astonishingly obvious. How could they, in their decline from 1941 to 1945, fail to secure any guarantees whatever of the independence of Eastern Europe? How could they give away broad regions of Saxony and Thuringia in exchange for the preposterous toy of a four-zone Berlin, their own future Achilles' heel? And what was the military or political sense in their surrendering to destruction at Stalin's hands hundreds of thousands of armed Soviet citizens determined not to surrender? They say it was the price they paid for Stalin's agreeing to enter the war against Japan. With the atom bomb already in their hands, they paid Stalin for not

handed over many wagonloads of old people, women, and children who did not want to return to their native Cossack rivers. This great hero, monuments to whom will in time cover all England, ordered that they, too, be surrendered to their deaths.

In addition to the hurriedly created Vlasov divisions, quite a few Russian subunits went right on turning sour in the depths of the German Army, wearing standard German uniforms. They finished out the war on various sectors and in different ways.

I myself fell under Vlasov fire a few days before my arrest. There were Russians in the East Prussian "sack" which we had surrounded, and one night at the end of January their unit tried to break through our position to the west, without artillery preparation, in silence. There was no firmly delineated front in any case, and they penetrated us in depth, catching my sound-locator battery, which was out in front, in a pincers. I just barely managed to pull it back by the last remaining road. But then I went back for a piece of damaged equipment, and, before dawn, I watched as they suddenly rose from the snow where they'd dug in, wearing their winter camouflage cloaks, hurled themselves with a cheer on the battery of a 152-millimeter gun battalion at Adlig Schwenkitten, and knocked out twelve heavy cannon with hand grenades before they could fire a shot. Pursued by their tracer bullets, our last little group ran almost two miles in fresh snow to the bridge across the Passarge River. And there they were stopped.

Soon after that I was arrested. And now, on the eve of the Victory Parade, here we all were sitting together on the board bunks of the Butyrki. I took puffs from their cigarettes and they took puffs from mine. And paired with one or another of them, I used to carry out the six-bucket tin latrine barrel.

Many of the Vlasov men, like the "spies for hire," were

---

refusing to occupy Manchuria, for strengthening Mao Tse-tung in China, and for giving Kim Il Sung control of half Korea! What bankruptcy of political thought! And when, subsequently, the Russians pushed out Mikolajczyk, when Benes and Masaryk came to their ends, when Berlin was blockaded, and Budapest flamed and fell silent, and Korea went up in smoke, and Britain's Conservatives fled from Suez, could one really believe that those among them with the most accurate memories did not at least recall that episode of the Cossacks?

young, born, say, between 1915 and 1922, that same "young and unknown tribe" which hustling-bustling Lunacharsky had hurried to greet in the name of Pushkin. Most of them got into Vlasov military units through that same blind chance which led their comrades in a neighboring camp to get into the spy thing —it all depended on which recruiter had gone where.

The recruiters had explained to them jeeringly—or rather, it would have been jeering if it hadn't been the truth: "Stalin has renounced you! Stalin doesn't give a damn about you!"

Soviet law had outlawed them even before they outlawed themselves.

So they signed up—some of them simply to get out of a death camp, others with the hope of going over to the partisans. (And some of them did! And fought side by side with the partisans! But according to Stalin's rules that didn't soften their sentences in the least.) However, in the case of some, the shame of 1941, that stunning defeat after long, long years of braggadocio, ate at their hearts. Some believed that the primary guilt for those in-human POW camps belonged to Stalin. They, too, wanted the chance to speak out about themselves and their awful experi-ence: to affirm that they, too, were particles of Russia, and wanted to influence Russia's future, and not to be the puppets of other people's mistakes.

But fate played them an even bitterer trick, and they became more abject pawns than before. The Germans, in their shallow stupidity and self-importance, allowed them only to die for the German Reich, but denied them the right to plan an independent destiny for Russia.

And the Allies were two thousand versts away—and anyway, what kind of allies would they indeed turn out to be?

The term "Vlasovite" in our country has the same force as the word "sewage." We feel we are dirtying our mouths merely by pronouncing it, and therefore no one dares utter a sentence with "Vlasovite" as its subject.

But that is no way to write history. Now, a quarter of a cen-tury later, when most of them have perished in camps and those who have survived are living out their lives in the Far North, I would like to issue a reminder, through these pages, that this was a phenomenon totally unheard of in all world history: that several hundred thousand young men,[13] aged twenty to thirty, took up arms against their Fatherland as allies of its most evil enemy. Perhaps there is something to ponder here: Who was more to blame, those youths or the gray Fatherland? One cannot explain this treason biologically. It has to have had a social cause.

Because, as the old proverb says: *Well-fed horses don't rampage.*

Then picture to yourself a field in which starved, neglected, crazed horses are rampaging back and forth.

■

That same spring many Russian émigrés were also in those cells.

It was very like a dream: the resurrection of buried history. The weighty tomes on the Civil War had long since been completed and their covers shut tight. The causes for which people fought in it had been decided. The chronology of its events had been set down in textbooks. The leaders of the White movement were, it appeared, no longer our contemporaries on earth but mere ghosts of a past that had melted away. The Russian émigrés had been more cruelly dispersed than the tribes of Israel. And, in our Soviet imagination, if they were still dragging out their lives somewhere, it was as pianists in stinking little restaurants, as lackeys, laundresses, beggars, morphine and cocaine addicts, and virtual corpses. Right up to 1941, when the war came, it would have been impossible to find out from any hints in our newspapers, our lofty literature, our criticism of the arts (nor did our own well-fed masters of art and literature help us find out) that Russia Abroad was a great spiritual world, that in it Russian philosophy was living and developing; that out there were philosophers like Bulgakov, Berdyayev, and Lossky; that Russian art had enchanted the world; that Rachmaninoff, Chaliapin, Benois, Diaghilev, Pavlova, and the Don Cossack Chorus of Jaroff were out there; that profound studies of Dostoyevsky were being undertaken (at a time when he was anathema in the

13. This, in fact, is the number of Soviet citizens who were in the Wehrmacht—in pre-Vlasov and Vlasov formations, and in the Cossack, Moslem, Baltic, and Ukrainian units and detachments.

Soviet Union); that the incredible writer Nabokov-Sirin also existed out there; that Bunin himself was still alive and had been writing for all these twenty years; that journals of the arts were being published; that theatrical works were being produced; that Russians from the same areas of Russia came together in groups where their mother tongue could be heard; and that émigré men had not given up marrying émigré women, who in turn presented them with children, which meant young people our own age.

The picture of emigration presented in our country was so falsified that if one had conducted a mass survey to ask which side the Russian émigrés were on in the Spanish Civil War, or else, perhaps, what side they were on in the Second World War, with one voice everyone would have replied: For Franco! For Hitler! Even now people in our country do not know that many more White émigrés fought on the Republican side in Spain. That both the Vlasov divisions and the Cossack corps of von Pannwitz (the "Krasnov" corps) were made up of Soviet citizens and not of émigrés. The émigrés did not support Hitler. They ostracized Merezhkovsky and Gippius, who took Hitler's part, leaving them to alienated loneliness. There was a joke—except it wasn't a joke—to the effect that Denikin wanted to fight for the Soviet Union against Hitler, and that at one time Stalin planned to arrange his return to the Motherland, not for military reasons, obviously, but as a symbol of national unity. During the German occupation of France, a horde of Russian émigrés, young and old, joined the Resistance. And after the liberation of Paris they swarmed to the Soviet Embassy to apply for permission to return to the Motherland. No matter what kind of Russia it was—it was still Russia! That was their slogan, and that is how they proved they had not been lying previously about their love for her. (Imprisoned in 1945 and 1946, they were almost happy that these prison bars and these jailers were their own, Russian. And they observed with surprise the Soviet boys scratching their heads and saying: "Why the hell did we come back? Wasn't there room enough for us in Europe?")

But, given that Stalinist logic which said that every Soviet person who had lived abroad had to be imprisoned in camp, how could the émigrés possibly escape the same lot? In the Balkans, Central Europe, Harbin, they were arrested as soon as the Soviet armies arrived. They were arrested in their apartments and on the street, just like Soviet citizens. For a while State Security arrested only men, and not all of them, only those who had in one or another way revealed a political bias. Later on, their families were transported to exile in Russia, but some were left where they were in Bulgaria and Czechoslovakia. In France they were welcomed into Soviet citizenship with honors and flowers and sent back to the Motherland in comfort; and only when they got to the U.S.S.R. were they raked in. Things dragged out longer for the Shanghai émigrés. In 1945 Russian hands didn't reach that far. But a plenipotentiary from the Soviet government went to Shanghai and announced a decree of the Presidium of the Supreme Soviet extending forgiveness to all émigrés. Well, now, how could one refuse to believe that? The government certainly couldn't lie! Whether or not there actually was such a decree, it did not, in any case, tie the hands of the *Organs*. The Shanghai Russians expressed their delight. They were told they could take with them as many possessions as they wanted and whatever they wanted. They went home with automobiles—the country could put them to good use. They were told they could settle wherever they wanted to in the Soviet Union and, of course, work at any profession or trade. They were transported from Shanghai in steamships. The fate of the passengers varied. On some of the ships, for some reason, they were given no food at all. They also suffered various fates after reaching the port of Nakhodka (which was, incidentally, one of the main transit centers of Gulag). Almost all of them were loaded into freight cars, like prisoners, except that they had, as yet, no strict convoy, and there were no police dogs. Some of them were actually delivered to inhabited places, to cities, and allowed to live there for two or three years. Others were delivered in trainloads straight to their camps and were dumped out somewhere off a high embankment into the forest beyond the Volga, together with their white pianos and their jardinieres. In 1948–1949, the former Far Eastern émigrés who had until then managed to stay out of camps were scraped up to the last man.

As a nine-year-old boy I had read the small dark-blue books of V. V. Shulgin with more interest than I had read Jules Verne. At that time they were sold openly in our book stalls. His was

a voice from a world that had disappeared with such finality
that not even the most extravagant fantasy could have projected
that invisible point in the soundless corridors of the Big Lubyanka where his steps would intersect my own before twenty years
had passed. True, I would not meet the man himself until another twenty years had gone by. But I had time to study attentively
many émigrés, old and young, in the spring of 1945.

I underwent a medical examination with Captain Borshch and
Colonel Mariyushkin. And the pitiful sight of their naked,
wrinkled, dark-yellow bodies, not bodies any longer but mummies, has always remained before my eyes. They were arrested
five minutes this side of the grave, so to speak, and brought to
Moscow from several thousand miles away, and there in Moscow, in 1945, an interrogation was proceeding in the most
serious way on . . . their struggle against Soviet power in 1919!

We have become so used to the piling up of injustices during
interrogation and trial that we have ceased drawing any distinctions of degree between them. This captain and this colonel
were veteran officers of the Tsar's Russian Army. They had both
been over forty, and they had both served in the army for
twenty years, when the telegraph brought them news that the
Tsar had been overthrown in Petrograd. For twenty years they
had served the Tsar according to their oath. And now, against
their wills—for all we know, possibly muttering "Beat it! Scram!"
to themselves—they swore loyalty to the Provisional Government. After that, no one asked them to swear any more oaths
because the whole army fell apart. They didn't like the new
scheme of things, wherein soldiers tore shoulder boards off officers and killed them, and it was natural for them to join other
officers to fight against it. And it was natural for the Red Army
to fight against them and push them into the sea. But in a country in which at least the rudiments of jurisprudence exist, what
basis was there for *putting them on trial,* and a quarter of a century later at that? (They had lived as private persons all that
time . . . Mariyushkin up to the very moment of his arrest.
Borshch, to be sure, had turned up in a Cossack wagon train in
Austria, but in a transport, with the old men and women, not in
an armed unit.)

However, in 1945, in the very center of Soviet jurisdiction, they were charged with: actions directed toward the *overthrow* of the government of the workers' and peasants' soviets; armed *incursion* into Soviet territory, in other words, not having immediately left Russia when Petrograd was declared Soviet; aiding the international bourgeoisie (which they had never seen even in their dreams); serving counterrevolutionary governments (i.e., their own generals, to whom they had been subordinate all their lives). And all these sections—Nos. 1, 2, 4, 13—of Article 58 were included in a Criminal Code adopted in 1926, that is, six to seven years *after the end* of the Civil War. This was a classic and unconscionable example of the *ex post facto* application of a law! In addition, Article 2 of the Code specified that it applied *only* to citizens taken into custody on the territory of the Russian Republic. But State Security's strong right arm had grabbed people who were in no wise Soviet citizens from all the countries of Europe and Asia.[14] And we won't even bring up the question of *statutes of limitations*. This question was provided for very flexibly—no statutes of limitations applied to Article 58. (*"Why stir up the past indeed?"*) Such statutes are invoked only in the case of our home-grown executioners, who have destroyed many, many more of their compatriots than did the whole Civil War.

Mariyushkin, at least, remembered everything clearly. He told us the details of being evacuated from Novorossisk. But Borshch had already descended into second childhood and prattled on and on about celebrating Easter in the Lubyanka: he had eaten only half his bread ration during Palm Sunday week and Holy Week and had set the rest of it aside, gradually replacing the stale pieces with fresh ones. Thus he had accumulated seven full rations when it came time to break the Lenten fast—and he had "feasted" for the three days of Easter.

I do not know what kind of White Guards they were in the Civil War, either of them, whether they were among the exceptional few who hung every tenth worker without trial and whipped the peasants, or whether they were the other kind, the soldierly majority. The fact that they were being interrogated and sentenced in Moscow was no proof of anything nor a matter

14. On this basis no single African leader has any assurance that we will not, ten years from now, promulgate a law in accordance with which we will put him on trial for what he does today. Yes. The Chinese, in fact, will promulgate precisely such laws—just give them the chance to reach out that far.

of any consequence. But if, from that time on, they had lived for a quarter of a century, not as retired officers, on pensions and with honor, but as homeless exiles, then how could anyone point to any moral basis for trying them? That is the kind of dialectic Anatole France mastered, but which we cannot seem to grasp. According to Anatole France, by the time it's today, yesterday's martyr is already in the wrong—in fact, from the first minute the red shirt covered his body. And vice versa. But our version is: If they rode me for one short year, when I had just outgrown being a foal, then I am called a riding horse all my life, even though I have long since been used only as a cab horse.

Colonel Konstantin Konstantinovich Yasevich was very different from these helpless émigré mummies. For him, clearly, the end of the Civil War had not ended the struggle against Bolshevism. As to how he continued to struggle—where and with what—he did not enlighten me. But the sense that he was still in the service remained with him in the cell itself. In the midst of all the chaotic concepts, the blurred and broken lines of vision, in most of our heads, he had, evidently, a clear and exact view of everything around him; as a result of this reasoned point of view on life, his body, too, exhibited a steady strength, resiliency, and activity. He was certainly not less than sixty. His head was totally bald, without a single hair. He had already survived his interrogation and was awaiting his sentence, like the rest of us. He could expect no help from anywhere, of course. But he kept his young, even rosy skin. Among all of us in the cell, he alone did exercises every morning and washed himself at the faucet. The rest of us were trying not to squander the calories in our prison ration. He put his time to use, and whenever an aisle opened up between the rows of board bunks, he paced those fifteen to twenty feet with a precise stride and a precise profile, crossing his arms over his chest and staring through the walls with clear young eyes.

And the difference between us and him was that we were all astonished at what was happening to us, while nothing around him contradicted his expectations, and precisely for that reason he was absolutely alone in the cell.

A year later, I was able to appraise his conduct in prison. Once again I was in the Butyrki, and in one of those seventy cells I met some young codefendants of Yasevich who had already been sentenced to ten and fifteen years. The sentences given everyone in their group were typed out on cigarette paper, and for some reason they had it in their possession. Yasevich was first on the list, and his sentence was: to be shot. So that was what he saw—what he foresaw—through the wall with his still-young eyes as he paced back and forth from the table to the door! But his unimpaired consciousness of the correctness of his path in life lent him extraordinary strength.

Among the émigrés was one my own age, Igor Tronko. We became friends. Both of us were weak, dried out; our skin was grayish-yellow on our bones. (Why had we collapsed to such an extent? I think the main cause was spiritual confusion.) Both of us were thin and on the tall side, and we were shaken by the gusts of summer wind in the Butyrki courtyards. We always walked side by side, with the careful steps of old men, and discussed the parallels in our lives. He had been born in South Russia the same year as I. We were still nursing babes when fate stuck her hand into her well-worn purse and drew out a short straw for me and a long one for him. So it was that he rolled off across the sea, even though his White Guard father was just a rank-and-file, unpropertied telegrapher.

I found it interesting in the extreme to picture through his life all those compatriots of my generation who had landed outside Russia. They had grown up under good family supervision and in very modest, even meager, circumstances. They were all very well brought up and, within the range of existing possibilities, well educated. They grew up without knowing fear or repression, though the White organizations maintained a certain yoke of authority over them until they themselves grew strong. They grew up in such a way that the sins to which all European youth was subject in that period—a high crime rate, a frivolous attitude toward life, thoughtlessness, dissipation—did not touch them. That was because they grew up, so to speak, in the shadow of the indelible misfortune which had befallen their families. Whatever country they grew up in, they looked on Russia alone as their Motherland. Their spiritual upbringing was based on Russian literature, all the more beloved because to them it was the beginning and end of their Motherland, because for them their Motherland did not exist as a primary geographical and physical fact. The contemporary printed word was much more generally accessible to them than to us, but they received Soviet books in conspicuously small quantities. And they felt this lack all the more keenly; it seemed to them chiefly responsible for their inability to understand what was most important, highest, and most beautiful in Soviet Russia; and that the books they did receive presented a distortion, a lie; were incomplete. The picture they had of our real life was very, very faint, but their longing for their Motherland was such that if we had called on them in 1941 they would all have joined the Red Army, and it would have been even sweeter for them to die than to survive. These young people from twenty-five to twenty-seven already represented and firmly defended several points of view, in definite conflict with the opinions of the old generals and political leaders. Thus Igor's group was called the "nepredreshentsy"— the "non-prejudgers": they declared that anyone who had not shared with the Motherland the whole, complex burden of the past decades had no right to decide anything about the future of Russia, nor even to presuppose anything, but should simply go and lend his strength to whatever the people might decide.

We would often lie beside one another on the wooden bunks. I tried to understand his world as best I could, and our encounter revealed to me a concept confirmed by later encounters—that the outflow from Russia of a significant part of her spiritual forces, which occurred in the Civil War, had deprived us of a great and important stream of Russian culture. Everyone who really loves that culture will strive for the reunion of both streams, the one at home and the tributary abroad. Only then will our culture attain wholeness. Only then will it reveal its capacity for benign development.

And I dream of living until that day.

A human being is weak, weak. In the end, that spring, even the most stubborn of us wanted forgiveness and were ready to give up a lot for just a little bit more life. An anecdote was current among us: "What is your last word, accused?" "I beg you to send me wherever you please, just as long as it is under the Soviet government and the sun is there!" No one was threatening to deprive us of the Soviet government, of course: just of the sun. No one wanted to be sent beyond the Arctic Circle, to scurvy and malnutrition. For some reason, a legend about the Altai region in particular flourished in the cells. Those rare persons who had been there at one time or another, but especially those who had never been there, wove melodious dreams about the wonderful country of the Altai for their cellmates! It had the vast expanses of Siberia and a mild climate. Rivers of honey flowing between banks of wheat. The steppe and mountains. Herds of sheep, flocks of wildfowl, shoals of fish. Populous, rich villages.[15]

Oh, if only we could find a hiding place in that quiet! If only we could listen to the pure resounding of the cock crow in the unpolluted air! Or stroke the good, serious face of a horse! Curses on you, all you great problems! Let someone else beat his head against you, someone more stupid. Oh, just to rest there from the interrogator's mother oaths and the monotonous un-winding of your whole life, from the crash of the prison locks, from the suffocating stuffiness of the cell. Only one life is allotted us, one small, short life! And we had been criminal enough to push ours in front of somebody's machine guns, or drag it with us, still unsullied, into the dirty rubbish heap of politics. There, in the Altai, it appeared, one could live in the lowest, darkest hut on the edge of the village, next to the forest. And one could go into the woods, not for brushwood and not for mushrooms, but just to go, for no reason, and hug two tree trunks: Dear ones, you're all I need.

And the spring itself sounded a summons to mercy. It was the spring that marked the ending of such an enormous war! We saw that millions of us prisoners were flowing past and knew that millions more would greet us in the camps. It just couldn't be that so many people were to remain in prison after the greatest

15. Does not the prisoner's dream of the Altai simply continue the old peasant dream about it? The so-called lands of His Majesty's Cabinet were in the Altai, and because of this the area was closed to colonization much longer than the rest of Siberia. But it was there that the peasants wanted most of all to settle—and where they actually settled. Is it not from this that the enduring legend has arisen?

victory in the world! It was just to frighten us that they were holding us for the time being: so that we might remember and take heed. Of course, there would soon be a total amnesty and all of us would be released. Someone even swore that he had read in a newspaper that Stalin, replying to some American correspondent (whose name I cannot remember), said that after the war there would be an amnesty the like of which the world had never seen. And one of the interrogators had actually said to someone else that there would soon be a general amnesty. (These rumors were a help to the interrogators because they weakened the prisoners' will: The hell with him, let's sign—it isn't going to be for long anyway.)

But . . . *for mercy one must have wisdom.* This has been a truth throughout our history and will remain one for a long time to come.

We did not heed the few sober minds among us who croaked out that never, in a whole quarter-century, had there been an amnesty for political prisoners—and that there never would be one. Some cell expert among the stool pigeons leaped up with an answer: "Yes, there was! In 1927. For the tenth anniversary of the Revolution. All the prisons were emptied, and *white flags were flown on all of them.*" This astonishing vision of white flags on the prisons—why white?—was particularly striking.[16] We brushed aside those wise individuals among us who explained that millions of us were imprisoned precisely because the war had ended. We were no longer needed at the front. We were dangerous in the rear. And, were it not for us, not one brick would ever get laid at the remote construction projects. We were too self-absorbed even to grasp Stalin's simple economic calculations—let alone his malice. Just who this year, after being demobilized, would want to leave his family and home and go off to the Kolyma, to Vorkuta, to Siberia, where there were neither roads

16. Vyshinsky, *Ot Tyurem k Vospitatelnym Uchrezhdeniyam,* p. 396, presents the figures. In the 1927 amnesty, 7.3 percent of the prisoners were amnestied. This is a credible figure. Pretty poor for a tenth anniversary. Among the political prisoners, women with children were freed and those who had only a few months left to serve. In the Verkhne-Uralsk Prison Isolator, for example, twelve out of the two hundred prisoners there were released. But, in the middle of it, they regretted even this wretched amnesty and began to *block it:* they delayed some releases, and some people who were freed were given a "minus" restriction instead of full freedom to go where they pleased.

nor houses? It was virtually the job of the State Planning Commission to assign to the MVD the number of workers required for plan fulfillment and thus the number to be arrested. An amnesty, a broad and generous amnesty, was what we waited for and thirsted for! Somebody said that in England prisoners were amnestied on the anniversary of the coronation, in other words, every year. Many politicals had been amnestied on the three hundredth anniversary of the Romanovs, in 1912. Could it really be possible that now, after we had won a victory which would resound throughout our entire era and even longer, the Stalin government would be petty and vengeful and would hang onto its resentment of every stumble and slip of each of its minuscule subjects?

There is a simple truth which one can learn only through suffering: in war not victories are blessed but defeats. Governments need victories and the people need defeats. Victory gives rise to the desire for more victories. But after a defeat it is freedom that men desire—and usually attain. A people needs defeat just as an individual needs suffering and misfortune: they compel the deepening of the inner life and generate a spiritual upsurge.

The Poltava victory was a great misfortune for Russia: it resulted in two centuries of great strain and stress, ruin, the absence of freedom—and war and war again. The Poltava victory spelled salvation for the Swedes. Having lost the appetite for war, the Swedes became the most prosperous and the freest people in Europe.[17]

We are so used to taking pride in our victory over Napoleon that we leave out of account the fact that because of it the emancipation of the serfs did not take place a half-century sooner. Because of it, the strengthened monarchy destroyed the Decembrists. (The French occupation was never a reality for Russia.) But the Crimean War, and the Japanese War, and our war with Germany in the First World War—all those defeats brought us freedom and revolution.

We believed in amnesty that spring, we weren't being at all original in this. Talking with old prisoners, one gradually discovers that this thirst for mercy and this faith in mercy is never absent within gray prison walls. For decades and decades, wave

17. Perhaps, only in the twentieth century, if one is to believe the stories one hears, has their stagnating well-being led to moral indigestion.

after wave of prisoners has thirsted for and believed in either an amnesty, or a new Code, or a general review of cases. And the rumors about these things have always been supported by the Organs with skilled caution. The prisoner's imagination sees the ardently awaited arrival of the angel of liberation in just about anything: the next anniversary of the October Revolution, Lenin's anniversaries, Victory Day, Red Army Day, Paris Commune Day, every new session of the All-Russian Central Executive Committee—the VTsIK—the end of every Five-Year Plan, every Plenary Session of the Supreme Court! And the wilder the arrests, the more Homeric and mind-boggling the scale of the waves of prisoners, the more they inspired not sober-mindedness but faith in amnesty!

All sources of light can to some degree be compared with the Sun. And the Sun cannot be compared with anything. So it is that all the expectations in the world can be compared with the expectation of amnesty, but the expectation of amnesty cannot be compared with anything else.

In the spring of 1945, every newcomer to the cell was asked first of all what he had heard about an amnesty. And if two or three prisoners were taken from their cells *with their things,* the cell experts immediately compared *cases* and drew the conclusion that theirs were the *least serious* cases and they had clearly been taken out to be released. *It had begun!* In the toilet and in the baths—the prisoners' post offices—our "activists" looked everywhere for signs and graffiti about the amnesty. And one day at the beginning of July, in the famous lavender vestibule of the Butyrki baths, we read the enormous prophecy written in soap on a glazed lavender slab far higher than a man's head—which meant that one man had stood on another's shoulders in order to write it in a place where it would take longer to erase:

"Hurrah!! Amnesty on July 17!"[18]

What a celebration went on! ("After all, if they hadn't known for sure, they wouldn't have written it!") Everything that beat, pulsed, circulated in the body came to a stop beneath the wave of happiness, the expectation that the doors were about to swing open.

But . . . *for mercy one must have wisdom.*

18. Indeed, the bastards were wrong by only one digit! For more details on the great Stalin amnesty of July 7, 1945, see Part III, Chapter 6.

In the middle of July, the corridor jailer sent one old man from our cell to wash down the toilet, and while they were there eye to eye—for he wouldn't have dared in the presence of witnesses—he looked sympathetically at the prisoner's gray head and asked: "What's your article, father?" "Fifty-eight!" The old man lit up. At home three generations were mourning his arrest. "You're not included," sighed the jailer. Nonsense, we decided in the cell: just an illiterate jailer.

There was also a young man from Kiev in the cell, Valentin. I can't remember his family name. He had big eyes that were beautiful in a feminine way, and he was terrified by the interrogation. There is no doubt that he had the gift of precognition—perhaps only in his then current state of excitement. More than once, he went around the cell in the morning and pointed: Today they are going to come for you and you. I saw it in my dream. And they came and got them . . . the very individuals he had pointed out. One might add that a prisoner's heart is so inclined toward mysticism that he accepts precognition almost without surprise.

On July 27 Valentin came up to me: "Aleksandr! Today it is our turn." And he told me a dream that had all the characteristics of prison dreams: a bridge across a muddy stream, a cross. I began to get my things together. And it was not for nothing either. He and I were summoned after morning tea. Our cellmates saw us off with noisy good wishes, and many of them assured us we were going off to freedom. They had figured it out by comparing our *less serious* cases.

Perhaps you honestly don't believe it. Perhaps you won't allow yourself to believe. You can try to brush it aside with jokes. But flaming pincers, hotter than anything else on earth, suddenly close around your heart. They just do. Suppose it's true?

They assembled twenty of us from various cells and took us to the baths first. Before every big change in his life, the prisoner has first of all to take a bath. We had time enough there, an hour and a half, to exchange our hunches and ideas. At that point, all steamed up, our skins tender, we were taken through the little emerald park in the Butyrki's interior courtyard, where the birds sang deafeningly, although they were probably only sparrows, and the green of the trees seemed unbearably bright to eyes no longer used to it. Never had my eyes seen the green of the leaves with such intensity as they did that spring! And never in my life had I seen anything closer to God's paradise than that little Butyrki park, which never took more than thirty seconds to cross on the asphalt path.[19]

They took us to the Butyrki *station*—a very well-chosen nickname for that reception and dispatch point, especially because its main hall was really like a good railroad station. They pushed us into a large, spacious box. It was half-dark inside and the air was clean and fresh, since its one and only little window was very high up and had no "muzzle." And it opened on that same sunny little park, and through the transom the birds' twitter deafened us, and in the opening a little bright-green twig hung, promising us all freedom and home. (We had never been imprisoned in such a good box—and that couldn't be a matter of chance!)

And we were all cases for the OSO's—the Special Boards attached to the GPU-NKVD. And it turned out that each of us had been imprisoned for nothing much.

No one touched us for three hours. No one opened the doors. We paced up and down the box and, finally, tired out, we sat down on the slab benches. And the little twig kept bobbing and bobbing outside the opening, and the sparrows screamed as if they were possessed.

Suddenly the door crashed open, and one of us was summoned, a quiet bookkeeper, thirty-five years old. He went out. The door was locked. We started running about our box even more agitatedly than before. We were on hot coals.

Once more the crash of the door. They called another one out and readmitted the first. We rushed to him. But he was not the same man! The life had gone out of his face. His wide-open eyes were unseeing. His movements were uncertain as he stumbled across the smooth floor of the box. Was he in a state of shock? Had they swatted him with an ironing board?

"Well? Well?" we asked him, with sinking hearts. (If he had not in fact just gotten up from the electric chair, he must at the

19. Many years later, this time as a tourist, I saw another, similar park, except that it was even smaller, in the Trubetskoi bastion of the Peter and Paul Fortress in Leningrad. The other tourists exclaimed over the darkness of the corridors and cells, but I kept thinking to myself that with *such* a park to walk in, the prisoners of the Trubetskoi bastion were not lost men. *We* were taken out to walk only in deathly cell-like stone enclosures.

very least have been given a death sentence.) And in the voice of one reporting the end of the universe, the bookkeeper managed to blurt out:

"Five . . . years!"

And once more the door crashed. That was how quickly they returned, as if they were only being taken to the toilet to urinate. The second man returned, all aglow. Evidently he was being released.

"Well, well, come on?" We swarmed around him, our hopes rising again. He waved his hand, choking with laughter.

"Fifteen years!"

It was just too absurd to be believed.

Chapter 7

■

In the Engine Room

The box adjacent to the so-called Butyrki "station" was the famous *frisking* box, where new arrivals were searched. It had space enough for five or six jailers to process up to twenty zeks in one batch. Now, however, it was empty and the rough-hewn search tables had nothing on them. Over at one side of the room, seated behind a small nondescript table beneath a small lamp, was a neat, black-haired NKVD major. Patient boredom was what his face chiefly revealed. The intervals during which the zeks were brought in and led out one by one were a waste of his time. Their signatures could have been collected much, much faster.

He indicated that I was to sit down on the stool opposite him, on the other side of his table. He asked my name. To the right and left of the inkwell lay two piles of white papers the size of a half-sheet of typewriter paper, all looking much the same. In format they were just like the fuel requisitions handed out in apartment-house management offices, or warrants in official institutions for purchase of office supplies. Leafing through the pile on the right, the major found the paper which referred to me. He pulled it out and read it aloud to me in a bored patter. (I understood I had been sentenced to eight years.) Immediately, he began to write a statement on the back of it, with a fountain pen, to the effect that the text had been read to me on the particular date.

My heart didn't give an extra half-beat—it was all so everyday and routine. Could this really be my sentence—the turning point in my life? I would have liked to feel nervous, to experience this moment to the full, but I just couldn't. And the major had already pushed the sheet over to me, the blank side facing up. And a schoolchild's seven-kopeck pen, with a bad point that had lint on it from the inkwell, lay there in front of me.

"No, I have to read it myself."

"Do you really think I would deceive you?" the major objected lazily. "Well, go ahead, read it."

Unwillingly, he let the paper out of his hand. I turned it over and began to look through it with deliberate slowness, not just word by word but letter by letter. It had been typed, but what I had in front of me was not the original but a carbon:

EXTRACT
from a decree of the OSO of the NKVD of the U.S.S.R.
of July 7, 1945,[1] No. ———.

All of this was underscored with a dotted line and the sheet was vertically divided with a dotted line:

Case heard:	.	Decreed:
Accusation of so-and-so (name, year of birth, place of birth)	. . . . .	To designate for so-and-so (name) for anti-Soviet propaganda, and for an attempt to create an anti-Soviet organization, 8 (eight) years in corrective labor camps.

Copy verified. Secretary_____

Was I really just supposed to sign and leave in silence? I looked at the major—to see whether he intended to say something to me, whether he might not provide some clarification. No, he had no such intention. He had already nodded to the jailer at the door to get the next prisoner ready.

To give the moment at least a little importance, I asked him, with a tragic expression: "But, really, this is terrible! Eight years! What for?"

And I could hear how false my own words sounded. Neither he nor I detected anything terrible.

"Right there." The major showed me once again where to sign.

I signed. I could simply not think of anything else to do.

---

1. They had met to sentence me on the very day of the amnesty. The work must go on. . . .

"In that case, allow me to write an appeal right here. After all, the sentence is unjust."

"As provided by regulations," the major assented with a nod, placing my sheet of paper on the left-hand pile.

"Let's move along," commanded the jailer.

And I *moved along*.

(I had not really shown much initiative. Georgi Tenno, who, to be sure, had been handed a paper worth twenty-five years, answered: "After all, this is a life sentence. In olden times they used to beat the drums and assemble a crowd when a person was given a life sentence. And here it's like being on a list for a soap ration—twenty-five years and run along!"

Arnold Rappoport took the pen and wrote on the back of the verdict: "I protest categorically this terroristic, illegal sentence and demand immediate release." The officer who had handed it to him had at first waited patiently, but when he read what Rappoport had written, he was enraged and tore up the paper with the note on it. So what! The term remained in force anyway. This was just a copy.

Vera Korneyeva was expecting *fifteen* years and she saw with delight that there was a typo on the official sheet—it read only *five*. She laughed her luminous laugh and hurried to sign before they took it back. The officer looked at her dubiously: "Do you really understand what I read to you?" "Yes, yes, thank you very much. Five years in corrective-labor camps."

The ten-year sentence of Janos Rozsas, a Hungarian, was read to him in the corridor in Russian, without any translation. He signed it, not knowing it was his sentence, and he waited a long time afterward for his trial. Still later, when he was in camp, he recalled the incident very vaguely and realized what had happened.)

I returned to the box with a smile. It was strange. Each minute I became jollier and more relieved. Everyone was returning with "ten-ruble bills," including Valentin. The lightest term in our group that day had been given the bookkeeper who had gone out of his mind. He was still, in fact, beside himself. And the lightest term after his was mine.

In the splashes of sun and the July breeze, the little twig outside the window continued to bob up and down as gaily as before. We chattered boisterously. Here and there, more and more frequently, laughter resounded in the box. We were laughing because everything had gone off so smoothly. We were laughing at the shocked bookkeeper. We were laughing at our morning hopes and at the way our cellmates had seen us off and arranged secret signals with us to be transmitted via food parcels—four potatoes or two bagels!

"Well, anyway, there is going to be an amnesty!" several affirmed. "All this is just for form's sake and it doesn't mean anything. They want to give us a good scare so we'll keep in line. Stalin told an American correspondent—"

"What was his name?"

"I don't remember his name."

So they ordered us to take our things, formed us up by twos, and led us once again through that same marvelous little park filled with summer. And where did they take us? Once again to the *baths*.

And, oh, what a peal of laughter that got! My God, what silly nincompoops! Still roaring, we undressed, hung our duds on the same trolley hooks and rolled them into the same roaster they'd already been rolled into that very morning. Roaring, each of us took a small sliver of repulsive soap and went into the spacious, resonant shower room to wash off our girlish gaiety. We splashed about in there, pouring hot clean water on ourselves, and we got to romping about as if we were school kids who had come to the baths after their last exam. This cleansing, relieving laughter was, I think, not really sick but a living defense for the salvation of the organism.

As we dried ourselves off, Valentin said to me, reassuringly, intimately: "Well, all right. We are still young. We are going to live a long time yet. The main thing is not to make a misstep *now*. We are going to a camp—and we'll not say *one word* to anyone, so they won't plaster new terms on us. *We will work honestly—and keep our mouths shut.*"

And he really believed in his program, that naïve little kernel of grain caught between Stalin's millstones! He really had his hopes set on it. One wanted to agree with him, to serve out the term cozily, and then expunge from one's head what one had lived through.

But I had begun to sense a truth inside myself: if in order to live it is necessary *not to live,* then what's it all for?

■

One cannot really say that the OSO had been conceived after the Revolution. Catherine the Great had sentenced the journalist Novikov, whom she disliked, to fifteen years on, one might say, an OSO basis, since she didn't turn him over to a court. And all the Tsars once in a while, in a fatherly way, exiled without any trial those who had incurred their displeasure. In the 1860's, a basic court reform took place. It seemed as if rulers and subjects had both begun to develop something like a juridical view of society. And yet in the seventies and eighties Korolenko tracked down cases where administrative repression had usurped the role of judicial judgment. In 1872, he himself and two other students were exiled without trial, on the orders of the Deputy Minister of State Properties—a typical case of an OSO. Another time, he and his brother were exiled without trial to Glazov. Korolenko has also given us the name of one Fyodor Bogdan, an emissary from the peasants—a khodok—who got right up to the Tsar himself and was then exiled. And of Pyankov, too, who was acquitted by a court and yet exiled by order of the Tsar. And there were several others as well. And Vera Zasulich explained in a letter sent after she emigrated that she had not run away from the court and a trial but from nonjudicial administrative repression.

Thus the tradition of the "dotted line"—the administratively issued sentence—dragged on. But it was too lax; it was suitable for a drowsy Asiatic country, but not for a country that was rapidly advancing. . . . Moreover, it lacked any definite identity: *who* was the OSO? Sometimes it was the Tsar, sometimes the governor, sometimes the deputy minister. And if it was still possible to *enumerate* names and cases, this was not, begging your pardon, real scope.

Real scope entered the picture with the twenties, when *permanently* operating *Troikas*—panels of three, operating behind closed doors—were created to bypass the courts permanently. In the beginning they even flaunted it proudly—*the Troika of the GPU.* Not only did they not conceal the names of the members; they publicized them. Who on the Solovetsky Islands did not know the names of the famous Moscow Troika—Gleb Boky,

Vul, and Vasilyev? Yes, and what a word it was, in fact—
troika! It bore a slight hint of sleigh bells on the shaft bow; the
celebration of Shrovetide; and, interwoven with all this, a
mystery. Why "troika"? What did it mean? After all, a court
wasn't a quartet either! And a Troika wasn't a court! And the
biggest mystery of all lay in the fact that it was kept out of sight.
We hadn't been there. We hadn't seen it. All we got was a piece
of paper. Sign here! The Troika was even more frightening than
a Revolutionary Tribunal. It set itself even farther apart, muffled
itself up, locked itself in a separate room, and—soon—concealed
the names of its members. Thus we grew used to the idea that the
Troika members didn't eat or drink or move about among
ordinary people. Once they had isolated themselves in order to
go into session, they were shut off for good, and all we knew of
them were the sentences handed out through typists. (And they
had to be returned too. Such documents couldn't be left in the
hands of individuals!)

These Troikas (we use the plural just in case, because—as
with a deity—we never know where or in what form it exists)
satisfied a persistent need that had arisen: never to allow those
arrested to return to freedom (This was like an OTK—a Department for Quality Control in industry—but in this case it was
attached to the GPU—to prevent any *spoiled goods*.) If it turned
out that someone was innocent and could therefore not be tried
at all, then let him have his "minus 32" via the Troika—which
meant he couldn't live in any of the provincial capitals—or let
him spend two or three years in exile, after which he would have
a convict's clipped ear, would always be a marked man, and, from
then on, a recidivist.

(Please forgive us, reader. We have once more gone astray with
this rightist opportunism—this concept of "guilt," and of the
guilty or innocent. It has, after all, been explained to us that *the
heart of the matter is not personal guilt, but social danger*. One
can imprison an innocent person if he is socially hostile. And one
can release a guilty man if he is socially friendly. But lacking legal
training, we can be forgiven, for the 1926 Code, according to
which, my good fellow, we lived for twenty-five years and more,
was itself criticized for an "impermissible bourgeois approach,"
for an "insufficiently class-conscious approach," and for some

kind of "bourgeois weighing of punishments in relation to the gravity of what had been committed.")[2]

Alas, it is not for us to write the absorbing history of this particular *Organ*: how the Troikas turned into OSO's; or when they got renamed; or whether there were OSO's in provincial centers, or just one of them in the Great Palace; or which of our great and proud leaders were members; or how often they met and how long their sessions lasted; whether or not they were served tea while they worked, and if they were, what was served with the tea; and how the work itself proceeded—did they converse while it was going on or not? We are not the ones who will write this history—because we don't know. All that we have heard is that the essence of the OSO was triune. And even though it is still impossible to name its industrious members, yet we do know the three organs permanently represented there: one member represented the Central Committee of the Party, one the MVD, and one the Chief Prosecutor's office. However, it would not be a miracle if we should learn someday that there were never any sessions, and that there was only a staff of experienced typists composing extracts from nonexistent records of proceedings, and one general administrator who directed the typists. As for typists, there were certainly typists. That we can guarantee.

Up to 1924, the authority of the Troika was limited to sentences of three years, maximum. From 1924 on, they moved up to five years of camp; from 1937 on, the OSO could turn out "ten-ruble bills"; after 1948, they could rivet a "quarter"—twenty-five years—on you. And there are people—Chavdarov, for example—who know that during the war years the OSO even sentenced prisoners to execution by shooting. Nothing unusual about this.

The OSO was nowhere mentioned in either the Constitution or the Code. However, it turned out to be the most convenient kind of hamburger machine—easy to operate, undemanding, and requiring no legal lubrication. The Code existed on its own, and the OSO existed on its own, and it kept on deftly grinding without all the Code's 205 articles, neither invoking them nor even mentioning them.

2. Vyshinsky, *Ot Tyurem k Vospitatelnym Uchrezhdeniyam.*

As they used to joke in camp: "There is no court for nothing —for that there is an OSO."

Of course, the OSO itself also needed for convenience some kind of operational shorthand, but for that purpose it worked out on its own a dozen "letter" articles which made operations very much simpler. It wasn't necessary, when they were used, to cudgel your brains trying to make things fit the formulations of the Code. And they were few enough to be easily remembered by a child. Some of them we have already described:

ASA —Anti-Soviet Agitation
KRD —Counter-Revolutionary Activity
KRTD—Counter-Revolutionary Trotskyite Activity (And that "T" made the life of a zek in camp much harder.)
PSh —Suspicion of Espionage (Espionage that went beyond the bounds of suspicion was handed over to a tribunal.)
SVPSh—Contacts Leading (!) to Suspicion of Espionage
KRM —Counter-Revolutionary Thought
VAS —Dissemination of Anti-Soviet Sentiments
SOE —Socially Dangerous Element
SVE —Socially Harmful Element
PD —Criminal Activity (a favorite accusation against former camp inmates if there was nothing else to be used against them)

And then, finally, there was the very expansive category:

ChS —Member of a Family (of a person convicted under one of the foregoing "letter" categories)

It has to be remembered that these categories were not applied uniformly and equally among different groups and in different years. But, as with the articles of the Code and the sections in special decrees, they broke out in sudden epidemics.

There is one more qualification. The OSO did not claim to be handing down a *sentence*. It did not sentence a person but, instead, *imposed an administrative penalty*. And that was the whole thing in a nutshell. Therefore it was, of course, natural for it to have juridical independence!

But even though they did not claim that the administrative

penalty was a court sentence, it could be up to twenty-five years and include:

- Deprivation of titles, ranks, and decorations
- Confiscation of all property
- Imprisonment
- Deprivation of the right to correspond

Thus a person could disappear from the face of the earth with the help of the OSO even more reliably than under the terms of some primitive court sentence.

The OSO enjoyed another important advantage in that its penalty could not be appealed. There was nowhere to appeal to. There was no appeals jurisdiction above it, and no jurisdiction beneath it. It was subordinate only to the Minister of Internal Affairs, to Stalin, and to Satan.

Another big advantage the OSO had was speed. This speed was limited only by the technology of typewriting.

And, last but not least, not only did the OSO not have to confront the accused face to face, which lessened the burden on interprison transport: it didn't even have to have his photograph. At a time when the prisons were badly overcrowded, this was a great additional advantage because the prisoner did not have to take up space on the prison floor, or eat free bread once his interrogation had been completed. He could be sent off to camp immediately and put to honest work. The copy of the sentence could be read to him much later.

It used to be that in favorable conditions the prisoners were unloaded from freight cars at their destinations. And they were made to kneel down right there, next to the tracks—as a precaution against attempted escape. But it looked as if they were praying to the OSO. And then and there their sentences were read out to them. It could also happen differently. In 1938 those who arrived at Perebory on prisoner transports did not know either their Code articles or their sentences, but the clerk who met them knew, and he looked them up on the list: SVE—Socially Harmful Element—five years. That was during the time when there was an urgent need for many hands to work on the Moscow-Volga Canal.

Others worked in the camps for months without knowing their sentences. After this, as I. Dobryak reported, they were solemnly lined up—and not just on any old day, but on May 1, 1938, when the red flags were flying—and the Stalino Province Troika's sentences were announced. (This would indicate that the OSO did get decentralized in times of heavy load.) These sentences were from ten to twenty years apiece. And in that same year, my former camp foreman, Sinebryukhov, was sent off with a whole trainload of unsentenced prisoners from Chelyabinsk to Cherepovets. Months passed and the zeks worked away. And then one rest day in winter (Note the days? Another advantage of the OSO), when the frost was cracking, they were driven out into the courtyard and lined up. A newly arrived lieutenant appeared and introduced himself as having come to inform them of their OSO penalties. But he turned out to be a decent sort because he squinted at their thin footwear and at the sun's rays in the steaming frost and said:

"Well anyway, men, why should you freeze out here? The OSO gave you all ten years apiece. There are just a very, very few who got eight. You understand? Disssperse!"

■

But in view of the frankly mechanical operation of the Special Board, why have any courts at all? Why use a horsecar when there's a noiseless modern streetcar available, which no one can jump out of? Is it a matter of keeping the judges well fed?

Still, it is really quite indecent for a democratic state not to have courts. In 1919, the Eighth Congress of the Party proclaimed in its program: Efforts must be made *to involve all the working population* in the exercise of judicial duties. It did not prove possible to involve "all" the working population. Conducting a trial is a delicate business. But there was no question of getting along entirely without courts.

However, our political courts—the special collegia of provincial courts, the military tribunals (and why, actually, should there be military tribunals in peacetime anyway?), and all the supreme courts too—unanimously followed the path of the OSO. They, too, did not get stuck in the mud of public trials or in arguments between sides.

Their primary and principal distinguishing feature was closed doors. They were first of all *closed courts*—for their own convenience.

And by now we have become so accustomed to the fact that millions and millions of people were tried in closed sessions and have become used to this for so long that now and then some mixed-up son, brother, or nephew of a prisoner will even snort at you with conviction: "And what would you have wanted? . . . There's *information* here. Our enemies will find out! You can't do it!"

Thus the fear that our "enemies will find out" makes us clamp our head between our own knees. Who in our Fatherland, except some bookworms, remembers now that Karakozov, who fired at the Tsar, was provided with a defense lawyer? Or that Zhelyabov and all the Narodnaya Volya group were tried in public, without any fear that the "Turks would find out"? Or that Vera Zasulich, who attempted to kill the official who was, translated into Soviet terms, the Chief of the Moscow Administration of the MVD— although she missed, and the bullet went past his head—not only was not destroyed in a torture chamber but was *acquitted* in *open* court by a jury—no Troika—and then went off in triumph in a carriage?

Despite these comparisons, I do not at all mean to say that a perfect system of courts and justice ever existed in Russia. In all probability, an excellent judicial system is the last fruit of the most mature society, or else one needs a Solomon. Vladimir Dal notes that in the period before the emancipation of the serfs Russia had "not one single proverb containing any praise of the courts." And that really means something. It seems likely that they never had time to get around to making up a proverb praising the zemstvo chiefs either. But, nevertheless, the judicial reform of 1864 at least set the urban sector of our society on the road toward those English models which Herzen praised so highly.

Saying all this, I still have not forgotten what Dostoyevsky had to say in his *Diary of a Writer* against our trials by jury: about the excesses of some lawyers' eloquence ("Gentlemen of the jury! What kind of woman would she have been if she had not stabbed her rival? Gentlemen of the jury! Who among you would not have thrown the child out of the window?"); and the risk that a juror's momentary impulse might outweigh his civic responsibility. But spiritually Dostoyevsky far outstripped the realities of our life, and he worried about what he shouldn't have worried about! He believed that we had achieved open trials once and for all! (Indeed, who among his contemporaries could have believed in the OSO?) And somewhere else he writes: "It is better to err on the side of mercy than on that of the death penalty." Oh, yes, yes, yes!

Excesses of eloquence do not afflict exclusively a judicial system in process of being established; even more conspicuously, they afflict an already established democracy that has not yet discovered its moral goals. England again gives us examples, as when, for partisan advantage, the leader of the opposition does not hesitate to blame the government for a national predicament worse than actually exists.

Excesses of eloquence are a malady. But what word can we then use for the excessive use of closed doors? Dostoyevsky dreamed of a court in which everything essential to the *defense* of the accused would be set forth by the *prosecutor*. How many aeons will we have to wait for that? Our social experience has so far enriched us immeasurably with *defense lawyers* who *accuse* the defendant. ("As an honest Soviet person, as a true patriot, I cannot but feel repugnance at the disclosure of these evil deeds.")

And how comfortable it all is for the judges in a closed session! Judicial robes are not required and one can even roll up one's sleeves. How easy it is to work! There are no public-address systems, no newspapermen, and no public. (Well, there is a public, an audience, but it consists of *interrogators*. For example, they used to attend the Leningrad Province Court during the day to find out how their "protégés" were conducting themselves, and at night went calling on those prisoners who needed to have their *consciences appealed to*.)[3]

The second main characteristic of our political courts is the lack of ambiguity in their work, which is to say predetermined verdicts.[4] In other words, you, a judge, always know what the

---

3. Ch——n's group.
4. That same collection edited by A. Y. Vyshinsky, *Ot Tyurem k Vospitatelnym Uchrezhdeniyam,* includes materials indicating that the predetermination of verdicts is an old, old story. In 1924–1929, sentences were determined by joint administrative and economic considerations. Beginning in 1924, because of

higher-ups expect of you (furthermore there's a telephone if you still have any doubts). And, following the example of the OSO's, sentences might even be typed out ahead of time, with only the prisoner's name to be added later, by hand. And in 1942 Strakhovich cried out during a session of the military tribunal of the Leningrad Military District: "But I could not have been recruited by Ignatovsky when I was only ten years old!" But the presiding judge barked back: "Don't slander the Soviet intelligence service!" The whole thing had been predetermined long before: each and every one of the Ignatovsky group was to be sentenced to be shot. Some man named Lipov got included in the group, but *no one* from the group *knew him* and he knew *none* of them either. Well, so, all right, Lipov got ten years.

How hugely the predetermination of sentences contributed to easing the thorny life of a judge. It wasn't so much a mental relief, in the sense that one didn't have to think, as it was a moral relief. You didn't have to torture yourself with worry that you might make a mistake in a sentence and make orphans out of your own little children. And the predetermination of sentences could dispose even so immovable a judge as Ulrikh to good humor. (And what major execution had he not pronounced?) In 1945, the Military Collegium was hearing the case of the "Estonian separatists." Short, stocky, good-humored Ulrikh was presiding. He didn't pass up a single opportunity to joke not only with his colleagues but also with the prisoners. (After all, that's what humaneness is! A new trait—where had it ever been seen?) Having learned that Susi was a lawyer, he said to him with a smile: "Well, so now your profession can be of some use to you!" Well, there is no need to quarrel. Why be embittered? The court routine proceeded pleasantly. They smoked right at the judge's table, and at a con-

---

national *unemployment,* the courts reduced the number of verdicts which sentenced prisoners to corrective labor while they continued to live at home and increased short-term prison sentences. These cases involved only nonpolitical offenders, of course. As a result, prisons were overcrowded with short-termers serving sentences of up to six months, and not enough use was being made of them in labor colonies. At the beginning of 1929, the People's Commissariat of Justice of the U.S.S.R., in Circular No. 5, *condemned* short-term sentences and, on November 6, 1929, the eve of the twelfth anniversary of the October Revolution, when the country was supposedly entering on the construction of socialism, a decree of the Central Executive Committee and the Council of People's Commissars simply *forbade* all sentences of less than one year!

venient moment broke off for a good lunch. And when evening began to fall, they had to go and *confer*. But who confers at night? They left the prisoners to sit at their desks all night long and went on home. At nine in the morning they came in all brisk and freshly shaved: "Rise. The court is in session." And all the prisoners were given a "ten-ruble bill" apiece.

And if anyone should object that the OSO at least proceeded without hypocrisy, whereas there was hypocrisy in instances like the above—they pretended to be conferring but didn't really confer—we would certainly have to enter a strong—very strong—dissent!

Well, the third and final characteristic is *dialectics*. (Which used to be crudely described in the folk saying: "Whichever way you point a wagon tongue, that's the way it goes.") The Code cannot be a dead weight in the path of the judge. The articles of the Code had been around during ten, fifteen, twenty years of rapid change, and, just as Faust said:

> The whole world changes and everything moves forward,
> And why should I be afraid to break my word?

All the articles of the Code had become encrusted with interpretations, directions, instructions. And if the actions of the accused are not covered by the Code, he can still be convicted:

- By analogy (What opportunities!)
- Simply because of *origins* (7-35: belonging to a socially dangerous milieu)[5]
- For *contacts with dangerous persons*[6] (Here's scope for you! Who is "dangerous" and what "contacts" consist of only the judge can say.)

But one should not complain about the precise wording of our published laws either. On January 13, 1950, a decree was issued re-establishing capital punishment. (One is bound, of course, to

5. In the Republic of South Africa, terror has gone to such lengths in recent years that every *suspicious* (SDE—Socially Dangerous Element) black can be arrested and held for three *months* without investigation or trial. Anyone can see immediately the flimsiness of this: why not from three to ten years?

6. This is something we hadn't known, something the newspaper *Izvestiya* told us in July, 1957.

consider that capital punishment never did depart from Beria's cellars.) And the decree stated that the death sentence could be imposed on *subversives*—diversionists. What did that mean? It didn't say. Iosif Vissarionovich loved it that way: not to say all of it, just to hint. Did it refer only to someone who blew up rails with TNT? It didn't say. We had long since come to know what a "diversionist" was: someone who produced goods of poor quality was a diversionist. But what was a *subversive?* Was someone *subverting* the authority of the government, for example, in a conversation on a streetcar? Or if a girl married a foreigner—wasn't she *subverting* the majesty of our Motherland?

But it is not the judge who judges. The judge only takes his pay. The directives did the judging. The directive of 1937: ten years; twenty years; execution by shooting. The directive of 1943: twenty years at hard labor; hanging. The directive of 1945: ten years for everyone, plus five of disenfranchisement[7] (manpower for three Five-Year Plans). The directive of 1949: everyone gets twenty-five.[8]

The machine stamped out the sentences. The prisoner had already been deprived of all rights when they cut off his buttons on the threshold of State Security, and he couldn't avoid a stretch. The members of the legal profession were so used to this that they fell on their faces in 1958 and caused a big scandal. The text of the projected new "Fundamental Principles of Criminal Prosecution of the U.S.S.R." was published in the newspapers, and they'd *forgotten* to include any reference to *possible* grounds for acquittal. The government newspaper issued a mild rebuke: "*The impression might be created* that our courts only bring in convictions."[9]

But just take the jurists' side for a moment: why, in fact, should a trial be supposed to have *two* possible outcomes when our general *elections* are conducted on the basis of *one* candidate? An acquittal is, in fact, unthinkable from the economic point of view! It would mean that the informers, the Security officers, the inter-

7. Babayev, in fact a nonpolitical, shouted at them: "You can '*muzzle*' me for three hundred years! But I'll never lift my hand for you, you benefactors!"
8. Thus it was that a real spy (Schultz, in Berlin, in 1948) could get ten years, and someone who had never been a spy, Günther Waschkau, got twenty-five. Because he was in the wave of 1949.
9. *Izvestiya*, September 10, 1958.

292 | THE GULAG ARCHIPELAGO

rogators, the prosecutor's staff, the internal guard in the prison, and the convoy had all worked to no purpose.

Here is one straightforward and typical case that was brought before a military tribunal. In 1941, the Security operations branch of our inactive army stationed in Mongolia was called on to show its activity and vigilance. The military medical assistant Lozovsky, who was jealous of Lieutenant Pavel Chulpenyev because of some woman, realized this. He addressed three questions to Chulpenyev when they were alone: 1. "Why, in your opinion, are we retreating from the Germans?" (Chulpenyev's reply: "They have more equipment and they were mobilized earlier." Lozovsky's counter: "No, it's a *maneuver*. We're *decoying* them.") 2. "Do you believe the Allies will help?" (Chulpenyev: "I believe they'll help, but not from unselfish motives." Lozovsky's counter: "They are deceiving us. They won't help us at all.") 3. "Why was Voroshilov sent to command the Northwest Front?"

Chulpenyev answered and forgot about them. And Lozovsky wrote a denunciation. Chulpenyev was summoned before the Political Branch of the division and expelled from the Komsomol: for a defeatist attitude, for praising German equipment, for belittling the strategy of our High Command. The loudest voice raised against him belonged to the Komsomol organizer Kalyagin, who had behaved like a coward at the battle of Khalkhin-Gol, in Chulpenyev's presence, and therefore found it convenient to get rid of the witness once and for all.

Chulpenyev's arrest followed. He had one confrontation with Lozovsky. Their previous conversation *was not even brought up* by the interrogator. One question was asked: "Do you know this man?" "Yes." "Witness, you may leave." (The interrogator was afraid the charge might fall through.)[10]

Depressed by his month's incarceration in the sort of hole in the ground we have already described, Chulpenyev appeared before a military tribunal of the 36th Motorized Division. Present were Lebedev, the Divisional Political Commissar, and Slesarev, the Chief of the Political Branch. The witness Lozovsky was not even

10. Today Lozovsky holds the degree of candidate in medical sciences and lives in Moscow. Everything is going well with him. Chulpenyev drives a trolley bus.

summoned to testify. However, after the trial, to document the false testimony, they got Lozovsky's signature and that of Political Commissar Seryegin. The questions the tribunal asked were: Did you have a conversation with Lozovsky? What did he ask you about? What were your answers? Naïvely, Chulpenyev told them. He still couldn't understand what he was guilty of. "After all, many people talk like that!" he innocently exclaimed. The tribunal was interested: "Who? Give us their names." But Chulpenyev was not of their breed! He had the last word. "I beg the court to give me an assignment that will mean my death so as to assure itself once more of my patriotism"—and, like a simplehearted warrior of old—"Me and the person who slandered me—both of us together."

Oh, no! Our job is to kill off all those chivalrous sentiments in the people. Lozovsky's duty was to hand out pills and Seryegin's duty was to indoctrinate the soldiers.[11] Whether or not you died wasn't important. What was important was that *we* were on guard. The members of the military tribunal went out, had a smoke and returned: ten years plus three years' disenfranchisement.

There were certainly more than ten such cases in every division during the war. (Otherwise, the military tribunals would not have justified the cost of maintaining them.) And how many divisions were there in all? Let the reader count them up himself.

The sessions of the military tribunals were depressingly like one another. The judges were depressingly faceless and emotionless —rubber stamps. The sentences all came off the same assembly line.

Everyone maintained a serious mien, but everyone understood it was a farce, above all the boys of the convoy, who were the simplest sort of fellows. At the Novosibirsk Transit Prison in 1945 they greeted the prisoners with a roll call based on *cases.* "So and so! Article 58-1a, twenty-five years." The chief of the convoy guard was curious: "What did you get it for?" "For nothing at all." "You're lying. *The sentence for nothing at all is ten years.*"

When the military tribunals were under pressure, their "sessions" lasted one minute—the time it took them to go out and come in again. When their working day went on for sixteen con-

11. Viktor Andreyevich Seryegin lives in Moscow today and works in a Consumer Service Combine attached to the Moscow Soviet. He lives well.

secutive hours, one could see, through the door of the conference room, bowls of fruit on a table set with a white tablecloth. If they weren't in a hurry, they enjoyed delivering their sentence "with a psychological twist": ". . . sentenced to the supreme measure of punishment!" And then a pause. The judges would look the condemned man in the eye. It was interesting to see how he took it. What was he feeling at that moment? Only then would the verdict continue: ". . . but taking into consideration the sincere repentance . . ."

On the walls of the waiting room messages had been scratched with nails and scrawled in pencil: "I got execution," "I got twenty-five," "I got a 'tenner!' " They didn't clean off these graffiti; they served an educational purpose. Be scared; bow down; don't think that you can change anything by your behavior. Even if you were to speak in your own defense with the eloquence of Demosthenes, in a hall empty except for a handful of interrogators—like Olga Sliozberg in 1936, at the Supreme Court—it would not help you in the slightest. All you could do would be to increase your sentence from ten years to execution. For instance, if you were to shout: *"You are fascists!* I am ashamed to have been a member of your Party for several years!" (Nikolai Semyonovich Daskal did it in 1937, at the Special Collegium of the Azov–Black Sea Province at Maikop, presided over by Kholik.) In that situation what they did was fabricate a new *case* and do you in once and for all.

Chavdarov has described an incident in which the accused suddenly repudiated at their trial all the false testimony they had given during the interrogation. And what happened? If there was any hesitation while glances were exchanged, it lasted no more than a few seconds. The prosecutor asked for a recess, without explaining why. The interrogators and their tough-boy helpers dashed in from the interrogation prison. All the prisoners, distributed among separate boxes, were given a good beating all over again and promised another after the next recess. The recess came to an end. Once again the judges questioned all of them—and this time they all confessed.

Aleksandr Grigoryevich Karetnikov, the Director of the Textile Research Institute, provided an example of outstanding astuteness. Just before the session of the Military Collegium of the Supreme Court was to begin, he sent word through the guard that he wanted to give *supplementary* testimony. This, of course, provoked curiosity. He was received by the prosecutor. Karetnikov displayed his infected collarbone, broken by the interrogator who had struck him with a stool, and declared: "I signed everything under torture." By this time the prosecutor was cursing himself for having been so greedy to get "supplementary" testimony, but it was too late. Each of them is fearless only as long as he is an anonymous cog in the whole machine. But just as soon as the responsibility has become personalized, individualized, concentrated on him, just as soon as the searchlight is on him, he grows pale and realizes that he is nothing and can slip on any chance banana peel. So Karetnikov caught the prosecutor, and the latter was unwilling to suppress the whole business. The session of the Military Collegium began and Karetnikov repeated his statement in front of them. Now there was a case in which the Military Collegium went out and really conferred! But the only verdict they could have brought in was acquittal, which would have meant releasing Karetnikov on the spot. Therefore *they brought in no verdict at all!*

As if nothing at all had happened, they took Karetnikov back to prison, treated his collarbone, and kept him another three months. A very polite new interrogator entered the case, who wrote out a new warrant for Karetnikov's arrest. (If the Collegium had not twisted things, he might at least have spent those three months as a free man.) The interrogator asked the same questions as the first interrogator. Karetnikov, sensing freedom in the offing, conducted himself staunchly and refused to admit any guilt whatever. And what happened next? He got eight years from an OSO.

This example shows well enough the possibilities available to the prisoner and the possibilities available to the OSO. It was the poet Derzhavin who wrote:

> A partial court is worse than banditry.
> Judges are enemies; there sleeps the law.
> In front of you the citizen's neck
> Lies stretched out, quiet and without defense.

But it was a rare thing for such accidents to take place in the Military Collegium of the Supreme Court. For that matter, it was in general rare for it to rub clear its clouded eyes and take a look at any individual little tin soldier of a prisoner. In 1937, A.D.R., an electrical engineer, was taken up to the fourth floor, running upstairs with a convoy guard on either side of him. (In all probability, the elevator was working, but there were so many prisoners pouring in and out that the officials and employees would not have been able to use the elevator if the prisoners had been permitted to.) Meeting a convicted prisoner who had just left, they dashed into the court. The Military Collegium was in such a hurry they hadn't sat down yet, and all three members remained standing. Catching his breath with difficulty, for he had been weakened by his long interrogation, R. blurted out his full name. They muttered something, exchanged glances, and Ulrikh—the very same, no less—proclaimed: "Twenty years!" And they dragged R. out at a gallop and, at a gallop, dragged in the next prisoner.

It was all like a dream. In February, 1963, I, too, got to climb those stairs, but I was courteously accompanied by a colonel who was also a Communist Party organizer. And in that room with the circular colonnade, in which, they say, the Plenary Sessions of the Supreme Court of the U.S.S.R. meet—with an enormous horseshoelike table that had another round table inside it and seven antique chairs—seventy officials of the Military Collegium heard me out—that same Military Collegium which once sentenced Karetnikov, and R. and others and others, and so on and so forth. And I said to them: "What a remarkable day this is! Although I was first sentenced to camp and then to eternal exile, I never before saw a single judge face to face. And now I see all of you assembled here together!" (And they, rubbing their eyes open, for the first time saw a living zek.)

But it turned out that it had not been they! Yes. They said it had not been they. They assured me that *those others* were no longer present. Some had retired honorably on pensions. A few had been removed. (Ulrikh, the outstanding executioner of all, had been removed, it turned out, back in Stalin's time, in 1950, for, believe it or not, leniency.) Some of them—there were only a few of these—had even been tried under Khrushchev, and, in their role as defendants, *they* had threatened: "Today you are trying us. Tomorrow we will try you. Watch out!" But like all the starts made under Khrushchev, this effort, too, which had been very active at first, was soon abandoned. He dropped it before it got far enough to produce an irreversible change; which meant that things were left where they had been.

On that occasion, several veterans of the bench, all speaking up at the same time, gave voice to their recollections, unwittingly providing me with material for this chapter. (Oh, if only they had undertaken to remember and to publish! But the years pass; another five have gone by; and it has not become any brighter or lighter.) They recalled how certain judges, at conferences of their judicial colleagues, *took pride* when they spoke from the rostrum of *having succeeded* in not applying Article 51 of the Criminal Code, which specifies those circumstances that extenuate guilt, and thus had *succeeded* in handing down sentences of twenty-five years instead of ten. And how the *courts* had been humiliatingly *subservient to the Organs*. A certain judge was trying a case. A Soviet citizen who had returned from the United States had made the slanderous statement that there were good automobile roads in America—and nothing else. That was all there was to the case. The judge ventured to send the case back for further investigation *for the purpose* of getting "genuine anti-Soviet materials"— in other words, so that the accused could be beaten and tortured. But his praiseworthy intention wasn't taken into account. The angry answer came back: "You mean you don't trust our Organs?" And, in the upshot, the judge was exiled to the post of secretary of a military tribunal on Sakhalin! (Under Khrushchev, reproof was not so severe; judges who "made mistakes" were sent—where do you think?—to work as *lawyers*.)[12] The prosecutor's office was just as subservient to the Organs. When, in 1942, Ryumin's flagrant abuses in the counterintelligence section of the Northern Fleet became known, the prosecutor's office did not dare interfere on its own, but only reported *respectfully* to Abakumov that his boys were acting up. Abakumov had good reason to consider the Organs the salt of the earth! (This was the occasion when he called in Ryumin and promoted him—to his own eventual undoing.)

There just wasn't enough time that February day, or they

---

12. *Izvestiya,* June 9, 1964. This throws an interesting light on views of legal defense! In 1918, V. I. Lenin demanded that judges who handed down sentences that were too lenient be excluded from the Party.

would have told me ten times as much as they did. But this, too, provides food for thought. If both the courts and the prosecutor's office were simply pawns of the Minister of State Security, then maybe there isn't any need for a separate chapter to describe them.

They vied with each other in telling me things, and I kept looking around me in astonishment. They were people! Real *people!* They were smiling! They were explaining that their intentions were of the best. Well, and what if things turn full circle and it is once again up to them to try me? Maybe even in that very hall—and they were showing me the main hall.

Well, so they will convict me.

Which comes first—the chicken or the egg? The people or the system?

For several centuries we had a proverb: "Don't fear the law, fear the judge."

But, in my opinion, the *law* has outstripped people, and people have lagged behind in cruelty. It is time to reverse the proverb: "Don't fear the judge, fear the *law*."

Abakumov's kind of law, of course.

They stepped onto the rostrum and talked about *Ivan Denisovich*. They said happily that the book had eased their consciences (that's what they said . . .). They admitted that the picture I painted was decidedly on the bright side, that *every one of them* knew of camps worse than that. (Ah, so they did know?) Of the seventy people seated around that horseshoe, several turned out to be knowledgeable in literature, even to be readers of *Novy Mir*. They were eager for reform. They spoke forcefully about our social ulcers, about our neglect of our rural areas.

And I sat there and thought: If the first tiny droplet of truth has exploded like a psychological bomb, what then will happen in our country when whole waterfalls of Truth burst forth?

And they will burst forth. It has to happen.

Chapter 8

■

The Law as a Child

We forget everything. What we remember is not what actually happened, not history, but merely that hackneyed dotted line they have chosen to drive into our memories by incessant hammering.

I do not know whether this is a trait common to all mankind, but it is certainly a trait of our people, And it is a vexing one. It may have its source in goodness, but it is vexing nonetheless. It makes us an easy prey for liars.

Therefore, if they demand that we forget even the public trials, we forget them. The proceedings were open and were reported in our newspapers, but they didn't drill a hole in our brains to make us remember—and so we've forgotten them. Only things repeated on the radio day after day drill holes in the brain. I am not even talking about young people, since they, of course, know nothing of all this, but about people who were alive at the time of those trials. Ask any middle-aged person to enumerate the highly publicized open trials. He will remember those of Bukharin and Zinoviev. And, knitting his brow, that of the Promparty too. And that's all. There were no other public trials.

Yet in actual fact they began right after the October Revolution. In 1918, quantities of them were taking place, in many different tribunals. They were taking place before there were either laws or codes, when the judges had to be guided solely by the requirements of the revolutionary workers' and peasants' power. At the same time, they were regarded as blazing their own trail of bold legality. Their detailed history will someday be written by someone, and it's not for us even to attempt to include it in our present investigation.

However, we cannot do without a brief review. It is our duty, anyway, to probe some of the charred ruins which go all the way back to that gentle, misty, rose-colored dawn.

In those dynamic years, the sabers of war were not rusting in their scabbards, nor did the executioners' revolvers have time to grow cold in their holsters. Only later on did the custom develop of hiding executions in cellars under cover of night and of shooting the victims in the back of the head. In 1918, the famous Ryazan Chekist Stelmakh had those sentenced to death shot in the courtyard, during the day, so that prisoners awaiting execution could watch from the prison windows.

There was an official term current then: *extrajudicial reprisal* . . . not because there weren't any courts at the time, but because there was the Cheka.[1] Because it was more efficient. Certainly, there were courts, and they tried and convicted and executed people, but we need to remember that, parallel to them and independently of them, extrajudicial reprisal went on at the same time. How can one depict its scale? M. Latsis, in his popular review of the Cheka's activity,[2] gives us material for only a year and a half (1918 and half of 1919) and for only twenty provinces of Central Russia ("The figures presented here are *far from complete*,"[3] in part, perhaps, out of modesty): those shot by the Cheka (i.e., without trial, bypassing the courts) numbered 8,389 persons (eight thousand three hundred and eighty-nine);[4] counterrevolutionary organizations uncovered—412 (a fantastic figure, in view of our inadequate capacity for organization throughout our history and also the general isolation of individuals in those years and the general psychological depression); the total of those arrested—87,000[5] (and this figure smells of understatement).

1. This fledgling whose beak had not yet hardened was warmed and encouraged by Trotsky: "Terror is a powerful means of policy and one would have to be a hypocrite not to understand this." And Zinoviev rejoiced too, not yet foreseeing his own end: "The letters GPU, like the letters VChK, are the most popular in the world."
2. Latsis, *Dva Goda Borby na Vnutrennom Fronte*.
3. *Ibid.*, p. 74.
4. *Ibid.*, p. 75.
5. *Ibid.*, p. 76.

What comparison is available for purposes of evaluation? In 1907 a group of leftist leaders published a collection of essays entitled *Against Capital Punishment,*[6] in which are listed by name all those sentenced to death in Tsarist Russia from 1826 to 1906. The editors qualify their findings with the statement that there were some additional victims, whose names remain unknown, and that the list is incomplete. (However, it is certainly not so incomplete as Latsis' materials compiled during the Civil War.) The list totals 1,397—from which 233 persons have to be deducted because their death sentences were commuted, as do an additional 270, who were sentenced *in absentia* and never caught (for the most part Polish rebels who had fled to the West). That leaves 894, a figure covering eighty years, which is not even close to Latsis' total for only one and a half years, and not including all the provinces of Russia either. True, the editors of the collection cite another presumed statistic of 1,310 for those sentenced to death (although perhaps not executed) in 1906 alone, and a total of 3,419 for 1826 through 1906. But this, mind you, was right in the midst of the notorious Stolypin reaction, a period for which an additional figure is available: 950 executions over a period of six months.[7] (In fact, the Stolypin military field tribunals were in existence for six months all told.) It sounds awful, and yet it does not make much of an impression on our hardened nerves: even if we multiply by three this figure of 950 for six months, in order to compare it with the Latsis figure for eighteen months in the postrevolutionary period, we still come up with the fact that the terror after the Revolution was at least *three times more intense* than Stolypin's. And that was for just twenty provinces and *excluded courts and tribunals.*

And from November, 1917, on, the courts acted on their own. Despite all the difficulties at the time, *Guiding Principles of the Criminal Law of the R.S.F.S.R.* were issued for their use in 1919. (We have not read this work, could not obtain it, and know only that it included "imprisonment for an indefinite term"—in other words, pending a special order.)

The courts were of three kinds: the people's courts, the circuit courts, and the Revolutionary Tribunals—the *Revtribunals.*

6. M. N. Gernet (editor), *Protiv Smertnoi Kazni* (*Against Capital Punishment*), second edition, 1907, pp. 385–423.
7. The journal *Byloye,* No. 2/14, February, 1907.

The people's courts handled ordinary misdemeanors and non-political criminal cases. They were not empowered to impose death sentences, and, laughable as it seems, the people's court could not, in fact, impose sentences exceeding *two* years. Up to July, 1918, the heritage of the Left SR's still endured in our judicial proceedings. Only by special intervention of the government and only individually were impermissibly lenient sentences raised to *twenty* years.[8] From July, 1918, on, the people's courts were given the right to hand down sentences of up to *five* years. And in 1922, when all threats of war had died down, the people's courts got the right to impose sentences of up to *ten* years and lost the right to sentence anyone to *less* than six months.

From the beginning, the circuit courts and the *Revtribunals* had the power to impose the death sentence, but they lost it for a brief period: the circuit courts in 1920, and the *Revtribunals* in 1921. There were many tiny ups and downs in this period which only a historian pursuing all the details of those years would be able to trace.

Perhaps that historian will seek out the documents and unroll for us the scroll of tribunal sentences and also the statistics. (Though probably not. Whatever time and events failed to destroy was destroyed by persons interested in having such material disappear.) We know only that the *Revtribunals* were not asleep. They were handing down sentences right and left. And we know, too, that every time a city was captured during the Civil War the event was marked not only by gunsmoke in the courtyards of the Cheka, but also by sleepless sessions of the tribunal. And you did not have to be a White officer, a senator, a landowner, a monk, a Cadet, an SR, or an Anarchist in order to get your bullet. Soft white uncallused hands alone were sufficient in those years. But one can also hazard the guess that in Izhevsk or Votkinsk, Yaroslavl or Murom, Kozlov or Tambov, the uprisings were very costly as well to those who had callused workers' hands. And if those scrolls—of both the *extrajudicial* executions and those by tribunal—are unrolled for us someday, the most surprising thing will be the number of ordinary peasants we find on them. Because there was no end to the number of peasant uprisings and revolts from 1918 to 1921, even though they did not

8. See Part III, Chapter 1.

adorn the colored pages of the official *History of the Civil War,*
and even though no one photographed them, and no one filmed
motion pictures of those furious crowds attacking machine guns
with clubs, pitchforks, and axes and, later, lined up for execution
with their arms tied behind their backs—*ten for one!* The revolt
in Sapozhok is remembered only in Sapozhok; the one in Pitelino
only in Pitelino. We learn from Latsis the number of peasant
rebellions that were suppressed during that same year and a half
in twenty provinces—344.[9] (From 1918 on, peasant revolts were
already being called "kulak" revolts, for how could the *peasants*
revolt against the workers' and peasants' power! But how then
could one explain that in every instance it was not just three
peasant huts that revolted but the whole village? Why did the
masses of poor peasants not kill the insurgent "kulaks" with those
same pitchforks and axes, instead of marching with them against
the machine guns? Latsis claims: "The kulaks compelled the
rest of the peasants to take part in these revolts by promises,
slander, and threats."[10] But what could have been more laden
with promises than the slogans of the Committees of the Poor?
And what could have been more loaded with threats than the
machine guns of the Special Purpose Detachments, the CHON?

And how many wholly random people, completely random,
whose destruction inevitably accounts for half the casualties of
every real, shooting revolution, were caught between those millstones?

Here is an eyewitness description of a session of the Ryazan
Revtribunal which met in 1919 to hear the case of the Tolstoyan
I. Ye——v.

With the proclamation of universal and compulsory conscription into the Red Army (just one year after the slogans: "Down
with the war!"; "Stick your bayonets in the ground!"; "Go
home!"), "54,697 deserters were caught and sent to the front" by
September, 1919, in Ryazan Province alone.[11] (And how many
others were shot on the spot as examples?) Ye——v was not a
deserter at all but a man who simply and openly refused to enter
military service because of his religious convictions. He was con-

9. Latsis, *op. cit.,* p .75
10. *Ibid.,* p. 70.
11. *Ibid.,* p. 74.

scripted by main force, but in the barracks he refused to take up arms or undergo training. The enraged Political Commissar of the unit turned him over to the Cheka, saying: "He does not recognize the Soviet government." There was an interrogation. Three Chekists sat behind the desk, each with a Naguan revolver in front of him. "We have seen heroes like you before. You'll be on your knees to us in a minute! Either agree to fight immediately, or we'll shoot you!" But Ye———v was firm. He couldn't fight. He was a believer in free Christianity. And his case was sent to the *Revtribunal*.

It was an open session, with a hundred spectators in the hall. There was a polite elderly defense lawyer. The learned "accuser" —the term "prosecutor" was forbidden until 1922—was Nikolsky, another old jurist. One of the members of the *Revtribunal*— a juror—tried to elicit the views of the accused. (How can you, a representative of the working people, share the opinions of the aristocrat Count Tolstoi?) But the presiding judge interrupted the questioning and refused to permit it to continue. There was a quarrel.

Juror: "You do not want to kill people, and you try to persuade others to refrain from killing. But the Whites began the war, and you are preventing us from defending ourselves. We will send you to Kolchak, and you can preach your nonresistance there!"

Ye———v: "I will go wherever you send me."

Accuser: "This tribunal is not supposed to concern itself with any nondescript criminal actions but only with those which are counterrevolutionary. In view of the nature of this crime, I demand that the case be turned over to a people's court."

Presiding Judge: "Ha! Actions! What a pettifogger you are! We are guided not by the laws but by our revolutionary conscience!"

Accuser: "I insist that you include my demand in the record."

Defense Attorney: "I support the accuser. The case should be heard in an ordinary court."

Presiding Judge: "There's an old fool for you! Where did they manage to find him?"

Defense Attorney: "I have been a practicing lawyer for forty years and this is the first time I have heard such an insult. Enter it in the record."

Presiding Judge (laughing): "We'll enter it, we'll enter it!" Laughter in the hall. The court exits in order to confer. The sounds of a noisy argument come from the conference room. They return with the sentence: *to be shot.*

Loud indignation in the hall.

Accuser: "I protest against the sentence and will complain to the Commissariat of Justice!"

Defense Lawyer: "I join my voice to that of the accuser."

Presiding Judge: "Clear the hall!"

The convoy came and led Ye———v to jail, saying to him: "If everyone was like you, brother, how good it would be! There would be no war, and no Whites and no Reds!" They went back to their barracks and called a Red Army meeting. It condemned the sentence and sent a protest to Moscow.

In daily expectation of death, Ye———v waited for thirty-seven days, while, from the prison window, he watched executions taking place. They commuted his sentence to fifteen years of *strict detention.*

This is an instructive example. Although "revolutionary legality" won a partial victory, how enormous an effort it required on the part of the presiding judge! How much disorganization, lack of discipline, lack of political consciousness there still was! The prosecution stood firmly with the defense. The convoy guards stuck their noses into something that wasn't their business in order to send off a protest. Whew, the dictatorship of the proletariat and the new kind of court were not having things easy by any means! Of course, not all the sessions were anything like so turbulent, but this wasn't the only one of its kind. How many years it would take to reveal, direct, and confirm the necessary line, until the defense would stand as one with the prosecution and the court, and the accused would be in agreement with them too, and all the resolutions of the workers as well!

To pursue this enterprise of many years' duration is the rewarding task of the historian. As for us—how are we to make our way through that rosy mist? Whom are we to ask about it? Those who were shot aren't talking, and neither are those who have been scattered to the four winds. Even if the defendants, and the lawyers, and the guards, and the spectators have survived, no one will allow us to seek them out.

Evidently, the only help we will get is from the *prosecution.*

In this connection, I was given by well-wishers an intact copy of a collection of speeches for the prosecution delivered by that fierce revolutionary, the first People's Commissar of Military Affairs in the Workers' and Peasants' Government, the Commander in Chief, and later the organizer of the Department of Exceptional Courts of the People's Commissariat of Justice—where the personal rank of tribune was being readied for him, until Lenin vetoed the title[12]—the glorious accuser in the greatest trials, subsequently exposed as the ferocious enemy of the people, N. V. Krylenko.[13] And if, despite everything, we want to attempt a brief review of the public trials, if we are determined to try to get a feeling for the judicial atmosphere of the first postrevolutionary years, then we have to learn to read this Krylenko text. We have no other. And using it as a basis, we must try to picture to ourselves everything that is missing from it and everything that happened in the provinces too.

Of course, we would prefer to see the stenographic record of those trials, to listen to the dramatic voices from beyond the grave of those first defendants and those first lawyers, speaking at a time when no one could have foreseen in what implacable sequence all of it would be swallowed up—together with those *Revtribunal* members as well.

However, as Krylenko has explained, *for a whole series of technical reasons* "it was inconvenient to publish the stenographic records"[14] It was convenient only to publish his speeches for the prosecution and the sentences handed down by the tribunals, which by that time had already come to jibe completely with the demands of the accuser-prosecutor.

Krylenko claims that the archives of the Moscow Revtribunal and the Supreme Revtribunal turned out (by 1922) to be "far from orderly. . . . In a whole series of cases the stenographic records . . . were so incomprehensible that it was necessary either to cross out entire pages or else to try to restore the text from memory"! And a "series of the biggest trials"—including the trial which followed the revolt of the Left SR's, and the case of Ad-

12. Lenin, fifth edition, Vol. 36, p. 210.
13. Krylenko, *Za Pyat Let (1918–1922)*. Edition 7,000 copies. Prosecution speeches in the most important trials held before the Moscow and the Supreme Revolutionary Tribunals.
14. *Ibid.*, p. 4.

miral Shchastny—"were conducted entirely without stenographic records."[15]

This is strange. The condemnation of the Left SR's was not a trivial matter. It was, after the February and October revolutions, the third turning point in our history, signaling the transition to a one-party system in the state. Not a few of them were shot. And no stenographic record was made.

And the "Military Plot" of 1919 was "liquidated by the Cheka in an extrajudicial reprisal,"[16] which "was further proof of its existence."[17] (In this case more than one thousand people were arrested altogether,[18] and, really, how could trials have been set up for them all?)

So just try to produce a neat, orderly report on the trials of those years!

Nevertheless we can learn the important principles involved in them. For example, the supreme accuser—in other words, the Prosecutor General—informs us that the All-Russian Central Executive Committee had the right to intervene in any judicial proceeding. "VTsIK pardons and *punishes,* at its own discretion *without any limitation whatever*."[19] For example, a six-month sentence was changed to ten years. (And, as the reader understands, it was not necessary for the entire All-Russian Central Executive Committee to assemble at a plenary meeting to this end, since its Chairman, Sverdlov, for example, could correct a sentence without leaving his office.) All of this, Krylenko explains, "shows the superiority of our system over the false theory of the separation of powers,"[20] that is, the theory of the independence of the judiciary. (True, Sverdlov also said: "It is very good that the legislative and executive power are not divided by a thick wall as they are in the West. All problems *can be decided quickly.*" Especially on the phone.)

Krylenko formulated even more frankly and precisely *the general tasks of the Soviet courts* in his speeches before those tribunals, when the court was "at one and the same time both

15. *Ibid.,* pp. 4–5.
16. *Ibid.,* p. 7.
17. *Ibid.,* p. 44.
18. Latsis, *op. cit.,* p. 46.
19. Krylenko, *op. cit.,* p. 13. (My italics.)
20. *Ibid.,* p. 14.

the creator of the law [Krylenko's italics] . . . *and a political weapon.*"[21] (My italics.)

Creator of the law because, for four years, there were no codes. They had thrown out the Tsarist codes, and they had not composed their own. "Don't tell me our criminal courts ought to act exclusively on the basis of existing written norms. We live in the process of Revolution."[22] "A tribunal is not the kind of court in which fine points of jurisprudence and clever stratagems are to be restored. . . . We are creating a new law and *new ethical norms.*"[23] And also: "No matter how much is said here about the eternal law of truth, justice, etc., we know . . . how dearly these have cost us."[24]

(But if *your* prison terms are compared with *ours*, maybe it didn't cost you so dearly after all? Maybe eternal justice was somewhat more comfortable?)

The reason that fine points of jurisprudence are unnecessary is that there is no need to clarify whether the defendant is guilty or not guilty: the concept of *guilt* is an old bourgeois concept which has now been uprooted.[25]

And so we heard from Comrade Krylenko that a tribunal was *not that kind of court!* On another occasion we would hear from him that a tribunal was *not a court at all:* "A tribunal is an organ of the class struggle of the workers directed against their enemies" and must act "from the point of view of the interests of the revolution . . . having in mind *the most desirable results* for the masses of workers and peasants."[26] People are not people, but "carriers of specific ideas."[27] "No matter what the individual qualities [of the defendant], *only one* method of evaluating him is to be applied: evaluation from the point of view of *class expediency.*"[28]

In other words, you can exist only if it's expedient for the working class. And if "this expediency should require that the avenging sword should fall on the head of the defendants, then

21. *Ibid.*, p. 3.
22. *Ibid.*, p. 408.
23. *Ibid.*, p. 22. (My italics.)
24. *Ibid.*, p. 505.
25. *Ibid.*, p. 318.
26. *Ibid.*, p. 73. (The italics throughout are mine.)
27. *Ibid.*, p. 83.
28. *Ibid.*, p. 79.

no . . . verbal arguments can help."[29] (Such as arguments by lawyers, etc.) "In our revolutionary court we are guided not by articles of the law and not by the degree of extenuating circumstances; in the tribunal we must proceed on the basis of considerations of expediency."[30]

That was the way it was in those years: people lived and breathed and then suddenly found out that their existence was *inexpedient*.

And it must also be kept in mind that it was not what he had done that constituted the defendant's burden, but what he *might* do if he were not shot now. "We protect ourselves not only against the past but also against the future."[31]

Comrade Krylenko's pronouncements are clear and all-inclusive. They bring alive for us that whole period of the law in sharp relief. The clarity of autumn suddenly pierces the mists of spring and reaches us. And is it perhaps unnecessary to go further? Perhaps we aren't required to page through trial after trial. These pronouncements will be henceforth inexorably applied.

Close your eyes tight for a minute and picture a tiny courtroom—not yet gilded. Earnest members of the tribunal in simple field jackets, lean, not yet fat-faced. The *accusing power*—as Krylenko loved to style himself—wears an unbuttoned civilian jacket, with a glimpse of a sailor's striped undershirt just visible at the open throat.

The supreme accuser expresses himself in this sort of language: "The question of fact is interesting to me!"; "Define concretely the aspect of the tendency!"; "We are operating on the plane of analysis of objective truth." Sometimes, as you read, a quotation from the Latin shines out. (It is true that the same quotation turns up in case after case, but, after several years, a different one does appear.) And no wonder—he did, after all, complete the course in two faculties despite all his revolutionary running around. What attracts one to him are his frank opinions about the defendants: "Professional scoundrels!" And he isn't hypocritical in the least. If he didn't like the defendant's smile, he didn't hesitate to blurt out a threat, even before any sentence was imposed.

29. *Ibid.*, p. 81.
30. *Ibid.*, p. 524.
31. *Ibid.*, p. 82.

"And as for you and your smile, Citizeness Ivanova, we'll make you pay for it, and we'll find a way to fix it so that you *never laugh again!*"[32]

So, shall we begin?

A. The Case of "Russkiye Vedomosti"

In this case, one of the earliest, *free speech* was on trial. On March 24, 1918, this famous "professorial" newspaper published an article by Savinkov entitled "En Route." They would have much preferred to arrest Savinkov himself, but he really was *en route*, damn it, and where was he to be found? So instead they closed down the paper and brought the elderly editor, P. V. Yegorov, to court as a defendant, insisting that he explain how he had dared to publish the article. After all, the New Era was four months old, and it was time to get used to it!

Yegorov naïvely defended himself by saying that the article had been written by a "leading political figure whose opinion was of general interest whether or not the editors shared it." Furthermore, he saw nothing slanderous in Savinkov's having said: "Let us not forget that Lenin, Natanson, and Co. arrived in Russia via Berlin; i.e., that the German authorities helped them return to the homeland"—because that in actual fact was what had happened; Kaiser Wilhelm's embattled Germany had helped Comrade Lenin to return.

Krylenko retorted that he would not conduct a prosecution for slander (why not?), and that the newspaper was on trial *for attempting to influence people's minds!* (And how could any newspaper dare have such a purpose!?)

The formal charge did not include Savinkov's phrase: "One has to be criminally insane to affirm seriously that the international proletariat *will come to our aid*"—because it still would come to our aid.

For attempting to influence people's minds, the newspaper, which had been published since 1864 and had survived the most fiercely reactionary periods—those of Loris-Melikov, Pobedonostsev, Stolypin, Kasso, and all the rest—was ordered *closed down forever!* And Yegorov, the editor—and this is a shameful

32. *Ibid.,* p. 296.

thing to have to say—was given only three months of solitary— just as though we were in Greece or some such place. (It is not so shamefully lenient, however, if one stops to think that it was only 1918! And if the old man managed to survive, he would be imprisoned again, and many more times too!)

It may seem strange to us now, but it is a fact that in those thunderous years bribes were given and taken just as tenderly as they had been from time immemorial in Old Russia and as they will be in the Soviet Union from here to eternity. Bribery was particularly rife in the judicial organs. And, though we blush to say it, in the Cheka. The official histories in their red, gold-stamped bindings are silent about this, but the old folks and eyewitnesses remember that the fate of political prisoners in the first years of the Revolution, as distinct from Stalinist times, often depended on bribes: they were accepted uninhibitedly, and prisoners were honestly released as a result. Although Krylenko picked out only a dozen *cases* for the five-year period his book covers, he reports two cases of bribery. Alas, even the Moscow Tribunal and the Supreme Tribunal squeezed their way through to perfection along a crooked path, muddied themselves in improprieties.

B. The Case of the Three Interrogators of the Moscow Revtribunal— April, 1918

In March, 1918, a speculator in gold bars named Beridze was arrested. His wife tried to find a way to ransom her husband, which was the accepted thing to do. Through a series of connections she succeeded in getting to one of the interrogators, who brought two others in with him. Meeting secretly, they demanded a bribe of 250,000 rubles, but, after some bargaining, they reduced it to 60,000, half in advance. The deal was to be made through the lawyer Grin. Everything would have gone off without a fuss, as hundreds of similar deals had, and the case would have gotten into neither Krylenko's chronicle nor ours, nor even become a matter of concern to the Council of People's Commissars, had it not been that Beridze's wife began to get miserly, and brought Grin only 15,000 as an advance payment, instead of

30,000. But the main thing was that, in consequence of female fickleness, she changed her mind overnight, decided her lawyer wasn't good enough for her, and went off the next morning to find another, the attorney Yakulov. It is not stated anywhere, but it was evidently Yakulov who decided to turn in the interrogators.

It is of interest that all the witnesses in this trial, beginning with the unfortunate wife, tried to give testimony helpful to the accused and to befuddle the prosecution. (Which would have been impossible in a political trial!) Krylenko explained their conduct as the result of a narrow-minded, philistine attitude, because they felt like outsiders as far as the *Revtribunal* was concerned. (And might we ourselves be so audacious as to advance the philistine hypothesis that in the course of a year and a half the witnesses had already learned *to be afraid of* the dictatorship of the proletariat? After all, it took a lot of nerve to turn in the interrogators of the *Revtribunal*. What would happen to you after that?)

The accuser's line of argument is also of interest. After all, just a month earlier the defendants had been his associates, his comrades in arms, his assistants. They were people who had been inalienably dedicated to the interests of the Revolution, and one of them, Leist, was even "a stern accuser, capable of hurling thunder and lightning at anyone who attacked the foundations." What was he to say about them now? Where was he to look for the causes of their fall? (A bribe was not enough in itself.) And, of course, it is clear where he looked: in their *pasts,* in their biographies!

Declared Krylenko: "If we look closely" at this Leist, "we will find highly interesting information." This is intriguing. Was he an inveterate adventurer? No, but he was the son of a professor at Moscow University! And not an ordinary professor, but one who had survived twenty years of reaction by his indifference to political activity! (And who, notwithstanding that reaction, had been accepted by Krylenko as a consultant.) Was it surprising, then, that the son turned out to be a double-dealer?

As for Podgaisky, he was the son of an official in the law courts . . . beyond doubt one of the reactionary, pogrom-organizing Black Hundreds; otherwise how could he have served the Tsar for twenty years? And the son, too, had prepared for a career in the law courts, but then the Revolution had come—and he had wormed his way into the *Revtribunal*. Just yesterday all this had been depicted in a very favorable light, but it had suddenly become repulsive!

More repulsive than them both was, of course, Gugel. He had been a publisher. And what intellectual food had he been offering the workers and peasants? He was "nourishing the broad masses with low-quality literature," not Marx but, instead, books by bourgeois professors with world-famous names. (And we shall soon encounter these professors as defendants too.)

Krylenko is enraged and marvels at the kind of people who have sneaked into the tribunal. (Neither do we understand: What kind of people are the workers' and peasants' tribunals composed of? Why had the proletariat entrusted the task of striking down their enemies to people of this particular kind?)

And as for Grin, the lawyer, a man with an "in" on the investigating commission, who was quite able to get anybody off scot-free, he was a typical representative of that subspecies of the human race which Marx called *"leeches* on the capitalist structure"—a category including, in addition, all lawyers, gendarmes, priests, and also . . . notaries.[33]

It appears that Krylenko spared no effort in demanding mercilessly severe sentences, without reference to "the individual shadings of guilt." But some kind of lethargy, some sort of torpor, overcame the eternally vigorous tribunal, and it just barely managed to mumble six months in jail for the interrogators, and a fine for the lawyer. And only by availing himself of the authority of the All-Russian Central Executive Committee "to punish without limitation," did Krylenko, there in the Metropole, continue to hang ten-year sentences on the interrogators and five on the lawyer, plus full confiscation of his property. Krylenko thundered on about vigilance, and he almost managed, but not quite, to get the title of *Tribune* he so coveted.

We recognize that among the revolutionary masses at the time, as among our readers today, this unfortunate trial could not but undermine faith in the sanctity of the tribunal. And we therefore proceed with even greater timidity to the next case, which concerned an even loftier institution.

33. *Ibid.*, p. 500.

C. The Case of Kosyrev—February 15, 1919

F. M. Kosyrev and his pals Libert, Rottenberg, and Solovyev had first served on the Commission for Supply of the Eastern Front (back before Kolchak, when the enemy forces were the armies of the Constituent Assembly). It was discovered that there they had found ways to siphon into their own pockets from seventy thousand to a million rubles at a time; they rode around on fine horses and engaged in orgies with the nurses. Their Commission had acquired a house and an automobile, and their major-domo lived it up in the Yar Restaurant. (We aren't accustomed to picturing 1918 in this light, but all this was in the testimony of the Revtribunal.)

But none of this, to be sure, was the *case* against them. No charge had been brought against any of them in connection with their activities on the Eastern Front; they had even been forgiven all that. But wonder of wonders! Hardly had their Commission for Supply been disbanded than all four of them, with the addition of Nazarenko, a former Siberian tramp and convict pal of Kosyrev in criminal hard labor, were invited to constitute . . . the Control and Auditing Collegium of the VChK—the Cheka!

Here's what this Collegium was: *it had plenipotentiary powers to verify the legality of the actions of all the remaining organs of the Cheka,* the right to demand and review any case at any stage of its processing, and to reverse the decisions of all the remaining organs of the VChK, excepting only the Presidium of the Cheka!"[34] This was no small thing. This Collegium was second-in-command in the Cheka after the Presidium itself—it ranked immediately below Dzerzhinsky-Uritsky-Peters-Latsis-Menzhinsky-Yagoda!

The way of life of this comradely group remained just what it had been before. They didn't get swelled heads; they didn't get carried away. With certain individuals named Maximych, Lenka, Rafailsky, and Mariupolsky, "who had no connection at all with the Communist Party," they set up—in private apartments and in the Hotel Savoy—"lavish establishments where card games with table stakes as high as a thousand rubles a throw were the order of the day, along with heavy drinking and women." Kosyrev acquired a rich establishment of his own (costing 70,000 rubles)

34. *Ibid.,* p. 507.

and, in fact, did not even draw the line at hauling off silver spoons and goblets, and even ordinary glassware, from the Cheka. (And how did all these objects get to the Cheka?) "And this was where his attention was concentrated, rather than in the direction of ideas and ideology, and this was what he took from the revolutionary movement." (In the very act of repudiating the bribes he had accepted, this leading Chekist, without blinking, volunteered the lie that he possessed 200,000 rubles from an inheritance in a Chicago bank! Evidently, as far as he was concerned, there was no conflict between such a circumstance and world revolution!)

Now how did he propose to make proper use of his superhuman right to arrest anyone at all and release anyone at all? Clearly, one had to find a fish with golden roe—and in 1918 there were not a few such fish in the nets. (After all, the Revolution had been carried out too quickly; they hadn't found everything—how many precious stones, necklaces, bracelets, rings, and earrings the bourgeois ladies had managed to hide away!) Then one had to make contact with the relatives of those who had been arrested through some reliable middleman.

Such characters also pass before us at the trial. There was Uspenskaya, a woman of twenty-two. She had graduated from the St. Petersburg Gymnasium, but hadn't gone on to the university— the Soviets had come to power—and so, in the spring of 1918, Uspenskaya appeared at the Cheka to offer her services as an informer. She qualified on the basis of her appearance, and they accepted her.

Krylenko has this to say about informing, which in those days had a different label: "For *ourselves, we* see nothing shameful in it, we consider *this* to be our duty . . . the work itself is not disgraceful; once a person admits that this work is necessary in the interests of the Revolution, then he must do it."[35] But, alas, it turned out that Uspenskaya had no political credo! That's what was awful. She declared: "I agreed in order to be paid a fixed percentage" on the cases which were turned up, and, beyond that, "to split 50-50" with someone else . . . whom the court protected and instructed her not to identify. Krylenko put it in his own words: "Uspenskaya was not a staff member of the Cheka but worked at *piece rates*."[36] And, incidentally, the accuser, under-

35. *Ibid.,* p. 513. (My italics.)
36. *Ibid.,* p. 507.

standing her in a very human way, explains that she had grown used to having plenty of money, and that her insignificant salary of 500 rubles from the Supreme Council of the Economy was nothing at all, considering that one exercise in extortion—for example, helping a merchant get the seal removed from his store—would net her 5,000 rubles, and another—from Meshcherskaya-Grevs, wife of a prisoner—would bring in 17,000. For that matter, Uspenskaya served only briefly as a mere stool pigeon. Thanks to the help of certain big Chekists, in a few months she became a member of the Communist Party and an interrogator.

However, we don't seem to be getting to the essence of the *case*. Uspenskaya had arranged a meeting between this Meshch- erskaya-Grevs and a certain Godelyuk, a bosom pal of Kosyrev, in order to reach an agreement on her husband's ransom. (They had initially demanded 600,000 rubles!) But unfortunately, by some still unexplained means, the arrangements for that secret meeting became known to the same attorney, Yakulov, who had already done in the three bribe-taking interrogators and who, evidently, felt a class hatred for the whole proletarian system of judicial and extrajudicial processing. Yakulov denounced them to the Moscow Revtribunal,[37] and the presiding judge of the tribunal, recalling perhaps the wrath of the Council of People's Commissars in connection with the three interrogators, also blundered in terms of class premises. Instead of simply warning Comrade Dzerzhinsky and working it all out in the family, he hid a steno- grapher behind the curtain. And the stenographer took down all Godelyuk's references to Kosyrev, and to Solovyev and to other commissars, and all his stories about *who* in the Cheka *takes* how many thousands. Then, as per the stenographic record, Godelyuk received an advance payment of 12,000 rubles, and Meshcher- skaya-Grevs was given a pass to enter the Cheka that had already been filled out by the Control and Auditing Collegium, by Libert and Rottenberg. (The bargaining was to continue there, inside the Cheka.) Then and there Godelyuk was caught! In his con-

37. In order to temper the reader's indignation against this leechlike snake, Yakulov, we should point out that by the time of Kosyrev's trial he had already been arrested and was in custody. They had found a *case* to take care of him. He was brought in to testify accompanied by convoy, and we are certainly entitled to hope that he was shot soon afterward. (Today we are surprised: How did things reach such a pitch of illegality? Why did no one mount an offensive against it?)

fusion, he gave testimony against them! (And Meshcherskaya-Grevs had already gotten to the Control and Auditing Collegium, and they had already ordered her husband's case transferred there *for verification.*)

But just a moment! After all, an exposé like this sullies the heavenly blue uniforms of the Cheka! Was the presiding judge of the Moscow Revtribunal in his right mind? Was he really tending to his own business?

But it turns out that that was the nature of the *moment*—a moment totally hidden from us in the folds of our majestic history! It seems that the Cheka's first year of work had produced a somewhat repellent impression even on the Party of the proletariat, which still hadn't gotten used to it. Only its first year had passed; the Cheka had taken only the first step on its glorious path; and already, as Krylenko writes, although not very clearly, a "dispute" had arisen "between the court and its functions and the extrajudicial functions of the Cheka . . . a dispute which, at the time, split the Party and the workers' districts into two camps."[38] And that is how the Kosyrev case could come up—whereas everything had gone smoothly before—and reach all the way up to the topmost level of the whole state apparatus.

The Cheka had to be saved! Help! Save the Cheka! Solovyev asked the tribunal to allow him inside the Taganka Prison to visit Godelyuk (who, alas, was not in the Lubyanka) so as *to chat* with him. The tribunal declined the request. Then Solovyev managed to *penetrate into Godelyuk's cell* without the help of any tribunal, and—what a coincidence!—at that very point Godelyuk became seriously ill. ("One can hardly speak of evil intentions on Solovyev's part," Krylenko bows and scrapes.) Feeling the approach of death, Godelyuk shakily repented having slandered the Cheka and asked for a sheet of paper on which to write his recantation: it was all untrue; he had slandered Kosyrev and the other commissars of the Cheka, and everything the stenographer had taken down behind the curtain was also untrue![39]

38. Krylenko, *op. cit.,* p. 14.
39. Oh, how many themes we have here! Oh, where is Shakespeare? Solovyev passes through the walls, flickering shadows in the cell, Godelyuk recants with failing hand. And all we hear about the years of the Revolution in our plays and our films is the street singing of "Hostile Whirlwinds."

"And who filled out the passes for Meshcherskaya-Grevs?" Krylenko insisted. They hadn't materialized out of thin air, certainly? No, the chief accuser "does not wish to say that Solovyev was an accessory in this case, because . . . because there is insufficient evidence," but he advances the hypothesis that "citizens still at liberty who were in danger of being caught with their hands in the till" might have sent Solovyev to the Taganka jail.

This was the perfect time to question Libert and Rottenberg, and they were subpoenaed, but they didn't appear! Just like that! They didn't show up. They declined to. All right, in that case question Meshcherskaya-Grevs! And—can you imagine it?—this broken-down aristocrat, too, was so brazen as not to appear before the Revtribunal! And there was no way to force her to! Godelyuk had recanted—and was dying. Kosyrev refused to admit anything! Solovyev was not guilty of anything! So there was no one to question.

What witnesses, on the other hand, did indeed appear before the tribunal, and of their own free will! The Deputy Chief of the Cheka, Comrade Peters. And even Feliks Edmundovich Dzerzhinsky himself. He arrived in a state of alarm. His long, burning zealot's face confronted the tribunal—whose members sat with sinking hearts—and he testified passionately in defense of the totally innocent Kosyrev and his high moral, revolutionary, and professional qualities. This testimony, alas, has not been preserved for us, but Krylenko refers to it this way: "Solovyev and Dzerzhinsky portrayed Kosyrev's wonderful qualites."[40] (Alas, you careless shavetail, you! In twenty years' time, in the Lubyanka, they are going to remind you of that trial!) It is easy to guess what Dzerzhinsky could have said: that Kosyrev was an iron Chekist, merciless to their enemies; that he was a good *comrade*. A hot heart, a cool head, clean hands.

And from the garbage heap of slander, the bronze knight Kosyrev rises before our eyes. Furthermore, his whole biography testifies to his remarkable will. Before the Revolution he was convicted several times—most often for murder. In the city of Kostroma, he was convicted of worming his way by deception into the house of an old woman named Smirnova and *strangling her with his own hands;* then of an attempt to kill his own father;

40. Krylenko, *op. cit.,* p. 522.

and then of killing a comrade in order to use his passport. The rest of Kosyrev's convictions were for swindling, and in all he spent many years at hard labor. (One could understand his desire for a luxurious life.) And he had only been freed by the Tsarist amnesties.

At that point, the stern and righteous voices of the major Chekists interrupted the chief accuser; they pointed out to him that those courts which had convicted Kosyrev were courts of the bourgeoisie and landowners and did not merit being noticed in our new society. But what happened? The shavetail, going overboard, poured forth from the chief accuser's rostrum a tirade so ideologically faulty that in our exposition of this harmonious series of cases tried by the tribunals, citing it is to strike a discordant note.

"If there was anything good in the old Tsarist court system, it was only trial by jury. . . . One could always have confidence in the jurors' decisions and a minimum of judicial error was to be found in them."[41]

It was all the more vexing to hear this sort of thing from Comrade Krylenko because just three months before, at the trial of the provocateur R. Malinovsky, a former favorite of the Communist Party leadership, who, notwithstanding his four criminal convictions in the past, had been co-opted into the Central Committee by the leadership and appointed to the Duma, the accusing power had taken an impeccable class stand.

"Every crime is the result of a given social system, and in these terms criminal convictions under the laws of a capitalist society and in Tsarist times do not, in our eyes, constitute a fact branding a person with an indelible mark once and for all. . . . We know of *many examples* of persons *in our ranks* branded by *such facts in the past*, but we have *never* drawn the conclusion that it was necessary to remove such a person from our milieu. *A person who knows our principles* cannot fear that the existence of previous criminal convictions in his record will jeopardize his being included in the ranks of the revolutionaries."[42]

That is how Comrade Krylenko could speak when in a Party

41. *Ibid.*
42. *Ibid.*, p. 337.

vein. But in this other case, as a result of his mistaken judgment, the image of the knight in shining armor, Kosyrev, was being bespattered. And it created a situation in the tribunal wherein Comrade Dzerzhinsky was forced to say: "For just one second [Just one second!] the thought crossed my mind that citizen Kosyrev might be falling victim to the political passions which *in recent times have blazed up around the Extraordinary Commission*."[43]

And Krylenko suddenly took thought: "I do not wish, and I never have wished, that the present trial should turn into a trial of the Cheka rather than a trial of Kosyrev and Uspenskaya. Not only am I *unable to desire* such an outcome: I am obliged to fight against it with all available means!" And he went on: "The most responsible, honest, and self-controlled comrades were put at the head of the Extraordinary Commission, and they took on themselves the difficult task of striking down the enemy, *even though this involved the risk of error*. . . . For this the Revolution is obliged to say thank you. . . . I underline this aspect so that . . . no one can ever say to me later: 'He turned out to be an instrument of political treason!' "[44] (But that's what they will say!)

What a razor edge the supreme accuser was walking! But he evidently had certain contacts, going back to his days in the underground, through which he learned how things were going to move on the morrow. This is conspicuous in several trials, and came out here too. At the beginning of 1919, there were certain trends toward saying: "*It is enough!* It is time to bridle the Cheka!" And this moment was "beautifully caught in Bukharin's essay, in which he said that *revolutionary legality* must give way to *legalized revolutionality*."[45]

Wherever you look you see dialectics! And Krylenko burst out: "The Revtribunal is being called on to replace the Extraordinary Commission." (*To replace???*) Meanwhile, it "must be . . . no less fierce in implementing the system of terror, intimidation, and threat than was the Extraordinary Commission—the Cheka."[46]

Than it *was?* The past tense? Has he already buried it? Come

43. *Ibid.*, p. 509.
44. *Ibid.*, pp. 505–510. (My italics.)
45. *Ibid.*, p. 511.
46. *Ibid.*

now, you are going to replace it, and where are the Chekists supposed to go? Ominous days! That was reason enough to hurry to the tribunal, in a greatcoat down to one's heels, to testify as a witness.

But perhaps your sources of information, Comrade Krylenko, are false?

Yes, the heavens darkened over the Lubyanka in those days. And this whole book might have been very different. But I suppose that what happened was that iron Feliks Dzerzhinsky went to see Vladimir Ilyich Lenin, and talked it over and explained. And the skies cleared. And although two days later, on February 17, 1919, the Cheka was deprived of its judicial rights by special decree of the All-Russian Central Executive Committee— it was *"not for long."*[47]

Our day in court was further complicated by the fact that the objectionable Uspenskaya behaved abominably. From the defendants' bench she "threw mud at" leading Chekists who had not previously been touched by the trial, including Comrade Peters! (She turned out to have used his pure name in her blackmailing operations; she used to sit right in his office, without any ceremony, during his conversations with other intelligence agents.) Now she hinted at some dark prerevolutionary past of his in Riga. That's the kind of snake she had turned into in eight months, despite the fact that she had been with Chekists during those eight months! What was to be done with such a woman? Here Krylenko's position jibed completely with that of the Chekists: "Until a firm regime has been established, and we are a long way from that being the case [Are we really???] . . . in the interests of the defense of the Revolution . . . there is not and cannot be any sentence for citizeness Uspenskaya other than her *annihilation.*" He did not say "to be shot"—what he said was "annihilation"! But after all, Citizen Krylenko, she's just a young girl! Come on now, give her a "tenner," or maybe a "twenty-five," and maybe the system will be firmly established by then? How about it? But alas: "In the interests of society and of the Revolution there is no other answer, nor can there be one—and the question cannot be put any other way. *In the given case,* detention isn't going to bear any fruit!"

47. *Ibid.,* p. 14.

She had sure rubbed the salt in. . . . She knew too much. . . .

And Kosyrev had to be sacrificed too. They shot him. It was for the health of the others.

Can it really be that someday we will read the old Lubyanka archives? No, they will burn them. They already have.

As the reader can see for himself, this was a very unimportant case. We didn't have to dwell on it. But here is a different one.

D. The Case of the "Churchmen"—January 11–16, 1920

This case, in Krylenko's opinion, is going to have a "suitable place in the annals of the Russian Revolution." Right there in the annals, indeed! It took one day to wring Kosyrev's neck, but in this case they dragged things out for five whole days.

The principal defendants were: A. D. Samarin (a famous man in Russia, the former chief procurator of the Synod; a man who had tried to liberate the church from the Tsar's yoke, an enemy of Rasputin whom Rasputin had forced out of office);[48] Kuznetsov, Professor of Church Law at Moscow University; the Moscow archpriests Uspensky and Tsvetkov. (The accuser himself had this to say about Tsvetkov: "An important public figure, perhaps the best that the clergy could produce, a philanthropist.")

Their guilt lay in creating the "Moscow Council of United Parishes," which had in turn recruited, from among believers forty to eighty years old, a voluntary guard for the Patriarch (unarmed, of course), which had set up permanent day and night watches in his residence, who were charged with the responsibility, in the event of danger from the authorities to the Patriarch, of assembling the people by ringing the church alarm bells and by telephone, so that a whole crowd might follow wherever the Patriarch might be taken and *beg*—and there's your counter-revolution for you!—the Council of People's Commissars to release him!

What an ancient Russian—Holy Russian—scheme! To assemble the people by ringing the alarm bells . . . and proceed in a crowd with a petition!

48. But accuser Krylenko saw no difference whatever between Samarin and Rasputin.

And the accuser was astonished. What danger threatened the Patriarch? Why had plans been made to defend him?

Well, of course, it was really no more than the fact that the Cheka had for two years been conducting extrajudicial reprisals against undesirables, the fact that only a short while before four Red Army men in Kiev had killed the Metropolitan, the fact that the Patriarch's "case had already been worked up and completed, and all that remained was to bring it before the Revtribunal," and "it was only out of concern for the broad masses of workers and peasants, still under the influence of clerical propaganda, that we have left these, our class enemies, *alone for the time being.*"[49] How could Orthodox believers possibly be alarmed on the Patriarch's account? During those two years Patriarch Tikhon had refused to keep silent. He had sent messages to the People's Commissars, to the clergy, and to his flock. His messages were not accepted by the printers but were copied on typewriters (the first samizdat). They exposed the annihilation of the innocents, the ruin of the country. How, therefore, could anyone really be concerned for the Patriarch's life?

A second charge was brought against the defendants. Throughout the country, a census and requisition of church property was taking place (this was in addition to the closing of monasteries and the expropriation of church lands and properties; in question here were liturgical vessels, cups, and candelabra). And the Council of Parishes had disseminated an appeal to believers to resist the requisition, sounding the alarm on the church bells. (And that was natural, after all! That, after all, was how they had defended the churches against the Tatars too!)

And the third charge against them was their incessant, impudent *dispatching of petitions* to the Council of People's Commissars for relief from the desecration of the churches by local authorities, from crude blasphemy and violations of the law which guaranteed freedom of conscience. Even though no action was taken on these petitions (according to the testimony of Bonch-Bruyevich, administrative officer of the Council of People's Commissars), they had discredited the local authorities.

Taking into consideration all the violations committed by these defendants, what punishment could the accuser possibly demand

49. Krylenko, *op. cit.,* p. 61.

for these awful crimes? Will not the reader's revolutionary conscience prompt the answer? *To be shot*, of course. And that is
just what Krylenko did demand—for Samarin and Kuznetsov.

But while they were fussing around with these damned legal
formalities, and listening to too many long speeches from too
many bourgeois lawyers (speeches which "for technical reasons"
we will not cite here), it turned out that capital punishment had
been . . . abolished! What a fix! It just couldn't be! What had
happened? It developed that Dzerzhinsky had issued this order to
the Cheka (the Cheka, without capital punishment?). But had it
been extended to the tribunals by the Council of People's Commissars? Not yet. Krylenko cheered up. And he continued to demand execution by shooting, on the following grounds:

"Even if we suppose that the consolidation of the Republic has
removed the immediacy of threat from such persons, it seems
nonetheless indubitable that in this period of creative effort . . .
a purge . . . of the old turncoat leaders . . . is required by revolutionary necessity." And further: "Soviet power is proud of the
decree of the Cheka abolishing the death penalty." But this "still
does not force us to conclude that the question of the abolition of
capital punishment has been decided once and for all . . . for
the entire period of Soviet rule."[50]

That was quite prophetic! Capital punishment would return—
and very soon too! After all, what a long line still remained to
be rubbed out! (Yes, including Krylenko too, and many of his
class brothers as well.)

And, indeed, the tribunal was submissive and sentenced
Samarin and Kuznetsov to be shot, but they did manage to tack
on a recommendation for clemency: to be imprisoned in a concentration camp *until the final victory over world imperialism!*
(They would still be sitting there today!) And as for "the best
that the clergy could produce"—his sentence was fifteen years,
commuted to five.

Other defendants as well were dragged into this trial in order
to add at least a little substance to the charges. Among them
were some monks and teachers of Zvenigorod, involved in the
Zvenigorod affair in the summer of 1918, but for some reason
not brought to trial for a year and a half (or they might have
been, but were now being tried again, since it was expedient).

50. *Ibid.*, p. 81.

That summer some Soviet officials had called on Father Superior Ion[51] at the Zvenigorod monastery and ordered him ("Step lively there!") to turn over to them the holy relics of St. Savva. The officials not only smoked inside the church and evidently behind the altar screen as well, and, of course, refused to take off their caps, but one of them took Savva's skull in his hands and began to spit into it, to demonstrate that its sanctity was an illusion. And there were further acts of desecration. This led to the alarm bell being sounded, a popular uprising, and the killing of one or two of the officials. (The others denied having committed any acts of desecration, including the spitting incident, and Krylenko accepted their denials.)[52] Were these officials the ones on trial now? No, the monks.

We beg the reader, throughout, to keep in mind: from 1918 on, our judicial custom determined that every Moscow trial, except, of course, the unjust trial of the Chekists, was by no means an isolated trial of an accidental concatenation of circumstances which had converged by accident; it was a landmark of judicial policy; it was a display-window model whose specifications determined what product was good for the provinces too; it was a *standard;* it was like that one-and-only model solution up front in the arithmetic book for the schoolchildren to follow for themselves.

Thus, when we say, "the trial of the churchmen," this must be understood in the multiple plural . . . "many trials." And, in fact, the supreme accuser himself willingly explains: "Such trials *have rolled along through almost all the tribunals of the Republic.*" (What language!) They had taken place not long before in the tribunals in North Dvina, Tver, and Ryazan; in Saratov, Kazan, Ufa, Solvychegodsk, and Tsarevokokshaisk, trials were held of the clergy, the choirs, and the active members of the congrega-

51. Firguf, a former guards officer of the Tsar's household cavalry, who had "suddenly undergone a spiritual conversion, given all his goods to the poor, and entered a monastery, but I do not in fact know whether he actually did distribute his goods to the poor." Yes, and if one admits the possibility of spiritual conversion, what then remains of class theory?

52. But which of us doesn't remember similar scenes? My first memory is of an event that took place when I was, probably, three or four: The *peaked-heads* (as they called the Chekists in their high-peaked Budenny caps) invaded a Kislovodsk church, sliced through the dumbstruck crowd of worshipers, and, in their pointed caps, went straight through the altar screen to the altar and stopped the service.

tion—representatives of the ungrateful "Orthodox church, *liberated* by the October Revolution."[53]

The reader will be aware of a conflict here: why did many of these trials occur earlier than the Moscow model? This is simply a shortcoming of our exposition. The judicial and the extrajudicial persecution of the liberated church had begun well back in 1918, and, judging by the Zvenigorod affair, it had already reached a peak of intensity by that summer. In October, 1918, Patriarch Tikhon had protested in a message to the Council of People's Commissars that there was no freedom to preach in the churches and that "many courageous priests have already paid for their preaching with the blood of martyrdom. . . . You have laid your hands on church property collected by generations of believers, and you have not hesitated to violate their posthumous intent." (The People's Commissars did not, of course, read the message, but the members of their administrative staff must have had a good laugh: Now they've really got something to reproach us with—posthumous intent! We sh-t on your ancestors! We are only interested in descendants.) "They are executing bishops, priests, monks, and nuns who are guilty of nothing, on the basis of indiscriminate charges of indefinite and vaguely counterrevolutionary offenses." True, with the approach of Denikin and Kolchak, this was stopped, so as to make it easier for Orthodox believers to defend the Revolution. But hardly had the Civil War begun to die down than they took up their cudgels against the church again, and the cases started *rolling through* the tribunals once more. In 1920 they struck at the Trinity-St. Sergius Monastery and went straight to the holy relics of that chauvinist Sergius of Radonezh, and hauled them off to a Moscow museum.[54]

53. Krylenko, *op. cit.,* p. 61.
54. The Patriarch cited Klyuchevsky: "The gates of the monastery of the Saint will shut and the ikon lamps will be extinguished over his sepulcher only when we shall have lost every vestige of that spiritual and moral strength willed to us by such great builders of the Russian land as Saint Sergius." Klyuchevsky did not imagine that the loss would occur almost in his own lifetime. The Patriarch asked for an appointment with the Chairman of the Council of People's Commissars, in the hope of persuading him not to touch the holy monastery and the relics . . . for after all the church was separate from the state! The answer came back that the Chairman was occupied in discussing important business, and that the appointment could not be arranged for the near future.
Nor for the distant future either.

The People's Commissariat of Justice issued a directive, dated August 25, 1920, for the liquidation of relics of all kinds, since they were a significant obstacle to the resplendent movement toward a new, just society.

Pursuing further Krylenko's own selection of cases, let us also examine the case tried in the *Verkhtrib*—in other words, the Supreme Tribunal. (How affectionately they abbreviated words within their intimate circle, but how they roared out for us little insects: "Rise! The *court* is in session!")

E. The Case of the "Tactical Center"—August 16–20, 1920

In this case there were twenty-eight defendants present, plus additional defendants who were being tried *in absentia* because they weren't around.

At the very beginning of his impassioned speech, in a voice not yet grown hoarse and in phrases illumined by class analysis, the supreme accuser informs us that in addition to the land-owners and the capitalists "there existed and there continues to exist one additional social stratum, the social characteristics of which have *long since been under consideration* by the representatives of revolutionary socialism. [In other words: to be or not to be?] This stratum is the *so-called 'intelligentsia.'* In this trial, we shall be concerned with *the judgment of history on the activity of the Russian intelligentsia*"[55] and with the verdict of the Revolution on it.

The narrow limits of our investigation prevent our comprehending exactly the *particular manner* in which the representatives of revolutionary socialism were *taking under consideration* the fate of the so-called intelligentsia and what specifically they were planning for it. However, we take comfort in the fact that these materials have been published, that they are accessible to everyone, and that they can be assembled in any required detail. Therefore, solely to understand the over-all atmosphere of the Republic, we shall recall the opinion of the Chairman of the Council of People's Commissars in the years when all these tribunal sessions were going on.

55. Krylenko, *op. cit.*, p. 34.

In a letter to Gorky on September 15, 1919—which we have already cited—Vladimir Ilyich Lenin replied to Gorky's attempts to intercede in the arrests of members of the intelligentsia, among them, evidently, some of the defendants in this trial, and, commenting on the bulk of the Russian intelligentsia of those years (the "close-to-the-Cadets intelligentsia"), he wrote: "In actual fact *they are not [the nation's] brains, but shit.*"[56] On another occasion he said to Gorky: "If we break too many pots, it will be its [the intelligentsia's] fault."[57] If the intelligentsia wants justice, why doesn't it come over to us? "I've gotten one bullet from the intelligentsia myself."[58] (In other words, from Kaplan.)

On the basis of these feelings, he expressed his mistrust and hostility toward the intelligentsia: rotten-liberal; "pious"; "the slovenliness so customary among 'educated' people";[59] he believed the intelligentsia was always shortsighted, that it had *betrayed the cause of the workers.* (But when had the intelligentsia ever sworn loyalty *to the cause of the workers,* the dictatorship of the workers?)

This mockery of the intelligentsia, this contempt for the intelligentsia, was subsequently adopted with enthusiasm by the publicists and the newspapers of the twenties and was absorbed into the current of day-to-day life. And in the end, the members of the intelligentsia accepted it too, cursing their eternal thoughtlessness, their eternal *duality,* their eternal *spinelessness,* and their hopeless *lagging behind the times.*

And this was just! The voice of the accusing power echoed and re-echoed beneath the vaults of the Verkhtrib, returning us to the defendants' bench.

"This social stratum . . . has, during recent years, undergone the trial of universal re-evaluation." Yes, yes, re-evaluation, as was so often said at the time. And how did that re-evaluation occur? Here's how: "The Russian intelligentsia which entered the crucible of the Revolution with slogans of power for the people [so, it had something to it after all!] emerged from it an ally of the black [not even White!] generals, and a hired [!] and obedient

56. Lenin, fifth edition, Vol. 51, p. 48.
57 *V. I. Lenin i A. M. Gorky (V. I. Lenin and A. M. Gorky),* Moscow, Academy of Sciences Publishing House, 1961, p. 263.
58. *Ibid.*
59. Lenin, fourth edition, Vol. 26, p. 373.

agent of European imperialism. The intelligentsia trampled on its own banners [as in the army, yes?] and covered them with mud."[60]

How, indeed, can we not cry out our hearts in repentance? How can we not lacerate our chests with our fingernails?

And the only reason why *"there is no need to deal out the death blow to its individual representatives"* is that *"this social group has outlived its time."*[61]

Here, at the start of the twentieth century! What power of foresight! Oh, scientific revolutionaries! (However, the intelligentsia had to be *finished off* anyway. Throughout the twenties they kept finishing them off and finishing them off.)

We examine with hostility the twenty-eight individual allies of the black generals, the hirelings of European imperialism. And we are especially aroused by the stench of the word *Center*. Now we see a Tactical Center, now a National Center, and now a Right Center. (And in our recollection of the trials of two decades, Centers keep creeping in all the time, Centers and Centers, Engineers' Centers, Menshevik Centers, Trotskyite-Zinovievite Centers, Rightist-Bukharinite Centers, but all of them are crushed, all crushed, and that is the only reason you and I are still alive.) Wherever there is a *Center*, of course, the hand of imperialism can be found.

True, we feel a measure of relief when we learn that the Tactical Center on this occasion *was not an organization*; that it did not have: (1) statutes; (2) a program; (3) membership dues. So, what did it have? Here's what: *They used to meet!* (Goose-pimples up and down the back!) And when they met, *they undertook to familiarize themselves with one another's point of view!* (Icy chills!)

The charges were extremely serious and were supported by the evidence. There were two (2) pieces of evidence to corroborate the charges against twenty-eight accused individuals.[62] These were two letters from people who were not present in court because they were abroad: Myakotin and Fyodorov. They were absent, but until the October Revolution they had been members

60. Krylenko, *op. cit.*, p. 54.
61. *Ibid.*, p. 38.
62. *Ibid.*

of the same committees as those who were present, a circumstance that gave us the right to equate those who were absent with those who were present. And their letters dealt with their *disagreements* with Denikin on certain trivial questions: the peasant question (we are not told what these differences were, but they were evidently advising Denikin to give the land to the peasants); the Jewish question (they were evidently advising him not to return to the previous restrictions); the federated nationalities question (enough said: clear); the question of the structure of the government (democracy rather than dictatorship); and similar matters. And what conclusion did this evidence suggest? Very simple. It proved the fact of correspondence, and it also proved *the agreement, the unanimity, of those present with Denikin!* (Grrr! Grrrr!)

But there were also direct accusations against those present: that they had exchanged information with acquaintances who lived in outlying areas (Kiev, for example) which were not under the control of the central Soviet authorities! In other words, this used to be Russia, let's say, but then in the interests of world revolution we ceded this one piece to Germany. And people continued to exchange letters. How are you doing there, Ivan Ivanich? Here's how things are going with us. N. M. Kishkin, a member of the Central Committee of the Cadets, was so brazen as to try to justify himself right from the defendants' bench: "A man doesn't want to be blind. He tries to find out everything he can about what's going on everywhere."

To find out *everything* about what's going on *everywhere?* He doesn't want to be blind? Well, all one can say is that the accuser correctly described their actions as *treason, treason to Soviet power!*

But their most heinous acts were something else again. In the midst of the Civil War they wrote books, composed memoranda and projects. Yes, as experts in constitutional law, financial science, economic relationships, the system of justice, and education, they wrote *works!* (And, as one might easily guess, their works were not based on earlier works by Lenin, Trotsky, and Bukharin.) Professor Kotlyarevsky wrote on the federal structure of Russia; V. I. Stempkovsky on the agrarian question (no doubt, without collectivization); V. S. Muralevich on education in the future Russia; N. N. Vinogradsky on economics. And the (great) biologist N. K. Koltsov (who never received anything from the Motherland except persecution and execution) allowed all those bourgeois big shots to get together in his institute for their discussions. (N. D. Kondratyev was included here also. In 1931 he was condemned once and for all in connection with TKP—the fictitious Working Peasants Party.)

Our accuser's heart jumps right out of our chest, outrunning the sentence. Well, what punishment was adequate for these assistants to the general? Just one, of course—*to be shot!* That was not merely what the accuser demanded—it was the *sentence* of the tribunal. (Alas, it was later commuted to concentration camp until the end of the Civil War.)

And indeed the defendants' guilt consisted in the fact that they hadn't sat in their own corners, sucking on their quarter-pound of bread; that "they had talked things over and reached agreements as to what the state structure should be after the fall of the Soviet regime."

In contemporary scientific language, this is known as the study of the alternative possibility.

The voice of the accuser thundered, but we hear some kind of crack in it. As if his eyes were searching the rostrum, looking for another piece of paper? A quotation, perhaps? Give it to him *on tiptoe, quick, quick!* Give him one at random! From some other trial? It's not important! Wasn't this the one, Nikolai Vasilyevich Krylenko?

"For us . . . the concept of *torture* inheres in the very fact of holding political prisoners in prison. . . ."

So that's it! It is torture to keep political prisoners in prison! And the accuser said so! What a generous view! A new jurisprudence is arising! And further:

". . . Struggle against the Tsarist government was second nature to them [the politicals] and *not to struggle* against Tsarism was something of which *they were incapable.*"[63]

What's that? They *were incapable* of not studying alternative possibilities? Perhaps *thinking* was first nature to the intellectual?

Alas, through stupidity, they had shoved the wrong quotation at him. Now wasn't that a mix-up for you! But Nikolai Vasilyevich was already off to the races.

"*And even if* the defendants here in Moscow did not lift a

63. *Ibid.,* p. 17.

finger [and it looks very much as though that's the way it was] at such a moment, nevertheless . . . even a conversation over a teacup as to the kind of system that should replace the Soviet system, which is allegedly about to fall, is a counterrevolutionary act. . . . During the Civil War not only is any kind of action [against Soviet power] a crime . . . but the *fact of inaction is also criminal*."[64]

Well, now everything is comprehensible, everything is clear. They are being sentenced to death—for inaction. For a cup of tea.

The Petrograd intellectuals, for example, decided that in the event of Yudenich's taking the city, they would first of all "concern themselves with convening a democratic municipal Duma." (In other words, to safeguard the city against a possible dictatorship.)

Krylenko: "I would like to shout at them: 'It was your duty to think first of all *how you might die in battle,* so as not to allow Yudenich into the city!' "

But they didn't die in battle.

(Nor, in fact, did Nikolai Vasilyevich Krylenko.)

In addition, there were certain defendants *who knew about all this talk* and yet *kept silent,* did not write denunciations. (In our contemporary lingo: "He knew, but he didn't tell.")

And here is another real example not merely of inaction but of actively criminal action. Through L. N. Khrushcheva, a member of the Political Red Cross (and there she was, *on the defendants' bench*), some of the other defendants had raised money to *help the Butyrki prisoners.* (One can just picture that flood of capital—pouring into the prison commissary!) And they had supplied various articles too. (Yes, indeed. Just look. Woolens, too, perhaps?)

There were no bounds to their evil-doing! Nor would there be any limits to their proletarian punishment!

As when a cinema projector starts slowing down, twenty-eight prerevolutionary male and female faces flicker past us in a film that's fuzzy and askew. We didn't notice their expressions! Were they frightened? Contemptuous? Proud?

We don't have their answers! Their last words are missing—

64. *Ibid.*

because of "technical considerations." But, making up for this lack, the accuser croons to us: "From beginning to end, it was self-flagellation and repentance for the mistakes they committed. The political instability and the interim nature of the intelligentsia . . . [yes, yes, here comes another one: interim nature] completely justified that Marxist evaluation of the intelligentsia made by the Bolsheviks."[65]

I don't know. Perhaps they did engage in self-flagellation. Perhaps they didn't. Perhaps the passion to save one's life at any cost had *already* come into being. Perhaps the old dignity of the intelligentsia had *still* been maintained. . . . I don't know.

Who was that young woman flashing past?

That was Tolstoi's daughter, Alexandra. Krylenko asked her: "What did you do during these conversations?" And she answered: "I attended to the samovar." Three years of concentration camp!

And who was that man over there? His face was familiar. It was Savva Morozov. But listen here: after all, he gave the Bolsheviks all that money! And now he has handed a little to *these people?* Three years in prison, but released on probation. Let that be a lesson to him![66]

And that's how the sun of our freedom rose. It was as just such a well-nourished little imp that our Octobrist child—Law—began to grow.

Today we don't remember this at all.

---

65. *Ibid.*, p. 8.
66. He would soon cut his own throat.

Chapter 9

■

The Law Becomes a Man

Our review has already grown. Yet we have in fact hardly begun. All the big and famous trials are still ahead of us. But their basic lines have already been indicated.

So let us stick with our Law while it is still in its boy scout stage.

Let us recall one long-forgotten case which was not even political.

F. The Case of Glavtop—May, 1921

This case was important because it involved *engineers*—or, as they had been christened in the terminology of the times, "specialists," or spetsy. (Glavtop was the Main Fuels Committee.)

Nineteen twenty-one was the most difficult of all the four winters of the Civil War; nothing was left for fuel, and trains simply couldn't get to the next station; and there were cold and famine in the capitals, and a wave of strikes in the factories— strikes which, incidentally, have been completely wiped out of our history books by now. Who was to blame? That was a famous question: *Who is to blame?*

Well, obviously, *not* the Over-All Leadership. And not even the local leadership. That was important. If the "comrades who were often brought in from outside"—i.e., the Communist leaders —did not have a correct grasp of the business at hand, then it was the engineers, or spetsy, who were supposed to "outline for them the correct approach to the problem."[1] And this meant that "it was not the leaders who were to blame. . . . Those who had worked out the calculations were to blame, those who had refigured the calculations, those who had calculated the plan"—which consisted of how to produce food and heat with zeros. Those to blame weren't the ones who *compelled* but the ones who *calculated!* If the planning turned out to be inflated, the spetsy were the ones to blame. Because the figures did not jibe, "this was the fault of the spetsy, not of the Council of Labor and Defense" and "not even of the responsible men in charge of Glavtop—the Main Fuels Committee."[2]

If there was no coal, firewood, or petroleum, it was because the spetsy had "brought about a mixed-up, chaotic situation." And it was their own fault that they hadn't resisted the urgent telephonograms from Rykov and the government—and had issued and allotted fuels outside the scope of the plan.

The spetsy were to blame for everything. But the proletarian court was not merciless with them. Their sentences were lenient. Of course, an inner hostility to those cursed spetsy remains in proletarian hearts—but one can't get along without them; everything goes to rack and ruin. And the tribunal doesn't persecute them, and Krylenko even says that from 1920 on "there is no question of any sabotage." The spetsy are to blame, but not out of malice on their part; it's simply because they are inept; they aren't able to do any better; under capitalism, they hadn't learned to work, or else they were simply egotists and bribe-takers.

And so, at the beginning of the reconstruction period, a surprising tendency toward leniency could be observed in regard to the engineers.

The year 1922, the first year of peace, was rich in public trials, so rich that almost this entire chapter will be devoted to that year alone. (People are surprised: the war has ended, and yet there is an increase in court activity? But in 1945, too, and in 1948, the Dragon became very, very energetic. Is there not, perhaps, a simple sort of law in this?)

1. Krylenko, *Za Pyat Let,* p. 381.
2. *Ibid.,* pp. 382–383.

Although in December, 1921, the Ninth Congress of the Soviets decreed that *the authority of the Cheka be narrowed*[3] and, in consequence, its authority was indeed narrowed and it was renamed the GPU, as early as October, 1922, the powers of the GPU were broadened again, and in December Dzerzhinsky told a *Pravda* correspondent: "Now we need to keep watch *with particular vigilance* over anti-Soviet currents and groupings. The GPU has reduced its apparatus but strengthened it in terms of *quality*."[4]

And, at the beginning of 1922, we must not bypass:

G. The Case of the Suicide of Engineer Oldenborger
(Tried before the Verkhtrib—the Supreme Tribunal
—in February, 1922)

This case is forgotten, insignificant, and totally atypical. It was atypical because its entire scale was that of a single life that had already ended. And if that life hadn't ended, it would have been that very engineer, yes, and ten more with him, forming a *Center,* who would have sat before the *Verkhtrib;* in that event the case would have been altogether typical. But as it was, an outstanding Party comrade, Sedelnikov, sat on the defendants' bench and, with him, two members of the RKI—the Workers' and Peasants' Inspection—and two trade-union officials.

But, like Chekhov's far-off broken harp-string, there was something plaintive in this trial; it was, in its own way, an early predecessor of the Shakhty and Promparty trials.

V. V. Oldenborger had worked for thirty years in the Moscow water-supply system and had evidently become its chief engineer back at the beginning of the century. Even though the Silver Age of art, four State Dumas, three wars, and three revolutions had come and gone, all Moscow drank Oldenborger's water. The Acmeists and the Futurists, the reactionaries and the revolutionaries, the military cadets and the Red Guards, the Council of People's Commissars, the Cheka, and the Workers' and Peasants' Inspection—all had drunk Oldenborger's pure cold water. He had never married and he had no children. His whole life had consisted of that one water-supply system. In 1905 he refused

---

3. *Sobraniye Uzakonenii RSFSR (Collection of Decrees of the R.S.F.S.R.),* 1922, No. 4, p. 42.
4. *Pravda,* December 17, 1922.

to permit the soldiers of the guard near the water-supply conduits
—"because the soldiers, out of clumsiness, might break the pipes
or machinery." On the second day of the February Revolution
he said to his workers that that was enough, the revolution was
over, and they should all go back to their jobs; the water must
flow. And during the October fighting in Moscow, he had only
one concern: to safeguard the water-supply system. His colleagues went on strike in answer to the Bolshevik coup d'état
and invited him to take part in the strike with them. His reply
was: "On the operational side, please forgive me, I am not on
strike. . . . In everything else, I—well, yes, I am on strike." He
accepted money for the strikers from the strike committee, and
gave them a receipt, but he himself dashed off to get a sleeve to
repair a broken pipe.

But despite this, he was an enemy! Here's what he had said
to one of the workers: "The Soviet regime won't last two weeks."
(There was a new political situation preceding the announcement
of the New Economic Policy, and in this context Krylenko could
allow himself some frank talk before the *Verkhtrib*: "It was not
only the spetsy who thought that way at the time. *That is what
we ourselves thought more than once.*")

But despite this, Oldenborger was an enemy! Just as Comrade
Lenin had told us: to keep watch over the bourgeois specialists
we need a watchdog—the RKI—the Workers' and Peasants'
Inspection.

They began by assigning two such watchdogs to Oldenborger
on a full-time basis. (One of them, Makarov-Zemlyansky, a
swindler and a former clerk in the water system, had been fired
"for improper conduct" and had entered the service of the RKI
"because they paid better." He got promoted to the Central
People's Commissariat because "the pay there was even better"—
and, from that height, he had returned to check up on his former
chief and take hearty vengeance on the man who had wronged
him.) Then, of course, the local Party committee—that match-
less defender of the workers' interests—wasn't dozing either. And
Communists were put in charge of the water system. "Only
workers are to hold the top positions; there are to be only
Communists at leadership level; and the wisdom of this view was
confirmed by the given trial."[5]

5. Krylenko, *op. cit.,* p. 433.

The Moscow Party organization also kept its eyes on the water-supply system. (And behind it stood the Cheka.) "In our own time we built our army on the basis of *a healthy feeling of class enmity;* in its name, we do not entrust even one responsible position to people who do not belong to our camp, without assigning them . . . a commissar."[6] And so, they all immediately began to order the chief engineer about, to supervise him, to give him instructions, and to shift the engineering personnel around without his knowledge. ("They broke up the whole nest of businessmen.")

But they did not, even so, safeguard the water-supply system. Things didn't go better with it, but worse! So slyly had that gang of engineers contrived to carry out an evil scheme. Even more: overcoming his intellectual's interim nature, as a result of which he had never in his life expressed himself sharply, Oldenborger made so bold as to describe as stupid stubbornness the actions of the new chief of the water-supply system, Zenyuk (to Krylenko, "a profoundly likable person on the basis of his internal structure").

It was at this point that it became clear that "engineer Oldenborger was consciously betraying the interests of the workers and that he was a direct and open enemy of the dictatorship of the working class." They started bringing inspection commissions into the water-supply system, but the commissions found that everything was in good order and that water was being supplied on a normal basis. The RKI men, the "rabkrinovtsy," refused to be satisfied with this. They kept pouring report after report into the RKI. Oldenborger simply wanted to "ruin, spoil, break down the water-supply system for political purposes," but he was unable to. Well, they put what obstacles in his way that they could; they prevented wasteful boiler repairs and replacing the wooden tanks with concrete ones. At meetings of the water-supply-system workers, the leaders began saying openly that their chief engineer was the "soul of organized technical sabotage" and that he should not be believed, that he should be resisted at every point.

Despite all this, the operation of the water-supply system not only didn't improve, but deteriorated.

What was particularly offensive to the "hereditary proletarian

6. *Ibid.*, p. 434.

psychology" of the officials of the Workers' and Peasants' Inspection and of the trade unions was that the majority of the workers at the pumping stations "had been infected with petty-bourgeois psychology" and, unable to recognize Oldenborger's sabotage, had come to his defense. At this point, elections to the Moscow Soviet were being held and the workers nominated Oldenborger as the candidate of the water-supply system, against whom, of course, the Party cell backed its own Party candidate. However, this turned out to be futile because of the chief engineer's fraudulent authority with the workers. Nonetheless, the Party cell brought up the question with the District Party Committee, on all levels, and announced at a general meeting that "Oldenborger is the center and soul of sabotage, and will be our political enemy in the Moscow Soviet!" The workers responded with an uproar and shouts of "Untrue! Lies!" And at that point the secretary of the Party Committee, Comrade Sedelnikov, flung right in the faces of the thousand-headed proletariat there: "I am not even going to talk to such Black Hundred, reactionary pogrom-makers." That is to say: We'll talk to you somewhere else.

Party measures were also taken: they expelled the chief engineer from—no less—the collegium for administration of the water system, and kept him under constant investigation; continually summoned him before a multitude of commissions and subcommissions; kept interrogating him and giving him assignments that were to be urgently carried out. Every time he failed to appear, it was entered in the record "in case of a future trial." And through the Council of Labor and Defense (Chairman—Comrade Lenin) they got an "Extraordinary Troika" appointed to the water system. (It consisted of representatives of the RKI, the Council of Trade Unions, and Comrade Kuibyshev.)

And for the fourth year the water kept right on flowing through the pipes. And Moscovites kept on drinking it and didn't notice anything wrong.

Then Comrade Sedelnikov wrote an article for the newspaper *Ekonomicheskaya Zhizn*: "In view of the rumors disturbing the public in regard to the catastrophic state of the water mains . . ." and he reported many new and alarming rumors—even that the water system was pumping water underground and was *intentionally washing away the foundations of all Moscow*." (Set there by Ivan Kalita in the fourteenth century.) They summoned a

Commission of the Moscow Soviet. The Commission found that the "state of the water system was satisfactory and that its technical direction was efficient." Oldenborger denied all the accusations. And then Sedelnikov placidly declared: "I had set myself the task of *stirring up a fuss* about this matter in order to get the question of the spetsy taken up."

What remained for the leaders of the workers to do at this point? What was the final, infallible method? A denunciation to the Cheka! Sedelnikov resorted to just that! He "painted a picture of the conscious wrecking of the water system by Oldenborger." He did not have the slightest doubt that "a counterrevolutionary organization" existed "in the water system, in the heart of Red Moscow." And, furthermore, a catastrophic situation at the Rublevo water tower!

At this point, Oldenborger was guilty of a tactless act of rudeness, the outburst of a spineless, interim intellectual. They had refused to authorize his order for new boilers from abroad— and at the time, in Russia, it was quite impossible to fix the old ones. So Oldenborger committed suicide. (It had been just too much for one man—after all, he hadn't undergone the conditioning for that sort of thing.)

The cause was not lost, however. They could find a counterrevolutionary organization without him. RKI men would now undertake to expose the whole thing. Some concealed maneuvering went on for two months. But such was the spirit at the beginning of the NEP that "a lesson had to be taught both one side and the other." So there was a trial in the Supreme Tribunal. Krylenko was moderately severe. Krylenko was moderately merciless. He was understanding: "The Russian worker, of course, was right to see in every person *not of his own class* someone more likely to be an enemy than a friend."[7] Nevertheless: "Given the further change in our practical and general policy, perhaps we must be prepared for still greater concessions, for retreating and maneuvering. Perhaps the Party will be forced to adopt a tactical program of action which the primitive logic of *honest, dedicated warriors* is going to protest."[8]

Well, it's a fact, the workers who testified against Comrade

7. *Ibid.,* p. 435.
8. *Ibid.,* p. 438.

Sedelnikov and the RKI men were "easily brushed off" by the tribunal. And the defendant Sedelnikov replied brazenly to the threats of the accuser. "Comrade Krylenko! I know all those articles. But after all, *no one is judging class enemies here,* and those articles relate to class enemies."

However, Krylenko laid it on good and thick. Deliberately false denunciations to state institutions . . . in circumstances aggravating guilt, such as a personal grudge and the settling of personal accounts . . . the abuse of an official position . . . political irresponsibility . . . abuse of power and of the authority of government officials and members of the Russian Communist Party (Bolsheviks) . . . disorganization of the work of the water-supply system . . . injury done the Moscow Soviet and Soviet Russia, because there were few such specialists, and it was impossible to find replacements for them. *"And we won't even begin to speak of the individual, personal loss. . . .* In our time, when struggle is the chief content of our lives, we have somehow grown used to not counting these irrevocable losses."[9] The Supreme Revolutionary Tribunal must utter its weighty word: "Punishment must be assessed with all due severity! . . . We didn't come here just to crack jokes."

Good Lord, now what are they going to get? Could it really be? My reader has gotten used to prompting: *all of them to be sh——!*

And that is absolutely correct. All of them were to be publicly shamed—bearing in mind their sincere repentance! All of them to be sentenced to—ostracism and ridicule.

Two truths . . .

And Sedelnikov, allegedly, got one year in jail.

You will just have to forgive me if I don't believe it.

Oh, you bards of the twenties, painting your pictures of their bright and bubbling happiness! Even those who touched only their farthest edge, who touched them only in childhood, will never forget them. And those plug-uglies, those fat faces, busy persecuting engineers—in the twenties, too, they ate their bellies full.

And now we see also that they had been busy from 1918 on.

9. *Ibid.,* p. 458.

■

In the two trials following we will take leave of our favorite supreme accuser for a while: he is occupied with his preparations for the major trial of the SR's.[10] This spectacular trial aroused a great deal of emotion in Europe beforehand, and the People's Commissariat of Justice was suddenly taken aback: after all, we had been trying people for four years without any code, neither a new one nor an old one. And in all probability Krylenko himself was concerned about the code too. Everything had to be neatly tied up ahead of time.

The coming church trials were *internal*. They didn't interest progressive Europe. And they could be conducted without a code.

We have already had an opportunity to observe that the separation of church and state was so construed by the state that the churches themselves and everything that hung in them, was installed in them and painted in them, belonged to the state, and the only church remaining was that church which, in accordance with the Scriptures, lay *within the heart*. And in 1918, when political victory seemed to have been attained faster and more easily than had been expected, they had pressed right on to confiscate church property. However, this leap had aroused too fierce a wave of popular indignation. In the heat of the Civil War, it was not very intelligent to create, in addition, an internal front against the believers. And it proved necessary to postpone for the time being the dialogue between the Communists and the Christians.

At the end of the Civil War, and as its natural consequence, an unprecedented famine developed in the Volga area. They give it only two lines in the official histories because it doesn't add a very ornamental touch to the wreaths of the victors in that war. But the famine existed nonetheless—to the point of cannibalism, to the point at which parents ate their own children—such a famine as even Russia had never known, even in the Time of Troubles in the early seventeenth century. (Because at that time, as the historians testify, unthreshed ricks of grain survived intact

10. The provincial trials of the SR's took place even earlier, such as the one in Saratov in 1919.

beneath the snow and ice for several years.) Just one film about famine might throw a new light on everything we saw and everything we know about the Revolution and the Civil War. But there are no films and no novels and no statistical research—the effort is to forget it. It does not embellish. Besides, we have come to blame the *kulaks* as the *cause* of every famine—and just who were the kulaks in the midst of such collective death? V. G. Korolenko, in his *Letters to Lunacharsky* (which, despite Lunacharsky's promise, were never officially published in the Soviet Union),[11] explains to us Russia's total, epidemic descent into famine and destitution. It was the result of productivity having been reduced to zero (the working hands were all carrying guns) and the result, also, of the peasants' utter lack of trust and hope that even the smallest part of the harvest might be left for them. Yes, and someday someone will also count up those many carloads of food supplies rolling on and on for many, many months to Imperial Germany, under the terms of the peace treaty of Brest-Litovsk—from a Russia which had been deprived of a protesting voice, from the very provinces where famine would strike—so that Germany could fight to the end in the West.

There was a direct, immediate chain of cause and effect. The Volga peasants had to eat their children because we were so impatient about putting up with the Constituent Assembly.

But political genius lies in extracting success even from the people's ruin. A brilliant idea was born: after all, three billiard balls can be pocketed with one shot. *So now let the priests feed the Volga region!* They are Christians. They are generous!

1. If they refuse, we will blame the whole famine on them and destroy the church.
2. If they agree, we will clean out the churches.
3. In either case, we will replenish our stocks of foreign exchange and precious metals.

Yes, and the idea was probably inspired by the actions of the church itself. As Patriarch Tikhon himself had testified, back in August, 1921, at the beginning of the famine, the church had

11. Published in Paris in 1922, and in the Soviet Union in samizdat in 1967.

created diocesan and all-Russian committees for aid to the starving and had begun to collect funds. But to have permitted any *direct* help to go straight from the church into the mouths of those who were starving would have undermined the dictatorship of the proletariat. The committees were banned, and the funds they had collected were confiscated and turned over to the state treasury. The Patriarch had also appealed to the Pope in Rome and to the Archbishop of Canterbury for assistance—but he was rebuked for this, too, on the grounds that only the Soviet authorities had the right to enter into discussions with foreigners. Yes, indeed. And what was there to be alarmed about? The newspapers wrote that the government itself had all the necessary means to cope with the famine.

Meanwhile, in the Volga region they were eating grass, the soles of shoes, and gnawing at door jambs. And, finally, in December, 1921, Pomgol—the State Commission for Famine Relief —proposed that the churches help the starving by donating church valuables—not all, but those not required for liturgical rites. The Patriarch agreed. Pomgol issued a directive: all gifts must be strictly voluntary! On Febraury 19, 1922, the Patriarch issued a pastoral letter permitting the parish councils to make gifts of objects that did not have liturgical and ritual significance.

And in this way matters could again have simply degenerated into a compromise that would have frustrated the will of the proletariat, just as it once had been by the Constituent Assembly, and still was in all the chatterbox European parliaments.

The thought came in a stroke of lightning! The thought came— and a decree followed! A decree of the All-Russian Central Executive Committee on February 26: *all* valuables were to be requisitioned from the churches—for the starving!

The Patriarch wrote to Kalinin, who did not reply. Then on February 28 the Patriarch issued a new, fateful pastoral letter: from the church's point of view such a measure is sacrilege, and we cannot approve the requisition.

From the distance of a half-century, it is easy to reproach the Patriarch. Of course, the leaders of the Christian church ought not to have been distracted by wondering whether other resources might not be available to the Soviet government, and *who* it was who had driven the Volga to famine. They ought not to have clung to those treasures, since the possibility of a new fortress of faith arising—if it existed at all—did not depend on them. But one has also to picture the situation of that unfortunate Patriarch, not elected to his post until after the October Revolution, who had for a few short years led a church that was always persecuted, restricted, under fire, and whose preservation had been entrusted to him.

But right then and there a sure-fire campaign of persecution began in the papers, directed against the Patriarch and high church authorities who were strangling the Volga region with the bony hand of famine. And the more firmly the Patriarch clung to his position, the weaker it became. In March a movement to relinquish the valuables, to come to an agreement with the government, began even among the clergy. Their still undispelled qualms were expressed to Kalinin by Bishop Antonin Granovsky, a member of the Central Committee of Pomgol: "The believers fear that the church valuables may be used for *other purposes,* more limited and alien to their hearts." (Knowing the general principles of our Progressive Doctrine, the experienced reader will agree that this was indeed very probable. After all, the Comintern's needs and those of the East in the course of being liberated were no less acute than those of the Volga.)

The Petrograd Metropolitan, Veniamin, was similarly impelled by a mood of trust: "This belongs to God and we will give all of it by ourselves." But forced requisitions were wrong. Let the sacrifice be of our own free will. He, too, wanted verification by the clergy and the believers: to watch over the church valuables up to the very moment when they were transformed into bread for the starving. And in all this he was tormented lest he violate the censuring will of the Patriarch.

In Petrograd things seemed to be working out peacefully. The atmosphere at the session of the Petrograd Pomgol on March 5, 1922, was even joyful, according to the testimony of an eyewitness. Veniamin announced: "The Orthodox Church is prepared to give everything to help the starving." It saw sacrilege only in forced requisition. But in that case requisition was unnecessary! Kanatchikov, Chairman of the Petrograd Pomgol, gave his assurances that this would produce a favorable attitude toward the church on the part of the Soviet government. (Not very likely, that!) In a burst of good feeling, everyone stood up. The Metropolitan said: "The heaviest burden is division and enmity. But the time will come when the Russian people will unite. I myself, at the head of the worshipers, will remove the cover [of precious metals and precious stones] from the ikon of the Holy Virgin of Kazan. I will shed sweet tears on it and give it away." He gave his blessing to the Bolshevik members of Pomgol and they saw him to the door with bared heads. The newspaper *Petrogradskaya Pravda,* in its issues of March 8, 9, and 10,[12] confirmed the peaceful, successful outcome of the talks, and spoke favorably of the Metropolitan. "In Smolny they agreed that the church vessels and ikon coverings would be melted down into ingots in the presence of the believers."

Again things were getting fouled up with some kind of compromise! The noxious fumes of Christianity were poisoning the revolutionary will. *That kind of* unity and *that way of* handing over the valuables *were not* what the starving people of the Volga needed! The spineless membership of the Petrograd Pomgol was changed. The newspapers began to howl about the "evil pastors" and "princes of the church," and the representatives of the church were told: "We don't need your *donations!* And there won't be any *negotiations* with you! *Everything belongs to the government* —and the government will take whatever it considers necessary."

And so forcible requisitions, accompanied by strife, began in Petrograd, as they did everywhere else.

And this provided the legal basis for initiating trials of the clergy.[13]

H. The Moscow Church Trial—April 26–May 7, 1922

This took place in the Polytechnic Museum. The court was the Moscow Revtribunal, under Presiding Judge Bek; the prosecutors were Lunin and Longinov. There were seventeen defendants, including archpriests and laymen, accused of disseminating the Patriarch's proclamation. This charge was more important than

12. See the articles entitled "Tserkov i Golod" ("The Church and the Famine") and "Kak budut izyaty tserkovnye tsennosti" ("How the Church Valuables Will Be Requisitioned").
13. I have taken this material from *Ocherki po Istorii Tserkovnoi Smuty* (*Essays on the History of the Troubles of the Church*), by Anatoly Levitin, Part I, samizdat, 1962, and from the stenographic notes on the questioning of Patriarch Tikhon, Trial Record, Vol. V.

the question of surrendering, or not surrendering, church valuables. Archpriest A. N. Zaozersky *had surrendered all the valuables in his own church,* but he defended in principle the Patriarch's appeal regarding forced requisition as sacrilege, and he became the central personage in the trial—and would shortly be *shot.* (All of which went to prove that what was important was not to feed the starving but to make use of a convenient opportunity to break the back of the church.)

On May 5 Patriarch Tikhon was summoned to the tribunal as a witness. Even though the public was represented only by a carefully selected audience (1922, in this respect, differing little from 1937 and 1968), nonetheless the stamp of Old Russia was still so deep, and the Soviet stamp was still so superficial, that on the Patriarch's entrance more than half of those present rose to receive his blessing.

Tikhon took on himself the entire blame for writing and disseminating his appeal. The presiding judge of the tribunal tried to elicit a different line of testimony from him: "But it isn't possible! Did you really write it in your own hand? All the lines? You probably just signed it. And *who* actually *wrote* it? And *who* were your *advisers?*" and then: "Why did you mention in the appeal the persecution to which the newspapers are subjecting you? [After all, they are persecuting *you* and why should *we* hear about it?] What did you want to express?"

The Patriarch: "That is something you will have to ask the people who started the persecution: What objectives were they pursuing?"

The Presiding Judge: "But that after all has nothing to do with religion!"

The Patriarch: "It has historical significance."

The Presiding Judge: "Referring to the fact that the decree was published while you were in the midst of talks with Pomgol, you used the expression, *behind your back?*"

The Patriarch: "Yes."

Presiding Judge: "You therefore consider that the Soviet government acted incorrectly?"

A crushing argument! It will be repeated a million times more in the nighttime offices of interrogators! And we will never answer as simply and straightforwardly as:

The Patriarch: "Yes."

The Presiding Judge: "Do you consider the state's laws obligatory or not?"

The Patriarch: "Yes, I recognize them, *to the extent that they do not contradict the rules of piety.*"

(Oh, if only everyone had answered just that way! Our whole history would have been different.)

A debate about church law followed. The Patriarch explained that if the church itself surrendered its valuables, it was not sacrilege. But if they were taken away against the church's will, it was. His appeal had not prohibited giving the valuables at all, but had only declared that seizing them against the will of the church was to be condemned.

(But that's what we wanted—expropriation against the will of the church!)

Comrade Bek, the presiding judge, was astounded: "Which in the last analysis is more important to you—the laws of the church or the point of view of the Soviet government?"

(The expected reply: "The Soviet government.")

"Very well; so it was sacrilege according to the laws of the church," exclaimed the accuser, "but what was it from the point of view of *mercy?*"

(For the first and last time—for another fifty years—that banal word *mercy* was spoken before a tribunal.)

Then there was a philological analysis of the word "svyatotatstvo," meaning "sacrilege," derived from "svyato," meaning "holy," and "tat," meaning "thief."

The Accuser: "So that means that we, the representatives of the Soviet government, are thieves of holy things?"

(A prolonged uproar in the hall. A recess. The bailiffs at work.)

The Accuser: "So you call the representatives of the Soviet government, the All-Russian Central Executive Committee, thieves?"

The Patriarch: "I am citing only church law."

Then there is a discussion of the term "blasphemy." While they were requisitioning the valuables from the church of St. Basil the Great of Caesarea, the ikon cover would not fit into a box, and at that point they trampled it with their feet. But the Patriarch himself had not been present.

The Accuser: "How do you know that? *Give us the name of* the priest who told you that. [And we will arrest him immediately!]"

The Patriarch does not give the name.

That means it was a lie!

The Accuser presses on triumphantly: "No, *who* spread that repulsive slander?"

The Presiding Judge: "Give us the names of those who trampled the ikon cover! [One can assume that after doing it they left their visiting cards!] Otherwise the tribunal cannot believe you!"

The Patriarch cannot name them.

The Presiding Judge: "That means you have made an unsubstantiated assertion."

It still remained to be proved that the Patriarch wanted to overthrow the Soviet government. And here is how it was proved: "Propaganda is an attempt to prepare a mood preliminary to preparing a *revolt* in the future."

The tribunal ordered criminal charges to be brought against the Patriarch.

On May 7 sentence was pronounced: of the seventeen defendants, eleven were to be shot. (They actually shot five.)

As Krylenko said: "We didn't come here just to crack jokes."

One week later the Patriarch was removed from office and arrested. (But this was not the very end. For the time being he was taken to the Donskoi Monastery and kept there in strict incarceration, so that the believers would grow accustomed to his absence. Remember how just a short while before Krylenko had been astonished: what danger could possibly threaten the Patriarch? Truly, when the danger really does come, there's no help for it, either in alarm bells or in telephone calls.)

Two weeks after that, the Metropolitan Veniamin was arrested in Petrograd. He had not been a high official of the church before the Revolution. Nor had he even been appointed, like almost all Metropolitans. In the spring of 1917, for the first time since the days of ancient Novgorod the Great, they had *elected* a Metropolitan in Moscow and in Petrograd. A gentle, simple, easily accessible man, a frequent visitor in factories and mills, popular with the people and with the lower clergy, Veniamin had been elected by their votes. Not understanding the times, he had seen as his task the liberation of the church from politics "because it had suffered much from politics in the past." This was the Metropolitan who was tried in:

I. The Petrograd Church Trial—June 9–July 5, 1922

The defendants, charged with resisting the requisition of church valuables, numbered several dozen in all, including a professor of theology and church law, archimandrites, priests, and laymen. Semyonov, the presiding judge of the tribunal, was twenty-five years old and, according to rumor, had formerly been a baker. The chief accuser was a member of the collegium of the People's Commissariat of Justice, P. A. Krasikov—a man of Lenin's age and a friend of Lenin when he was in exile in the Krasnoyarsk region and, later on, in emigration as well. Vladimir Ilyich used to enjoy hearing him play the violin.

Out on Nevsky Prospekt, and at the Nevsky turn-off, a dense crowd waited every day of the trial, and when the Metropolitan was driven past, many of them knelt down and sang: "Save, O Lord, thy people!" (It goes without saying that they arrested overzealous believers right on the street and in the court building also.) Most of the spectators in the court were Red Army men, but even they rose every time the Metropolitan entered in his white ecclesiastical hood. Yet the accuser and the tribunal called him *an enemy of the people*. Let us note that this term already existed.

From trial to trial, things closed in on the defense lawyers, and their humiliating predicament was already very apparent. Krylenko tells us nothing about this, but the gap is closed by an eyewitness. The tribunal roared out a threat *to arrest* Bobrishchev-Pushkin *himself*—the principal defense lawyer—and this was already so in accord with the spirit of the times, and the threat was so real that Bobrishchev-Pushkin made haste to hand over his gold watch and his billfold to lawyer Gurovich. And right then and there the tribunal actually ordered the imprisonment of a witness, Professor Yegorov, because of his testimony on behalf of the Metropolitan. As it turned out, Yegorov was quite prepared for this. He had a thick briefcase with him in which he had packed food, underwear, and even a small blanket.

The reader can observe that the court was gradually assuming forms familiar to us.

Metropolitan Veniamin was accused of entering, with evil intent, into an agreement with . . . the Soviet government, no less, and thereby obtaining a relaxation of the decree on the requisition of valuables. It was charged that his appeal to Pomgol had been maliciously disseminated among the people. (Samizdat! —self-publication!) And he had also acted in concert with the world bourgeoisie.

Priest Krasnitsky, one of the principal "Living Church" schismatics, and GPU collaborator, testified that the priests had conspired to provoke a revolt against the Soviet government on the grounds of famine.

The only witnesses heard were those of the prosecution. Defense witnesses were not permitted to testify. (Oh, how familiar it all is! More and more!)

Accuser Smirnov demanded "sixteen heads." Accuser Krasikov cried out: "The whole Orthodox Church is a subversive organization. Properly speaking, *the entire church ought to be put in prison.*"

(This was a very realistic program. Soon it was almost realized. And it was a good basis for a *dialogue.*)

Let us make use of a rather rare opportunity to cite several sentences that have been preserved from the speech of S. Y. Gurovich, who was the Metropolitan's defense attorney.

"There are no proofs of guilt. There are no facts. There is not even an indictment. . . . What will history say? [Oh, he certainly had discovered how to frighten them! History will forget and say nothing!] The requisition of church valuables in Petrograd took place in a complete calm, but here the Petrograd clergy is on the defendants' bench, and somebody's hands keep pushing them toward death. The basic principle which you stress is the good of the Soviet government. But do not forget that the church will be nourished by the blood of martyrs. [Not in the Soviet Union, though!] There is nothing more to be said, but it is hard to stop talking. While the debate lasts, the defendants are alive. When the debate comes to an end, life will end too."

The tribunal condemned ten of them to death. They waited more than a month for their execution, until the trial of the SR's had ended. (It was as though they had processed them in order to shoot them at the same time as the SR's.) And after that, VTsIK, the All-Russian Central Executive Committee, pardoned six of them. And four of them—the Metropolitan Veniamin; the Archimandrite Sergius, a former member of the State Duma; Professor of Law Y. P. Novitsky; and the barrister Kovsharov—were shot on the night of August 12–13.

We insistently urge our readers not to forget the principle of provincial multiplicity. Where two church trials were held in Moscow and Petrograd, there were twenty-two in the provinces.

■

They were in a big hurry to produce a Criminal Code in time for the trial of the SR's—the Socialist Revolutionaries. The time had come to set in place the granite foundation stones of the Law. On May 12, as had been agreed, the session of VTsIK convened, but the projected Code had not yet been completed. It had only just been delivered for analysis to Vladimir Ilyich Lenin at his Gorki estate outside Moscow. Six articles of the Code provided for execution by shooting as the maximum punishment. This was unsatisfactory. On May 15, on the margins of the draft Code, Lenin added six more articles requiring execution by shooting (including—under Article 69—propaganda and agitation, particularly in the form of an appeal for passive resistance to the government and mass rejection of the obligations of military service or tax payments).[14] And one other crime that called for execution by shooting: unauthorized return from abroad (my, how the socialists all used to bob back and forth incessantly!). And there was one punishment that was the equivalent of execution by shooting: exile abroad. Vladimir Ilyich foresaw a time not far distant when there would be a constant rush of people to the Soviet Union from Europe, and it would be impossible to get anyone voluntarily to leave the Soviet Union for the West. Lenin went on to express his principal conclusion to the People's Commissar of Justice:

14. In other words, like the Vyborg appeal, for which the Tsar's government had imposed sentences of three months' imprisonment.

"Comrade Kursky! In my opinion we ought to extend the use of execution by shooting (allowing the substitution of exile abroad) to all activities of the Mensheviks, SR's, etc. We ought to find a formulation that would connect these activities *with the international bourgeoisie.*"[15] (Lenin's italics.)

To extend the use of execution by shooting! Nothing left to the imagination there! (And did they exile very many?) *Terror is a method of persuasion.*[16] This, too, could hardly be misunderstood.

But Kursky, nonetheless, still didn't get the whole idea. In all probability, what he couldn't quite work out was a way of formulating that formulation, a way of working in that very matter of *connection.* The next day, he called on the Chairman of the Council of People's Commissars, Lenin, for clarification. We have no way of knowing what took place during their conversation. But following it up, on May 17, Lenin sent a second letter from Gorki:

COMRADE KURSKY!

As a sequel to our conversation, I am sending you an outline of a supplementary paragraph for the Criminal Code. . . . The basic concept, I hope, is clear, notwithstanding all the shortcomings of the rough draft: openly to set forth a statute which is both principled and politically truthful (and not just juridically narrow) to supply the motivation for the *essence* and the *justification* of terror, its necessity, its limits.

The court must not exclude terror. It would be self-deception or deceit to promise this, and in order to provide it with a foundation and to legalize it in a principled way, clearly and without hypocrisy and without embellishment, it is necessary to formulate it as broadly as possible, for only revolutionary righteousness and a revolutionary conscience will provide the conditions for applying it more or less broadly in practice.

With Communist greetings,
LENIN[17]

We will not undertake to comment on this important document. What it calls for is silence and reflection.

The document is especially important because it was one of Lenin's last directives on this earth—he had not yet fallen ill—

15. Lenin, fifth edition, Vol. 45, p. 189.
16. *Ibid.,* Vol. 39, pp. 404–405.
17. *Ibid.,* Vol. 45, p. 190.

and an important part of his political testament. Ten days after this letter, he suffered his first stroke, from which he recovered only incompletely and temporarily in the autumn months of 1922. Perhaps both letters to Kursky were written in that light and airy white marble boudoir-study at the corner of the second floor, where the future deathbed of the leader already stood waiting.

Attached to this letter is the *rough draft* mentioned in it, containing two versions of the supplementary paragraph, out of which would grow in a few years' time both Article 58-4 and all of our dear little old mother, Article 58. You read it and you are carried away with admiration: that's what it really means *to formulate it as broadly as possible!* That's what is meant by *extending its use.* You read and you recollect how broad was the embrace of that dear little old mother.

". . . propaganda or agitation, or participation in an organization, or assistance (objectively assisting *or being capable of assisting*) . . . organizations or persons whose activity has the character . . ."

Hand me St. Augustine, and in a trice I can find room in that article for him too.

Everything was inserted as required; it was retyped; execution by shooting was extended—and the session of the All-Russian Central Executive Committee adopted the new Criminal Code shortly after May 20 and decreed it to be in effect from June 1, 1922, on.

And so began, on the most legal basis, the two-month-long

J. Trial of the SR's—June 8–August 7, 1922

The court was the Supreme Tribunal, the *Verkhtrib.* The usual presiding judge, Comrade Karklin (a good name for a judge—derived from the word meaning to "croak" or "caw"), was replaced for this important trial, which was being watched closely by the entire socialist world, by the resourceful Georgi Pyatakov. (Provident fate enjoys its little jokes—but it also leaves us time to think things over! It left Pyatakov fifteen years.) There were no defense lawyers. The defendants, all leading SR's, undertook their own defense. Pyatakov bore himself harshly, and interfered with the defendants' having their say.

If my readers and I were not already sufficiently informed to know that what was important in every trial was not the charges brought nor *guilt,* so called, but *expediency,* we would perhaps not be prepared to accept this trial wholeheartedly. But *expediency* works without fail: the SR's, as opposed to the Mensheviks, were considered still dangerous, not yet dispersed and broken up, not yet finished off. And on behalf of the fortress of the newly created dictatorship (the proletariat), it was expedient to finish them off.

Someone unfamiliar with this principle might mistakenly view the entire trial as an act of Party vengeance.

Involuntarily one ponders the charges set forth in this trial, placing them in the perspective of the long-drawn-out and still unfolding history of nations. With the exception of a very limited number of parliamentary democracies, during a very limited number of decades, the history of nations is entirely a history of revolutions and seizures of power. And whoever succeeds in making a more successful and more enduring revolution is from that moment on graced with the bright robes of Justice, and his every past and future step is legalized and memorialized in odes, whereas every past and future step of his unsuccessful enemies is criminal and subject to arraignment and a legal penalty.

The Criminal Code had been adopted only one week earlier, but five whole years of postrevolutionary experience had been compressed into it. Twenty, ten, and five years earlier, the SR's had been the party next door in the effort to overthrow Tsarism, the party which had chiefly taken upon itself, thanks to the particular character of its terrorist tactics, the burden of hard-labor imprisonment, which had scarcely touched the Bolsheviks.

Now the first charge against them was that the SR's had initiated the Civil War! Yes, they began it, *they* had begun it. They were accused of armed resistance to the October seizure of power. When the Provisional Government, which they supported and which was in part made up of their members, was lawfully swept out of office by the machine-gun fire of the sailors, the SR's tried altogether illegally to defend it,[18] and even returned shot for shot,

---

18. The fact that their efforts in defending it were very feeble, that they were beset by hesitations, and that they renounced it right away is another matter. For all that, their *guilt* was no less.

and even called into battle the military cadets of that deposed government.

Defeated in battle, they did not repent politically. They did not get down on their knees to the Council of People's Commissars, which had declared itself to be the government. They continued to insist stubbornly that the only legal government was the one which had been overthrown. They refused to admit right away that what had been their political line for twenty years was a failure,[19] and they did not ask to be pardoned, nor to have their party dissolved and cease to be considered a party.[20]

The second charge against them was that they had deepened the abyss of the Civil War by taking part in demonstrations—by this token, rebellions—on January 5 and 6, 1918, against the lawful authority of the workers' and peasants' government. They were supporting their illegal Constituent Assembly (elected by universal, free, equal, secret, and direct voting) against the sailors and the Red Guards, who legally dispersed both the Assembly and the demonstrators. (And what good could have come of peaceable sessions of the Constituent Assembly? Only the conflagration of a three-year-long Civil War. And that is why the Civil War began, because not all the people submitted simultaneously and obediently to the lawful decrees of the Council of People's Commissars.)

The third charge was that they had not recognized the peace treaty of Brest-Litovsk, that lawful, lifesaving peace of Brest-Litovsk, which had cut off not Russia's head but only parts of its torso. By this token, declared the official indictment, there were present "all the signs of *high treason* and criminal activity directed to drawing the country into war."

High treason! That is another club with two ends. It all depends on which end you have hold of.

From this followed the serious fourth charge: in the summer and fall of 1918, those final months and weeks when the Kaiser's Germany was scarcely managing to hold its own against the Allies, and the Soviet government, faithful to the Brest treaty,

19. And it had indeed been a failure, although this did not become clear immediately.

20. In the same way, all the local Russian governments, and those in outlying areas, were illegal—those in Archangel, Samara, Ufa or Omsk, the Ukraine, the Don, the Kuban, the Urals or Transcaucasia—inasmuch as they all declared themselves to be governments *after* the Council of People's Commissars had declared itself to be the government.

was supporting Germany in its difficult struggle with trainloads of foodstuffs and a monthly tribute in gold, the SR's traitorously prepared (well, they didn't actually prepare anything but, as was their custom, *did more talking* about it than anything—but what if they really had!) to blow up the railroad tracks in front of one such train, thus keeping the gold in the Motherland. In other words, they "prepared criminal destruction of our public wealth, the railroads."

(At that time the Communists were not yet ashamed of and did not conceal the fact that, yes, indeed, Russian gold had been shipped off to Hitler's future empire, and it didn't seem to dawn on Krylenko despite his study in two academic departments— history and law—nor did any of his assistants whisper the notion to him, that if steel rails are public wealth, then maybe gold ingots are too?)

From this fourth charge a fifth followed inexorably: the SR's had intended to procure the technical equipment for such an explosion with money received from Allied representatives. (They had wanted to *take* money from the Entente in order not to *give gold away* to Kaiser Wilhelm.) And this was the extreme of treason! (Just in case, Krylenko did mutter something about the SR's also having connections with Ludendorff's General Staff, but this stone had indeed landed in the wrong vegetable garden, and he quickly dropped the whole thing.)

From this it was only a very short step to the sixth charge: that the SR's had been Entente *spies* in 1918. Yesterday they had been revolutionaries, and today they were spies. At the time, this accusation probably sounded explosive. But since then, and after many, many trials, the whole thing makes one want to vomit.

Well, then, the seventh and tenth points concerned collaboration with Savinkov, or Filonenko, or the Cadets, or the "Union of Rebirth" (had it really ever existed?), and even with aristocratic, reactionary, dilettante—so-called "white-lining"—students, or even the White Guards.

This series of linked charges was well expounded by the prosecutor.[21] As a result of either hard thinking in his office, or a sudden stroke of genius on the rostrum, he managed in this trial to come up with that tone of heartfelt sympathy and friendly criticism which he would make use of in subsequent trials with

21. The title of "prosecutor" had by now been restored to him.

increasing self-assurance and in ever heavier doses, and which, in 1937, would result in dazzling success. This tone created a common ground—against the rest of the world—between those doing the judging and those who were being judged, and it played on the defendant's particular soft spot. From the prosecutor's rostrum, they said to the SR's: *"After all, you and we are revolutionaries!* [We! You and we—that adds up to us!] And how could you have fallen so low as to join with the Cadets? [Yes, no doubt your heart is breaking!] Or with the officers? Or to teach the aristocratic, reactionary, dilettante students your brilliantly worked-out scheme of conspiratorial operation?"

None of the defendants' replies is available to us. Did any of them point out that the particular characteristic of the October coup had been to declare war immediately on all the other parties and forbid them to join forces? ("They're not hauling you in, so don't you dare peep!") But for some reason one gets the feeling that some of the defendants sat there with downcast eyes and that some of them truly had divided hearts: just how could they have fallen so low? After all, for the prisoner who'd been brought in from a dark cell, the friendly, sympathetic attitude of the prosecutor in the big bright hall struck home very effectively.

And Krylenko discovered another very, very logical little path which was to prove very useful to Vyshinsky when he applied it against Kamenev and Bukharin: On entering into an alliance with the bourgeoisie, you accepted money from them. At first you took it *for the cause,* only *for the cause,* and in no wise for Party purposes. *But where is the boundary line? Who can draw that dividing line?* After all, isn't the *cause* a Party cause also? And so you sank to the level—you, the Socialist Revolutionary Party—of being supported by the bourgeoisie! Where was your revolutionary pride?

A full quota of charges—and then some—had been piled up. And the tribunal could have gone out to confer and thereupon nailed each of the prisoners with his well-merited execution—but, alas, there was a big mix-up:

   a. Everything the Socialist Revolutionary Party had been accused of related to 1918.

   b. Since then, on February 27, 1919, an amnesty had been declared for SR's exclusively, which pardoned all their past belligerency against the Bolsheviks on the sole stipulation that they would not continue the struggle into the future.

    c. *And they had not continued the struggle since that time*.

    d. And it was now 1922!

How could Krylenko get around that one?

Some thought had been given to this point. When the Socialist International asked the Soviet government to drop charges and not put its socialist brothers on trial, some thought had been given to it.

In fact, at the beginning of 1919, in the face of threats from Kolchak and Denikin, the SR's had renounced their task of revolt against the Bolsheviks and had abandoned all armed struggle against them. (And to aid their Communist brethren, the Samara SR's had even *opened up* a section of the Kolchak front . . . which was, in fact, why the amnesty had been granted.) And right at the trial the defendant Gendelman, a member of the Central Committee, said: "Give us the chance to make use of the whole gamut of so-called civil liberties, and we will not break the law." (Give it to them! The "whole gamut," to boot! What loud-mouths!)

And it wasn't just that they weren't engaged in any opposition: they had recognized the Soviet government! In other words, they had renounced their former Provisional Government, yes, and the Constituent Assembly as well. And all they asked was a *new election* for the soviets, with freedom for all parties to engage in electoral campaigning.

Now did you hear that? Did you hear that? That's where the hostile bourgeois beast poked his snout through. How could we? After all, this is a *time of crisis!* After all, we are *encircled by the enemy*. (And in twenty years' time, and fifty years' time, and a hundred years' time, for that matter, it will be exactly the same.) And you want freedom for the parties to engage in electoral campaigning, you bastards?

Politically sober people, said Krylenko, could only laugh in reply and shrug their shoulders. It had been a just decision "immediately and by all measures of state suppression to prevent these groups from conducting propaganda against the government."[22] And specifically: in reply to the renunciation by the SR's of armed opposition and to their peaceful proposals, *they*

22. Krylenko, *op. cit.*, p. 183.

had put the entire Central Committee of the Socialist Revolutionary Party in prison! (As many of them as they could catch.)

That's how we do it!

But to keep them in prison—and hadn't it already been three years?—wasn't it necessary to try them? And what should they be charged with? "This period had not been sufficiently investigated in the pretrial examination," our prosecutor complained.

But in the meanwhile one charge was correct. In that same February, 1919, the SR's had passed a resolution which they had not put into effect, though in terms of the new Criminal Code that didn't matter at all: to carry on secret agitation in the ranks of the Red Army in order to induce the soldiers *to refuse to participate in reprisals* against the peasants.

And that was a low-down, foul betrayal of the Revolution—to try to persuade men not to take part in reprisals.

And they could also be charged with everything that the so-called "Foreign Delegation of the Central Committee" of the SR's —those prominent SR's who had fled to Europe—had said, written, and done (mostly words).

But all that wasn't enough. So here's what they thought up: "Many defendants sitting here would not deserve to be indicted in the given case, were it not for the charge of having planned *terrorist acts.*" Allegedly, when the amnesty of 1919 had been published, "none of the leaders of Soviet Justice had imagined" that the SR's had also planned to use terrorism against the leaders of the Soviet state! (Well, indeed, who could possibly have imagined that! The SR's! And terrorism, all of a sudden? And if it had come to mind, it would have been necessary to include it in the amnesty too! Or else not accept the gap in the Kolchak front. It was really very, very fortunate indeed that no one had thought of it. Not until it was needed—then someone thought of it.) So *this* charge had *not* been amnestied (for, after all, *struggle* was the only offense that had been amnestied). And so Krylenko could now make the charge!

And, in all likelihood, they had discovered so very much! So very much!

In the first place, they had discovered what the SR leaders had *said*[23] back in the first days after the October seizure of power.

23. And what hadn't those chatterboxes said in the course of a lifetime?

Chernov, at the Fourth Congress of the SR's, had said that the Party would "counterpose all its forces against any attack on the rights of the people, as it had" under Tsarism. (And everyone remembered how it had done that.) Gots had said. "If the autocrats at Smolny also infringe on the Constituent Assembly . . . the Socialist Revolutionary Party will remember its old tried and true tactics."

Perhaps it did *remember,* but it didn't make up its mind to act. Yet apparently it could be tried for it anyway.

"In this area of our investigation," Krylenko complained, because of conspiracy "there will be little testimony from witnesses." And he continued: "This has made my task extremely difficult. . . . In this area [i.e., terrorism] it is necessary, at certain moments, to wander about in the shadows."[24]

What made Krylenko's task difficult was the fact that the use of terrorism against the Soviet government *was discussed* at the meeting of the SR Central Committee in 1918 and *rejected.* And now, years later, it was necessary to prove that the SR's had been engaged in self-deception.

The SR's had said at the time that they would not resort to terrorism until and unless the Bolsheviks began to execute socialists. Or, in 1920, they had said that if the Bolsheviks were to threaten the lives of SR hostages, then the party would take up arms.[25]

So the question then was: Why did they qualify their renunciation of terrorism? Why wasn't it absolute? And how had they even dared *to think* about taking up arms! "Why were there no statements equivalent to *absolute renunciation?*" (But, Comrade Krylenko, maybe terrorism was their "second nature"?)

The SR Party carried out no terrorist acts whatever, and this was clear even from Krylenko's summing up of the charges. But the prosecution kept stretching such facts as these: One of the defendants had in mind a plan for blowing up the locomotive of a train carrying the Council of People's Commissars to Moscow. That meant the Central Committee of the SR's was guilty of terrorism. And the terrorist Ivanova had spent one night near the railroad station with *one* charge of explosives—which meant

24. Krylenko, *op. cit.,* p. 236. (What lingo!)
25. It was evidently all right to shoot the other hostages.

there had been an attempt to blow up Trotsky's train—and therefore the SR Central Committee was guilty of terrorism. And further: Donskoi, a member of the Central Committee, warned Fanya Kaplan that she would be expelled from the Party if she fired at Lenin. But that wasn't enough! Why hadn't she been categorically forbidden to? (Or perhaps: why hadn't she been denounced to the Cheka?)

It was feathers of this sort that Krylenko kept plucking from the dead rooster—that the SR's had not taken measures to stop individual terrorist acts by their unemployed and languishing gunmen. That was the whole of their terrorism. (Yes, and those gunmen of theirs didn't do anything either. In 1922, two of them, Konopleva and Semyonov, with suspicious eagerness, enriched the GPU and the tribunal with their voluntary evidence, but their evidence couldn't be pinned on the SR Central Committee—and suddenly and inexplicably these inveterate terrorists were released scot-free.)

All the evidence was such that it had to be bolstered up with props. Krylenko explained things this way in regard to one of the witnesses: "If this person had really wanted to make things up, it is unlikely he would have done so in such a way as to hit the target merely by accident."[26] (Strongly put, indeed! This could be said about any piece of fabricated testimony whatever.) Or else, about Donskoi: Could one really "suspect him of possessing the special insight to testify to what the prosecution wanted"? It was just the other way around with Konopleva: the reliability of her testimony was evidenced by the fact that she had *not* testified *to everything* the prosecution needed. (But enough for the defendants to be shot.) "If we ask whether Konopleva concocted all this, then it is . . . clear: *if one is going to concoct, one must really concoct* [He should know!], and if one is going to expose someone, one should really expose him."[27] But she, you see, did not carry it through to the end. Then things are put still another way: "After all, it is unlikely that Yefimov needed to put Konopleva in danger of execution without cause."[28] Once more correct, once more strongly put! Or, even more strongly: "Could this encounter have taken place? Such a possibility is not ex-

26. Krylenko, *op. cit.*, p. 251.
27. *Ibid.*, p. 253.
28. *Ibid.*, p. 258.

cluded." *Not excluded?* That means *it did take place.* Off to the races!

Then, too, the "subversive group." They talked about this for a long time, and then suddenly: "Dissolved for lack of activity." So what was all the fuss about? There had been several expropriations of money from Soviet institutions (the SR's had nothing with which to work, to rent apartments, to move from city to city). But previously these had been the lovely, noble *"exes"*— as all the revolutionists called them. And now, in a Soviet court? They were "robbery and concealment of stolen goods."

Through the material adduced by the prosecution in this trial, the dull, unblinking, yellow streetlamps of the Law throw light on the whole uncertain, wavering, deluded history of this pathetically garrulous, essentially lost, helpless, and even inactive party which never was worthily led. And its every decision or lack of decision, its every casting about, upsurge, or retreat, was transformed into and regarded as total guilt . . . guilt and more guilt.

And if in September, 1921, ten months before the trial, the SR Central Committee, already sitting in the Butyrki, had written to the newly elected Central Committee that it did not agree to the overthrow of the Bolshevik dictatorship by any available means, but only through rallying the working masses and the dissemination of propaganda—all of which meant that, even as they languished in prison, they did not agree to being liberated through either terrorism or conspiracy—then that, too, was converted into their primary guilt: Aha! so that means that *you did agree* to its overthrow.

And what if they were, nevertheless, not guilty of overthrowing the government, and not guilty of terrorism, and if there had been hardly any "expropriations" at all, and if they had long since been forgiven for all the rest? Our favorite prosecutor pulled out his canonical weapon of last resort: "Ultimately, failure *to denounce* is a category of crime applying to all the defendants without exception, and it must be considered as having been proved."[29]

The Socialist Revolutionary Party was guilty of *not having squealed on itself!* Now there's something that couldn't miss! This represented a discovery that juridical thought had made in the new Code. It was a paved highway along which they would keep

29. *Ibid.,* p. 305.

driving and driving grateful descendants into Siberia!

And Krylenko burst out in a temper: "Hardened eternal enemies"—that's who the defendants are! In that case it's quite clear even without any trial what has to be done with them.

The Code was still so new that Krylenko could not even remember the main counterrevolutionary articles by their numbers —but how he slashed about with those numbers! How profoundly he cited and interpreted them! Just as if the blade of the guillotine had for decades hinged and dropped only on those articles. And especially new and important was the fact that *we did not draw* the distinction between *methods* and *means* the old Tsarist Code had drawn. Such distinctions had no influence either on the classification of the charges or on the penalties imposed! For us, intent and action were *identical!* A resolution had been passed—we would try them for that. And whether it "was carried out or not had no essential significance."[30] Whether a man whispered to his wife in bed that it would be a good thing to overthrow the Soviet government or whether he engaged in propaganda during elections or threw a bomb, it was all one and the same! *And the punishment was identical!!!*

And just as a foresighted painter proceeds from his first few brusquely drawn, angular strokes to create the whole desired portrait, so, for us, the entire panorama of 1937, 1945, and 1949 becomes ever clearer and more visible in the sketches of 1922.

But no, one thing is missing! What's missing is *the conduct of the defendants*. They have not yet become trained sheep. They are still people! We have been told little, very little, but from that little we can understand a great deal. Sometimes through carelessness, Krylenko cites what they said right at the trial. For example, the defendant Berg "accused the Bolsheviks of responsibility for the deaths of January 5"—shooting down those who were demonstrating on behalf of the Constituent Assembly. And what Liberov said was even more direct: "I admit I was guilty of failing to work hard enough at overthrowing the Bolshevik government in 1918.[31] Yevgeniya Ratner adhered to the same line, and Berg also declared: "I consider myself guilty before the workers' Russia for having been unable to fight with all my strength against the so-called workers' and peasants' government,

30. *Ibid.,* p. 185.
31. *Ibid.,* p. 103.

but I hope that my time has not yet gone."[32] (It has gone, darling, all gone!)

Of course, there is in all this an element of the ancient passion for the resounding phrase, but there is firmness too.

The prosecutor argued: the accused are dangerous to Soviet Russia because *they consider everything they did to have been a good thing.* "Perhaps certain of the defendants find their own consolation in the hope that some future chronicler will praise them or *their conduct at the trial.*"[33]

And a decree of the All-Russian Central Executive Committee issued after the trial declared: "At the trial itself they reserved to themselves the right to continue" their former activity.

The defendant Gendelman-Grabovsky (a lawyer himself) was conspicuous during the trial for his arguments with Krylenko on tampering with the testimony of witnesses and on "special methods of treating witnesses before the trial"—in other words, the obvious working-over they had gotten from the GPU. (It is all there! All the elements are there! There was only a little way to go before attaining the ideal.) Apparently the preliminary interrogation had been conducted under the supervision of the prosecutor—that same Krylenko. And during that process individual instances of a lack of consistency in testimony had been ironed out. Yet some testimony was presented *for the first time* only at the trial itself.

Well, so what! So there were some rough spots. So it wasn't perfect. But in the last analysis, "We have to declare altogether clearly and coldly that . . . we are not concerned with the question of *how the court of history is going to view our present deed.*"[34]

And as far as the rough spots are concerned, we will take them under advisement and correct them.

But as it was, Krylenko, squirming, had to bring up—probably for the first and last time in Soviet jurisprudence—the matter of *the inquiry,* the initial inquiry required before investigation. And here's how cleverly he handled this point: The proceeding which took place in the absence of the prosecutor and which you considered the investigation was actually *the inquiry.* And the proceeding in the presence of the prosecutor which you regarded

32. *Ibid.*
33. *Ibid.*, p. 325.
34. *Ibid.*

as the reinvestigation, when all the loose ends were gathered up
and all the bolts tightened, was really *the investigation*. The dis-
organized "materials provided by the Organs for inquiry and
unverified by the investigation have *much less value as proof*
than the materials provided by the skillfully directed investigation."[35]

Clever, wasn't it? Just try grinding that up in your mortar!

To be practical about it, Krylenko no doubt resented having
to spend half a year getting ready for this trial, then another two
months barking at the defendants, and then having to drag out
his summation for fifteen hours, when all these defendants "had
more than once been in the hands of the extraordinary Organs at
times when these Organs had extraordinary powers; but, thanks to
some circumstances or other, *they had succeeded in surviving*."[36]
So now Krylenko had to slave away to try and get them executed
legally.

There was, of course, "only one possible verdict—execution
for every last one of them"![37] But Krylenko qualifies this generously. Because this case is being watched by the whole world,
the prosecutor's demand "does not constitute a directive to the
court" which the latter would "be obliged to accept immediately
for consideration or decision."[38]

What a fine court, too, that requires such an explanation!

And, indeed, the tribunal did demonstrate its daring in the
sentences it imposed: it did not hand down the death penalty
for "every last one of them," but for fourteen only. Most of the
rest got prison and camp sentences, while sentences in the form
of productive labor were imposed on another hundred.

And just remember, reader, remember: "All the other courts
of the Republic watch what the Supreme Tribunal does. It provides them with guidelines."[39]

The sentences of the *Verkhtrib* are used "as directives for their
guidance."[40] As to how many more would now be railroaded in
the provinces, you can figure that out for yourself.

And, probably, on appeal the decision of the Presidium of the
All-Russian Central Executive Committee was worth the whole

35. *Ibid.,* p. 238.
36. *Ibid.,* p. 322.
37. *Ibid.,* p. 326.
38. *Ibid.,* p. 319.
39. *Ibid.,* p. 407.
40. *Ibid.,* p. 409.

trial: the death sentences were to remain in effect, but not to be carried out for the time being. The further fate of those condemned would depend, then, on the conduct of those SR's who had not yet been arrested, apparently including those abroad as well. In other words: If you move *against* us, we'll squash them.

In the fields of Russia they were reaping the second peacetime harvest. There was no shooting except in the courtyards of the Cheka. (Perkhurov in Yaroslavl, Metropolitan Veniamin in Petrograd. And always, always, always.) Beneath the azure sky our first diplomats and journalists sailed abroad across the blue waters. And the Central Executive Committee of Workers' and Peasants' Deputies thrust into its pockets eternal *hostages*.

The members of the ruling Party read all sixty issues of *Pravda* devoted to the trial—for they *all* read the papers—and all of them said: *"Yes, yes, yes."* No one mumbled: *"No!"*

What, then, were they surprised at in 1937? What was there to complain about? Hadn't all the foundations of lawlessness been laid—first by the extrajudicial reprisals of the Cheka, and then by these early trials and this young Code? Wasn't 1937 also *expedient* (expedient for Stalin's purposes and, perhaps, History's, too, for that matter)?

Prophetically, Krylenko let it slip that they were judging not the past but the future.

Only the first swath cut by the scythe is difficult.

■

On or about August 20, 1924, Boris Viktorovich Savinkov crossed the Soviet border. He was immediately arrested and taken to the Lubyanka.[41] In all, the interrogation lasted for just one

---

41. Many hypotheses were advanced about his return. Only a little while ago, a certain Ardamatsky, a person obviously connected with the archives and personnel of the Committee for State Security, published a story which, despite being adorned with pretentiously inflated literary gewgaws, is evidently close to the truth. (The magazine *Neva*, No. 11, 1967.) Having induced certain of Savinkov's agents to betray him and having deceived others, the GPU used them to set a foolproof trap, convincing Savinkov that inside Russia a large underground organization was languishing for lack of a worthy leader! It would have been impossible to devise a more effective trap! And it would have been impossible for Savinkov, after such a confused and sensational life, merely to spin it out quietly to the end in Nice. He couldn't bear not trying to pull off one more feat and not returning to Russia and his death.

session, which consisted solely of voluntary testimony and an evaluation of his activity. The official indictment was ready by August 23. The speed was totally unbelievable, but it had impact. (Someone had estimated the situation quite accurately: to have forced false and pitiful testimony out of Savinkov by torture would only have wrecked the authenticity of the picture.)

In the official indictment, couched in already-well-developed terminology that turned everything upside down, Savinkov was charged with just about everything imaginable: with being a "consistent enemy of the poorest peasantry"; with "assisting the Russian bourgeoisie in carrying out its imperialist ambitions" (in other words, he was in favor of continuing the war with Germany); with "maintaining relations with representatives of the Allied command" (this would have been when he was in charge of the Ministry of War!); with "becoming a member of soldiers' committees for purposes of provocation" (i.e., he was elected by the soldiers' committees); and, last but not least, something to make even the chickens cackle with laughter—with having had "monarchist sympathies."

But all that was old hat. There were some new items too— the standard charges for all future trials: money from the imperialists; espionage for Poland (they left out Japan, believe it or not); yes, and he had also wanted to poison the Red Army with potassium cyanide (but for some reason he did not poison even one Red Army soldier).

On August 26 the trial began. The presiding judge was Ulrikh —this being our earliest encounter with him. And there was no prosecutor at all, nor any defense lawyer.

Savinkov was lackadaisical in defending himself, and he raised hardly any objection at all to the evidence. He conceived of this trial in a lyrical sense. It was his last encounter with Russia and his last opportunity to explain himself in public. And to repent. (Not of these imputed sins, but of others.)

(And that theme song fitted well here, and greatly confused the defendant: "*After all, we are all Russians together*. You and we adds up to *us*. You love Russia beyond a doubt, and we respect your love—and do we not love Russia too? In fact, are we not at present the fortress and the glory of Russia? And you wanted to fight against us? Repent!")

But it was the sentence that was most wonderful: "Imposition of the death penalty is not required in the interests of preserving revolutionary law and order, and, on the grounds that motives of vengeance should not influence the sense of justice of the proletarian masses"—the death penalty was commuted to ten years' imprisonment.

Now that was a sensation! And it confused many minds too. Did it mean a relaxation? A transformation? Ulrikh even published in *Pravda* an apologetic explanation of why Savinkov had not been executed.

You see how strong the Soviet government has become in only seven years! Why should it be afraid of some Savinkov or other! (On the twentieth anniversary of the Revolution, it is going to get weaker, and don't be too hard on us because we are going to execute thousands.)

And so, on the heels of the first riddle of his return, there would have been the second riddle of his being spared capital punishment had it not been overshadowed in May, 1925, by a third riddle: in a state of depression, Savinkov jumped from an unbarred window into the interior courtyard of the Lubyanka, and the gaypayooshniki, his guardian angels, simply couldn't manage to stop him and hold on to his big, heavy body. However, just in case—so that there wouldn't be any scandal in the service —Savinkov left them a suicide letter in which he explained logically and coherently why he was killing himself—and this letter was so authentically phrased, so clearly written in Savinkov's style and vocabulary, that even Lev Borisovich, the son of the deceased, was fully convinced of its genuineness and explained to everyone in Paris that no one except his father could have written it and that he had ended his life because he realized his political bankruptcy.[42]

And all the major and most famous trials are still ahead of us.

42. And we, silly prisoners of a later Lubyanka, confidently parroted to one another that the steel nets hanging in the Lubyanka stairwells had been installed after Savinkov had committed suicide there. Thus do we succumb to fancy legends to the extent of forgetting that the experience of jailers is, after all, international in character. Such nets existed in American prisons as long ago as the beginning of the century—and how could Soviet technology have been allowed to lag behind?

In 1937, when he was dying in a camp in the Kolyma, the former Chekist Artur Pryubel told one of his fellow prisoners that he had been one of the four who *threw* Savinkov from a fifth-floor window into the Lubyanka courtyard! (And there is no conflict between that statement and Ardamatsky's recent account: There was a low sill; it was more like a door to the balcony than a window—they had picked the right room! Only, according to Ardamatsky, the guards were careless; according to Pryubel, they rushed him all together.)

Thus the second riddle, the unusually lenient sentence, was unraveled by the crude third "riddle."

The story ascribed to Pryubel could not be checked, but I had heard it, and in 1967 I told it to M. P. Yakubovich. He, with his still youthful enthusiasm and shining eyes, exclaimed: "I believe it. Things fit! And I didn't believe Blyumkin; I thought he was just bragging." What he had learned was this: At the end of the twenties, Blyumkin had told Yakubovich, after swearing him to secrecy, that *he* was the one who had written Savinkov's so-called suicide note, on orders from the GPU. Apparently Blyumkin was allowed to see Savinkov in his cell constantly while he was in prison. He kept him amused in the evenings. (Did Savinkov sense that death was creeping up on him . . . sly, friendly death, which gives you no chance to guess the form your end will take?) And this had helped Blyumkin acquire Savinkov's manner of speech and thought, had enabled him to enter into the framework of his last ideas.

And they ask: Why throw him out the window? Wouldn't it have been easier simply to poison him? Perhaps they showed someone the remains or thought they might need to.

And where, if not here, is the right place to report the fate of Blyumkin, who for all his Chekist omnipotence was fearlessly brought up short by Mandelstam. Ehrenburg began to tell Blyumkin's story, and suddenly became ashamed and dropped the subject. And there is a story to tell, too. After the 1918 rout of the Left SR's, Blyumkin, the assassin of the German Ambassador Mirbach, not only went unpunished, was not only spared the fate of all the other Left SR's, but was protected by Dzerzhinsky, just as Dzerzhinsky had wanted to protect Kosyrev. Superficially he converted to Bolshevism, and was kept on, one gathers, for particularly important assassinations. At one point, close to the thirties, he was secretly sent to Paris to kill Bazhenov, a member of the staff of Stalin's secretariat who had defected, and one night he succeeded in throwing him off a train. However, his gambler's blood, or perhaps his admiration of Trotsky, led Blyumkin to the Princes' Islands in Turkey, where Trotsky was living. He asked Trotsky whether there were any assignments he could carry out for him in the Soviet Union, and Trotsky gave him a package for Radek. Blyumkin delivered it, and his visit to Trotsky would have remained a secret had not the brilliant Radek already been a stool pigeon. Radek *brought down* Blyumkin, who was thereupon devoured by the maw of the monster his own hands had suckled with its first bloody milk.

Chapter 10

■

The Law Matures

But where were those mobs insanely storming the barbed-wire barricades on our western borders whom we were going to shoot, under Article 71 of the Criminal Code, for unauthorized return to the Russian Soviet Federated Socialist Republic? Contrary to scientific prediction, there were no such crowds, and that article of the Code dictated by Lenin to Kursky remained useless. The only Russian crazy enough to do it was Savinkov, and they had ducked applying that article even to him. On the other hand, the opposite penalty—exile abroad instead of execution —was tried out immediately on a large scale.

In those days when he was composing the Criminal Code, Vladimir Ilyich Lenin, developing his brilliant idea, wrote in the heat of the moment, on May 19:

Comrade Dzerzhinsky! On the question of exiling abroad writers and professors who aid the counterrevolution: this is a measure which must be prepared most carefully. Unless we prepare well, we can commit stupidities. . . . We must arrange the business in such a way as to catch these "military spies" and keep on catching them constantly and systematically and exiling them abroad. I beg you to show this secretly, and without making any copies of it, to members of the Politburo.[1]

The extreme secrecy was natural in view of the importance

1. Lenin, fifth edition, Vol. 54, pp. 265–266.

and instructive impact of the measure. The crystal-clear line-up of forces on the class front in Soviet Russia was, to put it simply, spoiled by the presence of this shapeless, jellylike stain of the old *bourgeois* intelligentsia, which in the ideological area genuinely played the role of *military spies*—and the very best solution one could imagine was to scrape off that stagnant scum of ideas and toss it out abroad.

Comrade Lenin had already been stricken by his illness, but the members of the Politburo had apparently given their approval, and Comrade Dzerzhinsky had done the catching. At the end of 1922, about three hundred prominent Russian humanists were loaded onto—a barge, perhaps? No, they were put on a steamer and sent off to the European garbage dump. (Among those who settled down in exile and acquired reputations were the philosophers N. O. Lossky, S. N. Bulgakov, N. A. Berdyayev, F. A. Stepun, B. P. Vysheslavtsev, L. P. Karsavin, S. L. Frank, I. A. Ilin; the historians S. P. Melgunov, V. A. Myakotin, A. A. Kizevetter, I. I. Lapshin, and others; the writers and publicists Y. I. Aikhenvald, A. S. Izgoyev, M. A. Osorgin, A. V. Peshekhonov. At the beginning of 1923, additional small groups were sent off, including for example V. F. Bulgakov, the secretary of Lev Tolstoi. And because of questionable associations some mathematicians also shared this fate, including D. F. Selivanov.)

However, it didn't work out *constantly and systematically*. Perhaps the roar with which the émigrés announced that they regarded it as a "gift" made it apparent that this punishment left something to be desired, that it was a mistake to have let go good material for the executioner, and that poisonous flowers might grow on that garbage dump. And so they abandoned this form of punishment. And all subsequent purging led to either *the executioner* or the Archipelago.

The improved Criminal Code promulgated in 1926, which, in effect, continued right into Khrushchev's times, tied all the formerly scattered political articles into one durable dragnet— Article 58—and the roundup was under way. The catch swiftly expanded to include the engineering and technical intelligentsia; it was especially dangerous because it occupied a firm position in the economy and it was hard to keep an eye on it with the help of the Progressive Doctrine alone. It now became clear that the trial in defense of Oldenborger had been a mistake—after all, a very nice little *center* had been organized there. And Krylenko's declaration that "there was no question of sabotage on the part of the engineers in 1920 and 1921"[2] had granted an all too hasty absolution. Now it was not sabotage but worse—*wrecking,* a word discovered, it appears, by a rank-and-file interrogator in the Shakhty case.

It had no sooner been established that wrecking was what had to be tracked down—notwithstanding the nonexistence of this concept in the entire history of mankind—than they began to discover it without any trouble in all branches of industry and in all individual enterprises. However, there was no unity of plan, no perfection of execution, in all these hit-or-miss discoveries, although Stalin, by virtue of his character, and of course the entire investigative branch of our judicial apparatus, evidently aspired to just that. But our Law had finally matured and could show the world something really perfect—a big, coordinated, well-organized trial, this time a trial of engineers. And that is how the Shakhty case came about.

K. The Shakhty Case—May 18–July 15, 1928

This case was tried before a Special Assize of the Supreme Court of the U.S.S.R., under Presiding Judge A. Y. Vyshinsky (who was still the Rector of First Moscow University); the chief accuser was N. V. Krylenko (what a significant encounter!—rather like a handing over of the juridical relay-baton).[3] There were fifty-three defendants and fifty-six witnesses. How spectacular!

Alas, in its spectacular aspect lay the weakness of this case. If one were to tie to each of the defendants only three threads of evidence, there would still have to be 159 of them. And meanwhile Krylenko had only ten fingers and Vyshinsky another ten. Of course, the "defendants strove to expose their heinous crimes

2. Krylenko, *Za Pyat Let,* p. 437.
3. And the members of the tribunal were the old revolutionaries Vasilyev-Yuzhin and Antonov-Saratovsky. The very simple folk sound of their family names inclines one to a favorable reaction. They are easy to remember. And when suddenly, in 1962, obituaries of certain victims of repression appeared in *Izvestiya,* whose signature was at the bottom? That of the long-lived Antonov-Saratovsky!

to society"—but not all of them did, only sixteen; thirteen wiggled back and forth, and twenty-four didn't admit their guilt at all.[4] This introduced an impermissible discord, and the masses could certainly not understand it. Along with its positive aspects —which had, incidentally, already been displayed in earlier trials —such as the helplessness of the defendants and of the defense attorneys, and their inability either to budge or to deflect the implacable boulder of the sentence—the shortcomings of the new trial were fully apparent. Someone less experienced than Krylenko might have been forgiven them—but not he.

On the threshold of the classless society, we were at last capable of realizing *the conflictless trial*—a reflection of the absence of inner conflict in our social structure—in which not only the judge and the prosecutor but also the defense lawyers and the defendants themselves would strive collectively to achieve their common purpose.

Anyway, the whole scale of the Shakhty case, comprising as it did the coal industry alone and the Donets Basin alone, was disproportionately paltry for this era.

It appears that then and there, on the day the Shakhty case ended, Krylenko began to dig a new, capacious pit. (Even two of his own colleagues in the Shakhty case—the public accusers Osadchy and Shein—fell into it.) And it goes without saying that the entire apparatus of the OGPU, which had already landed in Yagoda's firm hands, aided him willingly and adroitly. It was necessary to create and uncover an engineers' organization which encompassed the entire country. And for this purpose it was essential to have several strong, prominent "wreckers" at its head. And what engineer was unaware of just such an unequivocally strong and impatiently proud leader—Pyotr Akimovich Palchinsky? An important mining engineer from as far back as the beginning of the century, he had been the Deputy Chairman of the War Industry Committee during World War I—in other words, he had directed the war efforts of all Russian industry, which had managed, during the course of the war, to make up for the failures in Tsarist preparations. After February, 1917, he became the Deputy Minister of Trade and Industry. He had been persecuted under the Tsar for revolutionary activity. He had been imprisoned three times after October—in 1917, 1918, and 1922.

4. *Pravda*, May 24, 1928, p. 3.

From 1920 on, he had been a professor at the Mining Institute and a consultant to the Gosplan—the State Planning Commission. (For more details about him see Part III, Chapter 10.)

They picked this Palchinsky to be the chief defendant in a grandiose new trial. However, the thoughtless Krylenko, stepping into what was for him a new field—engineering—not only knew nothing about the resistance of materials but could not even conceive of the potential resistance of souls . . . despite ten years of already sensational activity as a prosecutor. Krylenko's choice turned out to be a mistake. Palchinsky resisted every pressure the OGPU knew—and did not surrender; in fact, he died without signing any sort of nonsense at all. N. K. von Meck and A. F. Velichko were subjected to torture with him, and they, too, appear not to have given in. We do not yet know whether they died while under torture or whether they were shot. But they proved it was *possible* to resist and that it was *possible* not to give in—and thus they left behind a spotlight of reproach to shine on all the famous subsequent defendants.

To cover up his defeat, on May 24, 1929, Yagoda published a brief GPU communiqué on the execution of the three for large-scale wrecking, which also announced the condemnation of many other unidentified persons.[5]

But how much time had been spent for nothing! Nearly a whole year! And how many nights of interrogation! And how much inventiveness on the part of the interrogators! And all to no avail. And Krylenko had to start over from the very beginning and find a leader who was both brilliant and strong, and at the same time utterly weak and totally pliable. But so little did he understand this cursed breed of engineers that another whole year was spent in unsuccessful tries. From the summer of 1929 on, he worked over Khrennikov, but Khrennikov, too, died without agreeing to play a dastardly role. They twisted old Fedotov, but he was too old, and furthermore he was a textile engineer, which was an unprofitable field. And one more year was wasted! The country was waiting for the all-inclusive wreckers' trial, and Comrade Stalin was waiting—but things just couldn't seem to fall into place for Krylenko.[6] It was only

5. *Izvestiya,* May 24, 1929.
6. And it is quite possible that this failure of his was held against him by the Leader and led to the symbolic destruction of the prosecutor—on the very same guillotine as his victims.

in the summer of 1930 that someone found or suggested Ramzin, the Director of the Thermal Engineering Institute! He was arrested, and in three months a magnificent drama was prepared and performed, the genuine perfection of our justice and an unattainable model for world justice.

L. The Promparty (Industrial Party) Trial—
November 25–December 7, 1930

This case was tried at a Special Assize of the Supreme Court, with the same Vyshinsky, the same Antonov-Saratovsky, and that same favorite of ours, Krylenko.

This time none of those "technical reasons" arose to prevent the reader's being offered a full stenographic report of the trial[7] or to prohibit the attendance of foreign correspondents.

There was a majesty of concept: all the nation's industry, all its branches and planning organs, sat on the defendants' benches. (However, only the eyes of the man who arranged it all could see the crevices into which the mining industry and railroad transportation had disappeared.) At the same time there was a thrift in the use of material: there were only eight defendants in all. (The mistakes of the Shakhty trial had been taken into account.)

You are going to exclaim: Can eight men represent the entire industry of the country? Yes, indeed; we have more even than we need. Three out of eight are solely in textiles, representing the industrial branch most important for national defense. But there were, no doubt, crowds of witnesses? Just seven in all, who were exactly the same sort of wreckers as the defendants and were also prisoners. But there were no doubt bales of documents that exposed them? Drawings? Projects? Directives? Summaries of results? Proposals? Dispatches? Private correspondence? No, not one! You mean to say, *Not even one tiny piece of paper?* How could the GPU let that sort of thing get by? They had arrested all those people, and they hadn't even grabbed one little piece of paper? "There had been a lot," but "it had all been destroyed." Because "there was no place to keep the files." At the

---

7. *Protsess Prompartii* (*The Trial of the Promparty*), Moscow, Sovetskoye Zakonodatelstvo (Soviet Legislation Publishing House), 1931.

trial they produced only a few newspaper articles, published in the émigré press and our own. But in that event how could the prosecution present its case? Well, to be sure, there was Nikolai Vasilyevich Krylenko. And, to be sure, it wasn't the first time either. "The best evidence, no matter what the circumstances, is the confessions of the defendants."[8]

But what confessions! These confessions were not forced but inspired—repentance tearing whole monologues from the breast, and talk, talk, and more talk, and self-exposure and self-flagellation! They told old man Fedotov, who was sixty-six, that he could sit down, that he had talked long enough, but no, he kept pouring out additional explanations and interpretations. For five sessions in a row, no questions were asked. The defendants kept talking and talking and explaining and kept asking for the floor again in order to supply whatever they had left out. They presented inferentially everything the prosecution needed without any questions whatever being asked. Ramzin, after extensive explanations, went on to provide brief résumés, for the sake of clarity, as if he were addressing slow-witted students. The defendants were afraid most of all that something might be left unexplained, that someone might go unexposed, that someone's name might go unmentioned, that someone's intention to wreck might not have been made clear. And how they reviled themselves! "I am a class enemy!" "I was bribed." "Our bourgeois ideology." And then the prosecutor: "Was that your error?" And Charnovsky replied: "And crime!" There was simply nothing for Krylenko to do. For five sessions he went on drinking tea and eating cookies or whatever else they brought him.

But how did the defendants sustain such an emotional explosion? There was no tape recorder to take down their words, but Otsep, the defense attorney, described them: "The defendants' words flowed in a businesslike manner, cold and professionally calm." There you are! Such a passion for confession—and businesslike at the same time? Cold? More than that: they appear to have mumbled their glib repentance so listlessly that Vyshinsky often asked them to speak louder, more clearly, because they couldn't be heard.

The harmony of the trial was not at all disturbed by the de-

8. *Ibid.,* p. 452.

fense, which agreed with all the prosecutor's proposals. The principal defense lawyer called the prosecutor's summation *historic* and described his own as narrow, admitting that in making it he had gone against the dictates of his heart, for "a Soviet defense lawyer is first of all a Soviet citizen" and "like all workers, he, too, is outraged" at the crimes of the defendants.[9] During the trial the defense asked shy and tentative questions and then instantly backed away from them if Vyshinsky interrupted. The lawyers actually defended only two harmless textile officials and did not challenge the formal charges nor the description of the defendants' actions, but asked only whether the defendants might avoid execution. Is it more useful, Comrade Judges, "to have their corpses or their labor?"

. . . How foul-smelling were the crimes of these bourgeois engineers? Here is what they consisted of. They planned to reduce the tempo of development, as, for instance, to an over-all annual increase in production of *only* 20 to 22 percent, whereas the workers were prepared to increase it by 40 to 50 percent. They slowed down the rate of mining local fuels. They were too slow in developing the Kuznetsk Basin. They exploited theoretical and economic arguments —such as whether to supply the Donets Basin with electricity from the Dnieper power station or whether to build a supertrunk-line between Moscow and the Donbas—in order to delay the solutions of important problems. (The work stops while engineers argue!) They postponed considering new engineering projects (i.e., they did not authorize them immediately). In lectures on the *resistance of materials*, they took an *anti-Soviet line*. They installed worn-out equipment. They tied up capital funds, for example, by using them for costly and lengthy construction projects. They carried out unnecessary (!) repairs. They misused metals (some grades of iron were wanting). They created an imbalance between the departments of a plant and between the supply of raw materials and the capacity for processing them industrially. (This was particularly notable in the textile industry, where they built one or two factories more than they needed to process the cotton harvest.) Then they leaped from minimal to maximal plans. And obvious wrecking began through the *accelerated* development of that same unfortunate textile industry. Most importantly, they planned sabotage in the field of electric power—even though none was ever carried out. Thus wrecking did not take the form of

9. *Ibid.*, p. 488.

actual damage done but remained within the area of operational planning, yet it was intended to lead to a nationwide crisis and even to economic paralysis in 1930! But it didn't—and only because of the competitive industrial and financial plans of the masses (doubling the figures!). . . .

"Yeah, yeah, yeah," begins the skeptical reader.

What? That isn't enough for you? But if, at the trial, we repeat every point and chew it over five or eight times, then perhaps it turns out not to be so negligible?

"Yeah, yeah, yeah." The reader of the sixties nonetheless sticks to his own view. "Mightn't all that have happened precisely because of those competing industrial and financial plans? Aren't things bound to be out of balance if any union meeting, without consulting Gosplan, can twist the ratios around as it pleases?"

Oh, the prosecutor's bread is bitter! After all, they decided to publish every last word! That meant that engineers would read it too. "You've made your bed, now lie in it." And Krylenko rushed in fearlessly to discuss and to question and cross-question engineering details! And the inside pages and inserts of the enormous newspapers were full of small print about fine technical points. The notion was that every reader would be overcome by the sheer mass of material, that he wouldn't have enough time, even if he used up all his evenings and his rest days too, and so he wouldn't read it all but would only notice the refrain following every few paragraphs: "We were wreckers, wreckers, wreckers."

But suppose someone did begin, and read every last line?

In that case, he would come to see, through the banality of self-accusations, composed with such ineptitude and stupidity, that the Lubyanka boa constrictor had gotten involved in something outside its competence, its own kind of work, that what breaks free of the crude noose is the strong-winged thought of the twentieth century. There the prisoners are: in the dock, submissive, repressed—but their thought leaps out. Even their terrified, tired tongues manage to name everything with its proper name and to tell us everything.

. . . Here is the situation in which they worked. Kalinnikov: "Well, to be sure, a situation of technical distrust was created." Larichev: "Whether we wanted to or not, we still had to produce that 42 millions of tons of petroleum [i.e., it had been thus ordered from on high] . . . because, no matter what, 42 million tons of petroleum could not have been produced under any circumstances whatever."[10]

All the work of that unhappy generation of our engineers was squeezed between two such impossibilities. The Thermal Engineering Institute was proud of its principal research achievement, which was the sharply improved coefficient of fuel consumption. On this basis, lower requirements for fuel production had been stipulated in the preliminary plan. *And that meant wrecking*—reducing fuel resources. In the transportation plan, they had provided for all freight cars to be equipped with automatic coupling. *And that meant wrecking:* they had tied up capital funds. After all, it takes a long time to introduce automatic coupling, and the capital investment involved in installing it can only be recouped over a long period, and we want everything immediately! In order to make more efficient use of single-track railroads, they decided to increase the size of the locomotives and freight cars. And was that considered modernization? *No, it was wrecking.* Because in that case it would have been necessary to invest funds in strengthening the roadbeds and the superstructures of the bridges. From the profound economic consideration that in America capital is cheap and labor dear, and that the situation here is just the opposite, and that we therefore ought not to borrow things with monkeylike imitativeness, Fedotov concluded that it was useless for us to purchase expensive American assembly-line machinery. For the next ten years it would be more profitable for us to buy less sophisticated English machinery and to put more workers on it, since it was inevitable that in ten years' time whatever we had purchased would be replaced anyway, no matter what. And we could then buy more expensive machinery. So that, too, was *wrecking.* Alleging economy as his reason, what he really wanted, they charged, was to avoid having the most advanced type of machinery in Soviet industry. They began to build new factories out of reinforced concrete, instead of cheaper ordinary concrete, on the grounds that over a hundred-year period reinforced concrete would recoup the additional investment many times over. So that, too, was *wrecking:* tying up capital; using up scarce reinforcing rods when iron was in short supply. (What was it supposed to be kept for—false teeth?)

From among the defendants, Fedotov willingly conceded: Of course, if every kopeck must be counted today, then it could be considered wrecking. The English say: I'm not rich enough to buy cheap goods.

10. *Ibid.,* p. 325.

He tries softly to explain to the hardheaded prosecutor: "Theoretical approaches of every kind project norms which in the final analysis are [they will be considered to be] wrecking. . . ."[11]

Well, tell me now: how much more clearly could a frightened defendant speak out? What is theory to us is wrecking to you! Because you are compelled to grab today, without any thought for tomorrow.

Old Fedotov tries to explain where thousands and millions of rubles are lost in the insane rush of the Five-Year Plan: Cotton is not sorted where it is grown so that every factory can be sent that grade and kind of cotton it requires; instead, it is shipped any old way, all mixed up. But the prosecutor doesn't listen to him. With the stubbornness of a block of stone he keeps coming back again and again—ten times—to the more obvious question he has put together out of children's building blocks: Why did they begin to build the so-called "factory-palaces," with high ceilings, broad corridors, and unnecessarily good ventilation? Was that not the most obvious sort of *wrecking?* After all, that amounted to tying up capital irrevocably! The bourgeois wreckers explain to him that the People's Commissariat of Labor wanted to build factories for the workers in the land of the proletariat which were spacious and had good air. [That means there are also *wreckers* in the People's Commissariat of Labor. Make a note of that!] The doctors had insisted on thirty feet of space between floors, and Fedotov reduced it to twenty—so why not to sixteen? Now that was *wrecking*! (If he had reduced it to fifteen, that would have been flagrant wrecking: he would have wanted to create the nightmare conditions of a capitalist factory for free Soviet workers.) They explain to Krylenko that in relation to the entire cost of the factory and its equipment, this difference accounted for 3 percent of the total— but no, again and again and again, he keeps on about the height of the ceilings! And how did they dare install such powerful ventilators? They took into account the hottest summer days. Why the hottest days? So what! Let the workers sweat a little on the hottest days!

And in the meantime: "The disproportions were inherent. . . . Bungling organization saw to that before there was any 'Engineers Center.' " (Charnovsky.)[12] "No wrecking activities were ever necessary. . . . All one had to do was carry out the *appropriate actions* and everything would happen on its own." (Charnovsky again.)[13] He could not have expressed himself more clearly. And he said this after many months in the Lubyanka and from the defendants' bench in

11. *Ibid.,* p. 365.
12. *Ibid.,* p. 204.
13. *Ibid.,* p. 202.

382 | THE GULAG ARCHIPELAGO

court. The *appropriate actions*—i.e., those imposed by bungling *higher-ups*—were quite enough: carry them out and the unthinkable plan would destroy itself. Here was their kind of wrecking: "We *had the capability* of producing, say, 1,000 tons and *we were ordered* [in other words, by a nonsensical plan] to produce 3,000, so we took no steps to produce them."[14] . . .

You must admit that for an official, double-checked, spruced-up stenographic record in those years, this is not so little.

On many occasions Krylenko drives his actors to tones of exhaustion, thanks to the nonsense they are compelled to grind out over and over again . . . like a bad play in which the actor is ashamed for the dramatist, and yet has to go on and on anyway, to keep body and soul together.

Krylenko: "Do you agree?"

Fedotov: "I agree . . . even though in general I do not think . . ."[15]

Krylenko: "Do you confirm this?"

Fedotov: "Properly speaking . . . in certain portions . . . and so to speak, in general . . . yes."[16]

For the engineers (those who were still free, not yet imprisoned, and who had to face the necessity of working cheerfully after the defamation at the trial of their whole class), there was no way out. They were damned if they *did* and damned if they *didn't*. If they went forward, it was wrong, and if they went backward, it was wrong too. If they hurried, they were hurrying for the purpose of wrecking. If they moved methodically, it meant wrecking by slowing down tempos. If they were painstaking in developing some branch of industry, it was intentional delay, sabotage. And if they indulged in capricious leaps, their intention was to produce an imbalance for the purpose of wrecking. Using capital for repairs, improvements, or capital readiness was tying up capital funds. And if they allowed equipment to be used until it broke down, it was a diversionary action! (In addition, the interrogators would get all this information out of them by subjecting them to sleeplessness and punishment cells and then de-

14. *Ibid.,* p. 204.
15. *Ibid.,* p. 425.
16. *Ibid.,* p. 356.

manding that they give convincing examples of how they might have carried on wrecking activities.)

"Give us a clear example! Give us a clear example of your wrecking activity!" the impatient Krylenko urges them on.

(They will give you outstanding examples! Just wait! Soon someone will write *the history of the technology* of those years! He will give you examples—and negative examples. He will evaluate for you all the convulsions of your epileptic "Five-Year Plan in Four Years." Then we will find out how much of the people's wealth and strength was squandered. Then we will find out how all the best projects were destroyed, and how the worst projects were carried out by the worst means. Well, yes, if the Mao Tse-tung breed of Red Guard youths supervise brilliant engineers, what good can come of it? Dilettante enthusiasts— they were the ones who egged on their even stupider leaders.)

Yes, full details are a disservice. Somehow the more details provided, the less the evil deeds seem to smell of execution.

But just a moment! We've not had everything yet! The most important crimes all lie ahead! Here they are, here they come, comprehensible and intelligible to every illiterate! The Promparty (1) prepared the way for the Intervention; (2) took money from the imperialists; (3) conducted espionage; (4) assigned cabinet posts in a future government.

And that did it! All mouths were shut. And all those who had been expressing their reservations fell silent. And only the tramping of demonstrators could be heard, and the roars outside the window: *"Death! Death! Death!"*

What about some more details? Why should you want more details? Well, then, if that's the way you want it; but they will only be more frightening. They were all acting under orders from the French General Staff. After all, France doesn't have enough worries, or difficulties, or party conflicts of its own, and it is enough just to whistle, and, lo and behold, divisions will march. . . . Intervention! First they planned it for 1928. But they couldn't come to an agreement, they couldn't tie up all the loose ends. All right, so they postponed it to 1930. But once more they couldn't agree among themselves. All right, 1931 then. And, as a matter of fact, here's how it was to go: France herself would not fight but, as her commission for organizing the deal, would take the Ukraine right bank as her share. England wouldn't fight either, of course, but, in order to raise a scare, promised to send her fleet into the Black Sea and into the Baltic—in return, she would get Caucasian oil. The actual warriors would, for the most part, be the following: 100,000 émigrés (true, they had long since scattered to the four winds, but it would take only a whistle to gather them all together again immediately); Poland —for which she would get half the Ukraine; Rumania (whose brilliant successes in World War I were famous—she was a formidable enemy). And then there were Latvia and Estonia. (These two small countries would willingly drop all the concerns of their young governments and rush forth en masse to do battle.) And the most frightening thing of all was the direction of the main blow. How's that? Was it already known? Yes! It would begin from Bessarabia, and from there, *keeping to* the right bank of the Dnieper, it would move *straight* on Moscow.[17] And at that fateful moment, would not all our railroads certainly be blown up? No, not at all. *Bottlenecks would be created!* And the Promparty would also yank out the fuses in electric power stations, and the entire Soviet Union would be plunged into darkness, and all our machinery would come to a halt, including the textile machinery! And sabotage would be carried out. (Attention, defendants! You must not name your methods of sabotage, nor the factories which were your objectives, nor the geographic sites involved, until the closed session. And you must not name names, whether foreign or our own!) Combine all this with the fatal blow which will have been dealt the textile industry by that time! Add the fact that the saboteurs will have constructed two or three textile factories in Byelorussia which will serve as *a base of operations for the interventionists.*[18] With the textile factories already in their hands, the interventionists would march implacably on Moscow. But here was the cleverest part of the whole plot: though they didn't succeed in doing so, they had wanted to drain the Kuban marshes and the Polesye swamps, and the swamp near Lake Ilmen (Vyshinsky had forbidden them to name the exact places, but one of the witnesses blurted them

17. Who drew that arrow for Krylenko on a cigarette pack—was it not drawn by the same hand that thought up our entire defense strategy in 1941?
18. *Protsess Prompartii,* p. 356. This was not intended as a joke.

out), and then the interventionists would open up the shortest routes and would get to Moscow without wetting their feet or their horses' hoofs. (And why was it so hard for the Tatars? Why was it that Napoleon didn't reach Moscow? Yes! It was because of the Polesye and the Ilmen swamps. And once those swamps were drained, the capital would lie exposed.) On top of that, don't forget to add that hangars had been built there under the guise of sawmills (places not to be named!) so that the planes of the interventionists would not get wet in the rain and could be taxied into them. And *housing for the interventionists* had also been built (do not name the places!). (And where had all the homeless occupation armies been quartered in previous wars?) The defendants had received all the directives on these matters from the mysterious foreign gentlemen K. and R. (It is strictly forbidden to name their names—or to name the countries they come from!)[19] And most recently they had even begun "the preparation of treasonable actions by individual units of the Red Army." (Do not name the branches of the service, nor the units, nor the names of any persons involved!) True, they hadn't done any of this; but they had also intended (though they hadn't done that either) to organize within some central army institution a cell of financiers and former officers of the White armies. (Ah, the White Army? Write it down! Start making arrests!) And cells of anti-Soviet students. (Students? Write it down! Start making arrests!)

(Incidentally, don't push things too far. We wouldn't want the workers to get despondent and begin to feel that everything is falling apart, that the Soviet government has been caught napping. And so they also threw a good deal of light on that side of it: that *they had intended to do a lot and had accomplished very little, that not one industry had suffered serious losses!*)

But why didn't the Intervention take place anyway? For various complex reasons. Either because Poincaré hadn't been elected in France, or else because our émigré industrialists decided that their former enterprises had not yet been sufficiently restored by the Bolsheviks—let the Bolsheviks do more. And then, too, they couldn't seem to come to terms with Poland and Rumania.

19. *Ibid.*, p. 409.

So, all right, there hadn't been any intervention, but there was, at least, a Promparty! Do you hear the tramp of marching feet? Do you hear the murmur of the working masses: *"Death! Death! Death!"*? And the marchers were "those who in the event of war would have to atone with their deaths, and deprivations and sufferings, for the work of these men."[20]

(And it was as if he had looked into a crystal ball: it was indeed with their deaths, and deprivations and sufferings, that those trusting demonstrators would atone in 1941 for the work . . . *of these men!* But where is your finger pointing, prosecutor? At whom is your finger pointing?)

So then—why was it the Industrial *Party*? Why a party and not an Engineering-Technical Center? We are accustomed to having a *Center!*

Yes, there was a Center too. But they had decided to reorganize themselves into a party. It was more respectable. That way it would be easier to fight over cabinet posts in the future government. It would "mobilize the engineering-technical masses for the struggle for power." And whom would they be struggling against? Other parties, of course. Against the Working Peasants Party—the TKP—in the first place, for after all they had 200,000 members! Against the Menshevik Party in the second place! And as for a *Center,* those three parties together were to have constituted a United Center. But the GPU had destroyed them. "And it's a good thing they destroyed us." (All the defendants were glad!)

(And it was flattering to Stalin to annihilate three more *parties*. Would there have been any glory, indeed, in merely adding another three "Centers" to his list?)

And having a party instead of a Center meant having another Central Committee—yes, the Promparty's own Central Committee! True, there had not been any party conferences, nor had there been any elections, not even one. Whoever wanted to be on the Central Committee just joined up—five people all told. They all made way for one another, and they all yielded the post of chairman to one another too. There were no meetings—either of the Central Committee (no one else would remember this, but Ramzin would remember it very well indeed, and he

20. *Ibid.,* p. 437.

would name names) or of the groups from various branches of industry. There seemed even to be some dearth of members. As Charnovsky said, "There *never was* any formal organization of a Promparty." And how many members had there been? Larichev: "A count of members would have been difficult; the exact composition was unknown." And how had they carried out their wrecking? How had directives been communicated? Well, it was just a matter of whoever met whomever in some particular institution—directives were passed on orally. From then on everyone would carry out his own wrecking on his own conscience. (Well, now, Ramzin confidently named two thousand members. And whenever he named two, they arrested five. According to the documents in the trial, there were altogether thirty to forty thousand engineers throughout the U.S.S.R. That meant they would arrest every seventh one, and terrify the other six.) And what about contacts with the Working Peasants Party? Well, they might meet in the State Planning Commission, or else in the Supreme Council of the Economy, and "plan systematic acts against village Communists."

Where have we seen all this before? Aha! In *Aïda*. They are seeing Radames off on his campaign, and the orchestra is thundering, and eight warriors are standing there in helmets and with spears—and two thousand more are painted on the backdrop.

That's your Promparty.

But that's all right. It works. The show goes on! (Today it is quite impossible to believe just how threatening and serious it all looked at the time.) And it is hammered in by repetition, and every individual episode is gone over several times. And because of this the awful visions multiply. And, in addition, so that things won't become too bland, the defendants suddenly "forget" something terribly unimportant, or else they "try to renounce testimony"—and right then and there "they pin them down with cross-questioning," and it all winds up being as lively as the Moscow Art Theatre.

But Krylenko pressed too hard. On the one hand he planned to disembowel the Promparty—to disclose its social basis. That was a question of class, and his analysis couldn't go wrong. But Krylenko abandoned the Stanislavsky method, didn't assign the roles, relied on improvisation. He let everyone tell his own story of his own life, and what his relationship to the Revolution had been, and how he was led to participate in wrecking.

And, in one fell swoop, that thoughtless insertion, that human picture, spoiled all five acts.

The first thing that we learn to our astonishment is that all eight of these big shots of the bourgeois intelligentsia came from poor families: the son of a peasant; one of the many children of a clerk; the son of an artisan; the son of a rural schoolteacher; the son of a peddler. At school, they were all impoverished and earned the money for their education themselves, from the ages of twelve, thirteen, and fourteen. Some gave lessons, and some worked on locomotives. And here was what was monstrous: no one barred their way to an education! They all completed the courses in high school and in higher technological institutions, and they became important and famous professors. (How could that have been? They always told us that under Tsarism only the children of landowners and capitalists . . . Those calendars certainly couldn't have been lying!)

And here and *now,* in the Soviet period, engineers were in a very difficult position. It was almost impossible for them to provide their children with a higher education (after all, the children of the intelligentsia had the lowest priority, remember!). The court didn't argue, nor did Krylenko. (And the defendants themselves hastened to qualify what they had said, asserting that, against the background of the general and over-all victories, this, of course, was unimportant.)

Here we begin to distinguish bit by bit among the defendants, who, up to this point, had talked very much like one another. Their age differential also divided them with respect to probity. Those close to sixty and older made statements that aroused a friendly, sympathetic reaction. But forty-three-year-old Ramzin and Larichev, and thirty-nine-year-old Ochkin (the same one who had denounced Glavtop—the Main Fuels Committee—in 1921), were glib and shameless. And all the major testimony about the Promparty and intervention comes from them. Ramzin was the kind of person (as a result of his early and extraordinary successes) who was shunned by the entire engineering profession, and he endured it. At the trial he caught Krylenko's hints on the wing and volunteered precise statements. All the charges were founded on Ramzin's recollections. He possessed such self-control and force that he might very well have conducted plenipotentiary talks in Paris about intervention (on assignment from the GPU, obviously). Ochkin, too, was a fast climber: at twenty-nine he had already possessed "the unlimited trust of the Council of Labor and Defense and the Council of People's Commissars."

One couldn't say the same about sixty-two-year-old Professor Charnovsky: Anonymous students had persecuted him in the wall newspapers. After twenty-three years of lecturing, he had been summoned to a general students' meeting to "give an account of his work." He hadn't gone.

And in 1921 Professor Kalinnikov had headed an open struggle against the Soviet government—specifically a professors' strike. What it amounted to was this: Back in the days of the Stolypin repression, the Moscow Higher Technical School had won academic autonomy (including the right to fill important posts, elect a rector, etc.). In 1921 the professors in this school had re-elected Kalinnikov to a new term as rector, but the People's Commissariat didn't want him there and had designated its own candidate. However, the professors went on strike and were supported by the students—at that time there were no truly proletarian students—and Kalinnikov was rector for a whole year despite the wishes of the Soviet government. (It was only in 1922 that they had wrung the neck of that autonomy, and even then, in all probability, not without arrests.)

Fedotov was sixty-six years old and he had been a factory engineer eleven years longer than the whole life span of the Russian Social Democratic Workers' Party—from which the Soviet Communist Party had sprung. He had worked at all the spinning mills and textile factories in Russia. (How hateful such people are, and how desirable it is to get rid of them as quickly as possible!) In 1905 he had left his position as a director of the Morozov textile firm and the high salary which went with it because he preferred to attend the "Red Funerals" which followed the caskets of the workers killed by the Cossacks. And now he was ill, had poor eyesight, and was too weak to leave home at night even to go to the theater.

And such people organized intervention? And economic ruin? Charnovsky had not had any free evenings for many years because he had been so busy with his teaching and with developing new sciences—such as the science of the organization of production and the scientific principles of rationalization. I recall from my own childhood the engineering professors of those years, and that's exactly what they were like. Their evenings were given up to their students at all levels, and they didn't get home to their families until 11 P.M. After all, at the beginning of the Five-Year Plan there were only thirty thousand of them for the whole country. They were all strained to the breaking point.

And it was these people who were supposed to have contrived a crisis, to have spied in exchange for handouts?

Ramzin uttered just one honest phrase during the whole trial: "The path of wrecking is alien *to the inner structure* of engineering."

Throughout the trial Krylenko forced the defendants to concede apologetically that they were "scarcely conversant" with or were "illiterate" in politics. After all, politics is much more difficult and much loftier than some kind of metallurgy or turbine design. In politics your head won't help you, nor will your education. Come on! Answer me! What was your attitude toward the October Revolution when it happened? Skeptical. *In other words,* immediately hostile. Why? Why? Why?

Krylenko hounded them with his theoretical questions—and as a result of simple human slips of the tongue inconsistent with their assigned roles, the nucleus of the truth is disclosed to us— as to *what really had taken place* and from what the entire bubble had been blown.

What the engineers had first seen in the October coup d'état was ruin. (And for three years there had truly been ruin and nothing else.) Beyond that, they had seen the loss of even the most elementary freedoms. (And these freedoms never returned.) How, then, could engineers *not have wanted* a democratic republic? How could *engineers* accept the *dictatorship of the workers,* the dictatorship of their subordinates in industry, so little skilled or trained and comprehending neither the physical nor the economic laws of production, but now occupying the top positions, from which they supervised the *engineers?* Why shouldn't the engineers have considered it more natural for the structure of society to be headed by those who could intelligently direct its activity? (And, excepting only the question of the *moral* leadership of society, is not this precisely where all social cybernetics is leading today? Is it not true that professional politicians are boils on the neck of society that prevent it from turning its head and moving its arms?) And why shouldn't engineers have political views? After all, politics is not even a science, but is an empirical area not susceptible to description by any mathematical apparatus; furthermore, it is an area subject to human egotism and blind passion. (Even in the trial Charnovsky speaks out: "Politics must, nonetheless, be guided to some degree by the findings of technology.")

The wild pressures of War Communism could only sicken the engineers. An engineer cannot participate in irrationality, and until 1920 the majority of them did nothing, even though they were barbarically impoverished. When NEP—the New Economic Policy—got under way, the engineers willingly went back to work. They accepted NEP as an indication that the government had come to its senses. But, alas, conditions were not what they had been. The engineers were looked on as a socially suspicious element that did not even have the right to provide an education for its own children. Engineers were paid immeasurably low salaries in proportion to their contribution to production. But while their superiors demanded successes in production from them, and discipline, they were deprived of the authority to impose this discipline. Any worker could not only refuse to carry out the instructions of an engineer, but could insult and even strike him and go unpunished—and as a representative of the ruling class the worker was *always right* in such a case.

Krylenko objects: "Do you remember the Oldenborger trial?" (In other words, how we, so to speak, defended him.)

Fedotov: "Yes. He had to lose his life in order to attract some attention to the predicament of the engineer."

Krylenko (disappointed): "Well, that was not how the matter was put."

Fedotov: "He died and *he was not the only one to die. He died voluntarily, and many others were killed.*"[21]

Krylenko was silent. That meant it was true. (Leaf through the Oldenborger trial again, and just imagine the persecution. And with the additional final line: "Many other were killed.")

21. *Ibid.,* p. 228.

So it was that the engineer was to blame for everything, even when he had done nothing wrong. But if he actually had made a real mistake, and after all he was a human being, he would be torn to pieces unless his colleagues could manage to cover things up. For would *they* value honesty? So the engineers then were forced at times to lie to the Party leadership?

To restore their authority and prestige, the engineers really had to unite among themselves and help each other out. They were all in danger. But they didn't need any kind of conference, any membership cards, to achieve such unity. Like every kind of mutual understanding between intelligent and clear-thinking people, it was attained by a few quiet, even accidental words; no kind of voting was called for. Only narrow minds need resolutions and the Party stick. (And this was something Stalin could never understand, nor could the interrogators, nor their whole crowd. They had never had any experience of human relationships of that kind. They had never seen anything *like that* in Party history!) In any case, that sort of unity had long existed among Russian engineers in their big illiterate nation of petty tyrants. It had already been tested for several decades. But now a new government had discovered it and become alarmed.

Then came 1927. And the rationality of the NEP period went up in smoke. And it turned out that the entire NEP was merely a cynical deceit. Extravagantly unrealistic projections of a super-industrial forward leap had been announced; impossible plans and tasks had been assigned. In those conditions, what was there for the collective engineering intelligence to do—the engineering leadership of the State Planning Commission and the Supreme Council of the Economy? To submit to insanity? To stay on the sidelines? It would have cost them nothing. One can write any figures one pleases on a piece of paper. But "our comrades, our colleagues in actual production, will not be able to fulfill these assignments." And that meant it was necessary to try to introduce some moderation into these plans, to bring them under the control of reason, to eliminate entirely the most outrageous assignments. To create, so to speak, their own State Planning Commission of engineers in order to correct the stupidities of the leaders. And the most amusing thing was that this was in *their* interests—the interests of the leaders—too. And in the interests of all industry and of all the people, since ruinous decisions could be avoided, and squandered, scattered millions could be picked up from the ground. To defend *quality*—"the heart of technology"—amid the general uproar about *quantity,* planning, and overplanning. And to indoctrinate students with this spirit.

That's what it was, the thin, delicate fabric of the truth. *That is what it really was.*

But to utter such thoughts aloud in 1930 meant being shot.

And yet it was still too little and too invisible to arouse the wrath of the mob.

It was therefore necessary to reprocess the silent and redeeming collusion of the engineers into crude wrecking and intervention.

Thus, in the picture they substituted, we nonetheless caught a fleshless—and fruitless—vision of the truth. The work of the stage director began to fall apart. Fedotov had already blurted out something about sleepless nights (!) during the eight months of his imprisonment; and about some important official of the GPU who had recently *shaken his hand* (?) (so there must have been a deal: you play your roles, and the GPU will carry out its promises?). And even the witnesses, though their role was incomparably less important, began to get confused.

Krylenko: "Did you participate in this group?"

Witness Kirpotenko: "Two or three times, when questions of intervention were being considered."

And that was just what was needed!

Krylenko (encouragingly): "Go on."

Kirpotenko (a pause): *"Other than that nothing is known."*

Krylenko urges him on, tries to give him his cue again.

Kirpotenko (stupidly): *"Other than intervention nothing is known to me."*[22]

Then, when there was an actual confrontation with Kupriyanov, the facts no longed jibed. Krylenko got angry, and he shouted at the inept prisoners:

"Then you just have to fix things so you come up with the same answers."

And in the recess, behind the scenes, everything was once more brought up to snuff. All the defendants were once again nervously awaiting their cues. And Krylenko prompted all eight

22. *Ibid.,* p. 354.

of them at once: the émigré industrialists had published an article abroad to the effect that they had held no talks at all with Ramzin and Larichev and knew nothing whatever about any Promparty, and that the testimony of the witnesses had in all likelihood been forced from them by torture. Well, what are you going to say to that?

Good Lord! How outraged the defendants were! They clamored for the floor without waiting their turns. What had become of that weary calm with which they had humiliated themselves and their colleagues for seven days? Boiling indignation at those émigrés burst from them. They demanded permission to send a written declaration to the newspapers *in defense of GPU methods*. (Now, wasn't that an embellishment? Wasn't that a jewel?) And Ramzin declared: "Our presence here is sufficient proof that we were not subjected to tortures and torments!" (And what, pray tell, would be the use of tortures that made it impossible for the defendants to appear in court!) And Fedotov: "Imprisonment did me *good* and not only me. . . . I even feel *better* in prison than in freedom." And Ochkin: "Me too. I feel better too!"

It was out of sheer generosity that Krylenko and Vyshinsky declined their offer of a collective declaration. They certainly would have written one! And they certainly would have signed it!

But maybe someone had some lingering suspicions still? Well, in that case, Comrade Krylenko vouchsafed them a flash of his brilliant logic. "If we should admit even for one second that these people were telling untruths, then *why were they arrested* and why did they all at once start *babbling* their heads off?"[23]

Now that is the power of logic for you! For a thousand years prosecutors and accusers had never even imagined that the fact of arrest might in itself be a proof of guilt. If the defendants were innocent, then why had they been arrested? And once they had been arrested, that meant they were guilty!

And, indeed, *why had they started babbling away?*

"The question of torture we discard! . . . But let us put the question psychologically: Why did they confess? And I ask you: *What else could they have done?*"[24]

23. *Ibid.*, p. 452.
24. *Ibid.*, p. 454.

Well, how true! How psychological! If you ever *served* time in that institution, just recollect: what else was there to do?

(Ivanov-Razumnik wrote[25] that in 1938 he was imprisoned in the same cell in the Butyrki as Krylenko, and that Krylenko's place in the cell was under the board bunks. I can picture that vividly—since I have crawled there myself. The bunks were so low that the only way one could crawl along the dirty asphalt floor was flat on one's stomach, but newcomers could never adapt and would try to crawl on all fours. They would manage to get their heads under, but their rear ends would be left sticking out. And it is my opinion that the supreme prosecutor had a particularly difficult time adapting, and I imagine that his rear end, not yet grown thin, used to stick out there for the greater glory of Soviet justice. Sinful person that I am, I visualize with malice that rear end sticking out there, and through the whole long description of these trials it somehow gives me solace.)

Yes, the prosecutor expounded, continuing along the same line, if all this about tortures was true, then it was impossible to understand what could have induced all the defendants to confess, unanimously and in chorus, without any arguments and deviations. Just where could such colossal collusion have been carried out? After all, they had no chance to communicate with each other during the interrogation period.

(Several pages further along, a witness who survived will tell us *where*.)

Now it is not for me to tell the reader but for the reader to tell me just what the notorious "riddle of the Moscow trials of the thirties" consisted of. At first people were astounded at the *Promparty* trial, and then that riddle was transferred to the trials of the Party leaders.

After all, they didn't put on trial in open court the two thousand who had been dragged into it, or even two or three hundred, but only eight people. It is not as hard as all that to direct a chorus of eight. And *as for his choices*, Krylenko was free to *choose* from thousands over a period of two years. Palchinsky had not been broken, but had been shot—and posthumously named "the leader of the Promparty," which is what he was called in the testimony, even though no word of his survived.

25. Ivanov-Razumnik, *Tyurmy i Ssylki* (*Prisons and Exiles*), New York, Chekhov Publishing House, 1953.

And they had hoped to beat what they wanted out of Khrenni-kov, and Khrennikov didn't yield to them either; therefore he appeared just once in the record—in a footnote in small type: "Khrennikov died during the course of his interrogation." The small type you are using is for fools, but we at least know, and we will write it in double-sized letters: TORTURED TO DEATH DURING INTERROGATION. He, too, was posthum-ously named a leader of the Promparty, but there wasn't one least little fact from him, not one tiny piece of testimony in the general chorus, not one. *Because he did not give even one!* (And then all at once Ramzin appeared! He was a find. What energy and what a grasp! And he was ready to do anything in order to *live!* And what talent! He had been arrested only at the end of the summer, just before the trial really—and he not only man-aged to enter fully into his role, but it seemed as though he had written the whole play. He had absorbed a whole mountain of interrelated material, and he could serve it up spick-and-span, any name at all, any fact at all. And sometimes he manifested the languid ornateness of a *bigwig* scientist: "The activity of the Promparty was so widespread that even in the course of an eleven-day trial there is no opportunity to disclose it in total detail.") (In other words, go on and look for it, look further!) "I am firmly convinced that a small anti-Soviet stratum *still exists* in engineering circles." (Go get 'em, go get 'em, grab some more!) And how capable he was: he knew that it was a *riddle,* and that a riddle must be given an artistic explanation. And, unfeeling as a stick of wood, he found then and there within himself "the traits of the Russian criminal, for whom purification lay in public recantation before all the people."[26]

So what it comes down to is that all Krylenko and the GPU had to do was select the right people. But the risk was small. Goods spoiled in interrogation could always be sent off to the grave. And whoever managed to get through both the frying pan and the fire could always be given medical treatment and be fattened up, and put on public trial!

26. Ramzin has been undeservedly neglected in Russian memories. In my view, he fully deserved to become the prototype of a cynical and dazzling traitor. The Bengal fire of betrayal! He wasn't the only such villain of this epoch, but he was certainly a prominent case.

So then where is the riddle? How they were *worked over?* Very simply: Do you want to *live?* (And even those who don't care about themselves care about their children or grandchildren.) Do you understand that it takes absolutely no effort to have you shot, without your ever leaving the courtyards of the GPU? (And there was no doubt whatever about that. Whoever hadn't yet learned it would be given a course in being ground down by the Lubyanka.) But it is useful both for you and for us to have you act out a certain drama, the text for which you, as specialists, are going to write yourselves, and we, as prosecutors, are going to learn by heart . . . and we will try to remember the technical terms. (Krylenko sometimes made mistakes during the trial. He said "freight car axle" instead of "locomotive axle.") It will be unpleasant to perform and you will feel ashamed, but you just have to suffer through it. After all, it is better to *live*. And what assurance have we that you won't shoot us afterward? Why should we take vengeance on you? You are excellent specialists and you have not committed any crimes and we value you. Look at how many wrecking trials there have been; you'll see that no one who behaved has been shot. (Mercy for the defendants who cooperated in one trial was an important prerequisite for the success of the next. And hope was transmitted via this chain right up to Zinoviev and Kamenev themselves.) But the understanding is that you have to carry out *all* our conditions to the very last! The trial must work for the good of socialist society.

And the defendants would fulfill *all* the conditions.

Thus they served up all the subtlety of engineers' intellectual opposition as dirty wrecking on a level low enough to be comprehensible to the last illiterate in the country. (But they had not yet descended to the level of ground glass in the food of the workers. The prosecutors had not yet thought that one up.)

A further theme was ideological motivation. Had they begun to wreck? It was the result of a hostile motivation. And now they jointly collaborated in confessing? It was once again the result of ideological motivation, for they had been converted (in prison) by the blazing blast-furnace face of the third year of the Five-Year Plan! Although in their last words they begged for their lives, that wasn't the main thing for them. (Fedotov: "There is no forgiveness for us. The prosecutor is right!") The main

398 | THE GULAG ARCHIPELAGO

thing for these strange defendants right at that moment, on the threshold of death, was to convince the people and the whole world of the infallibility and farsightedness of the Soviet government. Ramzin, in particular, glorified the "revolutionary consciousness of the proletarian masses and their leaders," who had been "able to find immeasurably more dependable paths of economic policy" than the scientists, and who had calculated the tempos of economic growth rate far more correctly. And then: "I had come to understand it was necessary to make a jump ahead, and that it was necessary to make a *leap* forward,[27] that it was necessary to capture by storm," etc., etc. And Larichev declared: "The Soviet Union is invincible against the weakening capitalist world." And Kalinnikov: "The dictatorship of the proletariat is an inevitable necessity." And further: "The interests of the people and the interests of the Soviet government merge into one purposeful whole." Yes, and in addition, in the countryside "the general line of the Party, the destruction of the kulaks, is correct." They had time, while awaiting execution, to deliver themselves of judgments about everything. And the repenting intellectuals even had enough voice for such a prophecy as this: "In proportion to the development of society, individual life is going to become more circumscribed. . . . Collective will is the highest form."[28]

Thus it was that with eight-horse traction all the goals of the trial were attained:

1. All the shortages in the country, including famine, cold, lack of clothing, chaos, and obvious stupidities, were blamed on the engineer-wreckers.

2. The people were terrified by the threat of imminent intervention from abroad and therefore prepared for new sacrifices.

3. Leftist circles in the West were warned of the intrigues of their governments.

4. The solidarity of the engineers was destroyed; all the intelligentsia was given a good scare and left divided within itself. And so that there should be no doubt about it, this purpose of the trial was once more clearly proclaimed by Ramzin:

27. *Protsess Prompartii,* p. 504. And that is how they were talking here in the Soviet Union, *in our own country,* in 1930, when Mao Tse-tung was still a stripling.
28. *Ibid.,* p. 510.

"I would like to see that, in consequence of the present trial of the Promparty, *the dark and shameful past of the entire intelligentsia* will be buried once and for all."[29]

Larichev joined in: "This caste must be *destroyed!* . . . There is not and *there cannot be loyalty among engineers!*"[30] And Ochkin too: The intelligentsia "is some kind of mush. As the state accuser has said, it has no backbone, and this constitutes unconditional spinelessness. . . . How immeasurably superior is the sensitivity of the proletariat."[31]

So now just why should such diligent collaborators be shot?

And that was the way the history of our intelligentsia has been written for decades—from the anathema of 1920 (the reader will remember: "not the brains of the nation, but shit," and "the ally of the black generals," and "the hired agent of imperialism") right up to the anathema of 1930.

So should anyone be surprised that the word "intelligentsia" got established here in Russia as a term of abuse.

That is how the public trials were manufactured. Stalin's searching mind had once and for all attained its ideal. (Those blunderheads Hitler and Goebbels would come to envy it and rush into their shameful failure with the burning of the Reichstag.)

The standard had been set, and now it could be retained perennially and performed over again every season—according to the wishes of the Chief Producer. And in fact the Chief wanted another within three months. The rehearsal time was very short, but that was all right. Come and see the show! Only in our theater! A premiere.

M. The Case of the All-Union Bureau of the Mensheviks— March 1–9, 1931

The case was heard by a Special Assize of the Supreme Court, the presiding judge in this case, for some reason, being N. M. Shvernik. Otherwise everyone was in his proper place—Antonov-Saratovsky, Krylenko, and his assistant Roginsky. The pro-

29. *Ibid.,* p. 49.
30. *Ibid.,* p. 508.
31. *Ibid.,* p. 509. For some reason, the main thing about the proletariat is always, believe it or not, *sensitivity.* Always via the nostrils.

ducers were sure of themselves. For after all, the subject wasn't technical but was Party material, ordinary stuff. So they brought fourteen defendants onto the stage.

And it all went off not just smoothly but brilliantly.

I was twelve at the time. For three years I had been attentively reading everything about politics on the enormous pages of *Izvestiya*. I read the stenographic records of these two trials line by line. In the Promparty case, I had already felt, in my boyish heart, superfluity, falsehood, fabrication, but at least there were spectacular stage sets—universal intervention, the paralysis of all industry, the distribution of ministerial portfolios! In the trial of the Mensheviks, all the same stage sets were brought out, but they were more pallid. And the actors spoke their lines without enthusiasm. And the whole performance was a yawning bore, an inept, tired repetition. (Could it be that Stalin felt this, too, through his rhinoceros hide? How else can one explain his calling off the case of the Working Peasants Party after it had already been prepared, or why there were no more trials for several years?)

It would be boring to base our interpretations once again on the stenographic record. In any case, I have fresher evidence from one of the principal defendants in this case—Mikhail Petrovich Yakubovich. At the present moment, his petition for rehabilitation, exposing all the dirty work which went on, has filtered through to samizdat, our savior, and people are reading it just as it happened.[32] His story offers material proof and explanation of the whole chain of Moscow trials of the thirties.

How was the nonexistent "Union Bureau" created? The GPU had been given an assignment: they had been told to prove that the Mensheviks had adroitly wormed their way into—and seized —many important government jobs for counterrevolutionary purposes. The genuine situation did not jibe with this plan. There were no real Mensheviks in important posts. But then there were no real Mensheviks on trial either. (True, they say V. K. Ikov

32. He was refused rehabilitation. After all, the case in which he was tried had entered the golden tables of our history. After all, one cannot take back even one stone, because the entire building might collapse. Thus it is that M.P.Y. still has his conviction on his record. However, for his consolation, he has been granted a *personal* pension for his revolutionary activity! What monstrosities exist in our country.

actually was a member of the quiet, do-nothing illegal Moscow Bureau of the Mensheviks—but they didn't know that at the trial. He was processed in the second echelon and received a mere *eight*.) The GPU had its own design: two from the Supreme Council of the Economy, two from the People's Commissariat of Trade, two from the State Bank, one from the Central Union of Consumer Cooperatives, one from the State Planning Commission. (What a boring and unoriginal plan! Back in 1920, they had ordered, in the matter of the "Tactical Center," that it include two from the Union of Rebirth, two from the Council of Public Figures, two from this and that, etc.) Therefore they *picked* the individuals who suited them on the basis of their positions. And whether they were Mensheviks or not depended on whether one believed rumors. Some who got caught this way were not Mensheviks at all, but directives had been given to consider them Mensheviks. The genuine political views of those accused did not interest the GPU in the least. Not all the defendants even knew each other. And they raked in Menshevik witnesses, too, wherever they could find them.[33] (All the witnesses, without exception, were later given prison terms too.) Ramzin testified prolifically and obligingly at this trial also. But the GPU pinned its hopes on the principal defendant, Vladimir Gustavovich Groman (with the idea that he would *help* work up this *case* and be amnestied in return), and on the provocateur Petunin. (I am basing all this on Yakubovich's report.)

Let us now introduce M. P. Yakubovich. He had begun his revolutionary activity so early that he had not even finished the gymnasium. In March, 1917, he was already Chairman of the Smolensk Soviet. Impelled by the strength of his convictions, which continued to lead him on, he became a strong and successful orator. At the Congress of the Western Front, he impetuously called those journalists who were demanding that the war continue *enemies of the people*. And this was in April, 1917. He was

33. One was Kuzma A. Gvozdev, a man whose fate was bitter. This was the same Gvozdev who had been chairman of the workers' group in the War Industry Committee, and whom the Tsarist government, in an excess of stupidity, had arrested in 1916, and the February Revolution had made Minister of Labor. Gvozdev became one of the martyr *long-termers* of Gulag. I do not know how many years he had been imprisoned before 1930, but from 1930 on he was in prison continuously, and my friends knew him in Spassk Camp, in Kazakhstan, as late as 1952.

nearly hauled from the rostrum, and he apologized, but thereafter in his speech he maneuvered so adroitly and so won over
his listeners that at the end he called them enemies of the people
again, and this time to stormy applause. He was elected to the
delegation sent to the Petrograd Soviet, and hardly had he
arrived there than—with the informality of those days—he was
named to the Military Commission of the Petrograd Soviet. There
he exerted a strong influence on the appointment of army commissars,[34] and in the end he became an army commissar on the
Southwestern Front and personally arrested Denikin in Vinnitsa
(after the Kornilov revolt), and regretted very much indeed
(during the trial as well) that he had not shot him on the spot.

Clear-eyed, always sincere, and always completely absorbed
in his own ideas—whether they were right or wrong—he was
counted as—and was—one of the younger members of the Menshevik Party. This did not prevent him, however, from presenting
his own projects to the Menshevik leadership with boldness and
passion, such as, in the spring of 1917, proposing the formation
of a Social Democratic government, or, in 1919, recommending
that the Mensheviks enter the Comintern. (Dan and the others
invariably rejected all his plans and their variations, and quite
condescendingly, for that matter.) In July, 1917, he was very
pained by the action of the socialist Petrograd Soviet in approving the Provisional Government's calling up army units for use
against other socialists, considering it a fatal error even though
the other socialists were using armed force. Hardly had the October coup taken place than Yakubovich proposed to his party
that it should support the Bolsheviks wholeheartedly and work
to improve the state structure they were creating. In the upshot,
he was finally ostracized by Martov, and by 1920 he had left the
ranks of the Mensheviks once and for all, convinced that he
could not get them to follow the Bolsheviks' path.

I have gone into all this detail to make it quite clear that
throughout the Revolution Yakubovich had been not a Menshevik but a Bolshevik, and one who was entirely sincere and
disinterested. In 1920 he was still one of the Smolensk food-
supply commissars, and the only one of them who was not a

34. He is not to be confused with Colonel Yakubovich of the General Staff,
who, at the same time and the same meetings, represented the War Ministry.

Bolshevik. He was even honored by the People's Commissariat
of Food Supply as the *best*. (He claims that he got along without
reprisals against the peasantry, but I do not know whether or
not this is true. At his trial he did, however, recall that he had
organized "antispeculation" detachments.) In the twenties he
had edited the *Torgovaya Gazeta* (*The Trade Gazette*) and had
occupied other important posts. He had been arrested in 1930
when just such Mensheviks as he, "who had wormed their way
in," were to be rounded up in accordance with the GPU plans.

He had immediately been called in for questioning by Krylenko, who, earlier and always, as the reader already knows, *was
organizing* the chaos of the preliminary inquiry into efficient
interrogation. It turned out that they knew one another very
well, for in the years between the first trials Krylenko had gone
to that very Smolensk Province *to improve food-requisition work*.
And here is what Krylenko now said:

"Mikhail Petrovich, I am going to talk to you frankly: I consider you a Communist! [His words encouraged Yakubovich and
raised his spirits greatly.] *I have no doubt of your innocence.
But it is our Party duty, yours and mine, to carry out this trial.*
[Krylenko had gotten his orders from Stalin, and Yakubovich
was all atremble for the sake of the cause, like a zealous horse
rushing into the horse collar.] I beg you to help me in every
possible way, and to assist the interrogation. And in case of unforeseen difficulties during the trial, at the most difficult moments,
I will ask the chairman of the court to give you the floor."

!!!!

And Yakubovich promised. Conscious of his duty, he
promised. Indeed, the Soviet government had never before given
him such a responsible assignment.

And thus there was not the slightest need even to touch
Yakubovich during the interrogation. But that was too subtle
for the GPU. Like everyone else, Yakubovich was handed over
to the butcher-interrogators, and they gave him *the full treatment*
—the freezing punishment cell, the hot box, beating his genitals.
They tortured him so intensively that Yakubovich and his fellow
defendant Abram Ginzburg opened their veins in desperation.
After they had received medical attention, they were no longer
tortured and beaten. Instead, the *only* thing to which they were

subjected was two weeks of sleeplessness. (Yakubovich says: "Just to be allowed to sleep! Neither conscience nor honor matters any longer.") And then they were confronted with others who had already given in and who urged them to "confess" . . . to utter nonsense. And the interrogator himself, Aleksei Alekseyevich Nasedkin, said: "I know, I know, none of this actually happened! But they insist on it!"

On one occasion when Yakubovich had been summoned to interrogation, he found there a prisoner who had been tortured. The interrogator smiled ironically: "Moisei Isayevich Teitelbaum begs you to take him into your anti-Soviet organization. You can speak as freely as you please. I am going out for a while." He went out. Teitelbaum really did beg: "Comrade Yakubovich! I beg you, please take me into your Union Bureau of Mensheviks! They are accusing me of taking 'bribes from foreign firms' and threatening me with execution. But I would rather die a counterrevolutionary than a common criminal!" (It was likelier that they had promised him that as a counterrevolutionary he wouldn't be shot! And he wasn't wrong either: they gave him a juvenile prison term, a "fiver.") The GPU was so short on Mensheviks they had to recruit defendants from volunteers! (And, after all, Teitelbaum was being groomed for an important role—communication with the Mensheviks abroad and with the Second International! But they honorably kept the deal they had made with him—a "fiver.") And with the interrogator's approval Yakubovich *accepted* Teitelbaum as a member of the Union Bureau.

Several days before the trial began, the *first* organizing session of the Union Bureau of the Mensheviks convened in the office of the senior interrogator, Dmitri Matveyevich Dmitriyev—so as to coordinate things, and so that each should understand his own role better. (That's how the Central Committee of the Promparty convened too! That's *where* the defendants "could have met"—to answer Krylenko's earlier leading question.) But such a mountain of falsehood had been piled up that it was too much to absorb in one session and the participants got things mixed up, couldn't master it in one rehearsal, and were called together a second time.

What did Yakubovich feel as he went into the trial? Should

he not, in revenge for all the tortures to which he had been subjected, for all the falsehood shoved into his breast, create a sensational scandal and startle the world? But still:

1. To do so would be to stab the Soviet government in the back! It would be to negate his entire purpose in life, everything he had lived for, the whole path he had taken to extricate himself from mistaken Menshevism and become a right-minded Bolshevik.

2. After a scandal like that they wouldn't just allow him to die; they wouldn't just shoot him; they would torture him again, but this time out of vengeance, and drive him insane. But his body had already been exhausted by tortures. Where could he find the moral strength to endure new ones? Where could he unearth the required heroism?

(I wrote down his arguments as his heated words rang out— this being a most extraordinary chance to get, so to speak, a "posthumous" explanation from a participant in such a trial. And I find that it is altogether as though Bukharin or Rykov were explaining the reasons for their own mysterious submissiveness at their trials. Theirs were the same sincerity and honesty, the same devotion to the Party, the same human weakness, the same lack of the moral strength needed to fight back, because they had no *individual* position.)

And at the trial Yakubovich not only repeated obediently all the gray mass of lies which constituted the upper limit of Stalin's imagination—and the imagination of his apprentices and his tormented defendants. But he also played out his inspired role, as he had promised Krylenko.

The so-called Foreign Delegation of the Mensheviks—in essence the entire top level of their Central Committee—formally dissociated themselves from the defendants in a statement published in *Vorwärts*. They declared there that the trial was a shameful travesty, built on the testimony of provocateurs and unfortunate defendants forced into it by terror; that the overwhelming majority of the defendants had left the Party more than ten years earlier and had never returned; and that absurdly large sums of money were referred to at the trial, representing more than the party had ever disposed of.

And Krylenko, having read the article, asked Shvernik to

permit the defendants to reply—the same kind of pulling-all-strings-at-once he had resorted to at the trial of the Promparty. They all spoke up, and they all defended the methods of the GPU against the Menshevik Central Committee.

But what does Yakubovich remember today about his "reply" and his last speech? He recalls that he not only spoke as befitted his promise to Krylenko, but that instead of simply getting to his feet, he was seized and lifted up—like a chip on a wave—by a surge of anger and oratory. Anger against whom? After having learned what torture meant, and attempting suicide and coming close to death more than once, he was at this point in a real, honest-to-God rage. But not at the prosecutor or the GPU! Oh, no! At the Foreign Delegation of the Mensheviks!!! Now there's a psychological switch for you! There they sat, unscrupulous and smug, in security and comfort—for even the poverty of émigré life was, of course, comfort in comparison with the Lubyanka. And how could they refuse to pity *those* who were on trial, their torture and suffering? How could they so impudently dissociate themselves from them and deliver these unfortunates over to their fate? (The reply Yakubovich delivered was powerful, and the people who had cooked up the trial were delighted.)

Even when he was describing this in 1967, Yakubovich shook with rage at the Foreign Delegation, at their betrayal, their repudiation, their treason to the socialist Revolution—exactly as he had reproached them in 1917.

I did not have the stenographic record of the trial at the time. Later I found it and was astonished. Yakubovich's memory—so precise in every little detail, every date, every name—had in this instance betrayed him. He had, after all, said at the trial that the Foreign Delegation, on orders from the Second International, *had instructed them to carry out wrecking activities.* He no longer remembered this. The foreign Mensheviks' statement was neither unscrupulous nor smug. They had indeed *pitied* the unfortunate victims of the trial but did point out that they had not been Mensheviks for a long time—which was quite true. What was it, then, that made Yakubovich so unalterably and sincerely angry? And exactly how could the Foreign Delegation *not* have consigned the defendants to their fate?

We like to take our anger out on those who are weaker, those who cannot answer. It is a human trait. And somehow the arguments to prove we are right appear out of nowhere.

Krylenko said in his summation for the prosecution that Yakubovich was a fanatic advocate of counterrevolutionary ideas and demanded therefore that he be *shot*.

And Yakubovich that day felt a tear of gratitude roll down his cheek, and he feels it still to this day, after having dragged his way through many camps and detention prisons. Even today he is grateful to Krylenko for not humiliating him, for not insulting him, for not ridiculing him as a defendant, and for calling him correctly a *fanatic* advocate (even of an idea contrary to his real one) and for demanding simple, noble execution for him, that would put an end to all his sufferings! In his final statement, Yakubovich agreed with Krylenko himself: "The crimes to which I have confessed [he endowed with great significance his success in hitting on the expression *'to which I have confessed'*—anyone who understood would realize that he meant 'not those *which I committed'*] deserve the highest measure of punishment—and I do not ask any forgiveness! I do not ask that my life be spared!" (Beside him on the defendants' bench, Groman got excited! "You are insane! You have to consider your comrades. You don't have the right!")

Now wasn't he a find for the prosecutor?

And can one still say the trials of 1936 to 1938 are unexplained?

Was it not through this trial that Stalin came to understand and believe that he could readily round up all his loud-mouth enemies and get them organized for just such a performance as this?

And may my compassionate reader now have mercy on me! Until now my pen sped on untrembling, my heart didn't skip a beat, and we slipped along unconcerned, because for these fifteen years we have been firmly protected either by legal revolutionality or else by revolutionary legality. But from now on things will be painful: as the reader will recollect, as we have had explained to us dozens of times, beginning with Khrushchev, "from approximately 1934, violations of Leninist norms of legality began." And how are we to enter this abyss of illegality now? How are we to drag our way along yet another bitter stretch of the road?

However, *these* trials which follow were, because of the fame of the defendants, a cynosure for the whole world. They did not escape the attention of the public. They were written about. They were interpreted and they will be interpreted again and again. It is for us merely to touch lightly on their *riddle*.

Let us make one qualification, though not a big one; the published stenographic records did not coincide completely with what was said at the trials. One writer who received an entrance pass—they were given out only to selected individuals—took running notes and subsequently discovered these differences. All the correspondents also noted the snag with Krestinsky, which made a recess necessary in order to get him back on the track of his assigned testimony. (Here is how I picture it. Before the trial a chart was set up for emergencies: in the first column was the name of the defendant; in the second, the method to be used during the recess if he should depart from his text during the open trial; in the third column, the name of the Chekist responsible for applying the indicated method. So if Krestinsky departed from his text, then who would come on the run and what that person would do had already been arranged.)

But the inaccuracies of the stenographic record do not change or lighten the picture. Dumfounded, the world watched three plays in a row, three wide-ranging and expensive dramatic productions in which the powerful leaders of the fearless Communist Party, who had turned the entire world upside down and terrified it, now marched forth like doleful, obedient goats and bleated out everything they had been ordered to, vomited all over themselves, cringingly abased themselves and their convictions, and confessed to crimes they could not in any wise have committed.

This was unprecedented in remembered history. It was particularly astonishing in contrast with the recent Leipzig trial of Dimitrov. Dimitrov had answered the Nazi judges like a roaring lion, and, immediately afterward, his comrades in Moscow, members of that same unyielding cohort which had made the whole world tremble—and the greatest of them at that, those who had been called the "Leninist guard"—came before the judges drenched in their own urine.

And even though much appears to have been clarified since then—with particular success by Arthur Koestler—the *riddle* continues to circulate as durably as ever.

People have speculated about a Tibetan potion that deprives a man of his will, and about the use of hypnosis. Such explanations must by no means be rejected: if the NKVD possessed such methods, clearly *there were no moral rules* to prevent resorting to them. Why not weaken or muddle the will? And it is a known fact that in the twenties some leading hypnotists gave up their careers and entered the service of the GPU. It is also reliably known that in the thirties a school for hypnotists existed in the NKVD. Kamenev's wife was allowed to visit her husband before his trial and found him not himself, his reactions retarded. (And she managed to communicate this to others before she herself was arrested.)

But why was neither Palchinsky nor Khrennikov broken by the Tibetan potion or hypnosis?

The fact is that an explanation on a higher, psychological plane is called for.

One misunderstanding in particular results from the image of these men as old revolutionaries who had not trembled in Tsarist dungeons—seasoned, tried and true, hardened, etc., fighters. But there is a plain and simple mistake here. These defendants were *not those* old revolutionaries. They had acquired that glory by inheritance from and association with the Narodniks, the SR's, and the Anarchists. They were the ones, the bomb throwers and the conspirators, who had known hard-labor imprisonment and real prison *terms*—but even *they* had never in their lives experienced a *genuinely merciless interrogation* (because such a thing did not exist at all in Tsarist Russia). And *these others,* the Bolshevik defendants at the treason trials, had never known either interrogation or real prison terms. The Bolsheviks had never been sentenced to special "dungeons," any Sakhalin, any special hard labor in Yakutsk. It is well known that Dzerzhinsky had the hardest time of them all, that he had spent all his life in prisons. But, according to our yardstick, he had served *just a normal "tenner,"* just a simple *"ten-ruble bill,"* like any ordinary collective farmer in our time. True, included in that tenner were three years in the hard-labor central prison, but that is nothing special either.

The Party leaders who were the defendants in the trials of 1936 to 1938 had, in their revolutionary pasts, known short, easy imprisonment, short periods in exile, and had never even had a whiff of hard labor. Bukharin had many petty arrests on his record, but they amounted to nothing. Apparently, he was never imprisoned anywhere for a whole year at a time, and he had just a wee bit of exile on Onega.[35] Kamenev, despite long years of propaganda work and travel to all the cities of Russia, spent only two years in prison and one and a half years in exile. In our time, even sixteen-year-old kids got *five* right off. Zinoviev, believe it or not, *never spent as much as three months in prison.* He never received *even one sentence!* In comparison with the ordinary natives of our Archipelago they were all *callow youths;* they didn't know what prison was like. Rykov and I. N. Smirnov had been arrested several times and had been imprisoned for five years, but somehow they went through prison very easily, and they either escaped from exile without any trouble at all or were released because of an amnesty. Until they were arrested and imprisoned in the Lubyanka, they hadn't the slightest idea what a real prison was nor what the jaws of unjust interrogation were like. (There is no basis for assuming that if Trotsky had fallen into those jaws, he would have conducted himself with any less self-abasement, or that his resistance would have proved stronger than theirs. He had had no occasion to prove it. He, too, had known only easy imprisonment, no serious interrogations, and a mere two years of exile in Ust-Kut. The terror Trotsky inspired as Chairman of the Revolutionary Military Council was something he acquired very cheaply, and does not at all demonstrate any true strength of character or courage. Those who have condemned many others to be shot often wilt at the prospect of their own death. The two kinds of toughness are not connected.) And as for Radek—he was a plain provocateur. (And he wasn't the only one in these three trials!) And Yagoda was an inveterate, habitual criminal.

35. All the information here comes from Volume 41 of the *Granat Encyclopedia*, in which either autobiographical or reliable biographical essays on the leaders of the Russian Communist Party (Bolsheviks) are collected.

(This murderer of millions simply could not imagine that his superior Murderer, up top, would not, at the last moment, stand up for him and protect him. Just as though Stalin had been sitting right there in the hall, Yagoda confidently and insistently begged him directly for mercy: "I appeal to you! *For you* I built two great canals!" And a witness reports that at just that moment a match flared in the shadows behind a window on the second floor of the hall, apparently behind a muslin curtain, and, while it lasted, the outline of a pipe could be seen. Whoever has been in Bakhchisarai may remember that Oriental trick. The second-floor windows in the Hall of Sessions of the State Council are covered with iron sheets pierced by small holes, and behind them is an unlit gallery. It is never possible to guess down in the hall itself whether someone is up there or not. The Khan remained invisible, and the Council always met as if in his presence. Given Stalin's out-and-out Oriental character, I can readily believe that he watched the comedies in that October Hall. I cannot imagine that he would have denied himself this spectacle, this satisfaction.)

And, after all, our entire failure to understand derives from our belief in the unusual nature of these people. We do not, after all, where ordinary confessions signed by ordinary citizens are concerned, find their reasons for denouncing themselves and others so fulsomely baffling. We accept it as something we understand: a human being is weak; a human being gives in. But we consider Bukharin, Zinoviev, Kamenev, Pyatakov, I. N. Smirnov to be supermen to begin with—and, in essence, our failure to understand is due to that fact alone.

True, the directors of this dramatic production seem to have had a harder task in selecting the performers than they'd had in the earlier trials of the engineers: in those trials they had forty barrels to pick from, so to speak, whereas here the available troupe was small. Everyone knew who the chief performers were, and the audience wanted to see them in the roles and them only.

Yet there was a choice! The most farsighted and determined of those who were doomed did not allow themselves to be arrested. They committed suicide first (Skrypnik, Tomsky, Gamarnik). It was the ones who *wanted to live* who allowed themselves to be arrested. And one could certainly braid a rope from the ones who wanted to live! But even among them some behaved differently during the interrogations, realized what was happening, turned stubborn, and died silently but at least not shamefully. For some reason, they did not, after all, put on public trial Rudzutak, Postyshev, Yenukidze, Chubar, Kosior, and, for that matter, Krylenko himself, even though their names would have embellished the trials.

They put on trial the most compliant. A selection was made after all.

The men selected were drawn from a lower order, but, on the other hand, the mustached Producer knew each of them very well. He also knew that on the whole they were *weaklings,* and he knew, one by one, the particular weaknesses of each. Therein lay his dark and special talent, his main psychological bent and his life's achievement: to see people's weaknesses on the lowest plane of being.

And the man who seems, in the perspective of time, to have embodied the highest and brightest intelligence of all the disgraced and executed leaders (and to whom Arthur Koestler apparently dedicated his talented inquiry) was N. I. Bukharin. Stalin saw through him, too, at that lowest stratum at which the human being unites with the earth; and Stalin held him in a long death grip, playing with him as a cat plays with a mouse, letting him go just a little, and then catching him again. Bukharin wrote every last word of our entire existing—in other words, nonexistent—Constitution, which is so beautiful to listen to. And he flew about up there, just below the clouds, and thought that he had outplayed Koba: that he had thrust a constitution on him that would compel him to relax the dictatorship. And at that very moment, he himself had already been caught in those jaws.

Bukharin did not like Kamenev and Zinoviev, and way back when they had first been tried, after the murder of Kirov, he had said to people close to him: "Well, so what? That's the kind of people they were; maybe there was something to it. . . ." (That was the classic formula of the philistine in those years: "There was probably something to it. . . . In our country they don't arrest people for nothing." And that was said in 1935 by the leading theoretician of the Party!) He spent the period of the second trial of Kamenev and Zinoviev, in the summer of 1936, hunting in the Tien Shan, and knew nothing about it. He came down from the mountains to Frunze—and there he read that the death sentence had been imposed on both men, and read the newspaper articles which made clear what annihilating testimony they had given against him. But did he hasten to stop that act of repression? And did he protest to the Party that something monstrous was being done? No, all he did was send Koba a telegram asking him to postpone the execution of Kamenev and Zinoviev so that he, Bukharin, could get there to confront them and prove himself innocent.

It was too late! Koba had enough of the sworn testimony; why did he need living confrontations?

However, they still didn't arrest Bukharin for a long time. He lost his job as editor-in-chief of *Izvestiya* and all his other Party assignments and jobs, and he lived for half a year in his Kremlin apartment—in the Poteshny Palace of Peter the Great—as if in prison. (However, in the autumn he used to go to his dacha—and the Kremlin guards would salute him as though nothing at all had changed.) No one visited him or phoned him any longer. And all during these months he wrote endless letters: "Dear Koba! Dear Koba! Dear Koba!" And he got not one reply.

He was still trying to establish friendly contact with Stalin!

And *Dear Koba,* squinting, was already staging rehearsals. For many long years Koba had been holding tryouts for various roles, and he knew that *Bukharchik* would play his part beautifully. He had, after all, already renounced those of his pupils and supporters who had been arrested and exiled—they were few in number in any case—and had allowed them to be destroyed.[36] He had stood by and allowed his own line of thinking to be wiped out and pilloried before it was fully developed and born. And more recently, while he was still editor-in-chief of *Izvestiya* and a member of the Politburo, he had accepted as legal the execution of Kamenev and Zinoviev. Neither at the top of his lungs nor even in a whisper had he expressed any indignation over that. And yet these had all been tryouts for his own future role.

Way back in the past, when Stalin had threatened to expel him (and all the rest of them) from the Party, Bukharin (like all the rest) had renounced his views in order to remain in the Party. And that, too, had been a tryout for his role. If that was how

36. The only one he defended was Yefim Tseitlin—but not for long.

they acted while still in freedom and still at the height of honor and power, then they could certainly be depended on to follow the script of the play faultlessly when their body, their food, and their sleep were in the hands of the Lubyanka prompters.

And what did Bukharin fear most in those months before his arrest? It is reliably known that above all he feared expulsion from the Party! Being deprived of the Party! Being left alive but outside the Party! And *Dear Koba* had played magnificently on this trait of his (as he had with them all) from the very moment he had himself become the Party. Bukharin (like all the rest of them) did not have his own *individual point of view*. They didn't have their own genuine ideology of opposition, on the strength of which they could step aside and on which they could take their stand. Before they became an opposition, Stalin declared them to be one, and by this move he rendered them powerless. And all their efforts were directed toward staying in the Party. And toward not harming the Party at the same time!

These added up to too many different obligations for them to be independent.

In essence, Bukharin had been allotted the starring role, and nothing was to be overlooked or abridged in the Producer's work with him, in the working of time on him, and in his own getting used to the role. Even sending him to Europe the previous winter to acquire manuscripts by Marx had been essential—not just superficially, for the sake of the whole network of accusations about his establishing contacts, but so that the aimless freedom of life on tour might all the more insistently demand his return to the main stage. And now, beneath black thunderclouds of accusations, came the long, the interminable state of nonarrest, of exhausting housebound lethargy, which ground down the will power of the victim even more effectively than the direct pressure of the Lubyanka. (Nor would the Lubyanka run away either—it, too, would last for a year.)

On one occasion, Bukharin was summoned by Kaganovich, who arranged a confrontation between him and Sokolnikov in the presence of high-ranking Chekists. Sokolnikov gave testimony about "the parallel Rightist Center" (parallel, in other words, to that of the Trotskyites), and about Bukharin's underground activity. Kaganovich conducted the interrogation aggressively

and then ordered Sokolnikov to be taken away. And he said to
Bukharin in a friendly tone: "He lies in his teeth, the whore!"

Despite that, the newspapers continued to report the indignation of the masses. Bukharin telephoned the Central Committee.
Bukharin wrote letters beginning "Dear Koba," in which he
begged that the accusations against him be publicly denied. And
then the prosecutor's office published a roundabout declaration:
"Objective proofs for the indictment of Bukharin have not been
found."

Radek telephoned him in the fall, wanting to see him. Bukharin
shunned him: We are both being accused; why add another
cloud? But their *Izvestiya* country houses were next to each other,
and Radek dropped in on him one evening: "No matter what I
may say later on, please know that I am not to blame for anything.
And anyway you will come out of it whole: you were not connected with the Trotskyites."

And Bukharin believed he would come out of it whole and
that he would not be expelled from the Party. For that would be
monstrous! In actuality, he had always been hostile to the
Trotskyites: they had put themselves outside the Party and look
what had come of it! They had to stick together. Even if they
made mistakes, they had to stick together on that too.

At the November demonstration (his farewell to Red Square),
he and his wife went to the reviewing stand for guests on his
newspaper editor's press card. All at once an armed soldier came
up to him. His heart stopped! They were going to do it here? At
a time like this? No. The soldier saluted: "Comrade Stalin is surprised at your being here. He asks you to take your place on the
mausoleum."

And that's the way they tossed him back and forth from hot
to cold for the entire half-year. On December 5 they adopted the
Bukharin constitution with fanfare and celebration and named
it the Stalinist Constitution for all eternity. At the December
Plenum of the Central Committee, they brought in Pyatakov,
with his teeth knocked out, and not a bit like himself. Behind
his back stood silent Chekists (Yagoda men, and Yagoda, after
all, was also being tested and prepared for a role). Pyatakov
delivered himself of the most repulsive sort of testimony against
Bukharin and Rykov, both of whom were sitting right there

among the leaders. Ordzhonikidze put his hand up to his ear
(he was hard of hearing): "See here, are you giving all this
testimony *voluntarily?*" (Note that down! Ordzhonikidze will get
a bullet of his own!) "Absolutely voluntarily"—and Pyatakov
swayed on his feet. And during the recess, Rykov said to Bukharin: "Tomsky had will power. He understood it all back in
August, and he ended his own life. While you and I, like fools,
have gone on living."

At this point Kaganovich made an angry, condemnatory speech
(he wanted so much to believe in Bukharchik's innocence, but
he couldn't any longer). And then Molotov. And then Stalin!
What a generous heart! What a memory for the good things!
"Nonetheless, I consider that Bukharin's guilt has not yet been
proven. Perhaps Rykov is guilty, but not Bukharin." (Someone
had drawn up charges against Bukharin against his will!)

From cold to hot. That's how will power collapses. That's how
to grow used to the role of a ruined hero.

And then they began to bring to his home day after day the
records of interrogations: the depositions of young ex-students in
the Institute of Red Professors, of Radek, and all the rest of
them. And they all provided the gravest proofs of Bukharin's
black treason. They took these documents to his home, not as
if he were a defendant—oh, by no means! Merely in his position
as a member of the Central Committee—merely for his information.

Usually, when he received a new batch of these materials, Bukharin would say to his twenty-two-year-old wife, who only that
spring had given him a son: "You read them. I can't." And he
would bury his head in his pillow. He had two revolvers at home.
(Stalin was giving him time too.) And yet he did not commit
suicide.

Is it not clear that he had grown used to his ordained role?

And one more public trial took place. And they shot one more
batch of defendants. And yet they continued to be merciful to
Bukharin. They had not taken Bukharin.

At the beginning of February, 1937, he decided to go on a
hunger strike at home, in order to force the Central Committee
to hold a hearing and clear him of the charges against him. He
announced it in a letter to "Dear Koba," and he honestly went

through with it too. Then a Plenum of the Central Committee was convened with the following agenda: (1) the crimes of the Rightist *Center;* (2) the anti-Party conduct of Comrade Bukharin, as evidenced by his hunger strike.

Bukharin hesitated. Had he perhaps really insulted the Party in some particular way? Unshaven, thin, wan, already a prisoner in appearance, he dragged himself along to the Plenum. "What on earth were you thinking of?" Dear Koba asked him cordially. "But what was I to do in the face of such accusations? They want to expel me from the Party." Stalin made a wry face at the absurdity: "Come on, now. No one is going to expel you from the Party!"

Bukharin believed him and revived. He willingly assured the Plenum of his repentance, and immediately abandoned his hunger strike. (At home he said: "Come on now, cut me some sausage! Koba said they wouldn't expel me.") But in the course of the Plenum, Kaganovich and Molotov (impudent fellows they were, indeed!—paid no attention to Stalin's opinion!)[37] both called Bukharin a Fascist hireling and demanded that he be shot.

And once again Bukharin's spirits fell, and in his last days he began to compose his "Letter to the Future Central Committee." Committed to memory and thereby preserved, it recently became known to the whole world. However, it did not shake the world to its foundations.[38] For what were the last words this brilliant theoretician decided to hand down to future generations? Just one more cry of anguish and a plea to be restored to the Party. (He paid dearly in shame for that devotion!) And one more affirmation that he "fully approved" everything that had happened up to and including 1937. And that included not only all the previous jeeringly mocking trials, but also all the foul-smelling waves of our great prison sewage disposal system.

And that is how he himself certified that he, too, deserved to plunge into those waves.

So, at long last, he had matured to the point of being turned over to the prompters and the assistant producers—this muscular man, this hunter and wrestler! (In playful tussles in the presence of the Central Committee, how many times had he landed Stalin

---

37. See what a wealth of information we are deprived of because we're protecting Molotov's noble old age.
38. Nor did it shake the "Future Central Committee" either.

flat on his back! And this, too, was probably something Koba couldn't forgive him.)

And in the case of one so fully prepared, so demolished, that no torture was called for, how was his position any stronger than that of Yakubovich in 1931? How could he not be susceptible to the same two arguments? He was in fact much weaker, because Yakubovich longed for death, and Bukharin dreaded it.

There remained an easy dialogue with Vyshinsky along set lines:

"Is it true that every opposition to the Party is a struggle against the Party?" "In general it is, factually it is." "But a struggle against the Party cannot help but grow into a war against the Party." "According to the logic of things—yes, it must." "And that means that in the end, given the existence of oppositionist beliefs, any foul deeds whatever might be perpetrated against the Party [espionage, murder, sellout of the Motherland]?" "But wait a minute, none were actually committed." "But they *could have been?*" "Well, theoretically speaking." (Those are your theoreticians for you!) "But for us the highest of all interests are those of the Party?" "Yes, of course, of course!" "So you see, only a very fine distinction separates us. We are required to concretize the eventuality: in the interest of discrediting for the future any idea of opposition, we are required to accept as *having taken place* what *could* only theoretically have taken place. After all, it *could* have, couldn't it?" "It could have." "And so it is necessary to recognize as actual what was possible; that's all. It's a small philosophical transition. Are we in agreement? . . . Yes, and one thing more, and it's not for me to explain to you, but if you retreat and say something different during the trial, you understand that it will only play into the hands of the world bourgeoisie and will only do the Party harm. Well, and it's clear that in that case you yourself will not die an easy death. But if everything goes off all right, we will, of course, allow you to go on living. We'll send you in secret to the island of Monte Cristo, and you can work on the economics of socialism there." "But in previous trials, as I understand it, you did shoot them all?" "But what comparison is there between *you* and *them!* And then, we also left many of them alive too. They were shot only in the newspapers."

And so perhaps there isn't any insoluble riddle?

It was all that same invincible theme song, persisting with only minor variations through so many different trials: *"After all, we and you are Communists!* How could you have gotten off the track and come out against us? Repent! After all, you and we together—is *us!"*

Historical comprehension ripens slowly in a society. And when it does ripen, it is so simple. Neither in 1922, nor in 1924, nor in 1937 were the defendants able to hang onto their own point of view so firmly that they could raise their heads and shout, in reply to that bewitching and anesthetizing melody:

"No, we are not revolutionaries *with you!* No, we are not Russians *with you!* No, we are not Communists *with you!"*

It would seem that if only that kind of shout had been raised, all the stage sets would have collapsed, the plaster masks would have fallen off, the Producer would have fled down the backstairs, and the prompters would have sneaked off into their ratholes. And out of doors it would have been, say, 1967!

But even the most superbly successful of these theatrical productions was expensive and troublesome. And Stalin decided not to use open trials any longer.

Or rather in 1937 he probably did have a plan for holding public trials on a wide scale in the *local districts*—so the black soul of the opposition would be made visible to the *masses*. But he couldn't find producers who were good enough. It wasn't practical to prepare things so carefully, and the mental processes of the accused weren't so complex, and Stalin only got into a mess, although very few people know about it. The whole plan broke down after a few trials, and was abandoned.

It's appropriate here to describe one such trial—the Kady case, detailed reports of which the Ivanovo provincial newspapers published initially.

At the end of 1934, a new local administrative district was created in the remote wilds of Ivanovo Province at the point where it joined Kostroma and Nizhni Novgorod Provinces, and its center was situated in the ancient, slow-moving village of Kady. New leaders were sent there from various localities, and they made one another's acquaintance right in Kady. There they found a remote, sad, impoverished region, badly in need of money, machines, and intelligent economic management, but, instead, starved by grain procurements. It happened that Fyodor Ivanovich Smirnov, the First Secretary of the District Party Committee, was a man with a strong sense of justice; Stavrov, the head of the District Agricultural Department, was a peasant through and through, one of those peasants known as the intensivniki—in other words, the hard-working, zealous, and literate peasants who in the twenties had run their farms on a scientific basis, for which they were at that time rewarded by the Soviet government, since it had not yet been decided that all these intensivniki must be destroyed. Because Stavrov had entered the Party he had survived the liquidation of the kulaks. (And maybe he even took part in the liquidation of the kulaks?) These men tried to do something for the peasants in their new district, but directives kept pouring down from above and each one ran counter to some initiative of theirs; it was as if, up there, they were busy thinking up what they could do to make things worse and more desperate for the peasants. And at one point the leaders in Kady wrote the province leadership that it was necessary to *lower* the plan for procurement of breadgrains because the district couldn't fulfill the plan without becoming impoverished well below the danger point. One has to recall the situation in the thirties (and maybe not only the thirties?) to realize what sacrilege against the plan and what rebellion against the government this represented! But, in accordance with then current style, measures were not taken directly from above, but were left to local initiative. When Smirnov was on vacation, his deputy, Vasily Fyodorovich Romanov, the Second Secretary, arranged to have a resolution passed by the District Party Committee: "The successes of the district would have been even more brilliant [?] if it were not for the Trotskyite Stavrov." This set in motion the "individual case" of Stavrov. (An interesting approach: *Divide* and rule! For the time being, Smirnov was merely to be frightened, neutralized, and compelled to retreat; there would be time enough later on to get to him. And this, on a small scale, was precisely the Stalinist tactic in the Central Committee.) At stormy Party meetings, however, it became clear that Stavrov was about as much of a Trotskyite as he was a Jesuit. The head of the District Consumer Cooperatives, Vasily Grigoryevich Vlasov, a man with a ragtag, haphazard education but one of those native talents others are so surprised to find among Russians, a born retail trade executive, eloquent, adroit in an argument, who could get fired to red heat about anything he believed to be right, tried to persuade the Party meeting to *expel* Romanov from the Party for slander. And they actually did give Romanov an official Party rebuke! Romanov's last words in this dispute were typical of this kind of person, demonstrating his assurance in regard to the general situation: "Even though they proved Stavrov was not a Trotskyite, *nonetheless* I am sure he is a Trotskyite. *The Party will investigate,* and it will also investigate the rebuke to me." And the Party did investigate: the District NKVD arrested Stavrov almost immediately, and one month later they also arrested Univer, the Chairman of the District Executive Committee and an Estonian. And Romanov took over Univer's job as Chairman of the District Executive Committee. Stavrov was taken to the Provincial NKVD, where he confessed he was a Trotskyite, that he had acted in coalition with the SR's all his life, that he was a member of an underground *rightist* organization in his district (this is a bouquet worthy of the times, the only thing missing being a connection with the Entente). Perhaps he never really did confess these things, but no one is ever going to know, since he died from torture during interrogation in the internal prison of the Ivanovo NKVD. The pages of his deposition were there in full. Soon afterward, they arrested Smirnov, the secretary of the District Party Committee, as the head of the supposed rightist organization; and Saburov, the head of the District Financial Department, and someone else as well.

Of interest is the way in which Vlasov's fate was decided. He had only recently demanded the expulsion from the Party of Romanov, now the new Chairman of the District Executive Committee. He had also fatally offended Rusov, the district prosecutor, as we have already reported in Chapter 4, above. He had offended N. I. Krylov, the Chairman of the District NKVD, by protecting two of his energetic and resourceful executives from being arrested for supposed wrecking—both of them had black marks on their records because of their social origins. (Vlasov always hired all kinds of "former" people for his work—because they mastered the business effectively and, in addition, tried hard; people promoted from the ranks of the proletariat knew nothing and, more importantly, didn't want to know anything.) Nonetheless the NKVD was prepared to make its peace with the trade cooperative! Sorokin, the Deputy Chairman of the District NKVD, came in person to see Vlasov with a peace proposal: to give the NKVD 700 rubles' worth of materials without charging them for it (and later on we will somehow write it off). (The ragpickers! And that was two months' wages for Vlasov, who had never taken anything illegally for himself.) "And if you don't give it to us, you are going to regret it." Vlasov kicked him out: "How do you dare offer me, a Communist, a deal like that?" The very next day Krylov paid a call on the District Consumer Cooperative, this time as the representative of the District Committee of the Party. (This masquerade, like all these tricks, was in the spirit of 1937.) And this time he *ordered* the convening of a Party meeting; the agenda: "On the wrecking activities of Smirnov and Univer in the Consumers' Cooperatives," the report to be delivered by Comrade Vlasov. Well, now, that's a gem of a trick for you! No one at that point was making charges against Vlasov. But it would be quite enough for him to say two little words about the wrecking activities of the former secretary of the District Party Committee in his, Vlasov's, field, and the NKVD would interrupt: "And where were *you?* Why didn't you come to us in time?" In a situation of this sort many others would have lost their heads and allowed themselves to be trapped. But not Vlasov! He immediately replied: "I won't make the report! Let Krylov make the report—after all, he arrested Smirnov and Univer and is handling their case." Krylov refused: "I'm not familiar with the evidence." Vlasov replied: "If even *you* aren't familiar with the evidence, that means they were arrested without cause." So the Party meeting simply didn't take place. But how often did people dare to defend themselves? (We will not have a complete picture of the atmosphere of 1937 if we lose sight of the fact that there were still strong-willed people capable of difficult decisions, and if we fail to recall that late that night T., the senior bookkeeper of the District Consumer Cooperative, and his deputy N. came to Vlasov's office with 10,000 rubles: "Vasily Grigoryevich! Get out of town tonight! Don't wait for tomorrow. Otherwise you are finished!" But Vlasov thought it did not befit a Communist to run away.) The next morning there was a nasty article in the district paper on the work of the District Consumer Cooperative. (One has to point out that in 1937 the *press* always played hand in glove with the NKVD.) By evening Vlasov had been asked to give the District Party Committee an accounting of his own work. (Every step of the way, this was how things were in the entire Soviet Union.)

This was 1937, the second year of the so-called "Mikoyan prosperity" in Moscow and other big cities. And even today, in the reminiscences of journalists and writers, one gets the impression that at the time there was already plenty of everything. This concept seems to have gone down in history, and there is a danger of its staying there. And yet, in November, 1936, two years after the abolition of bread rationing, a secret directive was published in Ivanovo Province (and in other provinces) *prohibiting the sale of flour*. In those years many housewives in small towns, and particularly in villages, still used to bake their own bread. Prohibiting the sale of flour meant: Do not eat bread! In the district center of Kady, long bread lines formed such as had never before been seen. (However, they attacked that problem, too, by forbidding the baking of black bread in district centers, permitting only expensive white bread to be baked.) The only bakery in the whole Kady District was the one in the district center, and people began to pour into the center from the villages to get black bread. The warehouses of the District Consumer Cooperative had flour, but the two parallel prohibitions blocked off all avenues by which it could be made available to the public! Vlasov, however, managed to find a way out of the impasse, and despite the clever government rulings he kept the district fed for a whole year: he went out to the collective farms and got eight of them to agree to set up public bakeries in empty "kulak" huts (in other words, they would simply bring in firewood and set the women to baking in ordinary Russian peasant ovens, but, mind you, ovens which were now socialized, publicly not privately owned). The District Consumer Cooperative would undertake to supply them with flour. There is eternal simplicity to a solution once it has been discovered! Without building any bakeries (for which he had no funds), Vlasov set them up in one day. Without carrying on a trade in flour, he released flour from the warehouse continuously and proceeded to order more from the provincial center. Without selling black bread in the district center, he gave the district black bread. Yes, he did not violate the letter of the instructions, but he violated their *spirit*—for their essence was to compel a reduction in flour consumption by starving the people. And so, of course, there were good grounds for *criticizing* him at the District Party Committee.

After that criticism he remained free overnight and was arrested the next morning. He was a tough little bantam rooster. He was short, and he always carried his head slightly thrown back, with a touch of aggressiveness. He tried to avoid surrendering his Party membership card, because no decision expelling him from the Party had been reached at the District Party Committee the night before. He also refused to give up his identification card as a deputy of the district soviet, since he had been elected by the people, and the District Executive Committee had not taken any decision depriving him of his deputy's immunity. But the police did not appreciate such formalities and overpowered him, and took them away by main force. They took him from the District Consumer Cooperative down the main street of Kady in broad daylight, and his young merchandise manager, a Komsomol member, saw him from the window of the District Party Committee headquarters. At that time not everyone, especially in the villages, because of their naïveté, had learned to keep quiet about what they thought. The merchandise manager shouted: "Look at those bastards! Now they've taken away my boss too!" Right then and there, without leaving the room, they expelled him from both the District Party Committee and from the Komsomol, and he slid down the well-known pathway into the bottomless pit.

Vlasov was arrested very late in comparison with the others who were charged in the same case. The case had been nearly completed without him, and it was in process of being set up as an open trial. They took him to the Ivanovo NKVD Internal Prison, but, since he was the last to be involved, he was not subjected to any heavy pressure. He was interrogated twice. There was no supporting testimony from witnesses. And the file of his interrogation was filled with summary reports of the District Consumer Cooperative and clips from the district newspaper. Vlasov was charged with: (1) initiating bread lines; (2) having an inadequate minimum assortment of merchandise (just as though the unavailable merchandise existed somewhere else and someone had offered it to Kady); (3) procuring a surplus of salt (but this was the obligatory "mobilization" reserve: ever since ancient times people in Russia have been afraid of being without salt in the event of war).

At the end of September, the defendants were brought to Kady for public trial. It was not a short trip. (Remember how cheap the OSO's and the closed courts were!) From Ivanovo to Kineshma they went in a Stolypin railway car; then seventy miles from Kineshma to Kady in automobiles. There were more than ten cars, an unusual file along an old, deserted road, and one that aroused astonishment, fear, and the expectation of war in the villages. Klyugin, the Chief of the Special Secret Department of the Provincial NKVD for Counter-Revolutionary Organizations, was responsible for the faultless organization of the whole trial and for terrifying the public with it. Their convoy consisted of forty guards from the reserves of the mounted police, and every day from September 24 to 27, with swords unsheathed and Naguan revolvers at the ready, they took the prisoners from the District NKVD to the still unfinished club building and back, through the village where they had until recently been the government. Windows had already been installed in the club, but the stage had not yet been finished. There was no electricity. There was no electricity in Kady at all. After nightfall the court met by the light of kerosene lamps. The spectators were brought in from the collective farms in rotation. And all Kady crowded in as well. Not only did they sit on window sills and benches, but they stood packed in the aisles, seven hundred of them at a time. (Russians have always loved spectacles.) The forward benches were regularly reserved for Communists to provide the court with dependable support.

A Special Assize of the provincial court had been constituted, consisting of Deputy Chairman of the Provincial Court Shubin, who presided, and members Biche and Zaozerov. The provincial prosecutor Karasik, a graduate of Dorpat University, was in charge of the prosecution. And even though all the accused declined defense lawyers, a government lawyer was forced on them so that the case wouldn't be left without a prosecutor. The formal indictment, solemn, menacing, and lengthy, came down in essence to the charge that an underground Rightist Bukharinite group had existed in Kady District, which had been formed in Ivanovo (in other words, you could expect arrests in Ivanovo too), and had as its purpose the overthrow by wrecking of the Soviet government in the village of Kady (and this was about the remotest boondock in all Russia the *rightists* could have found for a starting point!).

The prosecutor petitioned the court to have Stavrov's testimony, given before his death in prison, read to the court and accepted as evidence. In fact, the whole charge against the group was based on Stavrov's evidence. The court agreed to include the testimony of the deceased, just as if he were alive. (With the advantage, however, that none of the defendants could refute it.)

But darkest Kady did not appreciate these scholarly fine points. It waited to see what came next. The testimony of Stavrov, who had been killed under interrogation, was read to the court and once again became part of the record. The questioning of the defendants began—and immediately there was chaos. *All* of them *repudiated* the testimony they had given during the interrogation.

It is not clear how, in such an event, things would have been arranged in the October Hall of the House of the Unions in Moscow—but here, at any rate, it was decided shamelessly to continue. The judge rebuked the defendants: How could you have given different testimony during the interrogation? Univer, very weak, replied in a barely audible voice: "As a Communist I cannot, in a public trial, describe the interrogation methods of the NKVD." (Now there was a model for the Bukharin trial! Now that's what keeps them together! More than anything else, they are worried that people might think ill of the Party. Their judges had long since stopped worrying about that.)

During the recess, Klyugin visited the cells of the defendants. He said to Vlasov: "You've heard how Smirnov and Univer played the whore, the bastards? You've got to admit your guilt and tell the whole truth!" "The truth and nothing but the truth," willingly agreed Vlasov, who had not yet weakened. "The truth and nothing but the truth that you are every bit as bad as the German Fascists!" Klyugin flew into a rage: "Listen here, you whore, you'll pay with your blood!"[39] From that moment Vlasov was pushed forward from a back seat among the defendants to a leading role in the trial—as the *ideological leader* of the group.

The crowd jamming the aisles grew interested whenever the court fearlessly broke into questions about bread lines—about things that touched everyone present to the quick. (And, of course, bread had been put on unrestricted sale just before the trial, and there were no bread lines that day.) A question to the accused Smirnov: "Did you know about the bread lines in the district?" "Yes, of course. They stretched from the store itself right up to the building of the District Party Committee." "And what did you do about them?" Notwithstanding the tortures he had endured, Smirnov had preserved his resounding voice and tranquil righteousness. This broad-shouldered man with a simple face and light-brown hair answered slowly, and the whole hall heard every word he said: "Since all appeals to organizations in the provincial capital had failed, I instructed Vlasov to write a report to Comrade Stalin." "And why didn't you write it?" (They hadn't yet known about it! They had certainly missed that one!) "We did write it, and I sent it by courier directly to the Central Committee, bypassing the provincial leaders. A copy was kept in the District Committee files."

The whole courtroom held its breath. The court itself was in a commotion. They shouldn't have continued questioning, but nonetheless someone asked: "And what happened?"

And, indeed, that question was on the lips of everyone in the courtroom: "What happened?"

Smirnov did not sob, did not groan over the death of his ideal (and that's what was missing in the Moscow trials!). He replied loudly and calmly:

"Nothing. *There was no answer.*"

And his tired voice seemed to say: Well, that, in fact, was just what I expected.

There was no answer. From the Father and Teacher there was no answer! The public trial had already reached its zenith! It had already shown the masses the black heart of the Cannibal! And

39. Your own blood, too, is going to flow soon, Klyugin! Caught in the Yezhov gang of gaybisty, Klyugin will have his throat cut by the stool pigeon Gubaidulin.

the trial could have been called off right then and there. But, oh no, they didn't have sense enough for that, or tact enough for that, and they kept rubbing away at the befouled spot for three more days.

The prosecutor raised a hue and cry: Double-dealing! That's what it was. They engaged in wrecking with one hand and with the other they dared write Comrade Stalin. And they even expected a reply from him. Let the defendant Vlasov tell us how he pulled off such a nightmarish piece of wrecking that he stopped the sale of flour and the baking of rye bread in the district center.

Vlasov, the bantam rooster, didn't have to be asked to rise—he had already jumped up, and he shouted resoundingly through the hall:

"I agree to give a full answer to the court, but on condition that you, the prosecutor, Karasik, leave the accuser's rostrum and sit down here next to me!" It was incomprehensible. Noise, shouting. Call them to order! What was going on?

Having gotten the floor with this maneuver, Vlasov explained willingly.

"The prohibitions on selling flour and baking rye bread were instituted by a decree of the Provincial Executive Committee. One of the permanent members of its presidium is Provincial Prosecutor Karasik. If that's wrecking, then why didn't you veto it as prosecutor? That means you were a wrecker even before I was!"

The prosecutor choked. It was a swift, well-placed blow. The court was also at a loss. The judge mumbled.

"If necessary [?] we will try the prosecutor too. But today we are trying you."

(Two truths: it all depends on your rank.)

"I demand that he be removed from the prosecutor's rostrum," insisted the indefatigable, irrepressible Vlasov.

Recess.

Now, in terms of indoctrinating the masses, just what significance could such a trial have?

But they kept on and on. After questioning the defendants they began to question the witnesses. The bookkeeper N.

"What do you know about Vlasov's wrecking activities?"

"Nothing."

"How can that be?"

"I was in the witnesses' room and I didn't hear what was said in here."

"You don't have to hear! Many documents passed through your hands. You couldn't help but know."

"The documents were all in proper order."

"But here is a stack of district newspapers, and even there they were writing about Vlasov's wrecking activities. And you claim you don't know anything?"

"Well, go ask the people who wrote the articles."

Then there was the manager of the bread store.

"Tell me, does the Soviet government have much bread?"

(Well, now! Just how could you answer that? Who was going to say: "I didn't count it"?)

"A lot."

"Why are there bread lines at your store?"

"I don't know."

"Who was in charge?"

"I don't know."

"What do you mean, you don't know? Who was in charge of your store?"

"Vasily Grigoryevich."

"What the devil! What do you mean calling him Vasily Grigoryevich? Defendant Vlasov! That means he was in charge."

The witness fell silent.

The judge of the court dictated to the stenographer: "The answer: 'As a consequence of the wrecking activity of Vlasov, bread lines resulted, notwithstanding the Soviet government's enormous stocks of bread.'"

Repressing his own fears, the prosecutor delivered a long and angry speech. The defense lawyer for the most part defended only himself, emphasizing that the interests of the Motherland were as dear to him as they were to any honest citizen.

In his final words to the court, Smirnov asked for nothing and expressed no repentance for anything. Insofar as we can reconstruct it now, he was a firm person and too forthright to have lasted through 1937.

When Saburov begged that his life be spared—"not for me, but for my little children"—Vlasov, out of vexation, pulled him back by the jacket: "You're a fool."

Vlasov himself did not fail to take advantage of his last chance to talk back impudently.

"I consider you not a court but actors pretending to be a court in a stage farce where roles have already been written for you. You are engaged in a repulsive provocation on the part of the NKVD. You are going to sentence me to be shot no matter what I say. I believe one thing only: the time will come when you will be here in my place."[40]

The court spent from 7 P.M. to 1 A.M. composing the verdict, and all the while the kerosene lamps were burning in the hall, and the defendants sat beneath drawn sabers, and there was a hum of conversation among the spectators who had not left.

And just as it took them a long time to compose the verdict, it took them a long time to read it, piling up on top of one another all kinds of fantastic wrecking activities, contacts, and plans. Smirnov, Univer, Saburov, and Vlasov were sentenced to be shot; two others to ten years; one to eight years. In addition, the verdict of the court led to the exposure of an additional wrecking organization in the Komsomol in Kady (whose members were, of course, immediately arrested. Remember the young merchandise manager?). And of a center of underground organizations in Ivanovo, which was, of course, in its turn, subordinate to Moscow. (One more nail in Bukharin's coffin.)

After the solemn words "To be shot!" the judges paused for applause. But the mood in the hall was so gloomy, with the sighs and tears of people who had no connection with the defendants, and the screams and swooning of their relatives, that no applause was to be heard even from the first two benches, where the Party members were sitting. This, indeed, was totally improper. "Oh, good Lord, what have you done?" someone in the hall shouted at the members of the court. Univer's wife dissolved in tears. In the half-darkness, the crowd began to stir. Vlasov shouted at the front benches:

"Come on, you bastards, why aren't you clapping? Some Communists you are!"

The political commissar of the guards platoon ran up to him and shoved his revolver in his face. Vlasov reached out to grab the revolver, but a policeman ran up and pushed back his political commissar, who had been guilty of a blunder. The chief

40. Generally speaking, he was wrong just on this one point.

of the convoy gave the command: "Arms at the ready!" And thirty police carbines and the pistols of the local NKVD men were aimed at the defendants and at the crowd. (It seemed at the time as though the crowd would rush forward to free the defendants.)

The hall was lit only by a few kerosene lamps, and the semi-darkness heightened the general confusion and fear. The crowd, finally convinced, not so much by the trial as by the carbines now leveled at it, pushed in a panic against the doors and windows. The wood cracked and broke; glass tinkled. Univer's wife, in a dead faint, was almost trampled to death and was left lying beneath the chairs until morning.

And there never was any applause.[41]

And not only couldn't the condemned prisoners be shot then and there, but they had to be kept under even stricter guard, because now they really had nothing at all to lose, and they had to be taken to the provincial capital for execution.

They managed to cope with the first problem—sending them off by night to the NKVD along the main street—by having each condemned man guarded by five men. One of the guards carried a lantern. One went ahead with a pistol at the ready. Two held the condemned prisoner by the arms and kept their pistols in their free hands. The fifth brought up the rear, with his pistol pointed at the condemned man's back.

The rest of the police were ranged in formation in order to prevent any attack by the crowd.

Every reasonable man will now agree that the NKVD could never have carried out its great assignment if they had fussed about with open trials.

And that is why public political trials never really put down roots in our country.

---

41. One little note on eight-year-old Zoya Vlasova. She loved her father intensely. She could no longer go to school. (They teased her: "Your papa is a wrecker!" She would get in a fight: "My papa is good!") She lived only one year after the trial. Up to then she had never been ill. During that year *she did not once smile;* she went about with head hung low, and the old women prophesied: "She keeps looking at the earth; she is going to die soon." She died of inflammation of the brain, and as she was dying she kept calling out: "Where is my papa? Give me my papa!" When we count up the millions of those who perished in the camps, we forget to multiply them by two, by three.

Chapter 11

■

The Supreme Measure

Capital punishment has had an up-and-down history in Russia. In the Code of the Tsar Aleksei Mikhailovich Romanov there were fifty crimes for which capital punishment could be imposed. By the time of the Military Statutes of Peter the Great there were two hundred. Yet the Empress Elizabeth, while she did not repeal those laws authorizing capital punishment, never once resorted to it. They say that when she ascended the throne she swore an oath never to execute anyone—and for all twenty years of her reign she kept that oath. She fought the Seven Years' War! Yet she still got along without capital punishment. It was an astounding record in the mid-eighteenth century—fifty years before the guillotine of the Jacobins. True, we have taught ourselves to ridicule all our past; we never acknowledge a good deed or a good intention in our history. And one can very easily blacken Elizabeth's reputation too; she replaced capital punishment with flogging with the knout; tearing out nostrils; branding with the word "thief"; and eternal exile in Siberia. But let us also say something on behalf of the Empress: how could she have changed things more radically than she did in contravention of the social concepts of her time? And perhaps the prisoner condemned to death today would voluntarily consent to that whole complex of punishments if only the sun would continue to shine on him; but we, in our humanitarianism, don't offer him that chance. And perhaps the reader will come to feel in the course of this book that twenty or even ten years in our camps are harder to bear than were the punishments of Elizabeth?

In today's terms, Elizabeth had a universally human point of view on all this, while the Empress Catherine the Great had, on the contrary, a class point of view (which was consequently more correct). Not to execute anyone at all seemed to her appalling and indefensible. She found capital punishment entirely appropriate to defending herself, her throne, and her system—in other words, in political cases, such as those of Mirovich, the Moscow plague mutiny, and Pugachev. But for *habitual criminals,* for *nonpolitical offenders,* why not consider capital punishment abolished?

Under Paul, the abolition of capital punishment was confirmed. (Despite his many wars, there were no military tribunals attached to military units.) And during the whole long reign of Alexander I, capital punishment was introduced only for war crimes that took place during a campaign (1812). (Right at this point, some people will say to us: What about deaths from running the gantlet? Yes, indeed, there were, of course, hidden executions— for that matter, one can literally drive a person to death with a trade-union meeting!) But the yielding up of one's God-given life because others, sitting in judgment, have so voted simply did not take place in our country even for *crimes* of state for an entire half-century—from Pugachev to the Decembrists.

The blood of the five Decembrists whetted the appetite of our state. From then on, execution for crimes of state was no longer prohibited nor was it forgotten, right up to the February Revolution in 1917. It was confirmed by the Statutes of 1845 and 1904, and further reinforced by the criminal statutes of the army and navy.

And how many people were executed in Russia during that period? We have already, in Chapter 8 above, cited the figures given by liberal leaders of 1905–1907. Let us add to them the verified figures of N. S. Tagantsev, the expert on Russian criminal law.[1] Up until 1905, the death penalty was an exceptional measure in Russia. For a period of thirty years—from 1876 to 1904 (the period of the Narodnaya Volya revolutionaries and the use of terrorism—a terrorism which did not consist merely

1. N. S. Tagantsev, *Smertnaya Kazn (Capital Punishment)*, St. Petersburg, 1913.

of *intentions* murmured in the kitchen of a communal apartment —a period of mass strikes and peasant revolts; the period when the parties of the future revolution were created and grew in strength)—486 people were executed; in other words, about seventeen people per year for the whole country. (This figure includes executions of ordinary, nonpolitical criminals!)[2] During the years of the first revolution (1905) and its suppression, the number of executions rocketed upward, astounding Russian imaginations, calling forth tears from Tolstoi and indignation from Korolenko and many, many others: from 1905 through 1908 about 2,200 persons were executed—forty-five a month. This, as Tagantsev said, was an *epidemic of executions.* It came to an abrupt end.

When the Provisional Government came to power, it abolished capital punishment entirely. In July, 1917, however, it was reinstated in the active army and front-line areas for military crimes, murder, rape, assault, and pillage (very widespread in those areas at that time). This was one of the most unpopular of the measures which destroyed the Provisional Government. The Bolsheviks' slogan before the Bolshevik coup d'état was: "Down with capital punishment, reinstated by Kerensky!"

A story has come down to us that on the night of October 25–26 a discussion arose in Smolny as to whether one of the first decrees shouldn't be the abolition of capital punishment in perpetuity—whereupon Lenin justly ridiculed the idealism of his comrades. He, at any rate, knew that without capital punishment there would be no movement whatever in the direction of the new society. However, in forming a coalition government with the Left SR's, he gave in to their faulty concepts, and on October 28, 1917, capital punishment was abolished. Nothing good, of course, could come from that "goody-goody" position. (Yes, and how did they get rid of it? At the beginning of 1918, Trotsky ordered that Aleksei Shchastny, a newly appointed admiral, be brought to trial because he had refused to scuttle the Baltic Fleet. Karklin, the Chairman of the Verkhtrib, quickly sentenced him in broken Russian: "To be shot within twenty-four hours." There was a stir in the hall: But it has been abolished! Prosecutor

2. Thirteen people were executed in Schlüsselburg from 1884 to 1906. An awesome total—for Switzerland perhaps!

Krylenko explained: "What are you worrying about? Executions have been abolished. But Shchastny is not being executed; he is being shot." And they did shoot him.)

If we are to judge by official documents, capital punishment was restored in all its force in June, 1918. No, it was not "restored"; instead, a *new* era of executions was inaugurated. If one takes the view that Latsis[3] is not deliberately understating the real figures but simply lacks complete information, and that the Revtribunals carried on approximately the same amount of judicial work as the Cheka performed in an extrajudicial way, one concludes that in the twenty central provinces of Russia in a period of sixteen months (June, 1918, to October, 1919) more than sixteen thousand persons were shot, which is to say *more than one thousand a month.*[4] (This, incidentally, is when they shot both Khrustalev-Nosar, the Chairman of the 1905 St. Petersburg Soviet—the first Russian soviet—and the artist who designed the legendary uniform worn by the Red Army throughout the Civil War.)

However, it may not even have been these individual executions, with or without formally pronounced death sentences, which added up to thousands and inaugurated the new era of executions in 1918 that stunned and froze Russia. Still more terrible to us was the practice—initially followed by both warring sides and, later, by the victors only—of *sinking barges* loaded with uncounted, unregistered hundreds, unidentified even by a roll call. (Naval officers in the Gulf of Finland, in the White, Caspian, and Black seas, and, as late as 1920, hostages in Lake Baikal.) This is outside the scope of our narrow history of courts and trials, but it belongs to the history of *morals,* which is where everything else originates as well. In all our centuries, from the first Ryurik on, had there ever been a period of such cruelties and so much killing as during the post-October Civil War?

We would omit from view one of the characteristic ups-and-downs of the Russian capital-punishment story if we neglected to mention that capital punishment was abolished in January,

3. Latsis, *Dva Goda Borby na Vnutrennom Fronte,* p. 75.
4. Now that we have started to make comparisons, here is another: during the eighty years of the Inquisition's peak effort (1420 to 1498), in all of Spain ten thousand persons were condemned to be burned to death at the stake—in other words, about ten a month.

1920. Yes, indeed! And some students of the subject might conceivably be at a loss to interpret the credulity and helplessness of a dictatorship that deprived itself of its avenging sword when Denikin was still in the Kuban, Wrangel still in the Crimea, and the Polish cavalry were saddling up for a campaign. But, in the first place, this decree was quite sensible: *it did not extend to the decisions of military tribunals,* but applied only to extrajudicial actions of the Cheka and the decisions of tribunals in the rear. In the second place, the way was *prepared* for it by first *cleaning out the prisons* by the wholesale execution of prisoners who might otherwise have come "under the decree." And, in the third place, it was in effect for a brief period—four months. (It lasted only until the prisons had filled up again.) By a decree of May 28, 1920, capital punishment was restored to the Cheka.

The Revolution had hastened to rename everything, so that everything would seem new. Thus the death penalty was rechristened "the supreme measure"—no longer a "punishment" but a means of *social defense.* From the groundwork of the criminal legislation of 1924 it is clear that the supreme measure was introduced only *temporarily, pending its total abolition by the All-Russian Central Executive Committee.*

And in 1927 they actually did begin to *abolish* it. It was retained *solely* for crimes against the state and the army—Article 58 and military crimes—and, true, for banditry also. (But the broad political interpretation of "banditry" was as well known then as it is now: from a Central Asian "Basmach," right up to a Lithuanian forest guerrilla, every armed nationalist who doesn't agree with the central government is a "bandit," and how could one possibly get along without that article? Similarly, any participant in a camp rebellion and any participant in an urban rebellion is also a "bandit.") But where articles protecting private individuals were concerned, capital punishment was abolished to commemorate the tenth anniversary of the Revolution.

And for the fifteenth anniversary, the law of *Seven-eighths* was added to the roster of capital punishment—that law so vitally important to advancing socialism, which guaranteed the Soviet subject a bullet for each crumb stolen from the state's table.

As always happens at the start, they hurried to apply this

law in 1932–1933 and shot people with special ferocity. In this time of *peace* in December, 1932 (while Kirov was still alive), *at one time 265 condemned prisoners* were *awaiting* execution in Leningrad's Kresty Prison alone.[5] And during the whole year, it would certainly seem that more than a thousand were shot in Kresty alone.

And what kind of evildoers were these condemned men? Where did so many plotters and troublemakers come from? Among them, for example, were six collective farmers from nearby Tsarskoye Selo who were guilty of the following crime: After they had finished mowing the collective farm with their own hands, they had gone back and mowed a second time along the hummocks to get a little hay for their own cows. The All-Russian Central Executive Committee *refused to pardon all six of these peasants, and the sentence of execution was carried out.*

What cruel and evil Saltychikha, what utterly repulsive and infamous serf-owner would have *killed* six peasants for their miserable little clippings of hay? If one had dared to beat them with birch switches even once, we would know about it and read about it in school and curse that name.[6] But now, heave the corpses into the water, and pretty soon the surface is all smooth again and no one's the wiser. And one must cherish the hope that someday documents will confirm the report of my witness, who is still alive. Even if Stalin had killed no others, I believe he deserved to be drawn and quartered just for the lives of those six Tsarskoye Selo peasants! And yet they still dare shriek at us (from Peking, from Tirana, from Tbilisi, yes, and plenty of big-bellies in the Moscow suburbs are doing it too): "How could you dare expose him?" "How could you dare disturb his great shade?" "Stalin belongs to the world Communist movement!" But in my opinion all he belongs to is the Criminal Code. "The peoples of all the world remember him as a friend." But not those on whose backs he rode, whom he slashed with his knout.

5. Testimony of B., who brought food to the cells of the prisoners condemned to be shot.
6. What isn't known in our schools is the fact that Saltychikha, by a verdict of her own peers, was imprisoned for eleven years in the subterranean crypt of the Ivanovsky Monastery in Moscow for the atrocities inflicted on her serfs. (Prugavin, *Monastyrskiye Tyurmy [Monastery Prisons]*, Posrednik Publishers, p. 39.)

However, let us return to being dispassionate and impartial once more. Of course, the All-Russian Central Executive Committee would certainly have "completely abolished" the supreme measure, as promised, but unfortunately what happened was that in 1936 the Father and Teacher "completely abolished" the All-Russian Central Executive Committee itself. And the *Supreme Soviet* that succeeded it had an eighteenth-century ring. "The supreme measure" became a *punishment* once again, and ceased to be some kind of incomprehensible "social defense." Even to the Stalinist ear the executions of 1937–1938 could hardly fit into any framework of "defense."

What legal expert, what criminal historian, will provide us with verified statistics for those 1937–1938 executions? Where is that *Special Archive* we might be able to penetrate in order to read the figures? There is none. There is none and there never will be any. Therefore we dare report only those figures mentioned in rumors that were quite fresh in 1939–1940, when they were drifting around under the Butyrki arches, having emanated from the high- and middle-ranking Yezhov men of the NKVD who had been arrested and had passed through those cells not long before. (And they really knew!) The Yezhov men said that during those two years of 1937 and 1938 a *half-million* "political prisoners" had been shot throughout the Soviet Union, and 480,-000 *blatnye*—habitual thieves—in addition. (The thieves were all shot under Article 59-3 because they constituted "a basis of Yagoda's power"; and thereby the "ancient and noble companionship of thieves" was pruned back.)

How improbable are these figures? Taking into consideration that the mass executions went on not for two full years but only for a year and a half, we would have to assume (under Article 58—in other words, the politicals alone) an average of 28,000 executions per month in that period. For the whole Soviet Union. But at how many different locations were executions being carried out? A figure of 150 would be very modest. (There were more, of course. In Pskov alone, the NKVD set up torture and execution chambers in the basements of many churches, in former hermits' cells. And even in 1953 tourists were still not allowed into these churches, on the grounds that "archives" were kept there. The cobwebs hadn't been swept out for ten years at a stretch: those were the "archives" they kept there. And before beginning restoration work on these churches, they had to haul away the bones in them by the truckload.) On the basis of this calculation, an average of six people were shot in the course of one day at each execution site. What's so fantastic about that? It is even an understatement! (According to other sources, 1,700,000 had been shot by January 1, 1939.)

During the years of World War II, the use of capital punishment was occasionally extended for various reasons (as, for example, by the militarization of the railroads), and, at times, was broadened as to method (from April, 1943, on, for example, with the decree on *hanging*).

All these events delayed to a certain extent the promised full, final, and perpetual repeal of the death penalty. However, the patience and loyalty of our people finally earned them this reward. In May, 1947, Iosif Vissarionovich inspected his new starched dickey in his mirror, liked it, and dictated to the Presidium of the Supreme Soviet the Decree on the Abolition of Capital Punishment in peacetime (replacing it with a new maximum term of twenty-five years—it was a good pretext for introducing the so-called *quarter*).

But our people are ungrateful, criminal, and incapable of appreciating generosity. Therefore, after the rulers had creaked along and eked out two and a half years without the death penalty, on January 12, 1950, a new decree was published that constituted an about-face: "In view of petitions pouring in from the national republics [the Ukraine?], from the trade unions [oh, those lovely trade unions; they always know what's needed], from peasant organizations [this was dictated by a sleepwalker: the Gracious Sovereign had stomped to death all peasant organizations way back in the Year of the Great Turning Point], and also from cultural leaders [now, *that* is quite likely]," capital punishment was restored for a conglomeration of "traitors of the Motherland, spies, and subversives-diversionists." (And, of course, they forgot to repeal the *quarter,* the twenty-five-year sentence, which remained in force.)

And once this return to our familiar friend, to our beheading blade, had begun, things went further with no effort at all: in 1954, for premeditated murder; in May, 1961, for theft of state property, and counterfeiting, and terrorism in places of imprisonment (this was directed especially at prisoners who killed informers and terrorized the camp administration); in July, 1961, for violating the rules governing foreign currency transactions; in February, 1962, for threatening the lives of (shaking a fist at) policemen or Communist vigilantes, the so-called "druzhinniki"; then for rape; and immediately thereafter for bribery.

But all of this is simply temporary—until complete abolition. And that's how it's described today too.[7]

And so it turns out that Russia managed longest of all without capital punishment in the reign of the Empress Elizabeth Petrovna.

■

In our happy, blind existence, we picture condemned men as a few ill-fated, solitary individuals. We instinctively believe that we could never end up on death row, that it would take an outstanding career if not heinous guilt for that to happen. A great deal has still to be shaken up inside our heads for us to get the real picture: a mass of the most ordinary, average, gray people have languished in death cells for the most ordinary, everyday misdemeanors, and, although some were lucky and had their death sentences commuted, which was purely a matter of chance, they very often got the *super* (which is what the prisoners called "the supreme measure," since they hate lofty words and manage somehow to give everything a nickname that is both crude and short).

The agronomist of a District Agricultural Department got a death sentence for his mistaken analysis of collective farm grain! (Maybe it was because his analysis wasn't what his chiefs wanted from him?) That was in 1937.

Melnikov, the chairman of a handicraft artel that made spools for thread, was sentenced to death because a spark from a steam engine in his artel had caused a fire! That was in 1937. (True, his death sentence was commuted to a "tenner.")

7. "Osnovy Ugolovnogo Zakonodatelstva SSSR" ("Fundamental Principles of Criminal Legislation of the U.S.S.R."), Article 22, in *Vedomosti Verkhovnogo Soveta SSSR* (*Bulletin of the Supreme Soviet of the U.S.S.R.*), 1959, No. 1.

In that same Kresty Prison in Leningrad, in 1932, two of the men in death cells were Feldman, convicted of possessing foreign currency, and Faitelevich, a student at the conservatory, for having sold steel ribbon for pen points. Primordial commerce, the bread and butter and pastime of the Jew, had also become worthy of the death penalty.

Ought we to be surprised then that the Ivanovo Province village lad Geraska got the death penalty? In honor of the spring St. Nicholas holiday, he went off to the next village to celebrate; he drank heavily and, with a stick, he hit the rear end—no, not of the policeman himself, but of the policeman's horse. (True, in a rage at the police he ripped a piece of board off the village soviet building and then yanked out the village soviet telephone by the cord, shouting: "Smash the devils!")

Whether our destiny holds a death cell in store for us is not determined by what we have done or not done. It is determined by the turn of a great wheel and the thrust of powerful external circumstances. For example, Leningrad was under siege and blockade. And what would its highest-ranking leader, Comrade Zhdanov, think if there were no executions among the *cases* in Leningrad State Security during such difficult times? He would think the Organs were lying down on the job, would he not? Were there not big underground plots, directed from outside by the Germans, to be discovered? Why were such plots discovered under Stalin in 1919 and not under Zhdanov in 1942? No sooner ordered than done. Several ramified plots were discovered. You were asleep in your unheated Leningrad room, and the sharp claws of the black hand were already hovering over you. And yet none of this depended on you. Notice was taken of a Lieutenant General Ignatovsky, whose windows looked out on the Neva; he had pulled out a white handkerchief to blow his nose. Aha, a signal! Furthermore, because Ignatovsky was an engineer, he liked to talk about machinery with the sailors. And that clinched it! Ignatovsky was arrested. The time for reckoning came. Come on now, name forty members of your organization. He named them. And so, if you happened to be an usher at the Aleksandrinsky Theatre, your chances of being named as one of his particular forty were minimal. But if you were a professor at the Technological Institute, there you were on that list (once more, that accursed intelligentsia). So how could it depend on you? To be on such a list amounted to execution for each one.

And so they shot all of them. But here is how Konstantin Ivanovich Strakhovich, a very important Russian scientist in hydrodynamics, remained alive: Some even higher bigwigs in State Security were dissatisfied because the list was too small and not enough people were being shot. Therefore Strakhovich was selected as a suitable center for uncovering a new organization. He was summoned by Captain Altshuller: "What's this all about? Did you rush to confess everything so that you'd get shot and thereby conceal the underground government? What was your role in it?" Thus Strakhovich found himself in a new round of interrogations while he remained on death row. He proposed that they consider him the underground Minister of Education. (He wanted to get it over with as soon as possible!) But that wasn't good enough for Altshuller. The interrogation continued, and by this time Ignatovsky's group was being executed. During one of the interrogation sessions Strakhovich got angry. It wasn't that he wanted to live but that he was tired of dying, and, more than anything else, the lies made him sick. And so while he was being cross-questioned in the presence of some Security police bigwig, he pounded on the table: "*You* are the ones who ought to be shot. I am not going to lie any longer. I take back all my testimony." And his outburst helped! Not only did they stop interrogating him, but they forgot about him in his death cell for a long time.

In all probability an outburst of desperation in the midst of general submissiveness will always help.

Thus many were shot—thousands at first, then hundreds of thousands. We divide, we multiply, we sigh, we curse. But still and all, these are just numbers. They overwhelm the mind and then are easily forgotten. And if someday the relatives of those who had been shot were to send one publisher photographs of their executed kin, and an album of those photographs were to be published in several volumes, then just by leafing through them and looking into the extinguished eyes we would learn much that would be valuable for the rest of our lives. Such reading, almost without words, would leave a deep mark on our hearts for all eternity.

In one household I am familiar with, where some former zeks live, the following ceremony takes place: On March 5, the day of the death of the Head Murderer, they spread out on the table all the photographs of those who were shot and those who died in camps that they have been able to collect—several dozen of them. And throughout the day solemnity reigns in the apartment —somewhat like that of a church, somewhat like that of a museum. There is funeral music. Friends come to visit, to look at the photographs, to keep silent, to listen, to talk softly together. And then they leave without saying good-bye.

And that is how it ought to be everywhere. At least these deaths would have left a small scar on our hearts.

So that they should not have died *in vain!*

And I, too, have a few such chance photographs. Look at these at least:

Viktor Petrovich Pokrovsky—shot in Moscow in 1918.

Aleksandr Shtrobinder, a student—shot in Petrograd in 1918.

Vasily Ivanovich Anichkov—shot in the Lubyanka in 1927.

Aleksandr Andreyevich Svechin, a professor of the General Staff—shot in 1935.

Mikhail Aleksandrovich Reformatsky, an agronomist—shot in Orel in 1938.

Yelizaveta Yevgenyevna Anichkova—shot in a camp on the Yenisei in 1942.

How does *all that* happen? What is it like for people to *wait* there? What do they feel? What do they think about? And what decisions do they come to? And what is it like when they are *taken away?* And what do they feel in their last moments? And how, actually, do they . . . well . . . do they . . . ?

The morbid desire to pierce that curtain is natural. (Even though it is, of course, never going to happen to any of *us.*) And it is natural that those who have survived cannot tell us about the very end—because, after all, they were pardoned.

What happens *next* is something the executioners know about. But the executioners are not about to talk. (Take, for instance, that famous *Uncle Lyosha* in the Kresty Prison in Leningrad, who twisted the prisoner's hands behind his back and put handcuffs on him, and then, if the prisoner shouted down the nighttime corridor, "Farewell, brothers!" crammed a rolled-up rag into his mouth—just why should he tell you about it? He is probably still walking around Leningrad, well dressed. But if you happen to run into him in a beer parlor on the islands or at a soccer game, ask him!)

However, even the executioner doesn't know about everything right to the very end. While a motor roars its accompaniment, he fires his pistol bullets, unheard, into the back of a head, and he is himself stupidly condemned not to understand what he has done. He doesn't know about *the very end!* Only those who have been killed know it all to the very end—and that means no one.

It's true, however, that the artist, however obliquely and unclearly, nevertheless knows some part of what happens right up to the actual bullet, the actual noose.

So we are going to construct—from artists and from those who were pardoned—an approximate picture of the death cell. We know, for example, that they do not sleep at night but lie there *waiting*. That they calm down again only in the morning.

Narokov (Marchenko) in his novel, *Imaginary Values,*[8] a work much spoiled by the author's self-assigned task of describing everything as though he were Dostoyevsky, of tearing at the reader's heartstrings and trying to move him even more than Dostoyevsky, nevertheless in my opinion described the death cell and the scene of the execution itself very well. One cannot verify it, of course, but somehow one believes it.

The interpretations of earlier artists, for example, Leonid Andreyev, seem today somehow to belong willy-nilly to Krylov's time, a century and a half ago. And for that matter, what fantasist could have imagined the death cells of 1937? Of necessity, he would have woven his psychological threads: what it was like to wait, how the condemned man kept listening, and the like. But who could have foreseen and described such unexpected sensations on the part of prisoners condemned to death as:

1. Prisoners awaiting execution suffered from the *cold*. They had to sleep on the cement floor under the windows, where it was 28 degrees Fahrenheit. (Strakhovich.) You could freeze to death while you were waiting to be shot.

8. N. Narokov, *Mnimyye Velichiny, Roman v 2-kh Chastyakh* (*Imaginary Values; a Novel in Two Parts*), New York, Chekhov Publishing House, 1952.

2. They suffered from being in *stuffy, overcrowded cells*. Into a cell intended for solitary confinement they would shove seven (*never* fewer), sometimes ten, fifteen, even *twenty-eight* prisoners awaiting execution. (Strakhovich in Leningrad, 1942.) And they remained packed in this way for weeks or even *months!* What kind of nightmare was your *seven* to be hanged? People in these circumstances don't think about execution, and it's not being shot they worry about, but how to move their legs, how to turn over, how to get a gulp of air.

In 1937, when up to forty thousand prisoners were being held at one time in the prisons of Ivanovo—the internal prison of the NKVD, No. 1, No. 2, and the cells for preliminary detention —although they were just barely designed to hold three to four thousand, Prison No. 2 held a mixture of prisoners under inter-rogation, prisoners condemned to camp, prisoners sentenced to be executed, prisoners whose death sentences had been com-muted, and ordinary thieves—and all of them *stood for several days so jammed in against each other* in one big cell that it was impossible either to raise or lower an arm and those who were shoved up against the bunks could easily break their legs on the edges. It was winter, but in order not to be suffocated the prisoners broke the glass in the windows. (It was in this cell that the old Bolshevik Alalykin, with his snow-white head of hair—he had joined the Party in 1898 and had quit the Party in 1917 after the April Theses—waited for his death sentence to be carried out.)

3. Prisoners sentenced to death also suffered from *hunger*. They waited such a long time after the death sentence had been imposed that their principal sensation was no longer the fear of being shot but the pangs of hunger: where could they get something to eat? In 1941 Aleksandr Babich spent seventy-five days in a death cell in the Krasnoyarsk Prison. He had already reconciled himself to death and awaited execution as the only possible end to his unsuccessful life. But he *began to swell up from starvation*. At that point, they commuted his death sentence to ten years, and that was when he began his camp career. And what was the record stay in a death cell? Who knows? Vsevolod Petrovich Golitsyn, the *elder* of a death cell, so to speak, spent 140 days in it in 1938. But was that a record? The glory of Russian science, famed geneticist N. I. Vavilov, waited several

months for his execution—yes, *maybe even a whole year*. As a prisoner still under death sentence he was evacuated to the Saratov Prison, where he was kept in a basement cell that had no window. When his death sentence was commuted in the summer of 1942, he was transferred to a general cell, and he could not even walk. Other prisoners carried him to the daily outdoor walk, supporting him under the arms.

4. Prisoners sentenced to death were given no medical attention. Okhrimenko was kept in a death cell for a long time in 1938, and he became very ill. Not only did they refuse to put him in the hospital, but the doctor took forever to come to see him. When she finally did come, she didn't go into the cell; instead, without examining him or even asking him any questions, she handed him some powders through the bars. And fluid began to accumulate in Strakhovich's legs—dropsy. He told the jailer about it—and they sent him, believe it or not, a dentist.

And when a doctor did enter the picture, was it right for him to cure the prisoner under sentence of death—in other words, to prolong his expectation of death? Or did humanitarianism dictate that the doctor should insist on execution as quickly as possible? Here is another little scene from Strakhovich: The doctor entered and, talking with the duty jailer, he pointed a finger at the prisoners awaiting execution: "He's a dead man! He's a dead man! He's a dead man!" (He was pointing out to the jailer the victims of malnutrition and insisting that it was wrong to torment people so, that it was time to shoot them.)

What, in fact, was the reason for holding them so long? Weren't there enough executioners? One must point out that the prison authorities often suggested to and even asked many of the condemned prisoners to sign appeals for commutation; and when prisoners objected strongly and refused, not wanting any more "deals," *they signed appeals in the prisoners' names.* And at the very least it took months for the papers to move through the twists and turns of the machine.

A clash between two different institutions was probably involved. The interrogatory and judicial apparatus—as we learned from the members of the Military Collegium, they were one and the same—anxious to expose nightmarish and appalling cases, could not impose anything less than a deserved penalty on the criminals—death. But as soon as the sentences had been pronounced and entered into the official record of interrogation and trial, the scarecrows now called condemned men no longer interested them. And, in actual fact, there hadn't been any sedition involved, nor would the life of the state be affected in any way if these condemned men remained alive. So they were left entirely to the prison administration. And that administration, which was closely associated with Gulag, looked at prisoners from the economic point of view. To them the important *figures* were not an increase in the number of executions but an increase in the manpower sent out to the Archipelago.

And that is exactly the light in which Sokolov, the chief of the internal prison of the Big House in Leningrad, viewed Strakhovich, who finally became *bored* in the death cell and asked for paper and pencil for his scientific work. In a notebook he first composed "On the Interaction of a Liquid and a Solid Moving in It," and then "Calculations for Ballistas, Springs and Shock Absorbers," and then "Bases of the Theory of Stability." They had already allotted him an individual "scientific" cell and fed him better, and questions began to come to him from the Leningrad Front. He worked out for them "Volumetric Weapons' Fire Against Aircraft." And it all ended with Zhdanov's commuting his death sentence to fifteen years. (The mail from the mainland was slow, but soon his regular *commutation* order came from Moscow, and it was more generous than Zhdanov's: merely a *tenner*.)[9]

And N.P., a mathematician with the rank of assistant professor, was exploited by the interrogator Kruzhkov (yes, yes, that same thief) for his personal ends. Kruzhkov was taking correspondence courses. And so he *summoned P. from the death cell* and gave him problems to solve in the theory of functions of a complex variable for Kruzhkov's assignments (and probably they weren't even his either).

So what did world literature understand about pre-execution suffering?

9. Strakhovich has all his prison notebooks even now. And his "scientific career" outside the bars only began with them. He was destined later on to head up one of the first projects in the U.S.S.R. for a turbojet engine.

Finally, we learn from a story of Ch———v that a death cell can be used as *an element in interrogation,* as a method of coercing a prisoner. Two prisoners in Krasnoyarsk who had refused to confess were suddenly summoned to a "trial," "sentenced" to the death penalty, and taken to the death cell. (Ch———v said: "They were subjected to a staged trial." But in a context in which every trial is staged, what word can we use to distinguish this sort of pseudo trial from the rest? A stage on a stage, or a play within a play, perhaps?) They let them get a good swallow of that deathlike life. And then they put in stoolies who were allegedly sentenced to die also and who suddenly began to repent having been so stubborn during interrogation and begged the jailer to tell the interrogator that they were now ready to sign everything. They were given their confessions to sign and then taken out of the cell during the *day*—in other words, not to be shot.

And what about the *genuine* prisoners in that cell who had served as the raw material for the interrogators' game? They no doubt experienced reactions of their own when people in there "repented" and were pardoned? Well, of course, but those are the producer's costs, so to speak.

They say that Konstantin Rokossovsky, the future marshal, was twice taken into the forest at night for a supposed execution. The firing squad leveled its rifles at him, and then they dropped them, and he was taken back to prison. And this was also making use of "the supreme measure" as an interrogator's trick. But it was all right; nothing happened; and he is alive and healthy and doesn't even cherish a grudge about it.

And almost always a person obediently allows himself to be killed. Why is it that the death penalty has such a hypnotic effect? Those pardoned recall hardly anyone in their cell who offered any resistance. But there were such cases. In the Leningrad Kresty Prison in 1932, the prisoners sentenced to execution took the jailers' revolvers away and opened fire. Following this, a different approach was adopted: After peering through the peephole to locate the person they wanted to take, they swarmed into the cell—five armed jailers at a time—and rushed to grab their man. There were eight prisoners under sentence of death in the cell, but every one of them, after all, had sent a petition to Kalinin and every one expected a commutation, and therefore: "You today, me tomorrow." They moved away and looked on indifferently while the condemned man was tied up, while he cried out for help, while they shoved a child's rubber ball into his mouth. (Now, looking at that child's ball, could one really guess all its possible uses? What a good example for a lecturer on the dialectical method!)

Does hope lend strength or does it weaken a man? If the condemned men in every cell had ganged up on the executioners as they came in and choked them, wouldn't this have ended the executions sooner than appeals to the All-Russian Central Executive Committee? When one is already on the edge of the grave, why not resist?

But wasn't everything foredoomed anyway, from the moment of arrest? Yet all the arrested crawled along the path of hope on their knees, as if their legs had been amputated.

■

Vasily Grigoryevich Vlasov remembers that night after he'd been sentenced when he was being taken through dark Kady, and four pistols were brandished on four sides of him. His main thought was: "What if they shoot right now, as a provocation, claiming I was trying to escape?" Obviously he didn't yet believe in his sentence. He still hoped to live.

They confined him in the police room. He was allowed to lie down on the desk to sleep, and two or three policemen kept continuous guard by the light of a kerosene lamp. They talked among themselves: "I kept listening and listening for four days, and I never could understand what they were being condemned for." "It's not for us to understand."

Vlasov lived in this room for five days: they were waiting for an official confirmation of the verdict in order to execute them right there in Kady; it was not easy to convoy the condemned men to some other point. Someone sent a telegram for Vlasov requesting pardon: "I do not admit my guilt, and I request that my life be spared." There was no reply. During these days Vlasov's hands shook so that he could not lift his spoon to his mouth and, instead, picked up his bowl and drank directly from it. Klyugin visited him to jeer. (Soon after the Kady case, he was transferred from Ivanovo to Moscow. That year saw swift ascendancies and swift declines among those crimson stars of the Gulag heaven. The time was approaching when they, too, would be hurled into that same pit, but they didn't know it.)

Neither confirmation nor commutation of the sentence arrived, so they had to take the four condemned men to Kineshma. They took them in four one-and-a-half-ton trucks, with one condemned man guarded by seven policemen in each truck.

In Kineshma they were put in the crypt of a monastery. (Monastery architecture, liberated from monkish ideology, was very useful for us.) At this point some other condemned prisoners were added to their group, and they were all taken in a prisoners' railroad car to Ivanovo.

In the freight yard in Ivanovo they separated three from the rest—Saburov, Vlasov, and one of the men from the other group —and immediately took the others away—to be shot—so as not to crowd the prison any further. And thus it was that Vlasov said farewell to Smirnov.

The three others were put in the courtyard of Prison No. 1 in the dank and raw October air and held there for four hours while they led out, led in, and searched other groups of prisoners in transit. There still was no actual proof that they wouldn't be shot that very day. During those four hours, they had to sit there on the ground and think about it. At one point Saburov thought they were being taken to be shot, but they were actually taken to a cell instead. He did not cry out, but he gripped his neighbor's arm so hard that the latter yelled with pain. The guards had to drag Saburov and prod him with their bayonets.

There were four death cells in this prison—in the same corridor as the juvenile cells and the hospital cells! The death cells had two doors: the customary wooden door with a peephole and a door made of iron grating; each door had two locks, and the jailer and the block supervisor each had a key to a different one, so the doors could be opened only by the two together. Cell 43 was on the other side of a wall of the interrogator's office, and at night, while the condemned men were waiting to be executed, their ears were tormented by the screams of prisoners being tortured.

Vlasov was put into Cell 61. This was a cell intended for solitary confinement, sixteen feet long and a little more than three feet wide. Two iron cots were anchored to the floor by thick iron bolts, and on each cot two condemned men were lying, their heads at opposite ends. Fourteen other prisoners were lying crosswise on the cement floor.

Though it has long been well known that even a corpse has a right to *three arshins* of earth (and even that seemed too little to Chekhov), in this cell each of the condemned had been allotted, while waiting for death, a little less than a third of that!

Vlasov asked whether executions were carried out immediately. "See for yourself. We've been here for ages and we're still alive."

The time of waiting began—of the well-known kind: the prisoners didn't sleep all night long; in a state of total depression, they waited to be led out to death; they listened for every rustling in the corridor. (And the worst thing was that endless waiting destroys the will to resist.) Particularly nerve-racking were the nights following a day on which someone received a commutation of sentence. He went off with cries of happiness, and fear thickened in the cell. After all, rejections as well as commutation had rolled down from the high mountain that day. And at night they would come for someone.

Sometimes the locks rattled at night and hearts fell: Is it for me? Not me! ! And the turnkey would open the wooden door for some nonsense or other: "Take your things off the window sill." That unlocking of the door probably took a year off the lives of all nineteen inmates; maybe if that door was unlocked a mere fifty times, they wouldn't have to waste bullets! But how grateful to him everyone was because everything was all right: "We'll take them off right away, citizen chief!"

After the morning visit to the toilet, they went to sleep, liberated from their fears. Then the jailer brought in the pail of gruel and said: "Good morning!" According to prison rules, the inner, iron door was supposed to be opened only in the presence of the duty officer for the prison. But, as is well known, human beings are better and lazier than their rules and instructions, and in the morning the jailer came in without the duty officer and greeted them quite humanly—no, it was even more precious than that: "Good morning!"

To whom else on all the earth was that morning as good as it was to them! Grateful for the warmth of that voice and the warmth of that dishwater, they drifted off to sleep until noon. (They ate only in the morning!) Many were unable to eat when they woke during the day. Someone had received a parcel. Relatives might or might not know about the death sentence. Once in the cell, these parcels became common property, but they lay and rotted there in the stagnant damp.

By day there was still a little life and activity in the cell. The block supervisor might come around—either gloomy Tarakanov or friendly Makarov—and offer paper on which to write petitions, and ask whether any of them who had some money wanted to buy smokes from the commissary. Their questions seemed either too outrageous or extraordinarily human: the pretense was being made that they weren't condemned men at all, was that it?

The condemned men broke off the bottoms of matchboxes, marked them like dominoes, and played away. Vlasov eased his tension by telling someone about the Consumer Cooperatives, and his narrative always took on a comic touch.[10] Yakov Petrovich Kolpakov, the Chairman of the Sudogda District Executive Committee, a Bolshevik since the spring of 1917 who joined up at the front, sat for dozens of days without changing his position, squeezing his head in his hands, his elbows on his knees, always staring at the same spot on the wall. (It must have been so jolly to recall the spring of 1917.) Vlasov's garrulity irritated him: "How can you?" And Vlasov snapped back at him: "And what are you doing? Preparing yourself for heaven?" Vlasov spoke with round "o's" even in a fast retort. "For myself, I've decided one thing only. I'm going to tell the executioner: 'You alone, not the judges, not the prosecutors, you alone are guilty of my death, and you are going to have to live with it! If it weren't for you willing executioners, there would be no death sentences!' So then let him kill me, the rat!"

Kolpakov was shot. Konstantin Sergeyevich Arkadyev, the former Manager of the Aleksandrov District Agricultural Department in Vladimir Province, was shot. Somehow, in his case,

10. His stories about the consumer cooperatives are remarkable and deserve to be published.

the farewells were particularly hard. During the night six guards came tramping in for him, making a big rush of it, while he, gentle, well mannered, kept turning around, twisting his cap in his hands, putting off the moment of his leavetaking—from the last people on earth for him. And when he said his final "Farewell," you could hardly hear his voice.

At the very first moment, when the victim has been pointed out, the rest are relieved (It's not me!). But right after he has been taken away, the ones left behind are in a state that is hardly any easier to bear than his. All the next day, those left behind are destined to silence and they won't want to eat.

However, Geraska, the young fellow who broke up the building of the village soviet, ate well and slept a lot, getting used to things, even here, with typical peasant facility. He somehow couldn't believe they would shoot him. (And they didn't. They commuted his sentence to a *tenner*.)

Several of the inmates turned gray in three or four days before their cellmates' eyes.

When people wait so long for execution, their hair grows, and orders are given for the whole cell to get haircuts, for the whole cell to get baths. Prison existence goes on, without regard to sentences.

Some individuals lost the ability to speak intelligibly and to understand. But they were left there to await their fate anyway. Anyone who went insane in the death cell was executed insane.

Many sentences were commuted. It was right then, in that fall of 1937, that fifteen- and twenty-year terms were introduced for the first time since the Revolution, and in many cases they replaced the executioners' bullets. There were also commutations to ten-year sentences. And even to *five* years. In the country of miracles even such miracles as this were possible: yesterday he deserved to be executed, and this morning he gets a juvenile sentence; he is a minor criminal, and in camp he may even be able to move around without convoy.

V. N. Khomenko, a sixty-year-old Cossack captain from the Kuban, was also imprisoned in their cell. He was the "soul of the cell," if a death cell can be said to have a soul: he cracked jokes; he smiled to himself; he didn't act as if things were bad. He had become unfit for military service way back after the Japanese

War, had studied horse breeding, and then served in the provincial local self-government council; by the thirties he was attached to the Ivanovo Provincial Agricultural Department as "inspector of the horse herd of the Red Army." In other words, he was supposed to see to it that the best horses went to the army. He was arrested and sentenced to be shot for wrecking—for recommending that stallions be gelded before the age of three, by which means he allegedly "subverted the fighting capacity of the Red Army." Khomenko appealed the verdict. Fifty-five days later the block supervisor came around and pointed out to him that he had addressed his appeal to the wrong appeals jurisdiction. Right then and there, propping the paper against the wall and using the block supervisor's pencil, Khomenko crossed out one jurisdiction and substituted another, as if it were a request for a pack of cigarettes. Thus clumsily corrected, the appeal made the rounds for another sixty days, so Khomenko had been awaiting death for four months. (As for waiting a year or two, after all, we spend year after year waiting for the angel of death! Isn't our whole world just a death cell?) And one day *complete rehabilitation* for Khomenko arrived. (In the interval since his sentence, Voroshilov had given orders that gelding should be done before age three.) Die one minute and dance the next!

Many sentences were commuted, and many prisoners had high hopes. But Vlasov, comparing his case with those of the others, and keeping in mind his conduct at the trial as the principal factor, felt that things were likely to go badly for him. They had to shoot someone. They probably had to shoot at least half of those condemned to death. So he came to believe they would shoot him. And he wanted just one thing—not to bow his head when it happened. That recklessness which was one of his characteristics returned to him and increased within him, and he was all set to be bold and brazen to the very end.

And an opportunity came his way. Making the rounds of the prison for some reason—most likely just to give himself a thrill —the Chief of the Investigation Department of Ivanovo State Security, Chinguli, ordered the door of their cell opened and stood on the threshold. He spoke to someone and asked: "Who is here from the Kady case?"

He was dressed in a short-sleeved silk shirt, which had just begun to appear in Russia and therefore still seemed effeminate.

And either he or his shirt was doused in a sweetish perfume that drifted into the cell.

Vlasov swiftly jumped up on the cot and shouted shrilly: "What kind of colonial officer is this? Get out of here, you murderer!" And from that height he spat juicily full into Chinguli's face.

And he hit his mark.

Chinguli wiped his face and retreated. Because he had no right to enter the cell without six guards, and maybe not even with six guards either.

A reasonable rabbit ought not to behave in that fashion. What if Chinguli had been dealing with your case at that moment and was the one to decide whether to commute or not? After all, he must have had a reason for asking: "Who is here from the Kady case?" That was probably why he came.

But there is a limit, and beyond it one is no longer willing, one finds it too repulsive, to be a reasonable little rabbit. And that is the limit beyond which rabbits are enlightened by the common understanding that all rabbits are foredoomed to become only meat and pelts, and that at best, therefore, one can gain only a postponement of death and not life in any case. That is when one wants to shout: "Curse you, hurry up and shoot!"

It was this particular feeling of rage which took hold of Vlasov even more intensely during his forty-one days of waiting for execution. In the Ivanovo Prison they had twice suggested that he write a petition for pardon, but he had refused.

But on the forty-second day they summoned him to a box where they informed him that the Presidium of the Supreme Soviet had commuted the supreme measure of punishment to twenty years of imprisonment in corrective-labor camps with disenfranchisement for five additional years.

The pale Vlasov smiled wryly, and even at that point words did not fail him:

"It is strange. I was condemned for lack of faith in the victory of socialism in our country. But can even Kalinin himself believe in it if he thinks camps will still be needed in our country twenty years from now?"

At the time it seemed quite inconceivable: after twenty years. Strangely, they were still needed even after thirty.

Chapter 12

■

Tyurzak

Oh, that good Russian word "ostróg"—meaning "jail." What a powerful word it is and how well put together. One senses in it the strength of those thick, impenetrable walls from which one cannot escape. And it is all expressed in just six letters. And it has so many interesting connotations deriving from words that are close to it in sound: as, for instance, strógost—meaning "severity"; and ostrogá—meaning "harpoon"; and ostrotá—meaning "sharpness" (the sharpness of the porcupine's quills when they land in your snout, the sharpness of the blizzard lashing your frozen face, the sharpness of the pointed stakes of the camp perimeter, and the sharpness of the barbed wire too); and the word "ostorózhnost"—meaning "caution" (a convict's caution)—is somewhere close too; and then the word "rog"—meaning "horn." Yes, indeed, the horn juts out boldly and is pointed forward! It is aimed straight at us.

And if one glances over all Russia's jail customs and conduct, at the entire institution during, say, the last ninety years, then you'll see not just one horn really, but two horns. The Narodnaya Volya ("People's Will") revolutionaries began at the tip of one horn, right where it gores, right where it's too excruciatingly painful to take even on the breastbone. They kept wearing it down gradually until it got rounded off, shrank to a stump, and was hardly a horn any longer, and finally became just a woolly open spot (this was the beginning of the twentieth century). But then, after 1917, the first swelling of a new knob could be felt, and there, there, splaying out and with the slogan "You don't have the right!"—it began to thrust upward again, and to narrow to a point and harden, to acquire a horny surface—until by 1938 it was pinning the human being right in that gap between the collarbone and the neck: *tyurzak!*[1] And once a year, the single stroke of a watchman's bell could be heard in the night in the distance: "TONnnnnn!"[2]

If we pursue this parabola with the help of one of the prisoners in the Schlüsselburg Fortress near St. Petersburg, we find that initially things were pretty bad.[3] The prisoner had a number, and no one called him by his family name; the gendarmes acted as if they had been trained in the Lubyanka. They didn't speak a word on their own. If you stammered out: "We . . . ," the reply came: "Speak only for yourself!" The silence of the grave. The cell was in eternal shadows, the windows were frosted glass, the floor asphalt. The hinged ventilation pane in the window was open for forty minutes a day. The food consisted of grits and cabbage soup without meat. They would not allow you any scholarly books from the library. You wouldn't see another human being for two years at a stretch. Only after three years would they let you have sheets of paper—numbered.[4] And then, little by little, things got to be more lenient as the point of the horn got rounded off; there was white bread; and then the prisoners were allowed tea and sugar; one could have money and could buy things in addition to the rations; smoking was permitted; they put transparent glass in the windows; and the transom could be kept open all the time; they painted the walls a light color; in no time at all you could get books by *subscribing* to the St. Petersburg library; there were gratings between the garden plots; one could converse through them, and prisoners even delivered lectures to other prisoners. By then the prisoners were urging the prison administration: "Give us more land to work on, more!" So they planted

1. Tyurzak=TYURemnoye ZAKlyucheniye=prison confinement. Tyurzak is an official term.
2. TON=Tyurma Osobogo Naznacheniya=Special Purpose Prison. TON is likewise an official abbreviation.
3. Vera Figner, *Zapechatlenny Trud: Vospominaniya v Dvukh Tomakh* (*Impressed Labor: Memoirs in Two Volumes*), Moscow, "Mysl," 1964.
4. According to the account of M. Novorussky, from 1884 to 1906 three prisoners in Schlüsselburg committed suicide and five others went insane.

two large prison courtyards in flowers and vegetables—no fewer than 450 varieties! And then there were scientific collections, a carpentry shop, a smithy, and they could earn money and buy books, even Russian political books,[5] and also magazines from abroad. And they wrote their families and got letters from them. And they could go out to walk the whole day long if they liked.

And gradually, as Figner recollects, "it was no longer the superintendent who shouted at the prisoners, but we who shouted at him." In 1902, because he refused to forward a protest of hers, *she ripped the shoulder boards off his uniform*. And the result was that a *military investigator* came and *apologized* profusely to Figner for the ignoramus superintendent!

How did that horn come to shrink and broaden? Figner explains it to some extent by the humanitarian attitudes of individual prison superintendents, and also by the fact that the "gendarmes became friendly with the prisoners," got used to them. One significant factor certainly was the prisoners' determination and dignity and adroitness in conducting themselves. But nonetheless I myself believe that it was the temper of the times: this moisture and freshness in the air which drove away the thundercloud; this breeze of freedom, which was sweeping through society, it was decisive. Without it one could have given the gendarmes instructions from the *Short Course* every Monday, and kept tightening things up, kept putting the screws on. And instead of "impressed labor," Vera Nikolayevna Figner, for tearing off an officer's shoulder boards, would have gotten *nine grams* in the back of her head in a cellar.

The weakening and shaking up of the Tsarist prison system did not come about on its own, of course, but because all society, in concert with the revolutionaries, was shaking it up and ridiculing it in every possible way. Tsarism lost its chance to survive not in the street skirmishes of February but several decades earlier, when youths from well-to-do families began to consider a prison term an honor; when army officers (even guard officers) began to regard it as dishonorable to shake the hand of a gendarme. And the more the prison system weakened, the more clearly

5. P. A. Krasikov, who, as we have seen, later condemned the Metropolitan Veniamin to death, read Marx's *Capital* in the Peter and Paul Fortress. (But he was there only a year, and then they let him out.)

evident were the triumphant *ethics of the political prisoners,* and the more visibly did the members of the revolutionary parties realize their strength and regard their own laws as superior to those of the state.

And that was how Russia of 1917 arrived, bearing 1918 on its shoulders. The reason we have proceeded immediately to 1918 is that the subject of our investigation does not permit us to dwell on 1917. In February, 1917, all political prisons, both those used for interrogation and those in which sentences were served, and all hard-labor prisons as well were emptied. It is a wonder that all the jailers managed to get through the year. Perhaps to make ends meet they simply set to work raising potatoes in their vegetable gardens. (But from 1918 on, things began to get much better for them, and at Shpalernaya Prison they were still serving the new regime even in 1928, and why not!)

In December, 1917, it had already become clear that it was altogether impossible to do without prisons, that some people simply couldn't be left anywhere except behind bars (see Chapter 2, above), because—well, simply because there was no place for them in the new society. And so it was that the new rulers managed to feel their way across the space between the two horns and grope for the budding of the second horn.

Of course, they proclaimed immediately that the horrors of the Tsarist prisons would not be repeated; that *fatiguing correction* would not be permitted; that there would be no compulsory silence in prison, no solitary confinement, no separating the prisoners from one another during outdoor walks, no marching in step and single file, not even any locked cells.[6] Go ahead, dear guests, get together, and talk as much as you like and complain about the Bolsheviks. And the attention of the new prison authorities was directed toward the combat readiness of the prison guards outside the walls and the takeover of the stock of prisons inherited from the Tsar. (This was *one particular part* of the machinery of state that did not have to be destroyed and rebuilt from its foundations.) Fortunately, it turned out that the Civil War had not resulted in the destruction of all the principal *central prisons* and jails. What was really necessary, however, was to repudiate all those old, besmirched words. So now they called

6. Vyshinsky, *Ot Tyurem k Vospitatelnym Uchrezhdeniyam.*

them *political isolators*—political detention centers—demonstrating with this phrase their view of the members of once revolutionary parties as political enemies and stressing not the punitive role of the bars but only the necessity of isolating (and only temporarily, it appeared) these old-fashioned revolutionaries from the onward march of the new society. So that was how the arches of the old central prisons (evidently including the one in Suzdal from the very beginning of the Civil War) came to receive SR's, Social Democrats, and Anarchists.

They all returned to prison with a consciousness of their rights as convicts and a long-established tradition of how to stand up for them. They accepted as their legal due a special *political ration* (conceded by the Tsar and confirmed by the Revolution), which included half a pack of cigarettes a day; purchases from the market (cottage cheese, milk); unrestricted walks outdoors during most hours of the day; being addressed with the formal personal pronoun by prison personnel and not having to stand up when addressed by them; confinement of husband and wife in the same cell; the right to have newspapers, magazines, books, writing materials, and personal articles, even including razors and scissors; sending and receiving letters three times a month; visits from relatives once a month; windows without bars, of course (at that time the concept of the "muzzle" did not exist); unrestricted visits from cell to cell; courtyards with greenery and lilacs for outdoor walks; the freedom to choose companions for outdoor walks and to toss small mailbags from one courtyard to another; and the dispatching of pregnant women from prison into exile two months before they were due to give birth.[7]

All this was just the *politregime*—the prison regimen for political prisoners. But the political prisoners of the twenties remembered well something even more important: *self-government for political prisoners,* and hence even in prison the sense of oneself as part of a whole, a member of a community. Self-government (the free election of spokesmen who represented all the interests of all the prisoners in negotiations with the prison administration) weakened the pressure on the individual because all shoulders bore it together; and it augmented each protest because all voices spoke as one.

7. From 1918 on, they did not hesitate to imprison women SR's, even when they were pregnant.

They undertook to defend all this! And the prison authorities undertook to take it all away from them. And a silent battle began in which no artillery shells were fired, and rifle shots only rarely, and the crash of broken glass wasn't audible even half a verst away. A mute struggle went on for vestiges of freedom, for vestiges of the right to have individual opinions, and it went on for almost twenty years—but no large, richly illustrated volumes describing it have ever been published. And all its ups-and-downs, its catalogue of victories and of defeats, are almost lost to us now, because, after all, there is no written language in the Archipelago and oral communication is broken off when people die. And only random particles of that struggle have occasionally come down to us, illuminated by moonlight that is indirect and indistinct.

And since that time we have grown so supercilious! We are familiar with tank battles; we know about nuclear explosions. What kind of struggle is it over the question of whether cells are kept locked and whether prisoners, to exercise their right to communicate, can openly spell out messages to each other by knocking on the walls, shout from window to window, drop notes from floor to floor on threads, and insist that at least the elected spokesmen of the various party fractions be allowed to move freely among the cells? What sort of a struggle is it to us when the chief of the Lubyanka goes into the cell and the Anarchist Anna G———va (in 1926) or the SR Katya Olitskaya (1931) refuses to stand up when he enters? And that savage beast thought up a punishment for Katya: to deprive her of the right to go to the toilet. What kind of struggle was it when two girls, Shura and Vera (in 1925), in protest against the Lubyanka rule—intended to stifle personality—that conversations may be carried on only in whispers, sang loudly in their cell (only about lilacs and the spring), and thereupon the prison chief, the Latvian Dukes, dragged them through the corridor to the toilet by their hair? Or when the students in a Stolypin car en route from Leningrad (1924) sang revolutionary songs and the convoy thereupon deprived them of water? They yelled out: "A Tsarist convoy wouldn't have done that!" and the convoy beat them. Or when the SR Kozlov, at the transit prison in Kem, loudly called the guards "executioners"—and because of that was dragged off and beaten?

After all, we have gotten used to regarding as *valor* only valor in war (or the kind that's needed for flying in outer space), the kind which jingle-jangles with medals. We have forgotten another concept of *valor*—*civil valor*. And that's all our society needs, just that, just that, just that! That's all we need and that's exactly what we haven't got.

In 1923, in Vyatka Prison, the SR Struzhinsky and his comrades (how many were there? who were they? what were they protesting against?) barricaded themselves in a cell, poured kerosene over all the mattresses, and *incinerated themselves*. Now that was an act altogether in the tradition of Schlüsselburg before the Revolution; and, not to go further, what an uproar such an act provoked *then,* before the Revolution, and how all Russian society was aroused! But this time around neither Vyatka knew about them, nor Moscow, nor history. And yet the human flesh crackled in the flames in exactly the same way.

That was the initial purpose of imprisonment on the Solovetsky Islands (nicknamed Solovki): it was such a good place, cut off from communication with the outside world for half a year at a time. You couldn't be heard from there no matter how loud you shouted, and you could even burn yourself up for all anyone would know. In 1923 the imprisoned socialists were transported there from Pertominsk on the Onega Peninsula—and split up among three isolated monasteries.

Take Savvatyevsky Monastery, consisting of the two buildings which had formerly been guest quarters for religious believers on pilgrimage. Part of the lake was included in the prison compound. In the early months everything seemed to be all right: they had their special political regimen, several relatives succeeded in getting there for visits, and three spokesmen from the three parties were wholly responsible for negotiating with the prison administration. And the monastery compound was a free zone. Inside it the prisoners could talk, think, and do as they pleased without hindrance.

But even then, at the dawn of the Archipelago, there were insistent unpleasant *latrine rumors* (not yet so called) to the effect that the special political regimen was going to be liquidated.

And, in reality, having waited until the middle of December, until the White Sea was no longer navigable, with the consequent cutoff in all communication with the outside world, the chief of the Solovetsky Camp, Eichmans,[8] announced that new instructions had indeed been received regarding the regimen. They wouldn't, of course, take everything away, not by any means! They would cut down on correspondence, and then on something else, too, and, as the most keenly felt measure of the lot, from that day on, December 20, 1923, the right to go in and out of prison buildings twenty-four hours a day would be curtailed— limited to the daylight hours up to 6 P.M.

The party fractions decided to protest, and the SR's and Anarchists called for volunteers: on the first day of the new prohibition they would go outside exactly at 6 P.M. But, as it turned out, Nogtyev, the chief of the Savvatyevsky Monastery Prison, had such an itchy trigger finger that even *before* the appointed hour of 6 (and maybe their watches showed different times; after all, there was no checking it by radio in those days), the guards entered the compound with rifles and opened fire on the prisoners there, who were out of doors quite legally. Three volleys killed six and critically wounded three.

The next day Eichmans himself showed up: there had been an unfortunate misunderstanding. Nogtyev was removed (transferred and promoted). A funeral was held for the victims. They sang in chorus across the Solovetsky wilderness:

> You fell a victim in a fateful fray.

(Was not this perhaps the last occasion when that long-drawn-out melody was permitted for newly dead victims?) They pushed a great boulder onto the common grave and carved on it the names of those who had been killed.[9]

One cannot say that the press concealed this event. *Pravda,* for example, carried a report in small type: the prisoners had *attacked* the convoy, and six had been killed. The honest newspaper *Rote Fahne* reported *revolt* on Solovki.[10]

8. How like Eichmann, is it not?
9. In 1925 the stone was overturned, and the names on it were thus buried too. Any of you who clamber about Solovki—seek it out and gaze upon it!
10. One of the SR's in the Savvatyevsky Monastery was Yuri Podbelsky. He collected the medical documents on the Solovetsky massacre—for publication at some future date. But a year later, at the Sverdlovsk Transit Prison, they discovered a false bottom in his suitcase and confiscated the material he'd hidden. And that is how Russian history stumbles and falls.

Yet the prisoners had defended the regimen successfully! And for a whole year no one spoke of changing it.

For the whole of 1924, yes. But toward the end of the year, insistent rumors circulated again that they were planning to introduce a new system in December. The Dragon had grown hungry again. He wanted new victims. So even though the three monasteries in which socialists were confined—Savvatyevsky, Troitsky, and Muksalmsky—were on separate islands, they managed, by conspiratorial methods, to reach an agreement that all the party fractions in all three monasteries would on one and the same day deliver an ultimatum to Moscow and to the Solovki administration: They must either be removed from the Solovetsky Islands before navigation stopped or else the previous political regimen must be left unchanged. The ultimatum stipulated a time limit of two weeks, and then all three prisons would go on a hunger strike.

This kind of unity compelled attention. It wasn't the sort of thing you could allow to go in one ear and out the other. One day before the time limit expired, Eichmans visited each monastery and announced that Moscow had refused. And on the appointed day a hunger strike began (not a dry hunger strike—water was allowed) in all three monastery prisons (which were now unable to communicate with each other). In Savvatyevsky, about two hundred people struck. Those who fell ill were exempted from striking. A doctor from among the prisoners examined the strikers every day. A collective hunger strike is always more difficult to carry out than an individual one; after all, the weakest rather than the strongest of the strikers can determine its outcome. The only point to a hunger strike is to carry it out with implacable determination and in such a way that everyone knows everyone else involved personally and trusts them fully. Given various party fractions, given several hundred people, both disagreements and moral anguish on other people's behalf were inevitable. After fifteen days, it was necessary to vote by secret ballot in Savvatyevsky—the urn with the ballots was taken from room to room—whether to continue or to lift the hunger strike.

And Moscow and Eichmans waited them out! After all, they were well fed, and there wasn't a peep from the capital newspapers about the hunger strike, and there were no student protest meetings at Kazan Cathedral. *Silence* was already confidently shaping our history.

The monasteries lifted the hunger strike. They had not won out, but they hadn't lost either. The political regimen was left intact for the winter, except that cutting firewood in the forests was added, but that was logical enough. And in the spring of 1925 it looked as though the hunger strike had brought victory: the prisoners from all three monastery prisons were removed from Solovki! To the mainland! No more Arctic night and no more half-year cut off from communication!

But both the convoy and their rations en route were very harsh for that time. And soon they were all perfidiously tricked: On the pretext that their spokesmen would be more comfortable in the "staff" car with the stores and equipment, they were deprived of their leaders. The "staff" car was detached at Vyatka, and the spokesmen were taken to the Tobolsk Isolator. Only at that point did it become clear that the hunger strike of the previous fall had failed. The strong and influential spokesmen had been taken away so as to tighten up on the rest. Yagoda and Katanyan personally directed the incarceration of the former Solovetsky Islands prisoners in the long-standing but until then unused buildings of the Verkhne-Uralsk Isolator, which they thus "opened" in the spring of 1925 (under Chief Dupper). It was destined to be a particular bugbear to prisoners for many decades ahead.

The relocated former Solovki prisoners immediately lost their freedom to move about. The cells were locked. They succeeded in electing spokesmen nonetheless, but the spokesmen didn't have the right to go from cell to cell. The unlimited circulation between cells of money, personal articles, and books, which had existed earlier, was now forbidden. They shouted back and forth from window to window—until the guard fired from his tower into the cells. In reply they organized a protest—they broke windowpanes and destroyed prison equipment. (And, after all, breaking a windowpane is something to think about twice. They might just *not* replace it all winter, and there would be no big surprise in that. It was under the Tsar that the glaziers used to come on the run.) The struggle continued, but it was now being carried on in desperation and under grave handicaps.

In the year 1928 (according to Pyotr Petrovich Rubin) some

466 | THE GULAG ARCHIPELAGO

event or other precipitated a new joint hunger strike by the entire
Verkhne-Uralsk Isolator. But this time the earlier stern and
solemn atmosphere was absent, as were the approval of friends
and a doctor of their own. On a certain day of the strike, the
jailers came bursting into the cells in overwhelming numbers,
and simply began to *beat* the weakened prisoners with clubs and
boots. They beat them to within an inch of their lives—and the
hunger strike ended.

■

From our experience of the past and our literature of the past we
have derived a naïve faith in the power of a hunger strike. But the
hunger strike is a purely moral weapon. It presupposes that the
jailer has not entirely lost his conscience. Or that the jailer is
afraid of public opinion. Only in such circumstances can it be
effective.

The Tsarist jailers were still inexperienced. They got nervous
if one of their prisoners went on a hunger strike; they exclaimed
over it; they looked after him; they put him in the hospital. There
are many examples, but this work is not about them. It is even
humorous to note that it was enough for Valentinov to go on a
hunger strike for twelve days: as a result, he not only achieved
some relaxation in the regimen but was *totally released* from interrogation—whereupon he went to Lenin in Switzerland. Even
in the Orel central hard-labor prison the strikers always won.
They got the regimen relaxed in 1912 and further relaxed in
1913, to the point of general access to outdoor walks for all
political hard-labor prisoners—who were obviously so unrestricted by their supervisors that they managed to compose and
send out to freedom their appeal "to the Russian people." (And
this from the hard-labor prisoners of a central prison!) Furthermore, it was *published*. (It's enough to make one's eyes pop out
of one's head! Someone has to have been crazy!) It was published
in 1914 in issue No. 1 of the *Vestnik Katorgi i Ssylki*—the *Hard-
Labor and Exile Herald*.[11] (And what about that *Herald* itself?

11. M. N. Gernet, *Istoriya Tsarskoi Tyurmy* (*A History of Czarist Prisons*),
Moscow, Yuridicheskaya Literatura (Legal Literature Publishers), 1960–1963,
Vol. V, Ch. 8.

Should we, too, perhaps try to publish one like it?) In 1914, after only *five* days of a hunger strike—admittedly, without water —Dzerzhinsky and four of his comrades obtained *all* their numerous demands (which had to do with living conditions).[12]

In those years, there were no dangers or difficulties for the prisoner beyond the torments of hunger. They could not beat him up for going on a hunger strike, nor sentence him to a second term, nor increase his term, nor shoot him, nor send him off on a prisoner transport. (All this was to come later on.)

In the Revolution of 1905 and the years following it, the prisoners felt themselves to be masters of the prison to such an extent that they did not even go to the trouble of declaring a hunger strike; they simply destroyed prison property (so-called "obstructions"), or went so far as to declare a *strike,* although it might seem that for prisoners this would have hardly any meaning. Thus in the city of Nikolayev in 1906, 197 prisoners in the local prison declared a "strike" in conjunction with people *outside.* Outside the prison, leaflets in support of their strike were published and daily meetings assembled in front of the prison. These meetings (and it goes without saying that the prisoners were at the windows, which had, of course, no "muzzles") forced the administration to accept the demands of the "striking" prisoners. After this, some people on the street and others behind the bars joined in singing revolutionary songs. And things went on that way for *eight* days. (And nobody stopped them! It was, after all, a year of postrevolutionary repression.) On the ninth day all the demands of the prisoners were satisfied! Similar incidents occurred at the time in Odessa, in Kherson, and in Yelizavetgrad. That's how easily victory was attained then.

It would be interesting, incidentally, to compare the effectiveness of hunger strikes under the Provisional Government, but those few Bolsheviks imprisoned from the July days until the Kornilov episode (Kamenev, Trotsky, and Raskolnikov for a while longer) evidently had no reason to go on a hunger strike.

In the twenties, the lively picture of hunger strikes grows clouded (though that depends, of course, on the point of view . . .). This widely known weapon, which had justified itself so gloriously, was, of course, taken over not only by recognized

12. *Ibid.*

"politicals" but also by those who were not recognized as such—the *KR's* (Article 58—Counter-Revolutionaries) and all other kinds of riffraff. However, those arrows which used to be so piercing had been blunted somehow, or else some iron hand had checked them in midflight. True, written declarations of impending hunger strikes were still accepted, and nothing subversive was seen in them as yet. But unpleasant new rules were trotted out: The hunger striker had to be isolated in a special solitary cell (in the Butyrki it was in the Pugachev Tower). It was essential to keep any knowledge about the hunger strike not only from *people outside,* who might protest publicly, and from prisoners in cells nearby, but even from those in the cell in which the hunger striker had been imprisoned until that day—for that, too, constituted a public, and it was necessary to separate him from it. This measure had as its nominal justification the argument that the prison administration had to make sure that the hunger strike was going on honestly—that others in the cell weren't sneaking food to the hunger striker. (And how had that been verified previously? Through honest, "cross my heart" word of honor?)

Still, it was possible in those years to achieve at least one's personal demands by this means.

From the thirties on, state thinking about hunger strikes took a new turn. What did the state want with even such watered-down, isolated, half-suppressed hunger strikes? Wasn't the ideal picture one of prisoners who had no will of their own, nor the capacity to make their own decisions—and of a prison administration that did their thinking and their deciding for them? These are, if you will, the only prisoners who can exist in the new society. And so from the beginning of the thirties, they stopped accepting declarations of hunger strikes as legal. "The hunger strike as a method of resistance *no longer exists,"* they proclaimed to Yekaterina Olitskaya in 1932, and they said the same thing to many others. The government has abolished your hunger strikes—and that's that. But Olitskaya refused to obey and began to fast. They let her go on fasting in solitary for *fifteen* days. Then they took her to the hospital and put milk and dried crusts in front of her to tempt her. But she stood firm, and on the *nineteenth* day she won her victory: she got an extended outdoor period and newspapers and parcels from the Political Red Cross. (That's how one had to moan and groan in order to receive those legitimate relief parcels!) Overall, however, it was an insignificant victory and paid for too dearly. Olitskaya recalls such foolish hunger strikes on the part of others too: people starved up to twenty days in order to get delivery of a parcel or a change of companions for their outdoor walk. Was it worth it? After all, in the *New Type Prison* one's strength, once lost, could not be restored. The religious-sect member Koloskov fasted until he died on the twenty-fifth day. Could one in general permit oneself to fast in the New Type Prison? After all, the new prison heads, operating in secrecy and silence, had acquired several powerful methods of combating hunger strikes:

1. Patience on the part of the administration. (We have seen enough of what this meant from preceding examples.)

2. Deception. This, too, can be practiced thanks to total secrecy. When every step is reported by the newspapers, you aren't going to do much deceiving. But in our country, why not? In 1933, in the Khabarovsk Prison, S. A. Chebotaryev, demanding that his family be informed of his whereabouts, fasted for seventeen days. (He had come from the Chinese Eastern Railroad in Manchuria and then suddenly disappeared, and he was worried about what his wife might be thinking.) On the seventeenth day, Zapadny, the Deputy Chief of the Provincial GPU, and the Khabarovsk Province prosecutor (their ranks indicate that lengthy hunger strikes were really not so frequent) came to see him and showed him a telegraph receipt (There, they said, they had informed his wife!), and thus persuaded him to take some broth. And the receipt was a fake! (Why had these high-ranking officials gone to this trouble? Not, certainly, for Chebotaryev's life. Evidently, in the *first* half of the thirties there was still some sort of personal responsibility on the part of higher-ups for long-drawn-out hunger strikes.)

3. Forced artificial feeding. This method was adapted, without any question, from experience with wild animals in captivity. And it could be employed only in total secrecy. By 1937 artificial feeding was, evidently, already in wide use. For example, in the group hunger strike of socialists in the Yaroslavl Central Prison, artificial feeding was forced on everyone on the fifteenth day.

Artificial feeding has much in common with rape. And that's what it really is: four big men hurl themselves on one weak being and deprive it of its one interdiction—they only need to do it once and what happens to it next is not important. The element of rape inheres in the violation of the victim's will: "It's not going to be the way you want it, but the way I want it; lie down and submit." They pry open the mouth with a flat disc, then broaden the crack between the jaws and insert a tube: "Swallow it." And if you don't swallow it, they shove it farther down anyway and then pour liquefied food right down the esophagus. And then they massage the stomach to prevent the prisoner from resorting to vomiting. The sensation is one of being morally defiled, of sweetness in the mouth, and a jubilant stomach gratified to the point of delight.

Science did not stand still, and other methods were developed for artificial feeding: an enema through the anus, drops through the nose.

4. A new view of the hunger strike: that hunger strikes are a continuation of counterrevolutionary activity in prison, and must be punished with a new *prison term*. This aspect promised to give rise to a very rich new category in the practices of the New Type Prison, but it remained essentially in the realm of threats. And it was not, of course, any sense of humor that cut it short, but most likely simple laziness: why bother with all that when patience will take care of it? Patience and more patience—the patience of a well-fed person vis-à-vis one who is starving.

Approximately in the middle of 1937, a new directive came: From now on the prison administration *will not in any respect be responsible for those dying on hunger strikes!* The last vestige of personal responsibility on the part of the jailers had disappeared! (In these circumstances, the prosecutor of the province would not have come to visit Chebotaryev!) Furthermore, so that the interrogator shouldn't get disturbed, it was also announced that days spent on hunger strike by a prisoner under interrogation should be crossed off the official interrogation period. In other words, it should not only be considered that the *hunger strike had not taken place,* but the prisoner should be regarded as not having been in prison at all during the period of the strike. Thus the interrogator would not be to blame for being behind schedule. Let the only perceptible result of the hunger strike be the prisoner's exhaustion!

And that meant: If you want to kick the bucket, go ahead!

Arnold Rappoport had the misfortune to declare a hunger strike in the Archangel NKVD Internal Prison at the very moment when this directive arrived. It was a particularly severe form of hunger strike, and that ought, it would seem, to have given it more impact. His was a "dry" strike—without fluids— and he kept it up for thirteen days. (Compare the five-day "dry" strike of Dzerzhinsky, who probably wasn't isolated in a separate cell. And who in the end won total victory.) And during those *thirteen* days in solitary, to which Rappoport had been moved, only a medical assistant looked in now and then. No doctor came. And no one from the administration took the slightest interest in *what he was demanding* with his hunger strike. They never even asked him. The only attention the administration paid him was to search his cell carefully, and they managed to dig out some hidden makhorka and several matches. What Rappoport wanted was to put an end to the interrogator's humiliation of him. He had prepared for his hunger strike in a thoroughly scientific way. He had received a food parcel earlier, and so he ate only butter and ring-shaped rolls, baranki, and he quit eating black bread a week before his strike. He starved until he could see the light through his hands. He recalls experiencing a sensation of lightheadedness and clarity of thought. At a certain moment, a kindly, compassionate woman jailer named Marusya came to his cell and whispered to him: "Stop your hunger strike; it isn't going to help; you'll just die! You should have done it a week earlier." He listened to her and called off his hunger strike without having gotten anywhere at all. Nevertheless, they gave him hot red wine and a roll, and afterward the jailers took him back to the common cell in a hand-carry. A few days later, his interrogation began again. But the hunger strike had not been entirely useless: the interrogator had come to understand that Rappoport had will power enough and no fear of death, and he eased up on the interrogation. "Well, now, it turns out you are quite a wolf," the interrogator said to him. "A wolf!" Rappoport affirmed. "And I'll certainly never be your dog."

Rappoport declared another hunger strike later on, at the

Kotlas Transit Prison, but it turned out somewhat comically. He announced that he was demanding a new interrogation, and that he would not board the prisoner transport. They came to him on the third day: "Get ready for the prisoner transport." "You don't have the right. I'm on a hunger strike!" At that point four young toughs picked him up, carried him off, and tossed him into the bath. After the bath, they carried him to the guardhouse. With nothing else left to do, Rappoport stood up and went to join the column of prisoners boarding the prisoner transport—after all, there were dogs and bayonets at his back.

And that is how the New Type Prison defeated bourgeois hunger strikes.

Even a strong man had no way left him to fight the prison machine, except perhaps suicide. But is suicide really resistance? Isn't it actually submission?

The SR Yekaterina Olitskaya thinks that the Trotskyites, and, subsequently, the Communists who followed them into prison, did a great deal to weaken the hunger strike as a weapon for fighting back: they declared hunger strikes too easily and lifted them too easily. She says that even the Trotskyite leader I. N. Smirnov, after going on a hunger strike four days before their Moscow trial, quickly surrendered and lifted it. They say that up to 1936 the Trotskyites rejected any hunger strike *against the Soviet government* on principle, and never supported SR's and Social Democrats who were on hunger strikes.[13]

Let history say how true or untrue that reproach is. However, no one paid for hunger strikes so much and so grievously as the Trotskyites. (We will come to their hunger strikes and their strikes in camps in Part III.)

Excessive haste in declaring and lifting hunger strikes was probably characteristic of impetuous temperaments which reveal their feelings too quickly. But there were, after all, such natures, such characters, among the old Russian revolutionaries, too, and there were similar temperaments in Italy and France, but no-

---

13. But they always demanded support for themselves from the SR's and Social Democrats. On a prisoner transport to Karaganda and the Kolyma in 1936, they addressed as traitors and provocateurs all those who refused to sign their telegram to Kalinin protesting "against sending the *vanguard of the Revolution* [i.e., themselves] to the Kolyma." (The story was told by Makotinsky.)

where, either in prerevolutionary Russia, in Italy, or in France, were the authorities so successful in discouraging hunger strikes as in the Soviet Union. There was probably no less physical sacrifice and no less spiritual determination in the hunger strikes in the second quarter of our century than there had been in the first. But there was no public opinion in the Soviet Union. And on that basis the New Type Prison waxed and grew strong. And instead of easy victories, the prisoners suffered hard-earned defeats.

Decades passed and time produced its own results. The hunger strike—the first and most natural weapon of the prisoner—in the end became alien and incomprehensible to the prisoners themselves. Fewer and fewer desired to undertake them. And to prison administrations the whole thing began to seem either plain stupidity or else a malicious violation.

When, in 1960, Gennady Smelov, a nonpolitical offender, declared a lengthy hunger strike in the Leningrad prison, the prosecutor went to his cell for some reason (perhaps he was making his regular rounds) and asked him: "Why are you torturing yourself?"

And Smelov replied: "Justice is more precious to me than life."

This phrase so astonished the prosecutor with its irrelevance that the very next day Smelov was taken to the Leningrad Special Hospital (i.e., the insane asylum) for prisoners. And the doctor there told him:

"We suspect you may be a schizophrenic."

■

Along the rings of the horn, where it began to narrow to its point, the former central prisons arose, rechristened, by the beginning of 1937, the "special isolators." The last little weaknesses were now being squeezed out of the system, the last vestiges of light and air. And the hunger strike of the tired socialists, their numbers sparse by now, in the Yaroslavl Penalty Isolator at the beginning of 1937 was one of their last, desperate efforts.

They were still demanding that everything should be restored to what it once had been. They were demanding both the election of spokesmen and free communication between cells, but it is unlikely that even they had hopes of this any longer. By a fifteen-day hunger strike, even though it ended with their being force-fed through a tube, they had apparently succeeded in defending some portions of their regimen: a one-hour period outdoors, access to the provincial newspaper, notebooks for their writing. These they kept. But the authorities promptly took away their personal belongings and threw at them the common prison cloth-ing of the special isolator. And a little while later, they cut half an hour off their time outdoors. And then they reduced it by another fifteen minutes.

These were the same people who were being dragged through a sequence of prisons and exiles according to the rules of the Big Solitaire. Some hadn't lived an ordinary, decent human life for ten years; some for fifteen; all they had was this meager prison life, with hunger strikes to boot. A few who had gotten used to winning out over the prison administrations before the Revolu-tion were still alive. However, before the Revolution they were marching in step with Time against a weakening enemy. And now Time was against them and allied with an enemy growing steadily stronger. Among them were young people too (how strange that seems to us nowadays)—those who considered them-selves SR's, Social Democrats, or Anarchists even after the parties themselves had been battered out of existence—and the only future these new recruits had to look forward to was life in prison.

The loneliness surrounding the entire prison struggle of the socialists, which became more hopeless with every year that passed, grew more and more acute, approaching a vacuum in the end. That was not how it had been under the Tsar: Throw open the prison doors and the public greeted them with flowers. Now they leafed through the newspapers and saw that they were being drenched in vituperation, with slops even. (For it was the socialists, after all, whom Stalin saw as the most dan-gerous enemies of his socialism.) And the people were silent. And what could give them any reason to dare suppose that the people had any kindly feelings left toward those they had not long before elected to the Constituent Assembly? And finally the newspapers stopped showering profanity on them because Rus-sian socialists had by that time come to seem so unimportant and so impotent and even nonexistent. By this time these socialists were remembered outside in freedom only as something belonging to the past—the distant past. And young people hadn't the slightest idea that SR's and Mensheviks were still alive somewhere. And in the sequence of Chimkent and Cherdyn exile, and the Verkhne-Uralsk and Vladimir isolators—how could they not tremble in their dark solitary-confinement cells, cells with "muzzles" by this time, and feel that perhaps their program and their leaders had been mistaken, that perhaps their tactics and actions had been mistaken too? And all their actions began to seem nothing but inaction—and their lives, devoted only to suffering, a fatal delusion.

Their lonely prison struggle had been essentially undertaken for all of us, for all future prisoners (even though they themselves might not think so, nor understand this), for *how* we would exist in imprisonment and how we would be kept there. And if they had won out, then probably nothing of what happened to us would have happened, nothing of what this book is about, all seven of its parts.

But they were beaten. They failed to protect either themselves or us.

In part, too, the canopy of loneliness spread over them because, in the very first postrevolutionary years, having naturally accepted from the GPU the well-merited identification of *politicals,* they naturally agreed with the GPU that all who were "to the right"[14] of them, beginning with the Cadets, were not politicals but KR's —*Counter-Revolutionaries*—the manure of history. And they also regarded as KR's those who suffered for their faith in Christ. And whoever didn't know what "right" or "left" meant —and that, in the future, would be all of us—they considered to be KR's also. And thus it was that, in part voluntarily, in part involuntarily, keeping themselves aloof and shunning others, they gave their blessing to the future "Fifty-eight" into whose maw they themselves would disappear.

Objects and actions change their aspect quite decisively depending on the position of the observer. In this chapter we have been describing the prison stand of the socialists from their point of view. And, as you see, it is illuminated by a pure and tragic light. But those KR's whom the politicals treated so con-

14. I do not like these "left" and "right" classifications; they are conditional concepts, they are loosely bandied about, and they do not convey the essence.

temptuously on Solovki, those KR's recall the politicals in their own way! *"The politicals?* What a nasty crowd they were: they looked down their noses at everyone else; they stuck to their own group; they demanded their own special rations all the time and their own special privileges. And they kept quarreling among themselves incessantly." And how can one but feel that there is truth here too? All those fruitless and endless arguments which by now are merely comical. And those demands for additional rations for themselves in comparison with the masses of the hungry and impoverished? In the Soviet period, the honorable appellation of *politicals* turned out to be a poisoned gift. And then another reproach followed immediately: Why was it that the socialists, who used to *escape* so easily under the Tsar, had become so soft in Soviet prisons? Where are their *escapes?* In general there were quite a few escapes, but who can remember any socialists among them?

And, in turn, those prisoners "to the left" of the socialists—the Trotskyites and the Communists—shunned the socialists, considering them exactly the same kind of KR's as the rest, and they closed the moat of isolation around them with an encircling ring.

The Trotskyites and the Communists, each considering their own direction more pure and lofty than all the rest, despised and even hated the socialists (and each other) who were imprisoned behind the bars of the same buildings and went outdoors to walk in the same prison courtyards. Yekaterina Olitskaya recalls that in 1937, at the transit prison on Vanino Bay, when the socialists called to each other across the fence between the men's and women's compounds, looking for fellow socialists and reporting news, the Communists Liza Kotik and Mariya Krutikova were indignant because they might bring down punishment on them all by such irresponsible behavior. They said: "All our misfortunes are due to those socialist rats! [A profound explanation, and so dialectical too!] They should be choked!" And those two girls in the Lubyanka in 1925, whom I have already mentioned, sang about spring and lilacs only because one of them was an SR and the second a member of the Communist opposition, and they had no political song in common, and in fact the Communist-deviationist girl shouldn't really have joined the SR girl in her protest at all.

And if in a Tsarist prison the different parties often joined forces in a common struggle (let us recall in this connection the escape from the Sevastopol Central Prison), in Soviet prisons each political group tried to ensure its own purity by steering clear of the others. The Trotskyites struggled on their own, apart from the socialists and Communists; the Communists didn't struggle at all, for how could one allow oneself to struggle against one's own government and one's own prison?

It turned out in consequence that the Communists in isolators and in prisons for long-termers were restricted earlier and more cruelly than others. In 1928, in the Yaroslavl Central Prison, the Communist Nadezhda Surovtseva went outdoors for fresh air in a single-file column that was forbidden to engage in conversation, while the socialists were still chattering in their own groups. She was not permitted to tend the flowers in the courtyard —because they had been left by previous prisoners who had struggled for their rights. And they deprived her of newspapers too. (However, the Secret Political Department of the GPU permitted her to have complete sets of Marx and Engels, Lenin and Hegel in her cell.) Her mother's visit to her took place virtually in the dark, and her downcast mother died soon afterward. (What must she have thought of her daughter's circumstances in prison?)

The difference between the treatment of socialist prisoners and that of the Communists persisted many years, went far beyond this, and extended to a difference in rewards: in 1937–1938 the socialists were imprisoned like the rest and they all got their *tenners* too. But, as a rule, they were not forced to denounce themselves: they had, after all, never hidden their own, *special*, individual views—which were quite enough to get them sentenced. But a Communist had no *special*, individual views, so what, then, was he to be sentenced for if a self-denunciation wasn't forced out of him?

■

Even though the enormous Archipelago was already spreading across the land, the prisons for long-termers didn't fall into decay. The old jail tradition was being zealously carried on. Everything new and invaluable which the Archipelago had contributed to the indoctrination of the masses was still not enough in itself.

The deficiency was provided for by the complementary existence of the TON's—the Special Purpose Prisons—and prisons for long-termers in general.

Not everyone swallowed up by the Great Machine was allowed to mingle with the natives of the Archipelago. Well-known foreigners, individuals who were too famous or who were being held secretly, purged gaybisty, could not by any means be seen openly in camps; their hauling a barrow did not compensate for the disclosure and the consequent *moral-political*[15] damage. In the same way, the socialists, who were engaged in a continuous struggle for their prison rights, could not conceivably be permitted to mingle with the masses but had to be kept separately and, in fact, suffocated separately—in view of their special privileges and rights. Much later on, in the fifties, as we shall learn later in this work, the Special Purpose Prisons were also needed to isolate camp rebels. And in the last years of his life, disappointed in the possibilities of "reforming" thieves, Stalin gave orders that various *ringleaders of the thieves* should also get *tyurzak* rather than camp. And then, to be sure, it was necessary for the state to support free of charge in prison those prisoners who because of their feebleness would have immediately died off in camp and would thus have shirked their duty to serve out their terms. And others who couldn't possibly be used in camp work—like the blind Kopeikin, a man of seventy who used to sit all day long in the market in Yuryevets on the Volga. His songs and facetious comments won him ten years for KRD—Counter-Revolutionary Activity—but in his case they had to substitute prison for camp.

The inventory of old jails, inherited from the Romanov dynasty, was, of necessity, looked after, remodeled, strengthened, and perfected. Certain central prisons, like the one in Yaroslavl, were so well and suitably appointed (doors plated with iron; table, stool, and cot permanently anchored in each cell) that the only thing required to bring them up to date was the installation of "muzzles" on the windows and the fencing in of the courtyards where the prisoners walked in order to reduce them to the size of a cell (by 1937 all the trees on prison grounds had been cut down, all vegetable gardens plowed under, and all grassy areas paved with asphalt). Others, like the one in Suzdal, required new

15. This term actually exists! And it has a sky-blue swampy coloration!

equipment, and the monastery arrangement had to be remodeled, but, after all, self-incarceration of a body in a monastery and its incarceration in a prison by the state serve physically similar purposes, and therefore the buildings were always easy to adapt. One of the buildings of the Sukhanovka Monastery was adapted for use as a prison for long-termers. Of course, it was also necessary to make up for losses from the Tsarist inventory: the conversion of the Peter and Paul Fortress in Leningrad and of Schlüsselburg near Leningrad into museums for tourists. The Vladimir Central Prison was expanded and added to—with a big new building constructed under Yezhov. It was heavily used and garnered many prisoners over those decades. We have already mentioned how the Tobolsk Central Prison was inaugurated, and that Verkhne-Uralsk was opened in 1925 for continuous and abundant use. (To our misfortune, all these isolators are still in use and are *in operation* at the moment these lines are being written.) From Tvardovsky's poem "Distance Beyond Distance" one can draw the conclusion that the Aleksandrovsk Central Prison wasn't empty in Stalin's time either. We have less information about the one in Orel: it is feared that it suffered serious damage during World War II. But not far from it was the well-equipped prison for long-termers in Dmitrovsk-Orlovsky.

During the twenties the prisoner's *food* was very decent in the isolators for politicals (still called "politizakrytki"—"political lock-ups"—by the prisoners): the lunches always included some meat; fresh vegetables were served; milk could be bought in the commissary. In 1931–1933 the food deteriorated sharply, but things were no better out in freedom at that time. Both scurvy and dizziness from lack of food were no rarity in the prisons for politicals in those years. Later on the food improved, but it was never the same as before. In 1947, in the Vladimir TON, I. Korneyev was constantly hungry: one pound of bread, two pieces of sugar, two hot dishes which were not at all filling; the only thing available in unlimited quantities was boiling water. (It will, of course, be said once more that this was not a typical year and there was hunger outside in freedom, too, at the time. This was when they generously allowed freedom to feed prison: unlimited parcels were permitted.) The *light* in cells was always "rationed," so to speak, in both the thirties and the forties: the "muzzles" on the windows and the frosted reinforced glass created a permanent twilight in the cells (darkness is an important factor in causing depression). They often stretched netting above the window "muzzle," and in the winter it was covered with snow, which cut off this last access to the light. Reading became no more than a way of ruining one's eyes. In the Vladimir TON, they made up for this lack of light at night: bright electric lights burned all night long, preventing sleep. And in the Dmitrovsk Prison in 1938 (N. A. Kozyrev), there was light in the evenings and at night—a kerosene lamp on a little shelf way up near the ceiling, that burned away and smoked up the last air; in 1939 there were electric lights that glowed red at half-voltage. *Air* was "rationed" too. The hinged panes for ventilation were kept locked, and opened only during the interval of the prisoners' trip to the toilet, as prisoners recall from both Dmitrovsk and Yaroslavl prisons. (Y. Ginzburg: The bread grew moldy between morning and lunchtime; the sheets were damp, and the walls green.) In Vladimir in 1948 there was no lack of air, because the transom was open permanently. *Walks outdoors* ranged from fifteen to forty-five minutes at various hours in various prisons. There was no such thing as the communication with the soil that had existed in Schlüsselburg or Solovki; everything that grew had been torn up by the roots, trampled, covered with concrete and asphalt. They even forbade lifting up one's head to the heavens during the walks: "Look at your feet!" This was the command both Kozyrev and Adamova remember from the Kazan Prison. *Visits* from relatives were forbidden in 1937 and never renewed. *Letters* could be sent to close relatives twice a month and could be received from them in most years. (But in Kazan they had to be returned to the administration the day after they had been read.) Access to the *commissary* to make purchases with the money sent in specifically limited amounts was usually permitted. *Furniture* was no unimportant part of the prison regimen. Adamova wrote eloquently of her happiness at finding a simple wooden cot with a straw mattress and a simple wooden table in her cell in Suzdal, after having had only cots that folded into the wall and chairs anchored to the floor. In the Vladimir TON, I. Korneyev experienced two different prison *regimens:*

Under one, in 1947–1948, personal articles were not removed from the cell; one could lie down during the day; and the turnkey very seldom looked through the peephole. But under the other, in 1949–1953, the cell was locked with two locks (the responsibility of the turnkey and duty officer respectively); one was forbidden to lie down, forbidden to talk in a normal voice (in Kazan, only in a whisper); personal articles were all taken away; a uniform of striped mattress ticking was issued; correspondence was permitted only twice a year and only on those days announced without warning by the chief of the prison (anyone who missed that day couldn't write), and only a sheet of paper half the size of a postal sheet could be used; violent *searches* and unscheduled visits were frequent, requiring the complete turning out of one's belongings and undressing down to one's skin. Communication between cells was prohibited to such an extent that the jailers went through the toilets with a portable lantern after each toilet visit and searched in each hole. The entire cell would get *punishment cells* for graffiti in the toilets. The punishment cells were a scourge in the Special Purpose Prisons. One could get into a punishment cell for coughing. ("Cover your head with your blanket. Then you can cough!") Or for *walking around the cell* (Kozyrev: "It was considered to be rebellious"); for the noise made by one's shoes. (In the Kazan Prison women had been issued men's shoes that were much too large for women's feet— size 10½.) Incidentally, Ginzburg was correct in concluding that periods in a punishment cell were meted out not for any particular misdemeanor but *according to a schedule:* every prisoner was required to spend some time there in order to learn what it was like. And the rules included another generally applicable point: "In the event of any display of unruliness in a punishment cell [?], the chief of the prison has the right to extend the term of incarceration there *to twenty days.*" Just what was meant by unruliness? Here's what happened to Kozyrev. (The descriptions of the punishment cell and much else in the prison regimen tally to such an extent among all sources that the stamp of a single system of administrative rules can be detected.) He was given another five days in the punishment cell for pacing back and forth. In the autumn, the building containing the punishment cells was unheated, and it was very cold. They forced prisoners to undress down to their underwear and to take off their shoes. The floor was bare earth and dust (it might be wet dirt; and in the Kazan Prison it might even be covered with water). Kozyrev had a stool in his. (Ginzburg had none in hers.) He immediately concluded that he would perish, that he would freeze to death. But some kind of mysterious inner warmth gradually made itself felt, and it was his salvation. He learned to sleep sitting on his stool. They gave him a mug of hot water three times a day; it made him drunk. One of the duty officers, in violation of the rules, pressed a piece of sugar into his ten-and-a-half-ounce bread ration. On the basis of the rations issued him, and by observing the light from some faraway, tiny, labyrinthine window, Kozyrev kept count of the days. His five days had come to an end, but he had not been released. His sense of hearing had become extremely acute and he heard whispers in the corridor—having to do with either "the sixth" or "six days." This was a provocation: they were waiting for him to say that his five days were over and that it was time to let him out. That would have constituted unruliness, for which his stay in the punishment cell would have been prolonged. But he sat silent and obedient for another day, and then they let him out, just as if everything had been the way it was supposed to be. (Perhaps the chief of the prison used this method for testing all the prisoners in turn for submissiveness? And then he could sentence all those who weren't yet submissive enough to further terms in the punishment cell.) After the punishment cell the ordinary cell seemed like a palace. Kozyrev became deaf for half a year, and he began to get abscesses in his throat. His cellmate went insane from frequent imprisonment in the punishment cell, and Kozyrev was kept locked up with an insane man for more than a year, with just the two of them there. (Nadezhda Surovtseva recalls many cases of insanity in political isolators—she herself recalls as many as Novorussky totaled up in the whole chronicle of Schlüsselburg.)

Does it not at this point seem to the reader that we have gradually, step by step, mounted to the very point, the peak, of the second horn—and that it is probably really higher than the first? And probably sharper too?

But opinions are divided. With one voice the old camp veterans consider the Vladimir TON of the fifties a *resort*. That is how

Vladimir Borisovich Zeldovich, sent there from Abez Station, regarded it, and Anna Petrovna Skripnikova, who was sent there in 1956 from the Kemerovo camps. Skripnikova was particularly astonished at the regular dispatch, every ten days, of petitions and declarations (she even began to write, believe it or not, to the United Nations) and by the excellent library, including books in foreign languages: they used to bring the complete catalogue to the cell and you made out a list for a whole year ahead.

It is also necessary to keep in mind how elastic our law is: thousands of women ("wives") were sentenced to prison, to tyurzak. And then one fine day someone whistled—and they were transferred to camps. (The Kolyma hadn't fulfilled the gold plan.) And so they switched them, without any trial or any court.

In fact, does tyurzak actually *exist* at all, or is it only the vestibule for the camps?

■

And only here, right here, is where our chapter ought to have begun. It ought to have examined that glimmering light which, in time, the soul of the lonely prisoner begins to emit, like the halo of a saint. Torn from the hustle-bustle of everyday life in so absolute a degree that even counting the passing minutes puts him intimately in touch with the Universe, the lonely prisoner has to have been purged of every imperfection, of everything that has stirred and troubled him in his former life, that has prevented his muddied waters from settling into transparency. How gratefully his fingers reach out to feel and crumble the lumps of earth in the vegetable garden (but, alas, it is all asphalt). How his head rises of itself toward the Eternal Heavens (but, alas, this is forbidden). And how much touching attention the little bird on the window sill arouses in him (but, alas, there is that "muzzle" there, and the netting as well, and the hinged ventilation pane is locked). And what clear thoughts, what sometimes surprising conclusions, he writes down on the paper issued him (but, alas, only if you buy it in the commissary, and only if you turn it in to the prison office when you have used it up—for eternal safekeeping . . .).

But our peevish qualifications somehow interrupt our line of thought. The plan of our chapter creaks and cracks, and we no longer know the answer to the question: Is the soul of a person in the New Type Prison, in the Special Purpose Prison (the TON), purified or does it perish once and for all?

If the first thing you see each and every morning is the eyes of your cellmate who has gone insane, how then shall you save yourself during the coming day? Nikolai Aleksandrovich Kozyrev, whose brilliant career in astronomy was interrupted by his arrest, saved himself only by thinking of the eternal and infinite: of the order of the Universe—and of its Supreme Spirit; of the stars; of their internal state; and what Time and the passing of Time really are.

And in this way he began to discover a new field in physics. And only in this way did he succeed in surviving in the Dmitrovsk Prison. But his line of mental exploration was blocked by forgotten figures. He could not build any further—he had to have a lot of figures. Now just where could he get them in his solitary-confinement cell with its overnight kerosene lamp, a cell into which not even a little bird could enter? And the scientist prayed: "Please, God! I have done everything I could. Please help me! Please help me continue!"

At this time he was entitled to receive one book every ten days (by then he was alone in the cell). In the meager prison library were several different editions of Demyan Bedny's *Red Concert,* which kept coming around to each cell again and again. Half an hour passed after his prayer; they came to exchange his book; and as usual, without asking anything at all, they pushed a book at him. It was entitled *A Course in Astrophysics!* Where had it come from? He simply could not imagine such a book in the prison library. Aware of the brief duration of this coincidence, Kozyrev threw himself on it and began to memorize everything he needed immediately, and everything he might need later on. In all, just two days had passed, and he had eight days left in which to keep his book, when there was an unscheduled inspection by the chief of the prison. His eagle eye noticed immediately. "But you are an astronomer?" "Yes." "Take this book away from him!" But its mystical arrival had opened the way for his further work, which he then continued in the camp in Norilsk.

And so now we should begin the chapter on the conflict between the soul and the bars.

But what is this? The jailer's key is rattling brazenly in the lock. The gloomy block superintendent is there with a long list. "Last name, first name, patronymic? Date of birth? Article of the Code? Term? End of term? Get your *things* together. Be quick about it!"

Well, brothers, a prisoner transport! A prisoner transport! We're off to somewhere! Good Lord, bless us! Shall we gather up our bones?

Well, here's what: If we are still alive, then we'll finish this story another time. In Part IV. If we are still alive . . .

END OF PART I

PART II

Perpetual Motion

■

And then we see it in the wheels,
    the wheels!
Which never like to rest,
    the wheels! . . .
How heavy are the stones themselves,
    the millstones!
They dance in merry ranks . . .
    the millstones!

W. Müller

Viktor Petrovich Pokrovsky

Aleksandr Shtrobinder

Vasily Ivanovich Anichkov

Aleksandr Andreyevich Svechin

Mikhail Aleksandrovich Reformatsky

Yelizaveta Yevgenyevna Anichkova

Chapter 1

■

The Ships of the Archipelago

Scattered from the Bering Strait almost to the Bosporus are thousands of islands of the spellbound Archipelago. They are invisible, but they exist. And the invisible slaves of the Archipelago, who have substance, weight, and volume, have to be transported from island to island just as invisibly and uninterruptedly.

And by what means are they to be transported? On what?

Great ports exist for this purpose—transit prisons; and smaller ports—camp transit points. Sealed steel ships also exist: railroad cars especially christened *zak cars* ("prisoner cars"). And out at the anchorages, they are met by similarly sealed, versatile *Black Marias* rather than by sloops and cutters. The *zak cars* move along on regular schedules. And, whenever necessary, whole caravans—trains of red cattle cars—are sent from port to port along the routes of the Archipelago.

All this is a thoroughly developed system! It was created over dozens of years—not hastily. Well-fed, uniformed, unhurried people created it. The Kineshma convoy waits at the Moscow Northern Station at 1700 hours on odd-numbered days to accept Black Marias from the Butyrki, Krasnaya Presnya, and Taganka prisons. The Ivanovo convoy has to arrive at the station at 0600 hours on even-numbered days to receive and hold in custody transit prisoners for Nerekhta, Bezhetsk, and Bologoye.

All this is happening right next to you, you can almost touch it, but it's invisible (and you can shut your eyes to it too). At the big stations the loading and unloading of the dirty faces takes place far, far from the passenger platform and is seen only by switchmen and roadbed inspectors. At smaller stations a blind alleyway between two warehouses is preferred, into which the Black Marias can back so that their steps are flush with the steps of the zak car. The convict doesn't have time to look at the station, to see you, or to look up and down the train. He gets to look only at the steps. (And sometimes the lower step is waist-high, and he hasn't the strength to climb up on it.) And the convoy guards, who have blocked off the narrow crossing from the Black Maria to the zak car, growl and snarl: "Quick, quick! Come on, come on!" And maybe even brandish their bayonets.

And you, hurrying along the platform with your children, your suitcases, and your string bags, are too busy to look closely: Why is that second baggage car hitched onto the train? There is no identification on it, and it is very much like a baggage car —and the gratings have diagonal bars, and there is darkness behind them. But then why are soldiers, defenders of the Fatherland, riding in it, and why, when the train stops, do two of them march whistling along on either side and peer down under the car?

The train starts—and a hundred crowded prisoner destinies, tormented hearts, are borne along the same snaky rails, behind the same smoke, past the same fields, posts, and haystacks as you, and even a few seconds sooner than you. But outside your window even less trace of the grief which has flashed past is left in the air than fingers leave in water. And in the familiar life of the train, which is always exactly the same—with its slit-openable package of bed linen, and tea served in glasses with metal holders—could you possibly grasp what a dark and suppressed horror has been borne through the same sector of Euclidean space just three seconds ahead of you? You are dissatisfied because there are four of you in your compartment and it is crowded. And could you possibly believe—and will you possibly believe when reading these lines—that in the same size compartment as yours, but up ahead in that zak car, there are fourteen people? And if there are twenty-five? And if there are thirty?

The *zak car*—what a foul abbreviation it is! As, for that matter, are all the executioners' abbreviations. They meant to indicate that this was a railroad car for prisoners—for *zaklyuchennye.* But nowhere, except in prison documents, has this term caught on and stuck. The prisoners got used to calling this kind of railroad car a *Stolypin* car, or, more simply, just a *Stolypin.*

As rail travel was introduced more widely in our Fatherland, prisoner transports changed their form. Right up to the nineties of the last century the Siberian prisoner transports moved on foot or by horse cart. As far back as 1896, Lenin traveled to Siberian exile in an ordinary third-class passenger car (with free people all around him) and shouted to the train crew that it was intolerably crowded. The painting by Yaroshenko which everyone knows, *Life Is Everywhere*, shows a fourth-class passenger car re-equipped in very naïve fashion for prisoner transport: everything has been left just as it was, and the prisoners are traveling just like ordinary people, except that double gratings have been installed on the windows. Cars of this type were used on Russian railroads for a very long time. And certain people remember being transported as prisoners in just such cars in 1927, except that the men and women were separated. On the other hand, the SR Trushin recalls that even during Tsarist times he was transported as a prisoner in a "Stolypin" car, except that —once again going back to legendary times—there were six people in a compartment.

Probably this type of railroad car really was first used under Stolypin, in other words before 1911. And in the general Cadet revolutionary embitterment, they christened it with his name. However, it really became the favorite means of prisoner transport only in the twenties; and it became the universal and exclusive means only from 1930 on, when everything in our life became uniform. Therefore it would be more correct to call it a *Stalin* car rather than a *Stolypin* car. But we aren't going to argue with the Russian language here.

The Stolypin car is an ordinary passenger car divided into compartments, except that five of the nine compartments are allotted to the prisoners (here, as everywhere in the Archipelago, half of everything goes to the auxiliary personnel, the guards), and compartments are separated from the corridor not by a solid barrier but by a grating which leaves them open for inspection. This grating consists of intersecting diagonal bars, like the kind one sees in station parks. It rises the full height of the car, and because of it there are not the usual baggage racks projecting from the compartments over the corridor. The windows on the corridor sides are ordinary windows, but they have the same diagonal gratings on the outside. There are no windows in the prisoners' compartments—only tiny, barred blinds on the level of the second sleeping shelves. That's why the car has no exterior windows and looks like a baggage car. The door into each compartment is a sliding door: an iron frame with bars.

From the corridor side all this is very reminiscent of a menagerie: pitiful creatures resembling human beings are huddled there in cages, the floors and bunks surrounded on all sides by metal grilles, looking out at you pitifully, begging for something to eat and drink. Except that in menageries they never crowd the wild animals in so tightly.

According to the calculations of nonprisoner engineers, six people can sit on the bottom bunks of a Stolypin compartment, and another three can lie on the middle ones (which are joined in one continuous bunk, except for the space cut out beside the door for climbing up and getting down), and two more can lie on the baggage shelves above. Now if, in addition to these eleven, eleven more are pushed into the compartment (the last of whom are shoved out of the way of the door by the jailers' boots as they shut it), then this will constitute a normal complement for a Stolypin prisoners' compartment. Two huddle, half-sitting, on each of the upper baggage shelves; another five lie on the joined middle level (and they are the lucky ones—these places are won in battle, and if there are any prisoners present from the underworld companionship of thieves—the blatnye—then it is they who are lying there); and this leaves thirteen down below: five sit on each of the bunks and three are in the aisle between their legs. Somewhere, mixed up with the people, on the people and under the people, are their belongings. And that is how they sit, their crossed legs wedged beneath them, day after day.

No, it isn't done especially to torture people. A sentenced prisoner is a laboring soldier of socialism, so why should he be tortured? They need him for construction work. But, after all, you will agree he is not off on a jaunt to visit his mother-in-law, and there is no reason in the world to treat him so well that people out in *freedom* would envy him. We have problems with our transportation: he'll get there all right, and he won't die on the way either.

Since the fifties, when railroad timetables were actually straightened out, the prisoners haven't had to travel in this fashion for very long at a time—say, a day and a half or two days. During and after the war, things were worse. From Petropavlovsk (in Kazakhstan) to Karaganda, a Stolypin car might be *seven days* en route (with twenty-five people in a compartment). From Karaganda to Sverdlovsk it could be *eight days* (with up to twenty-six in a compartment). Even just going from Kuibyshev to Chelyabinsk in August, 1945, Susi traveled in a Stolypin car for several days, and their compartment held *thirty-five* people lying on top of one another, floundering, fighting.[1] And in the autumn of 1946 N. V. Timofeyev-Ressovsky traveled from Petropavlovsk to Moscow in a compartment that had *thirty-six* people in it! For several days he *hung* suspended between other human beings and his legs did not touch the floor. Then they started to die off—and the guards hauled the corpses out from under their feet. (Not right away, true; only on the second day.) That way things became less crowded. The whole trip to Moscow continued in this fashion for *three weeks.*[2]

Was thirty-six the upper limit for a Stolypin compartment? I have no evidence available on thirty-seven or higher, and yet, adhering to our one-and-only scientific method, and remembering the necessity to struggle against "the limiters," we are compelled to reply: No, no, no! It is not a limit! Perhaps in some other country it would be an upper limit, but not here! As long as there are any cubic centimeters of unbreathed air left in the compartment, even if it be beneath the upper shelves, even if between shoulders, legs, and heads, the compartment is ready to take additional prisoners. One might, however, conditionally accept

1. Does this perhaps satisfy those who are astonished and reproachful because people *didn't fight?*

2. When he got to Moscow, a miracle took place in accordance with the laws of the country of miracles. *Officers* carried Timofeyev-Ressovsky from the prisoner transport in their arms, and he was driven away in an ordinary automobile: he was off to advance science!

494 | THE GULAG ARCHIPELAGO

as the upper limit the number of unremoved corpses which can be contained in the total volume of the compartment, given the possibility of packing them in at leisure.

V. A. Korneyeva traveled from Moscow in a compartment that held *thirty women*—most of them withered old women, exiled for their religious beliefs (on arrival *all* these women, except two, were immediately put in the hospital). Nobody died in the compartment because several of the prisoners were young, well-developed, good-looking girls, arrested "for going out with foreigners." These girls took it upon themselves to shame the convoy: "You ought to be ashamed to transport them this way! These are your own mothers!" It probably wasn't so much their moral argument as their attractive appearance which produced a reaction in the convoy guards, and they did move several of the old women out —*to the punishment cell*. But the punishment cell in a Stolypin car is no punishment; it is a blessing. Of five prisoner compartments, four are used as general cells, and the fifth is set aside and divided in two halves—two narrow half-compartments with one lower and one upper berth, like those the conductors have. These punishment cells serve to isolate prisoners; three or four travel in them at a time, and this gives both comfort and space.

No, it is not intentionally to torture them with thirst that the exhausted and overcrowded prisoners are fed not soup but salt herring or dry smoked Caspian carp for the whole of their trip in the Stolypin car. (This was exactly how it was in *all* the years, the thirties and the fifties, winter and summer, in Siberia and the Ukraine, and it isn't even necessary to cite examples.) It was not to torture them with thirst—but just you tell me what these ragamuffins were to be fed anyway while being moved around. They were not supposed to get hot meals in prisoner-transport railroad cars. (True, there was a kitchen in one of the Stolypin car compartments, but that was only for the convoy.) You couldn't just give the prisoners raw grits, and you couldn't give them raw codfish either, nor could you give them canned meat because they might stuff themselves. Herring was just the thing, with a piece of bread—and what else did they need?

Go ahead, take your half a herring while they are handing it out, and be glad you got it. If you're smart, you aren't going to eat that herring; just be patient, wait, hide it in your pocket, and you can eat it at the next transit point where there is water to be had. It's worse when they issue you wet Sea of Azov anchovies, covered with coarse salt. You can't keep them in your pocket; so scoop them up in the flaps of your pea jacket, or in your handkerchief, in the palm of your hand—and eat them. They divide up these Azov anchovies on somebody's pea jacket, whereas the convoy guards dump the dried carp right on the floor of the compartment, and it is divided up on the benches, on the prisoners' knees.[3]

But once they've given you a fish, they aren't going to hold back on the bread, and maybe they'll even throw in a bit of sugar. Things are much worse when the convoy comes over and announces: "We aren't going to be feeding you today; *nothing was issued* for you." And it could very well be that nothing was actually issued: someone in one or another prison accounting office made a mistake in the figures. And it could also be that it was issued but that the convoy was short on rations—after all, they aren't exactly overfed either—and so they decided *to snag* a bit of your bread for themselves; and in that case to hand over half a herring by itself would seem suspicious.

And, of course, it is not for the purpose of intentionally torturing the prisoner that after his herring he is given neither hot water (and he never gets that here in any case) nor even plain, unboiled water. One has to understand the situation: The convoy staff is limited; some of them have to be on watch in the corridor; some are on duty on the platform; at the stations they clamber all over the car, under it, on top of it, to make sure that there aren't any holes in it. Others are kept busy cleaning guns, and then, of course, there has to be time for political indoctrination and their catechism on the articles of war. And the third shift is sleeping. They insist on their full eight hours—for, after all, the war is over. And then, to go carry water in pails—it has to be hauled a long

3. P. F. Yakubovich (*V Mire Otverzhennykh* [*In the World of the Outcasts*], Vol. 1, Moscow, 1964), writing about the nineties of the last century, recounts that in those terrible years they gave out ten-kopecks-a-day mess money per person in Siberian prisoner transports, when the price of a loaf of wheat bread (weighing ten and a half ounces?) was five kopecks; a pot of milk (two quarts?) three kopecks. "The prisoners were simply in clover," he writes. But then in Irkutsk Province the prices were higher. A pound of meat cost ten kopecks there and the "prisoners were simply famished!" One pound of meat per day per person—it's not half a herring, is it?

way, too, and it's insulting: why should a Soviet soldier have to carry water like a donkey for enemies of the people? And there are also times when they spend half a day hauling the Stolypin cars way out from the station in order to reshuffle or recouple the cars (it will be farther away from prying eyes), and the result is that you can't get water even for your own Red Army mess. True, there is one way out. You can go dip up some water from the locomotive tender. It's yellow and murky, with some lubricating grease mixed in with it. But the zeks will drink it willingly. It doesn't really matter that much anyway, since it isn't as if they could see what they are drinking in the semidarkness of their compartment. They don't have their own window, and there isn't any light bulb there either, and what light they get comes from the corridor. And there's another thing too: it takes a long time to dole out that water. The zeks don't have their own mugs. Whoever did have one has had it taken away from him—so what it adds up to is that they have to be given the two government issue mugs to drink out of, and while they are drinking up you have to keep standing there and standing, and dipping it out and dipping it out some more and handing it to them. (Yes, and then, too, the prisoners argue about who's to drink first; they want the healthy prisoners to drink first, and only then those with tuberculosis, and last of all those with syphilis! Just as if it wasn't going to begin all over again in the next cell: first the healthy ones . . .)

But the convoy could have borne with all that, hauled the water, and doled it out, if only those pigs, after slurping up the water, didn't ask to go to the toilet. So here's the way it all works out: if you don't give them water for a day, then they don't ask to go to the toilet. Give them water once, and they go to the toilet once; take pity on them and give them water twice—and they go to the toilet twice. So it's pure and simple common sense: just don't give them anything to drink.

And it isn't that one is stingy about taking them to the toilet because one wants to be stingy about the use of the toilet itself, but because taking prisoners to the toilet is a responsible—even, one might say, a combat—operation: it takes a long, long time for one private first class and two privates. Two guards have to be stationed, one next to the toilet door, the other in the corridor on the opposite side (so that no one tries to escape in that direction), while the private first class has to push open and then shut the door to the compartment, first to admit the returning prisoner, and then to allow the next one out. The statutes permit letting out only one at a time, so that they don't try to escape and so that they can't start a rebellion. Therefore, the way it works out is that the one prisoner who has been let out to go to the toilet is holding up 30 others in his own compartment and 120 in the whole car, not to mention the convoy detail! And so the command resounds: "Come on there, come on! Get a move on, get a move on!" The private first class and the soldiers keep hurrying him all the way there and back and he hurries so fast that he stumbles, and it's as though they think he is going to steal that shithole from the state. (In 1949, traveling in a Stolypin car between Moscow and Kuibyshev, the one-legged German Schultz, having understood the Russian hurry-up by this time, jumped to the toilet and back on his one leg while the convoy kept laughing and ordering him to go faster. During one such trip, one of the convoy guards pushed him when he reached the platform at the end of the corridor, and Schultz fell down on the floor in front of the toilet. The convoy guard went into a rage and began to beat him, while Schultz, who couldn't get up because of the blows raining down on him, crawled and crept into the dirty toilet. The rest of the convoy roared with laughter.)[4]

So that the prisoner shouldn't attempt to escape during the moment he was in the toilet, and also for a faster turnaround, the door to the toilet was not closed, and the convoy guard, watching the process from the platform of the car, could encourage it: "Come on, come on now! That's plenty, that's enough for you!" Sometimes the orders came before you even started: "All right, number one only!" And that meant that from the platform they'd prevent your doing anything else. And then, of course, you couldn't wash your hands. There was never enough water in the tank there, and there wasn't enough time either. If the prisoner even so much as touched the plunger of the washstand, the convoy guard would roar: "Don't you touch that, move along." (And if someone happened to have soap or a towel among his belongings, he wouldn't dare take it out anyway, simply out of shame:

4. This, it seems, is what is meant by the phrase "Stalin's cult of personality"?

that would really be *acting like a sucker*.) The toilet was filthy. Quicker, quicker! And tracking back the liquid mess on his shoes, the prisoner would be shoved back into the compartment, where he would climb up over somebody's arms and shoulders, and then, from the top row, his dirty shoes would dangle to the middle row and drip.

When women were taken to the toilet, the statutes of the convoy service, and common sense as well, required that the toilet door be kept open, but not every convoy insisted on this and some allowed the door to be shut: Oh, all right, go ahead and shut it. (Later on one of the women was sent in to wash out the toilet, and the guard again had to stand right there beside her so that she didn't try to escape.)

And even at this fast tempo, visits to the toilet for 120 people would take more than two hours—more than a quarter of the entire shift for three convoy guards! And in spite of that, you still couldn't make them happy. In spite of that, some old sandpiper or other would begin to cry half an hour later and ask to go to the toilet, and, of course, he wouldn't be allowed to go, and then he would soil himself right there in the compartment, and once again that meant trouble for the private first class: the prisoner had to be forced to pick it up in his hands and carry it away.

So that was all there was to it: fewer trips to the toilet! And that meant less water, and less food too—because then they wouldn't complain of loose bowels and stink up the air; after all, how bad could it be? A man couldn't even breathe.

Less water! But they had to hand out the herring anyway, just as the regulations required! No water—that was a reasonable measure. No herring—that was a service crime.

No one, no one at all, ever set out to torture us on purpose! The convoy's actions were quite reasonable! But, like the ancient Christians, we sat there in the cage while they poured salt on our raw and bleeding tongues.

Also the prisoner-transport convoys did not often deliberately (though sometimes they did) mix the thieves—blatari—and non-political offenders in with Article 58 politicals in the same compartment. But a particular situation existed: There were a great many prisoners and very few railroad cars and compartments, and time was always short, and so when was there time enough to sort them out? One of the four compartments was kept for women, and if the prisoners in the other three were to be sorted out on one basis or another, the most logical basis would be by destination so that it would be easier to unload them.

After all, was it because Pontius Pilate wanted to humiliate him that Christ was crucified between two thieves? It just happened to be crucifixion day that day—and there was only one Golgotha, and time was short. And so *he was numbered with the transgressors.*

■

I am afraid even to think what I would have had to suffer if I had been in the position of a common convict. . . . The convoy and the transport officers dealt with me and my comrades with cautious politeness. . . . Being a political, I went to hard labor in relative comfort—on the transports, I had quarters separate from the criminal prisoners, and my pood—my thirty-six pounds —of baggage was moved about on a cart. . . .

. . . I left out the quotation marks around the above paragraph to enable the reader to understand things a little better. After all, quotation marks are always used either for irony or to set something apart. And without quotation marks the paragraph sounds wild, does it not?

It was written by P. F. Yakubovich about the nineties of the last century. His book was recently republished as a sermon on that dark and dismal age. We learn from it that even on a barge the political prisoners had special quarters and a special section set aside for their walks on deck. (The same thing appears in Tolstoi's *Resurrection,* in which, furthermore, an outsider, Prince Nekhlyudov, is allowed to visit the political prisoners in order to interview them.) And it was only because the *"magic word 'political'* had been left out by mistake" opposite Yakubovich's name on the list (his own words) that he was met at Ust-Kara "by the hard-labor inspector . . . like an ordinary criminal prisoner— rudely, provocatively, impudently." However, this misunderstanding was all happily cleared up.

What an unbelievable time! It was almost a crime to mix politicals with criminals! Criminals were teamed up and driven along the streets to the station so as to expose them to public disgrace. And politicals could go there in carriages. (Olminsky, in 1899.) Politicals were not fed from the common pot but were given a food allowance instead and had their meals brought from public eating houses. The Bolshevik Olminsky didn't want even the hospital rations because he found the food too coarse.[5] The Butyrki Prison superintendent apologized to Olminsky for the jailer's having addressed him too familiarly: You see, we seldom get politicals here, and the jailer didn't know any better!

Seldom get politicals in the Butyrki? What kind of dream is this? Then where were they? The Lubyanka didn't exist as a prison at the time, and neither did Lefortovo!

The writer Radishchev was taken to the prisoner transport in shackles, and when the weather got cold they threw over him a "repulsive, raw sheepskin coat," which they had taken from a watchman. However, the Empress Catherine immediately issued orders that his shackles be removed and that he be provided with everything he required for his journey. But in November, 1927, Anna Skripnikova was sent on a transport from the Butyrki to the Solovetsky Islands in a straw hat and a summer dress. (That was what she had been wearing when she was arrested in the summer, and since that time her room had been sealed and no one was willing to give her permission to get her winter things out of it.)

To draw a distinction between political prisoners and common criminals is the equivalent of showing them respect as equal opponents, of recognizing that people may have *views of their own.* Thus a political prisoner is conscious of political *freedom* even when under *arrest.*

But since the time when we all became *KR's* and the socialists failed to retain their status as *politicals,* since then any protest that as a *political* you ought not to be mixed up with ordinary criminals has resulted only in laughter on the prisoners' part and bewilderment on the part of the jailers. "All are criminals here," the jailers reply—sincerely.

This mingling, this first devastating encounter, takes place either in the Black Maria or in the Stolypin car. Up to this

5. Because of all of this the ordinary criminal mob christened the professional revolutionaries "mangy swells." (P. F. Yakubovich.)

moment, no matter how they have oppressed, tortured, and tormented you during the interrogation, it has all originated with the bluecaps, and you have never confused them with human beings but have seen in them merely an insolent branch of the service. But at the same time, even if your cellmates have been totally different from you in development and experience, and even if you have quarreled with them, and even if they have *squealed on you,* they have all belonged to that same ordinary, sinful, everyday humanity among which you have spent your whole life.

When you were jammed into a Stolypin compartment, you expected that here, too, you would encounter only colleagues in misfortune. All your enemies and oppressors remained on *the other* side of the bars, and you certainly did not expect to find them on *this* side. And suddenly you lift your eyes to the square recess in the middle bunk, to that one and only heaven above you, and up there you see three or four—oh, no, not faces! They aren't monkey muzzles either, because monkeys' muzzles are much, much decenter and more thoughtful! No, and they aren't simply hideous countenances, since there must be something human even in them. You see cruel, loathsome snouts up there, wearing expressions of greed and mockery. Each of them looks at you like a spider gloating over a fly. Their web is that grating which imprisons you—and you have been had! They squinch up their lips, as if they intend to bite you from one side. They hiss when they speak, enjoying that hissing more than the vowel and consonant sounds of speech—and the only thing about their speech that resembles the Russian language is the endings of verbs and nouns. It is gibberish.

Those strange gorilloids were usually dressed in sleeveless undershirts. After all, it is stuffy in the Stolypin car. Their sinewy purple necks, their swelling shoulder muscles, their swarthy tattooed chests have never suffered prison emaciation. Who are they? Where do they come from? And suddenly you see a small cross dangling from one of those necks. Yes, a little aluminum cross on a string. You are surprised and slightly relieved. That means there are religious believers among them. How touching! So nothing terrible is going to happen. But immediately this "believer" belies both his cross and his faith by cursing (and they curse partly in Russian), and he jabs two protruding fingers, spread into the "V" of a slingshot, right in your eyes—not even pausing to threaten you but starting to punch them out then and there. And this gesture of theirs, which says, "I'll gouge out your eyes, crowbait!" covers their entire philosophy and faith! If they are capable of crushing your eyeballs like worms, what is there on you or belonging to you that they'll spare? The little cross dangles there and your still unsquashed eyes watch this wildest of masquerades, and your whole system of reckoning goes awry: Which of you is already crazy? And who is about to go insane?

In one moment, all the customs and habits of human intercourse you have lived with all your life have broken down. In your entire previous life, particularly before your arrest but even to some degree afterward, even to some degree during interrogation, too, you spoke *words* to other people and they answered you in *words*. And those words produced actions. One might persuade, or refuse, or come to an agreement. You recall various human relationships—a request, an order, an expression of gratitude. But what has overtaken you here is beyond all these words and beyond all these relationships. An emissary of the ugly snout descends, most often a vicious boy whose impudence and rudeness are thrice despicable, and this little demon unties your bag and rifles your pockets—not tentatively, but treating them like his very own. From that moment, nothing that belongs to you is yours any longer. And all you yourself are is a rubber dummy around which superfluous things are wrapped which can easily be taken off. Nor can you explain anything in words, nor deny, nor prohibit, nor plead with that evil little skunk or those foul snouts up above. They are not people. This has become clear to you in one moment. The only thing to be done with them is to *beat* them, to beat them without wasting any time flapping your tongue. Either that juvenile there or those bigger vermin up above.

But how can you hit those three up top from down below? And the kid there, even though he's a stinking polecat, well, it doesn't seem right to hit him either. Maybe you can push him away soft like? No, you can't even do that, because he'll bite your nose right off, or else they'll break your head from above (and they have knives, too, but they aren't going to bother to pull them out and soil them on you).

You look at your neighbors, your comrades: Let's either resist or protest! But all your comrades, all your fellow Article 58's, who have been plundered one by one even before you got there, sit there submissively, hunched over, and they stare right past you, and it's even worse when they look at you the way they always do look at you, as though no violence were going on at all, no plundering, as though it were a natural phenomenon, as though it were the grass growing and the rain falling.

And the reason why, gentlemen, comrades, and brothers, is that the proper time was allowed to slip by! You ought to have got hold of yourselves and remembered who you were back when Struzhinsky burned himself alive in his Vyatka cell, and even before that, when you were declared "counterrevolutionaries."

And so you allow the thieves to take your overcoat and paw through your jacket and snatch your twenty rubles from where it was sewn in, and your bag has already been tossed up above and checked out, and everything your sentimental wife collected for your long trip after you were sentenced stays up there, and they've thrown the bag back down to you with . . . your toothbrush.

Although not everyone submitted just like that, 99 percent did in the thirties and forties.[6] And how could that be? Men, officers, soldiers, front-line soldiers!

To strike out boldly, a person has to be ready for that battle, waiting for it, and has to understand its purpose. All these conditions were absent here. A person wholly unfamiliar with the thieves'—the blatnoi—milieu didn't anticipate this battle and, most importantly, failed totally to understand its vital necessity. Up to this point he had assumed (incorrectly) that his only enemies were the bluecaps. He needed still more education to arrive at the understanding that the tattooed chests were merely the rear ends of the bluecaps. This was the revelation the bluecaps never utter aloud: "You today, me tomorrow." The new prisoner wanted to consider himself a political—in other words, on the side of the people—while the state was against the people. And at that point he was unexpectedly assaulted from behind and both sides by quick-fingered devils of some kind, and all the

6. I have heard of a few cases in which three seasoned, young, and healthy men stood up against the thieves—not to defend justice in general, but to protect, not those who were being plundered right next to them, but themselves only. In other words: armed neutrality.

categories got mixed up, and clarity was shattered into fragments. (And it would take a long time for the prisoner to put two and two together and figure out that this horde of devils were hand in glove with the jailers.)

To strike out boldly, a person has to feel that his rear is defended, that he has support on both his flanks, that there is solid earth beneath his feet. All these conditions were absent for the Article 58's. Having passed through the meat grinder of political interrogation, the human being was physically crushed in body: he had been starved, he hadn't slept, he had frozen in punishment cells, he had lain there a beaten man. But it wasn't only his body. His soul was crushed too. Over and over he had been told and had had demonstrated to him that his views, and his conduct in life, and his relationships with people had all been wrong because they had brought him to ruin. All that was left in that scrunched-up wad the engine room of the law had spewed out into the prisoner transport was a greed for life, and no understanding whatever. To crush him once and for all and *to cut him off from all others* once and for all—that was the function of interrogation under Article 58. The convicted prisoner had to learn that his worst guilt out in freedom had been his attempt somehow to get together or unite with others by any route but the Party organizer, the trade-union organizer, or the administration. In prison this fear went so far as to become fear of all kinds of *collective action:* two voices uttering the same complaint or two prisoners signing a complaint on one piece of paper. Gun-shy now and for a good long time to come of any and every kind of collaboration or unification, the pseudo politicals were not prepared to unite even against the thieves. Nor would they even think of bringing along a weapon—a knife or a bludgeon—for the Stolypin car or the transit prison. In the first place, why have one? And against whom? In the second place, if you did use it, then, considering the aggravating circumstance of your malevolent Article 58, you might be shot when you were retried. In the third place, even before that, your punishment for having a knife when they searched you would be very different from the thief's. For him to have a knife was mere misbehavior, tradition, he didn't know any better. But for you to have one was "terrorism."

Finally, many of the people imprisoned under Article 58 were peaceful people (very often elderly, too, and often ill), and they had gotten along all their lives with words and without resorting to fisticuffs, and they weren't any more prepared for them now than they had been before.

Nor had the thieves ever been put through the same kind of interrogation. Their entire interrogation had consisted of two sessions, an easy trial, and an easy sentence, and they wouldn't have to serve it out. They would be released ahead of time: either they would be amnestied or else they would simply escape.[7] Even during interrogation, no one ever deprived a thief of his legitimate parcels—consisting of abundant packages from the loot kept by his underworld comrades who were still on the loose. He never grew thin, was never weak for a single day, and in transit he ate at the expense of the innocent nonthieves, whom he called, in his own jargon, the frayera[8]—"frayers," or "innocents," or "suckers." Not only did the articles of the Code dealing with thieves and bandits not oppress the thief; he was, in fact, proud of his convictions under them. And he was supported in this pride by all the chiefs in blue shoulder boards and blue piping. "Oh, that's nothing. Even though you're a bandit and a murderer, you are not a traitor of the Motherland, you *are one of our own people;* you will reform." There was no *Section Eleven*—for organization— in the thieves' articles in the Code. Organization was not forbidden the thieves. And why should it be? Let it help develop in them the feelings of collectivism that people in our society need so badly. And disarming them was just a game. They weren't punished for having a weapon. Their thieves' *law* was respected ("They can't be anything but what they are"). And a new murder in the cell would not increase a murderer's sentence, but instead would bring him new laurels.

And all that went very deep indeed. In works of the last century, the lumpenproletariat was criticized for little more than a certain lack of discipline, for fickleness of mood. And Stalin was always partial to the thieves—after all, who robbed the banks for

7. V. I. Ivanov (now from Ukhta) got Article 162 (thievery) nine times and Article 82 (escape) five times, for a total of thirty-seven years in prison— and he "served out" five to six years for all of them.

8. "Frayer" is a blatnoi—underworld—word meaning *nonthief*—in other words, not a *Chelovek* ("Human being," with a capital letter). Well, even more simply: the *frayera* were all nonthief, nonunderworld mankind.

him? Back in 1901 his comrades in the Party and in prison accused him of using common criminals against his political
enemies. From the twenties on, the obliging term *"social ally"*
came to be widely used. That was Makarenko's contention too:
these could be reformed. According to Makarenko, the origin of
crime lay solely in the "counterrevolutionary underground."[9]
(*Those* were the ones who couldn't be reformed—engineers,
priests, SR's, Mensheviks.)

And why shouldn't they steal, if there was no one to put a stop
to it? Three or four brazen thieves working hand in glove could
lord it over several dozen frightened and cowed pseudo politicals.

With the approval of the administration. On the basis of the
Progressive Doctrine.

But even if they didn't drive off the thieves with their fists,
why didn't the victims at least make complaints? After all, every
sound could be heard in the corridor, and a convoy guard was
marching slowly back and forth right out there.

Yes, that is a question! Every sound and every complaining
cry can be heard, and the convoy just keeps marching back and
forth—why doesn't he interfere? Just a yard away from him, in
the half-dark cave of the compartment, they are plundering a
human being—why doesn't the soldier of the government police
interfere?

For the very same reason: he, too, has been indoctrinated.

Even more than that: after many years of favoring thieves, the
convoy has itself slipped in their direction. The convoy *has itself
become a thief.*

From the middle of the thirties until the middle of the forties,
during that ten-year period of the thieves' most flagrant debauches
and most intense oppression of the politicals, no one at all can
recall a case in which a convoy guard intervened in the plundering of a political in a cell, in a railroad car, or in a Black Maria.
But they will tell you of innumerable cases in which the convoy
accepted stolen goods from the thieves and, in return, bought
them vodka, snacks (sweeter than the rations, too), and smokes.
The examples are so numerous as to be typical.

The convoy sergeant, after all, hasn't anything either: he has
his gun, his greatcoat roll, his mess tin, his soldier's ration. It

9. A. S. Makarenko, *Flagi na Bashnyakh* (*Flags on the Towers*).

would be cruel to require him to escort an enemy of the people in an expensive overcoat or chrome-leather boots or with a *swag* of luxurious city articles—and to reconcile himself to that inequality. Was not taking these things just one additional form of the class struggle, after all? And what other norms were there?

In 1945–1946, when prisoners streamed in not just from anywhere but from Europe, and wore and had in their bags unheard-of European articles, even the convoy officers could not restrain themselves. Their service had kept them from the front, but at the end of the war it also kept them from the harvest of booty—and, I ask you, was that just?

And so, in these circumstances, the convoy guard systematically mixed the thieves and the politicals in each compartment of their Stolypin, not through lack of space for them elsewhere and not through haste, but out of greed. And the thieves did not let them down: they stripped the *beavers*[10] of everything, and then those possessions migrated into the suitcases of the convoy.

But what could be done if the *beavers* had been loaded into the Stolypin cars, and the train was moving, and there simply weren't any thieves at all—they simply hadn't put any aboard? What if they weren't being shipped out on prisoner transports that day, even from one of the stations along the way? This could and did happen—several such cases are known.

In 1947 they were transporting from Moscow to the Vladimir Central Prison a group of foreigners who had opulent possessions —as could be seen the very first time their suitcases were opened. At that point, the convoy *itself* began a systematic confiscation of their belongings right there in the railroad car. So that nothing should be missed, the prisoners were forced to undress *down to their bare skin* and to sit on the floor of the car near the toilet while their things were examined and taken away. But the convoy guard failed to take into account that they were taking these prisoners not to a camp but to a genuine prison. On their arrival there, I. A. Korneyev handed in a written complaint, describing exactly what had happened. They found the particular unit of convoy guards and searched them. Some of the things were

10. A *beaver* in the blatnoi—underworld—jargon was any rich zek who had "trash"—meaning good clothes—and "bacilli"—meaning fats, sugar, and other goodies.

recovered and returned to their owners, who also received compensation in money for those that weren't recovered. They say that the convoy guards got from ten to fifteen years. However, this is something that cannot be checked, and anyway they would have been convicted under an ordinary nonpolitical article of the Code, and they wouldn't have had to spend a long time in prison.

However, that was an exceptional case, and if he had managed to restrain his greed in time, the chief of the convoy would have realized that it was better not to get involved in it. And here is another, less complicated case, which probably means that it happened often. In August, 1945, in the Moscow-Novosibirsk Stolypin car (in which A. Susi was being transported), it turned out that there weren't any thieves. And the trip was a long one, and the Stolypins just crawled along at that time. Without hurrying in the least, all in good time, the convoy chief declared a search—one prisoner at a time in the corridor with his things. Those summoned were made to undress in accordance with prison rules, but that wasn't why the search was being conducted, for each prisoner who had been searched was, in fact, put right back into his own crowded compartment, and any knife, anything forbidden, could simply have been passed from hand to hand. The real purpose of the search was to examine their personal articles —the clothes they were wearing and whatever was in their bags. And right there, beside the bags, not in the least bored by the whole protracted search, the chief of the convoy guard, an officer, stood with a haughty poker face, with his assistant, a sergeant, beside him. Sinful greed kept trying to pop out, but the officer kept it hidden under a pretended indifference. It was the same situation as an old rake looking over little girls but embarrassed by the presence of outsiders—yes, and by that of the girls too— and not knowing exactly how to proceed. How badly he needed just a few thieves! But there were no thieves in the transport.

There were no thieves aboard, but there were individuals among the prisoners who had already been infected by the thief-laden atmosphere of the prison. After all, the example of thieves is instructive and calls forth imitations: it demonstrates that there is an easy way to live in prison. Two recent officers were in one of the compartments—Sanin (from the navy) and Merezhkov. They were both 58's, but their attitudes had already changed. Sanin, with Merezhkov's support, proclaimed himself the monitor of the compartment and, through a convoy guard, requested a meeting with their chief. (He had fathomed that haughtiness and its need of a pimp!) This was unheard of, but Sanin was summoned, and they had a chat somewhere. Following Sanin's example, someone in the second compartment also asked for a meeting. And that person was similarly received.

And the next morning they issued not twenty ounces of bread —the prisoner-transport ration at the time—but no more than nine ounces.

They gave out the ration, and a quiet murmur began. A murmur, but in fear of any "collective action," these politicals did not speak up. In the event, only one among them loudly asked the guard distributing the bread: "Citizen chief! How much does this ration weigh?"

"The correct weight," he was told.

"I demand a reweighing; otherwise I will not accept it!" the dissatisfied prisoner declared loudly.

The whole car fell silent. Many waited before beginning to eat their ration; expecting that theirs, too, would be reweighed. And at that moment, in all his spotlessness, the officer appeared. Everyone fell silent, which made his words all the weightier and all the more irresistible.

"Which one here spoke out against the Soviet government?"

All hearts stopped beating. (People will protest that this is a universal approach, that even out in freedom every little chief declares himself to be the Soviet government, and just try to argue with him about it. But for those who are panicky, who have just been sentenced for anti-Soviet propaganda, the threat is more frightening.)

"Who was starting *a mutiny* over the bread ration?" the officer demanded.

"Citizen lieutenant, I only wanted . . ." The guilty rebel was already trying to explain it all away.

"Aha, you're the bastard? You're the one who doesn't like the Soviet government?"

(And why rebel? Why argue? Wasn't it really easier to eat that little underweight ration, to suffer it in silence? And now he had fallen right in it!)

"You stinking shit! You counterrevolutionary! You ought to be hanged, and you have the nerve to demand that the bread ration be reweighed! You rat—the Soviet government gives you food and drink, and you have the brass to be dissatisfied? Do you know what you're going to get for that?"

Orders to the guard: "Take him out!" The lock rattles. "Come on out, you! Hands behind your back!" They bring out the unfortunate.

"Now who else is dissatisfied? Who else wants his bread ration reweighed?"

(And it's not as if you could prove anything anyway. It's not as if they'd take your word against the lieutenant's if you were to complain somewhere that there were only nine ounces instead of twenty.)

It's quite enough to show a well-beaten dog the whip. All the rest turned out to be satisfied, and that was how the penalty ration was confirmed for *all the days* of the long journey. And they began to withhold the sugar too. The convoy had appropriated it.

(And this took place during the summer of our two great victories—over Germany and Japan—victories which embellish the history of our Fatherland and which our grandsons and great-grandsons will learn about in school.)

The prisoners went hungry for a day and then a second day, by which time several of them began to get a bit wiser, and Sanin said to his compartment: "Look, fellows: If we go on this way, we're lost. Come on now, all of you who have some good stuff with you, let me have it, and I'll trade it for something to eat." With great self-assurance he accepted some articles and turned down others. (Not all the prisoners were willing to let their things go—and, you see, no one forced them to either.) And then he and Merezhkov asked to be allowed to leave the compartment, and, strangely enough, the convoy let them out. Taking the things, they went off toward the compartment of the convoy guard, and they returned from there with sliced loaves of bread and with makhorka. These very loaves constituted the eleven ounces missing from the daily rations. Now, however, they were not distributed on an equal basis but went only to those who had handed over their belongings.

And that was quite fair: after all, they had all admitted they were satisfied with the reduced bread ration. It was also fair because the belongings were, after all, worth something, and it was right that they should be paid for. And it was also fair in the long view because those things were simply too good for camp and were destined anyway to be taken away or stolen there.

The makhorka had belonged to the guard. The soldiers shared their precious makhorka with the prisoners. And that was fair, too, since they had eaten the prisoners' bread and drunk up their sugar, which was too good for enemies anyway. And, last, it was only fair, too, that Sanin and Merezhkov took the largest share for themselves even though they'd contributed nothing—because without them all this would not have been arranged.

And so they sat crammed in there, in the semidarkness, and some of them chewed on their neighbors' chunks of bread and their neighbors sat there and watched them. The guard permitted smoking only on a collective basis, every two hours—and the whole car was as filled with smoke as if there'd been a fire. Those who at first had clung to their things now regretted that they hadn't given them to Sanin and asked him to take them, but Sanin said he'd only take them later on.

This whole operation wouldn't have worked so well and so thoroughly had it not been for the slow trains and slow Stolypin cars of the immediate postwar years, when they kept unhitching them from one train and hitching them to another and held them waiting in the stations. And, at the same time, if it hadn't been the immediate postwar period, neither would there have been those greed-inspiring belongings. Their train took a week to get to Kuibyshev—and during that entire week they got only nine ounces of bread a day. (This, to be sure, was twice the ration distributed during the siege of Leningrad.) And they did get dried Caspian carp and water, in addition. They had to ransom their remaining bread ration with their personal possessions. And soon the supply of these articles exceeded the demand, and the convoy guards became very choosy and reluctant to take more things.

They were received at the Kuibyshev Transit Prison, given baths, and returned as a group to that very same Stolypin. The convoy which took them over was new—but, in passing on the relay baton, the previous crew had evidently told them how to put the squeeze on, and the very same system of ransoming their own rations functioned all the way to Novosibirsk. (It is easy to see how this infectious experiment might have spread rapidly through whole units of the convoy guards.)

And when they were unloaded on the ground between the tracks in Novosibirsk, some new officer came up and asked them: "Any complaints against the convoy?" And they were all so confused that nobody answered.

The first chief of convoy had calculated accurately—this was Russia!

■

Another factor which distinguishes Stolypin passengers from the rest of the train is that they do not know where their train is going and at what station they will disembark: after all, they don't have tickets, and they don't read the route signs on the cars. In Moscow, they sometimes load them on so far from the station platform that even the Muscovites among them don't know which of the eight Moscow stations they are at. For several hours the prisoners sit all squeezed together in the stench while they wait for a switching engine. And finally it comes and takes the zak car to the already made-up train. If it is summertime, the station loudspeakers can be heard: "Moscow to Ufa departing from Track 3. Moscow to Tashkent still loading at Platform 1 . . ." That means it's the Kazan Station, and those who know the geography of the Archipelago are now explaining to their comrades that Vorkuta and Pechora are out: *they* leave from the Yaroslavl Station; and the Kirov and Gorky camps[11] are out too. They never send people from Moscow to Byelorussia, the Ukraine, or the Caucasus anyway. They have no room there even for their own. Let's listen some more: the Ufa train has left, and ours hasn't moved. The Tashkent train has started, and we're still here. "Moscow to Novosibirsk departing. All those seeing passengers off, disembark. . . . All passengers show their tickets. . . ." We have started.

11. Thus it is that weeds get into the harvest of fame. But are they weeds? After all, there are no Pushkin, Gogol, or Tolstoi camps—but there are Gorky camps, and what a nest of them too! Yes, and there is a separate mine "named for Maxim Gorky" (twenty-five miles from Elgen in the Kolyma)! Yes, Aleksei Maximovich Gorky . . . "with your heart and your name, comrade . . ." If the enemy does not surrender . . . You say one reckless little word, and look— you're not in literature any longer.

Our train! And what does that prove? Nothing so far. The middle Volga area is still open, and the South Urals. And Kazakhstan with the Dzhezkazgan copper mines. And Taishet, with its factory for creosoting railroad ties (where, they say, creosote penetrates the skin and bones and its vapors fill the lungs—and that is death). All Siberia is still open to us—all the way to Sovetskaya Gavan. The Kolyma too. And Norilsk.

And if it is wintertime, the car is battened down and the loud-speakers are inaudible. If the convoy guards obey their regulations, then you'll hear nary a whisper from them about the route either. And thus we set out, and, entangled in other bodies, fall asleep to the clacking of the wheels without knowing whether we will see forest or steppe through the window tomorrow. Through that window in the corridor. From the middle shelf, through the grating, the corridor, the two windowpanes, and still another grating, you can still see some switching tracks and a piece of open space hurtling by the train. If the windowpanes have not frosted over, you can sometimes even read the names of the stations— some Avsyunino or Undol. Where are these stations? No one in the compartment knows. Sometimes you can judge from the sun whether you are being taken north or east. Or at some place called Tufanovo, they might shove some dilapidated nonpolitical offender into your compartment, and he would tell you he was being taken to Danilov to be tried and was scared he'd get a couple of years. In this way you would find out that you'd gone through Yaroslavl that night, which meant that the first transit prison on your route would be Vologda. And some know-it-alls in the compartment would savor gloomily the famous flourish, stressing all the "o's," of the Vologda guards: "The Vologda convoy guards don't joke!"

But even after figuring out the general direction, you still haven't really found out anything: transit prisons lie in clusters on your route, and you can be shunted off to one side or another from any one of them. You don't fancy Ukhta, nor Inta, nor Vorkuta. But do you think that Construction Project 501—a railroad in the tundra, crossing northern Siberia—is any sweeter? It is worse than any of them.

Five years after the war, when the waves of prisoners had finally settled within the river banks (or perhaps they had merely expanded the MVD staffs?), the Ministry sorted out the millions of piles of *cases* and started sending along with each sentenced prisoner a sealed envelope that contained his *case file* and, visible through a slot in the envelope, his route and destination, inserted for the convoy (and the convoy wasn't supposed to know anything more than that—because the contents of the *file* might have a corrupting influence). So then, if you were lying on the middle bunk, and the sergeant stopped right next to you, and you could read upside down, you might be fast enough to read that someone was being taken to Knyazh-Pogost and that you were being sent to Kargopol.

So now there would be more worries! What was Kargopol Camp? Who had ever heard of it? What kind of *general-assignment* work did they have there? (There did exist general-assignment work which was fatal, and some that was not that bad.) Was this a death camp or not?

And then how had you failed to let your family know in the hurry of leaving, and they thought you were still in the Stalinogorsk Camp near Tula? If you were very nervous about this and very inventive, you might succeed in solving that problem too: you might find someone with a piece of pencil lead half an inch long and a piece of crumpled paper. Making sure the convoy doesn't see you from the corridor (you are forbidden to lie with your feet toward the corridor; your head has to be in that direction), hunched over and facing in the opposite direction, you write to your family, between lurches of the car, that you have suddenly been taken from where you were and are being sent somewhere else, and you might be able to send only one letter a year from your new destination, so let them be prepared for this eventuality. You have to fold your letter into a triangle and carry it to the toilet in the hope of a lucky break: they might just take you there while approaching a station or just after passing a station, and the convoy guard on the car platform might get careless, and you can quickly press down on the flush pedal and, using your body as a shield, throw the letter into the hole. It will get wet and soiled, but it might fall right through and land between the rails. Or it might even get through dry, and the draft beneath the car will catch and whirl it, and it will fall under the wheels or miss them and land on the downward slope of the embankment. Perhaps it will lie there until it rains, until it snows, until it disintegrates, but perhaps a human hand will pick it up. And if this person isn't a stickler for the Party line, he will make the address legible, he will straighten out the letters, or perhaps put it in an envelope, and perhaps the letter will even reach its destination. Sometimes such letters do arrive—postage due, half-blurred, washed out, crumpled, but carrying a clearly defined splash of grief.

■

But it is better still to stop as soon as possible being a *sucker*—that ridiculous greenhorn, that prey, that victim. The chances are ninety-five out of a hundred that your letter won't get there. But even if it does, it will bring no happiness to your home. And you won't be measuring your life and breath by hours and days once you have entered this epic country: arrivals and departures here are separated by decades, by a quarter-century. *You will never return* to your former world. And the sooner you get used to being without your near and dear ones, and the sooner they get used to being without you, the better it will be. And the easier!

And keep as few things as possible, so that you don't have to fear for them. Don't take a suitcase for the convoy guard to crush at the door of the car (when there are twenty-five people in a compartment, what else could he figure out to do with it?). And don't wear new boots, and don't wear fashionable oxfords, and don't wear a woolen suit: these things are going to be stolen, taken away, swept aside, or switched, either in the Stolypin car, or in the Black Maria, or in the transit prison. Give them up without a struggle—because otherwise the humiliation will poison your heart. They will take them away from you in a fight, and trying to hold onto your property will only leave you with a bloodied mouth. All those brazen snouts, those jeering manners, those two-legged dregs, are repulsive to you. But by owning things and trembling about their fate aren't you forfeiting the rare opportunity of observing and understanding? And do you think that the freebooters, the pirates, the great privateers, painted in such lively colors by Kipling and Gumilyev, were not simply these same blatnye, these same thieves? That's just what they were. Fascinating in romantic literary portraits, why are they so repulsive to you here?

Understand them too! To them prison is *their native home*. No matter how fondly the government treats them, no matter how it softens their punishments, no matter how often it amnesties them, their inner destiny brings them back again and again. Was not the first word in the legislation of the Archipelago for them? In our country, the right to own private property was at one time just as effectively banished out *in freedom* too. (And then those who had banished it began to enjoy *possessing* things.) So why should it be tolerated in prison? You were too slow about it; you didn't eat up your fat bacon; you didn't share your sugar and tobacco with your friends. And so now the thieves empty your *bindle* in order to correct your moral error. Having given you their pitiful worn-out boots *in exchange* for your fashionable ones, their soiled coveralls in return for your sweater, they won't keep these things for long: your boots were merely something to lose and win back five times at cards, and they'll *hawk* your sweater the very next day for a liter of vodka and a round of salami. They, too, will have nothing left of them in one day's time —just like you. This is the principle of the second law of thermodynamics: all differences tend to level out, to disappear. . . .

Own nothing! Possess nothing! Buddha and Christ taught us this, and the Stoics and the Cynics. Greedy though we are, why can't we seem to grasp that simple teaching? Can't we understand that with property we destroy our soul?

So let the herring keep warm in your pocket until you get to the transit prison rather than beg for something to drink here. And did they give us a two-day supply of bread and sugar? In that case, eat it in one sitting. Then no one will steal it from you, and you won't have to worry about it. And you'll be free as a bird in heaven!

Own only what you can always carry with you: know languages, know countries, know people. Let your memory be your travel bag. Use your memory! Use your memory! It is those bitter seeds alone which might sprout and grow someday.

Look around you—there are people around you. Maybe you will remember one of them all your life and later eat your heart out because you didn't make use of the opportunity to ask him questions. And the less you talk, the more you'll hear. Thin strands of human lives stretch from island to island of the Archipelago. They intertwine, touch one another for one night only in just such a clickety-clacking half-dark car as this and then separate once and for all. Put your ear to their quiet humming and the steady clickety-clack beneath the car. After all, it is the spinning wheel of life that is clicking and clacking away there.

What strange stories you can hear! What things you will laugh at.

Now that fast-moving little Frenchman over there near the grating—why does he keep twisting around, what is he so surprised at? Explain things to him! And you can ask him at the same time how he happened to land here. So you've found some-one who knows French, and you learn that he is Max Santerre, a French soldier. And he used to be just as alert and curious out in freedom, in his douce France. They told him politely to stop hanging around the transit point for Russian repatriates, but he kept doing it anyway. And then the Russians invited him to have a drink with them, and from a certain moment after that he remembers nothing. He came to on the floor of an airplane to find himself dressed in a Red Army man's field shirt and britches, with the boots of a convoy guard looming over him. They told him he was sentenced to ten years in camp, but that, of course, as he very clearly understood, was just a nasty joke, wasn't it, and everything would be cleared up? Oh, yes, it will be cleared up, dear fellow; just wait.[12] Well, there was nothing to be surprised at in such cases in 1945–1946.

That particular story was Franco-Russian, and here is one which is Russo-French. But no, really just pure Russian, be-cause no one but a Russian would play this kind of trick! Through-out our history there have been people *who just couldn't be con-tained*, like Menshikov in Berezovo in Surikov's painting. Now take Ivan Koverchenko, average height, wiry, and yet he couldn't be contained either. Because he was a stalwart fellow with a healthy countenance—but the devil threw in a bit of vodka for good measure. He would talk about himself quite willingly and

12. Ahead of him lay another sentence—for twenty-five years—that he was given in camp, and he would not get out of Ozerlag until 1957.

laugh at himself too. Such stories as his are a treasure. They are meant to be heard. True, it took a long time to figure out why he had been arrested and why he was considered a political. But there's no real need to make a fetish of the category "political" either. Does it matter a damn what rake they haul you in with?

As everyone knows very well, the Germans were preparing for chemical warfare and we weren't. Therefore, it was most unfortunate that because of some dunderheads in the quartermaster's department we left whole stacks of mustard-gas bombs at a certain airdrome when we fled the Kuban—and the Germans could have turned this fact into an international scandal. At that point, Senior Lieutenant Koverchenko, a native of Krasnodar, was assigned twenty parachutists and dropped behind the German lines to bury all those invidious bombs. (Those hearing this story have already guessed how it ends and are yawning: next he was taken prisoner, and he has now become a traitor of the Motherland. Nothing at all like that!) Koverchenko carried out his assignment brilliantly and returned through the front with his entire complement of men, having lost not one, and was nominated to receive the order of Hero of the Soviet Union.

But it takes a month or two for the official nomination to be confirmed—and what if you can't be contained within that Hero of the Soviet Union either? "Heroes" are awarded to quiet boys who are models of military and political preparedness—but what if your soul is afire and you want a drink, and there isn't anything to drink? And why, if you're a Hero of the whole Union, are the rats being so stingy as to refuse you an extra liter of vodka? And Ivan Koverchenko mounted his horse and, even though it's true that he had never heard of Caligula, he rode his horse upstairs to the second floor to see the city's military commissar— the commandant: Come on now, issue me some vodka. (He figured this would be more imposing, more in the style of a Hero, and harder to turn down.) Did they arrest him for that? No, of course not! But his award was reduced from Hero to the Order of the Red Banner.

Koverchenko had a large thirst, and vodka wasn't always available, and so he had to be inventive. In Poland, he had gone in and prevented the Germans from blowing up a certain bridge —and he got the feeling this bridge really belonged to him and so, for the time being, before our commandant's headquarters arrived, he exacted payment from the Poles for crossing the bridge. After all, without me you wouldn't have this bridge, you pests! He collected tolls for a whole day (for vodka), and then got bored with it, and this wasn't in any case the place for him to stick around. So Captain Koverchenko offered the nearby Poles his equitable solution: that they *buy* the bridge from him. (Was he arrested for this! Nooo!) He didn't ask very much for it, but the Poles protested and refused. Pan Captain abandoned the bridge: All right then, to hell with you, take your bridge and cross it for nothing.

In 1949 he was chief of staff of a parachute regiment in Polotsk. Major Koverchenko was very much disliked by the Political Branch of the division because he had *failed* the political indoctrination course. He had once asked them to recommend him for admission to the Military Academy, but when they gave him the recommendation, he took one look at it and threw it back across the table at them: "With that kind of recommendation the place for me to go is not the Academy but to the *Banderovtsy* [the Ukrainian nationalist rebels]." (Was he arrested for that? He might very well have gotten a *tenner* for it, but he got away with it.) At that point, on top of all the rest, it turned out that he had given one of his men an unwarranted leave. And then he himself drove a truck at breakneck speed while drunk and wrecked it. And so they gave him ten—ten days in the guardhouse. However, his own men, who loved him with absolute devotion, were the guards, and they let him out of the guardhouse to go and have fun in the village. So he could have been patient through that guardhouse stretch too. But the Political Branch began to threaten him with a trial! Now that threat shocked and insulted Koverchenko; it meant: for burying bombs—Ivan, we need you; but for a lousy one-and-a-half-ton truck—off to prison with you? He crawled out the window at night, went over to the Dvina River, where a friend's motorboat was hidden, and off he went in it.

And it turned out that he wasn't just one more drunk with a short memory: he wanted to avenge himself for everything the Political Branch had done to him; and in Lithuania he left his boat and went to the Lithuanians, saying: "Brothers, take me to your partisans! Accept me and you won't be sorry; we'll twist their tails." But the Lithuanians decided he was being planted on them.

Ivan had a letter of credit sewn in his clothes. He got a ticket to the Kuban. However, en route to Moscow he got very drunk in a restaurant. Consequently, he squinched up his eyes at Moscow as they were leaving the station, and told the taxi driver: "Take me to an embassy!" "Which one?" "Who the hell cares? Any one." And the driver took him to one: "Which one is that?" "The French." "All right."

Perhaps his thoughts got mixed up, and his original intentions in going to an embassy had changed into something else, but his cleverness and his strength had in no wise lapsed: without alerting the policemen at the embassy entrance, he went quietly down a side street and climbed to the top of a smooth wall double a man's height. In the embassy yard it was easier: no one discovered him or detained him, and he went on inside, walked through one room, then another, and he saw a table set. There were many things on the table, but what astonished him most was the pears. He felt a yen for them, and he stuffed all the pockets in his field jacket and trousers with them. At that moment, the members of the household came in to dine. Koverchenko began to attack them and shout at them before they could begin on him: "You Frenchmen!" According to him, France hadn't done anything good for the last century. "Why don't you start a revolution? Why are you trying to get de Gaulle into power? And you want us to send our Kuban wheat to you? It's no go." "Who are you? Where did you come from?" The French were astounded. Immediately adopting the right approach, Koverchenko kept his wits about him: "A major of the MGB." The French were frightened. "But even so, you are not supposed to burst in here. What is your business here?" "——— you in the mouth!" Koverchenko bellowed at them straight from the heart. And, after playing the hoodlum for them a while longer, he noticed that in the next room they were already telephoning about him. He was still sober enough to begin his retreat, but the pears started to fall out of his pockets—and he was pursued by mocking laughter.

And in actual fact, he had enough strength left not only to leave the embassy safe and sound but to move on. The next morning he woke up in Kiev Station (was he not planning to go on to the West Ukraine?), and they soon picked him up there.

During his interrogation he was beaten by Abakumov personally. And the scars on his back swelled up to a hand's breadth.

The Minister beat him, of course, not because of the pears and not because of his valid rebuke to the French, but to find out by whom and when he had been recruited. And, of course, the prison term they handed him was twenty-five years.

There are many such stories, but like every railroad car, the Stolypin falls silent at night. At night there won't be any fish, nor water, nor going to the toilet.

And the car is filled then with the steady noise of the wheels, which doesn't in the least break the silence. And if, in addition, the convoy guard has left the corridor, one can talk quietly from the third compartment for men with the fourth, or women's, compartment.

A conversation with a woman in prison is quite special. There is something noble about it, even if one talks only about articles of the Code and prison terms.

One such conversation went on all night long, and here are the circumstances in which it took place. It was in July, 1950. There were no passengers in the women's compartment except for one young girl, the daughter of a Moscow doctor, sentenced under Article 58-10. And there was a big to-do in the men's compartment. The convoy guards began to drive all the zeks out of three compartments into two (and don't even ask how many they piled up in there). And they brought in some offender who was not at all like a convict. In the first place, he hadn't had his head shaved and his wavy blond locks, real *curls*, lay seductively on his big, thoroughbred head. He was young, dignified, and dressed in a British military uniform. He was escorted through the corridor with an air of deference (the convoy itself had been a little awed by the instructions on the envelope containing his *case file*). And the girl had managed to catch a glimpse of the whole episode. But he himself had not seen her. (And how much he regretted that later!)

From the noise and the commotion she realized that the compartment next to hers had been emptied for him. It was obvious that he was not supposed to communicate with anyone—all the more reason for her to want to talk with him. It wasn't possible in a Stolypin to see from one compartment into another, but when everything was still, you could hear between them. Late at night, when things had begun to quiet down, the girl sat on the edge of her bunk, right up against the grating, and called to him quietly. (And perhaps she first sang softly. The convoy guard was supposed to punish her for all this, but the guard itself had settled down for the night, and there was no one in the corridor.) The stranger heard her and, following her instructions, sat in the same position. They were now sitting with their backs to each other, braced against the same one-inch partition, and speaking quietly through the grating at the outer edge of the partition. Their heads were as close as if their lips were kissing, but they could neither touch one another nor see each other.

Erik Arvid Andersen understood Russian tolerably well by this time, made many mistakes when he spoke it, but, in the end, could succeed in communicating his thoughts. He told the girl his astonishing story (and we, too, will hear about it at the transit prison center). She, in turn, told him the simple story of a Moscow student who had gotten 58-10. But Arvid was fascinated. He asked her about Soviet youth and about Soviet life, and what he heard was not at all what he had learned earlier in leftist Western newspapers and from his own official visit here.

They talked all night long. And that night everything came together for Arvid: the strange prisoners' car in an alien country; the rhythmic nighttime clicking of the wheels, which always finds an echo in our hearts; and the girl's melodic voice, her whispers, her breath reaching his ear—his very ear, yet he couldn't even look at her. (And for a year and a half he hadn't heard a woman's voice.)

And for the first time, through that invisible (and probably, and, of course, necessarily beautiful) girl, he began to see the real Russia, and the voice of Russia told him the truth all night long. One can learn about a country for the first time this way too. (And in the morning he would glimpse Russia's dark straw-thatched roofs through the window—to the sad whispering of his hidden guide.)

Yes, indeed, all this is Russia: the prisoners on the tracks refusing to voice their complaints, the girl on the other side of the Stolypin partition, the convoy going off to sleep, pears falling out of pockets, buried bombs, and a horse climbing to the second floor.

■

"The gendarmes! The gendarmes!" the prisoners cried out happily. They were happy that they would be escorted the rest of the way by the attentive gendarmes and not by the convoy.

Once again I have forgotten to insert quotation marks. That was Korolenko who was telling us this.[13] We, it is true, were not happy to see the bluecaps. But anyone who ever got caught in what the prisoners christened the *pendulum* would have been glad to see even them.

An ordinary passenger might have a difficult time *boarding* a train at a small way station—but not getting off. Toss your things out and jump off. This was not the case with a prisoner, however. If the local prison guard or police didn't come for him or was late by even two minutes, toot-toot, the whistle would blow, and the train would get under way, and they would take the poor sinner of a prisoner all the way to the next transit point. And it was all right if it was actually a transit point that they took you to, because they would begin to feed you again there. But sometimes it was all the way to the end of the Stolypin's route, and then they would keep you for eighteen hours in an empty car and take you back with a whole new group of prisoners, and then once again, maybe, they wouldn't come for you—and once again you'd be in a blind alley, and once again you'd wait there and during all that time they *wouldn't feed you*. Your rations, after all, were issued only until your first stop, and the accounting office isn't to blame that the prison messed things up, for you are, after all, listed for Tulun. And the convoy isn't responsible for feeding you out of its own rations. So they swing you back and forth *six times* (it has actually happened!): Irkutsk to Krasnoyarsk, Krasnoyarsk to Irkutsk, Irkutsk to Krasnoyarsk, etc., etc., etc., and when you do see a blue visor on the Tulun platform, you are ready to throw your arms around him: Thank you, beloved, for saving me.

You get so worn down, so choked, so shattered in a Stolypin, even in two days' time, that before you get to a big city you

13. V. G. Korolenko, *Istoriya Moyego Sovremennika* (*A History of My Contemporary*), Moscow, 1955, Vol. III, p. 166.

yourself don't know whether you would rather keep going in torment just to get there sooner, or whether you'd rather be put in a transit prison to recover a little.

But the convoy guards begin to hustle and bustle. They come out with their overcoats on and knock their gunstocks on the floor. That means they are going to unload the whole car.

First the convoy forms up in a circle at the car steps, and no sooner have you dropped, fallen, tumbled down them, than the guards shout at you deafeningly in unison from all sides (as they have been taught): "Sit down, sit down, sit down!" This is very effective when several voices are shouting it at once and they don't let you raise your eyes. It's like being under shellfire, and involuntarily you squirm, hurry (and where is there for you to hurry to?), crouch close to the ground, and sit down, having caught up with those who disembarked earlier.

"Sit down!" is a very clear command, but if you are a new prisoner, you don't yet understand it. When I heard this command on the switching tracks in Ivanovo, I ran, clutching my suitcase in my arms (if a suitcase has been manufactured out in freedom and not in camp, its handle always breaks off and always at a difficult moment), and set it down on end on the ground and without looking around to see how the first prisoners were sitting, sat down on the suitcase. After all, to sit down right on the ties, on the dark oily sand, in my officer's coat, which was not yet so very dirty and which still had uncut flaps! The chief of the convoy—a ruddy mug, a good Russian face—broke into a run, and I hadn't managed to grasp what he wanted and why until I saw that he meant, clearly, to plant his sacred boot in my cursed back but something restrained him. However, he didn't spare his polished toe and kicked the suitcase and smashed in the top. "Sit down!" he gritted by way of explanation. Only at that point did it dawn on me that I towered over the surrounding zeks, and without even having the chance to ask: "How am I supposed to sit down?" I already understood how, and sat down in my precious coat, like everybody else, just as dogs sit at gates and cats at doors.

(I still have that suitcase, and even now when I chance to come upon it, I run my fingers around the hole torn in it. It is a wound which cannot heal as wounds heal on bodies or on hearts. Things have longer memories than people.)

And forcing prisoners to sit down was also a calculated maneuver. If you are sitting on your rear end on the ground, so that your knees tower in front of you, then your center of gravity is well back of your legs, and it is difficult to get up and impossible to jump up. And more than that, they would make us sit as tightly massed together as possible so that we'd be in each other's way. And if all of us wanted to attack the convoy together, they would have mowed us down before we got moving.

They had us sitting there to wait for the Black Maria (it transports the prisoners in batches, you couldn't get them all in at once), or else to be herded off on foot. They would try to sit us down someplace hidden so that fewer free people would see us, but at times they did make the prisoners sit right there awkwardly on the platform or in an open square. (That is how it was in Kuibyshev.) And it is a difficult experience for the free people: we stare at them quite freely and openly with a totally sincere gaze, but how are they supposed to look at us? With hatred? Their consciences don't permit it. (After all, only the Yermilovs believe that people were imprisoned "for cause.") With sympathy? With pity? Be careful, someone will take down your name and they'll set you up for a prison term too; it's that simple. And our proud free citizens (as in Mayakovsky: "Read it, envy me, I am a citizen") drop their guilty heads and try not to see us at all, as if the place were empty. The old women are bolder than the rest. You couldn't turn them bad. They believe in God. And they would break off a piece of bread from their meager loaf and throw it to us. And old camp hands—nonpolitical offenders, of course—weren't afraid either. All camp veterans knew the saying: "Whoever hasn't been there yet will get there, and whoever was there won't forget it." And look, they'd toss over a pack of cigarettes, hoping that someone might do the same for them during their next term. And the old woman's bread wouldn't quite carry far enough, what with her weak arm, and it would fall short, whereas the pack of cigarettes would arch through the air right into our midst, and the convoy guards would immediately work the bolts of their rifles—pointing them at the old woman, at kindness, at the bread: "Come on, old woman, run along."

And the holy bread, broken in two, was left to lie in the dust while we were driven off.

In general, those minutes of sitting on the ground there at the station were among our very best. I remember that in Omsk we were made to sit down on the railroad ties between two long freight trains. No one from outside entered this alleyway. (In all probability, they had stationed a soldier at either end: "You can't go in there." And even in freedom our people are taught to take orders from anyone in a uniform.) It began to grow dark. It was August. The oily station gravel hadn't yet completely cooled off from the sun and warmed us where we sat. We couldn't see the station, but it was very close by, somewhere behind the trains. A phonograph blared dance music, and the crowd buzzed in unison. And for some reason it didn't seem humiliating to sit on the ground in a crowded dirty mass in some kind of pen; and it wasn't a mockery to hear the dances of young strangers, dances we would never dance; to picture someone on the station platform meeting someone or seeing someone off—maybe even with flowers. It was twenty minutes of near-freedom: the twilight deepened, the first stars began to shine, there were red and green lights along the tracks, and the music kept playing. Life was going on without us—and we didn't even mind any more.

Cherish such moments, and prison will become easier to bear. Otherwise you will explode from rage.

And if it was dangerous to herd the zeks along to the Black Maria because there were streets and people right next to them, then the convoy statutes provided another good command: "Link arms!" There was nothing humiliating in this—link arms! Old men and boys, girls and old women, healthy people and cripples. If one of your hands is hanging onto your belongings, your neighbor puts his arm under that arm and you in turn link your other arm with your other neighbor's. So you have now been compressed twice as tightly as in ordinary formation, and you have immediately become heavier and are hampered by being thrown out of balance by your belongings and by your awkward-ness with them, and you sway steadily as you limp. Dirty, gray, clumsy creatures, you move ahead like blind men with an ostensible tenderness for one another—a caricature of humanity.

It may well be that no Black Maria at all is there to fetch you. And the chief of convoy is perhaps a coward. He is afraid he will fail to deliver you safely—and in this state, weighed down, jouncing as you go, knocking into things, you trudge all the way through the city to the prison itself.

There is one more command which is a caricature of geese: "Take hold of your heels!" This meant that anyone whose hands were free had to grab both his legs at about ankle height. And now: "Forward march." (Well, now, reader, put this book aside, try going around the room that way! How does it work? And at what speed? How much looking around could you do? And what about escaping?) Picture the way three or four dozen such geese look from the side. (Kiev, 1940.)

And it is not necessarily August out; it might be December, 1946, and, there being no Black Maria, you are being herded at 40 degrees below zero to the Petropavlovsk Transit Prison. And it is easy to guess that during the last hours before arriving the Stolypin convoy refused to go to the trouble of taking you to the toilet, so as to avoid getting it dirty. Weakened from interrogation, gripped by the cold, you have a very hard time holding it—women especially. Well, and so what! It's for horses to stand stock-still and loose the floodgates! It's for dogs to go lift a leg against a fence. But as for people, you can do it right there, while you keep moving. No need to be shy in your own fatherland. It will dry at the transit prison. . . . Vera Korneyeva stooped down to adjust her shoe and fell one step behind, and the convoy immediately set the police dog on her and the dog bit her in the buttocks through all her winter clothing. Don't fall behind! And an Uzbek fell down, and they beat him with their gunstocks and jackboots.

Well, that's no tragedy: it won't be photographed for the *Daily Express.* And the chief of convoy will live to a ripe old age and never be tried by anyone.

■

And the *Black Marias,* too, came down to us from history. In what respect does the prison carriage described by Balzac differ from a Black Maria? Only that the prison carriage was drawn along more slowly, and prisoners weren't packed so tightly.

True, in the twenties columns of prisoners were still being driven afoot through our cities, even Leningrad. They brought traffic to a halt at intersections. ("So you got caught stealing?" came the reproaches from the sidewalks. No one had yet grasped the great plan for sewage disposal.)

But, always alert to technological trends, the Archipelago lost no time in adopting the *black ravens,* more familiarly known simply as *ravens*—Black Marias. These first Black Marias appeared at the same time as the very first trucks on our still cobblestoned streets. Their suspension was poor, and it was very rough riding in them, but then the prisoners weren't made of crystal either. On the other hand, they were very tightly corked even at that time, in 1927: there wasn't one little crack; and there wasn't one little electric light bulb, and there wasn't any air to breathe, and it was impossible to see out. And even in those days they stood so tightly packed inside that there wasn't any room left at all. And it wasn't that all this was intentionally planned; there simply weren't enough wheels to go around.

For many years the Black Marias were steel-gray and had, so to speak, prison written all over them. But in the biggest cities after the war they had second thoughts and decided to paint them bright colors and to write on the outside, "Bread" (the prisoners were the bread of construction), or "Meat" (it would have been more accurate to write "bones"), or even, simply, "Drink Soviet Champagne!"

Inside, the Black Marias might consist of a simple armored body or shell, an empty enclosure. Or perhaps there were benches against the walls all the way around. This was in no sense a convenience, but the reverse: they would push in just as many prisoners as could be inserted standing up, but in this case they would be piled on top of each other like baggage, one bale on another. The Black Maria might also have a *box* in the rear— a narrow steel closet for one prisoner. Or it might be *boxed* throughout: single closets that locked like cells along the right- and left-hand walls, with a corridor in the middle for the turnkey.

One was hardly likely to imagine that interior like a honeycomb when looking at that laughing maiden on the outside: "Drink Soviet Champagne!"

They drive you into the Black Marias to the tune of the same shouts coming from the convoy from all sides at once: "Come on there, get a move on, quick!" And so that you shouldn't have time to look around and figure out how to escape, you are shoved and pushed so that you and your bag get stuck in the narrow little door and you knock your head against the lintel. The steel rear door slams shut with a bang—and off you go.

It was rare, of course, to spend hours in a Black Maria; twenty to thirty minutes were more likely. But you got flung around, it was a bone-breaker, it crushed all your insides during those half-hours, your head stooped if you were tall, and you remembered the cozy Stolypin with longing.

And the Black Maria means one thing further—it is a re-shuffling of the deck, new encounters, and among them those which stand out most clearly are, of course, your encounters with the thieves. You may never happen to be in the same compartment with them, and maybe they won't put you in the same cell with them even at the transit prison, but here in the Black Maria you are in their hands.

Sometimes it is so crowded that even the thieves, the urki, find it awkward *to filch*. Your legs and your arms are clamped between your neighbors' bodies and bags as tightly as if they were in stocks. Only when all of you are tossed up and down and all your insides are shaken up by ruts and bumps can you change the position of your legs and arms.

Sometimes, in less crowded circumstances, the thieves can check out the contents of all the bags in just half an hour and appropriate all the "bacilli"—the fats and goodies—and the best of the "trash"—the clothing. Cowardly and sensible considerations most likely restrain you from putting up a fight against them. (And crumb by crumb you are already beginning to lose your immortal soul, still supposing that the main enemies and the main issues lie somewhere ahead and that you must save yourself for them.) And you might just throw a punch at them once and get a knife in the ribs then and there. (There would be no investigation, and even if there should be one, it wouldn't threaten the thieves in any way: they would only *be delayed* at the transit prison instead of going to the far-off camp. You must concede that in a fight between a socially friendly prisoner and a socially hostile prisoner the state simply could not be on the side of the latter.)

In 1946, retired Colonel Lunin, a high-ranking official in

Osoaviakhim—the Society for Assistance to Defense and to Aviation-Chemical Construction of the U.S.S.R.—recounted in a Butyrki cell how the thieves in a Moscow Black Maria, on March 8, International Women's Day, during their transit from the City Court to Taganka Prison, gang-raped a young bride in his presence (and amid the silent passivity of everyone else in the van). That very morning the girl had come to her trial a free person, as attractively dressed as she could manage (she was on trial for leaving her work without official permission—which in itself was a repulsive fabrication worked up by her chief in revenge for her refusal to live with him). A half-hour before the Black Maria, the girl had been sentenced to five years under the decree and had then been shoved into this Black Maria, and right there in broad daylight, somewhere on the Park Ring ("Drink Soviet Champagne!"), had been turned into a camp prostitute. And are we really to say that it was the thieves who did this to her and not the jailers? And not her chief?

And thief tenderness too! Having raped her, they robbed her. They took the fashionable shoes with which she had hoped to charm the judges, and her blouse—which they shoved through to the convoy guards, who stopped the van and went off to get some vodka and handed it in so the thieves could drink at her expense too.

And when they got to the Taganka Prison, the girl sobbed out her complaint. And the officer listened to her, yawned, and said: "The government can't provide each of you with individual transportation. We don't have such facilities."

Yes, the Black Marias are a "bottleneck" of the Archipelago. If there is no possibility of separating the politicals from the criminals in the Stolypins, then it isn't possible to keep women separate from men in the Black Marias. And just how could one expect the thieves not to live it up en route from one jail to another?

Well, and if it weren't for the thieves, we would have to be grateful to the Black Marias for our brief encounters with women! Where, if not here, is one to see them, hear them, and touch them in a prison existence?

Once in 1950 they were transporting us from the Butyrki to the station in a not at all crowded van—fourteen people in a

Black Maria with benches. Everyone sat down, and suddenly they pushed in one more—a woman, alone. She sat down beside the rear door, fearfully at first. After all, she was totally defenseless against fourteen men in a dark cell. But it became clear after a few words that all those present were comrades. Fifty-eights.

She gave us her name—Repina, a colonel's wife, and she had been arrested right after he had. And suddenly a silent military man, so young and thin that it seemed he had to be a lieutenant, said to her: "Tell me, weren't you arrested with Antonina I.?" "What? Are you her husband? Oleg?" "Yes!" "Lieutenant Colonel I.? From the Frunze Academy?" "Yes!"

What a *yes* that was! It emerged from a trembling throat, and in it there was more fear of finding out something bad than there was happiness. He sat down next to her. Twilight shafts of summer daylight, diffused through two microscopic gratings in the two rear doors, flickered around the interior as the van moved along and across the faces of the woman and the lieutenant colonel. "She and I were imprisoned in the same cell for four months while she was undergoing interrogation." "Where is she now?" "All that time she lived only for you! Her fears weren't for herself but were all for you. First that they shouldn't arrest you. And then later that you should get a lighter sentence." "But what has happened to her now?" "She blamed herself for your arrest. Things were so hard for her!" "Where is she now?" "Just don't be frightened"—and Repina put her hands on his chest as if he were her own kin. "She simply couldn't endure the strain. They took her away from us. She, you know, became—well, a little confused. You understand?"

And that tiny storm boxed in sheets of steel rolled along so peacefully in the six-lane automobile traffic, stopped at traffic lights, and signaled for a turn.

I had met Oleg I. in the Butyrki just a few moments before— and here is how it happened. They had herded us into the station "box" and had brought us our things from the storage room. They called him and me to the door at the same moment. Through the opened door into the corridor we could see a woman jailer rifling the contents of his suitcase, and she flung out of it and onto the floor a golden shoulder board with the stars of a lieutenant colonel that had survived until then all by itself, heaven only knows how; she herself hadn't noticed it, and she had accidentally stepped on its big stars with her foot.

She had trampled it with her shoe—exactly as in a film shot.

I said to him: "Direct your attention to that, Comrade Lieutenant Colonel!"

And he glowered. After all, he still had his ideas about the spotlessness of the service.

And now here was the next thing—about his wife.

And he had had only one hour to fit all this in.

Chapter 2

■

The Ports
of the Archipelago

Spread out on a large table the enormous map of our Motherland. Indicate with fat black dots all provincial capitals, all railroad junctions, all transfer points where the railroad line ends in a river route, and where rivers bend and trails begin. What is this? Has the entire map been speckled by infectious flies? What it is, in fact, is precisely the majestic map of the ports of the Archipelago. These are not, to be sure, the enchanted ports to which Aleksandr Grin enticed us, where rum is drunk in taverns and men pay court to beautiful women.

It is a rare zek who has not known from three to five transit prisons and camps; many remember a dozen or so, and *the sons of Gulag* can count up to fifty of them without the slightest difficulty. However, in memory they get all mixed up together because they are so similar: in the illiteracy of their convoys, in their inept roll calls based on *case files;* the long waiting under the beating sun or autumn drizzle; the still longer *body searches* that involve undressing completely; their haircuts with unsanitary clippers; their cold, slippery baths; their foul-smelling toilets; their damp and moldy corridors; their perpetually crowded, nearly always dark, wet cells; the warmth of human flesh flanking you on the floor or on the board bunks; the bumpy ridges of bunk heads knocked together from boards; the wet, almost liquid, bread; the gruel cooked from what seems to be silage.

And whoever has a good sharp memory and can recollect

precisely what distinguishes one from another has no need to travel about the country because he knows its geography full well on the basis of transit prisons. Novosibirsk? I know it. I was there. Very strong barracks there, made from thick beams. Irkutsk? That was where the windows had been bricked over in several stages, you could see how they had been in Tsarist times, and each course had been laid separately, and only small slits had been left between them. Vologda? Yes, an ancient building with towers. The toilets right on top of one another, the wooden partitions rotten, and the ones above leaking down into the ones underneath. Usman? Of course. A lice-ridden stinking hole of a jail, an ancient vaulted structure. And they used to pack it so full that whenever they took prisoners out for a transport you couldn't imagine where they'd put them all—a line strung out halfway through the city.

You had better not tell such a connoisseur that you know some city without a transit prison. He will prove to you conclusively that there are no such cities, and he will be right. Salsk? Well, there they keep transit prisoners in the KPZ—cells for preliminary detention—along with prisoners under interrogation. And what do you mean, no transit prison in every district center too? In Sol-Iletsk? Of course there's one. In Rybinsk? What about Prison No. 2, a former monastery? It's a quiet one, too, with empty courtyards paved with old, mossy flagstones and clean wooden tubs in the bath. In Chita? Prison No. 1. In Naushki? Not a prison but a transit camp, which is the same thing. In Torzhok? Up the hill, also in a monastery.

You must realize, dear sir, that every town has to have its own transit prison. After all, the courts operate everywhere. And how are prisoners to be delivered to camp? By air?

Of course, no transit prison is the equal of another. But which is better and which worse is something that can't be settled in an argument. If three or four zeks get together, each of them feels bound *to praise* his "own." Let us listen for a while to such a discussion:

"Well, even if the Ivanovo Transit Prison isn't one of the more famous, my friends, just ask anybody imprisoned there in the winter of 1937–1938. The prison was *unheated*—and the prisoners not only didn't freeze to death, but on the upper bunks they lay there undressed. And they knocked out all the windowpanes so as not to suffocate. Instead of the twenty men Cell 21 was supposed to contain, there were *three hundred and twenty-three!* There was water underneath the bunks, and boards were laid in the water and people lay on those boards. That was right where the frost poured in from the broken windows. It was like Arctic night down under the bunks. There was no light down there either because it was cut off by the people lying on the bunks above and standing in the aisle. It was impossible to walk through the aisle to the latrine tank, and people crawled along the edges of the bunks. They didn't distribute rations to individuals but to units of ten. If one of the ten died, the others shoved his corpse under the bunks and kept it there until it started to stink. They got the corpse's ration. And all that could have been endured, but the turnkeys seemed to have been oiled with turpentine—and they kept driving the prisoners endlessly from cell to cell, on and on. You'd just get yourself settled when 'Come on, get a move on! You're being moved!' And you'd have to start in again trying to find a place! And the reason for such overcrowding was that they hadn't taken anyone to the bath for three months, the lice had multiplied, and people had abscesses from the lice on their feet and legs—and typhus too. And because of the typhus the prison was quarantined and no prisoner transports could leave it for four months."

"Well, fellows, the problem there wasn't Ivanovo, but the year. In 1937–1938, of course, not just the zeks but the very stones of the transit prisons were screaming in agony. Irkutsk was no special transit prison either, but in 1938 the doctors didn't even dare look into the cells but would walk down the corridor while the turnkey shouted through the door: '*Anyone unconscious, come out.*'"

"In 1937, fellows, it was that way all across Siberia to the Kolyma, and the big bottleneck was in the Sea of Okhotsk, and in Vladivostok. The steamships could transport only thirty thousand a month, and they kept driving them on and on from Moscow without taking that into account. Well, and so a hundred thousand of them piled up. Understand?"

"Who counted them?"

"Whoever was supposed to, counted."

"If you're talking about the Vladivostok Transit Prison, then in February, 1937, there weren't more than forty thousand there."

"People were stuck there for several months at a time. The bedbugs infested the board bunks like locusts. Half a mug of water a day; there wasn't any more!—no one to haul it. There was one whole compound of Koreans, and they all died from dysentery, every last one of them. They took a hundred corpses out of our own compound every morning. They were building a morgue, so they hitched the zeks to the carts and hauled the stone that way. Today you do the hauling, and tomorrow they haul you there yourself. And in autumn the typhus arrived. And we did the same thing: we didn't hand over the corpses till they stank—and took the extra rations. No medication whatever. We crawled to the fence and begged: 'Give us medicine.' And the guards fired a volley from the watchtowers. Then they assembled those with typhus in a separate barracks. Some didn't make it there, and only a few came back. The bunks there had two stories. And anyone on an upper who was sick and running a fever wasn't able to clamber down to go to the toilet—and so it would all pour down on the people underneath. There were fifteen hundred sick there. And all the orderlies were thieves. They'd pull out the gold teeth from the corpses. And not only from the corpses."

"Why do you keep going on and on about 1937? What about 1949 on Vanino Bay, in the fifth compound? What about that? There were 35,000! And for several months too! There was another bottleneck in transport to the Kolyma. And every night for some reason they kept driving people from one barracks to another and from one compound to another. Just as it was with the Fascists: Whistles! Screams! 'Come on out there *without the last one!*'[1] And everyone went on the run! Always on the run! They'd drive a hundred to get bread—on the run! For gruel—on the run! No bowls to eat from. Take the gruel in whatever you could—the flap of your coat, your hands! They brought water in big tanks and there was nothing to distribute it in, so they shot it out in sprays. And whoever could get his mouth in front of one

---

1. "Without the last one!"—a menacing command to be understood literally. It meant: "I will kill the last man" (literally or at least warm his hide with a club). And so all piled out so as not to be last.

got some. Prisoners began to fight in front of the tanks—and the guards fired on them from the towers. Exactly like under the Fascists! Major General Derevyanko, the Chief of Administration of the Northeast [i.e., Kolyma] Corrective Labor Camps, came, and while he was there an air force aviator stepped out in front of the crowd and ripped his field shirt down the front: 'I have seven battle decorations! Who gave you the right to shoot into the compound?' And Derevyanko replied: 'We shot and *we will go on shooting* until you learn how to behave.' "[2]

"No, boys, none of those are real transit prisons. Now take Kirov! That was a real one! Let's not take any special year, but, say, 1947. Even then in Kirov two turnkeys had to work together with their boots to jam people into a cell, that being the only way they could get the door shut. In September (and Kirov—formerly Vyatka—isn't on the Black Sea either) everyone was sitting naked on the three-story bunks because of the heat. They were *sitting* because there was no place to lie down: one row sat at the heads of the bunks and one row at the feet. And two rows sat on the floor in the aisle, and others stood between them, and they took turns. They kept their knapsacks in their hands or on their knees because there was nowhere to put them down. Only the thieves were in their *lawful* places, the second-story bunks next to the windows, and they spread out as they pleased. There were so many bedbugs that they went right on biting in the daytime, and they dive-bombed straight from the ceiling. And people had to suffer through that for a week or even a month."

I myself would like to interrupt in order to tell about Krasnaya Presnya[3] in August, 1945, in the Victory summer, but I am shy: after all, in Krasnaya Presnya we could somehow stretch out our legs at night, and the bedbugs were moderate, and flies bit us all night long as we lay naked and sweaty under the bright lights, but of course that's nothing at all, and I would be ashamed to boast about it. We streamed with sweat every time we moved,

2. Say there, Bertrand Russell's "War Crimes Tribunal"! Why don't you use this bit of material? Or doesn't it suit you?

3. This transit prison with its glorious revolutionary name is little known to Muscovites. There are no excursions to it, and how could there be when it is still *in operation?* But to get a close look at it, you don't have to travel any distance at all. It's a mere stone's throw from the Novokhoroshevo Highway on the circle line.

and it simply poured out of us after we ate. There were a hundred of us in a cell a little larger than the average room in an apartment, and we were packed in, and you couldn't find a place on the floor for your feet. And two little windows on the south side were blocked with "muzzles" made of steel sheets. They not only kept the air from circulating, but they got very hot from the sun and radiated heat into the cell.

Just as all transit prisons are pointless, talk about transit prisons is pointless, and, in all probability, this chapter, too, will turn out to be the same: one doesn't know what to take hold of first, what particular thing to talk about, what to lead off with. And the more people that are crowded into transit prisons, the more pointless it all becomes. It is unbearable for a human being, and it is inexpedient for Gulag—but people sit there month after month. And the transit prison becomes a straight factory: bread rations are lugged in, stacked up in hand barrows like those in which bricks are hauled. And the steaming gruel is brought in six-bucket wooden casks that have holes knocked in them with a crowbar.

The transit prison at Kotlas was tenser and more aboveboard than many. Tenser because it opened the way to the whole Northeast of European Russia, and more aboveboard because it was already deep in the Archipelago, and there was no need to pretend to anybody. It was simply a piece of land divided into cages by fencing and the cages were all kept locked. Although it had been thickly settled by peasants when they were exiled in 1930 (one must realize that they had no roofs over their heads, but nobody is left to tell about it), even in 1938 there simply wasn't room for everyone in the frail one-story wooden barracks made of discarded end-pieces of lumber and covered with . . . tarpaulin. Under the wet autumn snow and in freezing temperatures people simply lived there on the ground, beneath the heavens. True, they weren't allowed to grow numb from inactivity. They were being counted endlessly; they were invigorated by check-ups (twenty thousand people were there at a time) or by sudden night searches. Later on tents were pitched in these cages, and log houses two stories high were built in some of them, but to reduce the construction costs sensibly, no floor was laid between the stories—six-story bunks with stepladders were simply built into the sides, up and down which prisoners on their last legs, on the verge of dying, had to clamber like sailors (a structure which would have adorned a ship more appropriately than a port). In the winter of 1944–1945, when everyone had a roof over his head, there was room for only 7,500 prisoners, and fifty of them died every day, and the stretchers on which they were carried to the morgue were never idle. (People will object that this was quite acceptable—a death rate of less than one percent per day—and that, given that sort of turnover, a person might manage to last five months. Yes, but the main killer was camp labor, and that hadn't even begun yet for transit prisoners. This loss of two-thirds of one percent per day represents sheer *shrinkage,* and it would be intolerably high even in some vegetable warehouses.)

The deeper into the Archipelago one got, the more obviously did the concrete docks of the Archipelago become transformed into wharves made of wooden pilings.

In the course of several years, half a million people passed through *Karabas,* the transit camp near Karaganda, whose name became a byword in the language. (Yuri Karbe was there in 1942 and was already registered in the 433rd thousand.) The transit prison consisted of low rammed-earth barracks with earthen floors. Daily recreation there consisted in driving all the prisoners out with their things and putting artists to work whitewashing the floor and even painting carpets on it, and then in the evening the zeks would lie down on it, and their bodies would rub out both the whitewash and the carpets.[4]

The Knyazh-Pogost transit point (latitude 63 degrees north) consisted of shacks built on a swamp. Their pole frames were covered with torn tarpaulin tenting that didn't quite reach the ground. The double bunks inside them were also made of poles (from which, incidentally, the branches had been only partially removed), and the aisle was floored with poles also. During the day, the wet mud squelched through the flooring, and at night it froze. In various parts of the area, the walkways were laid on frail and shaky poles and here and there people whom weakness

4. Of all the transit prisons Karabas was worthiest of becoming a museum. But, alas, it no longer exists: in its place there is a factory for reinforced-concrete products.

had made clumsy fell into the water and ooze. In 1938 they fed the prisoners in Knyazh-Pogost the same thing every day: a mash made of crushed grits and fish bones. This was convenient because there were no bowls, spoons, or forks at the transit prison and the prisoners had none of their own either. They were herded to the boiler by the dozens and the mash was ladled into their caps or the flaps of their jackets.

And in the transit prison of Vogvozdino (several miles from Ust-Vym), where five thousand prisoners were kept at a time (now who ever heard of Vogvozdino before this sentence? how many such unknown transit prisons were there? and then multiply that by 5,000), the food was liquid, but they had no bowls either. However, they managed without them (what is there that our Russian ingenuity cannot overcome?) by distributing the gruel in *washbasins* for ten people at a time, leaving them to race each other gulping it down.[5]

True, no one was imprisoned in Vogvozdino longer than a year. (The kind of prisoner who would have been imprisoned there that long was a prisoner on his last legs whom all the camps had refused to accept.)

The imagination of writers is poverty-stricken in regard to the native life and customs of the Archipelago. When they want to write about the most reprehensible and disgraceful aspect of prison, they always accuse the *latrine bucket*. In literature the latrine bucket has become the symbol of prison, a symbol of humiliation, of stink. Oh, how frivolous can you be? Now was the latrine bucket really an evil for the prisoner? On the contrary, it was the most merciful device of the prison administration. The actual horror began the moment there was *no* latrine bucket in the cell.

In 1937 *there were no latrine buckets* in certain Siberian prisons, or there weren't enough. Not enough of them had been made ahead of time—Siberian industry hadn't caught up with the full scope of arrests. There were no latrine barrels in the warehouses for the newly created cells. There were old latrine buckets in the

---

5. Galina Serebryakova! Boris Dyakov! Aldan-Semyonov! Did you ever gulp from a washbasin, ten at a time? And if you had, you would never, of course, have descended to the "animal needs" of Ivan Denisovich, would you? And in the midst of the mob scene at the washbasin you would have continued to think only about your dear Party?

cells, but they were antiquated and small, and the only reasonable thing to do at that point was to remove them, since they amounted to nothing at all for the new reinforcements of prisoners. So if long ago the Minusinsk Prison had been built for five hundred people (Vladimir Ilyich Lenin was never inside it; he moved about freely), and there were now ten thousand in it, it meant that each latrine bucket ought to have become twenty times bigger. But it had not.

Our Russian pens write only in large letters. We have lived through so very much, and almost none of it has been described and called by its right name. But, for Western authors, peering through a microscope at the living cells of everyday life, shaking a test tube in the beam of a strong light, this is after all a whole epic, another ten volumes of *Remembrance of Things Past:* to describe the perturbation of a human soul placed in a cell filled to twenty times its capacity and with no latrine bucket, where prisoners are taken out to the toilet only once a day! Of course, much of the texture of this life is bound to be quite unknown to Western writers; they wouldn't realize that in this situation one solution was to urinate in your canvas hood, nor would they at all understand one prisoner's advice to another to urinate in his boot! And yet that advice was the fruit of wisdom derived from vast experience, and it didn't involve spoiling the boot and it didn't reduce the boot to the status of a pail. It meant that the boot had to be taken off, turned upside down, the boot tops turned inside out and up—and thus a cylindrical vessel was formed that constituted the much-needed container. But, at the same time, with what psychological twists and turns Western writers could enrich their literature (without in the least risking any banal repetition of the famous masters) if they only knew about the scheme of things in that same Minusinsk Prison: there was only one food bowl for every four prisoners; and one mug of drinking water per day was issued to each (there were enough mugs to go around). And it could happen that one of the four contrived to use the bowl allotted to him and three others to relieve his internal pressure and then refuse to hand over his daily water ration to wash it out before lunch. What a conflict! What a clash of four personalities! What nuances! (And I am not joking. That is when the rock bottom of a human being is revealed. It is only that

Russian pens are too busy to write about it, and Russian eyes don't have time to read about it. I am not joking—because only doctors can tell us how months in such a cell will ruin a human being's health for his entire life, even if he wasn't shot under Yezhov and was rehabilitated under Khrushchev.)

And just to think that we had dreamed of resting and loosening up a bit in port! After being squashed and doubled up for several days in the Stolypin, how we had dreamed of the transit prison! That we could stretch out a bit there and straighten up. That we would be able to go to the toilet there without hurrying! That we would drink as much water there as we wanted, and get as much hot water for tea. That there we wouldn't be forced to ransom our own bread rations from the convoy with our own belongings. That we would be fed hot food there. And that at last we would be taken to the bath, that we could drench ourselves in hot water and stop itching. We had had elbows stuck into our sides and been tossed from side to side in the Black Maria; and they had shouted at us: "Link arms!" "Take hold of your heels!" But we were in good spirits anyway: it was all right, all right, soon we would be at the transit prison! And now we were there.

And even if some part of our dreams came true in the transit prison, something else would foul it all up anyway.

What awaits us in the bath? You can never be sure. They begin suddenly to shave all the women's hair off. (In Krasnaya Presnya, in November, 1950.) Or a line of us naked men is clipped by women barbers only. In the Vologda steam room, portly Aunt Motya used to shout: "Stand up, men!" And she'd let the whole line have it from the steam pipe. And the Irkutsk Transit Prison argued differently: it's more natural for the entire service staff in the bath to be male and for a man to smear on the medicinal tar ointment between the women's legs. Or during the winter, in the cold soaping-up room of the Novosibirsk Transit Prison only cold water comes from the faucets; the prisoners make up their minds to ask higher-ups, and a captain comes, puts his own hand unfastidiously under a faucet: "I say this water is hot, get it?" I have already wearied of reporting that there are baths which have no water at all, that they scorch clothes in the roaster, that after the bath they compel people to run naked and barefoot through the snow to get their things (the counterintelligence of the Second Byelorussian Front in Brodnica in 1945).

From your very first steps in the transit prison you realize that here you are not in the hands of the jailers or the officers of the prison administration, who at least adhere some of the time to some kind of written law. Here you are in the hands of *the trusties.* That surly bath attendant who comes to meet your prisoner transport: "Well, go wash, gentlemen Fascists!" And that work-assignment clerk with a plywood writing board who looks over your formation searchingly and hurries you up. And that *instructor,* clean-shaven except for a prominent forelock, who slaps his leg with that rolled-up newspaper and at the same time gives your bags a once-over. And then other transit-prison trusties, whom you don't recognize, penetrate your suitcases with X-ray eyes—oh, how alike they all are! And where in your brief prisoner-transport journey have you seen them all before? Not so clean-looking, not so well washed, but the same kind of ugly-mug swine with pitiless, bare-toothed grins?

Baaaah! These are the same blatnye, the thieves, again. Those same urki crooks, whom Leonid Utyosov glorifies in his songs. Here again are Zhenka Zhogol, Seryoga-Zver, and Dimka Kishkenya, but not behind bars this time; they have been cleaned up, dressed up as representatives of the state. And *putting on airs* of great importance, they see to it that discipline is observed—by us. And if one peers into those snouts, one can even, with imagination, picture that they sprang from the same Russian roots as the rest of us—that once upon a time they were village boys whose fathers bore such names as Klim, Prokhor, Guri, and that their general structure is even similar to our own: two nostrils, two irises in the eyes, a rosy tongue with which to swallow food and utter certain Russian sounds, which, however, shape totally new words.

Every chief of a transit prison has enough presence of mind to realize that he can send his relatives back home the wages for all staff positions or else he can divvy them up with the other prison officers. And all you have to do is whistle to get as many volunteers as you want from among the *socially friendly* prison elements to carry out all that work just in return for being allowed to *cast anchor* at the transit prison and not have to go on to a mine or to the taiga. All these work-assignment clerks, office clerks, bookkeepers, instructors, bath attendants, barbers, stockroom clerks, cooks, dishwashers, laundresses, tailors who repair underwear and linens—are permanent transit-prison residents. They receive prison rations and are registered in cells, and they swipe the rest of their soup and chow on their own out of the common food pot or out of the *bundles* of the transit zeks. All these transit-prison trusties regard it as certain that they will never be better off in any camp. We arrive in their hands still not completely plucked, and they bamboozle us to their hearts' content. It is they and not the jailers who search us and our belongings here, and before the search they suggest we turn in our money for safekeeping, and they seriously write down a list—we never see the list or the money again. "We turned in our money." "Who to?" the officer who has arrived on the scene asks in surprise. "Well, it was one of them." "Who exactly?" The trusties hadn't noticed which one. "Why did you turn it over to him?" "We thought . . ." "That's what the turkey thought! Think less and you'll be better off." And that's that. They suggest we leave our things in the vestibule to the bath: "No one's going to take them. Who needs them?" We leave them, for after all we can't take them into the bath with us anyway. We return and there are no sweaters left and no fur-lined mittens. "What kind of a sweater was it?" "Grayish." "Well, that means it went to the laundry." They also take things from us *honestly:* in return for taking a suitcase into the storage room for safekeeping; for putting us in a cell without the thieves; for sending us off on prisoner transports as soon as possible; for not sending us off as long as possible. The only thing they don't do is rob us by main force out in the open.

"But those aren't thieves!" the connoisseurs among us explain. "These are the *bitches*—the ones who work for the prison. They are enemies of the *honest thieves*. And the honest thieves are the ones imprisoned in cells." But somehow this is hard for our rabbity brains to grasp. Their ways are the same; they have the same kind of tattoos. Maybe they really are enemies of *those others,* but after all they are not our friends either, that's how it is. . . .

And by this time they have forced us to sit down in the yard right underneath the cell windows. The windows all have "muzzles" on them and you can't look in, but from inside, hoarse, friendly voices advise: "Hey, fellows! You know what they do here? When they search you, they take away everything loose like tea and tobacco. If you have any, toss it in here, through our window. We'll give it back later." So what do you know? We are suckers and rabbits. Maybe they do take tea and tobacco away. We have read about universal prisoner solidarity in all our great literature, that one prisoner won't deceive another. The way they spoke to us was friendly. "Hey, fellows!" And so we *toss* them our tobacco pouches. And the genuine pure-bred thieves on the other side catch them and guffaw: "You Fascist stupes."

And here are the slogans with which the whole transit prison welcomes us even though they don't actually hang them on the walls: "Don't look for justice here!" "You're going to have to hand over everything you've got to us." "You'll have to give it all up." This is repeated to you by the jailers, the convoy, and the thieves. You are overwhelmed by your unbearable prison term, and you are trying to figure out how to catch your breath, while everyone around you is figuring out how to plunder you. Everything works out so as to oppress the political prisoner, who is already depressed and abandoned without all that. "You will have to give it all up." The jailer at the Gorky Transit Prison shakes his head hopelessly; and with a sense of relief, Ans Bernshtein gives him his officer's greatcoat—not free, but in exchange for two onions. And why should you complain about the thieves if you see all the jailers at Krasnaya Presnya wearing chrome-leather boots they were never issued? They were all *lifted* by the thieves in the cells and then *pushed* to the jailers. Why complain about the thieves if the *instructor of the Cultural and Educational Department* of the camp administration is a blatnoi, a thief, himself and writes *reports* on the politicals? (The Kem Transit Prison.) And how are you ever going to get justice against the thieves in the Rostov Transit Prison when this is their ancient native tribal den?

They say that in 1942 at the Gorky Transit Prison some officer prisoners (including Gavrilov, the military engineer Shchebetin, and others) nonetheless rebelled, beat up the thieves, and forced them to stay in line. But this is always regarded as a legend; did the thieves capitulate in just one of the cells? For long? And how was it that the bluecaps allowed the socially *hostile* elements to beat up the socially *friendly* ones? And when they say that at the Kotlas Transit Prison in 1940 the thieves started to grab money right out of the hands of the politicals lined up at the commissary, and the politicals began to beat them up so badly that they couldn't be stopped, and the perimeter guards entered the compound with machine guns to defend the thieves—now there's something that rings true. That's the way it really was.

Foolish relatives! They dash about in freedom, borrow money (because they never have that kind of money at home), and send you foodstuffs and things—the widow's last mite, but also a poisoned gift, because it transforms you from a free though hungry person into one who is anxious and cowardly, and it deprives you of that newly dawning enlightenment, that toughening resolve, which are all you need for your descent into the abyss. Oh, wise Gospel saying about the camel and the eye of the needle! These material things will keep you from entering the heavenly kingdom of the liberated spirit. And you see that others in the police van have the same kind of bags as you. "Ragbag bastards!" the thieves have already snarled at you in the Black Maria—but there were only two of them and there were fifty of you and so far they haven't touched you. And now they were holding us for the second day at the Krasnaya Presnya *station* with our legs tucked beneath us on the dirty floor because we were so crowded. However, none of us was observing the life going on around us, because we were all too concerned with how to turn in our suitcases for safekeeping. Even though we were supposed to have the right to turn in our things for safekeeping, nonetheless the only reason the work-assignment clerks permitted us to do it was because the prison was a Moscow prison and we ourselves hadn't yet lost our Moscow look.

What a relief—our things had been checked. (And that meant we would have to *give them up* not at this transit prison but later on.) The only things left dangling from our hands were our bundles with our ill-fated foodstuffs. Too many of us *beavers* had been assembled in one place. They began to distribute us among different cells. I was shoved into a cell with that same Valentin whom I had been with the day I signed for my OSO sentence, and who had proposed with touching sentiment that we begin a new life in camp. It was not yet packed full. The aisle was free. There was plenty of space under the bunks. According to the traditional arrangement, the thieves occupied the second tier of bunks: their senior members were beside the windows, their juniors farther back. A neutral gray mass was on the lower bunks. No one attacked us. Without looking around and without thinking ahead, inexperienced as we were, we sat down on the asphalt floor and crawled under the bunks. We would even be cozy there. The bunks were low for big men to get under, and we had to slide in on our bellies, inching along the asphalt floor. We did. And we were going to lie there quietly and talk quietly. Not a chance! In the semidarkness, with a wordless rustling, from all sides *juveniles* crept up on us on all fours, like big rats. They were still boys, some twelve-year-olds even, but the Criminal Code accepted them too. They had already been *processed* through a thieves' trial, and they were continuing their apprenticeship with the thieves here. They had been unleashed on us. They jumped us from all sides and six pairs of hands stripped from us and wrenched from under us all our wealth. And all this took place in total silence, with only the sound of sinister sniffing. And we were trapped: we couldn't get up, we couldn't move. It took no more than a minute for them to seize the bundles with the fat bacon, sugar, and bread. They were gone. We lay there feeling stupid. We had given up our food without a fight. And we could go on lying there now, but that was utterly impossible. Creeping out awkwardly, rear ends first, we got up from under the bunks.

Am I a coward? I had thought I wasn't one. I had pushed my way into the heat of a bombing in the open steppe, I hadn't been afraid to drive over a trail obviously mined with antitank mines. I had remained coolheaded when I led my battery out of encirclement and went back in for a damaged command car. Why, then, at that moment didn't I grab one of those human rats and grate his rosy face on the black asphalt? Was he too small? Well then, go for their leaders. But no. At the front we are strengthened by some kind of supplementary awareness (and quite false, too, perhaps): is it a sense of our military unity? The sense of being in the right place at the right time? Of duty? But in this new situation nothing is clear, there are no rules, and everything has to be learned by feel.

Getting to my feet, I turned to their senior, the pakhan, the ringleader of the thieves. All the stolen victuals were there in front of him beside the window on the second tier of bunks: the juvenile rats hadn't eaten a thing themselves. They were disciplined. Nature had sculpted the front part of the ringleader's head, in bipeds usually called a face, with nausea and hate. Or perhaps it had come to be what it was from living the life of a beast of prey. It sagged crookedly and loosely, with a low forehead, a savage scar, and modern steel crowns on the front teeth. His little eyes were exactly large enough to see all familiar objects and yet not take delight in the beauties of the world. He looked at me as a boar looks at a deer, knowing he could always knock me off my feet.

He was waiting. And what did I do? Leap forward to smash my fist in that ugly mug at least once and then go down in the aisle? Alas, I did not.

Am I a scoundrel? Until that moment I had always thought that I wasn't. But now, plundered and humiliated, I found it offensive to get down flat on my stomach again and crawl back beneath the bunks. And so I addressed the ringleader of the thieves indignantly and told him that since he had taken our food away from us he might at least give us a place on the bunks. (Now just tell me, wasn't that a natural complaint for a city dweller and an officer?)

And what happened then? The ringleader of the thieves agreed. After all, I was thereby surrendering any claim to the fat bacon; and I was thereby recognizing his superior authority; and I was revealing a point of view in common with his—he, too, would have driven off the weakest. And he gave orders for two of the gray neutrals to get off the lower bunks beside the window and free a space for us. They obeyed submissively. And we lay down in the best places. For a while we still grieved over our loss. (The thieves paid no attention to my military breeches. They weren't their kind of uniform. But one of the thieves was already fingering Valentin's woolen trousers. He liked them.) And it was only at night that the reproachful whisper of our neighbors reached us: how could we ask the thieves to help us by driving two *of our own people* under the bunks in our place? And only then did awareness of my own meanness prick my conscience and make me blush. (And for many years thereafter I blushed every time I remembered it.) The gray prisoners on the lower bunks were my own brothers, 58-1b, the POW's. Had I not just a short while ago sworn to assume the burden of their fate? And then I had shunted them off under the bunks. True, they hadn't done anything to defend us against the thieves. But why should they have fought for our fat bacon if we ourselves didn't? They had had enough cruel fights back in POW camps to destroy their faith in decency. But they hadn't done me any harm, and I had them.

And thus it is that we have to keep getting banged on flank and snout again and again so as to become, in time at least, human beings, yes, human beings. . . .

■

But even for the newcomer whom the transit prison cracks open and shucks, it is very, very necessary. It gives him some gradual preparation for camp life. Such a change all in one step would be more than the heart could bear. His consciousness would be unable to orient itself in that murk all at once. It has to happen gradually.

Then, too, the transit prison gave the prisoner the semblance of communicating with home. It was there he wrote the first letter he was permitted to: reporting that he hadn't been shot and, sometimes, the direction of his prisoner transport, and these were always the first unfamiliar words home of a man who had been plowed over by interrogation. At home they continued to remember him as he had been, but he would never be that person again. And that could suddenly, like a stroke of lightning, become apparent in one or another clumsily written line. Clumsily written because, even though letters could be sent from transit prisons, and there was a mailbox in the yard, it was impossible to get either paper or pencils—or anything to sharpen a pencil with. However, a makhorka wrapper or one from a sugar packet could turn up and be smoothed out, and someone in the cell would have a pencil—and so lines would be written in an undecipherable scrawl which would determine the family's future peace or discord.

Women driven out of their minds by receiving such a letter would sometimes precipitately rush off and try to get to their husbands at the transit prison—even though visits were never allowed and they would have succeeded only in burdening him with things. One such woman provided, in my opinion, the theme for a monument to all wives—and even indicated the place for it.

This was in the Kuibyshev Transit Prison in 1950. The prison was situated in a low-lying area (from which, however, the Zhiguli Gates of the Volga River could be seen). And right above the prison, bordering it on the east, rose a high, long, grassy hill. It was outside the camp compound and above it; and from the inside and down below we couldn't see the approach to it. Very rarely did anyone ever appear up there, although sometimes goats were pastured there or children played. And one cloudy summer day a city woman appeared on its ridge. Shading her eyes with her hand and barely moving, she began to scan our compound from above. At the time, three heavily populated cells were taking their outdoor walk in three separate exercise yards—and there in the abyss among those three hundred depersonalized ants she hoped to catch sight of her man! Did she hope that her heart would tell her which one he was? In all probability they had refused to allow her a visit with him and so she had climbed that hill. Everyone noticed her from the courtyards and everyone stared at her. Down below in the hollow there was no wind, but it was blowing hard up above. It made her long dress, her jacket, and her long hair stream out and billow, expressing all that love and anxiety which possessed her.

I think that a statue of such a woman, right there on that spot, on the hill overlooking the transit prison, with her face to the Zhiguli Gates, just as she actually stood, might explain at least a little something to our grandchildren.[6]

---

6. After all, someday the hidden and all but lost story of our Archipelago will be portrayed in monuments too! And I visualize, for example, one more such project: somewhere on a high point in the Kolyma, a most enormous Stalin, just such a size as he himself dreamed of, with mustaches many feet long and the bared fangs of a camp *commandant*, one hand holding the reins and the other wielding a knout with which to beat his team of hundreds of people harnessed in fives and all pulling hard. This would also be a fine sight on the edge of the Chukchi Peninsula next to the Bering Strait. (I had written this before I read "The Bas-Relief on the Cliff." And that means there is something to the idea. They say that on Mogutova Hill at the Zhiguli Gates on the Volga, a mile from the camp, there used to be an enormous oil portrait of Stalin which had been painted on the cliff for the benefit of passing steamers.)

She was there for a long time and they didn't drive her off, probably because the guards were too lazy to climb the hill. But finally a soldier climbed up and began to shout and wave his hands at her—and chased her away.

The transit prison also gives the prisoner some kind of over-all view, some breadth of outlook. As they say: even though there's nothing to eat, still it's a gay life. In the incessant traffic here, in the comings and goings of dozens and hundreds of people, in the frankness of the stories and conversations (in camp they don't talk so freely because they are always afraid there of stepping into the trap of the *Oper,* the Security officer), you are refreshed, you are aired out, you become more lucid, and you begin to understand better what is happening to you, to your people, even to the world. Even one single eccentric who turns up in your cell can tell you things you'll never in your life read about.

All of a sudden they introduce into the cell some kind of miracle: a tall young military man with a Roman profile, curly and unclipped flaxen locks, in a British uniform—just as if he had come straight from the Normandy landing, an officer of the invading army. He enters as proudly as if he expected everyone to rise to their feet in his presence. And it turns out that he had simply not expected to be among friends at this point: he had already been imprisoned for two years, but he had never yet been in a cell and he had been brought secretly, right to the transit prison itself, in an individual Stolypin compartment. And then, unexpectedly, either by mistake or else with special intent, he had been admitted to our common stable. He looked around the cell, saw a Wehrmacht officer there in German uniform, and started to argue with him in German; and there they were arguing heatedly, ready, it seemed, to resort to weapons if they'd had any. Five years had passed since the war, and it had been drummed into us that in the West the war had been waged only for the sake of appearances, and to us it was strange to observe their mutual outrage: the German had been with us for a long time, and we Russians hadn't argued with him; for the most part we had laughed with him.

No one would have believed the story of Erik Arvid Andersen had it not been for his unshorn locks—a miracle unique in all

Gulag. And that foreign bearing of his. And his fluent English, German, and Swedish speech. According to him he was the son of a rich Swede—not merely a millionaire but a billionaire. (Well, let's assume he embellished a little.) On his mother's side he was a nephew of the British General Robertson, who commanded the British Zone in occupied Germany. A Swedish subject, he had served as a volunteer in the British Army and had actually landed in Normandy, and after the war he had become a Swedish career officer. However, the investigation of social systems remained one of his principal interests. His thirst for socialism was stronger than his attachment to his father's capital. He looked upon Soviet socialism with feelings of profound sympathy, and he had even had the chance to become convinced of its flourishing state with his own eyes when he had come to Moscow as a member of a Swedish military delegation. They had been given banquets and taken to country homes and there they had encountered no obstacles at all to establishing contact with ordinary Soviet citizens—with pretty actresses who for some reason never had to rush off to work and who willingly spent time with them, even tête-à-tête. And thus convinced once and for all of the triumph of our social system, Erik on his return to the West wrote articles in the press defending and praising Soviet socialism. And this proved to be his undoing. In those very years, in 1947 and 1948, they were roping in from all sorts of nooks and crannies progressive young Westerners prepared to renounce the West publicly (and it appeared that if they could only have collected another dozen or so the West would shudder and collapse). Erik's newspaper articles caused him to be regarded as suitable for this category. At the time he was serving in West Berlin, and he had left his wife in Sweden. And out of pardonable male weakness he used to visit an unmarried German girl in East Berlin. And it was there that he was bound and gagged one night (and is not this the significance of the proverb which says: "He went to see his cousin, and he ended up in prison"? This had probably been going on for a long time, and he wasn't the first). They took him to Moscow, where Gromyko, who had once dined at his father's home in Stockholm and who knew the son also, not only returned the hospitality but proposed to the young man that he renounce publicly both capitalism and his own father. And in return he was promised full and complete capitalist maintenance to the end of his days here in our country. But to Gromyko's surprise, although Erik would not have suffered any material loss, he became indignant and uttered some very insulting words. Since they didn't believe in his strength of mind, they locked him up in a dacha outside Moscow, fed him like a prince in a fairy tale (sometimes they used "awful methods of repression" on him: they refused to accept his orders for the following day's menu and instead of the spring chicken he ordered they simply brought him a steak, just like that), surrounded him with the works of Marx-Engels-Lenin-Stalin, and waited a year for him to be re-educated. To their surprise it didn't happen. At that point they quartered with him a former lieutenant general who had already served two years in Norilsk. They probably calculated that by relating the horrors of camp the lieutenant general would persuade Erik to surrender. But either he carried out that assignment badly or else he didn't want to carry it out. After ten months of their being imprisoned together, the only thing he had taught Erik was broken Russian, and he had bolstered Erik's growing repugnance for the bluecaps. In the summer of 1950 they once more summoned Erik to Vyshinsky and he once more refused (in so doing, he made existence contingent on consciousness, thereby violating all the Marxist-Leninist rules!). And then Abakumov himself read Erik the decree: twenty years in prison (what for???). They themselves already regretted having gotten mixed up with this ignoramus, but at the same time they couldn't release him and let him go back to the West. And so they transported him in a separate compartment, and it was there that he had heard the story of the Moscow girl through the partition and seen through the train window in the dawn light the rotting straw-thatched roofs of the age-old Russia of Ryazan.

Those two years had very strongly confirmed him in his loyalty to the West. He believed blindly in the West. He did not want to recognize its weaknesses. He considered Western armies unbeatable and Western political leaders faultless. He refused to believe us when we told him that during the period of his imprisonment Stalin had begun a blockade of Berlin and had gotten away with it perfectly well. Erik's milky neck and creamy cheeks blushed with indignation whenever we ridiculed Churchill and

Roosevelt. And he was also certain that the West would not
countenance his, Erik's, imprisonment; that on the basis of information from the Kuibyshev Transit Prison the Western intelligence services would immediately learn that Erik had not
drowned in the Spree River but had been imprisoned in the Soviet
Union—and either he would be ransomed or someone would be
exchanged for him. (This faith of his in the individual importance
of *his own* fate among other prisoners' fates was reminiscent of
our own well-intentioned orthodox Soviet Communists.) Notwithstanding our heated arguments, he invited my friend and me
to Stockholm whenever we could come. ("Everyone knows us
there," he said with a tired smile. "My father virtually maintains
the Swedish King's whole court.") For the time being, however,
the son of the billionaire had nothing to dry himself with, and I
presented him with an extra tattered towel as a gift. And soon
they took him away on a prisoner transport.[7]

And the movement of people was endless. Prisoners were
brought in and taken away, singly and in groups, and driven off
in prisoner transports. Appearing so businesslike on the surface,
so planned, this movement was marked by such stupidity that
one can hardly believe it.

In 1949 the Special Camps were created. And then and there,
on the basis of some summit decision, masses of women were
driven from camps in the European North and the Trans-Volga
area, through the Sverdlovsk Transit Prison, to Siberia, to Taishet,
to Ozerlag. But in 1950 someone found it convenient to assemble

7. Since that time I have asked Swedes I have met or travelers going to
Sweden how to find his family. Have they heard anything about such a missing
person? The only reply I have received is a smile. The name Andersen in
Sweden is like Ivanov in Russia—and there is no such billionaire. And it is
only now, twenty-two years later, rereading this book for the last time,
that I have suddenly realized: of course, they must have *forbidden* him to
give his real name! He must have been warned by Abakumov, of course, that
he would be *destroyed* if he did. And so he traveled through the transit prisons
in the guise of a Swedish Ivanov. And it was only through unforbidden, secondary details of his biography that he was able to leave behind in the
memories of those he encountered by chance some trace of his ruined life.
More likely he still thought it could be saved—which was only human—like
millions of other rabbits in this book. He thought he would be imprisoned for
a while and that thereupon the indignant West would free him. He did not
understand the strength of the East. And he did not understand that such a
witness as himself, who had displayed *such* firmness of will, unheard of in the
soft West, could never be released.
Yet perhaps he is still alive even today. (Author's note, 1972.)

all the women not in Ozerlag, but in Dubrovlag—in Temnikov, in Mordvinia. And so all those same women, enjoying all the conveniences of Gulag travel, were dragged through this same Sverdlovsk Transit Prison—to the west. In 1951 new Special Camps were set up in Kemerovo Province (Kamyshlag)—and that turned out to be where the women's labor was required. And those ill-fated women were again put to the torment of being sent to the Kemerovo camps through that same accursed Sverdlovsk Transit Prison. The time came for liberation—but not for all of them. All those women who were left to drag out their terms in the midst of the general Khrushchev relaxation were once again swung out of Siberia through the Sverdlovsk Transit Prison—into Mordvinia: it was thought better to have them all together.

Well, after all, we have our own self-contained economy. The isles are all our own. And the distances aren't so very great for a Russian.

And the same sort of thing happened to individual zeks, the more unfortunate ones. Shendrik was a big, merry, open-faced fellow, and he *labored honestly,* as they say, in one of the Kuibyshev camps and had no intimation of the evil fate overtaking him. But this evil fate struck nonetheless. An urgent order arrived at the camp—not just from anybody but from the Minister of Internal Affairs himself! (And how could the Minister know of Shendrik's existence?) The order was to deliver this Shendrik to Prison No. 18 in Moscow immediately. They grabbed him, dragged him off to the Kuibyshev Transit Prison, and from there to Moscow with no delay. But not to some Prison No. 18; instead, with all the rest, he went to the widely known Krasnaya Presnya Prison. (Shendrik didn't know about any Prison No. 18. No one had told him.) But his misfortune did not drowse. No more than two days had passed before they *jerked* him onto a prisoner transport again and this time took him all the way to Pechora. The landscape outside the train window grew ever sparser and grimmer. Shendrik was alarmed: he knew there was an order from the Minister, and here they were rapidly hauling him off to the North, and that meant that the Minister had some awful *evidence* against him. In addition to all the other torments of the trip, they stole three days of bread rations from him while he was en route. And by the time he got to Pechora he was staggering. Pechora greeted him inhospitably. They drove him out to work in the wet snow, hungry and unsettled. In two days he never had a chance to dry out his shirts nor even a chance to stuff his mattress with pine needles. And right then they ordered him to turn in everything he had that was government issue and once again they scooped him up and whisked him still farther—to Vorkuta. It seemed quite evident from everything that had happened that the Minister was determined to destroy Shendrik, and not him alone but the entire group in his prisoner transport. At Vorkuta they didn't touch Shendrik for a whole month. He went out *to general-assignment work,* even though he had not yet recovered from his travels, but he had begun to reconcile himself to his Arctic fate. And then suddenly one day they called him out of the mine, and chased him off breathless to the camp to turn in everything he had that was government issue, and in one hour's time he was being carried off to the south. Now by this time it had already begun to smell of personal vengeance! They took him to Moscow Prison No. 18. They held him in the cell there for one month. And then he was summoned to some lieutenant colonel who asked him: "Where the hell have you been? Are you really a mechanical engineer?" And Shendrik confessed that he was. And then they took him off to none other than, yes, the Paradise Islands! (Yes, there are such islands in the Archipelago!)

This coming and going of people, these destinies, and these stories greatly enliven the transit prisons. And the old camp veterans advise newcomers: Lie down and take it easy. They feed you the guaranteed minimum here,[8] and you don't have to tire your back. And when it's not crowded you can sleep as much as you want to. So just stretch out and lie there from one handout of gruel to the next. The food is sparse, but the sleeping is good. Only those who know what *general-assignment* work is in the camps will understand that a transit prison is a rest home, a happiness on our path. And one more advantage too: when you sleep in the daytime the hours pass more quickly. If you can just kill off the day, the night will go away on its own.

True, recalling that labor created the human being and that only labor can reform the criminal, and sometimes having auxiliary projects, and sometimes acting as subcontractors in order

8. The rations guaranteed by Gulag when no work is being done.

to keep up their financial end, the bosses of transit prisons might sometimes even drive their loafing transit manpower out to labor.

The work at that same Kotlas Transit Prison before the war was not the least bit easier than in a regular camp. In the course of a winter day six or seven weakened prisoners were harnessed to a tractor (!) sledge and had to drag it *seven* miles along the Dvina River to the mouth of the Vychegda. They got stuck in snow and fell down, and the sledges got stuck. And it would seem that any work more wearing and debilitating could hardly have been thought up! But it turned out that this wasn't the actual work, but merely the warm-up. There at the mouth of the Vychegda, they had to load *thirteen* cubic yards of firewood on the sledges—and the same people harnessed in the same way (Repin is no longer with us, and this is no subject for our new artists; it is merely a crude reproduction from nature) had to haul the sledges back to their transit-prison home. Now what does a camp have to offer after that! You wouldn't even survive to get there. (The work-brigade leader for that task was Kolupayev, and the work horses were electrical engineer Dmitriyev, quartermaster corps Lieutenant Colonel Belyayev, and Vasily Vlasov, who is already familiar to us; but not all the other names can be collected at this date.)

During the war the Arzamas Transit Prison fed its prisoners beet tops and at the same time put them to work on a permanent basis. There were garment shops, a footgear-felting shop (where woolen fibers were fulled in hot water and acids).

In the summer of 1945 we went out of the stiflingly stagnant cells of Krasnaya Presnya to work as volunteers: for the right to breathe air the whole day long; for the right to sit unhurried and unhindered in a quiet plank latrine (an incentive that is often overlooked!) heated by the August sun (and these were the days of Potsdam and Hiroshima), listening to the peaceful buzzing of a lonely bee; and, last, for the right to get an extra quarter-pound of bread at night. They took us to the wharves of the Moscow River, where timber was being unloaded. It was our job to roll the logs off some of the piles, carry them over and stack them in other piles. We spent a good deal more strength than we received extra food in compensation. Nonetheless we enjoyed going out to work there.

I often have to blush at my recollections of my younger years (and that's where my younger years were spent!). But whatever casts you down also teaches you a lot. And it turned out that as a residue of the officer's shoulder boards, which had trembled and fluttered on my shoulders for two years in all, some kind of poisonous golden dust had settled in the empty space between my ribs. On that river wharf, which was a camplet too, there was also a compound with watchtowers surrounding it. We were merely transient, temporary work sloggers, and there had been no talk at all, no rumor, that we might be allowed to stay and serve out our terms there. But when they formed us up for the first time, and the work-assignment foreman looked down the line to pick out temporary work-brigade leaders, my worthless heart was bursting under my woolen field shirt: Me, me, pick me!

I was not chosen. But why did I want it? I would only have made further shameful mistakes.

Oh, how hard it is to part with power! This one has to understand.

■

There was a time when Krasnaya Presnya became the virtual capital of Gulag—in the sense that no matter where you went, you couldn't bypass it, just like Moscow. Just as when one travels in the Soviet Union it is more convenient to proceed from Tashkent to Sochi and from Chernigov to Minsk via Moscow, they dragged the prisoners there from all over and sent them off all over via Presnya. And that was the way it was when I was there. Presnya was at the point of breakdown from overcrowding. They built a supplementary building. Only the through trains of cattle cars carrying those who had been sentenced right at counterintelligence bypassed Moscow on the circle line around it, which, as it happened, went right past Presnya, perhaps even saluting it with a whistle on the way.

But we do have a ticket when we come to Moscow as free passengers in transit, and we hope sooner or later to proceed in the desired direction. At Presnya at the end of the war and just after, not only the prisoners who arrived there but even the very highest-ranking officials and even the heads of Gulag itself were unable to predict who would proceed where. At that time the prison system had not yet crystallized as it had by the fifties, and there were no routes and no destinations were indicated for anybody—except perhaps for service instructions: "Keep under strict guard"; "To be employed only on general-assignment work." The convoy sergeants carried the bundles of prison *cases,* torn folders tied somehow with twine or ersatz cotton string made of paper, into a separate wooden building that housed the prison offices, and tossed them onto shelves, on tables, under tables, under chairs, and simply on the floor in the aisle (just as their subject prisoners lay in the cells). They became untied and got scattered and mixed up. One room, a second, and a third got filled with those mixed-up *cases.* Secretaries from the prison office, well-fed, lazy, free women in bright-colored dresses, sweated in the heat, fanned themselves and flirted with prison and convoy officers. None of them wanted to or had the strength to pick a way through that chaos. And yet the trainloads had to be dispatched in the red trains—several times a week. And every day a hundred people had to be sent out on trucks to nearby camps. The *case* of every zek had to be sent with him. So just who was going to work on all that long-drawn-out mess? Who was there to sort out the cases and select the prisoners for the transports?

It was entrusted to several work-assignment supervisors from among the transit-prison trusties—who were either *"bitches"* or *"half-breeds."*[9] They moved freely through the prison corridors, entered the prison office, and were the ones who decided whether your *case* would be put in a *bad* prisoner transport or whether they would really exert themselves, search long and hard, and put it in a *good* one. (The newcomers were not mistaken in thinking that there were whole camps which were death camps, and they were right about that, but their idea that there were some that were "good" was simply a delusion. There were no good camps, but only certain easier duties within them—and they could only be sorted out on the spot.) The fact that the prisoner's whole future depended on such another prisoner, with whom one ought perhaps to find the chance *to talk* (even if via the bath attendant),

9. "Half-breeds" or "mulattoes" (polutsvetnye in Russian) were prisoners who had grown spiritually close to the thieves and tried to imitate them, but who had nonetheless not been accepted by the thieves' *law*.

and whose hand one ought perhaps *to grease* (even if via the storage room keeper), was worse than if his fortunes had simply been determined blindly by a roll of the dice. This invisible and unrealized opportunity—to go south to Nalchik instead of north to Norilsk in return for a leather jacket, to go to Serebryanny Bor outside Moscow instead of Taishet in Siberia for a couple of pounds of fat bacon (and perhaps to lose both the leather jacket and the fat bacon for nothing at all)—only aggravated and fatigued tired souls. Maybe someone did manage to arrange it, maybe someone got himself fixed up that way, but most blessed of all were those who had nothing to give or who spared themselves all that anxiety.

Submissiveness to fate, the total abdication of your own will in the shaping of your life, the recognition that it was impossible to guess the best and the worst ahead of time but that it was easy to take a step you would reproach yourself for—all this freed the prisoner from any bondage, made him calmer, and even ennobled him.

And thus it was that the prisoners lay in rows in the cells, and their fates lay in undisturbed piles in the rooms of the prison office. And the assignment supervisors took the files from the particular corner where it was easiest to get at them. And some zeks had to spend two or three months gasping in this accursed Presnya while others would whiz through it with the speed of a shooting star. As a result of all that congestion, haste, and disorder with the *cases,* sometimes *sentences got switched* at Presnya (and at other transit prisons as well). This didn't affect the 58's, because their prison terms, in Maxim Gorky's phrase, were "Terms" with a capital letter, were intended to be long, and even when they seemed to be nearing their end they just never got there anyway. But it made sense for big thieves and murderers to switch with some stupid nonpolitical offender. And so they or their accomplices would inch up to such an individual and question him with interest and concern. And he, not knowing that a short-termer at a transit prison isn't supposed to disclose anything about himself, would innocently tell them that his name was, for example, Vasily Parfenych Yevrashkin, that he was born in 1913, that he lived in Semidubye and had been born there. And his term was one year, Article 109, "Negligence." And then Yevrashkin was asleep or maybe not even asleep, but there was such a racket in the cell and there was such a crowd at the swill trough in the door that he couldn't make his way there and listen, while on the other side of it in the corridor they were rapidly muttering a list of names for a prisoner transport. Some of the names were shouted from the door into the cell, but not Yevrashkin's because hardly had the name been read out in the corridor than an urka, a thief, had obsequiously (and they *can* be obsequious when it's necessary) shoved up his snout and answered quickly and quietly: "Vasily Parfenych, born 1913, village of Semidubye, 109, one year," and ran off to get his things. The real Yevrashkin yawned, lay back on his bunk, and patiently waited to be called the next day, and the next week, and the next month, and then he made so bold as to bother the prison superintendent: why hadn't he been taken in a prisoner transport? (And every day in all the cells they kept calling out the name of some Zvyaga.) And when a month later or a half-year later they got around to combing through all the *cases* by calling the roll, what they had left was just one file—belonging to Zvyaga, a multiple offender, sentenced for a double murder and robbing a store, ten years—and one shy prisoner who was trying to tell everybody that he was Yevrashkin, although you couldn't make anything out from the photo, and so he damn well was Zvyaga and he had to be tucked away in a penalty camp, Ivdellag—because otherwise it would have been necessary to confess that the transit prison had made a mistake. (And as for that other Yevrashkin who had been sent off on a prisoner transport, you wouldn't even be able to find where he had gone—because none of the lists were left. And anyway he had only had a one-year term and had been sent to do farm work without being under guard and got three days off his sentence for every day he worked, or else he had simply run away, and was long since home or, more likely, was already imprisoned again on a new sentence.) There were also eccentrics who *sold* their short terms for a kilo or two of fat bacon. They figured that in any case the authorities would check up and establish their correct identities. And sometimes they did.[10]

10. And, as P. Yakubovich writes in reference to the so-called "cadgers," the sale of prison terms took place in the last century too. It is an ancient prison trick.

During the years when the prisoners' *cases* didn't carry any indication of their final destination, the transit prisons turned into slave markets. The most desired guests at the transit prisons were the *buyers*. This word was heard more and more often in the corridors and cells and was used without any shadow of irony. Just as it became intolerable everywhere in industry simply to sit and wait until things were sent from the center on the basis of allocations, and it was more satisfactory to send one's own "pushers" and "pullers" to get things done—the same thing happened in Gulag: the natives on the islands kept dying off; and even though they cost not one ruble, a count was kept of them, and one had to worry about getting more of them for oneself so there wouldn't be any failure in fulfilling the plan. The *buyers* had to be sharp, have good eyes, and look carefully to see what they were taking so that last-leggers and invalids didn't get shoved off on them. The buyers who picked a transport on the basis of case files were poor buyers. The conscientious merchants demanded that the *merchandise* be displayed alive and bare-skinned for them to inspect. And that was just what they used to say—without smiling—*merchandise*. "Well, what merchandise have you brought?" asked a buyer at the Butyrki station, observing and inspecting the female attributes of seventeen-year-old Ira Kalina.

Human nature, if it changes at all, changes not much faster than the geological face of the earth. And the very same sensations of curiosity, relish, and sizing up which slave-traders felt at the slave-girl markets twenty-five centuries ago of course possessed the Gulag bigwigs in the Usman Prison in 1947, when they, a couple of dozen men in MVD uniform, sat at several desks covered with sheets (this was for their self-importance, since it would have seemed awkward otherwise), and all the women prisoners were made to undress in the box next door and to walk in front of them bare-footed and bare-skinned, turn around, stop, and answer questions. "Drop your hands," they ordered those who had adopted the defensive pose of classic sculpture. (After all, these officers were very seriously selecting bedmates for themselves and their colleagues.)

And so it was that for the new prisoner various manifestations foreshadowed the camp battle of the morrow and cast their pall over the innocent spiritual joys of the transit prison.

For just two nights they put a *special-assignment prisoner* in our cell in Krasnaya Presnya. And he was next to me in the bunk. He traveled about with special-assignment orders, which meant that an invoice had been filled out in Central Administration indicating that he was a construction technician and could be used only in that capacity in his new location, and this went with him from camp to camp. The special-assignment prisoner was traveling in the common Stolypin cars and was kept in the common cells of the transit prisons, but he wasn't nervous; he was protected by his personal document, and he wouldn't be driven out to fell timber. A cruel and determined expression was the principal trait of this camp veteran's face. He had already served out the greater part of his term. (And I did not yet realize that this exact expression would in time etch itself on all our faces, because a cruel and determined expression is the national hallmark of the Gulag islanders. People with soft, conciliatory expressions die out quickly on the islands.) He observed our naïve floundering with an ironic smile, just as people look at two-week-old puppies.

What should we expect in camp? Taking pity on us, he taught us:

"From your very first step in camp everyone will try to deceive and plunder you. Trust no one but yourself. Look around quickly: someone may be sneaking up on you to bite you. Eight years ago I arrived at Kargopollag just as innocent and just as naïve as you are now. They unloaded us from two trains, and the convoy prepared to lead us the six miles to the camp through the deep, crumbly snow. Three sleds came up beside us. Some hefty chap whom the convoy didn't interfere with came over to us and said: 'Brothers, put your things on the sleds and we will carry them there for you.' We remembered reading in books that prisoners' belongings were carried on carts. And we thought: It isn't going to be all that inhuman in camp; they are concerned about us. And we loaded our things on the sleds. They left. And we never saw them again, not even an empty wrapper."

"But how can that happen? Isn't there any law there?"

"Don't ask idiotic questions. There is a law there. The law of the taiga, of the jungle. But as for *justice*—there never has been any in Gulag and there never will be. That Kargopol incident was simply a symbol of Gulag. And you have to get used to something else too: in camp no one ever does anything for nothing, no

one ever does anything out of the generosity of his heart. You
have to pay for everything. If someone proposes something to
you that is unselfish, disinterested, you can be sure it's a dirty
trick, a provocation. The main thing is: avoid *general-assignment
work*. Avoid it from the day you arrive. If you land in *general-
assignment work* that first day, then you are lost, and this time
for keeps."

"*General-assignment* work?"

"General-assignment work—that is the main and basic work
performed in any given camp. Eighty percent of the prisoners
work at it, and they all die off. All. And then they bring new ones
in to take their places and they again are sent to general-assignment work. Doing this work, you expend the last of your strength.
And you are always hungry. And always wet. And shoeless. And
you are given short rations and short everything else. And put in
the worst barracks. And they won't give you any treatment when
you're ill. The only ones who *survive* in camps are those who
try at any price not to be put on general-assignment work. From
the first day."

"At any price?"

"At any price!"

At Krasnaya Presnya I assimilated and accepted this altogether unexaggerated advice of the cruel special-assignment prisoner, forgetting only to ask him one thing: How do you measure
that price? How high do you go?

Chapter 3

■

The Slave Caravans

It was painful to travel in a Stolypin, unbearable in a Black Maria, and the transit prison would soon wear you down—and it might just be better to skip the whole lot and go straight to camp in the red cattle cars.

As always, the interests of the state and the interests of the individual coincided here. It was also to the state's advantage to dispatch sentenced prisoners straight to the camps by direct routing and thus avoid overloading the city trunk-line railroads, automotive transport, and transit-camp personnel. They had long since grasped this fact in Gulag, and it had been taken to heart: witness the caravans of *red cows* (red cattle cars), the caravans of barges, and, where there were no rails and no water, the caravans on foot (after all, prisoners could not be allowed to exploit the labor of horses and camels).

The red trains were always a help when the courts in some particular place were working swiftly or the transit facilities were overcrowded. It was possible in this way to dispatch a large number of prisoners in one batch. That is how the millions of peasants were transported in 1929–1931. That is how they exiled Leningrad from Leningrad. That is how they populated the Kolyma in the thirties: every day Moscow, the capital of our country, belched out one such train to Sovetskaya Gavan, to Vanino Port. And each provincial capital also sent off red train-loads, but not on a daily schedule. That is how they removed the Volga German Republic to Kazakhstan in 1941, and later all

565

the rest of the exiled nations were sent off in the same way. In 1945 Russia's prodigal sons and daughters were sent from Germany, from Czechoslovakia, from Austria, and simply from western border areas—whoever had gotten there on his own—in such trains as these. In 1949 that is how they collected the 58's in Special Camps.

The Stolypins follow routine railroad schedules. And the red trains travel on imposing waybills, signed by important Gulag generals. The Stolypins cannot go to an empty site, to "nowhere"; their destination must always be a station, even if it's in some nasty little two-bit town with some preliminary detention cells in an attic. But the red trains can go into emptiness: and wherever one does go, there immediately rises right next to it, out of the sea of the steppe or the sea of the taiga, a new island of the Archipelago.

Not every red cattle car is ready as is to transport prisoners. First it has to be prepared. But not in the sense some of our readers might expect: that the coal or lime it carried before it was assigned to carry people has to be swept out and the car cleaned—that isn't always done. Nor in the sense that it needs to be calked and have a stove installed if it is winter. (When the section of the railroad from Knyazh-Pogost to Ropcha was being built and wasn't yet part of the general railroad network, they immediately began to transport prisoners on it—in freight cars without either stoves or bunks. In winter the zeks lay on the icy, snowy floor and weren't even given any hot food, because the train could make it all the way through this section in less than a day. Whoever can in imagination lie there like them and survive those eighteen to twenty hours shall indeed survive! Here is what was involved in preparing a red cattle car for prisoners: The floors, walls, and ceilings had to be tested for strength and checked for holes or faults. Their small windows had to be barred. A hole had to be cut in the floor to serve as a drain, and specially protected by sheet iron firmly nailed down all around it. The necessary number of platforms on which convoy guards would stand with machine guns had to be evenly distributed throughout the train, and if there were too few, more had to be built. Access to the roofs of the cars had to be provided. Sites for searchlights had to be selected and supplied with uninterrupted electric power.

Long-handled wooden mallets had to be procured. A passenger car had to be hooked on for the staff, and if there wasn't one, then instead heated freight cars had to be prepared for the chief of convoy, the Security officer, and the convoy. Kitchens had to be built—for the convoy and for the prisoners. And only after all this had been done was it all right to walk along the cattle cars and chalk on the sides: "Special Equipment" or "Perishable Goods." (In her chapter, "The Seventh Car," Yevgeniya Ginzburg described a transport of red cars very vividly, and her description largely obviates the necessity of presenting details here.)

The preparation of the train has been completed—and ahead lies the complicated combat operation of *loading* the prisoners into the cars. At this point there are two important and obligatory *objectives:*

- to conceal the loading from ordinary citizens
- to terrorize the prisoners

To conceal the loading from the local population was necessary because approximately a thousand people were being loaded on the train simultaneously (at least twenty-five cars), and this wasn't your little group from a Stolypin that could be led right past the townspeople. Everyone knew, of course, that arrests were being made every day and every hour, but no one was to be horrified by the sight of large numbers of them *together.* In Orel in 1938 you could hardly hide the fact that there was no home in the city where there hadn't been arrests, and weeping women in their peasant carts blocked the square in front of the Orel Prison just as in Surikov's painting *The Execution of the Streltsy.* (Oh, who one day will paint this latter-day tragedy for us? But no one will. It's not fashionable, not fashionable. . . .) But you don't need to show our Soviet people an entire trainload of them collected in one day. (And in Orel that year there were.) And young people mustn't see it either—for young people are our future. Therefore it was done only at night—and every night, too, each and every night, and that was the way it went for several months. The black line of prisoners to be transported was driven from the prison to the station on foot. (Meanwhile the Black Marias were busy making new arrests.) True, the women realized, the women somehow found out, and at night they came to the station from all over the city and kept watch over the trains on the siding. They ran along the cars, tripping over the ties and rails, and shouting at every car: "Is So-and-so in there?" "Is So-and-so in there?" And they ran on to the next one, and others ran up to this one: "Is So-and-so in there?" And suddenly an answer would come from the sealed car: "I'm in here. I'm here!" Or else: "Keep looking for him. He's in another car." Or else: "Women! Listen! My wife is somewhere out there, near the station. Run and tell her."

These scenes, unworthy of our contemporary world, testify only to the then inept organization of train embarkations. The mistakes were noted, and after a certain night the trains were surrounded in depth by cordons of snarling and barking police dogs.

And in Moscow, the loading into red cattle cars from the old Sretenka Transit Prison (which prisoners no longer remember) or from Krasnaya Presnya took place only at night; that was the rule.

However, although the convoy had no use for the superfluous light of the sun by day, on the other hand they made use of suns by night—the searchlights. They were more efficient since they could be concentrated on the necessary area, where the prisoners were seated on the earth in a frightened pack awaiting the command: "Next unit of five—stand up! To the car—on the run!" (Only on the run, so as not to have time to look around, to think things over, to run as though chased by the dogs, afraid of nothing so much as falling down.) On that uneven path. Up the loading ramp, scrambling. And clear, hostile searchlight beams not only provided light but were an important theatrical element in terrorizing the prisoners, along with yells, threats, gunstock blows on those who fell behind, and the order: "Sit down." (And sometimes, as in the station square of that same Orel: "Down on your knees." And like some new breed of believers at prayer, the whole thousand would get down on their knees.) Along with that running to the car, quite unnecessary except for intimidation— for which it was very important. Along with the enraged barking of the dogs. Along with the leveled gun barrels (rifles or automatic pistols, depending on the decade). And the main thing was to undermine, to crush the prisoner's will power so he wouldn't think of trying to escape, so that for a long time he wouldn't notice his new advantage: the fact that he had exchanged a stone-walled prison for a railroad car with thin plank walls.

But in order to load one thousand prisoners into railroad cars at night so precisely, the prison had to start jerking them out of their cells and processing them for transport the morning before, and the convoy had to spend the entire day on a long-drawn-out and strict procedure of checking them in while still in prison and then holding those who'd been checked in for long hours, not, of course, in the cells by now, but in the courtyard, on the ground, so as not to mix them up with the prisoners still belonging in the prison. Thus for the prisoner the loading at night was only a relief after a whole day of torment.

Besides the ordinary counts, verifications, hair clipping, clothing roasting, and baths, the core of the preparation for the prisoner transport was general *frisking*. This search was carried out not by the prison but by the convoy receiving the prisoners. The convoy was expected, in accordance with the directives regarding the red transports and in accordance with their own operational requirements, to carry out this search so that the prisoners would not be left in possession of anything that might help them to escape; to take away: everything that could saw or cut; all powders (tooth powder, sugar, salt, tobacco, tea) so they could not be used to blind the convoy; all string, cord, twine, belts, and straps because they could all be used in escaping (and that meant all kinds of straps! and so they cut off the straps which held up the artificial limb of a one-legged man—and the cripple had to carry his artificial leg on his shoulder and hop with the help of those on either side of him). The rest of the things—all "valuables" and suitcases too—were, according to instructions, supposed to be checked and carried in a special baggage car and returned to their owners at the end of the journey.

Yet the power of the Moscow directive was weak and might be ignored by the Vologda or the Kuibyshev convoy, while the power of the convoy over the prisoners was very corporeal, very real. And this fact was crucial to the third objective of the loading operation:

- in simple justice to take all the good things they possess from enemies of the people for the use of its sons

"Sit down." "On your knees!" "Strip!" In these statutory orders of the convoy lay the basic power one could not argue with. After all, a naked person loses his self-assurance. He cannot straighten up proudly and speak as an equal to people who are still clothed. A search begins. (Kuibyshev, summer of 1949.) Naked prisoners approach, carrying their possessions and the clothes they've taken off. A mass of armed soldiers surrounds them. It doesn't look as though they are going to be led to a prisoner transport but as though they are going to be shot immediately or put to death in a gas chamber—and in that mood a human being ceases to concern himself with his possessions. The convoy does everything with intentional brusqueness, rudely, sharply, not speaking one word in an ordinary human voice. After all, the purpose is to terrify and dishearten. Suitcases are shaken apart, and things fall all over the floor and are then stacked up in separate piles. Cigarette cases, billfolds, and other pitiful "valuables" are all taken away and thrown without any identifying marks into a *barrel* that is standing nearby. (And, for some reason, the fact that this particular receptacle isn't a safe, or a trunk, or a box, but a barrel particularly depresses the naked prisoners there, and it seems so terribly futile to protest.) The naked prisoner has all he can do simply to snatch up his well-searched rags from the floor and knot them together or tie them up in a blanket. Felt boots? You can check them, throw them over there, sign for them on the list! (You aren't the one who gets the receipt, but *you* are the one who signs for having surrendered them, certifying that you threw them onto the pile!) And when at dusk the last truck leaves the prison yard with the prisoners, they see the convoy guards rushing to grab the best leather suitcases from the pile and select the best cigarette cases from the barrel. And after them, the jailers scurry for their booty, too, and last of all the transit prison *trusties*.

That is what it cost to spend one day to get to the cattle car. And now the prisoners have clambered with relief up onto the splintered planks of the bunks. But what kind of relief is this, what kind of heated cattle car is this? Once again they are squeezed in a nutcracker between cold and starvation, between the thieves and the convoy.

If there are thieves in a cattle car (and they are, of course, not kept separate in the red trains either) they take the best places, as is traditional—on the upper bunks by the window. That's in summer. So we can guess where their places are in winter. Next to the stove, of course, in a tight ring around the stove. As the former thief Minayev recalls: in 1949, during a severe cold wave, they were issued only *three pails* of coal for their car for the entire journey from Voronezh to Kotlas, lasting several days.[1] And in this crisis, the thieves not only occupied the places around the stove, and not only took all the *suckers'* warm things away from them and put them on, but didn't even hesitate to take their *footcloths* out of their shoes and wind them around their own feet. You today, me tomorrow. It was somewhat worse with food —the thieves took charge of the whole ration for the car and then kept the best for themselves along with whatever else they needed. Loshchilin recalls a three-day prisoner transport from Moscow to Perebory in 1937. They didn't cook anything hot on the train for such a short journey and handed out only dry rations. The thieves took the best for themselves but gave the others permission to divide up the bread and the herring; and that meant they weren't hungry. When the ration was hot and the thieves were *in charge of distributing it,* they divided up the gruel among themselves. (A three-week transport from Kishinev to Pechora in 1945.) With all this, the thieves didn't scruple to engage also in plain and simple robbery en route: they noticed an Estonian's gold teeth and they pushed him down and knocked out the teeth with a poker.

The zeks considered the hot food the real advantage of the red trains: at remote stations (again where people couldn't see them) the trains stopped and gruel and porridge were doled out to the cars. But they even managed to give out the hot food in such a way that things went wrong. They might (as on that same Kishinev train) pour out the gruel in the same pails in which they issued coal—there being nothing to wash them out with. Because drinking water was also rationed on the train and was in even shorter supply than gruel. And so you gulped down the gruel, your teeth gritting on pieces of coal. Or they brought the gruel and the hot cereal to the car and didn't issue enough bowls

1. In a letter to me in the *Literaturnaya Gazeta*, November 29, 1963.

—twenty-five instead of forty—and promptly ordered: "Come on, come on, faster, faster. We have other cars to feed too, not just you." How then could you eat, how could you divide it up? You couldn't dish it out equitably on the basis of bowls, and that meant you had to estimate each portion so as not to give out too much. And those to be served first would shout: "Stir it! Stir it!" And the last kept silent: there would be more on the bottom. The first were eating and the last waiting. They would have liked the others to eat faster, because they were hungry, and meanwhile the gruel would be getting cold in the barrel and they were also being hurried from outside: "Well, have you finished? Come on now, get a move on!" And then they served the second contingent —not more and not less and not thicker and not thinner than the first. And then came estimating the leftovers correctly and pouring them out two portions to a bowl. And all this time forty people don't so much eat as watch the sharing out and suffer.

They don't heat the car, they don't protect the other prisoners from the thieves, they don't give you enough to drink, and they don't give you enough to eat—but on the other hand they don't let you sleep either. During the day the convoy can see the whole train very clearly and the tracks behind them, and can be sure that no one has jumped out the side or slipped down on the rails. But at night vigilance possesses them. With long-handled wooden mallets (the standard Gulag equipment) they knock resoundingly on every board of the car at every stop: maybe someone has sawed through it. And at certain stops the door of the car is thrown open. The light of the lantern or the beam of the search-light: "Checkup!" And this means: Get on your feet and be ready to go where they tell you—everyone run to the left or to the right. The convoy guards jump inside with their mallets (others have ranged themselves in a semicircle outside with automatic pistols), and they point: to the left! That means that those on the left are in place and those on the right must get over there on the jump like fleas hopping over each other and landing where they can. And whoever isn't nimble, whoever gets caught daydreaming, gets whacked on the ribs and back with the mallets to give him more energy. And by this time the convoy jackboots are already trampling your pauper's pallet and all your lousy *duds* are being thrown in every direction and everywhere there are lights and hammering: Have you sawed through any place? No. Then the convoy guards stand in the middle and begin to shift you from left to right, counting: "First . . . second . . . third." It would be quite enough to count simply with a wave of the finger, but if that were done, it wouldn't be terrifying, and so it is more vivid, less subject to error, more energetic and faster, to beat out that count with the same mallet on your ribs, shoulders, heads, wherever it happens to land. They have counted up to forty. So now they will go about their tossing, lighting up, and hammering at the other end of the car. It's all over finally and the car is locked up. You can go back to sleep till the next stop. (And one can't really say that the anxiety of the convoy guard is entirely un-founded—because those who know how can escape from the red cattle cars. For instance, they knock on a board to test it and find it has been partially sawed through. Or suddenly in the morning, when the gruel is being distributed, they see that there are several shaved faces among the unshaven ones. And they surround the car with their automatic pistols: "Hand over your knives!" And this is really just petty bravado on the part of the thieves and their allies: they got tired of being unshaven, and now they are going to have to turn in their razor.)

The red train differs from other long-distance trains in that those who have embarked on it do not know whether or not they will disembark. When they unloaded a trainload from the Lenin-grad prisons (1942) in Solikamsk, the entire embankment was covered with corpses, and only a few got there alive. In the winters of 1944–1945 and 1945–1946 in the village of Zhelez-nodorozhny (Knyazh-Pogost), as in all the main rail junctions in the North, the prisoner trains from liberated territories (the Baltic states, Poland, Germany) arrived with one or two car-loads of corpses tacked on behind. That meant that en route they had carefully taken the corpses out of the cars that contained the living passengers and put them in the dead cars. But not always. There were many occasions when they found out who was still alive and who was dead only when they opened up the car after arriving at the Sukhobezvodnaya (Unzhlag) Station. Those who didn't come out were dead.

It was terrifying and deadly to travel this way in winter be-cause the convoy, with all its bother about security, wasn't able to haul coal for twenty-five stoves. But it wasn't so cushy to travel this way in hot weather either. Two of the four tiny windows were tightly sealed and the car roof would overheat and the convoy wasn't about to exert itself in hauling water for a thousand prisoners—after all, they couldn't even manage to give just one Stolypin car enough to drink. The prisoners considered April and September the best months for transports. But even the best of seasons was too short if the train was en route for *three months*. (Leningrad to Vladivostok in 1935.) And if such a long trip is in prospect, then arrangements have been made for both political indoctrination of the convoy soldiers and spiritual care of the imprisoned souls: in a separate railroad car attached to such a train travels a "godfather"—a Security officer. He has made his preparations for the prisoner-transport train back in prison, and prisoners are assigned to cars not simply at random but according to lists he has validated. He is the one who appoints the monitor in each car and who has instructed and assigned a stool pigeon to each. At long stops he finds some pretext for summoning both from the car and asks what the people are talking about in there. And any such Security chief would be ashamed to finish the journey without signed and sealed results. And so right there en route he puts someone under interrogation, and lo and behold! by the time they reach their destination, the prisoner has been handed a new prison term.

No, damn that red cattle car train too, even though it did carry the prisoners straight to their destination without changing trains. Anyone who has ever been in one will never forget it. Just as well get to camp sooner! Just as well arrive sooner.

A human being is all hope and impatience. As if the Security officer in camp will be any more humane or the stoolies any less unscrupulous. It's just the other way around. As if they won't force us to the ground with those same threats and those same police dogs when we arrive: "Sit down!" As if there will be less snow on the ground in camp than what has sifted through into the cattle cars. As if it means that we've already gotten to where we're going when they begin to unload us and won't be carried farther in open flatcars on a narrow-gauge track. (And how can they carry us in open flatcars? How can we be kept under guard? That's a problem for the convoy. And here is how they do it: They order us to lie down all huddled together and they cover us with one big tarpaulin, like the sailors in the motion picture *Potemkin* before they're to be executed. And say thank you for the tarpaulin too. In the North, in October, Olenyev and his comrades had the luck to have to sit in open flatcars all day long. They had already embarked, but no locomotive had come. First it rained. Then it froze. And the zeks' rags froze on them.) The tiny train will jerk and toss as it moves, and the sides of the flatcar will begin to crack and break, and the bouncing will hurl someone off the car and under the wheels. And here is a riddle: If one is traveling sixty miles from Dudinka through Arctic frost in open flatcars on the narrow-gauge track, then where are the thieves going to be? Answer: In the middle of each flatcar, so the livestock around them will keep them warm and keep them from falling under the train themselves. Right answer! Question: What will the zeks see at the end of this narrow-gauge track (1939)? Will there be any buildings there? No, not a one. Any dugouts? Yes, but already occupied, not for them. And does that mean that the first thing they do will be to dig themselves dugouts? No, because how can they dig in the Arctic winter? Instead, they will be sent out to mine metal. And where will they live? What—live? Oh, yes, live . . . They will live in tents.

But will there always be a narrow-gauge track? No, of course not. The train arrived: Yertsovo Station, February, 1938. The railroad cars were opened up at night. Bonfires were lit alongside the train and disembarkation took place by their light; then a count-off, forming up, and a count-off again. The temperature was 32 degrees below zero Centigrade. The prisoners' transport train had come from the Donbas, and all the prisoners had been arrested back in the summer and were wearing low shoes, oxfords, even sandals. They tried to warm themselves at the fires, but the guards chased them away: that's not what the fires were there for; they were there to give light. Fingers grew numb almost instantly. The snow filled the thin shoes and didn't even melt. There was no mercy and the order was given: "Fall in! Form up! One step to the right or left and we'll fire without warning. Forward march!" The dogs on their chains howled at their favorite command, at the excitement of the moment. The convoy guards marched ahead in their sheepskin coats—and the doomed prisoners in their summer clothes marched through deep snow on a totally untraveled road somewhere into the dark taiga, nary a light ahead. The northern lights gleamed—for them it was their first and probably their last view of them. The fir trees crackled in the frost. The ill-shod prisoners paced and trod down the snow, their feet and legs growing numb from the cold.

Or, as another example, here is a January, 1945, arrival at Pechora. ("Our armies have captured Warsaw! Our armies have cut off East Prussia!") An empty snowy field. The prisoners were tossed out of the cars, made to sit down in the snow by sixes, painstakingly counted off, miscounted, and counted again. They were ordered to stand up and then were harried through a snowy virgin waste for four miles. This prisoner transport was also from the south—from Moldavia. And everyone was wearing leather shoes. The police dogs were right on their heels, and the dogs pushed the zeks in the last row with their paws on their backs, breathing on the backs of their heads. (Two priests were in that row—old gray-haired Father Fyodor Florya and young Father Viktor Shipovalnikov, who was helping to hold him up.) What a use for police dogs? No, what self-restraint it showed on the dogs' part! After all, they wanted to bite so badly!

Finally they arrived. There was a camp reception bath; they had to undress in one cabin, run across the yard naked, and wash in another. But all this was bearable now: the worst was over. They had *arrived*. Twilight fell. And all of a sudden it was learned there was no room for them; the camp wasn't ready to receive the prisoner transport. And after the bath, the prisoners were again formed up, counted, surrounded by dogs, and were marched *back* to their prisoner-transport train all those four miles, but this time in the dark. And the car doors had been left open all those hours, and had lost even their earlier, pitiful measure of warmth, and then all the coal had been burned up by the end of the journey and there was nowhere to get any more now. And in these circumstances, they froze all night and in the morning were given dried carp (and anyone who wanted to drink could chew snow), and then marched back along the same road again.

And this, after all, was an episode with a *happy* ending. In this case, the camp at least *existed*. If it couldn't accept them today, it would tomorrow. But it was not at all unusual for the red trains to arrive nowhere, and the end of the journey often marked the opening day of a *new* camp. They might simply stop somewhere in the taiga under the northern lights and nail to a fir tree a sign reading: "FIRST OLP."[2] And there they would chew on dried fish for a week and try to mix their flour with snow.

But if a camp had been set up there even two weeks earlier, that already spelled comfort; hot food would have been cooked; and even if there were no bowls, the first and second courses would nonetheless be mixed together in washbasins for six prisoners to eat from at the same time; and this group of six would form a circle (there were no tables or chairs yet), and two of them would hold onto the handles of the washbasin with their left hands and would eat with their right hands, taking turns. Am I repeating myself? No, this was Perebory in 1937, as reported by Loshchilin. It is not I who am repeating myself, but Gulag.

Next they would assign the newcomers brigade leaders from among the camp veterans, who would quickly *teach them to live,* to make do, to submit to discipline, and to cheat. And from their very first morning, they would march off to work because the chimes of the clock of the great Epoch were striking and could not wait. The Soviet Union is not, after all, some Tsarist hard-labor Akatui for you, where prisoners got three days' rest after they arrived.[3]

■

Gradually the economy of the Archipelago prospered. New railroad branch lines were built. And soon they were transporting prisoners by train to many places that had been reached only by water not long before. But there are natives of the Archipelago still alive who can tell you how they went down the Izhma River in genuine ancient Russian river galleys, one hundred to a boat, and the prisoners themselves did the rowing. They can tell you how they traveled in fishing smacks down the northern rivers of Ukhta, Usa, and Pechora to their native camp. Zeks were shipped to Vorkuta in barges: on large barges to Adzvavom,

2. OLP = *Otdelny Lagerny Punkt* = Separate Camp Site.
3. P. F. Yakubovich, *V Mire Otverzhennykh.*

where there was a transshipping point for Vorkutlag, and from there only a stone's throw, let's say, to Ust-Usa, on a flat-bottomed barge for ten days. The whole barge was alive with lice, and the convoy allowed the prisoners to go up on deck one by one and brush the parasites off into the water. The river transports did not proceed directly to their destination either, but were sometimes interrupted to transfer for transshipment, or for portage, or for stretches covered on foot.

And they had their own transit prisons in this area—built out of poles or tents—Ust-Usa, Pomozdino, Shchelya-Yur, where they had their own special system of regulations. They had their own convoy rules, and of course, their own special commands, and their own special convoy tricks, and their own special methods of tormenting the zeks. But it's already clear that it is not our task to describe those particular exotica, so we won't even begin.

The Northern Dvina, the Ob, and the Yenisei know when they began to haul prisoners in barges—during the liquidation of the "kulaks." These rivers flowed straight north, and their barges were potbellied and capacious—and it was the only way they could cope with the task of carting all this gray mass from living Russia to the dead North. People were thrown into the trough-like holds and lay there in piles or crawled around like crabs in a basket. And high up on the deck, as though atop a cliff, stood guards. Sometimes they transported this mass out in the open without any cover, and sometimes they covered it with a big tarpaulin—in order not to look at it, or to guard it better, but certainly not to keep off the rain. The journey in such a barge was no longer prisoner transport, but simply death on the installment plan. Anyway, they gave them hardly anything to eat. Then they tossed them out in the tundra—and there they didn't give them anything at all to eat. They just left them there to die, alone with nature.

Prisoner transport by barge on the Northern Dvina (and on the Vychegda) had not died out even by 1940. That was how A. Y. Olenyev was transported. Prisoners in the hold *stood* tightly jammed against each other, and not just for a day either. They urinated in glass jars which were passed from hand to hand and emptied through the porthole. And anything more substantial went right in their pants.

Barge transport on the Yenisei came to be a regular and permanent feature for whole decades. In Krasnoyarsk in the thirties, open-sided sheds were built on the bank, and in the cold Siberian winters the prisoners would shiver there for a day or two while they waited for transportation.[4] The Yenisei prisoner-transport barges were permanently equipped with dark holds three decks deep. The only light was what filtered in through the companionway for the ship's ladder. The convoy lived in a little cabin on deck. Sentries kept watch over the exits from the hold and over the river to make sure that no one escaped by swimming. They didn't go down into the hold, no matter what groans and howls for help might come from there. And the prisoners were never taken up on deck for fresh air. In the prisoner transports of 1937 and 1938, and 1944 and 1945 (and we can guess it must have been the same in the interval), no medical assistance whatever was provided in the hold. The prisoners lay there lined up in two rows, one with their heads toward the side of the barge and the heads of the other row at their feet. The only way to get to the latrine barrels was to walk over them. The latrine barrels were not always emptied in time (imagine lugging that barrel full of sewage up the steep ship's ladder to the deck). They overflowed, and the contents spilled along the deck and seeped down on those below. And people lay there. They were fed gruel from casks hauled along the deck. The servers were prisoners too, and there, in the eternal darkness (today, perhaps, there is electricity), by the light of a portable "Bat" kerosene lamp, they ladled out the food. Such a prisoner transport to Dudinka sometimes took a month. (Nowadays, of course, they can do it in a week.) It sometimes happened that the trip dragged out much longer because of sand bars and other hazards of river travel, and they wouldn't have enough food with them, in which case they just stopped giving out the food for several days at a time. (And later on, of course, they never made up for the days they missed.)

At this point the alert reader can without the author's help add that the thieves were on the upper level inside the hold and closer to the ship's ladder—in other words, to light and air. They had what access they required to the distribution of the bread

4. And V. I. Lenin in 1897 boarded the *St. Nicholas* in the passenger port like a free person.

ration, and if the trip in question was a hard one, they didn't hesitate to *whip away* the *holy crutch* (in other words, they took the gray cattle's rations from them). The thieves whiled away the long journey playing cards, and they made their own decks.[5] They got the stakes for their card games by *frisking* the suckers, searching everyone lying in a particular section of the barge. For a certain length of time they won and lost and rewon and relost their loot, and then it floated up to the convoy. Yes, the reader has now guessed everything: the thieves had the convoy *on the hook;* the convoy either kept the stolen things for themselves or sold them at the wharves and brought the thieves something to eat in exchange.

And what about resistance? It happened—but only rarely. One case has been preserved. In 1950 on such a barge as I have described, except that it was larger—a seagoing barge en route from Vladivostok to Sakhalin—seven unarmed 58's resisted the thieves (in this case *bitches*), who numbered about eighty in all (some with knives, as usual). These *bitches* had searched the whole transport back at Vladivostok transit point *three-ten,* and they had searched it very thoroughly, in no way less efficiently than the jailers; they knew all the hiding places, but no search can ever turn up *everything.* Aware of this, when they were already in the hold they treacherously announced: "Whoever has money can buy makhorka." And Misha Grachev got out three rubles he had hidden in his quilted jacket. And the bitch Volodka Tatarin shouted at him: "You crowbait, why don't you *pay your taxes?*" And he rushed in to take it away. But Master Sergeant Pavel (whose last name has not been recorded) pushed him away. Volodka Tatarin aimed a slingshot—a "V" fork—at Pavel's eyes, and Pavel knocked him off his feet. Immediately twenty to thirty *bitches* moved in on him. And around Grachev and Pavel gathered Volodya Shpakov, a former army captain, Seryezha Potapov, Volodya Reunov, a former army sergeant, Volodya Tretyukin, another former sergeant, and Vasa Kravtsov. And what happened? The whole thing ended after only a few blows had been exchanged. This may have been a matter of the age-old and very real cowardice of the thieves (always concealed behind feigned toughness and devil-may-care insolence); or else

5. V. Shalamov tells about this in detail in his *Ocherki prestupnogo mira* (*Sketches of the Criminal World*).

the proximity of the guard held them back (this being right beneath the hatchway). Or it may have been that on this trip they were saving themselves for a more *important* social task—to seize control of the Aleksandrovsk Transit Prison (the one Chekhov described) and a Sakhalin construction project (seizing control of it, of course, not in order to *construct*) before the *honest thieves* could; at any rate they pulled back, restricting themselves to the threat: "On dry land we'll make *garbage* out of you!" (The battle never took place, and no one made "garbage" out of the boys. And at the Aleksandrovsk transit point the *bitches* met with misfortune: it was already firmly held by the *honest thieves*.)

In steamships to the Kolyma everything was the same as on the barges except that everything was on a larger scale. Strange as it seems, some of the prisoners sent to the Kolyma in several over-age old tubs on the famous expedition led by the ice-breaker *Krasin* in the spring of 1938 are still alive today. On the steamers *Dzhurma, Kulu, Nevostroi, Dneprostroi,* for which the *Krasin* was breaking the way through the spring ice, there were also three decks in the cold, dirty holds, and on these decks, in addition, there were two-story bunks made out of poles. It was not completely dark: there were some kerosene lanterns and lamps. The prisoners were allowed up on deck in batches for fresh air and walks. Three to four thousand prisoners were in each steamer. The voyage took more than a week, and before it was over all the bread brought aboard in Vladivostok got moldy and the ration was reduced from twenty-one to fourteen ounces a day. They also gave out fish, and as for drinking water . . . Well, there's no reason to gloat here, because there were *temporary difficulties* with the water. Here, in contrast to the river transports, there were heavy seas, storms, seasickness. The exhausted, enfeebled people vomited, and didn't have the strength to get up out of their vomit, and all the floors were covered with the nauseating mess.

There was one political incident on the voyage. The steamers had to pass through La Pérouse Strait, very close to the Japanese islands. And at that point the machine guns disappeared from the watchtowers and the convoy guards changed to civilian clothes, the hatches were battened down, and access to the decks was forbidden. According to the ships' papers, foresightedly prepared back in Vladivostok, they were transporting, God save us, not prisoners but volunteers for work in the Kolyma. A multitude of Japanese small craft and boats hovered about the ships without suspecting. (And on another occasion, in 1938, there was an incident involving the *Dzhurma*: The thieves aboard got out of the hold and into the storage room, plundered it, and set it afire. The ship was very close to Japan when this occurred. Smoke was pouring from it, and the Japanese offered help, but the captain refused to accept it and *even refused to open the hatches.* When Japan had been left behind, the corpses of those suffocated by smoke were thrown overboard, and the half-burned, half-spoiled food aboard was sent on to camp as rations for the prisoners.)[6]

Short of Magadan the ship caravan got caught in the ice and not even the *Krasin* could help (it was too early for navigation, but they had been in a hurry to deliver laborers). On May 2 they disembarked the prisoners on the ice, some distance from the shore. The newly arrived prisoners got a look at the cheerless panorama of the Magadan of that time: dead hillocks, neither trees, nor bushes, nor birds, just a few wooden houses and the two-story building of "Dalstroi." Nonetheless, continuing to play out the farce of *correction,* in other words, pretending they had brought not simply bones with which to pave the gold-bearing Kolyma but temporarily isolated Soviet citizens who would yet return to creative life, they were greeted by the Dalstroi orchestra. The orchestra played marches and waltzes, and the tormented, half-dead people strung along the ice in a gray line, dragging their Moscow belongings with them (and this enormous prisoner transport consisted almost entirely of politicals who had hardly encountered a single thief yet) and carrying on their shoulders other half-dead people—arthritis sufferers or prisoners without legs. (And the legless, too, got prison terms.)

But here I note that I am again beginning to repeat myself. And this will be boring to write, and boring to read, because the

6. Decades have passed since then, but how many times Soviet citizens have met with misfortune on the world's oceans—and in circumstances where it seems that zeks were not being transported—yet because of that same *secretiveness* disguised as national pride they have refused help! Let the sharks devour us, so long as we don't have to accept your helping hand! *Secretiveness* —that is our cancer.

reader already knows everything that is going to happen ahead of time: The prisoners would be trucked hundreds of miles, and driven dozens of miles more on foot. And on arriving they would occupy new camp sites and immediately be sent out to work. And they would eat fish and flour, chased down with snow. And sleep in tents.

Yes, it was like that. But first the authorities would put them up in Magadan, also in Arctic tents, and would *commission* them there too—in other words, examine them naked to determine their fitness for labor from the condition of their buttocks (and all of them would turn out to be fit). In addition, of course, they would be taken to a bath and in the bath vestibule they would be ordered to leave their leather coats, their Romanov sheepskin coats, their woolen sweaters, their suits of fine wool, their felt cloaks, their leather boots, their felt boots (for, after all, these were no illiterate peasants this time, but the Party elite—editors of newspapers, directors of trusts and factories, responsible officials in the provincial Party committees, professors of political economy, and, by the beginning of the thirties, all of them understood what good merchandise was). "And who is going to guard them?" the newcomers asked skeptically. "Oh, come on now, who needs your things?" The bath personnel acted offended. "Go on in and don't worry." And they did go in. And the exit was through a different door, and after passing through it, they received black cotton breeches, field shirts, camp quilted jackets without pockets, and pigskin shoes. (Oh, this was no small thing! This was farewell to your former life—to your titles, your positions, and your arrogance!) "Where are our things?" they cried. "*Your* things you left at home!" some chief or other bellowed at them. "In camp nothing belongs to *you*. Here in camp we have *communism!* Forward march, leader!"

And if it was "communism," then what was there for them to object to? That is what they had dedicated their lives to.

■

And there are also prisoner transports in carts and simply *on foot*. Do you remember in Tolstoi's *Resurrection* how on a sunny day they drove them on foot from the prison to the railroad station? Well, in Minusinsk in 194–, after the prisoners hadn't been taken into the fresh air for a whole year, they had forgotten how to walk, to breathe, to look at the light. And then they took them out, put them in formation, and drove them the *fifteen* miles to Abakan on foot. About a dozen of them died along the way. And no one is ever going to write a great novel about it, not even one chapter: if you live in a graveyard, you can't weep for everyone.

A prisoner transport on foot—that was the grandfather of prisoner transport by rail, of the Stolypin car, and of the red cattle cars too. In our time it is used less and less, and only where mechanical transportation is still impossible. Thus in one sector of Lake Ladoga, the prisoners were sent on foot from besieged Leningrad to the *red cars,* nicknamed "red *cows.*" They led the women together with the German POW's, and used bayonets to keep our men away from them so they couldn't take their bread. Those who fell by the wayside were immediately tossed up into a truck alive or dead, after their shoes were removed. And in the thirties, each day they sent off on foot from the Kotlas Transit Prison to Ust-Vym (about 185 miles) and sometimes to Chibyu (more than 300 miles) a transport of a hundred prisoners. Once in 1938 they sent off a women's prisoner transport the same way. These transports covered 15 miles a day. The convoy marched along with one or two dogs, and those who fell behind were urged on with gunstocks. True, the prisoners' possessions as well as the cooking pot and the food brought up the rear in carts, and this transport thus recalled the classic prisoner transports of the past century. There were also prisoner-transport huts —the ruined houses of liquidated kulaks, with windows broken and doors ripped off. The accounting office of the Kotlas Transit Prison had issued provisions to the transport based on a theoretical estimate of the time the journey would take, provided nothing went wrong on the way, without allowing for even one extra day. (The basic principle of all our accounting.) Whenever delays occurred en route, they had to stretch out the provisions, and fed the prisoners a mash of rye flour without salt and sometimes nothing at all. In this respect they departed from the classic model.

In 1940 Olenyev's prisoner transport, after disembarking from the barge, was herded on foot through the taiga (from Knyazh-

Pogost to Chibyu) without anything to eat at all. They drank swamp water and very quickly got dysentery. Some fell by the wayside out of weakness, and the dogs tore the clothes off those who had fallen. In Izhma they caught fish by using their trousers as nets and ate them alive. (And in a certain meadow they were told: Right here is where you are going to build a railroad from Kotlas to Vorkuta.)

And in other areas of our European North, prisoner transports on foot were standard until the time when, on those same routes and roadbeds built by those earlier zeks, the jolly red cattle cars rolled along carrying later prisoners.

A particular technique for prisoner transports on foot was worked out where such transports were frequent and abundant. When a transport is being taken through the taiga from Knyazh-Pogost to Veslyana, and suddenly some prisoner falls by the wayside and can go no farther, what is to be done with him? Just be reasonable and think about it: what? You aren't going to stop the whole transport. And you aren't going to leave one soldier behind for everyone who falls. There are many prisoners and only a few soldiers. And what does that mean? The soldier stays behind for a little while with the fallen prisoner and then hurries on to catch up with the rest—alone.

Regular transports on foot from Karabas to Spassk were retained for a long time. It was only twenty to twenty-five miles, but it had to be covered in one day, with one thousand prisoners in each transport, many of them very weak. It was expected in cases like these that many would simply either drop in their tracks or else fall behind through the indifference and apathy of dying men—you may shoot at them but they still can't go on. They are not afraid of death, but what about clubs, the indefatigable beating of the clubs wherever they hit? They are afraid of clubs, and they will keep going. This is a tested method—that's how it works. And so in these cases the transport column is surrounded not only by the ordinary chain of machine gunners at a distance of fifty yards, but also by an inner chain of soldiers armed only with clubs. Those who have fallen behind get beaten. (As, in fact, Comrade Stalin prophesied.) They are beaten again and again. And even when they have no strength at all with which to go farther, they keep going. And many do miraculously get to the destination. They don't know that this is a *testing by clubs,* and that those who lie down and stay lying down and don't go on despite the clubs are picked up by carts following behind. That's organizational experience for you! (And one can ask: Why, then, didn't they take them all on carts in the first place? But where could enough carts be found? And horses? After all, we have tractors. What about the price of oats nowadays?) Such transports as these were still common in 1948–1950.

And in the twenties, transport on foot was one of the basic methods. I was a small boy, but I remember very well how they drove them down the streets of Rostov-on-the-Don without any qualms. And the famous order: ". . . will open fire without warning!" had a different ring at that time, again because of a difference in technology: after all, the convoy often had only sabers. They used to deliver orders like this: "One step out of line and the convoy guard *will shoot and slash!*" That had a very powerful sound: "shoot and slash!" You could imagine them cutting off your head from behind.

Yes, and even in February, 1936, they drove on foot through Nizhni Novgorod a transport of long-bearded old men from the other side of the Volga, in their homespun coats and in real lapty —bast sandals—wrapped around with onuchi—Russian peasant footcloths—"Old Russia disappearing." And all of a sudden, right across their path, came three automobiles, in one of which rode the Chairman of the Central Executive Committee, President of the Soviet Union, this is to say, Kalinin. The prisoner transport halted. Kalinin went on through. He wasn't interested.

Shut your eyes, reader. Do you hear the thundering of wheels? Those are the Stolypin cars rolling on and on. Those are the red cows rolling. Every minute of the day. And every day of the year. And you can hear the water gurgling—those are prisoners' barges moving on and on. And the motors of the Black Marias roar. They are arresting someone all the time, cramming him in somewhere, moving him about. And what is that hum you hear? The overcrowded cells of the transit prisons. And that cry? The complaints of those who have been plundered, raped, beaten to within an inch of their lives.

We have reviewed and considered all the methods of delivering prisoners, and we have found that they are all . . . *worse*. We have examined the transit prisons, but we have not found any that were good. And even the last human hope that there is something better ahead, that it will be better in camp, is a false hope.

In camp it will be . . . worse.

Chapter 4

■

From Island to Island

And zeks are also moved from island to island of the Archipelago simply in solitary skiffs. This is called *special convoy.* It is the most unconstrained mode of transport. It can hardly be distinguished from free travel. Only a few prisoners are delivered in this way. I, in my own career as a prisoner, made three such journeys.

The special convoy is assigned on orders from high officials. It should not be confused with the *special requisition,* which is also signed by someone high up. A special-requisition prisoner usually travels on the general prisoner transports, though he, too, meets up with some amazing interludes on his trip (which are all the more extraordinary in consequence). For example, Ans Bernshtein was traveling on a special requisition from the North to the lower Volga, to join an agricultural mission. He was exposed to all the overcrowded conditions and humiliations I have described, snarled at by dogs, surrounded by bayonets, threatened with "One step out of line . . ." And then suddenly he was unloaded at the small station at Zenzevatka and met by one single, calm, unarmed jailer. The jailer yawned: "All right, you'll spend the night at my house, and you can go out on the town as you like till morning. Tomorrow I'll take you to the camp." And Ans did go out. Can you understand what *going out on the town* means to a person whose term is ten years, who has already said good-bye to life countless times, who was in a Stolypin car that very morning and will be in camp the next day? And he immediately went out to watch the chickens scratching around in the station master's garden and the peasant women getting ready to leave the station with their unsold butter and melons. He moved three, four, five steps to the side and no one shouted "Halt!" at him. With unbelieving fingers he touched the leaves of the acacias and almost wept.

And the special convoy is precisely that sort of miracle from beginning to end. You won't see the common prisoner transports this time. You don't have to keep your hands behind your back. You don't have to undress down to your skin, nor sit on the earth on your rear end, and there won't be any search at all. Your convoy guards approach you in a friendly way and even address you politely. They warn you, as a general precaution, that in case of any attempt to escape—We do, as usual, shoot. Our pistols are loaded and we have them in our pockets. However, let's go *simply*. Act natural. Don't let everyone see that you're a prisoner. (And I urge you to note how here, too, as always, the interests of the individual and the interests of the state coincide completely.)

My camp life was totally transformed the day I went out to line up forlornly in the carpenters' brigade, my fingers cramped (they had gotten stiff holding onto tools and wouldn't straighten out), and the work-assignment supervisor took me aside and with unexpected respect said to me: "Do you know that on orders of the Minister of Internal Affairs . . . ?"

I was stupefied. The line-up dispersed and the trusties in the camp compound surrounded me. Some of them said: "They are going to hang a new stretch on you." And others said: "To be released." But everyone agreed on one thing—that there was no escaping Minister of Internal Affairs Kruglov. And I, too, swayed between a new term and being released. I had quite forgotten that half a year before, some character had come to our camp and distributed Gulag registration cards. (After the war they had begun this registration in all the nearby camps, but it seems unlikely that it was ever completed.) The most important question on it was: "Trade or Profession." And the zeks would fill in the most precious Gulag trades to enhance their own value: "barber," "tailor," "storekeeper," "baker." As for me, I had frowned and filled in "nuclear physicist." I had never been a nuclear physicist in my life, and what I knew of the field I had heard in the university before the war—just a little bit, the names of the atomic particles and their parameters. And I had decided to write down "nuclear physicist." This was in 1946. The atom bomb was desperately needed. But I didn't assign any importance to that Gulag registration card and, in fact, forgot about it.

There was a vague, unverified legend, unconfirmed by anybody, that you might nevertheless hear in camp: that somewhere in this Archipelago were tiny *paradise islands*. No one had seen them. No one had been there. Whoever had, kept silent about them and never let on. On those islands, they said, flowed rivers of milk and honey, and eggs and sour cream were the least of what they fed you; things were neat and clean, they said, and it was always warm, and the only work was mental work—and all of it super-supersecret.

And so it was that I got to those paradise islands myself (in convict lingo they are called "sharashkas") and spent half my sentence on them. It's to them I owe my survival, for I would never have lived out my whole term in the camps. And it's to them I owe the fact that I am writing this investigation, even though I have not allowed them any place in this book. (I have already written a novel about them.) And it was from one to another of those islands, from the first to the second, and from the second to the third, that I was transported on a special-convoy basis: two jailers and I.

If the souls of those who have died sometimes hover among us, see us, easily read in us our trivial concerns, and we fail to see them or guess at their incorporeal presence, then that is what a special-convoy trip is like.

You are submerged in the mass of *freedom,* and you push and shove with the others in the station waiting room. You absentmindedly examine announcements posted there, even though they can hardly have any relevance for you. You sit on the ancient passenger benches, and you hear strange and insignificant conversations: about some husband who beats up his wife or has left her; and some mother-in-law who, for some reason, does not get along with her daughter-in-law; how neighbors in communal apartments make personal use of the electric outlets in the corridor and don't wipe their feet; and how someone is in someone else's way at the office; and how someone has been offered a good job but can't make up his mind to move—how can he move bag and baggage, is that so easy? You listen to all this, and the goose pimples of rejection run up and down your spine: to you the true measure of things in the Universe is so clear! The measure of all weaknesses and all passions! And these sinners aren't fated to perceive it. The only one there who is alive, truly alive, is incorporeal you, and all these others are simply mistaken in thinking themselves alive.

And an unbridgeable chasm divides you! You cannot cry out to them, nor weep over them, nor shake them by the shoulder: after all, you are a disembodied spirit, you are a ghost, and they are material bodies.

And how can you bring it home to them? By an inspiration? By a vision? A dream? Brothers! People! Why has life been given you? In the deep, deaf stillness of midnight, the doors of the death cells are being swung open—and great-souled people are being dragged out to be shot. On all the railroads of the country this very minute, right now, people who have just been fed salt herring are licking their dry lips with bitter tongues. They dream of the happiness of stretching out one's legs and of the relief one feels after going to the toilet. In Orotukan the earth thaws only in summer and only to the depth of three feet—and only then can they bury the bones of those who died during the winter. And you have the right to arrange your own life under the blue sky and the hot sun, to get a drink of water, to stretch, to travel wherever you like without a convoy. So what's this about unwiped feet? And what's this about a mother-in-law? What about the main thing in life, all its riddles? If you want, I'll spell it out for you right now. Do not pursue what is illusory—property and position: all that is gained at the expense of your nerves decade after decade, and is confiscated in one fell night. Live with a steady superiority over life—don't be afraid of misfortune, and do not yearn after happiness; it is, after all, all the same: the bitter doesn't last forever, and the sweet never fills the cup to overflowing. It is enough if you don't freeze in the cold and if thirst and hunger don't claw at your insides. If your back isn't broken, if your feet can walk, if both arms can bend, if both eyes see, and if both ears hear, then whom should you envy? And why? Our envy of others devours us most of all. Rub your eyes and purify your heart—and prize above all else in the world those who love you and who wish you well. Do not hurt them or scold them, and never part from any of them in anger; after all, you simply do not know: it might be your last act before your arrest, and that will be how you are imprinted in their memory!

But the convoy guards stroke the black handles of the pistols in their pockets. And we sit there, three in a row, sober fellows, quiet friends.

I wipe my brow. I shut my eyes, and then I open them. And once again I see this dream: a crowd of people unaccompanied by guards. I remember clearly that I spent last night in a cell and will be in a cell again tomorrow. But here comes some kind of conductor to punch my ticket: "Your ticket!" "My friend there has it!"

The cars are full. (Well, "full" in free people's terms—no one is lying under the benches, and no one is sitting on the floor in the aisles.) I was told to behave naturally, and I have been behaving very naturally indeed: I noticed a seat bèside a window in the next compartment, and got up and took it. And there were no empty seats for my guards in that compartment. They sat where they were and kept their loving eyes on me from there. In Perebory, the seat across the table from me was vacated, but before my guard could get to it and sit down, a moon-faced fellow in a sheepskin coat and a fur cap, with a plain but strong wooden suitcase, sat down there. I recognized his suitcase: it was camp work, "made in the Archipelago."

"Whew!" he puffs. There was very little light, but I could see he was red in the face and that he had had a hassle to get on the train. And he got out a bottle: "How about a beer, comrade?" I knew that my guards were close to a nervous breakdown in the next compartment: I was not allowed anything alcoholic. But still . . . I was supposed to conduct myself as naturally as possible. And so I said carelessly: "All right, why not?" (Beer! It's a whole poem! For three years I hadn't had even one swallow. And tomorrow in my cell I would brag: "I got beer!") The fellow poured it, and I drank it down with a shiver of pleasure. It was already dark. There was no electricity in the car. This was postwar dislocation. One tiny candle end was burning in an ancient lantern at the door, one for four compartments: two in front and two behind. I talked amiably with the fellow even though we could hardly see each other. No matter how far forward my guard leaned, he couldn't hear a thing because of the clickety-clack of the wheels. In my pocket I had a postcard addressed to my home. And I was about to explain who I was to my simple friend across the table and ask him to drop the card in a mailbox. Judging by his suitcase he had been in stir himself. But he beat me to it: "You know, I just barely managed to get some leave. They haven't given me any time off for two years; it's a dog's branch of the service." "What kind?" "Don't you know? I'm an MVD man, an asmodeus, blue shoulder boards, haven't you ever seen them?" Hell! Why hadn't I guessed right off? Perebory was the center for Volgolag, and he had gotten his suitcase out of the zeks, they had made it for him for free. How all this had permeated our life! Two MVD men, two asmodei, weren't enough in two compartments. There had to be a third. And perhaps there was also a fourth concealed somewhere? And maybe they were in every compartment? And maybe someone else there was traveling by special convoy like me.

My fellow kept on whining and complaining of his fate. And at that point, I decided to enter a somewhat mystifying demurrer. "And what about the ones you're guarding, the ones who got ten years for nothing—is it any easier for them?" He immediately subsided and remained silent until morning: earlier, in the semi-darkness, he had noticed that I was wearing some kind of semimilitary overcoat and field shirt. And he had thought I was simply a soldier boy, but now the devil only knew what I might be: Maybe I was a police agent? Maybe I was out to catch escapees? Why was I in this particular car? And he had criticized the camps there in my presence.

By this time the candle end in the lantern was floating but still burning. On the third baggage shelf some youth was talking in a pleasant voice about the war—the real war, the kind you don't read about in books: he had been with a unit of field engineers and was describing incidents that were true to life. And it was so pleasant to realize that unvarnished truth was, despite everything, pouring into someone's ears.

I could have told tales too. I would even have liked to. But no, I didn't really want to any more. Like a cow, the war had licked away four of my years. I no longer believed that it had all actually happened and I didn't want to remember it. Two years *here,* two years in the Archipelago, had dimmed in my mind all the roads of the front, all the comradeship of the front line, had totally darkened them.

One wedge knocks out another.

And after spending a few hours among *free people,* here is what I feel: My lips are mute; there is no place for me among them; my hands are tied here. I want free speech! I want to go back to my native land! I want to go home to the Archipelago!

In the morning I deliberately *forgot* my postcard on an upper shelf: after all, the conductor will get around to cleaning up the car; she will carry it to a mailbox—if she is a human being.

We emerge onto the square in front of the Northern Station in Moscow. Again my jailers are newcomers to Moscow, and don't know the city. We travel on streetcar "B," and I make the decisions for them. There is a mob at the streetcar stop in the middle of the square; everyone is on the way to work at this hour. One jailer climbs up to the streetcar motorman and shows him his MVD identity card. We are allowed to stand imposingly on the front platform for the whole trip, as if we were deputies of the Moscow Soviet, and we don't bother to get tickets. An old man isn't allowed to board there—he isn't an invalid and he has to board in the rear like the others.

We approach Novoslobodskaya and disembark—and for the first time I see Butyrki Prison from the outside, even though it's the fourth time I've been brought there and I can draw its interior plan without difficulty. Oof, what a grim, high wall stretches for two blocks there! The hearts of the Muscovites shiver when they see the steel maw of its gates slide open. But I leave the sidewalks of Moscow behind me without regret, and as I enter that tower of the gatehouse I feel I am returning home. I smile at the first courtyard and recognize the familiar main doors of carved wood. And it's nothing at all to me that they are now going to make me face the wall—and they already have—and ask me: "Last name? Given name and patronymic? Year of birth?"

My name? I am the Interstellar Wanderer! They have tightly bound my body, but my soul is beyond their power.

I know: after several hours of inevitable processing of my body—confinement in a box, search, issuing receipts, filling out the admissions card, after the roaster and the bath—I shall be taken to a cell with two domes, with a hanging arch in the middle (all the cells are like that), with two large windows and a long combination table and cupboard. And I shall be greeted by strangers who are certain to be intelligent, interesting, friendly people, and they will begin to tell me their stories, and I will begin to tell them mine, and by night we will not even feel like going off to sleep right away.

And on the bowls will be stamped (so we shouldn't make off with them on the prisoner transport) the mark "Bu-Tyur"—for *Bu*tyrskaya *Tyur*ma, Butyrki Prison. The "BuTyur" Health Resort, as we mocked it last time. A health resort, incidentally, very little known to the paunchy bigwigs who want so badly to lose weight. They drag their stomachs to Kislovodsk, and go out for long hikes on prescribed trails, do push-ups, and sweat for a whole month just to lose four to six pounds. And there in the "BuTyur" Health Resort, right near them, anyone of them could lose seventeen or eighteen pounds just like that, in one week, without doing any exercises at all.

This is a tried and true method. It has never failed.

■

One of the truths you learn in prison is that the world is small, very small indeed. True, the Gulag Archipelago, although it extended across the entire Soviet Union, had many fewer inhabitants than the Soviet Union as a whole. How many there actually were in the Archipelago one cannot know for certain. We can assume that *at any one time* there were not more than twelve million in the camps[1] (as some departed beneath the sod, the Machine kept bringing in replacements). And not more than half of them were politicals. Six million? Well, that's a small country, Sweden or Greece, and in such countries many people

1. According to the researches of the Social Democrats Nicolaevsky and Dallin, there were from fifteen to twenty million prisoners in the camps.

know one another. And quite naturally when you landed in any cell of any transit prison and listened and chatted, you'd be certain to discover you had acquaintances in common with some of your cellmates. (And so D., after having spent more than a year in solitary confinement, after Sukhanovka, after Ryumin's beatings and the hospital, could land in a Lubyanka cell and give his name, and then and there a bright chap named F. could greet him: "Aha, so now I know who you are!" "Where from?" D. shied away from him. "You are mistaken." "Certainly not. You are that very same American, Alexander D., whom the bourgeois press lied about, saying you had been kidnaped—and TASS denied it. I was free at the time and read about it.")

I love that moment when a newcomer is admitted to the cell for the first time (not a novice who has only recently been arrested and will inevitably be depressed and confused, but a veteran zek). And I myself love to enter a new cell (nonetheless, God grant I never have to do it again) with an unworried smile and an expansive gesture: "Hi, brothers!" I throw my bag on the bunks. "Well, so what's new this past year in Butyrki?"

We begin to get acquainted. Some fellow named Suvorov, a 58. At first glance there's nothing remarkable about him, but you probe and pry: at the Krasnoyarsk Transit Prison a certain Makhotkin was in his cell.

"Just a moment, wasn't he an Arctic aviator?"

"Yes. They named . . ."

" . . . an island after him in the Taimyr Gulf. And he's in prison for 58-10. So does that mean they let him go to Dudinka?"

"How do you know? Yes."

Wonderful! One more link in the biography of a man I don't know. I have never met him, and perhaps I never shall. But my efficient memory has filed away everything I know about him: Makhotkin got a whole "quarter"—twenty-five years—but the island named after him couldn't be renamed because it was on all the maps of the world (it wasn't a Gulag island). They had taken him on at the aviation sharashka in Bolshino and he was unhappy there: an aviator among engineers, and not allowed to fly. They split that sharashka in two, and Makhotkin got assigned to the Taganrog half, and it seemed as though all connection with him had been severed. In the other half of it, however, in Rybinsk,

I was told that he had asked to be allowed to fly in the Far North. And now I had just learned he had been given that permission. This was not information I needed, but I had remembered it all. And ten days later I turned up in the same Butyrki bath box (there are such lovely boxes in the Butyrki, with faucets and small washtubs so as not to tie up the big bath chambers) as a certain R. I didn't know this R. either, but it turned out he had been a patient in the Butyrki hospital for half a year and was about to leave for the Rybinsk sharashka. In another three days the prisoners in Rybinsk, too, a closed box where zeks are cut off from all ties with the outside world, would nevertheless learn that Makhotkin was in Dudinka, and they would also find out where I had been sent.

Now *this* is the prisoners' telegraph system: attentiveness, memory, chance meetings.

And this attractive man in horn-rimmed spectacles? He walked around the cell humming Schubert in a pleasant baritone.

> And youth again oppresses me,
> And the way to the grave is long.

"Tsarapkin, Sergei Romanovich."

"But look here, I know you very well indeed. You're a biologist? A nonreturnee? From Berlin?"

"How do you know?"

"But after all, it's a small world! In 1946 with Nikolai Vladimirovich Timofeyev-Ressovsky . . ."

Oh, what a cell that had been in 1946: The memories of it returned. It was perhaps the most brilliant cell in all my prison life. It was July. They had taken me from the camp to the Butyrki on those mysterious "instructions of the Minister of Internal Affairs." We arrived after lunch, but the prison was so overloaded that the reception processing took eleven hours, and it was not until 3 A.M. that, tired from the boxes, I was admitted to Cell 75. Lit by two bright electric bulbs below the two domes, the whole cell slept side by side, restless because of the stuffiness: the hot July air couldn't circulate through the windows blocked by the "muzzles." Sleepless flies kept buzzing, and the sleepers twitched when the flies lit on them. Some of the prisoners had put handkerchiefs over their faces to keep the light out of their eyes.

The latrine barrel smelled acrid—everything decayed more quickly in such heat. Eighty people were stuffed into a cell for twenty-five—and this was not the limit either. Prisoners lay tightly packed together on the bunks to left and right and also on the supplementary planks laid across the aisle, and everywhere feet were sticking out from under the bunks, and the traditional Butyrki table-cupboard was pushed back to the latrine barrel. That was where there was still a piece of unoccupied floor, and that was where I lay down. And thus it was that whoever got up to use the latrine barrel before morning had to step across me.

When the order "Get up!" was given, shouted through the swill trough in the door, everything started to stir: They began to take up the planks from across the aisles and push the table to the window. Prisoners came up to interview me—to find out whether I was a novice or a camp veteran. It turned out that two different waves had met in the cell: the ordinary wave of freshly sentenced prisoners being sent off to camp and a reverse wave of camp inmates who were all technical specialists—physicists, chemists, mathematicians, design engineers—all being sent to unknown destinations, to some sort of thriving scientific research institutes. (At this point I relaxed: the Minister was not going to *hang a new stretch* on me.) I was approached by a man who was middle-aged, broad-shouldered yet very skinny, with a slightly aquiline nose:

"Professor Timofeyev-Ressovsky, President of the Scientific and Technical Society of Cell 75. Our society assembles every day after the morning bread ration, next to the left window. Perhaps you could deliver a scientific report to us? What precisely might it be?"

Caught unaware, I stood before him in my long bedraggled overcoat and winter cap (those arrested in winter are foredoomed to go about in winter clothing during the summer too). My fingers had not yet straightened out that morning and were all scratched. What kind of scientific report could I give? And right then I remembered that in camp I had recently held in my hands for two nights the Smyth Report, the official report of the United States Defense Department on the first atom bomb, which had been brought in from outside. The book had been published that spring. Had anyone in the cell seen it? It was a useless question.

Of course no one had. And thus it was that fate played its joke, compelling me, in spite of everything, to stray into nuclear physics, the same field in which I had registered on the Gulag card.

After the rations were issued, the Scientific and Technical Society of Cell 75, consisting of ten or so people, assembled at the left window and I made my report and was accepted into the society. I had forgotten some things, and I could not fully comprehend others, and Timofeyev-Ressovsky, even though he had been in prison for a year and knew nothing of the atom bomb, was able on occasion to fill in the missing parts of my account. An empty cigarette pack was my blackboard, and I held an illegal fragment of pencil lead. Nikolai Vladimirovich took them away from me and sketched and interrupted, commenting with as much self-assurance as if he had been a physicist from the Los Alamos group itself.

He actually had worked with one of the first European cyclotrons, but for the purpose of irradiating fruit flies. He was a biologist, one of the most important geneticists of our time. He had already been in prison back when Zhebrak, not knowing that (or, perhaps, knowing it), had the courage to write in a Canadian magazine: "Russian biology is not responsible for Lysenko; Russian biology is Timofeyev-Ressovsky." (And during the destruction of Soviet biology in 1948 Zhebrak paid for this.) Schrödinger, in his small book *What Is Life?*, twice cited Timofeyev-Ressovsky, who had long since been imprisoned.

And there he was in front of us, and he was simply bursting with information concerning all possible sciences. He had that breadth of scope which scientists of later generations don't even want to have. (Or is it that the possibilities of encompassing knowledge have changed?) And even though at the moment he was so worn down by the starvation of the interrogation period that these exercises were very difficult for him. On his mother's side he was descended from impoverished Kaluga gentlefolk who had lived on the Ressa River, and on his father's side he was a collateral descendant of Stepan Razin, and that Cossack energy was very obvious in him—in his broad frame, in his basic soundness, in his determined struggle with his interrogator, and also in the fact that he suffered from hunger more than we did.

And his story was this: In 1922 the German scientist Vogt,

who had founded the Brain Institute in Moscow, had asked to have two talented graduate students sent abroad to work with him permanently. And that was how Timofeyev-Ressovsky and his friend Tsarapkin had been sent off on a foreign assignment with no time limit. And even though they did not have any ideological guidance there, they nonetheless achieved great things in science, and when in 1937 (!) they were instructed to return to their homeland, this seemed to them, since it meant interrupting their work, impossible. They could not abandon either the logical continuation of their own researches or their apparatus or their students. And, no doubt, they also couldn't do it because back in the Motherland they would have been compelled to pour shit publicly all over their fifteen years of work in Germany. And only that would have earned them the right to go on existing (and *would* it have earned it for them?). And so they became non-returnees, remaining patriots nevertheless.

In 1945 the Soviet armies entered Buch (a northeast suburb of Berlin), and Timofeyev-Ressovsky and his entire institute joyously welcomed them: everything had worked out in the best possible way, and now he would not have to be separated from his institute! Soviet representatives came to inspect it and said: "Hmm! hmm! Put everything in packing cases, and we'll take it all to Moscow." "That's impossible," Timofeyev objected. "Everything will die on the way. The installations have taken years to set up." "Hmm!" The bigwigs acted astonished. And very shortly after that Timofeyev and Tsarapkin were arrested and taken off to Moscow. They were naïve. They had thought that the institute would not be able to operate without them. Well, even if it didn't operate, the general line of the Party must triumph! In the Big Lubyanka it was very easily proven to the arrested individuals that they were traitors of the Motherland (or to it?), and they were sentenced to ten years, and now the President of the Scientific and Technical Society of Cell 75 took heart from the thought that he hadn't made any errors.

In the Butyrki cells, the arched metal frames supporting the bunks were very, very low. Even the prison administration had never thought of having prisoners sleep under them. Therefore, you first tossed your neighbor your coat so that he could spread it out for you under there, and then you lay face down in the aisle and crawled your way in. Prisoners walked through the aisle, the floor underneath the bunks was swept maybe once a month, and you could wash your hands only during the evening trip to the toilet, and even then without soap—and it was thus impossible to say that you could perceive your body as a Divine vessel. But I was happy! There, on the asphalt floor, under the bunks, in a dog's den, with dust and crumbs from the bunks falling in our eyes, I was absolutely happy, without any qualifications. Epicurus spoke truly: Even the absence of variety can be sensed as satisfaction when a variety of dissatisfactions has preceded it. After camp, which had already seemed endless, and after a ten-hour workday, after cold, rain, and aching back, oh, what happiness it was to lie there for whole days on end, to sleep, and nevertheless receive a pound and a half of bread and two hot meals a day—made from cattle feed, or from dolphin's flesh. In a word, the "BuTyur" Health Resort.

To sleep was so important! To lie there on one's belly, to cover one's back and just to sleep. When you were asleep, you didn't spend your strength nor torment your heart—and meanwhile your sentence was passing, passing. When our life crackles and sparks like a torch, we curse the necessity of spending eight hours uselessly in sleep. When we have been deprived of everything, when we have been deprived of hope, then bless you, fourteen hours of sleep!

But they kept me in that cell two months, and I slept enough to make up for the past year and the year ahead, and during that time I moved forward under the bunks to the window and then all the way back to the latrine barrel, but on the bunks this time, and then on the bunks I moved to the archway. I was sleeping very little by this time—I was gulping down the elixir of life and enjoying myself. In the morning the Scientific and Technical Society, then chess, books (oh, those itinerant books, there were only three or four for eight or ten people, and there was always a waiting list for them), then a twenty-minute walk outdoors—a major chord! We never refused our walk even when it was raining heavily. And the main thing was people, people, people! Nikolai Andreyevich Semyonov, one of the creators of the Dnieper Hydroelectric Dam and Power Station. His POW friend, the engineer F. F. Karpov. Witty, caustic Viktor Kagan, a physicist. The musician and conservatory student Volodya Klempner, a composer. A woodcutter and hunter from the Vyatka forests, as profound as a forest lake. An Orthodox preacher from Europe, Yevgeny Ivanovich Divnich. He did not confine himself to theology, but condemned Marxism, declaring that no one in Europe had taken it seriously for a long while—and I defended it, because after all I was a Marxist. And even a year ago I would have confidently demolished him with quotations; how disparagingly I would have mocked him! But my first year as a prisoner had left its mark inside me—and just when had that happened? I hadn't noticed: there had been so many new events, sights, meanings, that I could no longer say: "They don't exist! That's a bourgeois lie!" And now I had to admit: "Yes, they do exist." And right at that point my whole line of reasoning began to weaken, and so they could beat me in our arguments without half-trying.

And again the POW's kept coming and coming and coming—this was the second year of the wave of them that kept unceasingly coming from Europe. And once more there were Russian émigrés —from Europe, from Manchuria. One went about among the émigrés seeking news of acquaintances by first asking what country they had come from, and did they know so and so? Yes, of course, they did. (And that is how I learned of the execution of Colonel Yasevich.)

And the old German, that portly German, now emaciated and ill, whom I had once upon a time back in East Prussia (was it two hundred years ago?) forced to carry my suitcase. Oh, how small the world really is! Strange fate that brought us together again! The old man smiled at me. He recognized me too, and even seemed pleased by our meeting. He had forgiven me. He had been sentenced to ten years, but he certainly didn't have anywhere near that long to live. And there was another German there too— lanky and young, but unresponsive—perhaps because he didn't know one word of Russian. You wouldn't even take him for a German right off the bat: the thieves had torn off everything German he had on and given him a faded old Soviet field shirt in exchange. He was a famous German air ace. His first campaign had been in the war between Bolivia and Paraguay, his second in Spain, his third Poland, his fourth over England, his fifth Cyprus, his sixth the Soviet Union. Since he was an ace he could certainly not have avoided shooting down women and children from the air! That made him a war criminal and he got a prison sentence and a "muzzle" of five additional years. And, of course, there had to be one right-thinking person (like Prosecutor Kretov) in the cell: "They were right to imprison all you counterrevolutionary bastards! History will grind up your bones for fertilizer!" "You're going to be fertilizer yourself, you dog!" they shouted back. "No, they will reconsider my case. I am innocent!" And the whole cell howled and seethed. And a gray-haired Russian-language teacher stood up on the bunks, barefoot, and wrung his hands like a latter-day Jesus Christ: "Children of mine, make peace with one another! My children!" And they howled at him too: "Your children are in the Bryansk forests! We are nobody's children! All we are is the sons of Gulag."

After dinner and the evening trip to the toilet, night cloaked the window "muzzles" and the nagging electric lights below the ceiling lit up. Day divided the prisoners and night drew them closer together. There were no quarrels in the evening: lectures and concerts were given. And in this, too, Timofeyev-Ressovsky shone: he spent entire evenings on Italy, Denmark, Norway, Sweden. The émigrés spoke about the Balkans, about France. Someone delivered a lecture on Le Corbusier. Someone else delivered one on the habits of bees. Someone else on Gogol. This was when we smoked our lungs full. Smoke filled up the cell and hovered in the air like a fog, and there was no draft to pull it out the window because of the "muzzles." Kostya Kiula, twin to me in age, round-faced, blue-eyed, amusingly awkward, stepped up to the table and recited to us the verses he had composed in prison.[2] His voice broke with emotion. His verses were entitled, "My First Food Parcel," "To My Wife," "To My Son." When in prison you strain to get by ear verses written in prison, you don't waste a single thought on whether the author's use of syllabic stress is faulty and whether his lines end in assonances or full rhymes. These verses are the blood *of your own heart,* the tears *of your own wife.* The cell wept.

In that cell I myself set out to write verses about prison. And

2. Kostya Kiula doesn't respond, he's disappeared. I am afraid he is not among the living.

it was there that I recited the verses of Yesenin, who had almost but not quite been on the forbidden list before the war. And young Bubnov, a POW, and before that, apparently, a student who had not completed his studies, worshipfully gazed at those reciting, his face aglow. He was not a technical specialist and he hadn't come from camp, but was on his way there, and because of the purity and forthrightness of his character he would in all likelihood die there. People like him don't survive there. And for him and for others—their fatal descent braked for the moment —the evenings in Cell 75 were a sudden revelation of that beautiful world which exists and will continue to exist but which their own hard fate hadn't given them one little year of, not even one little year of their young lives.

The swill trough dropped down and the turnkey's mug barked at us: "Bed." No, even before the war, when I was studying at two higher educational institutions at the same time and earning my way by tutoring, and striving *to write* too, even then I had not experienced such full, such heart-rending, such completely filled days, as I did in Cell 75 that summer.

"But listen," I said to Tsarapkin, "I've heard since then from someone called Deul, a sixteen-year-old boy who got a *fiver* (not on a school report card) for 'anti-Soviet' propaganda. . . ."

"What, do you know him too? He was on our prisoner transport to Karaganda. . . ."

". . . I heard," I continued, "that you were given work as a laboratory assistant doing medical analyses and that Timofeyev-Ressovsky was constantly being sent out on *general-assignment work*. . . ."

"Yes, and he grew very weak. He was half-dead when they brought him from the Stolypin car here to the Butyrki. And he is in a hospital bed here right now, and the Fourth Special Department[3] is issuing him cream and even wine, but it's hard to say whether he will ever get back on his feet again."

"Did the Fourth Special Department summon you?"

"Yes. They asked us whether we considered it might still be possible after six months of Karaganda to start setting up our institute here, in the Fatherland."

3. The task of the Fourth Special Department of the MVD was to solve scientific problems, using prisoners.

"And you, of course, agreed enthusiastically."

"Most certainly! After all, we have come to understand our mistakes. And besides, all the equipment wrenched from its original place and put into packing cases got here even without us."

"What dedication to science on the part of the MVD! May I ask for a little more Schubert?"

And Tsarapkin sang softly, staring sadly at the window (his spectacles reflecting both their dark "muzzles" and their light upper sections):

> Vom Abendrot zum Morgenlicht
> ward mancher Kopf zum Greise.
> Wer glaubt es? Meiner ward es nicht
> auf dieser ganzen Reise.

■

Tolstoi's dream has come true: Prisoners are no longer compelled to attend pernicious religious services. The prison churches have been shut down. True, their buildings remain, but they have been successfully adapted to enlarge the prisons themselves. Two thousand additional prisoners have thereby been housed in the Butyrki church—and in the course of a year, estimating an average turnover of two weeks, another fifty thousand will pass through the cells in what was once the church.

On arriving at the Butyrki for the fourth or fifth time, hurrying confidently to my assigned cell, through the courtyard surrounded by prison buildings, and even outstripping the jailer by a shoulder (like a horse that hurries, without the urging of whip or reins, home to where the oats are waiting), I sometimes even forgot to glance at the square church rising into an octagon. It stood apart in the middle of the courtyard quadrangle. Its "muzzles" were not machine-made of glass reinforced with iron rods as they were in the main section of the prison. They were rotten, unplaned gray boards, pure and simple—and they indicated the building's second-rank priority. What they maintained there was a kind of intra-Butyrki transit prison, so to speak, for recently sentenced prisoners.

And at one time, in 1945, I had experienced it as a big, important step when they led us into the church after our OSO sentencing (and that was the right time to do it too!—it was a good time for prayer!), took us up to the second floor (and the third floor was also partitioned off), and from the octagonal vestibule distributed us among different cells. Mine was the southeast cell.

This was a large square cell in which, at the time, two hundred prisoners were confined. They were sleeping, as they did everywhere else there, on the bunks (and they were one-story bunks), under the bunks, and just simply on the tile floor, out in the aisles. Not only were the "muzzles" on the windows second-rate; everything else, too, was in a style appropriate not to true sons of Butyrki but to its stepsons. No books, no chess sets, no checkers were distributed to this swarming mass, and the dented aluminum bowls and beat-up wooden spoons were collected and removed from one mealtime to another for fear that in the rush they might get carried off on prisoner transports. They were even stingy with mugs for the stepsons. They washed the bowls after the gruel, and then the prisoners had to lap up their tea slops out of them. The absence of one's own dishes was particularly acute for those who experienced the mixed blessing of receiving a parcel from their families (despite their meager means, relatives made a special effort to provide parcels in those last days before the prisoner transports left). The families had had no prison education themselves, and they never got any good advice in the prison reception office either. And therefore they didn't send plastic dishes, the one and only kind prisoners were allowed to have, but glass or metal ones instead. All these honeys, jams, condensed milks were pitilessly poured and scraped out of their cans through the swill trough in the cell door into whatever the prisoner had, and in the church cells he had nothing at all, which meant that he simply got it in the palms of his hands, in his mouth, in his handkerchief, in the flaps of his coat—which was quite normal in Gulag terms, but not in the center of Moscow! And at the same time the jailer kept hurrying him as if he were late for his train. (The jailer hurried him because he was counting on licking out whatever was left in the jars.) Everything was temporary in the church cells, without that illusion of permanency which existed in the interrogation cells and in the cells where prisoners awaited sentencing. Ground meat, a semiprocessed product partially prepared for Gulag, the prisoners were unavoidably here those few days until a bit of space had been cleared for them at Krasnaya Presnya. They had just one special privilege here: three times a day they were allowed to go for their gruel themselves (no grits were given out here, but the gruel was served three times a day, and this was a merciful thing because it was more frequent, hotter, and stuck to the ribs better). This special privilege was allowed because there were no elevators in the church—as there were in the rest of the prison. And the jailers had no wish to exert themselves. The big heavy kettles had to be carried from a long way off, across the yard, and then up a steep flight of stairs. It was hard work, and the prisoners had very little strength for it, but they went willingly—just to get out into the green yard one more time and hear the birds singing.

The church cells had their own air: it held a fluttering presentiment of the drafts of future transit prisons, of the winds of the Arctic camps. In the church cells you celebrated the ritual of getting adjusted—to the fact that your sentence had been handed down and that it wasn't in the least a joke; to the fact that no matter how cruel the new era of your life might be, your mind must nevertheless digest and accept it. And you arrived at that with great difficulty.

And you had no permanent cellmates here as you did in the interrogation cells—which made the latter something like a family. Day and night, people were brought in and taken away singly and by tens, and as a result the prisoners kept moving ahead along the floor and along the bunks, and it was rare to lie next to any one neighbor for more than two nights. Once you met an interesting person there you had to question him immediately, because otherwise you would miss out for good and all.

And that is how I missed out on the automobile mechanic Medvedev. When I began to talk to him, I remembered that his name had been mentioned by the Emperor Mikhail. Yes, he had indeed been implicated in the same case as Mikhail, because he had been one of the first to read the "Manifesto to the Russian People"—and had failed to write a denunciation. Medvedev had been given an unforgivably, shamefully light sentence—three years. And under Article 58, too, for which even five years was considered a juvenile sentence. They had evidently decided the

Emperor was really insane, and had been easy on the rest of them because of *class* considerations. But I had hardly pulled myself together to ask how Medvedev regarded all this than they took him off "with his things." Certain circumstances led us to conclude that he had been taken off to be released. And this confirmed those first rumors of the Stalinist amnesty which reached our ears that summer, *the amnesty for no one*, an amnesty after which everything was just as crowded as before—even under the bunks.

They took my neighbor, an elderly Schutzbündler, off to a prisoner transport. (Here in the land of the world proletariat, all those Schutzbündlers who had been suffocating in conservative Austria had been *roasted* with "tenners," and on the islands of the Archipelago they met their end.) And there was a swarthy little fellow with coal-black hair and feminine-looking eyes like dark cherries, but with a broad, larger than usual nose that spoiled his whole face, turning it into a caricature. For a day he and I lay next to each other in silence, and on the second day he found occasion to ask me: "What do you think I am?" He spoke Russian correctly and fluently, but with an accent. I hesitated: there seemed to be something of Transcaucasia in him, Armenian presumably. He smiled: "I used to pass myself off very easily as a Georgian. My name was Yasha. Everyone laughed at me. I collected trade-union dues." I looked him over. His was truly a comical figure: a half-pint, his face out of proportion, asymmetrical, his smile amiable. And then suddenly he tensed up, his features sharpened, his eyes narrowed and cut me like the stroke of a black saber.

"I am an intelligence officer of the Rumanian General Staff! Lieutenant Vladimirescu!"

I started—this was real dynamite. I had met a couple of hundred fabricated spies, and I had never thought I might meet up with a real one. I thought they didn't exist.

According to his story, he was of an aristocratic family. From the age of three he had been destined to serve on the General Staff. At six he had entered the intelligence service school. Growing up, he had picked his own field of future activity—the Soviet Union, taking into account that here in Russia the most relentless counterintelligence service in the world existed and that it was particularly difficult to work here because everyone suspected everyone else. And, he now concluded, he had worked here not at all badly. He had spent several prewar years in Nikolayev and, it appears, had arranged for the Rumanian armies to capture a shipyard intact. Subsequently he had been at the Stalingrad Tractor Factory, and after that at the Urals Heavy Machinery Factory. In the course of collecting trade-union dues he had entered the office of the chief of a major division of the plant, had shut the door behind him, and his idiotic smile had promptly left his face, and that saber-sharp cutting expression had appeared: "Ponomaryev! [And Ponomaryev was using an altogether different name at the Urals Heavy Machinery Factory.] We have been keeping track of you from Stalingrad on. You left your job there. [He had been some kind of bigwig at the Stalingrad Tractor Factory.] And you have set yourself up here under an assumed name. You can choose—to be shot by your own people or to work with us." Ponomaryev chose to work with them, and that indeed was very much in the style of those supersuccessful pigs. The lieutenant supervised his work until he himself was transferred to the jurisdiction of the German intelligence officer resident in Moscow, who sent him to Podolsk *to work at his specialty*. As Vladimirescu explained to me, intelligence officers and saboteurs are given an all-round training, but each of them has his own *narrow* area of specialization. And Vladimirescu's special field was cutting the main cord of a parachute on the inside. In Podolsk he was met at the parachute warehouse by the chief of the warehouse guard (who was it? what kind of person was he?), who at night let Vladimirescu into the warehouse for eight hours. Climbing up to the piles of parachutes on his ladder and managing not to disturb the piles, Vladimirescu pulled out the braided main support-cord and, with special scissors, cut four-fifths of the way through it, leaving one-fifth intact, so that it would break in the air. Vladimirescu had studied many long years in preparation for this one night. And now, working feverishly, in the course of eight hours he ruined, according to his account, upwards of two thousand parachutes (fifteen seconds per parachute?). "I destroyed a whole Soviet parachute division!" His cherrylike eyes sparkled with malice.

When he was arrested, he refused to give any testimony for

eight whole months—imprisoned in the Butyrki, he uttered not
one word. "And didn't they torture you?" "No!" His lips twitched
as though to indicate he didn't even consider such a thing possible
in the case of a non-Soviet citizen. (Beat your own people so
foreigners will be more afraid of you! But a real spy's a gold
mine! After all, we may have to use him for an exchange.) The
day came when they showed him the newspapers: Rumania had
capitulated; come on, now, testify. He continued to keep silent:
the newspapers could have been forgeries. They showed him an
order of the Rumanian General Staff: under the conditions of the
armistice the General Staff ordered all its intelligence agents to
cease operations and surrender. He continued to keep silent.
(The order could have been a forgery.) Finally he was confronted with his immediate superior on the General Staff, who
ordered him to disclose his information and surrender. At this
point Vladimirescu coldbloodedly gave his testimony, and now,
in the slow passing of the cell day, it was no longer of any importance and he told me some of it too. They had not even tried
him! They had not even given him a sentence! (After all, he
wasn't one of our own! "I am a career man—and will remain one
until I die. And they won't waste me.")

"But you are revealing yourself to me," I pointed out. "I might
very well remember your face. Just imagine our meeting someday
in public."

"If I am convinced that you haven't recognized me, you will
remain alive. If you recognize me, I will kill you, or else force you
to work for us."

He had not the slightest desire to spoil his relationship with his
cell neighbor. He said this very simply, with total conviction.
I was really convinced that he wouldn't hesitate for a moment to
gun someone down or cut their throat.

In this whole long prisoners' chronicle, we will not again meet
such a hero. It was the only encounter of the sort I ever had in my
eleven years of prison, camp, and exile, and others didn't even
have one. And our mass-circulation comics try to dupe young
people into believing that these are the only people the *Organs*
catch.

It was enough to look around that church cell to grasp that it
was youth itself the Organs were catching in the first place. The

war had ended, and we could allow ourselves the luxury of arresting everyone who had been singled out: they were no longer needed as soldiers. They said that in 1944 and 1945 a so-called "Democratic Party" had passed through the cells of the Small (Moscow Province) Lubyanka. According to rumor, it had consisted of half a hundred boys, had its own statutes and its membership cards. The eldest of them was a pupil in the tenth grade of a Moscow school, and he was its "general secretary." Students were also glimpsed fleetingly in the prisons during the last year of the war. I met some here and there. I was presumably not old myself, but they at any rate were younger.

How imperceptibly all that crept up on us! While we—I, my codefendant, and others of our age—had been fighting for four years at the front, a whole new generation had grown up here in the rear. And had it been very long since we ourselves had tramped the parquet floors of the university corridors, considering ourselves the youngest and most intelligent in the whole country and, for that matter, on earth? And then suddenly pale youths crossed the tile floors of the prison cells to approach us haughtily, and we learned with astonishment that we were no longer the youngest and most intelligent—they were. But I didn't take offense at this; at that point I was already happy to move over a bit to make room. I knew so very well their passion for arguing with everyone, for finding out everything, I understood their pride in having chosen a worthy lot and in not regretting it. It gave me gooseflesh to hear the rustle of the prison halos hovering over those self-enamored and intelligent little faces.

One month earlier, in another Butyrki cell, a semihospital cell, I had just stepped into the aisle and had still not seen any empty place for myself—when, approaching in a way that hinted at a verbal dispute, even at an entreaty to enter into one, came a pale, yellowish youth, with a Jewish tenderness of face, wrapped, despite the summer, in a threadbare soldier's overcoat shot full of holes: he was chilled. His name was Boris Gammerov. He began to question me; the conversation rolled along: on one hand, our biographies, on the other, politics. I don't remember why, but I recalled one of the prayers of the late President Roosevelt, which had been published in our newspapers, and I expressed what seemed to me a self-evident evaluation of it:

"Well, that's hypocrisy, of course."

And suddenly the young man's yellowish brows trembled, his pale lips pursed, he seemed to draw himself up, and he asked me: "Why? Why do you not admit the possibility that a political leader might sincerely believe in God?"

And that is all that was said! But what a direction the attack *had* come from! To hear such words from someone born in 1923? I could have replied to him very firmly, but prison had already undermined my certainty, and the principal thing was that some kind of clean, pure feeling does live within us, existing apart from all our convictions, and right then it dawned upon me that I had not spoken out of conviction but because the idea had been implanted in me from outside. And because of this I was unable to reply to him, and I merely asked him: "Do you believe in God?"

"Of course," he answered tranquilly.

Of course? Of course . . . Yes, yes. The Komsomols were flying ahead of the flock—everywhere, but so far only the NKGB had noticed.

Notwithstanding his youth, Borya Gammerov had not only fought as a sergeant in an antitank unit with those antitank 45's the soldiers had christened "Farewell, Motherland!" He had also been wounded in the lungs and the wound had not yet healed, and because of this TB had set in. Gammerov was given a medical discharge from the army and enrolled in the biology department of Moscow University. And thus two strands intertwined in him: one from his life as a soldier and the other from the by no means foolish and by no means dead students' life at war's end. A circle formed of those who thought and reasoned about the future (even though no one had given them any instructions to do so), and the experienced eye of the Organs singled out three of them and pulled them in. (In 1937, Gammerov's father had been killed in prison or shot, and his son was hurrying along the same path. During the interrogation he had read several of his own verses to the interrogator *with feeling*. And I deeply regret that I have not managed to remember even one of them, and there is nowhere to seek them out today. Otherwise I would have cited them here.)

For a number of months after that my path crossed those of all three codefendants: right there in a Butyrki cell I met Vyacheslav D.—and there is always someone like him when young people

are arrested: he had taken an *iron stand* within the group, but
he quickly broke down under interrogation. He got less than any
of the others—five years—and it looked as though he were
secretly counting a good deal on his influential papa to get
him out.

And then in the Butyrki church I encountered Georgi Ingal,
the eldest of the three. Despite his youth, he was already a candi-
date-member of the Union of Soviet Writers. He had a very bold
pen. His style was one of strong contrasts. If he had been willing
to make his peace politically, vivid and untrodden literary paths
would have opened up before him. He had already nearly finished
a novel about Debussy. But his early success had not emasculated
him, and at the funeral of his teacher, Yuri Tynyanov, he had
made a speech declaring that Tynyanov had been persecuted—
and by this means had assured himself of an eight-year term.

And right then Gammerov caught up with us, and, while waiting to go to Krasnaya Presnya, I had to face up to their united
point of view. This confrontation was not easy for me. At the
time I was committed to that world outlook which is incapable
of admitting any new fact or evaluating any new opinion before
a label has been found for it from the already available stock:
be it the "hesitant duplicity of the petty bourgeoisie," or the
"militant nihilism of the déclassé intelligentsia." I don't recall
that Ingal and Gammerov attacked Marx in my presence, but
I do remember how they attacked Lev Tolstoi, and from what
direction the attack was launched! Tolstoi rejected the church?
But he failed to take into account its mystical and its organizing
role. He rejected the teachings of the Bible? But for the most part
modern science was not in conflict with the Bible, not even with
its opening lines about the creation of the world. He rejected the
state? But without the state there would be chaos. He preached
the combining of mental and physical work in one individual's
life? But that was a senseless leveling of capabilities and talents.
And, finally, as we see from Stalin's violence, an historical personage can be omnipotent, yet Tolstoi scoffed at the very idea.[4]

4. In my preprison and prison years I, too, had long ago come to the
conclusion that Stalin had set the course of the Soviet state in a fateful direction. But then Stalin died quietly—and did the ship of state change course
very noticeably? The personal, individual imprint he left on events consisted
of dismal stupidity, petty tyranny, self-glorification. And in all the rest he
followed the beaten path exactly as it had been signposted, step by step.

614 | THE GULAG ARCHIPELAGO

The boys read me their own verses and demanded mine in exchange, and I as yet had none. They read Pasternak particularly, whom they praised to the skies. I had once read "My Sister Life" and hadn't liked it, considering it precious, abstruse, and very, very far from ordinary human paths. But they recited to me Lieutenant Shmidt's last speech at his trial, and it touched me deeply because it applied so to us:

> For thirty years I have nurtured
> My love for my native land,
> And I shall neither expect
> Nor miss your leniency.

Gammerov and Ingal were just as shiningly attuned as that: We do not need your leniency! We are not languishing from *imprisonment;* we are proud of it. (But who is really capable of not languishing? After a few months Ingal's young wife renounced and abandoned him. Gammerov, because of his revolutionary inclinations, did not even have a sweetheart yet.) Was it not here, in these prison cells, that the great truth dawned? The cell was constricted, but wasn't *freedom* even more constricted? Was it not our own people, tormented and deceived, that lay beside us there under the bunks and in the aisles?

> Not to arise with my whole land
> Would have been harder still,
> And for the path that I have trod
> I have no qualms at all.

The young people imprisoned in these cells under the political articles of the Code were never the average young people of the nation, but were always separated from them by a wide gap. In those years most of our young people still faced a future of "disintegrating," of becoming disillusioned, indifferent, falling in love with an easy life—and then, perhaps, beginning all over again the bitter climb from that cozy little valley up to a new peak—possibly after another twenty years? But the young prisoners of 1945, sentenced under 58-10, had leaped that whole future chasm of indifference in one jump—and bore their heads boldly erect under the ax.

In the Butyrki church, the Moscow students, already sentenced, cut off and estranged from everything, wrote a song, and before twilight sang it in their uncertain voices:

> Three times a day we go for gruel,
> The evenings we pass in song,
> With a contraband prison needle
> We sew ourselves *bags* for the road.

> We don't care about ourselves any more,
> *We signed*—just to be quicker!
> And when will we ever return here again
> From the distant Siberian camps?

Good Lord, how could we have missed the main point of the whole thing? While we had been plowing through the mud out there on the bridgeheads, while we had been cowering in shell holes and pushing binocular periscopes above the bushes, back home a new generation had grown up and gotten moving. But hadn't it started moving in *another* direction? In a direction we wouldn't have been able and wouldn't have dared to move in? They weren't brought up the way we were.

Our generation would return—having turned in its weapons, jingling its heroes' medals, proudly telling its combat stories. And our younger brothers would only look at us contemptuously: Oh, you stupid dolts!

END OF PART II

Translator's Notes

These *translator's notes* are not intended to overlap the extensive explanatory and reference material contained in the author's own notes in the text and in the glossary which follows. They attempt to give that minimum of factual material about this book and the whole work of which it is a part which will enable the reader better to put it in perspective and understand what it is, and also to deal with several areas of special Russian terminology.

The *glossary* which follows these notes can be very useful. It gives in alphabetical order capsule identification of persons, institutions and their acronyms, political movements, and events mentioned in the text.

The *title* of the book in Russian—*Arkhipelag GULag*—has a resonance resulting from a rhyme which cannot be rendered in English.

The *image* evoked by this title is that of one far-flung "country" with millions of "natives," consisting of an *archipelago* of islands, some as tiny as a detention cell in a railway station and others as vast as a large Western European country, contained within another country—the U.S.S.R. This archipelago is made up of the enormous network of penal institutions and all the rest of the web of machinery for police oppression and terror imposed throughout the author's period of reference on all Soviet life. Gulag is the acronym for the Chief Administration of Corrective Labor Camps which supervised the larger part of this system.

The author's decision to publish this work was triggered by a tragedy of August, 1973: A Leningrad woman to whom the author had entrusted a portion of his manuscript for safekeeping broke down after 120 sleepless hours of intensive questioning by Soviet Security officers and revealed where she had hidden it—enabling them to seize it. Thereupon, in her desperation and depression, she committed suicide. It is to this event that the author refers in the statement that precedes the text: "Now that State Security has seized the book anyway, I have no alternative but to publish it immediately."

This present English-language edition of Parts I and II of *The Gulag Archipelago* differs very slightly, as a result of author's corrections and other corrections, from the Russian-language first edition of these parts which was published by the YMCA-Press in Paris in late December, 1973.

The Gulag Archipelago is a sweeping, panoramic work which consists in all of seven parts divided into three volumes—of which this present book, the first volume, contains two parts, representing about *one-third* of the whole.

One of the important aspects of Solzhenitsyn as a Russian literary figure is his contribution to the revival and expansion of the Russian literary language through introducing readers in his own country (and abroad) to the language, terminology, and slang of camps, prisons, the police, and the underworld. Millions of Soviet citizens became fully familiar with a whole new vocabulary through imprisonment. But this vocabulary did not find its way into Russian literature until Solzhenitsyn put it there—to the bewilderment of some of the uninitiated.

In this category there are terms in this book which require explanation.

Soviet Security services personnel, for example, are referred to in a variety of special epithets, some of them carrying overtones of contempt. Most of these have been manufactured from the various initials, at one time and another, of the basic Soviet secret police organization:

The oldest of these terms is, of course, "Chekíst"—pronounced "Che-keest," with the accent on the last syllable—from "Cheká." Though the name "Cheka" was replaced more than half a century ago, this label for Soviet Security personnel is still used—and is much beloved by the personnel of the *Organs* themselves.

"Gaybíst," which is pronounced "gay-beest," with the accent on the last syllable, is derived from the letters "g" and "b" standing for State Security.

Likewise "Gaybéshnik"—pronounced "gay-besh-neek," with the accent on the second syllable.

"Emvaydéshnik"—pronounced as it is spelled here, with the accent on the third syllable—is derived similarly from the Russian pronunciation of the letters "M" "V" "D"—for Ministry of Internal Affairs.

"Gaypayóoshnik"—accent also on the third syllable—comes from "G" "P" "U" or "Gaypayóo."

"Osobíst"—pronounced "oh-so-beest," with accent on the last syllable—is an officer of the Special Branch, representing State Security, usually in a military unit—the "Osóby Otdél."

All these terms have their pungent flavor, which comes through even to the English-speaking reader—and they have therefore often been used as is in the text of this translation.

In the Gulag world there was one particular type of police official who had special significance. This was the "operupolnomóchenny"—"óper" for short. Literally rendered, this title means "operations plenipotentiary"—the operations being Security operations, often in a forced-labor camp, where he had enormous power deriving from the fact that he represented State Security in an institution under the Ministry of Internal Affairs. His nickname among the prisoners was "Kum," which can be translated approximately as "godfather" or "father confessor." He was in charge of all camp stool pigeons and he had responsibility for the political supervision of all the prisoners. Throughout this work his title has been translated as "Security operations officer" or more usually just "Security officer," or "Security chief."

The Russian thieves are not just plain ordinary thieves, but constitute a whole underworld subculture which gets much attention and is well described in this book. The Russian thieves are "vóry"—meaning thieves. They are also the "blatnýe" (plural); "blatnói" is the masculine singular form and also the adjective, describing a thing or person attached to the underworld or to the law or companionship of thieves.

The Russian thieves are also the "blatarí" and the "úrki." They are also "tsvetnýe"—in other words "colored." And a person "polutsvetnói"—"half-colored" or "mulatto"—is a non-thief who has begun to take up the ways of the thieves.

By and large, to the extent that these and other terms appear in their original form in this translation they are clearly enough explained. But wherever the word "thief" appears it means one of the "blatnýe."

The language of the Russian thieves is used in this work to refer to much more than themselves.

Thus a nonthief in thief language is a "fráyer." By virtue of being a nonthief he is also naturally "a mark," "a cull," "a pigeon," "an innocent," "a sucker." In this translation, "fráyer" has been rendered throughout as "sucker."

Some other terms that relate to the world of Gulag require special explanation:

At times in the text "ugolóvniki" (which we have translated as "habitual criminals") and "bytovikí" (which we have translated as "nonpolitical offenders") have been grouped together in contrast to the political prisoners.

A "bytovík" is *any* prisoner who is *not* a political nor one of the Russian thieves—and the "bytovikí" or "nonpolitical offenders" make up the enormous main mass of the prisoners. The distinction here is just as much psychological as legal, and in English there is nothing that exactly translates this Russian term.

The "ugolóvniki" or "habitual criminals" are obviously professionals and therefore approximately the same as the thieves.

Chapter 3 in Part I is entitled in Russian "Slédstviye." The correct, legally formal rendering of this word into English would be "investigation." The official conducting the "investigation" is a "slédovatel" or, again in the formal rendering, "investigator." I have, however, chosen, deliberately and after consideration and consultation, generally to translate these Russian terms respectively as "interrogation" and "interrogator." The text of the book makes the reason amply clear. There was in the period and the cases described here no content of "investigation" in this process, nor was there anyone who could legitimately be called an "investigator." There *was* interrogation and there *were* interrogators.

In camps prisoners were divided into those who went out on general-assignment work every day—and therefore died off—and those who got "cushy" jobs within the camp compound at office work, as hospital orderlies, as cooks, bread cutters, assistants in the mess hall, etc., etc.—and thereby were in a better position to survive. These latter were contemptuously christened by the other prisoners "pridúrki"—derived from a verb meaning to shirk general-assignment work. I have here translated "pridúrki" as "trusties." As in many other cases there is no exact English equivalent, but this is certainly as close as there is.

Anyone who wishes to delve further into the lingo of Russian thieves and camps can well make use of the valuable book *Soviet Prison Camp Speech, a Survivor's Glossary,* compiled by Meyer Galler and Harlan E. Marquess, University of Wisconsin Press, 1972.

I wish to thank those who have given me invaluable assistance with this translation—and in the first place and in particular Frances Lindley, my experienced, able, and long-suffering editor at Harper & Row; Dick Passmore, my brilliant copy editor; Theodore Shabad, who has labored long and industriously over the glossary and details in footnotes and text; and also Nina Sobolev, for her long faithful hours of help of all kinds.

Michael Scammell, the well-known British translator and editor, was kind enough to come to New York during the final stages of the preparation of this manuscript and provide the benefit of his own considerable experience in giving the text one last thorough and most useful going over. I am deeply grateful to him.

There are several others who have done more for this project than I can possibly thank them for. But I can at least try—in the knowledge that they will know whom I mean when they read these lines.

Yet with all this, if there are faults in this translation, as no doubt there are, mine is the responsibility.

T.P.W.

Glossary

NAMES

Abakumov, Viktor Semyonovich (1894–1954). Stalin's Minister of State Security, 1946–1952. Executed in December, 1954, under Khrushchev.

Agranov, Yakov Savlovich (?–1939). Deputy People's Commissar of Internal Affairs under Yagoda and Yezhov. Played important role in preparing show trials of 1936–1938. Shot in purges.

Aikhenvald, Yuli Isayevich (1872–1928). Critic and essayist, translated Schopenhauer into Russian. Exiled in 1922.

Akhmatova (Gorenko), Anna Andreyevna (1889–1966). Acmeist poet, wife of Nikolai Gumilyev. Denounced in 1946 as "alien to the Soviet people." Long unpublished in Soviet Union; some works published after 1956.

Aldanov (Landau), Mark Aleksandrovich (1886–1957). Writer of historical novels; emigrated 1919 to Paris, and later to New York.

Aldan-Semyonov, Andrei Ignatyevich (1908–). Soviet writer; imprisoned in Far East camps, 1938–1953. Author of memoirs.

Aleksandrov, A. I. Head of Arts Section of All-Union Society for Cultural Relations with Foreign Countries; purged in 1935.

Alliluyevs. Family of Stalin's second wife, Nadezhda Sergeyevna.

Amfiteatrov, Aleksandr Valentinovich (1862–1938). Russian writer; emigrated 1920.

Anders, Wladyslaw (1892–1970). Polish general; formed Polish military units in Soviet Union and led them out to Iran in 1943.

Andreyev, Leonid Nikolayevich (1871–1919). Playwright and short story writer, close to Expressionism; died in Finland.

Andreyushkin, Pakhomi Ivanovich (1865–1887). Member of Narodnaya Volya terrorist group; executed after attempt to assassinate Alexander III in 1887.

Antonov-Saratovsky, Vladimir Pavlovich (1884–1965). Old Bolshevik, served as judge in Shakhty (1928) and Promparty (1930) trials.

Averbakh, I. L. Soviet jurist; associate of Vyshinsky.

Babushkin, Ivan Vasilyevich (1873–1906). Russian revolutionary.

Bakhtin, Mikhail Mikhailovich (1895–). Literary scholar, expert on Dostoyevsky. Unpublished in Soviet Union from 1930 to 1963.

Bakunin, Mikhail Aleksandrovich (1814–1876). A founder of Anarchism.

Bandera, Stepan (1909–1959). Ukrainian nationalist; led anti-Soviet forces in Ukraine after World War II until 1947; assassinated in Munich by a Soviet agent.

Bedny, Demyan (1883–1945). Soviet poet.

Belinsky, Vissarion Grigoryevich (1811–1848). Literary critic and ardent liberal, champion of socially-conscious literature.

Benois, Aleksandr Nikolayevich (1870–1960). Scenic designer; emigrated 1926 to Paris.

Berdyayev, Nikolai Aleksandrovich (1874–1948). Philosopher, religious thinker; opposed atheism and materialism. Expelled in 1922; lived in Paris after 1924.

Beria, Lavrenti Pavlovich (1899–1953). Georgian Bolshevik, became close Stalin associate in 1938, in charge of secret police and national security. Executed after Stalin's death.

Biron or Biren. Russian name of Count Ernst Johann Bühren (1690–1772). A favorite of Empress Anna Ivanovna, under whom he instituted a tyrannical rule.

Blok, Aleksandr Aleksandrovich (1880–1921). Symbolist poet.

Blücher, Marshal Vasily Konstantinovich (1890–1938). Commander of Far East Military District, 1929–1938; shot in purge.

Blyumkin, Yakov Grigoryevich (1898–1929). A Left Socialist Revolutionary; assassinated German Ambassador Mirbach in Moscow in 1918; later joined Cheka; executed after he took message from Trotsky to Radek.

Boky, Gleb Ivanovich (1879–1941). Secret police official; member of Supreme Court after 1927; arrested in 1937.

Bonch-Bruyevich, Vladimir Dmitriyevich (1873–1955). Bolshevik revolutionary; administrative officer of Council of People's Commissars, 1917–1920.

Bondarin, Sergei Aleksandrovich (1903–). Children's writer.

Budenny, Marshal Semyon Mikhailovich (1883–1973). Civil War hero; commander of Bolshevik cavalry; commander Southwest Front in early phase of World War II.

Bukharin, Nikolai Ivanovich (1888–1938). Prominent Party official and economic theorist; member of Politburo after 1924 and general secretary of Comintern after 1926; expelled from Party in 1929; executed after 1938 show trial.

Bulgakov, Mikhail Afanasyevich (1891–1940). Satirist, most of whose writings have not been published in Soviet Union.

Bulgakov, Sergei Nikolayevich (1871–1944). Religious philosopher; exiled in 1922, lived in Paris.

Bunin, Ivan Alekseyevich (1870–1953). Writer; emigrated 1920 to France; won Nobel Prize in 1933.

Bunyachenko, Sergei K. (?–1946). Commander of 1st Division of Vlasov's forces in World War II; executed in Soviet Union in 1946.

Charnovsky, N. F. (1868–?). Soviet economic official; among defendants in 1930 Promparty trial.

Chekhovsky, Vladimir Moiseyevich (1877–?). Ukrainian nationalist.

Chernov, Viktor Mikhailovich (1873–1952). Socialist Revolutionary Party leader; emigrated in 1920.

Chubar, Vlas Yakovlevich (1891–1939). High Soviet Ukrainian official; shot in purges.

Chukovskaya, Lidiya Korneyevna (1907–). Soviet literary critic and writer (samizdat).

Dal (Dahl), Vladimir Ivanovich (1801–1872). Lexicographer.

Dan (Gurvich), Fyodor Ilyich (1871–1947). Menshevik leader, physician; exiled in 1922.

Denikin, Anton Ivanovich (1872–1947). Tsarist military leader; commanded anti-Bolshevik (White) forces in south, 1918–1920; emigrated.

Derzhavin, Gavriil Romanovich (1743–1816). Poet and statesman under Catherine II.

Dimitrov, Georgi Mikhailovich (1882–1949). Bulgarian Communist leader; chief defendant in 1933 Reichstag trial in Leipzig.

Dolgun, Alexander M. (Alexander D.) (1926–). American-born former employee of United States Embassy in Moscow; spent eight years (1948–1956) in Soviet prisons and labor camps; allowed to leave Soviet Union in 1971.

Donskoi, D. D. (1881–1936). Right Socialist Revolutionary.

Doyarenko, Aleksei G. Soviet agronomist; a defendant in Working Peasants Party case of 1931.

Dukhonin, Nikolai Nikolayevich (1876–1917). Commander in Chief of Tsarist Army; slain by soldiers.

Dyakov, Boris Aleksandrovich (1902–). Author of labor-camp memoirs.

Dzerzhinsky, Feliks Edmundovich (1877–1926). First chief of the secret police (Cheka-GPU-OGPU); succeeded by Menzhinsky.

Ehrenburg, Ilya Grigoryevich (1891–1967). Soviet writer and journalist; spent many years in Paris; author of memoirs of Stalin era.

Etinger, Y. G. (?–1952). Soviet physician, arrested in 1952 in so-called "doctors' case." Died under interrogation.

Fedotov, A. A. (1864–?). A Soviet official; defendant in Shakhty trial.

Figner, Vera Nikolayevna (1852–1942). A leader of Narodnaya Volya group, took part in successful conspiracy to assassinate Alexander II in 1881.

Filonenko, Maksimilian Maksimilianovich. Right Socialist Revolutionary; led anti-Bolshevik forces in Archangel in 1918.

Frank, Semyon Lyudvigovich (1877–1950). Religious philosopher, pupil of Solovyev; exiled in 1922.

Fyodor Ivanovich (1557–1598). Halfwit son of Ivan the Terrible, whom he succeeded in 1584. His regent was Boris Godunov, who reigned as Tsar, 1598–1605.

Gaaz, Fyodor Petrovich (Haas, Friedrich-Joseph) (1780–1853). German-born physician of Moscow prison hospital; sought penal reforms.

Gamarnik, Yan Borisovich (1894–1937). Soviet military leader who committed suicide during purge.

Garin, N. (Mikhailovsky, Nikolai Georgiyevich) (1852–1906). Marxist writer, who depicted young Tsarist engineers.

Gernet, Mikhail Nikolayevich (1874–?). Writer on the death penalty.

Ginzburg, Yevgeniya Semyonovna (1911–). Author of labor-camp memoirs, *Journey into the Whirlwind.*

Gippius, Zinaida Nikolayevna (1869–1945). Writer, wife of Merezhkovsky; emigrated in 1920.

Golikov, Marshal Filipp Ivanovich (1900–). Soviet military leader; supervised repatriation of Red Army prisoners from Germany.

Golyakov, Ivan Terentyevich. Presiding judge of Supreme Court under Stalin.

Gorky, Maxim (Peshkov, Aleksei Maksimovich) (1868–1936). Writer; opposed Bolsheviks at first and lived abroad (1921–1928); returned to Russia in 1931; died under mysterious circumstances.

Gots, Abram Rafailovich (1882–1940). A Right Socialist Revolutionary leader; a defendant in 1922 trial.

Govorov, Marshal Leonid Aleksandrovich (1897–1955). Soviet military leader.

Griboyedov, Aleksandr Sergeyevich (1795–1829). Playwright and diplomat.

Grigorenko, Pyotr Grigoryevich (1907–). Former Red Army general, became a dissident in 1961; in mental asylums since 1969.

Grigoryev, Iosif Fyodorovich (1890–1949). Prominent Soviet geologist.

Grin (Grinovsky), Aleksandr Stepanovich (1880–1932). Writer of romantic, fantastic adventure stories.

Grinevitsky, Ignati Ioakhimovich (1856–1881). Revolutionary, member of Narodnaya Volya group. Threw bomb that killed Alexander II March 13, 1881; was himself mortally wounded.

Groman, Vladimir Gustavovich (1873–?). High Soviet economic official; a defendant in 1931 trial of Mensheviks.

Gromyko, Andrei Andreyevich (1909–). Soviet diplomat; former ambassador to United States and delegate to United Nations; Foreign Minister since 1957.

Gul (Goul), Roman Borisovich (1896–). Émigré writer of historical works; editor of *Novy Zhurnal,* a magazine published in New York.

Gumilyev, Nikolai Stepanovich (1886–1921). Acmeist poet, first husband of Akhmatova; accused in anti-Soviet plot and executed.

Herzen, Aleksandr Ivanovich (1812–1870). Liberal writer.

Ilin, Ivan Aleksandrovich (1882–1954). Mystic philosopher, exiled in 1922.

Ivan Kalita (?–1340). Founder of Grand Duchy of Muscovy.

Ivanov-Razumnik (Ivanov, Razumnik Vasilyevich) (1876–1946). Left Socialist Revolutionary; served in Tsarist prison (1901) and in Soviet labor camps; went to Germany in 1941.

Izgoyev (Lande), Aleksandr Solomonovich (1872–c.1938). A Right Cadet writer; expelled from Soviet Union in 1922.

Izmailov, Nikolai Vasilyevich (1893–). Soviet literary scholar, editor of Pushkin's works.

Kaganovich, Lazar Moiseyevich (1893–). Close associate of Stalin, in charge of railroads. Ousted from leadership in 1957.

Kalinin, Mikhail Ivanovich (1875–1946). Nominal President of Soviet Union (1919–1946), first as Chairman of All-Russian Central Executive Committee until 1922, then as Chairman of Central Executive Committee of U.S.S.R., and after 1938 as Chairman of Presidium of Supreme Soviet.

Kamenev (Rosenfeld), Lev Borisovich (1883–1936). Prominent Bolshevik leader, expelled from Party in 1927, readmitted and re-expelled; executed after 1936 show trial.

Kaplan, Fanya (Dora) (1888–1918). A Left Socialist Revolutionary; executed after unsuccessful attempt on Lenin's life in 1918.

Karakozov, Dmitri Vladimirovich (1840–1866). Revolutionary; executed after unsuccessful attempt on life of Alexander II in 1866.

Karsavin, Lev Platonovich (1882–1952). Mystic philosopher; expert on medieval history; exiled in 1922.

Kasso, Lev Aristidovich (1865–1914). Reactionary Minister of Education under Nicholas II.

Katanyan, Ruben Pavlovich (1881–1966). Soviet state prosecuting official in 1920's and 1930's; arrested 1938.

Kazakov, Ignati Nikolayevich (1891–1938). Physician accused of having murdered Soviet officials through use of "lysates" (antibodies); shot after 1938 show trial.

Kerensky, Aleksandr Fyodorovich (1881–1970). A Socialist Revolutionary leader; headed Provisional Government, July to November, 1917; fled to France; died in New York.

Khrustalev-Nosar, Georgi Stepanovich (1877–1918). Elected Chairman of St. Petersburg Soviet of Workers' Deputies in 1905; opposed Bolsheviks in Ukraine in 1918; shot by Bolsheviks.

Kirov (Kostrikov), Sergei Mironovich (1886–1934). Close Stalin associate; his murder in Leningrad, reputedly inspired by Stalin, set off wave of mass reprisals.

Kishkin, Nikolai Mikhailovich (1864–1930). A leader of Constitutional Democratic Party; a defendant in 1921 trial of famine-relief aides.

Kizevetter (Kiesewetter), Aleksandr Aleksandrovich (1866–1933). Cadet leader and historian; expelled in 1922; lived in Prague.

Klyuchevsky, Vasily Osipovich (1841–1911). Prominent historian.

Klyuyev, Nikolai Alekseyevich (1887–1937). Peasant poet; glorified ancient Russian values, opposing Western cultural influences; exiled to Siberia in early 1930's.

Kolchak, Aleksandr Vasilyevich (1873–1920). Tsarist admiral; led anti-Bolshevik forces in Siberia, 1918–1920; executed.

Koltsov, Nikolai Konstantinovich (1872–1940). Prominent biologist; founded experimental school in Russian biology.

Kondratyev, Nikolai Dmitriyevich (1892–?). Agricultural economist; figure in Working Peasants Party case in 1931.

Kornilov, Lavr Georgiyevich (1870–1918). Commander in Chief of Russian forces under Provisional Government; led revolt against Kerensky in August, 1917; fought Bolsheviks in Don area; killed in battle.

Korolenko, Vladimir Galaktionovich (1853–1921). Peasant democratic writer; persecuted under Tsars; viewed as bourgeois by Bolsheviks.

Kosarev, Aleksandr Vasilyevich (1903–1939). Leader of the Komsomol, 1929–1938.

Kosior, Stanislav Vikentyevich (1889–1939). Ukrainian Bolshevik leader; shot in purges.

Kozyrev, Nikolai Aleksandrovich (1908–). Astronomer; in prison, 1937–1948.

Krasikov, Pyotr Ananyevich (1870–1939). Old Bolshevik; prosecuting and justice official in 1920's and 1930's.

Krasnov (Levitin), Anatoly Emanuilovich (1915–). Religious writer; imprisoned under Stalin; in dissident movement after 1960.

Krasnov, Pyotr Nikolayevich (1869–1947). Don Cossack leader; emigrated in 1919; led pro-German Russian units in World War II; handed over by Allies after war and executed in Soviet Union.

Krestinsky, Nikolai Nikolayevich (1883–1938). Bolshevik Party official and diplomat; shot after 1938 show trial.

Kruglov, Sergei Nikiforovich (1903–). Minister of Interior, 1946–1956.

Krylenko, Nikolai Vasilyevich (1885–1938). Chief state prosecutor, 1918–1931; later People's Commissar of Justice; shot in 1938.

Krylov, Ivan Andreyevich (1769–1844). Noted fabulist.

Kuibyshev, Valerian Vladimirovich (1888–1935). Prominent economic planning official; died under mysterious circumstances.

Kupriyanov, G. N. Karelian Party official; arrested in 1949.

Kursky, Dmitri Ivanovich (1874–1932). People's Commissar of Justice, 1918–1928; envoy to Italy, 1928–1932.

Kuskova, Yekaterina Dmitriyevna (1869–1958). Cadet, later SR; figure in Famine Relief case 1921; exiled in 1922.

Kuznetsov, Aleksei Aleksandrovich (1905–1950). Lieutenant general, one of the organizers of the defense of Leningrad, Secretary of the Central Committee, convicted in connection with the Leningrad Affair.

Kuznetsov, Col. Gen. Vasily Ivanovich (1894–1964). Soviet military leader in World War II.

Lapshin, Ivan Ivanovich (1870–1948). Philosopher; exiled in 1922 to Prague, where he died.

Larichev, Viktor A. (1887–?). Chairman, Main Fuels Committee; figure in Promparty trial in 1930.

Larin, Y. (Lurye, Mikhail Aleksandrovich) (1882–1932). Agricultural economist; former Menshevik; helped found Soviet planning system.

Latsis (Lacis), Martyn Ivanovich (Sudrabs, Yan Fridrikhovich) (1888–1941). Early Cheka official, 1917–1921; director, Plekhanov Economics Institute, 1932–1937; arrested 1937.

Lelyushenko, Dmitri Danilovich (1901–). Soviet World War II leader.

Lermontov, Mikhail Yuryevich (1814–1841). Liberal poet.

Levina, Revekka Saulovna (1899–1964). Soviet economist.

Levitan, Yuri Borisovich (1914–). Soviet radio announcer noted for his sonorous voice, which became familiar through announcement of major Soviet successes in World War II and other news events.

Levitin. *See* Krasnov, A. E.

Likhachev, Nikolai Petrovich (1862–1935). Historian, specialist on ikon painting.

Lomonosov, Mikhail Vasilyevich (1711–1765). Universal scholar; in Russian spiritual history, prototype of scientific genius arising from the people.

Lordkipanidze, G. S. (1881–1937). Georgian writer; died in purge.

Loris-Melikov, Mikhail Tarpelovich (1825–1888). Powerful Tsarist Interior Minister, 1880–1881; initiator of unimplemented reforms.

Lorkh, Aleksandr Georgiyevich (1889–). Prominent potato breeder.

Lossky, Nikolai Onufriyevich (1870–1965). Philosopher; exiled in 1922.

Lozovsky, A. (Dridzo, Solomon Abramovich) (1878–1952). Revolutionary; chief of Trade Union International, 1921–1937; Deputy People's Commissar for Foreign Affairs and head of Sovinformburo in World War II; shot in anti-Jewish purge.

Lunacharsky, Anatoly Vasilyevich (1875–1932). Marxist cultural theorist; People's Commissar for Education, 1917–1929.

Lunin, Mikhail Sergeyevich (1787–1845). One of the Decembrists; wrote philosophical and political tracts in Siberian exile.

Lysenko, Trofim Denisovich (1898–). Agricultural biologist; virtual dictator of Soviet science after 1940 under Stalin, and of biology in the Khrushchev era until 1964.

Maisky, Ivan Mikhailovich (1884–). Historian and diplomat; former Menshevik; envoy to Britain, 1932–1943; Deputy Foreign Commissar, 1943–1946.

Makarenko, Anton Semyonovich (1888–1939). Educator; organized rehabilitation colonies for juvenile delinquents.

Malinovsky, Roman Vatslavovich (1876–1918). Tsarist police informer planted among Bolsheviks; emigrated in 1914; returned to Russia voluntarily in 1918, when he was tried and executed.

Mandelstam, Osip Emilyevich (1891–1938). Acmeist poet; died in transit camp.

Mariya, Mother. *See* Skobtsova.

Markos, Gen. Vafiades (1906–). Greek leftist rebel leader, 1947–1948.

Martov (Tsederbaum), Yuli Osipovich (1873–1923). A Menshevik leader; exiled by Lenin in 1921.

Mayakovsky, Vladimir Vladimirovich (1893–1930). Futurist poet; suicide.

Meck, Nikolai Karlovich von (1863–1929). Tsarist railroad industrialist; worked for Bolsheviks after 1917; accused of counterrevolutionary activities and shot.

Melgunov, Sergei Petrovich (1879–1956). Historian and Popular Socialist leader; exiled in 1923; lived in Paris.

Menshikov, Aleksandr Danilovich (1673–1729). Military leader and statesman; favorite of Peter the Great and Catherine I.

Menzhinsky, Vyacheslav Rudolfovich (1874–1934). Secret police official; headed OGPU, 1926–1934.

Meretskov, Marshal Kirill Afanasyevich (1897–1968). World War II leader.

Merezhkovsky, Dmitri Sergeyevich (1865–1941). Philosopher and novelist; founder of Symbolist movement; emigrated 1919 to Paris.

Mikhailov, Nikolai Aleksandrovich (1906–). Chief of Komsomol, 1938–1952; later envoy to Poland and Indonesia, Minister of Culture, chairman of State Publishing Committee; retired 1970.

Mikolajczyk, Stanislaw (1901–1966). Polish Peasant Party leader; in Polish government in exile during World War II; in Polish postwar government, 1945–1947.

Mikoyan, Anastas Ivanovich (1895–). Close associate of Stalin; in charge of consumer-goods area; foreign policy adviser to Khrushchev; retired 1966.

Milyukov, Pavel Nikolayevich (1859–1943). Leader of Constitutional Democratic Party and historian; emigrated in 1920; died in U.S.A.

Mirovich, Vasily Yakovlevich (1740–1764). Attempted palace coup under Catherine II in favor of pretender Ivan IV Antonovich.

Molotov (Skryabin), Vyacheslav Mikhailovich (1890–). Close associate of Stalin; served as Premier and Foreign Minister; ousted by Khrushchev after so-called 1957 anti-Party coup; retired.

Monomakh. *See* Vladimir II.

Myakotin, Venedikt Aleksandrovich (1867–1937). Historian and a founder of Popular Socialist Party; exiled in 1922.

Nabokov (Sirin), Vladimir (1899–). Russian-American writer; son of F. D. Sirin, a Cadet leader, who emigrated in 1919.

Narokov (Marchenko), Nikolai Vladimirovich (1887–1969). Émigré writer; left Soviet Union in World War II; lived in Monterey, Calif.

Natanson, Mark Andreyevich (1850–1919). Populist, later a Socialist Revolutionary; sided with Bolsheviks during World War I; died in Switzerland.

Nekrasov, Nikolai Alekseyevich (1821–1878). Civic poet.

Novikov, Nikolai Ivanovich (1744–1818). Writer and social critic; incarcerated in Schlüsselburg Fortress under Catherine II.

Novorussky, Mikhail Vasilyevich (1861–1925). Revolutionary, convicted with Aleksandr Ulyanov after abortive attempt to assassinate Alexander III in 1887; death sentence commuted to imprisonment in Schlüsselburg.

Obolensky, Yevgeny Petrovich (1796–1865). One of the Decembrists; death sentence commuted to 20 years' Siberian exile.

Olitskaya, Yekaterina Lvovna (1898–). Soviet dissident writer whose prison-camp memoirs circulated in samizdat and were published in 1971 by Possev, Russian-language publishing house of Frankfurt, West Germany.

Olminsky (Aleksandrov), Mikhail Stepanovich (1863–1933). Early professional revolutionary, journalist.

Ordzhonikidze, Grigory (Sergo) Konstantinovich (1886–1937). Close associate of Stalin, charged with heavy industry; a suicide during purges.

Osorgin (Ilin), Mikhail Andreyevich (1878–1942). Writer; exiled in 1922.

Palchinsky, Pyotr Akimovich (1878–1929). Economist and mining engineer; chief defendant in Shakhty trial of 1928; shot.

Pasternak, Boris Leonidovich (1890–1960). Poet and novelist; 1958 Nobel laureate.

Perkhurov, Aleksandr Petrovich (1876–1922). Anti-Bolshevik military commander; shot in Yaroslavl in 1922.

Peshekhonov, Aleksei Vasilyevich (1867–1933). Writer; exiled in 1922.

Peshkova-Vinaver, Yekaterina Pavlovna (1876–1965). First wife of Maxim Gorky; headed Political Red Cross.

Pestel, Pavel Ivanovich (1793–1826). One of the Decembrists, leader of radical wing; hanged.

Peters, Yakov Khristoforovich (1886–1942). Latvian revolutionary; high secret police official in 1920's; liquidated.

Petlyura, Simon Vasilyevich (1879–1926). Ukrainian nationalist leader; headed anti-Bolshevik forces in Ukraine, 1918–1919; assassinated in Paris exile.

Pilnyak (Vogau), Boris Andreyevich (1894–1937). Soviet writer; accused of distorting revolutionary events; died in prison.

Platonov, Sergei Fyodorovich (1860–1933). Historian; in official disfavor in early 1930's.

Plekhanov, Georgi Valentinovich (1856–1918). Marxist philosopher and historian, became a Menshevik leader; opposed Bolsheviks' 1917 coup.

Pletnev, Dmitri Dmitriyevich (1872–1953). Physician; sentenced to 25 years after 1938 show trial.

Pobedonostsev, Konstantin Petrovich (1827–1907). Lawyer and politician; Procurator of the Holy Synod; his reactionary Russian nationalist views were influential under Alexander III and in the early reign of Nicholas II.

Postyshev, Pavel Petrovich (1887–1940). Ukrainian Bolshevik leader; arrested in 1938; died in prison.

Potemkin, Grigory Aleksandrovich (1739–1791). Military leader and favorite of Catherine the Great.

Prokopovich, Sergei Nikolayevich (1871–1955). Economist and a Cadet leader; figure in 1921 Famine Relief Commission trial; expelled 1922.

Ptukhin, Lieut. Gen. Yevgeny Savvich (1900–1941). Soviet Air Force commander; executed after German attack against Soviet Union.

Pugachev, Yemelyan Ivanovich (1742–1775). Leader of a major peasant revolt against Catherine II; executed.

Radek, Karl Berngardovich (1885–1939). Comintern official, later journalist; shot after 1937 show trial.

Radishchev, Aleksandr Nikolayevich (1749–1802). Writer and social critic; exiled to Siberia by Catherine II.

Rakovsky, Khristian Georgiyevich (1873–1941). Bolshevik official who served as Ukrainian Premier, 1919–1923, and diplomat, 1923–1927; imprisoned after 1938 show trial; daughter Yelena arrested 1948.

Ramzin, Leonid Konstantinovich (1887–1948). Heat engineer; principal defendant in 1930 Promparty trial; death sentence commuted to 10 years; professionally active again during World War II.

Ransome, Arthur (1884–1967). British journalist; wrote on Bolshevik Revolution.

Raskolnikov (Ilin), Fyodor Fyodorovich (1892–1939). Bolshevik diplomat; defected in France; died under mysterious circumstances.

Rasputin, Grigory Yefimovich (1872–1916). Adventurer with strong influence over family of Nicholas II; killed by courtiers.

Razin, Stepan Timofeyevich (Stenka) (1630?–1671). Leader of a Cossack and peasant rebellion in the middle and lower Volga territories, he was defeated and executed; legendary figure in Russian national poetry.

Reilly, Sidney George (1874–1925). British intelligence officer; killed while crossing Soviet-Finnish border.

Repin, Ilya Yefimovich (1844–1930). Prominent painter; one of his works depicts the Volga boatmen.

Rokossovsky, Marshal Konstantin Konstantinovich (1896–1968). Soviet World War II leader; Defense Minister in Poland, 1949–1956.

Romanov, Panteleimon Sergeyevich (1884–1938). Soviet satirist.

Rudzutak, Yan Ernestovich (1887–1938). Associate of Stalin; arrested 1937; died in prison.

Ryabushinsky, Pavel Pavlovich (1871–1924). Russian industrialist and anti-Bolshevik leader; mentioned in 1930 Promparty trial.

Rykov, Aleksei Ivanovich (1881–1938). Close associate of Stalin; Premier of Soviet Union, 1924–1930; shot after 1938 show trial.

Ryleyev, Kondrati Fyodorovich (1795–1826). A Decembrist; hanged.

Rysakov, Nikolai Ivanovich (1861–1881). A revolutionary of Narodnaya Volya group; executed after assassination of Alexander II in 1881.

Ryumin, M. D. (?–1953). Secret police official who engineered the "doctors' case"; executed 1953.

Ryurik. Legendary Varangian prince who came to Novgorod in mid-ninth century and founded first Russian dynasty.

Sakharov, Col. Igor K. Émigré who commanded pro-German Russian military unit in World War II.

Saltychikha (Saltykova, Darya Nikolayevna) (1730–1801). Woman landowner in Moscow Province; noted for cruel treatment of serfs.

Samsonov, Aleksandr Vasilyevich (1859–1914). Tsarist general; suicide after his forces were defeated in East Prussia in World War I.

Savinkov, Boris Viktorovich (1879–1925). A Socialist Revolutionary leader; arrested after he re-entered Russia illegally in 1924.

Savva (1327–1406). Russian Orthodox saint; pupil of Sergius of Radonezh.

Sedin, Ivan K. People's Commissar for Petroleum in World War II.

Selivanov, Dmitri Fyodorovich (1885–?). Mathematician; emigrated 1922.

Serebryakova, Galina Iosifovna (1905–). Writer; author of camp memoirs.

Sergius of Radonezh (1321–1391). Russian Orthodox saint; founded monasteries, including Trinity-St. Sergius at Zagorsk, near his home town, Radonezh.

Serov, Ivan Aleksandrovich (1905–). Secret police official; chairman of KGB, 1954–1958.

Shalamov, Varlam Tikhonovich (1907–). Writer; spent 17 years in Kolyma camps; author of *Kolyma Stories* (Paris, 1969).

Shchastny, Captain Aleksei Mikhailovich (?–1918). Commander of Red Baltic Fleet; executed.

Shcherbakov, Alekandr Sergeyevich (1901–1945). Close associate of Stalin; Moscow city secretary, 1938–1945; Chief of Red Army's Political Department, 1942–1945.

Sheinin, Lev Romanovich (1906–1967). Soviet prosecuting and investigatory official; wrote spy stories after 1950.

Sheshkovsky, Stepan Ivanovich (1727–1793). Judicial investigator under Catherine II; known for harsh interrogatory techniques.

Shmidt, Pyotr Petrovich (1867–1906). Lieutenant in Black Sea Fleet; executed after Sevastopol revolt.

Sholokhov, Mikhail Aleksandrovich (1905–). Soviet writer; 1965 Nobel laureate.

Shulgin, Vasily Vitalyevich (1878–1965). Monarchist; emigrated after 1917 Revolution; caught by Red Army in Yugoslavia at end of World War II; served 10 years in labor camp.

Shvernik, Nikolai Mikhailovich (1888–1970). Associate of Stalin; trade-union chief, 1930–1944 and 1953–1956; President of Soviet Union, 1946–1953.

Sikorski, Wladyslaw (1881–1943). Military leader of Polish exiles.

Skobtsova, Yelizaveta Yuryevna (1892–1945). Acmeist poet; emigrated to Paris, where she became a nun (Mother Mariya); died in Nazi camp.

Skrypnik, Nikolai Alekseyevich (1872–1933). Ukrainian People's Commissar for Justice (1922–1927) and Education (1927–1933); suicide.

Skuratov, Malyuta (Belsky, Grigory Lukyanovich) (?–1572). Trusted aide of Ivan the Terrible; personifies Ivan's cruelties; headed Oprichnina, a policelike organization.

Smirnov, Ivan Nikitovich (1881–1936). Soviet People's Commissar for Communications, 1923–1927; expelled from Party; shot after 1936 trial.

Smushkevich, Yakov Vladimirovich (1902–1941). Soviet Air Force commander; executed after German invasion.

Sokolnikov, Grigory Yakovlevich (1888–1939). Soviet People's Commissar of Finance, 1922–1926; envoy to Britain, 1929–1934; sentenced to 10 years after 1937 show trial; died in prison.

Solovyev, Vladimir Sergeyevich (1853–1900). Religious philosopher; sought synthesis of Russian Orthodox faith and Western scientific thought and Roman Catholicism.

Stalin, Iosif Vissarionovich (1879–1953). Soviet political leader; named General Secretary of the Communist Party in 1922. After Lenin's death in 1924, he gradually eliminated political rivals in series of purges culminating in great trials of 1936–1938. His original family name was Dzhugashvili; revolutionary party name was Koba.

Stanislavsky, Konstantin Sergeyevich (1863–1938). Stage director; cofounder of the Moscow Art Theater in 1898; known in the West for the "Stanislavsky method" of acting technique.

Stepun, Fyodor Augustovich (1884–1965). Philosopher; expelled in 1922.

Stolypin, Pyotr Arkadyevich (1862–1911). Tsarist statesman; served as Minister of Interior after 1906; known for agrarian reform resettling poor peasants in Siberia; slain by an SR.

Sudrabs. *See* Latsis.

Sukhanov (Gimmer), Nikolai Nikolayevich (1882–1940). Menshevik historian; meeting at his apartment in Petrograd in October, 1917, the Bolsheviks decided to launch an armed uprising; figure in 1931 Menshevik trial; released after hunger strike; rearrested in purges of late 1930's; author of detailed account of the Bolshevik Revolution.

Surikov, Vasily Ivanovich (1848–1916). Historical painter of the realist school.

Suvorov, Aleksandr Vasilyevich (1729–1800). Military leader; led Italian and Swiss campaigns against Napoleon.

Svechin, Aleksandr Andreyevich (1878–1935). Military historian; shot.

Sverdlov, Yakov Mikhailovich (1885–1919). First Soviet President.

Tagantsev, Nikolai Stepanovich (1843–1923). Writer on criminal law.

Tarle, Yevgeny Viktorovich (1875–1955). Soviet historian; was briefly in official disfavor in early 1930's.

Tikhon, Patriarch (1865–1925). Head of Russian Orthodox Church after 1917; detained 1922–1923 on oppositionist charges.

Timofeyev-Ressovsky, Nikolai Vladimirovich (1900–). Soviet radiobiologist; worked in Germany, 1924–1945; spent 10 years in Stalin camps after return to Soviet Union.

Tolstoi, Alexandra Lvovna (1884–). Youngest dauthter of Lev Tolber of 1937 Supreme Soviet (national legislature).

Tolstoi, Alexandra Lvovna (1884–). Youngest daughter of Lev Tolstoi; author of a biography of her father; lives in the U.S., where she founded the Tolstoi Foundation for aid to refugees.

Tomsky, Mikhail Pavlovich (1880–1936). First Soviet chief of trade unions, until 1929; suicide in Stalin purges.

Trotsky (Bronshtein), Lev (Leon) Davidovich (1879–1940). Associate of Lenin; first Soviet Defense Commissar, until 1925; expelled from Party in 1927; deported to Turkey in 1929; slain in Mexico City by a Soviet agent.

Trubetskoi, Sergei Petrovich (1790–1860). One of the Decembrists; death sentence commuted to exile; amnestied in 1856.

Tsvetayeva, Marina Ivanovna (1892–1941). Poet; lived abroad 1922 to 1939; a suicide two years after return to Soviet Union.

Tukhachevsky, Mikhail Nikolayevich (1893–1937). Soviet military leader; shot in 1937 on trumped-up treason charges.

Tur Brothers. Pen names of two playwrights and authors of spy stories: Leonid Davydovich Tubelsky (1905–1961) and Pyotr Lvovich Ryzhei (1908–).

Tynyanov, Yuri Nikolayevich (1895–1943). Soviet writer and literary scholar.

Ulrikh, Vasily Vasilyevich (1889–1951). Supreme Court justice; presided over major trials of 1920's and 1930's.

Ulyanov, Aleksandr Ilyich (1866–1887). Lenin's older brother; executed after unsuccessful attempt to assassinate Alexander III in 1887.

Ulyanova (Yelizarova-Ulyanova), Anna Ilyinichna (1874–1935). Lenin's sister; journalist and editor.

Uritsky, Moisei Solomonovich (1873–1918). Revolutionary; chairman of the Petrograd Cheka; his assassination by an SR set off Red Terror.

Utyosov, Leonid Osipovich (1895–). Soviet orchestra leader and variety-stage star.

Valentinov (Volsky), Nikolai Vladislavovich (1879–1964). Journalist and philosopher; former Bolshevik turned Menshevik; emigrated 1930.

Vasilyev-Yuzhin, Mikhail Ivanovich (1876–1937). Revolutionary; secret police and justice official.

Vavilov, Nikolai Ivanovich (1887–1943). Prominent plant geneticist; Director of Institute of Applied Botany (1924–1940) and Institute of Genetics (1930–1940); arrested 1940; died in imprisonment.

Vereshchagin, Vasily Vasilyevich (1842–1904). Painter noted for battle scenes.

Vladimir II Monomakh. Ruler of Kievan Russia, 1113–1125.

Vladimirov (Sheinfinkel), Miron Konstantinovich (1879–1925). Early Soviet official in agriculture, finance and economic management.

Vlasov, Lieut. Gen. Andrei Andreyevich (1900–1946). Red Army officer; captured by Germans in 1942; led Russian forces against Soviet Union; handed over by Allies after war and executed.

Voikov, Pyotr Lazarevich (1888–1927). Bolshevik revolutionary; Soviet representative in Warsaw, 1924–1927; assassinated by an émigré.

Voloshin, Maksimilian Aleksandrovich (1878–1932). Symbolist poet and watercolorist; opposed Bolsheviks.

Voroshilov, Kliment Yefremovich (1881–1969). Close associate of Stalin; long Defense Commissar; Soviet President, 1953–1960.

Vysheslavtsev, Boris Petrovich (1877–1954). Philosopher; exiled in 1922.

Vyshinsky, Andrei Yanuaryevich (1883–1954). Lawyer and diplomat; former Menshevik turned Bolshevik; chief state prosecutor in show trials, 1936–1938; Deputy Foreign Commissar and Minister, 1939–1949 and 1953–1954; Foreign Minister, 1949–1953.

Wrangel, Pyotr Nikolayevich (1878–1928). Tsarist military commander; led anti-Bolshevik forces in South in 1920 after Denikin.

Yagoda, Genrikh Grigoryevich (1891–1938). Secret police official; People's Commissar of Internal Affairs, 1934–1936; shot after 1938 show trial.

Yakubovich, Pyotr Filippovich (1860–1911). Poet; translated Baudelaire; wrote memoirs about his Tsarist exile.

Yaroshenko, Nikolai Aleksandrovich (1846–1898). Painter.

Yenukidze, Avel Safronovich (1877–1937). Bolshevik official; Secretary of Central Executive Committee, 1918–1935; shot in purges.

Yermilov, Vladimir Vladimirovich (1904–1965). Soviet literary critic.

Yesenin, Sergei Aleksandrovich (1895–1925). Imagist poet; suicide.

Yezhov, Nikolai Ivanovich (1895–1939). Secret police official; People's Commissar of Internal Affairs, 1936–1938.

Yudenich, Nikolai Nikolayevich (1862–1933). Tsarist military commander; led anti-Bolshevik forces in Estonia, 1918–1920.

Zalygin, Sergei Pavlovich (1913–). Soviet writer.

Zamyatin, Yevgeny Ivanovich (1884–1937). Writer; returned 1917 from abroad, but opposed Bolsheviks; emigrated in 1932; his novel *We,* published in London in 1924, influenced Huxley, Orwell.

Zasulich, Vera Ivanovna (1849–1919). Revolutionary; acquitted after attempt to assassinate Mayor of St. Petersburg; emigrated 1880; returned 1905; became Menshevik.

Zavalishin, Dmitri Irinarkhovich (1804–1892). One of the Decembrists; sentenced to 20 years' Siberian exile; worked as journalist after 1863.

Zhdanov, Andrei Aleksandrovich (1896–1948). Close associate of Stalin; shaped cultural policy after World War II.

Zhebrak, Anton Romanovich (1901–1965). Soviet geneticist.

Zhelyabov, Andrei Ivanovich (1851–1881). Revolutionary; executed after his assassination of Alexander II in 1881.

Zhukov, Marshal Georgi Konstantinovich (1896–). World War II leader.

Zinoviev (Apfelbaum), Grigory Yevseyevich (1883–1936). Associate of Lenin; expelled from Party in 1927; shot after 1936 show trial.

INSTITUTIONS AND TERMS

All-Russian Central Executive Committee. *See* VTsIK.

April Theses. A programmatic statement issued by Lenin in April, 1917, calling for end of war with Germany and transfer of power to the Soviets.

Basmachi. Name given to anti-Bolshevik forces in Central Asia after 1917 Revolution.

Black Hundreds. Armed reactionary groups in Tsarist Russia; active from about 1905 to 1917 in pogroms of Jews and political assassinations of liberal personalities.

Butyrki. A major Moscow prison, named for a district of Moscow; often known also as Butyrka.

Cadet. *See* Constitutional Democratic Party.

Chechen. Ethnic group of Northern Caucasus; exiled by Stalin in 1944 on charges of collaboration with German forces.

Cheka. Original name of the Soviet secret police, 1917–1922; succeeded by GPU.

Chinese Eastern Railroad. A Manchurian rail system built (1897–1903) as part of original Trans-Siberian Railroad. Jointly operated by Chinese and Soviet authorities until 1935 (when it was sold to Japanese-dominated Manchukuo government) and again in 1945–1950. Russian acronym: KVZhD.

Codes. The 1926 Criminal Code and the 1923 Code of Criminal Procedure were repealed in 1958 with the adoption of new Fundamental Principles of Criminal Legislation and Criminal Procedure; in 1960 these were embodied in a new Criminal Code and a new Code of Criminal Procedure.

Collegium. Governing board of Soviet government departments and other institutions.

Comintern. Acronym for Communist International, the world organization of Communist parties that existed from 1919 to 1943.

Committee of the Poor, also known by the Russian acronym Kombed. A Bolshevik-dominated organization of poor peasants (1918).

Constituent Assembly. A multiparty legislative body with large anti-Bolshevik majority, elected in November, 1917, after the Bolshevik Revolution. It met in January, 1918, but was broken up when it refused to adopt Bolshevik proposals.

Constitutional Democratic Party. Founded in 1905 under the Tsars, advocating a constitutional monarchy; played a conservative role after overthrow of Tsar; members were known as Cadets, from a Russian acronym for the party.

Council of People's Commissars. Name given the Soviet cabinet (government) before 1946, when it became the Council of Ministers; also known by Russian acronym Sovnarkom.

Crimean Tatars. Exiled by Stalin to Central Asia in 1944 on charges of collaboration with Germans.

Dashnak. Anti-Bolshevik group in Armenia after 1917 Revolution.

Decembrists. Group of Russian officers who took part in unsuccessful liberal uprising against Nicholas I in December, 1825.

Doctors' case. The arrest of leading Kremlin physicians, most of them Jews, in 1952 on trumped-up charges of plotting against the lives of Soviet leaders. At least one, Y. G. Etinger, is believed to have died under interrogation; the others were released after Stalin's death in 1953.

Famine Relief, State Commission for. A Soviet governmental body, set up in 1921–1922; also known by the Russian acronym Pomgol.

GPU. Designation for Soviet secret police in 1922; acronym for Russian words meaning State Political Administration; continued to be used popularly after 1922, when the official designation became OGPU, acronym for United State Political Administration.

Gulag. The Soviet penal system under Stalin; a Russian acronym for Chief Administration of Corrective Labor Camps.

Hehalutz. Zionist movement that prepared young Jews for settling in Holy Land; it founded most of the kibbutzim.

Hiwi. German designation for Russian volunteers in German armed forces during World War II; acronym for Hilfswillige.

Industrial Academy. A Moscow school that served as training ground of industrial managers in late 1920's and early 1930's.

Industrial Party. *See* Promparty.

Informburo. *See* Sovinformburo.

Ingush. Ethnic group of Northern Caucasus; exiled by Stalin in 1944 on charges of collaboration with Germans.

Isolator. (1) Type of political prison established in early stage of Soviet regime for fractious Bolsheviks and other political foes. (2) In a labor camp, the designation for a building with punishment cells.

Kalmyks. Ethnic group of Northern Caucasus; exiled by Stalin in 1943 on charges of collaboration with German forces.

KGB. Acronym for Soviet secret police after 1953; stands for State Security Committee.

Khalkhin-Gol. River on border between China and Mongolia. Scene of Soviet-Japanese military clashes in 1939.

Khasan. Lake on Soviet-Chinese border, near Sea of Japan. Scene of Soviet-Japanese military clash in 1938.

Kolyma. Region of northeast Siberia; center of labor camps under Stalin.

Komsomol. Russian acronym for Young Communist League.

KVZhD. *See* Chinese Eastern Railroad.

Labor day. Accounting unit on collective farms.

Lubyanka. Popular designation for secret police headquarters and prison in central Moscow, named for adjacent street and square (now Dzerzhinsky Street and Square); housed Rossiya Insurance Company before the 1917 Revolution.

Makhorka. A coarse tobacco (*Nicotiana rustica*) grown mainly in the Ukraine.

Mensheviks. Democratic faction of Marxist socialists; split in 1903 from Bolshevik majority; repressed after 1917 Bolshevik Revolution.

MGB. Initials for Soviet secret police, 1946–1953; acronym for Ministry of State Security; succeeded by KGB.

MVD. Russian acronym for Ministry of Interior; performed secret police function briefly in 1953.

Narodnaya Volya (literal translation: People's Will). Secret terrorist society dedicated to overthrowing Tsarism; existed from 1879 until disbanded in 1881 after assassination of Alexander II.

Narodnik (Populist). Member of populist revolutionary movement under the Tsars.

NEP. Acronym for New Economic Policy, a period of limited private enterprise, 1921–1928.

Nine grams. A bullet.

NKGB. Designation of Soviet secret police, 1943–1946; acronym for People's Commissariat of State Security.

NKVD. Designation of Soviet secret police, 1934–1943; acronym for People's Commissariat of Internal Affairs.

OGPU. Designation of Soviet secret police, 1922–1934; acronym for United State Political Administration.

Okhrana. Name of Tsarist secret police from 1881 to 1917; Russian word means "protection," replacing the full designation Department for the Protection of Public Security and Order.

OSO. *See* Special Board.

People's Commissariat. Name of Soviet government departments from 1917 to 1946, when they were renamed "Ministry."

Petrograd. Official name of Leningrad, 1914–1924.

Polizei. German word for "police"; designation of Russians who served as police under German occupation in World War II.

Pomgol. *See* Famine Relief.

Popular Socialist Party. Founded in 1906, it favored general democratic reforms, opposed terrorism.

Promparty. Mixed Russian-English acronym for Industrial Party (in Russian, Promyshlennaya Partiya). Nonexistent underground to which the organization of industrial managers tried in 1930 allegedly belonged.

Provisional Government. Coalition government of Russia after overthrow of Tsarism, March to November, 1917; first under Prince Georgi Lvov, later under Kerensky; overthrown by Bolsheviks.

Revolutionary Tribunal (Revtribunal). Special Soviet courts (1917–1922), which tried counterrevolutionary cases.

Russkaya Pravda. Political program of the Decembrists; drafted by Pestel; the Russian words mean "Russian truth."

Sapropelite Committee. A scientific study group that sought to use bituminous lake-bottom ooze, or sapropel, as a fuel around 1920.

Schlüsselburg. Fortress on Lake Ladoga, at outlet of Neva River; used as political prison under Tsars; now called Petrokrepost.

Schutzbund. Armed contingents of Austrian Social Democrats; members sought refuge in Soviet Union in 1934 after defeat in civil war.

Sharashka. Russian prison slang for a special research center in which the research scientists, specialists, and technicians are all prisoners under prison discipline.

Short Course. Familiar title of the standard Stalinist version of the history of the Soviet Communist Party; used as the official text from 1938 until after Stalin's death in 1953.

SMERSH. Acronym for Soviet counterintelligence during World War II; stands for "death to spies."

Smolny. Former girls' school; Communist Party headquarters in Leningrad.

Socialist Revolutionary Party. Created in 1890's out of several populist groups; split at first congress held in Finland in December, 1905, into right wing, opposed to terrorism, and left wing, favoring terrorism; SR's played key role in Provisional Government; left wing cooperated briefly with Bolsheviks after Revolution.

Solovetsky Islands (colloquially known as **Solovki**). Island group in White Sea, with monasteries; used as place of exile for rebellious priests in Middle Ages; early forced-labor camp (SLON) after 1917 Revolution.

Sovinformburo. Soviet information agency in World War II.

Sovnarkom. *See* Council of People's Commissars.

Special Board (Russian acronym: **OSO**). Three-man boards of People's Commissariat of Internal Affairs, with powers to sentence "socially dangerous" persons without trial; abolished in 1953.

SR. *See* Socialist Revolutionary Party.

Stolypin car. A railroad car used to transport prisoners, named for P. A. Stolypin; also known in prison slang as vagonzak, for vagon zaklyuchennykh (prisoner car).

Supreme Council of the Economy. Highest industrial management agency in early years of Soviet regime; established in 1917; abolished 1932, when it was divided into industrial ministries.

Supreme Soviet. The national legislature of the Soviet Union, with counterparts in its constituent republics; meets usually twice a year to approve decisions taken by the Soviet leadership. Its lawmaking function is performed between sessions by the Presidium of the Supreme Soviet; nominally the highest state body in the Soviet Union.

Time of Troubles. A period of hardship and confusion during the Polish and Swedish invasions of Russia in the early seventeenth century.

Union Bureau. *See* Mensheviks.

UPK. Code of Criminal Procedure. *See* Codes.

Verkhtrib. Russian acronym for Supreme Tribunal (1918–1922), which tried the most important cases in the early Soviet period.

Vikzhel. Railroad workers union, opposed Bolsheviks after 1917 Revolution; acronym stands for All-Russian Executive Committee of Railroad Workers Union.

VSNKh. *See* Supreme Council of the Economy.

VTsIK. Acronym for All-Russian Central Executive Committee, the highest state body of the Russian Soviet Federated Socialist Republic, the largest Soviet state, from 1917 to 1937, when it was succeeded by the Presidium of the Republic's Supreme Soviet. The national equivalent of VTsIK was TsIK, the Central Executive Committee of the U.S.S.R. (1922–1938), which became the Presidium of the national Supreme Soviet.

Workers Opposition. Bolshevik faction that sought greater trade-union control of industry and greater democracy within Party; its activities were condemned at Tenth Party Congress in 1921, and some leaders were later expelled from Party and arrested.

Zek. Prison slang for prisoner, derived from zaklyuchenny, Russian word for "prisoner."

Zemstvo. Local government unit in prerevolutionary Russia.

Index

Page numbers in **boldface** refer to the Glossary.